Statistics and Econometrics

ECONOMICS INFORMATION GUIDE SERIES

Series Editor: Robert W. Haseltine, Associate Professor of Economics, State University College of Arts and Science at Geneseo, New York

Also in this series:

AMERICAN ECONOMIC HISTORY—*Edited by William K. Hutchinson*

EAST ASIAN ECONOMIES—*Edited by Molly K.S.C. Lee*

ECONOMIC EDUCATION—*Edited by Catherine A. Hughes*

ECONOMIC HISTORY OF CANADA—*Edited by Trevor J.O. Dick*

ECONOMICS OF MINORITIES—*Edited by Kenneth L. Gagala*

HEALTH AND MEDICAL ECONOMICS—*Edited by Ted J. Ackroyd*

HISTORY OF ECONOMIC ANALYSIS—*Edited by William K. Hutchinson*

LABOR ECONOMICS—*Edited by Ross E. Azevedo*

MATHEMATICAL ECONOMICS AND OPERATIONS RESEARCH—*Edited by Joseph Zaremba*

MONEY, BANKING, AND MACROECONOMICS—*Edited by James M. Rock*

REGIONAL STATISTICS—*Edited by M. Balachandran*

RUSSIAN ECONOMIC HISTORY—*Edited by Daniel R. Kazmer and Vera Kazmer*

SOVIET-TYPE ECONOMIC SYSTEMS—*Edited by Z. Edward O'Relley*

TRANSPORTATION ECONOMICS—*Edited by James P. Rakowski*

URBAN AND REGIONAL ECONOMICS—*Edited by Jean A. Shackelford*

The above series is part of the

GALE INFORMATION GUIDE LIBRARY

The Library consists of a number of separate series of guides covering major areas in the social sciences, humanities, and current affairs.

General Editor: Paul Wasserman, Professor and former Dean, School of Library and Information Services, University of Maryland

Managing Editor: Denise Allard Adzigian, Gale Research Company

VITA

Joseph Zaremba is professor of economics at State University College of Arts and Science, Geneseo, New York. He has degrees in forestry, economics, and mathematics, including a Ph.D. in economics from Harvard University. Zaremba began his teaching career on the faculty of the Yale School of Forestry and has taught at the State University of New York College of Forestry and Fordham University. He is the author of ECONOMICS OF THE AMERICAN LUMBER INDUSTRY (New York: Speller, 1963) and MATHEMATICAL ECONOMICS AND OPERATIONS RESEARCH: A GUIDE TO INFORMATION SOURCES, vol. 10 in the Economic Information Guide Series of the Gale Information Guide Library (Detroit: Gale Research Co., 1978).

CONTENTS

Contents

PREFACE

This guide is an annotated bibliography of more than 1,700 books which have been published in the English language, including English translations of foreign titles. It is divided into seventeen chapters on the basis of subject matter. Within each chapter, the books are arranged according to the author's last name, or the last name of the first author in the case of joint authorship. The relatively few books in which no author is listed are arranged alphabetically by title. The book's content generally serves as the main basis for classification. For example, "Multivariate Analysis," chapter 8, includes all books devoted to the study of the relationships among two or more random variables, and hence includes books on analysis of variance, principal component analysis, factor analysis, canonical analysis, cross-classification, and so on. In contrast, chapter 7, "Regression," includes all books devoted to the analysis of one random variable or, generally, all books on simple and multiple regression.

To qualify for inclusion a book must have a substantial portion of its analyses in terms of probability and/or statistical concepts. Moreover, book titles have been selected mainly from among those published since 1960. A few earlier works of outstanding importance are also included.

The search for books began with well-known examples and references from various sources, including journals and publishers' catalogues. These references contained new leads, and eventually certain categories became fairly well covered. The collections at various libraries were consulted, including those at the University of Rochester and the State University of New York. The interlibrary loan service of Milne Library at the State University of New York, College at Geneseo, provided an invaluable service in obtaining numerous books on loan from other libraries around the country. Without this service, it seems doubtful that this volume could have been completed.

The degree of coverage varies considerably among the seventeen chapters. Chapter 16, "Econometrics--Texts and References," is believed to be fairly well covered, in part because of the relatively small number of books available in this area. On the other hand, chapter 17, "Econometrics--Studies and Analyses," may contain numerous omissions because of the vastness of the field and also because of the differences in opinions among individuals as to what books naturally belong in this chapter. The coverage of books is also more thorough for publishers of hardcover books and monographs than it is for organizations which publish mainly paperbound reports and manuscripts. For example, publications in econometrics and statistics of such organizations as the United Nations and the Organization of European Economic Cooperation are, regrettably, almost entirely omitted.

In some cases American distributors of foreign titles are listed. For example, most books published by North-Holland are distributed by American Elsevier, and the distributor's name follows the title of the book. For American books, the location of the publisher's headquarters is given rather than the location of a branch office.

Each book was examined for content. The general form for each title is the routine publication details, followed by a list of appendixes, if any; indexes; and references. An attempt was made to include the following types of information in the annotations: (1) type of book, that is, monograph, textbook, or reference; (2) the audience for which the book is aimed, that is, student, practitioner, applied mathematician, and others; (3) a brief summary of the content of the book as reflected in the topics covered and applications made; (4) the mathematical and statistical prerequisites necessary for comprehension and the extent of mathematical and statistical reviews provided, if any; (5) availability of exercises, problems, references, and summaries; and (6) the style of presentation and the mathematical rigor employed. In some cases, some of the above information is conveyed implicitly in the book's title and length, and in the titles of the appendixes.

This volume complements MATHEMATICAL ECONOMICS AND OPERATIONS RESEARCH, volume 10 of the Economic Series of the Gale Information Guide Library published in 1978. In terms of topic coverage there is some overlap between these two books. For example, both volumes contain chapters devoted to probability and stochastic processes. In such cases, it was decided that no title would be listed in both volumes. Therefore, these two volumes together provide a more complete coverage of a given topic than either volume alone.

The annotations are formulated on the basis of the author's statements, views, and opinions as conveyed in the preface, table of contents, summaries, and introduction, and only rarely was a subjective opinion about a book offered. For example, no attempt was made to determine whether or not a given book succeeded in light of the author's expectations.

Joseph Zaremba
Geneseo, New York

LIST OF ABBREVIATIONS

The following abbreviations have been used in this guide.

CES	Constant Elasticity of Substitution
CPM	Critical Path Method
DOD	Department of Defense
EOQ	Economic Order Quantity
GERT	Graphic Evaluation and Review Techniques
GNP	Gross National Product
MIT	Massachusetts Institute of Technology
NASA	National Aeronautic and Space Administration
NBER	National Bureau of Economic Research
NSF	National Science Foundation
OBE	Office of Business Economics
OR	Operations Research
PERT	Program Evaluation and Review Techniques
Q-GERT	Queueing System Graphic Evaluation and Review Techniques
RPMS	Resource Planning and Management System
SIAM	Society for Industrial and Applied Mathematics
SRA	Science Research Associates
SSRC	Social Science Research Council

Part I

STATISTICS

Chapter 1

BASIC STATISTICS—BEHAVIORAL SCIENCE

Adkins, Dorothy C. STATISTICS: AN INTRODUCTION FOR STUDENTS IN THE BEHAVIORAL SCIENCES. Columbus, Ohio: Charles E. Merrill, 1964. xiv, 369 p. Appendix: Tables, pp. 349-56. Index, pp. 357-69.

> A text for a one-semester course for students with only a high school algebra background. Uses multiple-choice questions with a color-changing device to inform reader of correct answer. Topics include linear functions and graphs; descriptive statistics; standard scores; binomial and normal probability distributions; estimation and hypothesis testing of difference between two means and two proportions; chi-square; simple and multiple regression and correlation; and the following correlation coefficients: Spearman's rank-difference, biserial, point-biserial, phi, tetrachoric, and eta. Review questions appear at the ends of the chapters.

Afifi, A.A., and Azen, S.P. STATISTICAL ANALYSIS: A COMPUTER ORIENTED APPROACH. New York: Academic Press, 1972. xviii, 366 p. Appendix I: Review of Fundamental Concepts, pp. 285-332. Appendix II: Statistical Tables, pp. 333-53. References, pp. 354-58. Author Index, pp. 359-60. Subject Index, pp. 361-66.

> A text for courses in elementary and applied statistics, applied multivariate analysis, and data analysis assuming a college algebra background and one semester of basic statistics. Emphasizes application and interpretation of statistical tools with computations performed on a digital computer. Mathematical derivations kept to a minimum. Topics include computer terminology; data analysis, including descriptive statistics; contingency tables; regression, including stepwise regression; analysis of variance and covariance; multivariate statistical methods, including stepwise discriminant; principal component analysis; and factor analysis. Chapters conclude with problems for computations on a digital computer.

Anderson, Theodore R., and Zelditch, Morris, Jr. A BASIC COURSE IN STATISTICS WITH SOCIOLOGICAL APPLICATIONS. 3d ed., rev. International Series in Decision Processes. New York: Holt, Rinehart and Winston, 1975. xi, 372 p. Bibliography and References, pp. 348-51. Appendix: Tables, pp. 352-63. Index, pp. 364-72.

A text for a one-semester course for students who know only arithmetic. Emphasizes how to draw inference from data. Consists of three parts: "Summarizing and Describing Univariate Distributions"; "The Relationship Between Two or More Characteristics"; and "Introduction to Statistical Inference." Topics include simple regression and correlation; association between ordinal bivariate variables; multivariate analysis with interval variables; binomial sampling distributions; nonparametric tests; analysis of variance; and sequential sampling. Chapters conclude with problems.

Armore, Sidney J. INTRODUCTION TO STATISTICAL ANALYSIS AND INFERENCES FOR PSYCHOLOGY AND EDUCATION. New York: Wiley, 1966. xx, 546 p. Appendix A: Review of Basic Algebra, pp. 483-96. Appendix B: Tables, pp. 497-516. Answers to Even-Numbered Problems, pp. 517-25. Index, pp. 527-46.

A text for a one-year course for students with only a high school algebra background. Consists of the following five parts: "Orientation and Basic Concepts"; "Statistical Description and Analysis"; "Foundation for Statistical Inference"; "Applications of Statistical Inference"; and "Association and Prediction." Sections conclude with problems.

Arnoult, Malcolm D. FUNDAMENTALS OF SCIENTIFIC METHOD IN PSYCHOLOGY. 2d ed. Fundamentals of Psychology Series. Dubuque, Iowa: Wm. C. Brown, 1976. xvii, 209 p. Glossary, pp. 193-97. Suggested Readings for Further Study, p. 199. References, pp. 201-4. Index, pp. 205-9.

An introduction to the scientific method in psychology for use as a supplementary text or for self-study. Emphasizes both the philosophy and method of science. Topics include kinds of scientific theories; the experimental method; design of a representative psychological experiment; a psychological experiment in educational psychology; nominal, ordinal, and ratio scales; analysis of variance; distribution free methods; correlation; measurement of behavior and stimulus intensity; Pavlovian conditioning; operant conditioning; psychological tests; and theory construction on psychology. Attempts to clarify the relationship between scientific inquiry and observation. Chapters conclude with discussion items, true-false items, and true-false answers.

Baggaley, Andrew R. INTERMEDIATE CORRELATION METHODS. New York: Wiley, 1964. viii, 211 p. References, pp. 169-74. Appendix One: Tables, pp. 175-96. Appendix Two: Answers to Problems Given in the Text, p. 197.

Appendix Three: Derivations and More Advanced Material, pp. 198-203. Index, pp. 205-7.

A text for a course in intermediate statistics. Includes only the most useful formulas with others placed in footnotes and in the appendix. Topics include simple and multiple regression and correlation; reliability and validity of measurement (including significance tests); factor analysis; centroid method of factor extraction; graphic rotation of factors; and the diagonal method of factor extraction. Offers a good preparation for more advanced reading in factor analysis, test score theory, and multivariate statistical analysis. Chapters conclude with problem.

Bailey, Daniel Edgar. PROBABILITY AND STATISTICS: MODELS FOR RESEARCH. New York: Wiley, 1971. xviii, 686 p. Appendix: Tables and Charts, pp. 624-82. Index, pp. 683-86.

A text for a one-year course for graduates and undergraduates in the social and behavioral sciences who have knowledge of college algebra. Prepares students for reading contemporary literature in the social and behavioral sciences. Topics include events, sample spaces, and probability; conditional probability and independence; random experiments, discrete and continuous random variables and their probability distributions; moments of random variables; means and variances of samples; sampling distributions of means and variances; statistical inference, including one- and two-sample problems; many sample problems, including analysis of variance; simple and multiple regression and correlation; and chi-square. Chapters conclude with glossaries, references, and problems.

Bernstein, Allen L. A HANDBOOK OF STATISTICS SOLUTIONS FOR THE BEHAVIORAL SCIENCES. New York: Holt, Rinehart and Winston, 1964. xii, 145 p. Tables, pp. 99-145. No index.

A handbook which contains solution demonstrations for a variety of basic theoretical models. Demonstrations grouped into the following five chapters: "Calculation of Basic Statistics"; "Calculation of Confidence Intervals"; "Tests of Significance"; "Correlation"; and "Estimation of Sample Size Required in Advance of Experimentation." Concludes with a chapter containing practical problems with solutions."

Blakeslee, David W., and Chinn, William G. INTRODUCTORY STATISTICS AND PROBABILITY: A BASIS FOR DECISION MAKING. Boston: Houghton Mifflin, 1975. ix, 358 p. Appendix, pp. 281-338. Tables, pp. 339-51. Final Review, pp. 353-54. Index, pp. 355-58.

A text for a one-semester course for students in the behavioral sciences who know high school algebra. More rigorous than most basic texts with proofs of many theorems provided and many of the simpler results clearly derived. Includes a thorough treatment of random variables. Other topics include events and probability; conditional probability; Bayes' formula; functions of random variables; binomial distributions; sampling; interval estimation; and tests of hypothesis. Appendix devoted to summation notation, formulae, answers to problems which occur at the ends of the sections. Chapters conclude with summaries and review problems.

Blalock, Hubert M., Jr. SOCIAL STATISTICS. 2d ed., rev. McGraw-Hill Series in Sociology. New York: McGraw-Hill, 1972. xiv, 583 p. Appendix 1: Review of Algebraic Operations, pp. 533-40. Appendix 2: Tables, pp. 541-74. Name Index, pp. 575-76. Subject Index, pp. 577-83.

A text for a one-year course for graduates and undergraduates who intend to undertake social research. Emphasizes the logic of statistical inference, with motivation achieved by covering a wide range of applications. Consists of the following five parts: "Introduction"; "Univariate Descriptive Statistics"; "Inductive Statistics"; "Bivariate and Multivariate Statistics"; and "Sampling." Topics include nominal and interval scales; single sample tests involving means and proportions; two-sample tests; nonparametric tests; contingency problems; analysis of variance; simple and multiple regression; analysis of covariance and dummy variables; and stratified and cluster sampling. Chapters conclude with problems and references.

Blank, Stanley S. DESCRIPTIVE STATISTICS. New York: Appleton-Century-Crofts, 1968. viii, 158 p. No index.

A programmed text on descriptive statistics for use as a supplementary text in a basic statistics course for students of psychology and education. Topics include the calculation of frequency distributions, measures of central tendency, measures of variability, standard scores, percentiles, and correlations. Program requires ten to twelve hours for completion.

Blommers, Paul J., and Lindquist, E.F. ELEMENTARY STATISTICAL METHODS IN PSYCHOLOGY AND EDUCATION. Boston: Houghton Mifflin, 1959. xv, 528 p. Appendix A: Glossary of Symbols, pp. 469-78. Appendix B: Selected Formulas and Rules, pp. 479-90. Appendix C: Tables, pp. 492-518. Index, pp. 519-28.

A text for a one-semester course. Develops a relatively small number of techniques more thoroughly than is customary in most other basic texts. Topics include descriptive statistics; standard scores; normal curve; sampling theory; tests of hypotheses and interval estimation concerning difference between two means and two proportions; and simple correlation and regression.

Bradley, Jack I., and McClelland, James N. BASIC STATISTICAL CONCEPTS: A SELF-INSTRUCTIONAL TEXT. 2d ed., rev. Glenview, Ill.: Scott, Foresman, 1978. vii, 209 p. Index, pp. 208-9.

A supplemental text and a self-study for a course in basic statistics for students of psychology, education, and sociology. Requires twelve hours to complete. Left-hand page describes the material, while right-hand page contains completion-type questions. Topics include review of arithmetic and algebra; frequency distributions; measures of central tendency and of dispersion; normal distribution; correlation; probability; bivariate and multivariate analysis; reliability and validity of psychological measures; and individual differences and norms. Concludes with a comprehensive examination.

Bruning, James L., and Kintz, B.L. COMPUTATIONAL HANDBOOK OF STATISTICS. 2d ed., rev. and enl. Glenview, Ill.: Scott, Foresman, 1977. x, 308 p. Appendixes, pp. 238-304. Index, pp. 305-8.

A text and reference for a course in basic statistics for students in the behavioral and social sciences, education, business, medical research, and related areas who have knowledge of descriptive statistics. Based on the techniques of teaching by example with emphasis on applications. Appendixes include FORTRAN programs. Omits mathematical derivations and statistical theory. Consists of five parts: "Organizing Data and Some Simple Computations"; "Analysis of Variance"; "Supplemental Computations for Analysis of Variance"; "Correlation and Related Topics"; and "Nonparametric Tests, Miscellaneous Tests of Significance, and Indexes of Relationships." Topics include tests of significance for difference between two means; 2- and 3-level factorial designs; Latin square designs; tests for differences between two variances; Duncan's multiple-range test; simple and partial correlation measures, including point-biserial; reliability of measurement; tests for differences between correlations; Mann-Whitney U-tests; and chi-square. Also useful to instructors in beginning laboratory courses in experimental design.

Bugg, D.D.; Henderson, M.A.; Holden, K.; and Lund, P.J. STATISTICAL METHODS IN THE SOCIAL SCIENCES. Amsterdam: North Holland, 1968. xi, 315 p. Bibliography, pp. 309-10. Index, pp. 311-15.

A text for a one-semester course. Includes a set of hypothetical data (one hundred men with characteristics such as age and height) which forms the basis for much of the analysis found in the text. Topics include descriptive statistics; sampling and probability; normal distribution; statistical inference concerning two means and two proportions; chi-square; regression and correlation; and analysis of variance. Exercises included.

Champion, Dean J. BASIC STATISTICS FOR SOCIAL RESEARCH. Chandler Publications in Anthropology and Sociology. Scranton, Pa.: Chandler, 1970. xvi, 310 p. Some Answers to Selected Problems, pp. 235-37. Appendix A: Tables, pp. 239-96. Appendix B: Bibliography of Texts and Articles, pp. 297-300. Appendix C: Some Selected Symbols, pp. 301-2. Index, pp. 303-10.

> A text for a one-semester course assuming a high school algebra background. Achieves a balance between parametric and nonparametric statistical methods. Topics include standard scores and the normal curve; hypothesis testing and interval estimation; tests for k samples; chi-square; ordinal level tests, including Kolmogorov-Smirnov, Wilcoxon matched-pairs-signed-ranks, Mann-Whitney, Kruskal-Wallis, and Wald-Wolfowitz tests; and measures of association, including interval-level, nominal level, and ordinal-level measures. Chapters conclude with questions for review and problems.

Chase, Clinton I. ELEMENTARY STATISTICAL PROCEDURES. 2d ed., rev. New York: McGraw-Hill, 1976. viii, 277 p. Appendix A: Review of Arithmetic and Algebraic Processes, pp. 213-21. Appendix B: Mathematical Developments of Statistical Procedures, pp. 222-32. Appendix C: Tables, pp. 231-57. Appendix D: Introduction to Computer Usage, pp. 258-64. Appendix E: Answers to Practice Problems, pp. 265-74. Index, pp. 275-77.

> A text for a one-semester course in the social sciences with emphasis on the derivation of procedures based on the logical structure that underly the methods of analyzing data. Topics include normal curve and its application; simple correlation and regression; confidence interval estimation and hypothesis testing; one-way analysis of variance; chi-square and other nonparametric tests. Sections conclude with problems.

Clarke, Robert B.; Caladaci, Arthur P.; and Caffrey, John. STATISTICAL REASONING AND PROCEDURES. Columbus, Ohio: Charles E. Merrill, 1965. ix, 390 p. Appendixes: Tables, pp. 364-80. Index, pp. 381-90.

> A text for a one-semester course using simple examples to develop the concepts. Topics include normal curve; derived scores; Pearson and rank-order coefficient of correlation; simple regression; sampling distributions for means, proportions, differences between means and standard deviation; hypothesis testing; inferences about Pearson product-moment correlation coefficient; and normal approximation to the binomial. Chapters conclude with exercises and problems.

Cohen, Jacob. STATISTICAL POWER ANALYSIS FOR THE BEHAVIORAL SCIENCES. New York: Academic Press, 1969. xv, 415 p. Technical Appendix: Computational Procedures, pp. 398-406. References, pp. 407-9. Index, pp. 411-15.

> A handbook and supplementary text for intermediate courses

in applied statistics in the behavioral and social sciences. Assumes knowledge of one or two semesters of applied statistics, especially tests of significance. Introduces each test or research design in conjunction with power-analytic analysis, with illustrations from psychology, biology, sociology, political science, economics, education, and advertising. Topics include power analysis; t test for means; difference between correlation coefficients; sign test; difference between proportions; chi-square for goodness of fit and contingency tables; and F test in analysis of variance and covariance. Power and other tables comprise about 180 pages throughout the text. Omits use of computer program.

Cornell, Francis G. THE ESSENTIALS OF EDUCATIONAL STATISTICS. Wiley Series in Probability and Mathematical Statistics. New York: Wiley, 1965. xii, 375 p. Appendixes: Tables, pp. 351-69. Index, pp. 371-75.

A text for a one-year course with a prerequisite of algebra and the rudiments of calculus. Topics include probability distributions; estimation and hypothesis testing; regression and correlation; chi-square; two-sample problem; two-way analysis of variance; special correlation methods, including rank, biserial, and tetrachoric; and partial and multiple correlations. Chapters conclude with exercises and references.

Cotton, John W. ELEMENTARY STATISTICAL THEORY FOR BEHAVIORAL SCIENTISTS. Addison-Wesley Series in Foundations of Scientific Psychology. Reading, Mass.: Addison-Wesley, 1967. x, 86 p. Appendix: Tables, pp. 78-80. Answers to Exercises, pp. 81-82. Index, pp. 83-86.

A monograph intended as a supplement to texts in basic and intermediate statistics courses with emphasis on theory. Includes, in addition to conventional topics, a brief introduction to Chebyshev's inequality, Bayes' theorem, minimum variance unbiased estimators, central limit theorem, randomization tests, robustness, power of tests, credible Bayesian intervals, and likelihood ratio tests. Assumes knowledge of college algebra. Sections conclude with exercises, and chapters conclude with references.

Courts, Frederick A. PSYCHOLOGICAL STATISTICS: AN INTRODUCTION. Dorsey Series in Psychology. Homewood, Ill.: Irwin, 1966. x, 349 p. Appendix: Tables, pp. 319-44. Index, pp. 345-49.

A text for a one-semester course for students who know only arithmetic. Topics include linear relationships; product-moment correlation; probability and the normal curve; sampling distribution; confidence interval estimation for mean, proportion, and variance; testing the difference between two means and two variances; sign test; and analysis of variance. Sections conclude with problems; chapters, with references.

Darlington, Richard B. Assisted by Ronald G. Nathan. RADICALS AND SQUARES: STATISTICAL METHODS FOR THE BEHAVIORAL SCIENCES. Ithaca, N.Y.: Logan Hill Press, 1975. viii, 597 p. Appendix I: Review of Basic Algebra, pp. 571-73. Appendix II: Ranking Large Sets of Numbers, pp. 574-75. Appendix III: Finding Square Roots, pp. 576-78. Partial Answers to Selected Problems, pp. 588-89. Origins of Selected Methods, p. 590. Sources of Tables, p. 591. References, p. 592. Index, pp. 593-97.

> A text for a one-semester course and a reference for research workers. Includes numerous flow charts as an aid to computation and understanding concepts. Formulas, definitions, etc., placed in convenient tables. Consists of the following four parts: "Fundamentals"; "Description and Estimation"; "Hypothesis Testing"; and "Further Topics." Topics include univariate and bivariate statistics; standard scores; two-way analysis of variance; nonparametric tests; and regression. Chapters conclude with problems.

Dayton, Chauncy Mitchell, and Stunkard, Clayton L. STATISTICS FOR PROBLEM SOLVING. New York: McGraw-Hill, 1971. viii, 290 p. Technical Appendix, pp. 219-76. References, pp. 277-78. Solutions to Selected Problems, pp. 279-83. Index, pp. 285-90.

> A text for a one-semester course in applied statistics for students of education who have knowledge of algebra. Emphasizes the use of statistical procedures in the analysis of research data. Topics include probability; chi-square; analysis of variance; simple regression; and inferential methods for rank-order data. Technical appendix devoted to goodness-of-fit tests, normal distributions, t-test for the two-sample problem, theoretical distributions, and statistical tables. Chapters conclude with problems.

Diamond, Solomon. INFORMATION AND ERROR: AN INTRODUCTION TO STATISTICAL ANALYSIS. New York: Basic Books, 1959. xii, 308 p. Glossary of Symbols, pp. 263-68. Selected Formulas for Review and Reference, pp. 269-71. Appendix of Tables, pp. 272-97. Index, pp. 299-307. Answers to Computational Problems, p. 308.

> A text for a course in basic statistics for students in psychology who have knowledge of high school algebra. Topics include probability, normal distribution, and standard scores; sampling variance and confidence limits; comparison of two means; variance ratio; chi-square; product-moment correlation; uses of correlation; factor analysis; and nonparametric statistics. Chapters conclude with problems and references.

Downey, Kenneth J. ELEMENTARY SOCIAL STATISTICS. New York: Random House, 1975. x, 310 p. Appendix: Tables, pp. 283-95. Answers to Problems, pp. 297-303. Index, pp. 305-10.

A supplementary text for a course for sociologists. Uses an elementary approach to topics and formulae. Topics include probability; tests of difference between two means and two proportions; correlation; contingency tables and chi-square; analysis of variance; and Kendall's coefficient of concordance. Chapters conclude with readings and problems.

Downie, N.M., and Heath, R.W. BASIC STATISTICAL METHODS. 4th ed., rev. New York: Harper & Row, 1974. viii, 355 p. Appendixes A to N: Statistical Tables, pp. 277-325. Appendix O: Formulas, pp. 326-36. Appendix P: Answers to Exercises, pp. 337-44. References, pp. 345-47. Index, pp. 349-55.

A text for a one-semester course for students in the behavioral science. Omits derivations and de-emphasizes statistical theory. Topics include standard scores; correlation; regression; probability and probability distributions; sampling; tests of differences between two means and two proportions; analysis of variance; reliability, validity, and item analysis; and distribution-free tests. Chapters conclude with exercises.

Du Bois, Philip Hunter. AN INTRODUCTION TO PSYCHOLOGICAL STATISTICS. New York: Harper & Row, 1965. xi, 530 p. Appendix: Tables, pp. 483-507. Glossary of Symbols, pp. 509-13. Index, pp. 515-30.

A text for a one-year course for psychological students with a high school algebra background. Emphasizes the logic of statistical procedures and efficient methods of computation. Topics include chi-square; correlation and regression; multiple correlation; statistical control and partial correlation; probability and the normal curve; families of distributions, including binomial and Poisson; inferences about population parameters; analysis of variance; test construction; item analysis; factor analysis; and nonparametric tests. Chapters conclude with exercises and references.

Edgington, Eugene S. STATISTICAL INFERENCE: THE DISTRIBUTION-FREE APPROACH. McGraw-Hill Series in Psychology. New York: McGraw-Hill, 1969. xii, 211 p. References, pp. 203-5. Index, pp. 207-11.

A text for a one-semester course in distribution-free statistics for students in psychology who have a high school algebra background. Confined to finite, discrete populations of unknown shape. Topics include probability; sampling, including stratified and cluster sampling; confidence intervals for proportions, differences between totals, and for intervals; central limit theorem and binomial distribution arguments for normality; randomization tests for a difference between independent samples; paired comparisons; rank-order tests for independent samples and for paired comparisons; contingency tables; analysis of variance; experimental regression; and joint analysis of differences in central tendency and variability.

Edwards, Allen Louis. EXPECTED VALUES OF DISCRETE RANDOM VARIABLES AND ELEMENTARY STATISTICS. New York: Wiley, 1964. x, 146 p. Index, pp. 143-46.

A supplementary text for courses in applied statistics and experimental design requiring only elementary algebra. Topics include random variables and their distributions; expected values; moments of random variables; binomial populations; sampling from a finite population without replacement; mean and variance of a set of ranks; expectation of mean squares in a randomized-group design; factorial experiments; randomized block designs; Latin square designs; and infinite or continuous sample spaces. Presentation consists mostly of simple derivations and descriptions, with a few numerical examples.

______. STATISTICAL ANALYSIS. 3d ed., rev. New York: Holt, Rinehart and Winston, 1969. xi, 244 p. Answers to the Problems, pp. 197-204. Appendix: Tables, pp. 205-39. Index, pp. 240-44.

A text for a course for students in psychology, education, and the behavioral sciences. Places little stress on numerical calculations and presents elementary theory intuitively. Topics include variables and scales; simple correlation and regression; sample spaces and probability; random sampling distributions; sampling from a binomial population; the normal distribution; interval estimation and hypothesis testing; analysis of variance; chi-square; measures of association and tests of significance; random errors of measurement; and samples in research. Chapters conclude with reviews of terms, reviews of symbols, and questions and problems.

______. STATISTICAL METHODS. 2d ed., rev. New York: Holt, Rinehart and Winston, 1967. xvi, 462 p. References, pp. 375-80. Glossary, pp. 381-83. Appendix A: A Review of Some Elementary Mathematical Rules and Principles, pp. 385-94. Appendix B: Tables, pp. 395-440. Appendix C: Answers to the Examples, pp. 441-54. Index of Names, pp. 455-56. Subject Index, pp. 457-62.

A text for a course in basic statistics for students of psychology and the behavioral sciences who have knowledge of algebra. Topics include simple regression and correlation; biserial, tetrachoric, and rank correlation; sets and probability; random variables; binomial and normal probability distributions; small and large sample tests; analysis of variance; chi-square; and nonparametric tests. Includes proofs of theorems. Chapters conclude with problems, some of which call for proofs.

Elzey, Freeman F. AN INTRODUCTION TO STATISTICAL METHODS IN THE BEHAVIORAL SCIENCES. Monterey, Calif.: Brooks/Cole, 1976. xiii, 221 p. Answers to Group-A Exercises, pp. 179-206. Tables, pp. 207-15. Glossary of Symbols and Abbreviations, pp. 217-18. Index, pp. 219-21.

A text for a one-semester course for students who have knowledge of arithmetic. Excludes derivations. Topics include normal curve; probability; estimation and hypothesis testing; analysis of variance; simple correlation and regression; Spearman rank-order correlation; and chi-square. Chapters conclude with exercises.

Ericksen, Gerald L. SCIENTIFIC INQUIRY IN THE BEHAVIORAL SCIENCES: AN INTRODUCTION TO STATISTICS. Glenview, Ill.: Scott, Foresman, 1970. x, 372 p. Appendix A: Tables, pp. 301-30. Appendix B: Grouped Data Formulas for the Mean, Median, Mode, Percentile Tanks and Standard Deviation, pp. 331-34. Appendix C: Derivation of Computational Formulas for the One-way Analysis of Variance, pp. 335-36. Appendix D: Review of Basic Algebraic rules, pp. 337-38. Appendix E: Demonstration of the Variance Relationship for Independent Groups, pp. 339-41. Glossary of Symbols, pp. 343-45. References, pp. 347-49. Answers to Review Questions, pp. 351-65. Index, pp. 367-72.

A text for a one-semester course for students in the behavioral sciences. Emphasizes formulas necessary to define concepts, with little attention given to details of large computations. Numerous examples encourage the transition from intuitive thinking to systematic inquiry. Topics include set theory and probability; binomial, chi-square, and normal distributions; testing hypotheses; analysis of variance; simple regression and correlation; rank-order statistics; decision theory; and factor analysis. Chapters conclude with problems.

Ferguson, George Andrew. STATISTICAL ANALYSIS IN PSYCHOLOGY AND EDUCATION. McGraw-Hill Series in Psychology. New York: McGraw-Hill, 1976. x, 529 p. References, pp. 480-83. Appendix: Tables, pp. 484-516. Index, pp. 517-29.

A text for a one-year course for students who have an algebra background, and a reference for investigators in medicine, psychiatry, sociology, and related fields. Emphasizes the analysis and interpretation of data resulting from the conduct of experiments. Consists of the following four parts: "Basic Statistics"; "The Design of Experiments"; "Nonparametric Statistics"; and "Psychological Tests and Multivariate Statistics." Topics include three-way analysis of variance; orthogonal and other multiple comparison procedures; analysis of covariance; score transformation; and partial and multiple correlation. Chapters conclude with exercises.

Freeman, Linton C. ELEMENTARY APPLIED STATISTICS FOR STUDENTS IN BEHAVIORAL SCIENCE. New York: Wiley, 1965. viii, 298 p. Bibliography, pp. 229-30. Appendix A: Table of Statistical Symbols, pp. 231-32. Appendix B: Statistical Tables, pp. 233-56. Appendix C: Data for Problems, pp. 257-71. Problems and Exercises, pp. 273-85. Answers to Odd-Numbered Problems, pp. 286-93. Index, pp. 295-98.

A text for a one-semester course in statistics for students in the behavioral sciences who have knowledge of high school algebra. Emphasizes the logic of statistical inference, rather than derivations and computations. Topics include summarizing distributions on nominal, ordinal, and interval scales; describing associations between nominal, ordinal, and interval scales; descriptive associations between one nominal and one ordinal scale, between one normal and one interval scale, and between one cordial and one interval scale; and testing hypotheses about ordinal, nominal, and interval scales.

Fried, Robert. INTRODUCTION TO STATISTICS: SELECTED PROCEDURES FOR THE BEHAVIORAL SCIENCES. New York: Oxford University Press, 1969. xv, 304 p. Appendix: Tables, pp. 263-97. Bibliography, pp. 297-302. Index, 303-04.

A text for a one-semester course for students who have a high school algebra background. Assumes all inferential statistics represent elementary probability ratios. Order of presentation different from that found in most books. Discussion of probability located between empirical distributions and measures of central tendency. Topics include normal distribution and standard scores; hypothesis testing two population means; analysis of variance; simple regression; biserial and point-biserial correlations; tetrachoric correlation; nonparametric tests; and transformation of data from psychological populations. Chapters conclude with problems.

Games, Paul A., and Klare, George R. ELEMENTARY STATISTICS: DATA ANALYSIS FOR THE BEHAVIORAL SCIENCES. New York: McGraw-Hill, 1967. xiv, 564 p. Appendix A: Required and Optimal Skills for Using this Book, pp. 452-60. Appendix B: Squares, and Square Roots, pp. 461-73. Appendix C: Nominal, Ordinal, Interval, and Ratio Scales; Brief Description and Commentary, pp. 474-78. Appendix D: Tables, pp. 480-500. Appendix E: Computations of Chi-square, F Tests, and Simple Analysis of Variance, pp. 501-49. Index, pp. 551-64.

A text for a one-year course with emphasis on data analysis rather than on derivations. Provides a rigorous, yet largely verbal, statement of the more important concepts. Organized around a detailed set of objectives similar to those developed by writers of programmed learning materials. Consists of the following five parts: "Background"; "Univariate Descriptive Statistics"; "Statistical Inference"; "Bivariate Descriptive Statistics"; and "Experimental Design." Chapters conclude with problems, answers, and symbols.

Gellman, Estelle S. DESCRIPTIVE STATISTICS FOR TEACHERS. New York: Harper & Row, 1973. vi, 121 p. Appendix A: Table A. Squares and Square Roots of Numbers from 1 to 1,000, pp. 109-19. Bibliography, p. 120. Index, p. 121.

A supplementary text designed specifically for use by teachers in such courses as educational psychology or measurement and evaluation, as well as courses in the instructional area that deal with evaluation of student performance. Topics include organization and presentation of educational data; measure of relative performance; measures of variability in performance; and measures of the relationship between different sets of scores. Derivations omitted.

______. STATISTICS FOR TEACHERS. New York: Harper & Row, 1973. x, 239 p. Appendix: Tables, pp. 201-31. Bibliography, p. 233. Index, pp. 235-39.

A text for a one-semester course in pre-service and in-service teacher training programs. Designed to teach teachers elementary statistics with emphasis on inferential statistics for describing classroom performance and on testing hypotheses relevant to classroom conditions. Includes no derivations, and uses only algebra. Topics include classification of educational data; measures of performance; measures of variability in performance; correlation and prediction; sampling; and testing hypotheses about difference between two means.

Gilbert, Norman. STATISTICS. Philadelphia: W.B. Saunders, 1976. ix, 364 p. Appendix A: Symbols, pp. 327-30. Appendix B: Formulas, pp. 331-37. Appendix C: Tables, pp. 338-60. Index, pp. 361-64.

A text for a one-semester course for students in the social sciences who have a high school algebra background. Suitable for a self-paced approach as well as a lecture approach with 300 examples worked out in great detail. Chapters conclude with a list of vocabulary and symbols, as well as exercises. Topics include sample spaces, sets, and probability; discrete probability distributions; normal distribution and standard scores; hypothesis testing for differences between two means and two portions; chi-square; analysis of variance; simple regression and correlation; and nonparametric tests.

Glass, Gene V., and Stanley, Julian C. STATISTICAL METHODS IN EDUCATION AND PSYCHOLOGY. Prentice-Hall Series in Educational Measurement, Research, and Statistics. Englewood Cliffs, N.J.: Prentice-Hall, 1970. xii, 596 p. Appendix A: Statistical Tables, pp. 510-54. Appendix B: Answers to Problems and Exercises, pp. 555-69. Appendix C: Verification of Standard Solution to Least Squares Criterion, pp. 570-71. Bibliography, pp. 572-85. Author Index, pp. 586-88. Subject Index, pp. 589-96.

A text for a one-year course for students in education and psychology. Presents a more thorough coverage of analysis of variance techniques than that found in most. Topics include normal curve; product-moment correlation; simple regression and prediction; multiple and partial correlation; probability and random variables; properties of point estimators; tests of significance for population means, proportions, differences between two means, two proportions, and two correlation coefficients; two-way analysis of variance; multifactor analysis of variance; and analysis of covariance. Chapters conclude with exercises.

Gourevitch, Vivian. STATISTICAL METHODS: A PROBLEM-SOLVING APPROACH. Boston: Allyn and Bacon, 1965. x, 310 p. Appendix: Tables, pp. 280-303. Index, pp. 304-10.

A text for a one-semester course for students in psychology and related fields who have a high school algebra background. Emphasizes a careful scrutiny of research data, the interpretation of statistical results, and permissible conclusions. Topics include normal curve; linear correlation; probability and sampling from a binomial population; hypothesis testing concerning means and difference between two population means; chi-square; and analysis of variance. Chapters conclude with practice problems with detailed solutions.

Guilford, Joy Paul, and Fruchter, Benjamin. FUNDAMENTAL STATISTICS IN PSYCHOLOGY AND EDUCATION. New York: McGraw-Hill, 1978. x, 545 p. Appendix: Tables, pp. 491-35. Name Index, pp. 537-38. Subject Index, pp. 539-45.

A text for a one-semester course with emphasis on verbal description of concepts. Consists of the following four parts: "Basic Descriptive Statistics"; "Statistical Tests and Decisions"; "Relations and Prediction"; and "Psychological Measurements." Topics include probability and distributions; inferences concerning differences between two means, two proportions, and two correlation coefficients; chi-square; nonparametric tests; three-way analysis of variance; various correlation coefficients; prediction and accuracy; multiple predictions; reliability and validity of psychological measurements; and test scales and norms. Chapters conclude with exercises.

Haber, Audrey; Runyon, Richard P.; and Badia, Pietro, eds. READINGS IN STATISTICS. Reading, Mass.: Addison-Wesley, 1970. xii, 254 p. No Index.

Nineteen reprints of articles in contemporary statistical thinking grouped under the following three headings: "Problems of Measurement" (six articles); "Hypothesis Testing" (six articles); and "Nonparametric Statistical Techniques" (seven articles). Topics include degrees of freedom, statistical power, and the use of the A statistic as a substitute for the t. Useful as a supplement to basic statistics courses, particularly in psychology and sociology.

Hammond, Kenneth P., and Householder, James E. INTRODUCTION TO THE STATISTICAL METHOD: FOUNDATIONS AND USE IN THE BEHAVIORAL SCIENCES. Knopf Publications in Psychology. New York: Alfred A. Knopf, 1962. xvi, 426 p. An Index of Formulas and Symbols, pp. 389-96. Answers to Problems, pp. 397-412. Appendix: Tables, pp. 413-18. Indexes, pp. 419-25.

A monograph on the logic of the statistical method. Each chapter consists of two parts: the need for certain methods appropriate to the problems of the behavioral scientists and mathematical reasoning underlying the procedures described in the first part. The book consists of the following two parts: "The Description of Data" and "Inductive Inference." Topics include central tendency, variability, individual performance, correlation, random sampling distributions, and statistical decision. Chapters conclude with references and problems. Assumes knowledge of college algebra.

Handel, Judith D. INTRODUCTORY STATISTICS FOR SOCIOLOGY. Prentice-Hall Methods and Theories in the Social Sciences Series. Englewood Cliffs, N.J.: Prentice-Hall, 1978. xii, 387 p. Answers to Odd-Numbered Exercises, pp. 343-49. Appendix A: Statistical Tables, pp. 350-71. Appendix B: Glossary of Terms, pp. 372-79. Index, pp. 381-87.

A text for a one-semester course with emphasis on the most elementary statistical techniques. Examples use both real data and hypothetical data. Consists of the following five parts: "Introduction"; "Univariate Descriptive Statistics"; "Bivariate and Multivariate Descriptive Statistics"; "Probability"; and "Inferential Statistics." Topics include measuring association between partially and fully ordered variables; regression and correlation; multivariate contingency tables; probability; distributions; and tests of hypotheses concerning two population means. Chapters conclude with problems and questions.

Hardyck, Curtis D., and Petrinovich, Lewis F. INTRODUCTION TO STATISTICS FOR THE BEHAVIORAL SCIENCES. Saunders Books in Psychology. Philadelphia: W.B. Saunders, 1969. viii, 302 p. Appendix I: Coding Scores for Hand Computation, pp. 247-54. Appendix II: Statistical Tables, pp. 255-90. Appendix III: Answers to Odd-Numbered Exercises, pp. 291-94. Summary of Arithmetical Rules, pp. 295-97. Index, pp. 299-302.

A text for a one-semester course for students with limited mathematics background. Emphasizes the use of statistics in experimentation. Topics include probability and the normal curve; sampling distributions and confidence interval estimation; chi-square and proportions; distribution-free tests; regression and correlation; and applications to psychology. Chapters conclude with exercises.

Harshbarger, Thad R. INTRODUCTORY STATISTICS: A DECISION MAP. 2d ed., rev. New York: Macmillan, 1977. ix, 587 p. Appendix: Tables, pp. 519-73. Bibliography, pp. 575-78. Index, pp. 579-87.

A text for a one-semester course for students in psychology and education who have a college algebra background. Presents a general schema (a decision map) into which different kinds of problems might fit in an attempt to stimulate the kind of problem classification that might be used to determine the appropriate method of solution. Topics include transformation of scales; probability; distributions; comparing proportions of entire distributions; comparing variances; comparing means of three or more samples; hypothesis testing and ordinal scales; prediction; Pearson and related formulas for correlation; correlating three or more variables; two-way analysis of variance; Mann-Whitney U-test; Kruskal-Wallis test; and simple regression.

Hays, William L. BASIC STATISTICS. Basic Concepts in Psychology Series. Belmont, Calif.: Brooks/Cole, 1967. viii, 117 p. Appendix A: Normal-Curve Probabilities and Densities, pp. 108-12. Appendix B: Value of Chi-Square Significant at the .05 Level, p. 113. Appendix C: Significant Values of r, at .05 and .01, for Various Degrees of Freedom, p. 114. References, p. 115. Index, pp. 116-17.

A supplementary text for a basic course for psychology students. Topics include probability; random variables; normal curve; confidence limits; tests of hypotheses concerning difference between two means; simple correlation; and chi-square. Chapters conclude with problems.

______. STATISTICS FOR THE SOCIAL SCIENCES. 2d ed., rev. New York: Holt, Rinehart and Winston, 1973. xxi, 954 p. Appendix A: Rules of Summation, pp. 861-70. Appendix B: The Algebra of Expectations, pp. 871-77. Appendix C: Tables, pp. 878-907. References, pp. 908-12. Glossary of Symbols, pp. 913-21. Solutions to Selected Problems, pp. 922-47. Index, pp. 948-54.

A text for a one-year course for students of psychology and the social sciences who have a high school algebra background. More emphasis placed on theoretical than on applied and computational aspects. Topics include sets and functions; probability distributions; joint events and independence; discrete random variables; sampling distributions and point estimation; interval estimation and hypothesis testing; chi-square; analysis of variance; fixed and random effects models; individual comparisons among means; linear regression and correlation; order statistics; and Bayesian statistics. Chapters conclude with exercises.

Heermann, Emil F., and Proskamp, Larry A., eds. READINGS IN STATISTICS FOR THE BEHAVIORAL SCIENCES. Prentice-Hall Series in Educational

Measurement, Research, and Statistics. Englewood Cliffs, N.J.: Prentice-Hall, 1970. xii, 419 p. Appendix: Statistical Methods and Research Design: Index of Reviews and Notes in the PSYCHOLOGICAL BULLETIN, 1940-1966, by T.G. Andrews, pp. 399-409. Name Index, pp. 411-16. Subject Index, pp. 417-19.

> Thirty-one reprints of articles on the application and interpretation of statistical methods grouped under the following six headings: "History of the Application of Statistical Methods" (two articles); "Parametric vs Nonparametric Statistics" (six articles); "Randomization" (four articles); "Testing Statistical Hypotheses" (six articles); "Special Topics in Analysis of Variance" (nine articles); and "Correlation and Regression" (four articles). Useful as a supplementary text for graduate and undergraduate courses in statistics or as a text for a seminar course.

Hill, Joseph E., and Kerber, August. MODELS, METHODS, AND ANALYTICAL PROCEDURES IN EDUCATIONAL RESEARCH. Detroit: Wayne State University Press, 1967. xiv, 551 p. Note, pp. 529-32. Bibliography, pp. 533-45. Index, pp. 547-50. Colophon, p. 551.

> A text for a one-year course for graduate students and a reference for researchers who have limited backgrounds in mathematics, statistics, and research design. Consists of the following four parts: "Introduction to Research and Models"; "The General Analogue Model of Educational Research: Design Procedures"; "Adapting the General Model to Problems in Basic Types of Research"; and "Statistical Techniques and Models." The last part comprises about three-fourths of the book and considers such topics as probability; sampling procedures; simple and multiple regression and correlation; statistical inference; nonparametric tests; parametric tests, including analysis of variance and covariance; factor analysis; linear programming; and games. Extensive verbal discussion of the techniques and applications are included. Chapters conclude with references.

Hopkins, Kenneth D., and Glass, Gene V. BASIC STATISTICS FOR THE BEHAVIORAL SCIENCES. Englewood Cliffs, N.J.: Prentice-Hall, 1978. xiii, 436 p. Appendix: Tables, pp. 394-423. Bibliography, pp. 424-29. Name Index, pp. 431-32. Subject Index, pp. 432-36.

> A text for a one-year course with emphasis on the conceptual approach rather than on the mathematical approach. Topics include normal distribution and standard scores; rank and product-moment correlations; simple and multiple regression and correlation; sampling distributions; confidence intervals and inference concerning differences between two means; chi-square; analysis of variance; multiple comparisons; and factorial designs. Chapters conclude with tests, problems, and exercises.

Horowitz, Leonard M. ELEMENTS OF STATISTICS FOR PSYCHOLOGY AND EDUCATION. McGraw-Hill Series in Psychology. New York: McGraw-Hill, 1974. xv, 464 p. Glossary, pp. 427-30. Appendixes, pp. 431-62. Index, pp. 463-64.

A text for a one-semester course for students who have knowledge of high school algebra. Achieves a balance between theory and applications in the form of examples of experimental and correlation studies. Topics include the normal curve; Z scores and related topics; sets, combinatorial algebra and probability; binomial distribution; hypothesis testing, including testing for the difference between two means; analysis of variance; correlation and prediction; chi-square; and nonparametric tests. Chapters conclude with exercises, and the appendixes consist of tables and methodological and computational aids.

Huck, Schuyler W.; Cormier, William H.; and Bounds, William G., Jr. READING STATISTICS AND RESEARCH. New York: Harper & Row, 1974. x, 387 p. Index, pp. 379-87.

A text for a one-semester course for graduates and undergraduates in the behavioral sciences who are familiar with elementary concepts of statistics. Helps students learn to read journal articles. Consists of the following four parts: An Introduction; Statistics; Research Design; and Some Post Hoc Comments. Chapters include "Statistical Design"; "One-Way Analysis of Covariance"; "Multiple Correlation and Discriminate Function Analysis"; "Multivariate Analogs to the Quasi-experimental Designs"; and "Designs for Applied Behavioral Analysis." Includes a variety of excerpts from journal articles. Chapters conclude with review terms and questions.

Insko, Chester A., and Schoeninger, Douglas W. INTRODUCTORY STATISTICS FOR PSYCHOLOGY. 2d ed., rev. Boston: Allyn and Bacon, 1977. x, 450 p. Appendix A: Elementary Set Theory, pp. 385-94. Appendix B: An Introduction to Summation Algebra, pp. 395-99. Appendix C: Tables, pp. 401-24. References, pp. 425-26. Exercise Answers, pp. 427-41. Index, pp. 443-50.

A text for a one-semester course for students who have knowledge of high school algebra. Includes algebraic proofs in small print, with data from a single experiment to illustrate concepts, and a historical perspective at the end of each chapter. Topics include correlation, including point-biserial; probability; tests for the difference between two population means and two population proportions; analysis of variance; chi-square; and nonparametric tests. Chapters conclude with exercises.

Johnson, Allan G. SOCIAL STATISTICS WITHOUT TEARS. New York: McGraw-Hill, 1977. xvi, 270 p. Appendix A: A Glossary of Terms and Symbols, pp. 249-60. Appendix B: Answers to Selected Problems, pp. 261-63. Appendix C: Tables, pp. 264-66. Index, pp. 267-70.

A text for a one-semester course in basic statistics for behavioral science students in two parts: "Description and Explanation" and "Statistical Inference." Topics include probability; relation between variables, including Yule's Q; relations of more than two variables; multiple regression; estimation and hypothesis testing; and chi-square. Chapters conclude with problems and references.

Johnson, Palmer O., and Jackson, Robert W.B. MODERN STATISTICAL METHODS: DESCRIPTIVE AND INDUCTIVE. Chicago: Rand McNally, 1959. ix, 514 p. Appendixes: Tables, pp. 499-505. Index of Names, pp. 507-8. Subject Index, pp. 509-14.

An early text for a course in basic statistics for students in education, psychology, and the social sciences who have knowledge of high school algebra. Techniques presented as rigorously as possible with only arithmetic. Avoids lengthy verbal discussions. Includes real examples. Topics include tests of hypotheses for proportions; tests in terms of frequencies, including chi-square; tests concerning variances; analysis of variance; properties of point estimators; simple and multiple regression; analysis of covariance; regression matching and the Johnson-Neyman method; discriminant function; and design of experiments. Chapters conclude with exercises and references.

Kirk, Roger E. INTRODUCTORY STATISTICS. Monterey, Calif.: Brooks/Cole, 1978. x, 438 p. Appendix A: Review of Basic Mathematics, pp. 368-78. Appendix B: Glossary of Symbols, pp. 379-84. Appendix C: Answers to Starred Exercises, pp. 385-402. Appendix D: Tables, pp. 403-25. Appendix E: Recommended Supplemental Readings, pp. 426-27. References, pp. 428-31. Index, pp. 432-38.

A text for a one-semester course for students in the behavioral sciences and education who have knowledge of high school algebra. Includes detailed derivations in notes at the end of the chapters. Extensive coverage given to probability, including Bayes' theorem; the logic of hypothesis testing; and factors affecting the Pearson product-moment correlation. Other topics include two-way analysis of variance; two-sample statistical inference; multiple regression; chi-square, and nonparametric tests. Sections conclude with exercises, summaries, and technical notes.

______, ed. STATISTICAL ISSUES: A READER FOR THE BEHAVIORAL SCIENCES. Monterey, Calif.: Brooks/Cole, 1972. xii, 401 p. Glossary, pp. 387-94. Name Index, pp. 395-97. Subject Index, pp. 398-401.

A supplementary text for an intermediate or basic statistics course. Consists of forty-five articles previously published in journals grouped under the following ten headings: "Behavioral Statistics: Historical Perspective and Applications" (five articles); "Measurement" (five articles); "Probability and Theoretical Distributions" (one article); "Hypothesis Testing and Confidence Intervals" (nine articles); "Correlation" (one article); "The Design of Experiments" (six articles); "Analysis of Variance" (three articles); "Comparisons Among Means" (eight articles); "Nonparametric Methods" (three articles); and "The Likelihood Function and Bayesian Statistical Methods" (four articles). Topics include scale classification; statistical treatment of football numbers; relation between confidence intervals and tests of significance; uses of statistical levels of significance in social sciences; statistical inference and nonrandom samples; assumptions in correlation analysis and analysis of variance; multiple comparisons in psychological research; approximate randomization tests; and uses of the likelihood function in inference.

Klugh, Henry E. STATISTICS: THE ESSENTIALS FOR RESEARCH. New York: Wiley, 1970. xiv, 368 p. Answers, pp. 310-37. Appendix: Tables, pp. 338-64. Index, pp. 365-68.

A text for a one-semester course for students in the behavioral sciences, particularly psychology and education. Emphasizes analysis of variance and most of the important nonparametric tests. Little space devoted to confidence intervals, with regression and correlation contained in a brief chapter. Other topics include probability rules; binomial and normal distributions; and chi-square. Also emphasizes intuitive understanding of concepts rather than mathematical rigor. Chapters conclude with exercises.

Knopp, Thomas R. STATISTICS FOR EDUCATIONAL MEASUREMENT. Scranton, Pa.: Intext Educational Publishers, 1971. xi, 88 p. Appendix: Supplement, pp. 77-84. References, pp. 85-86. Index, pp. 87-88.

A supplementary text dealing with statistical concepts of measurement problems for graduates and undergraduates in education who take a course in educational or psychological measurement without having had a prior course in statistics. Topics include probability, reliability, validity, item analysis, and sampling and tests of significance. The appendix contains summation signs and proofs.

Koenker, Robert H. SIMPLIFIED STATISTICS FOR STUDENTS IN EDUCATION AND PSYCHOLOGY. Rev. ed. Totowa, N.J.: Littlefield, Adams, 1971. xii, 171 p. Appendix, pp. 130-66. Bibliography, pp. 167-68. Index, pp. 169-71.

A text for a one-semester course in basic statistics and a supplementary text for a course in tests and measurement or an intermediate or advanced statistics course. Illustrative exercises and problems selected on basis of simplicity, and assumes knowledge of high school algebra. Topics include standard scores; product-moment and other correlations; comparing means and proportions; and chi-square. Chapters conclude with references. Appendix contains glossaries, formulas, terms, answers to problems, and statistical tables.

Kolstoe, Ralph H. INTRODUCTION TO STATISTICS FOR THE BEHAVIORAL SCIENCES. Dorsey Series in Psychology. Homewood, Ill.: Dorsey Press, 1969. xiii, 299 p. Appendix A: Part A--Tables, pp. 268-90. Appendix B: Part B--List of Computing Formulas, pp. 291-94. Index, pp. 295-99.

A text for a course in applied statistics with emphasis on the logic of statistical concepts. Topics include nominal scales; interval scales; normal and binomial probability distributions; sampling theory; simple regression and correlation scores for nominal and ordinal, and interval data, tests of significance between groups with interval, nominal, and ordinal scaling; analysis of variance; and planning experiments. Chapters conclude with summaries and references.

Korin, Basil P. STATISTICAL CONCEPTS FOR THE SOCIAL SCIENCES. Cambridge, Mass.: Winthrop, 1975. 407 p. Appendix A: A Brief Review of Mathematics, pp. 345-52. Appendix B: Summation Notation, pp. 353-56. Appendix C: Linear Transformations, pp. 357-62. Appendix D: Statistical Tables, pp. 363-86. Appendix E: Answers to Odd-Numbered Problems, pp. 387-400. Index, pp. 401-7.

A text for a one-semester course for students who have a high school algebra background. Topics include measures of correlation for data measured on interval, ordinal, and nominal scales; probability and random variables, sampling distributions; tests of hypothesis for difference between two means; tests for ordinal scale variables; simple regression; and one- and two-way analysis of variance. Derivations kept to a minimum with numerous examples worked out in detail. Chapters conclude with summaries, formulas, references, and problems.

Kossack, Carl F., and Henschke, Claudia I. INTRODUCTION TO STATISTICS AND COMPUTER PROGRAMMING. San Francisco: Holden-Day, 1975. xviii, 651 p. Appendix A: The Mechanics of Handling Numerical Data, pp. 587-89. Appendix B: General Programs, pp. 591-99. Appendix C: Tables, pp. 600-623. Appendix D: Probability Programs, pp. 625-44. Index, pp. 645-51.

A text for a one-year course for undergraduates in the social, biological, management, and behavioral sciences. Emphasizes data analysis, with instruction in FORTRAN programming included. Illustrative examples taken from a variety of fields.

Assumes knowledge of high school algebra. Topics include discrete and continuous random variables; sampling theory; estimation and hypothesis testing; decision theory; regression and correlation; chi-square; two-way analysis of variance; sample survey designs; and statistical classification. Chapters conclude with exercises.

Levin, Jack. ELEMENTARY STATISTICS IN SOCIAL RESEARCH. 3d ed., rev. and enl. New York: Harper & Row, 1977. x, 293 p. Appendix A: A Review of Some Fundamentals of Mathematics, pp. 246-50. Appendix B: Tables, pp. 251-80. Appendix C: List of Formulas, pp. 281-84. References, pp. 285-86. Answers to Selected Problems, pp. 287-90. Index, pp. 291-93.

A text for a one-semester course for students with limited mathematics background. Excludes derivations, but contains step-by-step illustration of statistical procedures. Consists of three parts: "Description"; "From Description to Decision Making"; and "Decision Making." Topics include analysis of variance; chi-square; nonparametric tests; correlation, including gamma and Pearson r; and application of statistical procedures to research. Chapters conclude with summaries and problems.

Levy, Sheldon G. INFERENTIAL STATISTICS IN THE BEHAVIORAL SCIENCES. New York: Holt, Rinehart and Winston, 1968. xiv, 267 p. References, p. 243. Appendix: Tables, pp. 245-59. Index, pp. 261-67.

A text for a one-semester course for students with a high school algebra background. Begins with a discussion of statistical inferences, with descriptive statistics brought in only where necessary to continue the inferential argument. Emphasizes the translation of real world problems into mathematical statements and the reinterpretation of the mathematical conclusion in terms of the real world. Topics include sets and probability; probability distributions; the Z and t tests for true means and differences between two means; scaling; inferential tests for nominal data; binomial and chi-square distributions with applications; matched groups; and F test for one-way analysis of variance.

Lieberman, Bernhardt, ed. CONTEMPORARY PROBLEMS IN STATISTICS: A BOOK OF READINGS FOR THE BEHAVIORAL SCIENCES. New York: Oxford University Press, 1971. xviii, 446 p. Index, pp. 441-46.

Forty-five reprints of articles previously published in journals and elsewhere, grouped under the following seven headings: "Measurement and Scales" (eight articles); "Inference and Null-Hypothesis Testing" (eight articles); "The One-Tail, Two-Tail Controversy" (eleven articles); "Bayesian Statistics" (five articles); "The Use and Misuse of Chi-Square" (seven articles);

"Violations of Assumptions" (three articles); and "Current Interpretations" (three articles). An overview precedes each group of articles. Useful as a supplementary text for basic and intermediate statistics courses.

Loether, Herman J., and McTavish, Donald G. DESCRIPTIVE STATISTICS FOR SOCIOLOGISTS: AN INTRODUCTION. Boston: Allyn & Bacon, 1974. xiv, 388 p. Appendix: Statistical Tables, pp. 363-76. Indexes, pp. 377-88.

A text for a one-semester course in descriptive statistics. Consists of the following five parts: "Some Basic Consideration"; "Descriptive Statistics: One Variable"; and "Summary and Conclusions." Topics include bivariate and conditional distributions; measures of association for nominal, ordinal, and interval variables; regression and correlation; partial correlation coefficients; path analysis and multiple regression; and space analysis in sociology. Chapters conclude with concepts to know, questions and problems, general references, and other references.

______. INFERENTIAL STATISTICS FOR SOCIOLOGISTS: AN INTRODUCTION. Boston: Allyn & Bacon, 1974. xiv, 319 p. Appendix: Statistical Tables, pp. 287-307. Name Index, pp. 308-9. Subject Index, pp. 310-19.

A text for a one-semester course in inferential statistics for sociology students who have completed the first semester of basic statistics. Consists of the following four parts: "Introduction to Inferential Statistics"; "Sampling and Probability--Some Basic Concepts"; "Hypothesis Testing"; and "Summary and Conclusions." Topics include rules of probability; combinatorial rules; random sampling, including cluster and stratified; binomial sampling distribution; point and interval estimation of means, proportions, and variances; tests of hypothesis; testing two- and k-samples for means and proportions; chi-square; and nonparametric tests. Chapters conclude with references, questions, and problems.

Lohnes, Paul R., and Cooley, William W. INTRODUCTION TO STATISTICAL PROCEDURES: WITH COMPUTER APPLICATIONS. New York: Wiley, 1968. xv, 280 p. References, pp. 240-41. Appendix, pp. 243-76. Index, pp. 277-80.

A text for a one-semester course for graduates and undergraduates in the behavioral sciences and education with emphasis on how to read and use computer programs for data analysis. Computer laboratory experiments applying Monte Carlo simulation techniques provide empirical demonstration of basic principles and distributions, such as sampling, randomization, the law of large numbers, and the central limit theorems. Topics include statistical procedures in research, including a description of sample survey data for project TALENT covering 440,000 students in over 1,300 high schools; univariate distributions; variability in measurements; computing statistical data such as means and variances using FORTRAN Monte Carlo studies of the variance estimates, using FORTRAN programs to generate observations for analysis; theoretical distributions including normal and chi-square with applications to Monte Carlo results; Monte Carlo demonstrations of t distributions; and prediction and correlation. Chapters include summaries, exercises, and questions, and most chapters also conclude with computer programs. Appendix includes symbols, project TALENT data, answers to selected exercises, summary of mathematical concepts used for understanding elementary statistical concepts, and theoretical distributions. FORTRAN programs are kept simple for instructional purposes, and can be run on IBM 1620, IBM 7090, and IBM 360 computers.

Lordahl, Daniel S. MODERN STATISTICS FOR BEHAVIORAL SCIENCES. New York: Ronald Press, 1967. xii, 365 p. Appendix: Tables, pp. 325-46. Glossary, pp. 347-52. Answers to Exercises, pp. 353-60. Index, pp. 361-65.

A text for a one-semester course with emphasis on the potential use of computers to solve problems. Omits much of the computational schemes found in other tests. Topics include analysis of variance; scale transformations; sampling distributions; chi-square; probability; correlation; and nonparametric tests. Chapters conclude with exercises.

Loveday, Robert. A SECOND COURSE IN STATISTICS. New York: Cambridge University Press, 1961. xi, 155 p. Glossary of Terms Used in This Work, pp. 132-36. Index, pp. 137-38. Appendix: Tables, pp. 139-55.

A self-study for college students who are encountering statistics for the first time and a supplementary text for a basic statistics course. Topics include probability, combinations and permutations; binomial and Poisson distributions; chi-square and contingency tables; sampling and significance tests for a single mean and difference between two means; quality control; least squares; and correlation by product-moment and rank. Includes detailed examples and exercises. Concludes with a chapter containing exercises.

______. STATISTICAL MATHEMATICS: A COMPANION TO A SECOND COURSE IN STATISTICS. Cambridge, Engl.: Cambridge University Press, 1973. viii, 104 p. Answers to Exercises, pp. 90-93. Glossary, pp. 94-101. Some Suggestions for Further Reading, p. 102. Index, pp. 103-4.

A mathematical companion to the author's A SECOND COURSE IN STATISTICS (above); useful as an aid to a deeper involvement in the subject. Begins with twenty-five preliminary revision exercises, followed by definitions, examples, properties, derivations, and exercises dealing with the following topics: continuous distributions, expectation, estimation of parameters, binomial distribution, and Poisson and exponential distributions. Concludes with one chapter on examples and exercises indicating future developments, and one chapter containing thirty miscellaneous exercises.

Lovejoy, Elijah P. STATISTICS FOR MATH HATERS. New York: Harper & Row, 1975. x, 275 p. Appendix: Tables, pp. 237-52. Flash Cards, pp. 253-70. Index, pp. 271-75.

A text for a one-semester course in data analysis for psychology students who have a minimal mathematics background. Consists of the following three parts: "The Sign Test and the Logic of Statistical Inference"; "The Normal Distribution and the Z-Test"; and "The t-Test, Correlation, and Chi-Square." Emphasizes statistical inference as part of one's basic reasoning process by using only a portion of the statistical tools ordinarily covered in a basic text. Treatment is very elementary and topics include an extrasensory perception experiment; probability and coin toss experiments; sign test; variance and Z scores; sampling distribution of the mean; normal distribution and the central limit theorem; normal approximation to the binomial; testing for the mean of a set of difference scores; correlation; chi-square; and testing for the difference between two population means. Chapters conclude with problems.

Lyman, Howard B. TEST SCORES AND WHAT THEY MEAN. Englewood Cliffs, N.J.: Prentice-Hall, 1963. xv, 223 p. Bibliography, pp. 187-90. Appendix, pp. 191-223. No index.

A text for a short interpretation-oriented measurement course, a refresher course in testing, or for an in-service course on the meaning of test results. Also useful in a supplementary text for courses in psychology, measurement, and testing. Topics include types of tests; attributes of the test; descriptive statistics; norms; derived scores (Z, t, AGCT, CEEB, and IQ); interindividual comparison; and profiles. Appendix contains glossary of terms, conversion table for derived scores, and summary of score characteristics.

Lynch, Mervin D., and Huntsberger, David V. ELEMENTS OF STATISTICAL INFERENCE FOR EDUCATION AND PSYCHOLOGY. Boston: Allyn & Bacon, 1976. ix, 437 p. Answers to Odd-Numbered Problems, pp. 363-72. Appendix: Tables, pp. 373-426. Index, pp. 427-37.

A text for a one-semester course and a reference for research workers. Derivations kept to a minimum with problems and exercises used to illustrate concepts. Topics include transformations and Z scores; sets and probability; tests of hypothesis concerning two samples; chi-square; sampling; regression and correlation; phi and biserial correlation; nonparametric tests; and one-way analysis of variance. Chapters conclude with problems and references.

McCall, Robert B. FUNDAMENTAL STATISTICS FOR PSYCHOLOGY. 2d ed. New York: Harcourt, Brace Jovanovich, 1975. x, 406 p. Appendix I: Review of Basic Mathematics, pp. 335-48. Appendix II: Tables, pp. 349-80. Answers to the Exercises, pp. 381-95. Glossary, pp. 397-400. Index, pp. 401-6.

A text for a one-semester course for students who have a high school algebra and geometry background. Emphasizes concepts rather than techniques, with most examples from psychology and education. Mathematical derivations and proofs kept to a minimum and contained in tables. Topics include simple regression and correlation; sampling distributions; hypothesis testing; one- and two-way analysis of variance; and nonparametric tests.

McCollough, Celeste, and Van Atta, Loche. INTRODUCTION TO DESCRIPTIVE STATISTICS AND CORRELATION: A PROGRAM FOR SELF-INSTRUCTION. New York: McGraw-Hill, 1965. xii, 159 p. No index.

A supplementary programmed text and a self-study for courses in basic statistics for students in the social sciences with emphasis on interpretation of concepts rather than on computation and derivations. Portions of frames left incomplete for filling in by students. Topics include central tendency and dispersion; percentiles and standard scores; linear functions; regression and correlation; and interpretation of the correlation in terms of error reduction.

McNemar, Quinn. PSYCHOLOGICAL STATISTICS. 4th ed., rev. New York: Wiley, 1969. vii, 529 p. Exercises and Questions, pp. 467-500. Index, pp. 521-29.

A text for a one-year course with emphasis on interpretations and assumptions of statistical concepts. Topics include joint probabilities; hypothesis testing; simple and multiple regression and correlation; biserial, tetrachoric, four point, and rank correlation; chi-square and contingency tables; analysis of variance, including four-way classification; covariance analysis nonparametric tests; and variance components estimation. Assumes knowledge of high school algebra.

Malec, Michael B. ESSENTIAL STATISTICS FOR SOCIAL RESEARCH. Philadelphia: J.B. Lippincott, 1977. x, 235 p. Appendix: Tables, pp. 199-229. References, pp. 230-31. Index, pp. 233-35.

A text for a one-semester course for students with a limited mathematics background. Excludes derivations and emphasizes understanding concepts. Topics include probability; sampling and estimation; hypothesis testing for difference between two means; analysis of variance; chi-square; Goodman and Kruskal's Tau; Spearman's rank-order correlation coefficient rho; and simple and multiple regression and correlation. Chapters conclude with references and quick quizzes.

Malik, Henrick J., and Mullen, Kenneth. A FIRST COURSE IN PROBABILITY AND STATISTICS. Reading, Mass.: Addison-Wesley, 1973. xii, 361 p. Appendix: Tables, pp. 313-38. Answers to Exercises, pp. 339-52. Index, pp. 353-61.

A text for a one-semester course for students from a variety of disciplines who have a pre-calculus background. Emphasizes the use of examples from a broad range of disciplines. Uses the theorem-proof-example sequence. Topics include probability and Bayes' theorem; random variables and expectation; discrete probability distributions; organization and analysis of data; interval estimation and hypothesis testing for difference between two means and two proportions; chi-square; simple and multiple regression; analysis of variance; and nonparametric tests.

Marascuilo, Leonard A. STATISTICAL METHODS FOR BEHAVIORAL SCIENCE RESEARCH. McGraw-Hill Series in Psychology. New York: McGraw-Hill, 1971. xx, 578 p. Appendix A: List of Statistical Tables, pp. 521-57. Appendix B: List of Statistical Terms, pp. 558-63. Appendix C: Answer Key, pp. 564-71. Appendix D: Supplementary Readings in Related Tests, pp. 572-74. Index, pp. 575-78.

A text for a one-year course for students with little mathematics training. Topics include set theory and the set theoretic approach to probability; combinatorial analysis; Bernoulli variables; discrete and continuous probability; point estimators; interval estimation; chi-square; hypothesis testing in one- and two-sample models; F distribution and tests of variances; chi-square; regression and correlation; analysis of variance; and analysis of covariance. Uses no calculus. Presentation more rigorous than most tests with many theorems proved. Chapters conclude with exercises.

Mendenhall, William; McClave, James T.; and Ramey, Madelaine. STATISTICS FOR PSYCHOLOGY. 2d ed., enl. North Scituate, Mass.: Duxbury, 1977. ix, 502 p. Appendix I: Useful Statistical Tests and Confidence Intervals, pp. 449-52. Appendix II: Statistical Tables, pp. 453-89. Glossary, pp. 490-93. Answers to Exercises, pp. 494-99. Index, pp. 501-2.

A test for a one-semester course with emphasis on the role of inference and the relative frequency definition of probability. Excludes derivations. Topics include random variables and their distributions; binomial and normal distributions; nonparametric tests; estimation and hypothesis testing; design of experiments; two-way analysis of variance; linear regression and correlation; and chi-square. Sections conclude with exercises, and chapters conclude with references.

Minium, Edward W. STATISTICAL REASONING IN PSYCHOLOGY AND EDUCATION. 2d ed., rev. New York: Wiley, 1978. xii, 564 p. Appendix A: Review of Basic Mathematics, pp. 471-87. Appendix B: Summation Rules, pp. 488-89. Appendix C: List of Symbols, pp. 490-92. Appendix D: Useful Formulas, pp. 493-98. Appendix E: Answers to Problems and Exercises, pp. 499-519. Appendix F: Statistical Tables, pp. 520-51. Index, pp. 553-64.

A text for a one-year course. Emphasizes understanding statistical concepts and assumptions in the use of techniques. Topics include normal curve; regression, correlation, and prediction; hypothesis testing concerning the difference between two means; two-way analysis of variance; chi-square; and nonparametric tests. Chapters conclude with notes, problems, and exercises.

Moore, Peter Gerald. PRINCIPLES OF STATISTICAL TECHNIQUES: A FIRST COURSE, FROM THE BEGINNINGS, FOR SCHOOLS AND UNIVERSITIES. 2d ed., rev. New York: Cambridge University Press, 1969. viii, 288 p. Solutions to Exercises, pp. 278-84. Bibliography, p. 285. Index, pp. 286-88.

A reference for a course for students with a high school algebra background. Provides numerous examples from a wide range of reports, magazines, journals, and books. Coverage of topics is selective and includes probability and sampling; binomial theorem; rules of probability; normal curve and tests of significance; sampling techniques; simulation; time series; and pairs of characteristics.

Morrison, Denton E., and Henkel, Ramon E., eds. THE SIGNIFICANCE TEST CONTROVERSY: A READER. Methodological Perspectives. Chicago: Aldine, 1970. xviii, 333 p. References, pp. 313-24. Index, pp. 325-33.

Thirty-one reprints of articles previously published in journals and elsewhere which deal critically with the use of significance tests in behavioral research, grouped under the following headings: "Critical Historical Context" (three papers); "The Controversy in Sociology" (nineteen papers); "Criticism by Psychologists" (five papers); "Criticism From Other Quarters" (three papers); and "Epilogue" (one paper). Uses no mathematical formulas. Topics include significance as interpreted by R.A. Fisher, the significance of insignificant differences, the fallacy of the null hypothesis significance test, tests of significance considered as evidence, and the sacredness of .05.

Mosteller, Frederick; Kruskal, William H.; Pieters, Richard S.; Rising, Gerald R.; and Link, Richard F., eds. With the Assistance of Martha Zelinka. STATISTICS BY EXAMPLE: EXPLORING DATA. Addison-Wesley Innovative Series.

Reading, Mass.: Addison-Wesley, 1973. xvi, 125 p. Index, pp. 121-25.

Part one of a four-part series on teaching statistics through real life problems. Shows how to organize data tabularly and graphically and introduces probability in circumstances where simple counting is encountered in real life. Consists of fourteen problems, including organizing and reading population data; fractions on closing stock market prices; points and fouls in basketball; collegiate football series; ratings of typewriters; the cost of eating; testing beer tasters; Tom Paine and social security; and fruit flies. Includes examples and exercises. Useful as a supplementary text for basic statistics.

Mosteller, Frederick; Pieters, Richard S.; Kruskal, William H.; Rising, Gerald R.; and Link, Richard F., eds. With the Assistance of Roger Carlson and Martha Zelinka. STATISTICS BY EXAMPLE: WEIGHING CHANCES. Addison-Wesley Innovative Series. Reading, Mass.: Addison-Wesley, 1973. vix, 144 p. Index, pp. 141-44.

Part two of a four-part series on teaching statistics through real life examples. Develops probability concepts by means of random variables, simulations, and simple probability models, using the idea of scatter and residuals for developing ideas on the analysis of data. Contains fourteen real life problems, including plagiarism and probability; random digits and their uses; black and white survival in the United States; chi-square procedures; sample size; periodicities and moving averages; and prediction of election results from early returns. Includes examples and exercises.

Mosteller, Frederick; Rourke, Robert E.K.; and Thomas, George B., Jr. PROBABILITY WITH STATISTICAL APPLICATIONS. 2d ed., rev. Addison-Wesley Series in Statistics. Reading, Mass.: Addison-Wesley, 1970. xv, 527 p. Projects for High-Speed Computers, pp. 449-54. Appendix 1: Summations and Subscripts, pp. 457-64. Appendix 2: A Theorem on Independence, pp. 465-67. Bibliography, pp. 468-99. Answers to Even-Numbered Exercises, pp. 501-18. Index, pp. 521-27.

A text for a one-year course in elementary discrete probability for students from a variety of disciplines who have knowledge of high school algebra. Includes hypothetical examples and proofs of theorems. Topics include finite sample spaces with extensions to countably infinite sample spaces; discrete random variables and their distributions; normal distribution in probability and statistics; continuous random variables, joint probability distributions central limit theorem; estimation and hypothesis testing; operating characteristic curve; contingency tables; Bayesian approach; sampling theory; dependent random variables; least squares; and tests for the difference between two means. Sections conclude with exercises.

Mueller, John H.; Schuessler, Karl F.; and Costner, Herbert L. STATISTICAL REASONING IN SOCIOLOGY. 3d ed., rev. and enl. Boston: Houghton Mifflin, 1977. xvi, 544 p. Selected References, pp. 499-500. Appendix: Tables, pp. 501-34. Name Index, pp. 535-36. Subject Index, pp. 537-44.

A text for a two-semester course for students who have at least a high school algebra background. Falls naturally into two parts: descriptive statistics and inferential statistics. Formulas and results stated without proof. Topics include measurement of social variables; grouping of qualitative data; norming operations, including standardized scores; variation, including normal distribution; measures of association, including Kruskal's Tau and gamma for measuring relative reduction in prediction error; simple and multiple regression and correlation; path analysis; events and probability; binomial probabilities; sampling; interval estimation; hypothesis testing for difference between two means; distribution-free tests; component analysis; two-way analysis of variance; and multivariate contingency analysis. Problems deal with simple numerical applications and appear at the ends of sections. Chapters conclude with references.

Nemenyi, Peter; Dixon, Sylviak; and White, Nathaniel B., Jr. STATISTICS FROM SCRATCH. Holden-Day Series in Probability and Statistics. San Francisco: Holden-Day, 1977. vi, 630 p. Tables, pp. 555-630. No index.

A text for a one-semester course using an extremely elementary style, often folksy and friendly. Assumes knowledge of only one year of high school algebra. Order of presentation somewhat different from that found in other texts. For example, confidence intervals is taken up before probability. Topics include sets and probability; life insurance and the probability of dying; hypothesis testing, including the comparison of two sets of measurements; normal curve; quality control Mann-Whitney tests; simple regression and correlation; Kendall's correlation; and introduction to analysis of variance.

Noether, Gottfried Emanuel. INTRODUCTION TO STATISTICS: A FRESH APPROACH. Houghton Mifflin Series in Statistics. Boston: Houghton Mifflin, 1971. xvi, 253 p. Answers to Selected Problems, pp. 215-16. Tables, pp. 217-47. Bibliography, pp. 249-50. Index, pp. 251-53.

A text for a two-semester course which stresses basic ideas without becoming involved in technical and computational detail. Estimation and hypothesis testing discussed in terms of the binomial model, and one-, two-, and k-sample problems solved nonparametrically before the introduction of t-tests and the analysis of variance; rank correlation precedes least squares regression and product-moment correlation. Other topics include random variables, including joint and marginal distributions of two random variables and chi-square. Assumes knowledge of high school algebra. Chapters conclude with problems.

Novick, Melvin R., and Jackson, Paul H. STATISTICAL METHODS FOR EDUCATION AND PSYCHOLOGICAL RESEARCH. McGraw-Hill Series in Psychology. New York: McGraw-Hill, 1974. xviii, 456 p. Appendix: Tables, pp. 359-451. Index, pp. 453-56.

A text for a second course in basic statistics and data analysis for students who have already taken one or two semesters of introductory statistics. Consists of the following three parts: "Problems, Data, and Probability Models"; "Elementary Bayesian Methods"; and "Bayesian Methods for Comparing Parameters." Topics include Bayesian analysis of binary data; Bayesian inference for the normal model; Bayesian inference for two normal distributions; regression and the bivariate normal model; and Bayesian analysis of discrete data. Includes a large number of detailed examples. Chapters conclude with exercises.

Nunnally, Jum C. With the Collaboration of Robert L. Durham, L. Charles Lemond, and William H. Wilson. INTRODUCTION TO STATISTICS FOR PSYCHOLOGY AND EDUCATION. New York: McGraw-Hill, 1975. x, 432 p. Appendix A: List of Frequently Used Statistical Terms, pp. 308-15. Appendix B: Statistical Tables, pp. 317-38. References, p. 339. Index, pp. 340-42.

A comprehensive text for a one-semester terminal course with emphasis on understanding concepts rather than on developing a high level of skill in the actual use of statistics. Consists of the following four parts: "Fundamental Concepts"; "Descriptive Statistics"; "Inferential Statistics"; and "Nonparametric Statistics." Topics include nature and importance of statistics; history of quantification; research design; product-moment correlation; inferences regarding population means, variances, and correlation coefficients; analysis of variance; multiple comparisons; factorial designs; analysis of categorical data; and analysis of ranks. Chapters conclude with study questions, problems, and references.

Ott, Lyman; Mendenhall, William; and Larson, Richard F. STATISTICS: A TOOL FOR THE SOCIAL SCIENCES. 2d ed., rev. North Scituate, Mass.: Duxbury, 1978. xi, 531 p. Appendix: Tables, pp. 459-85. Glossary of Common Statistical Terms, pp. 487-90. Answers to Exercises, pp. 491-525. Index, pp. 527-31.

A text for a one-semester course which gives equal time to descriptive statistics and inferential statistics, reduces dependency on mathematics, and provides examples using actual data on individuals, groups, societies, and organizations. Topics include probability, inference, and sampling distributions; estimation and hypothesis testing concerning two samples; cross-classification of data; McNemar test; measures of association for nominal and ordinal data; regression and correlation; and analysis of variance. Chapters conclude with references and problems.

Palumbo, Dennis J. STATISTICS IN POLITICAL AND BEHAVIORAL SCIENCE. Rev. ed. New York: Columbia University Press, 1977. xv, 469 p. Appendix A: Exercises and Study Suggestions, pp. 403-30; Answers for Selected Exercises, pp. 431-38. Appendix B: Statistical Tables, pp. 439-64. Index, pp. 465-69.

A text for a course in basic statistics for students in political science. Includes mathematical proofs of some theorems. Consists of the following two parts: "Descriptive Statistics" and "Inferential Statistics." Topics include measures of association for nominal- and ordinal-scale data; simple linear correlation and regression; partial and multiple correlation and regression; time series; factor analysis; set theory and probability; sampling distributions; hypothesis testing, including tests for nominal- and ordinal-scale data; analysis of variance; sample design and elements of sampling theory. Chapters conclude with selected references.

Peatman, John Gray. INTRODUCTION TO APPLIED STATISTICS. New York: Harper and Row, 1963. xv, 458 p. References, pp. 387-90. Appendix: Tables, pp. 391-445. Index, pp. 447-58.

A text for a one-semester course in basic statistics for students in psychology who have knowledge of elementary algebra. Topics include normal probability; Pearson's r correlation and regression; Spearman's rank-difference method; point-biserial correlation; rank-difference correlation as a distribution-free method; probability, sampling, and inferential statistics; interval estimation of population means, variances, proportions, medians, and correlation coefficients; significance tests for means, variances, correlations, and differences between means and correlations; analysis of variance and experimental design; and nonparametric methods. Each chapter begins with an overview of its content.

Pine, Vanderlyn R. INTRODUCTION TO SOCIAL STATISTICS. Prentice-Hall Methods of Social Science Series. Englewood Cliffs, N.J.: Prentice-Hall, 1977. xiv, 415 p. Appendix: Statistical Tables, pp. 394-403. Index, pp. 405-15.

A text for a one-semester course for students who know only arithmetic. Consists of the following six parts: "Classificatory Descriptive Statistics"; "Univariate Descriptive Statistics"; "Bivariate Descriptive Statistics"; "Multivariate Descriptive Statistics"; "Inferential Statistics"; and "Multivariate Causal Analytic Statistics." Topics familiar in everyday life translated into statistics with results applied to less familiar concepts. Chapters conclude with exercises.

Popham, W. James, and Sirotnik, Kenneth A. EDUCATIONAL STATISTICS: USE AND INTERPRETATION. 2d ed. Exploration Series in Education. New York: Harper and Row, 1973. xii, 413 p. Answers to Exercises, pp. 342-53. Appendix: Tables, pp. 354-404.

A text for a one-semester course. Relies on the verbal and graphic techniques rather than on mathematical exposition. Topics include correlation; regression; t-test; analysis of variance and covariance; factor analysis; and nonparametric statistics. Chapters conclude with problems and references.

Ray, William S. STATISTICS IN PSYCHOLOGICAL RESEARCH. New York: Macmillan, 1962. xi, 303 p. Appendix: Tables, pp. 295-300. Index, pp. 301-3.

A text for a one-semester course for students who have knowledge of college algebra. Topics include index of summation; index of skewness; transformations; describing data by means of moments; product moments; partial and multiple correlation; multiple prediction with standard scores; analysis of variability; sampling theory; sampling distribution; statistical inference; and experimental inference. Emphasizes the distinction between descriptive and inferential statistics, between experimental and nonexperimental research, and between testing for significance and estimating parameters.

Runyon, Richard P. DESCRIPTIVE AND INFERENTIAL STATISTICS: A CONTEMPORARY APPROACH. Reading, Mass.: Addison-Wesley, 1977. viii, 354 p. Appendix: Tables, pp. 261-92. Answers, pp. 294-350. Index, pp. 351-54.

A text for a one-year course in basic statistics for students in the behavioral sciences. Also ideal for self-study because of the building block nature of the presentation. Emphasizes computational procedures. Topics include standard scores; correlation for quantitative and ordinal variables; regression and prediction; tests of hypotheses; interval estimation; Pearson r; power of a test; one- and two-way analysis of variance; and factorial designs. Exercises included; chapters conclude with tests.

Runyon, Richard P., and Haber, Audrey. FUNDAMENTALS OF BEHAVIORAL STATISTICS. 3d ed., rev. Addison-Wesley Series in Psychology. Reading, Mass.: Addison-Wesley, 1976. xvii, 446 p. References, pp. 351-56. Appendix I: Review of Basic Mathematics, pp. 357-66. Appendix II: Glossary of Symbols, pp. 367-72. Appendix III: Tables, pp. 373-410. Answers to Selected Exercises, pp. 411-34. Index, pp. 435-46.

A text for a one-semester course. Consists of three parts: "Descriptive Statistics"; "Parametric Tests of Significance"; and "Nonparametric Tests of Significance." Includes some proofs. Topics include regression and correlation; probability; inference and hypothesis testing; analysis of variance; power and efficiency of tests; inference with categorical variables; inference with ordinally scaled variables; Mann-Whitney U-test; and Wilsoxon matched-pair signed-rank test. Chapters conclude with exercises.

Schmidt, Marty J. UNDERSTANDING AND USING STATISTICS: BASIC CONCEPTS. Lexington, Mass.: Heath, 1975. x, 361 p. Appendixes: Tables, pp. 315-34. Glossary, pp. 335-52. Annotated Bibliography, pp. 353-54. Index, pp. 355-61.

A text for a one-semester course for students of psychology who know only arithmetic. Emphasizes principles and ideas rather than a large number of methods. Excludes derivations. Useful as a supplementary text for a more advanced course. Topics include nominal, ordinal, interval, ratio, and absolute level measurement; Z-scores; normal distribution; correlation; product-moment and rank-difference correlations; simple regression; frequency and axiomatic definitions of probability; hypothesis testing for difference between two means; and chi-square. Chapters conclude with problems.

Schuessler, Karl. ANALYZING SOCIAL DATA: A STATISTICAL ORIENTATION. Boston: Houghton Mifflin, 1971. xv, 476 p. Appendix: Tables, pp. 433-62. Answers, pp. 463-68. Index of Names, pp. 469-72. Index of Topics, pp. 473-76.

A text for an intermediate course for students who have gone through at least one semester of basic statistics. Emphasizes data analysis using examples, rather than causal analysis. Topics include correlations (simple, multiple, and partial); factors to correlations, including one-, two-, and multiple-factor models; correlations to factors, including the diagonal, centroid, and principal-factor methods; analysis of variance and covariance; multi-stage sampling; attitude measurement; the analysis of errors; and methods of transforming statistical data. Chapters conclude with exercises and references.

Schutle, Jerald G. EVERYTHING YOU ALWAYS WANTED TO KNOW ABOUT ELEMENTARY STATISTICS (BUT WERE AFRAID TO ASK). Englewood Cliffs, N.J.: Prentice-Hall, 1977. x, 230 p. Appendix 1: Historical Notes, pp. 187-96. Appendix 2: Glossary of Symbols, pp. 197-202. Appendix 3: Algebra, the Slide Rule, Calculators, and Other Forgotten Topics, pp. 203-12. Tables of Significance, pp. 213-26. Index, pp. 227-30.

A supplementary text for a basic statistics course for students in the social sciences. Employs the question and answer format and periodically introduces the mathematical logic behind formulas and derivations. Consists of four parts; "Introduction"; "Description"; "Inference"; and "Nonparametric Alternatives." Topics include probability and sampling; single- and two-sample tests; and multiple-sample tests.

Senders, Virginia L. MEASUREMENT AND STATISTICS: A BASIC TEXT EMPHASIZING BEHAVIORAL SCIENCE APPLICATIONS. New York: Oxford University Press, 1958. xvi, 594 p. Appendix: Tables, pp. 529-80. Index, pp. 581-94.

A text for one-year course for students with a high school algebra background. Topics include nomical and ordinal scales; frequency distributions; theoretical distributions; measures of correlation for interval and ratio scales; probability; tests of hypothesis; inferences from nominally scaled and ordinally scaled data; inferential statistics for data from interval and ratio scales; and analysis of variance for interval and ratio scales. Sections conclude with questions; chapters conclude with references and answers.

Senter, R.J. ANALYSIS OF DATA: INTRODUCTORY STATISTICS FOR THE BEHAVIORAL SCIENCES. Glenview, Ill.: Scott, Foresman, 1969. x, 512 p. Appendix A: A Brief Review of Basic Arithmetic Operations, pp. 458-70. Appendix B: Statistical Tables, pp. 471-506. Index, pp. 507-12.

A text for a one-semester course for students with a high school algebra background. Includes descriptive statistics, sampling statistics with emphasis on methods for examining differences between and among sets of data, and correlation techniques.

Smith, G. Milton. A SIMPLIFIED GUIDE TO STATISTICS FOR PSYCHOLOGY AND EDUCATION. 4th ed., enl. New York: Holt, Rinehart and Winston, 1970. x, 244 p. Selected Answers to Exercises, pp. 233-38. Index, pp. 239-44.

A text for a short introductory course and a supplementary text for more difficult courses. Presentation confined largely to a listing of formulas and a working out of applications with a minimum of explanation. Topics include distribution of scores; measures of central tendency; measures of variability; standard scores for comparing and combining test results; probabilities determined from a normal distribution; significance tests for the difference between the means of large and small samples; decision making and the power of significance tests; two-factor analysis of variance; correlation; chi-square; and tests based on the order of scores. Chapters conclude with exercises.

Spence, Janet T.; Cotton, John W.; Underwood, Benton J.; and Duncan, Carl P. ELEMENTARY STATISTICS. 3d ed., rev. and enl. Englewood Cliffs, N.J.: Prentice-Hall, 1976. vii, 282 p. Appendix I: List of Formulas, pp. 245-52. Appendix II: Tables, pp. 253-78. Index, pp. 279-82.

A text for a one-semester course with emphasis on sampling theory and design of experiments, nonparametric tests, and correlation. Omits derivations.

Sprowls, R. Clay. ELEMENTARY STATISTICS FOR STUDENTS OF SOCIAL SCIENCE AND BUSINESS. New York: McGraw-Hill, 1955. xiii, 392 p. Appendix A: Statistical Tables, pp. 369-82. Appendix B: Glossary of Symbols, pp. 383-85. Index, pp. 387-92.

A text for a one-semester course. Based on four fundamental exercises: an experiment in sampling a bead box, a random sampling experiment, a personal decision problem, and a term project. Supplemented by other exercises and problems in all sections. Topics include statistical inference using binomial distribution; acceptance sampling in industrial quality control; statistical-research methodology; descriptive statistics; inference; regression and correlation; and time series and index numbers. Chapters conclude with exercises and references.

Stahl, Sidney M., and Hennes, James D. READING AND UNDERSTANDING APPLIED STATISTICS: A SELF-LEARNING APPROACH. St. Louis, Mo.: C.V. Mosby, 1975. xvii, 318 p. Appendix A: Statistical Tables, pp. 288-303. Appendix B: Answers to Examinations, pp. 304-10. Appendix C: Formulas, pp. 311-13. References, pp. 314-15. Index, pp. 316-18.

A self-study for students of sociology, education, psychology, and health science who are seeking their own introduction and understanding of applied statistics, and for professionals who must be able to read critically the literature in their own fields. Also useful as a supplementary text in basic statistics. Covers both descriptive and inferential statistics, with an introduction to scientific methodology. Learning objectives and self-examinations provided in each chapter. Requires thirty hours to complete.

Steger, Joseph A. READINGS IN STATISTICS FOR THE BEHAVIORAL SCIENTIST. New York: Holt, Rinehart and Winston, 1971. ix, 406 p. Index, pp. 401-6.

Thirty-three reprints of articles designed as a supplementary text for basic courses in statistical methods and research design. Acquaints students with original articles and increases his awareness of the use, misuse, and limitations of statistics. Articles are grouped under the following five headings: "Measurement and Statistics" (four articles); "Chi-Square" (seven articles); "Parametric Techniques" (three articles); "Assumptions and Statistical Inference" (fifteen articles); and "Potpourri" (four articles). Topics include scales of measurement; use and misuse of chi-square; use of transformations; nature and use of analysis of covariance; one- and two-tailed tests; fallacy of the null hypothesis; relation between scientific and statistical hypotheses; effects of violations of assumptions; and degree of freedom.

Stilson, Donald W. PROBABILITY AND STATISTICS IN PSYCHOLOGICAL RESEARCH AND THEORY. San Francisco: Holden-Day, 1966. xii, 507 p. Appendixes, pp. 463-99. Index, pp. 501-7.

A text for a two-semester course for students familiar with college algebra who have had a brief introduction to statistical methods. Most chapters contain sections devoted to applications of probability and statistics to psychological theory, with both algebraic proofs and intuitive clarifications included. Topics include random variables, measurement; multivariate probability distributions; expected values and their distributions; matching theorem of Estes-Burke learning theory; covariance and correlation; sampling distribution; and estimation and hypothesis testing. Appendixes contain statistical tables and answers to odd-numbered problems. Chapters conclude with references.

Tai, Simon W. SOCIAL SCIENCE STATISTICS: ITS ELEMENTS AND APPLICATIONS. Santa Monica, Calif.: Goodyear, 1978. xiv, 426 p. Appendix: Tables, pp. 385-415. Index, pp. 416-26.

A text for a one-semester course. Consists of three parts: "Describing and Presenting Data"; "Inferences from Sample to Population"; and "Assessing Relationships Among Variables." Example oriented with illustrations of human behavior; excludes coin toss, dice throw, and animal experiments. Topics include sets and probability; rules of probability; sampling distributions and inferences; tests of hypotheses; chi-square; linear correlation and regression; measures of association for normal distributions; and Spearman's Rho coefficient. Chapters conclude with exercises and references.

Tanur, Judith M.; Mosteller, Frederick; Kruskal, William H.; Link, Richard F.; Pieters, Richard S.; Rising, Gerald R.; and Lehmann, E.L., eds. STATISTICS: A GUIDE TO POLITICAL AND SOCIAL ISSUES. Holden-Day Series in Probability and Statistics. San Francisco: Holden-Day, 1977. x, 141 p. Index, pp. 137-41.

Twelve nontechnical essays taken from STATISTICS: A GUIDE TO THE UNKNOWN and one new reprint taken from a journal all on simplified uses of statistics and probability in political science. Useful as an auxiliary text for an introductory course in basic statistics. Topics include calibrating college board scores; measuring the effects of social innovations by means of time series; opinion polling; traffic accidents; election; and registration and voting.

Taylor, Peter A. AN INTRODUCTION TO STATISTICAL METHODS. Itasca, Ill.: F.E. Peacock, 1972. xiv, 321 p. Bibliography and Suggestions for Further Reading, pp. 253-55. Appendix: Tables, pp. 257-318. Index, pp. 319-21.

A text (also work-text and supplementary text) for a one-semester course in basic statistics for students in the behavioral sciences who know only arithmetic. Descriptive statistics passed over quickly, and topics include product-moment correlation; probability; random sampling; chi-square; nonparametric tests; other types of correlations; regression and prediction; analysis of variance with random effects and mixed effects; and analysis of covariance. Chapters conclude with problems and answers.

Townsend, Edward Arthur, and Burke, Paul J. USING STATISTICS IN CLASSROOM INSTRUCTION. Current Topics in Classroom Instruction Series. New York: Macmillan, 1975. xiii, 94 p. Appendixes A to F, pp. 67-92. Index, pp. 93-94.

A pamphlet on procedures of using statistical data by classroom teachers for class sizes of twenty-five to thirty-five students using only arithmetic and hand calculations. Examples and charts provided. Chapter titles: "Scores"; "Central Tendency"; "Variability"; "Common Reporting Practices"; "Relationships Among Scores"; and "Interpreting Test Scores." Appendixes devoted to answers, tables, and references.

Turney, Billy L., and Roff, George P. SIMPLIFIED STATISTICS FOR EDUCATION AND PSYCHOLOGY: A WORK-TEXT WITH FEEDBACK. Scranton, Pa.: International Textbook, 1968. xi, 140 p. Suggested References, pp. 131-32. Calculation and Square Root, pp. 133-34. Appendix: Tables, pp. 135-38. Index, pp. 139-40.

A supplementary text for a course in basic statistics and self-study. Practical exercises and immediate feedback provided at the end of each chapter. Topics include graphic presentation; percentiles; measures of central tendency and dispersion; normal curve; sampling distribution and inference; significance of the difference between two means; and correlation.

Walker, Helen Mary. MATHEMATICS ESSENTIAL FOR ELEMENTARY STATISTICS: A SELF TEACHING MANUAL. Rev. ed. New York: Henry Holt, 1951. xiii, 382 p. Appendix, pp. 325-28. Tables, pp. 330-35. Answer Key, pp. 337-76. Index, pp. 377-82.

A review of mathematics essential for a self-study of statistics including decimals and fractions, algebraic symbols; directed numbers; simple functions and their graphs; inequalities; linear interpolation; square root; exponents and radicals; logarithms; the binomial expansion; and equations of second degree in two variables. Appendixes include the Greek alphabet and the metric and English systems.

Walker, Helen M[ary]., and Lev, Joseph. ELEMENTARY STATISTICAL METHODS. 3d ed., rev. International Series in Decision Processes. New York: Holt, Rinehart and Winston, 1969. xvi, 432 p. List of Tables in Appendix, p. 352. Appendix: Tables, pp. 353-81. Greek Alphabet, p. 382. List of Formulas, pp. 383-97. List of Figures in Text, pp. 398-400. List of Tables in Text, pp. 401-5. Glossary of Symbols, pp. 406-11. Answers, pp. 413-22. Index, pp. 423-32.

A text for a one-year course for students of education who have knowledge of high school algebra. Topics include normal distribution; estimation and hypothesis testing, simple regression and correlation; chi-square; inferences about populations on categorical variables; one-way analysis of variance; and multiple regression and correlation. Exercises at the ends of the sections intended to clarify concepts and encourage students to extend the concepts.

______. STATISTICAL INFERENCE. New York: Henry Holt, 1953. xi, 510 p. Tables and Charts, pp. 453-87. Glossary of Symbols, pp. 488-93. Answers to Problems, pp. 494-501. Index to Subject Matter, pp. 503-8. Index to Authors, pp. 509-10.

An early text for a course in inferential statistics for students who have taken a course in descriptive statistics. Omits derivations and emphasizes the verbal style with illustrative examples. Topics include probability distributions; inferences concerning standard deviations; chi-square; analysis of variance; simple and multiple regression and correlation; Latin squares; biserial correlation and other measures of association; transformation of scales; and nonparametric tests. Sections conclude with exercises, and chapters conclude with references.

Weinberg, George H., and Shumaker, John A. STATISTICS: AN INTUITIVE APPROACH. Belmont, Calif.: Wadsworth, 1962. xii, 338 p. Appendixes, pp. 307-30. Index, pp. 331-38.

A supplementary text for a basic statistics course for students in education, sociology, and psychology who have limited mathematics knowledge. Emphasizes developing insights into concepts using simple numerical examples. Self-contained and should be useful to anyone who wishes to develop statistical literacy without taking a statistical course. Topics include random and stratified random sampling; the abuse of statistics; measures of central tendency and variability; determining the shape of a distribution; normal distribution; probability and sampling from normal distributions; estimation and hypothesis testing; chi-square and independence; regression and correlation; prediction; and nonparametric tests. Chapters conclude with problems.

Weiss, Robert S. STATISTICS IN SOCIAL RESEARCH: AN INTRODUCTION. New York: Wiley, 1968. x, 369 p. Appendix 1: Tables, pp. 309-22. Appendix 2: Data, pp. 323-61. Index, pp. 363-69.

A text for a one-semester course for students in the social sciences and a guide for the professional embarking on quantitative research for the first time. More emphasis given to data collection, descriptive statistics, and tests for nominal and ordinal data, and less to correlation than customary.

Omits regression, errors of estimate, and curvilinear association. Appendix 2 contains data on one hundred respondents in a national sample survey that considered the attitudes of women toward childrearing. Useful for problem assignment. Other topics include measures of association based on nominal, ordinal, and metric data; sampling; and reporting results. Chapters conclude with problems.

Welkowitz, Joan; Ewen, Robert B.; and Cohen, Jacob. INTRODUCTORY STATISTICS FOR THE BEHAVIORAL SCIENCES. New York: Academic Press, 1971. xvi, 271 p. Appendix: Tables, pp. 243-66. Index, pp. 267-71.

A text for a one-semester course for students who know only arithmetic. Avoids a strictly cookbook approach, while explaining concepts clearly and verbally, with emphasis given to robustness of parametric procedures (i.e., t and F tests are shown to yield accurate results even if the assumptions of equal variance and normality are not met). Topics include Z and t scores; normal curve; hypothesis testing about differences between two means; linear regression and correlation; power curve analysis; one- and two-way analysis of variance; and chi-square.

Wike, Edward L. DATA ANALYSIS: A STATISTICAL PRIMER FOR PSYCHOLOGY STUDENTS. Chicago: Aldine-Atherton, 1971. x, 256 p. Answers to Even-Numbered Problems, pp. 177-79. References, pp. 181-85. Appendix: Tables, pp. 187-248. Index, pp. 249-56.

A reference on data analysis for undergraduate students who are trying to do research for the first time as well as a reference for graduate students and research workers. Examples based on real data from experiments with emphasis on techniques for performing multiple comparisons. Topics include the search for indicators; means of two and k independent groups; means of two matched groups; multiple comparisons for k matched groups; multiple comparison location tests; class frequencies of k independent groups and of k matched groups; multiple comparisons of class frequencies with k matched groups; and linear and curvilinear relationships. Chapters conclude with problems.

Willemsen, Eleanor Walker. UNDERSTANDING STATISTICAL REASONING: HOW TO EVALUATE RESEARCH LITERATURE IN THE BEHAVIORAL SCIENCES. San Francisco: Freeman and Co., 1974. xi, 223 p. Index, pp. 217-23.

A text and reference for students, teachers, and researchers who have had one year of basic statistics. Helps the reader understand statistical reasoning which arises in critical reading and interpretation of research literature in the behavioral sciences. Topics include the logic of drawing conclusions from empirical investigations; correlation, including Pearson product-moment coefficient; analysis of variance; multivariate analysis; nonparametric tests; and a checklist for individual articles. Useful to anyone writing a research report or planning a new research project.

Willoughby, Stephen S., and Vogeli, Bruce R. PROBABILITY AND STATISTICS. Morristown, N.J.: Silver Burdett Co., 1968. vi, 216 p. Appendix I: Sets, pp. 185-88. Appendix II: Summations, pp. 189-93. Tables, pp. 194-209. Index, pp. 210-16.

A text for a one-semester course in probability and statistics for students in the biological and social sciences who have knowledge of elementary set theory. Includes some derivations and proofs, with numerous examples for illustrating concepts. Unique in the large number of exercises at the ends of the sections and review exercises at the ends of the chapters. Topics include combinatorial concepts; axiomatic probability; Bayes' theorem; descriptive statistics; binomial and normal distributions; sampling distribution and estimation theory; hypothesis testing; statistical quality control; and game theory. Omits random variable concept.

Wyatt, Woodrow W., and Bridges, Charles M., Jr. STATISTICS FOR THE BEHAVIORAL SCIENCES. Boston: D.C. Heath, 1967. xv, 389 p. Appendix A: Tables, pp. 269-362. Appendix B: School and College Ability Test Scores, Verbal (X) and Quantitative (Y), for 995 College Freshman, pp. 363-68. Appendix C: Analysis-of-Data Sheet, pp. 369-70. Answers to Problems, pp. 371-80. Index, pp. 381-89.

A text for a one-year course for students who have knowledge of high school algebra and geometry. Introduces sample, population, and decision making early in order to prepare the student for the design of experiments, hypothesis testing, and statistical inference. Significance tests demonstrate how the student may determine real differences between sets of measures. Topics include two-way analysis of variance; simple linear regression and correlation; completely randomized block, Latin square, and factorial designs; analysis of covariance; and nonparametric tests. Chapters conclude with problems and references.

Yeomans, K.A. APPLIED STATISTICS: STATISTICS FOR THE SOCIAL SCIENTIST. Penguin Education X6 Studies in Applied Statistics, vol. 2. Baltimore: Penguin Books, 1968. 397 p. Bibliography, pp. 370-71. Suggestions for Further Reading, pp. 372-73. Appendix: Statistical Tables, pp. 374-82. Answers to Examples, pp. 383-89. Index, pp. 391-97.

A text for a one-semester course in inferential statistics for students who are familiar with probability and descriptive statistics. Topics include normal curve and other distributions; sampling procedures, including stratified sampling and sampling with probability proportionate to size; testing hypothesis using the t, F, and Z statistics; nonlinear simple and multiple regression and correlation; mathematical trend curves and exponential smoothing; nonparametric tests; quality control; and an introduction to econometrics and operational research. Chapters conclude with mathematical notes, proofs, and derivatives.

_____. INTRODUCING STATISTICS: STATISTICS FOR THE SOCIAL SCIENTIST. Baltimore: Penguin Education X5 Studies in Applied Statistics, vol. 1. Penguin, 1968. 258 p. Suggestions for Further Reading, pp. 245-46. Table 1: Logarithms, pp. 247-48. Table 2: Antilogarithms, pp. 249-50. Answers to Examples, pp. 251-54. Index, pp. 255-58.

A text for a one-semester course for students with limited mathematics background. Presents numerical and graphic methods for describing a set of statistical data in a form useful to both layman and student. Topics include averages and measures of dispersion; index numbers; simple linear regression and correlation; and time series. Numerical examples represent the United Kingdom's economic conditions. Chapters conclude with exercises.

Young, Robert K., and Veldman, Donald J. INTRODUCTORY STATISTICS FOR THE BEHAVIORAL SCIENCES. 3d rev. ed. New York: Holt, Rinehart & Winston, 1977. xii, 594 p. Answers to Problems, pp. 525-62. Appendix: Tables, pp. 563-83. Glossary of Symbols, pp. 585-86. Index, pp. 587-94.

A text for a one-semester course. Includes programmed exercises, with each chapter containing a large set of drill and practice exercises as well as problems. Examples drawn from a broad range of fields and topics. Useful to students of nursing, library science, and education as well as the social sciences. Topics include standard scores; normal distribution; tests of hypotheses concerning difference between two means; two-way analysis of variance; chi-square; correlation; and nonparametric tests.

Zeller, Richard A., and Carmines, Edward G. STATISTICAL ANALYSIS OF SOCIAL DATA. Chicago: Rand McNally, 1978. xix, 398 p. Appendixes, pp. 347-89. References, pp. 390-92. Index, pp. 393-98.

A text for a one-semester course in social statistics. Uses few formulas and no derivations. Includes lab assignments. Topics include variability, cross-tabulation, comparing means, multiple regression; probability; chi-square; and inference in bivariate correlation and regression. Appendixes contain a glossary of terms, a glossary of formulas, statistical tables, and instructions for computers.

Chapter 2

BASIC STATISTICS—ECONOMICS AND BUSINESS

Balsley, Howard Lloyd. BASIC STATISTICS FOR BUSINESS AND ECONOMICS. Columbus, Ohio: Grid, 1978. ix, 519 p. Appendixes: Tables, pp. 461-514. Index, pp. 515-19.

> A text for a one-year course in basic statistics for students of economics and business who have minimal mathematics background. Topics include index numbers, time series, and forecasting; probability; probability distributions; estimation and hypothesis testing; analysis of variance; nonparametric tests (one- two- and k-sample); statistical quality control; simple and multiple regression; decision theory; and Bayesian decision making. Style verbal with few derivations. Chapters conclude with solutions to problems and exercises.

_____. INTRODUCTION TO STATISTICAL METHODS WITH APPLICATIONS TO COMMERCIAL, ECONOMIC, AND INDUSTRIAL DATA. Paterson, N.J.: Littlefield, Adams, 1964. x, 347 p. Appendix A: Number Review, pp. 323-30. Appendixes B to D: Tables, pp. 331-42. Index, pp. 343-47.

> A text, reference, and self-study, as well as a supplementary text, for statistics courses, including mathematical statistics. Emphasizes use of statistics in the modern economy. Topics include estimation and hypothesis testing; sampling; linear correlation; time series; index numbers; and cyclical fluctuations. Excludes derivations, and includes detailed numerical examples.

_____. QUANTITATIVE RESEARCH METHODS FOR BUSINESS AND ECONOMICS. New York: Random House, 1970. viii, 339 p. Appendixes: Tables, 293-331. Index, pp. 333-39.

> A text for a graduate course in research methods. Omits derivations and proofs. Topics include statistical inference, tests of significance, experimental design, correlation and regression, time series, and linear programming. Chapters conclude with exercises and references.

Beals, Ralph E. STATISTICS FOR ECONOMISTS: AN INTRODUCTION. Chicago: Rand McNally, 1972. xi, 420 p. Appendix: Tables, pp. 393-402. Answers to Odd-Numbered Problems, pp. 403-16. Index, pp. 417-20.

A text for a one-semester course for advanced undergraduates who have knowledge of college algebra. Emphasizes the relation between theory and data. Consists of the following two parts: "Probability and Statistical Inference" and "Regression." Includes extensions of regression to analysis of variance and covariance, and the identification problem and simultaneous estimation in econometrics. Random variables and probability distributions developed in discrete terms.

Boot, John Cornelius Gerardus, and Cox, Edwin B. STATISTICAL ANALYSIS FOR MANAGERIAL DECISIONS. 2d ed., rev. New York: McGraw-Hill, 1974. xiv, 651 p. Appendix A: The Use of Computers, pp. 599-609. Appendix B: Statistical Tables, pp. 611-34. Bibliography, pp. 635-39. Index, pp. 641-51.

A text for a basic course requiring only high school mathematics, and a reference for practitioners in management. Uses simple computational procedures to illustrate concepts, with emphasis on applications; graphs set out in red. Exercises follow the sections; chapters conclude with answers. Topics include sets and probability, Bayes' formula, probability distributions, random variables, hypothesis testing and estimation, decision theory, regression and correlation, index numbers, statistical quality control, design of sample surveys, and nonparametric statistics.

Braverman, Jerome D. FUNDAMENTALS OF BUSINESS STATISTICS. New York: Academic Press, 1978. xiv, 597 p. Answers to Even-Numbered Problems, pp. 535-52. Appendixes: Tables, pp. 553-87. Index, pp. 589-97.

A text for a one-year course in basic statistics for students of economics and business who know only arithmetic. Topics include index numbers and time series; probability and Bayes' rule; random variables and expectation; estimation and hypothesis testing; two-sample tests; two-factor analysis of variance; chi-square; nonparametric tests; simple regression and correlation; and decision theory. Chapters conclude with problems.

Braverman, Jerome D., and Stewart, William C. STATISTICS FOR BUSINESS AND ECONOMICS. New York: Ronald Press, 1973. ix, 482 p. Appendix: Tables, pp. 445-78. Index, pp. 479-82.

A text for students who have only a high school algebra background. Emphasizes concepts and methods of analysis rather than derivations and computational details. Topics include review of mathematics; Chebyshev's inequality; Bayes' rule; probability distributions; sampling and sampling distributions;

point and interval estimation; estimation concerning means, proportions, and variances; hypothesis testing; simple regression and correlation; nonparametric statistics; time series; and Bayesian decision theory. Chapters conclude with problems.

Brite, Robert L. INTRODUCTION TO BUSINESS STATISTICS. Reading, Mass.: Addison-Wesley, 1977. xii, 365 p. Answers to Marginal Exercises, pp. 287-318. Answers to Odd-Numbered Problems, pp. 319-25. Appendix I: Statistical Tables, pp. 326-45. Appendix II: Index Numbers, pp. 347-50. Appendix III: Self-Tests, pp. 351-57. Index, pp. 359-65.

A work-text requiring virtually no mathematics. Presents topics in a more interesting and less traditional manner than most other texts using an intuitive rather than mathematical style. Organized around three basic areas: descriptive statistics; probability and statistical inference; and regression analysis and its application, chi-square, and analysis of variance. The objective stated at the beginning of each section serves as a summary and guide for review, and the marginal exercises give students the opportunity to work problems illustrating the concepts. Chapters conclude with problems.

Broster, Eric James. MANAGEMENT STATISTICS. Management Studies Series. London: Longman, 1972. xiv, 333 p. Index, pp. 329-33.

A practical guide to statistical techniques useful in business. Early chapters deal with concepts while later chapters demonstrate problems encountered in management statistics. Topics include statistical averages; sampling; including stratified and quota sampling; micro-economics and model building; correlation and regression; deriving demand elasticities; production functions; variable costing; index numbers; trend forecasting; business ratios; decision trees; stock market statistics; input-output analysis; and break-even analysis. Derivations kept to a minimum, and knowledge of college algebra sufficient. Includes numerical examples throughout.

Bryant, Edward Clark. STATISTICAL ANALYSIS. 2d ed., rev. New York: McGraw-Hill, 1966. ix, 321 p. Appendix: Tables, pp. 305-15. Index, pp. 317-21.

A text for a one-year course in management statistics with a prerequisite of college algebra. Emphasizes statistical inference by means of numerical examples, and topics include probability and Bayes' theorem; binomial, hypergeometric, and Poisson probability distributions; decision theory; estimation and hypothesis testing; normal approximation to the binomial; chi-square; nonparametric tests; regression and correlation; analysis of variance; time series; sampling populations, including cluster sampling; statistical quality control; and operating level problems. Uses matrix algebra to develop regression results. Chapters conclude with exercises.

Budin, Morris. STATISTICAL MEASUREMENTS FOR ECONOMICS AND ADMINISTRATION. London: Asia Publishing House, 1962. x, 404 p. Appendixes: Statistical Tables, pp. 344-96. List of References, pp. 397-99. Index, pp. 401-44.

A reference for research workers. Based on the author's experience in teaching, government service, and consulting in the United States and India. Topics include binomial, multinomial, Poisson, and normal probability distributions; hypothesis testing between two means and two proportions; chi-square; index numbers; time series; cyclical fluctuations; regression and correlation; and analysis of variance. Provides detailed and lengthy examples with derivations kept to a minimum. Omits use of matrix algebra in regression.

Burford, Roger L. STATISTICS: A COMPUTER APPROACH. Columbus, Ohio: Charles E. Merrill, 1968. xv, 397 p. Appendix, pp. 363-89. Index, pp. 391-97.

A text for a one-semester course for students who have a good background in algebra. Presentation more rigorous than that found in most comparable texts, and occasional use made of calculus. Emphasizes the use of the computer for solving problems with computational formulas presented in forms conducive to FORTRAN computer programming. Topics include Bayes' theorem; distributions of discrete and continuous random variables; sampling distributions; univariate estimation and hypothesis testing; tests of hypotheses for more than two universes, including chi-square and analysis of variance; joint density and conditional expectation; simple and multiple regression and correlation; and decision theory. Chapters conclude with exercises and references.

Cagelosi, Vincent E.; Taylor, Phillip H.; and Rice, Philip F. BASIC STATISTICS: A REAL WORLD APPROACH. New York: West Publishing Co., 1976. xiii, 432 p. Appendixes A to M: Tables, pp. 341-417. Answers to Odd-Numbered Problems, pp. 419-28. Index, pp. 429-32.

A text for a one-semester course with emphasis on real-world applications for students who have a background in algebra. Topics include counting techniques; random variables and probability distributions; sampling distributions; hypothesis testing; sample design; nonparametric statistics; regression and correlation; index numbers and time series; and decision theory. Chapters conclude with summaries of equations, review questions, and problems.

Caulcott, Evelyn. SIGNIFICANCE TESTS. Applied Statistics Series. Boston: Routledge and Kegan Paul, 1973. xviii, 145 p. Appendix: Statistical Tables, pp. 134-39. Answers to Exercises, pp. 140-42. Index, pp. 143-45.

A supplementary text and self-study for a basic course which deals comprehensively with significance tests. Assumes knowledge of algebra and descriptive statistics. Useful to those interested in the theory of sampling and the interpretation of sample results. Topics include binomial, normal, and Poisson distributions; theoretical basis for sampling; tests for difference between two population means and two population proportions; and chi-square. Chapters conclude with exercises and references.

Chao, Lincoln L. STATISTICS: METHODS AND ANALYSIS. 2d ed., rev. New York: McGraw-Hill, 1974. xii, 556 p. Supplements, pp. 465-75. Appendix: Tables, pp. 477-510. Answers to Odd-Numbered Problems, pp. 511-39. Index, pp. 541-56.

A text for a one-year course with a prerequisite of high school algebra. Bridges the gap between the predominately descriptive texts and the largely mathematical ones with emphasis on inferential statistics. Includes simple algebraic proofs throughout with the less essential proofs located in the supplements. Topics include sets and functions; counting rules and probability; Bayes' rule; probability distributions; estimation and hypothesis testing; chi-square; one- and two-way analysis of variance; regression and correlation; time series; nonparametric tests; and Bayesian decision theory. Sections conclude with exercises.

Chou, Ya-Lun. PROBABILITY AND STATISTICS FOR DECISION MAKING. New York: Holt, Rinehart and Winston, 1972. xv, 623 p. Appendix A: Sets, Permutations, Combinations, and Summations, pp. 569-86. Appendix B: Statistical Tables, pp. 587-618. Index, pp. 619-23.

A text for a one-year course requiring only freshman mathematics. Treatments of the concepts of probability theory, random variables, sampling, and decision making more thorough and rigorous than those found in most other basic texts. Topics include sample spaces; probability; random variables and their probability distributions, including continuous random variables; discrete probability models; Bayesian strategies and loss functions; descriptive statistics; theory of sampling; estimation and hypothesis testing; chi-square; simple and multiple regression and correlation; nonparametric tests; time series and index numbers; and analysis of variance. Emphasizes statistics as a way of thinking rather than as a set of rules employed to solve problems. Chapters conclude with exercises.

_____. STATISTICAL ANALYSIS: WITH BUSINESS AND ECONOMIC APPLICATIONS. Quantitative Methods Series. New York: Holt, Rinehart and Winston, 1969. xix, 794 p. Appendixes, pp. 737-85: A, the Summation Sign; B, Suggestions for Further Reading; C, Statistical Tables. Index, pp. 787-94.

A text for a one-year course based on a prerequisite of college algebra. More complete than most elementary texts, and achieves a balance between principles and applications. Topics include random variables and their distributions, including normal, multinomial, hypergeometric, uniform, Poisson, exponential, and binomial; joint probability; estimation and hypothesis testing; sampling distributions; chi-square; analysis of variance; nonparametric tests; index numbers and time series; simple and multiple regression and correlation; decision and game theories; queueing theory; and Monte Carlo simulation. Chapters conclude with glossaries of formulas and problems.

Clark, Charles T., and Schkade, Lawrence L. STATISTICAL ANALYSIS FOR ADMINISTRATIVE DECISIONS. 2d ed., rev. Cincinnati, Ohio: South-West, 1974. vii, 887 p. Appendix: Tables, pp. 735-61. Answers to Odd-Numbered Problems, pp. 862-77. Index, pp. 878-87.

A text for a one-year course requiring college algebra. Concepts and methods range from elementary to advanced in degree of sophistication and include a large part of what is called quantitative methods. Consists of the following six parts: "Statistical Data and Descriptive Measures"; "Probability and Probability Distributions"; "Sampling"; "Inference"; "Regression and Correlation"; and "Time Series and Index Numbers." Includes flow charts for many computational steps for those who wish to write their own programs and use the computer to solve problems. Chapters conclude with study questions, problems, and references.

______. STATISTICAL METHODS FOR BUSINESS DECISIONS. Cincinnati, Ohio: South-West, 1969. xii, 987 p. Glossary of Symbols, pp. 752-71. Glossary of Formulas, pp. 773-91. Appendix: Tables, pp. 792-968. Answers to Odd-Numbered Problems, pp. 969-78. Index, pp. 979-87.

Text for a one-year course and a reference for managers. Emphasizes the use of computer programs to solve problems and includes flow diagrams and statistical techniques appropriate for computer programming. Assumes knowledge of college algebra, but no previous knowledge of digital computers. Consists of the following seven parts: "A Review of Descriptive Statistics"; "The Computer and Statistical Analysis"; Probability and Probability Distributions"; "Sampling"; "Inference"; "Regression and Correlation"; and "Time Series and Index Numbers." Omits derivations and provides detailed solutions to examples. Chapters conclude with study questions, problems, and references.

Clelland, Richard C.; Brown, Francis E.; De Cani, John S.; Bursk, J. Parker; and Murray, Donald S. BASIC STATISTICS WITH BUSINESS APPLICATIONS. Wiley Series in Probability and Mathematical Statistics. New York: Wiley, 1966. xvi, 708 p. Appendix A: The Number e, p. 645. Appendix B: The

MacLaurin Series Expansion, pp. 646-47. Appendix: C: Multiple Integration, pp. 648-53. Appendix D: Review of Some Matrix Operations, pp. 654-63. Appendix E: Tables, pp. 665-77. Appendix F: Point of Division of An Interval, pp. 678-79. Appendix G: Convex Sets, pp. 680-83. Appendix H: Supporting and Separating Lines, pp. 684-86. Problem Solutions, pp. 687-704. Index, pp. 705-8.

A text for a three-semester course in basic statistics for students in business and economics who have had one year of mathematics which included calculus, linear algebra, and set theory. Emphasizes both theory and applications, with probability receiving more attention than usual. Topics include formulating a research project; random variables; moment-generating functions; sampling; estimation and tests of hypotheses; descriptive measures of bivariate distributions; maximum likelihood; regression and correlation; time series; econometric models, decision theory; and revised probability in decision making.

Costis, Harry G. STATISTICS FOR BUSINESS. Columbus, Ohio: Charles E. Merrill, 1972. xvi, 749 p. Appendix: Use of Logarithms and Square Roots, pp. 649-54. Tables, pp. 656-743. Index, pp. 744-49.

A text for a one-year course assuming knowledge of high school algebra. Topics include descriptive statistics, including time series and index numbers; probability; sampling theory and design; tests of hypotheses; regression; nonparametric tests; analysis of variance; and Bayesian statistics, including profit and loss functions and the expected value of perfect information. Chapters conclude with lists of terms and symbols, exercises, and references. Uses no matrix algebra in regression.

Croxton, Frederick Emory; Cowden, Dudley J.; and Bolch, Ben W. PRACTICAL BUSINESS STATISTICS. 4th rev. ed. Englewood Cliffs, N.J.: Prentice-Hall, 1969. xvi, 444 p. Appendixes 1 to 17, pp. 391-435. Index, pp. 437-44.

A text for a one-year course treating such topics as descriptive statistics, sample spaces and probability; normal curve; tests of hypotheses concerning differences between two means and two proportions; Bayesian decision theory; simple and multiple regression; two-way analysis of variance; and index numbers and time series. Appendixes consist of statistical tables and a review of elementary mathematics. Chapters conclude with problems.

Croxton, Frederick Emory; Cowden, Dudley J.; and Klein, Sidney. APPLIED GENERAL STATISTICS. 3d rev. ed. Englewood Cliffs, N.J.: Prentice-Hall, 1967. xviii, 754 p. Appendixes, pp. 638-742. Index, pp. 743-54.

A text for a one-year course assuming knowledge of high school algebra. Topics include fitting of time series by linear, nonlinear, and cyclical trends; index numbers; simple and multiple regression and correlation; significance tests for mean and proportions; chi-square; and two-way analysis of variance with more than one entry in a cell. Provides numerous examples in a variety of fields but no exercises. Appendixes consist of symbols, statistical tables, derivations of statistical formulas, and a discussion of rounding numbers.

Daniel, Wayne W., and Terrell, James C. BUSINESS STATISTICS: BASIC CONCEPTS AND METHODOLOGY. Boston: Houghton Mifflin, 1975. xv, 544 p. References, pp. 459-72. Appendix: Tables, pp. 473-528. Answers to Odd-Numbered Exercises, pp. 529-36. Index, pp. 537-44.

A text for a one-year course assuming a college algebra background. Emphasizes illustrating concepts with examples. Excludes derivations. Topics include sets and probability; discrete and continuous random variables; sampling distributions; interval estimation and hypothesis testing; Latin squares and factorial designs; simple and multiple regression and correlation; chi-square; nonparametric tests; time series and index numbers; survey sampling; decision theory; and statistical quality control. Chapters conclude with review questions, problems, and glossaries.

Dubois, Edward N. ESSENTIAL METHODS IN BUSINESS STATISTICS. New York: McGraw-Hill, 1964. xiv, 238 p. Appendix: Tables, pp. 211-33. Index, pp. 235-38.

Text for a one-semester course requiring only a high school algebra background. Emphasizes methods and applications rather than theory and includes the following topics: sampling distributions; point estimates and interval estimations; two-sample problems; analysis of variance; regression and correlation; and time series and index numbers. Chapters conclude with problems.

Dyckman, Thomas R., and Thomas, L. Joseph. FUNDAMENTAL STATISTICS FOR BUSINESS AND ECONOMICS. Englewood Cliffs, N.J.: Prentice-Hall, 1977. xv, 715 p. Appendix: Tables, pp. 667-93. Solutions to Starred Problems, pp. 694-705. Index, pp. 707-15.

A text for a one-year course for students who have a college background. Calculus used in some of the technical notes at the ends of the chapters to develop continuous-variable concepts. Emphasizes preparing potential managers to be consumers of statistics with examples taken from a variety of fields within business. Topics include probability and sample spaces; Bayes' theorem; random variables; sampling distributions; hypotheses testing; decision theory; two-factor analysis of variance; regression; index numbers and time series; and nonparametric tests. Chapters conclude with new symbols, key formulas and problems.

Dyckman, Thomas R.; Smidt, S.; and McAdams, A.K. MANAGEMENT DECISION MAKING UNDER UNCERTAINTY: AN INTRODUCTION TO PROBABILITY AND STATISTICAL DECISION THEORY. New York: Macmillan, 1969. xxiii, 662 p. Glossary, pp. 597-601. Bibliography, pp. 603-5. Appendix: Tables, pp. 607-51. Index, pp. 653-62.

Text for a one-year course for students interested in the solution of managerial problems. Knowledge of elementary calculus helpful but not essential, with presentation based on set theory concepts. Topics include probability and random variables; games; decision theory; Bayesian statistics; sampling and optimal sampling plans; and estimation and hypothesis testing. Chapters conclude with mathematical developments, computer applications, and exercises.

Ekeblad, Frederick A. THE STATISTICAL METHOD IN BUSINESS, APPLICATIONS OF PROBABILITY AND INFERENCE TO BUSINESS AND OTHER PROBLEMS. New York: Wiley, 1962. xii, 791 p. Appendix: Tables, pp. 735-79. Index, pp. 781-91.

A text for a one-year course with few derivations. Topics include sources of knowledge; probability calculations; inferences concerning differences between two means; Bayes' theorem; chi-square; regression; time series; and index numbers.

Enrick, Norbert Lloyd. CASES IN MANAGEMENT STATISTICS: WITH APPLICATIONS FROM ADMINISTRATION AND FINANCE, PRODUCTION AND ENGINEERING, SALES AND MARKETING, RESEARCH AND DEVELOPMENT. Introduction by W. Edwards Deming. Epilogue by Charles A. Bicking. New York: Holt, Rinehart and Winston, 1962. xvi, 159 p. Appendix: Tables, pp. 145-55. Epilogue, pp. 157-59. No index.

A supplementary text for a basic statistics course. Consists of a collection of practical problems from actual business conditions grouped under the following seven chapters: "Basic Statistical Analysis: Frequency Distributions, Averages, and Variability" (eleven cases); "Control Charts in Production, Management, and Administration" (nine cases); "Significance Tests for Simple Comparisons and Chi-Square" (eight cases); "Analysis of Variance in Production, Marketing, and Research" (twelve cases): "Regression and Correlation" (eight cases); "Sampling and Production, Administration, and Distribution" (ten cases); and "Time Series and Forecasting" (nine cases).

Erricker, Brinley Cenydd. ADVANCED GENERAL STATISTICS. London: English Universities Press, 1971. viii, 350 p. Answers to the Exercises, pp. 320-31. Tables, pp. 332-45. Index, pp. 347-50.

A self-study for well-prepared elementary school graduates from English universities who wish to prepare for university courses. Includes detailed solutions for examples. Topics include least squares; correlation; probability and chance; permutations and combinations; binomial, Poisson, normal, and chi-square distributions; sampling; F-distribution; quality control; and analysis of variance. Sections conclude with exercises. Useful to students in biology, economics, sociology, education, medicine, and other fields.

Finney, David John. AN INTRODUCTION TO STATISTICAL ANALYSIS IN AGRICULTURE. 4th ed., rev. New York: Wiley, Halsted Press, 1972. 290 p. Index, pp. 286-90.

A nontechnical presentation of statistical reasoning and methods of analysis for the interested layman. Enables the reader to converse more effectively with the statistician experienced in agricultural problems. Examples often oversimplified. Topics include frequencies and rates; probability; comparison of two variables; design of experiments; factorial design; sample surveys; regression and correlation; and statistical arithmetic. Chapters conclude with discussion of statistical theory and simple derivations.

Forester, John. STATISTICAL SELECTION OF BUSINESS STRATEGIES. Irwin Series in Quantitative Analysis for Business. Homewood, Ill.: Irwin, 1968. viii, 220 p. Appendix, pp. 175-209. Bibliography, pp. 213-15. Index, pp. 219-20.

An applications-oriented text for a one-semester course assuming a high school algebra background. Examples from many diverse industries. Topics include simple decision problems; graphic analysis of two-variable problems; Bayes' strategies; value of information; a priori and posterior probabilities; utility; binomial sampling; normal sampling; and the effect of sample information on distributions. The appendix presents tables, charts and diagrams, and useful formulas.

Fox, Karl A. INTERMEDIATE ECONOMIC STATISTICS. New York: Wiley, 1968. xi, 568 p. Appendix I: Glossary of Symbols and List of Important Equations, pp. 537-47. Appendix II: Reference Tables, pp. 548-59. Index, pp. 561-68.

A text for a one-year course in economic statistics for students who have a background in economic theory and introductory statistics covering descriptive statistics, hypothesis testing, and estimation. Emphasizes applications of statistical methods to the analysis of substantive economic problems. Many chapters contain appendixes devoted to derivations and applications. Topics include simple and multiple regression and correlation; index numbers and time series; analysis of variance; econometric models, including the Klein-Goldberger model of the U.S. economy, 1929-52, and the Brookings model; identification, including two-stage least squares; alternative methods of estimation, including indirect least squares, the k-class estimator, and three-stage least squares; maximum likelihood; Bayesian methods (by J.K. Sengupta and B.C. Sanya); multicollinearity; and the measurement of economic aggregates. Chapters conclude with exercises and references.

Freund, John E., and Williams, Frank J. ELEMENTARY BUSINESS STATISTICS: THE MODERN APPROACH. 3d ed., rev. Englewood Cliffs, N.J.: Prentice-Hall, 1972. xv, 560 p. Bibliography, pp. 506-9. Statistical Tables, pp. 511-38. Answers to Odd-Numbered Exercises, pp. 539-53. Index, pp. 555-60.

A text for a one-year course with emphasis on Bayesian procedures. Topics include index numbers; probability; expectation, games, and decisions; binomial, hypergeometric, and Poisson distributions; prior and posterior probabilities; Bayes' theorem and revision of probabilities; sampling distributions; two-way analysis of variance; nonparametric tests; regression and correlation; time series; survey methods; and introduction to operations research techniques. Concepts explained and illustrated in great detail with over 700 exercises based on real data given at the ends of the sections.

Guthrie, Harold Woodson. STATISTICAL METHODS IN ECONOMICS. Irwin Series in Economics. Homewood, Ill.: Irwin, 1966. xiv, 373 p. Appendixes: Tables, pp. 343-67. Index, pp. 371-73.

A text for a one-year course assuming a high school algebra background. Teaches both economics and statistics using real data in censuses, sample surveys, and scientific experiments. Consists of five parts: "Simple Methods of Description"; "Complex Methods of Description: Changes in Variables; Over Time" (including index numbers and curve fitting by least squares); "Statistical Inferences About a Single Variable" (including one-way analysis of variance); "Description of Relationships Between Two Variables" (including regression); and "Errors in Sample Survey Data." Mathematical results stated without extensive derivations. Exercises provided in a separate workbook.

Hadley, George F. INTRODUCTION TO BUSINESS STATISTICS. San Francisco: Holden-Day, 1968. xii, 463 p. Tables, pp. 447-58. Index, pp. 459-63.

A text for a one-semester course using only algebra. Probability covered in more depth than usual for texts of this level, with emphasis on the notion of a mathematical model. Bayesian statistics covered extensively. Topics include random variables; probability distributions; estimation and hypothesis testing; decision theory; quality control; regression and correlation; and time series and forecasting. Includes over 600 problems. Presentation more formal from a notational viewpoint than customary.

Hamburg, Morris. BASIC STATISTICS: A MODERN APPROACH. New York: Harcourt Brace Jovanovich, 1974. x, 451 p. Bibliography, pp. 386-88. Appendix A: Tables, pp. 389-415. Appendix B: Symbols, Subscripts, and Summations, pp. 416-19. Appendix C: Shortcut Formulas, pp. 420-22. Answers to Even-Numbered Exercises, pp. 423-46. Index, pp. 447-51.

> A text for a one-semester course. Employs mathematics at the lowest level consistent with the needs of modern statistics and emphasizes the appreciation of the effectiveness, scope, and versatility of statistical methods. Topics include probability rules and distributions; sampling, estimation, and hypothesis testing; chi-square; analysis of variance; simple regression and correlation; nonparametric statistics; time series and index numbers; decision making including posterior analysis. Omits use of random variables. Sections conclude with problems.

______. STATISTICAL ANALYSIS FOR DECISION MAKING. 2d ed., rev. New York: Harcourt Brace Jovanovich, 1977. xiii, 801 p. Bibliography, pp. 684-88. Appendix A: Statistical Tables, pp. 689-718. Appendix B: Symbols, Subscripts, and Summations, pp. 719-23. Appendix C: Properties of Expected Values and Variances, pp. 724-28. Appendix D: Shortcut Formulas, pp. 729-32. Solutions to Odd-Numbered Problems, pp. 733-93. Index, pp. 795-801.

> A text for a one-year course requiring only a high school algebra background. Clear presentation of concepts stressed. Applications, examples, and exercises selected from a variety of fields including market research, quality control, accounting, pollution control, and education. Mathematical derivations placed in footnotes and in appendix C. Topics include probability and discrete random variables; uniform, Poisson, multinomial, and hypergeometric distributions; sampling distributions; tests of hypotheses; chi-square; analysis of variance; simple and multiple regression; time series and index numbers; decision theory; sequential decision-making procedures; and comparison of classical and Bayesian statistics. Sections conclude with exercises.

Harnett, Donald L. INTRODUCTION TO STATISTICAL METHODS. 2d ed., rev. Reading, Mass.: Addison-Wesley, 1975. xi, 613 p. Selected Bibliography, pp. 550-51. Glossary of Undefined Symbols, p. 552. Appendix A: Calculus Review, pp. 553-61. Appendix B: Tables, pp. 562-97. Answers to Selected Exercises, pp. 598-609. Index, pp. 610-613.

> A text for a two-semester course assuming a prerequisite of college algebra and elementary calculus. Proofs given in simple terms and, in some cases, relegated to footnotes. Topics include discrete and continuous random variables; chi-square; sampling distributions; method of maximum likelihood; two-sample problem; estimation and hypothesis testing; simple and multiple regression; decision theory; time series and index numbers;

two-factor analysis of variance; and nonparametric tests. Chapters conclude with review problems and exercises, some of which involve extensions of the text material.

Harnett, Donald L., and Murphy, James L. INTRODUCTORY STATISTICAL ANALYSIS. 2d ed., rev. Reading, Mass.: Addison-Wesley, 1975. x, 564 p. Selected Bibliography, p. 524. Appendix A: Subscripts and Summations, pp. 525-27. Appendix B: Tables, pp. 528-54. Answers to Odd-Numbered Problems, pp. 555-61. Index, pp. 562-64.

A text for a one-year course with a prerequisite of college algebra. Uses no calculus but some explanations indicate how calculus may be used in certain concepts. Provides a mixture of intuitive explanation, examples, and mathematical rigor. Topics include probability and discrete sample spaces; discrete and continuous random variables and their distributions; sampling distributions; hypothesis testing; chi-square and analysis of variance; decision theory; regression; Bayes' rule; time series and index numbers; and multicollinearity, autocorrelation, heteroscedasticity, and nonparametric tests. Chapters conclude with review problems and exercises.

Hays, William L., and Winkler, Robert L. STATISTICS: PROBABILITY, INFERENCE, AND DECISION. Vol. 1. International Series in Decision Processes. New York: Holt, Rinehart and Winston, 1970. xviii, 650 p. Appendix: Some Common Differentiation and Integration Formulas, pp. 597-99. Tables, pp. 601-37. References and Suggestions for Further Reading, pp. 639-41. Index, pp. 643-50.

A text for a one-year course requiring elementary calculus. Emphasizes both mathematical and verbal styles. Uses set-theoretic approach to probability with both discrete and continuous random variables covered at length. Topics include sets and functions; moments of random variables; special probability distributions; frequency and sampling distributions; properties of point estimators; maximum likelihood estimation; chi-square; hypothesis testing for difference between two means; and Bayesian inference. Numerous problems, ranging from simple applications to theory, given at the ends of the chapters.

_____. STATISTICS: PROBABILITY, INFERENCE, AND DECISION. Vol. 2. International Series in Decision Processes. New York: Holt, Rinehart and Winston, 1970. xiv, 320 p. Appendix: Matrix Algebra, pp. 265-73. Tables, pp. 275-311. References and Suggestions for Further Reading, pp. 313-15. Index, pp. 317-20.

A continuation of volume 1 covering regression; experimental design; analysis of variance; and nonparametric methods.

Hey, John D. STATISTICS IN ECONOMICS. London: Martin Robertson and Co., 1974. x, 422 p. Appendix, pp. 401-11. Bibliography and References, pp. 413-16. Index, pp. 417-22.

A text for a one-year course requiring some knowledge of differential and integral calculus. Useful in introductory course in econometrics. Concepts explained in great detail and include many derivations not generally included in basic texts. Topics include joint probability; random variables and their distributions; asymptotic properties of point estimators; statistical inference; regression; Durbin-Watson statistics; and estimation of simultaneous equations. Chapters conclude with summaries and exercises. Appendixes devoted to summation notation, independence of uncorrelated normal variables, and statistical tables.

Hickman, Edgar P., and Hilton, James G. PROBABILITY AND STATISTICAL ANALYSIS. Scranton, Pa.: Intext Educational Publishers, 1971. x, 366 p. Appendixes: Tables, pp. 331-61. Index, pp. 363-66.

A text for a one-year course assuming some exposure to calculus. Includes probability theory, including random variables and their distributions; Bayes' formula; marginal and conditional probabilities; statistical analysis of one variable, including estimation, sampling, and hypothesis testing; and statistical analysis of more than one variable, including analysis of variance, goodness of fit, regression, and time series. Chapters conclude with problems and references.

Hoel, Paul G. ELEMENTARY STATISTICS. 4th ed., rev. New York: Wiley, 1976. xi, 361 p. Appendix: Tables, pp. 319-48. Answers to Odd-Numbered Exercises, pp. 349-58. Index, pp. 359-61.

A text for a one-year course requiring only high school algebra. Includes numerical data from journals in medicine and the social and life sciences. Emphasizes explanation and illustration of concepts, rather than mathematical theory. Topics include probability and Bayes' formula; discrete random variables and their moments; normal and binomial probability distributions; sampling; estimation and hypothesis; regression; chi-square; two-way analysis of variance; nonparametric tests; and decision theory.

Hoel, Paul G., and Jensen, Raymond J. BASIC STATISTICS FOR BUSINESS AND ECONOMICS. 2d ed., rev. New York: Wiley, 1977. xiv, 536 p. Appendixes: Tables, pp. 486-518. Answers, pp. 519-33. Index, pp. 535-36.

A text for a one-year course. Emphasizes simple explanations with mathematical derivations omitted. Topics include sample spaces and probability; Bayes' formula; random variables and their distributions, including exponential and hypergeometric;

sampling distributions; estimation and hypothesis testing; serial correlation; simple and multiple regression; chi-square; two-way analysis of variance; sample surveys; index numbers and time series; and decision theory. Chapters conclude with review illustrations and exercises.

Hughes, Ann, and Grawoig, Dennis. STATISTICS: A FOUNDATION FOR ANALYSIS. Reading, Mass.: Addison-Wesley, 1971. xvi, 525 p. A Brief Review of Important Mathematical Concepts, pp. 474-82. Statistical Tables, pp. 483-508. Answers to Selected Problems, pp. 509-16. Index, pp. 517-25.

A text for a one-year course requiring knowledge of the rudiments of integration and differentiation of polynomials and exponential functions. Includes examples worked out in detail and problems at the ends of both the sections and the chapters. Topics include events and probability; discrete and continuous random variables; two-dimensional random variables; binomial, Poisson, exponential, and normal probability laws; estimation and hypothesis; chi-square; inferences from a binomial population; analysis of variance; simple and multiple regression and correlation; nonparametric tests; and decision theory.

Huntsberger, David V.; Billingsley, Patrick; and Croft, D. James. STATISTICAL INFERENCE FOR MANAGEMENT AND ECONOMICS. Boston: Allyn and Bacon, 1975. xii, 507 p. Appendix: Tables, pp. 468-88. Answers to Odd-Numbered Problems, pp. 489-500. Index, pp. 501-7.

A text for a one-semester course requiring only high school algebra. Emphasizes understanding concepts and providing a base for more advanced work. Topics include probability and Bayes' theorem; population, samples, and distributions; two-sample problem; paired comparisons; multinomial distribution; regression and correlation; analysis of variance; nonparametric tests; time series and index numbers; and decision theory. Chapters conclude with problems and references.

Ingram, John A. INTRODUCTORY STATISTICS. Menlo Park, Calif.: Cummings, 1974. x, 443 p. Appendix A: Mathematics Essential for Statistics, pp. 343-58. Appendix B: Statistical Tables, pp. 359-401. Glossary, pp. 402-19. Selected Answers to Problems, pp. 420-37. Index, pp. 438-43.

A text for a one-semester course. Emphasizes problems that illustrate the use of statistics in everyday life. Includes three classes of problems: at the end of each section, more inclusive problems at the ends of the chapters, and review problems every two or three chapters. Formulas and computing procedures located in the glossaries. Topics include axioms of probability and Bayes' rule; random variables and probability distributions; random sampling; central limit theorem; estimation and hypothesis testing; chi-square; simple regression and correlation; two-way analysis of variance; and nonparametric tests.

INTRODUCTION TO MANAGEMENT STATISTICS: A PROGRAMME FOR MANAGERS AND MANAGEMENT TRAINEES WISHING TO ACHIEVE A BASIC UNDERSTANDING OF THE ELEMENTS OF STATISTICS. London: English Universities Press for International Tutor Machines, 1967. xii, 152 p. No index.

A programmed text for managers who wish to learn some statistics. Divided into sections grouped under the following four parts: "Methods of Presentation and Frequency Distribution"; "Measure of Central Tendency"; "Measure of Dispersion"; and "Probability and Curves." Includes pre-tests and post-tests with answers.

Jedamus, Paul, and Frame, Robert. BUSINESS DECISION THEORY. New York: McGraw-Hill, 1969. x, 290 p. Bibliography, p. 241. Appendix, pp. 243-83. Index, pp. 285-90.

A text for a one-semester course in statistical inference and decision theory including both classical and Bayesian approaches. Self-contained and makes an excellent prerequisite for courses in operations research, computer programming, and econometrics. The chapters conclude with exercises.

Jedamus, Paul; Frame, Robert; and Taylor, Robert. STATISTICAL ANALYSIS FOR BUSINESS DECISIONS. New York: McGraw-Hill, 1976. xii, 622 p. Appendix A: Tables, pp. 583-608. Appendix B: Glossary of Symbols and Abbreviations, pp. 609-11. Index, pp. 613-22.

A text for a one-year course in basic statistics for students of business who have knowledge of elementary algebra. Emphasizes intuitive explanation of concepts. Integrates both classical and Bayesian approaches. Topics include index numbers and time series; break-even analysis; forecasting, including time-series and exponential smoothing; rule of probability; interval estimation and hypothesis testing; simple and multiple regression and correlation; nonparametric tests; survey sampling; and decision theory. Order of presentation of topics does not follow that in other texts; for example, index numbers and time series precede probability and classical statistics.

Jolliffee, Flavia R. COMMONSENSE STATISTICS FOR ECONOMISTS AND OTHERS. Students Library of Economics. Boston: Routledge and Kegan Paul, 1974. xiii, 174 p. Appendix 1: Recommended Basic Statistical Sources for Community Use, pp. 157-58. Appendix 2: The Summation Sign, pp. 159-60. Solutions, pp. 161-72. References, pp. 173-74. No index.

A valuable introduction to statistics requiring little more than the ability to count and to use good judgment, although familiarity with certain algebraic notations, such as summation signs, helpful. Use made of both real and hypothetical data, with proofs included wherever possible. Topics include probability, distributions, sampling; interval estimation and hypothesis testing; and regression. Chapters conclude with exercises.

Kaplan, Lawrence J. ELEMENTARY STATISTICS FOR ECONOMICS AND BUSINESS. New York: Pitman, 1966. xv, 297 p. Appendix A: How to Use Logarithms, pp. 249-55. Appendix B: Steps in Computations of Square Roots, pp. 257-71. Appendix C: How to Solve Normal Equations Simultaneously, pp. 273-76. Appendix D: Selected Review of Economic and Business Data, pp. 277-82. Bibliography, pp. 283-86. Index, pp. 287-97.

A text for a one-semester course and a supplementary text for basic and intermediate statistics courses. Provides a nontechnical introduction to basic statistics using practical illustrations. Topics include permutations and combinations; probability; inference and hypothesis testing; chi-square; time series and index numbers; and simple regression. Chapters conclude with exercises.

Karmel, Peter Henry. APPLIED STATISTICS FOR ECONOMISTS: A COURSE IN STATISTICAL METHODS. 2d ed., rev. Melbourne, Australia: I. Pitman, 1963. xiii, 474 p. Appendix A: Statistical Tables, pp. 426-31. Appendix B: Sources of Australian Statistics, pp. 432-60. Appendix C: A Short List of References, pp. 461-64. Index, pp. 465-74.

A text for a one-year course providing a good prerequisite for the study of economics. Emphasizes understanding the reasoning underlying methods rather than the methods themselves. Topics include sampling and tests of hypotheses, including the two-sample problem; sample surveys; quality control; simple and multiple regression and correlation; time series; index numbers; social accounts and the measurement of national income; and demography. The numerical examples illustrate Australian experiences.

Kazmier, Leonard J. STATISTICAL ANALYSIS FOR BUSINESS AND ECONOMICS. 2d ed., rev. New York: McGraw-Hill, 1973. xv, 623 p. Appendix A: Application of the Computer in Statistical Analysis, pp. 480-518. Appendix B: Tables, pp. 519-47. Solutions to Exercises, pp. 548-99. Glossary of Symbols, pp. 600-604. Glossary of Formulas, pp. 605-15. Index, pp. 617-23.

A programmed text assuming only high school algebra. Includes frame-by-frame testing, key questions, and short sample problems designed to demonstrate progress of the student. Topics include probability and probability distributions; sampling and statistical inference; chi-square; decision theory; Bayesian inference; simple regression and correlation; time series and index numbers. Appendix A includes descriptions and examples of the application of eight computer programs. Instructor's manual includes complete FORTRAN programs for these eight applications. Chapters conclude with exercises.

Kim, Chaiho, STATISTICAL ANALYSIS FOR INDUCTION AND DECISION. Homewood, Ill.: Dryden, 1973. xv, 523 p. Bibliography, pp. 465-66. Appendix A: Sets and Their Properties, pp. 467-73. Appendix B: List of Tables, pp. 475-519. Index, pp. 521-23.

A text for a one-semester course for students of economics, management science, industrial engineering, operations research, and related fields. Concepts introduced by means of definitions and theorems, with examples of most theorems provided; proofs generally intuitive. Topics include sample spaces and probability; Bayes' theorem; random variables and their distributions; joint probability functions and covariance; central limit theorem; sampling distributions; maximum likelihood estimates; estimation and hypothesis testing, including admissible decision functions and loss functions; likelihood ratio tests; Neyman-Pearson lemma; composite hypotheses; decision theory; and regression. Sections conclude with exercises.

Koosis, Donald J. BUSINESS STATISTICS FOR SELF-STUDY OR CLASSROOM USE. Wiley Self-Teaching Guides. New York: Wiley, 1972. viii, 296 p. Tables, pp. 267-90. Text, pp. 291-94. Index, pp. 295-96.

A self-study for students who wish to review basic statistics and a supplementary text for basic statistics. Organized in frames, each frame consisting of a question and answer. Frames organized into nine chapters, each chapter requiring about two hours to complete. Each chapter concludes with a set of review problems, and the book concludes with a final examination. Chapter titles: "Basic Skills"; "Populations and Samples"; "Estimating"; "Hypothesis Testing"; "Difference Between Means"; "The Difference Between Two Variances or Several Means"; "The Relations Between Two Sets of Measures"; "Changes Over Time"; and "A Test of Distributions."

Korin, Basil P. STATISTICAL CONCEPTS FOR THE SOCIAL SCIENCES. Cambridge, Mass.: Winthrop Publishing, 1975. xii, 407 p. Appendix A: A Brief Review of Mathematics, pp. 345-52. Appendix B: Summation Notation, pp. 353-56. Appendix C: Linear Transformations, pp. 357-62. Appendix D: Statistical Tables, pp. 363-84. Appendix E: Selected References, pp. 385-86. Appendix F: Answers to Odd-Numbered Problems, pp. 387-400. Index, pp. 401-7.

A text for a one-semester course requiring only high school algebra. Derivations kept to a minimum with examples worked out in detail. Topics include normal distribution, linear regression, measures of correlation for data measured on interval, ordinal, and nominal scales; probability and random variables; sampling distributions; tests of hypotheses; binomial, multinomial, and goodness-of-fit tests; simple regression; and two-way analysis of variance. Chapters conclude with summaries, formulas, references, and problems.

Kurnow, Ernest; Glasser, Gerald J.; and Ottman, Frederick R. STATISTICS FOR BUSINESS DECISIONS. Homewood, Ill.: Irwin, 1959. xi, 523 p. Appendix: Tables, pp. 448-513. Index, pp. 515-23.

A text for a one-semester course. Emphasizes how to formulate a decision problem statistically so that data will serve as a basis for deciding upon a rational course of action. With some exceptions, treats only large sample theory. Each chapter ends with a summary, problems, and references. Topics include decision parameters; sample selection; probability; estimation of parameters; hypothesis testing; errors and bias; statistical control charts; comparison of two and of several populations (analysis of variance); regression and correlation; and time series.

Lapin, Lawrence L. STATISTICS: MEANING AND METHOD. New York: Harcourt Brace Jovanovich, 1975. xiii, 591 p. Appendix: Tables, pp. 542-69. Abbreviated Answers to Even-Numbered Exercises, pp. 571-78. Index, pp. 579-91.

A text for a one-semester course requiring only high school algebra. More accessible than most basic texts and generalizations arrived at by way of examples. Important formulas, graphs, and sentences set of in red. Topics include laws of probability; expected values; normal distribution; estimation and hypotheses testing; simple and multiple regression and correlation; inferences using two samples; chi-square; analysis of variance; and nonparametric tests. Sections conclude with exercises, and chapters conclude with review exercises.

______. STATISTICS FOR MODERN BUSINESS DECISIONS. 2d ed., rev. New York: Harcourt Brace Jovanovich, 1978. xxi, 857 p. Selected References, pp. 787-88. Appendix: Tables, pp. 789-829. Answers to Even-Numbered Exercises, pp. 830-40. Index, 841-57.

A text for a one-year course in basic statistics for students in business and economics who have knowledge of high school algebra. Topics introduced by carefully chosen examples that illustrate how they relate to present-day issues, such as health, conservation, the environment, accounting, marketing, finance, production, forecasting, and consumer behavior. Topics include sampling; sets and probability; probability distributions and expected value; normal distribution; estimation and hypothesis testing; regression and correlation; time series and forecasting; index numbers; inferences using two samples; chi-square; analysis of variance; goodness-of-fit tests; nonparametric tests; decision theory; and Bayesian methods. Sections conclude with exercises; chapters, with review exercises.

Leabo, Dick A. BASIC STATISTICS. 4th ed., rev. Homewood, Ill.: Irwin, 1972. xix, 668 p. Appendixes, pp. 571-650. Name Index, pp. 651-54. Subject Index, pp. 655-68.

A text for a one-year course requiring only high school algebra. Consists of the following eight parts: "The Nature of Statistical

Analysis"; "Fundamental Tools of Descriptive Statistics"; "Probability, the Basis for Statistical Inference"; "Basic Concepts of Statistical Inference--I"; "Measuring Economic Change"; "Basic Concepts of Statistical Inference--II"; "Nonparametric Statistics: Data Analysis with Less Restrictive Assumptions"; and "Elementary Decision Making Using Prior Information." Uses flowcharting where appropriate and a few computer printouts. Appendixes devoted to algebra, numbers, and ratios; the presentation of research data; and statistical tables. Chapters conclude with lists of new symbols, problems, and references.

L'Esperance, Wilford L. MODERN STATISTICS FOR BUSINESS AND ECONOMICS. New York: Macmillan, 1971. vii, 503 p. Appendix: Tables, pp. 481-96. Index, pp. 497-503.

A text for a one-year course assuming knowledge of college algebra. Topics include rules for probability, including Bayes' rule; random variables and their distributions; point and interval estimation; hypotheses testing and the two-sample problem; two-variable linear model with stochastic error; one-way analysis of variance; decision making under uncertainty; linear profit functions; revising probabilities of a random variable; index numbers and time series; and an introduction to econometrics.

Levin, Richard I. STATISTICS FOR MANAGEMENT. Englewood Cliffs, N.J.: Prentice-Hall, 1978. viii, 568 p. Appendix: Tables, pp. 538-59. Bibliography, pp. 560-62. Index, pp. 563-68.

A text for a one-year course requiring a minimum of mathematics. Includes intuitive proofs and no derivations. Explanations tend to be lengthy using large number of examples. Problems and examples reflect real life situations in both the public and private sectors. Topics include rules of probability; random variables and their distributions; sampling distributions; estimation and hypothesis testing; chi-square; simple and multiple regression; nonparametric tests; time series and index numbers; and decision theory. Chapters conclude with summaries of equations; sections, with exercises.

Lewis, Edward E. METHODS OF STATISTICAL ANALYSIS IN ECONOMICS AND BUSINESS. 2d ed., rev. Boston: Houghton and Mifflin, 1963. x, 726 p. Appendix, pp. 686-703. List of Charts, pp. 705-10. List of Tables, pp. 711-17. Index, pp. 719-26.

A text for a one-year course requiring knowledge of arithmetic. Consists of the following six parts: "Introduction to Statistical Analysis"; "Measures of Distributions"; "Statistical Inference"; "Index Numbers"; "Time Series Analysis"; and "Correlation." Chapters organized into relatively short sections each devoted to a single topic and followed by exercises. The appendix consists of tables and formulas.

Lowe, Cecil William. INDUSTRIAL STATISTICS. Vol. 1. London: Business Books Limited, 1968. xii, 316 p. Appendix: Statistical Tables, pp. 286-307. Bibliography, pp. 308-9. Index, pp. 311-16.

A reference for industrial statisticians who need methods, procedures, and techniques which can be applied quickly and simple. Includes charts and graphs, tests of significance, analysis of variance, correlation, analysis of covariance, sampling and testing, and chi-square. Chapters conclude with suggestions for further reading.

______. INDUSTRIAL STATISTICS. Vol. 2. London: Business Books Limited, 1970. x, 294 p. Bibliography, pp. 289-90. Index, pp. 291-94.

Topics include time series for forecasting; desirability coefficients for measuring maintenance performance and performance of manufacturing departments; evolutionary operation; linear programming; productivity analysis; business gaming, inventories, replacement and inspection; queues; and the use of the computer. Assumes knowledge of basic statistics and linear programming.

McAllister, Harry E. ELEMENTS OF BUSINESS AND ECONOMIC STATISTICS: LEARNING BY OBJECTIVES. New York: Wiley, 1975. viii, 556 p. Appendix A: The Use of Logarithms, pp. 483-90. Appendix B: Use of a Table of Square Roots, p. 491. Appendix C: The Principle of the Reciprocal, p. 492. Appendix D: Rounding Numbers, pp. 493-97. Appendix E: List of Tables, pp. 498-537. Answers to Selected Problems, pp. 538-48. Index, pp. 549-65.

A text for a one-semester course requiring only high school algebra. Consists of the following eight units each of which includes one or more chapters: "Frequency Distributions and Their Characteristics"; "Probability and Probability Distributions"; "Sampling and Sampling Distributions"; "Statistical Estimation and Decision Making"; "Linear Regression and Correlation"; "Data Collection and Presentation"; "Index Numbers"; and "Time Series." Chapters conclude with questions and problems, as well as references. Emphasizes clarity.

McClave, James T., and Benson, P. George. STATISTICS FOR BUSINESS AND ECONOMICS. Rev. ed. San Francisco: Dellen, 1979. xvii, 667 p. Appendix A: Basic Counting Rules, pp. 625-27. Appendix B: Tables, pp. 628-46. Answers to Selected Exercises, pp. 647-62. Index, pp. 663-67.

A text for a one-year course for students in business and economics who have an algebra background. Includes footnotes explaining the role of calculus. Includes simple derivations, and extensive coverage of multiple regression and model building. Topics include events and probability; discrete and continuous random variables; sampling distributions; estimation and hypothesis testing; time series and forecasting; analysis of variance; nonparametric statistics; contingency tables; and decision analysis. Sections conclude with exercises; chapters, with summaries and references.

McElroy, Elam E. APPLIED BUSINESS STATISTICS: AN ELEMENTARY APPROACH. San Francisco: Holden-Day, 1971. xi, 335 p. Appendixes A to F, pp. 307-24. Answers to Even-Numbered Problems, pp. 325-28. Index, pp. 329-35.

An applied text for a one-semester course requiring only a high school algebra background. Topics include binomial and normal distributions; hypotheses testing; chi-square; simple regression and correlation; and index numbers and time series. Chapters conclude with review questions and laboratory problems.

Malik, Henrick J., and Mullen, Kenneth. APPLIED STATISTICS FOR BUSINESS AND ECONOMICS. Reading, Mass.: Addison-Wesley, 1975. xiii, 470 p. A Selected List of Formulas, pp. 401-9. Selected Bibliography, pp. 411-12. Appendix: Tables, pp. A-1 to A-43. Answers to Odd-Numbered Exercises, pp. A-43 to A-52. Index, pp. I-1 to I-6.

A text for a one-year course in basic statistics for students of business and economics who have knowledge of high school algebra. Contains a large number of worked out examples, and a large number of exercises at the ends of the chapters. Topics include probability theory, including Bayes' rule; random variables and probability distributions; the binomial, Poisson, and normal distributions; sampling, including stratified and cluster sampling; estimation; time series; chi-square; two-factor analysis of variance; quality control; and decision making under uncertainty.

Mansfield, Edwin, ed. ELEMENTARY STATISTICS FOR ECONOMICS AND BUSINESS: SELECTED READINGS. New York: W.W. Norton, 1970. x, 290 p. Selected Readings, pp. 289-90. No index.

A supplement to basic statistics courses in economics and business consisting of nineteen reprints of articles dealing with applications of statistical techniques grouped under the following headings: "Economic Statistics"; "Nature, Limitations, and Pitfalls"; "Probability and Statistical Inference"; "Sampling and Applications of t, Chi-Square, and F Tests"; "Simple Regression: Demand and Cost"; "Simple Regression: Income, Employment, and Consumption." Topics include the consumer price index; objective and subjective probability; market surveys; application of statistics in auditing; sales forecasting; economies of scale; the great ratios of economics; tests of hypotheses regarding bilateral monopoly; Gibrat's law and the growth of firms; statistical cost functions; and fluctuations in the savings-income ratio.

Mason, Robert Deward. PROGRAMMED LEARNING AID FOR BUSINESS AND ECONOMIC STATISTICS. Foreword by Roger H. Hermanson. Homewood, Ill.: Irwin Learning Systems, 1970. xi, 164 p. Glossary of Terms and Formulas, pp. 152-54. Appendixes, pp. 155-62. Index, pp. 163-64.

A self-review of the techniques studied in most basic statistics courses. Illustrations business oriented, but the techniques applicable to other areas such as the social sciences, education, and engineering. Each chapter divided into segments called frames in which the reader can test his comprehension of the material by answering questions. Includes a final self-review (with answers) at the end of each chapter. Topics include averages, Bayes' theorem, chi-square, combination, correlation, cyclical variation, dispersion, graphs, hypothesis testing, indexes, permutations, probability, quality control, sampling, seasonal variation, skewness, and time series.

______. STATISTICAL TECHNIQUES IN BUSINESS AND ECONOMICS. 4th ed., rev. Irwin Series in Quantitative Analysis for Business. Homewood, Ill.: Irwin, 1978. xx, 596 p. Appendixes: Tables, pp. 554-92. Index, pp. 593-96.

A text for a one-year course requiring a minimum of mathematics. Derivations omitted entirely and examples used to illustrate concepts. Several computer printouts using the SPSS illustrate the computer's potential for problem solving. Topics include index numbers and time series; probability and probability distributions; inference and parametric tests of hypotheses, including the two-sample problem; two-way analysis of variance; nonparametric tests; statistical quality control; simple and multiple regression and correlation; decision theory; and Bayes' theorem. Chapters conclude with self-review examinations.

Mayes, Anne C., and Mayes, David G. INTRODUCTORY ECONOMIC STATISTICS. New York: Wiley, 1976. x, 223 p. Appendix 1: Index Numbers, pp. 200-207. Appendix 2: Elements of Matrix Algebra, pp. 208-13. Appendix 3: Statistical Tables, pp. 214-18. Index, pp. 219-23.

A text for a one-year course. More theoretically oriented than most texts and contains fewer numerical examples (based on United Kingdom data). Topics include probability and sampling, including the central limit theorem; estimation and hypothesis testing; regression and correlation; covariance; identification problem; indirect least squares; multicollinearity; autocorrelation; and simultaneous equation estimation. Uses matrix algebra for regression and econometric models. Includes flow charts.

Melnyk, Myron. PRINCIPLES OF APPLIED STATISTICS. Pergamon Management and Business Series. Elmsford, N.Y.: Pergamon, 1974. xiv, 619 p. Bibliography, pp. 567-68. Appendix: Statistical Tables, pp. 569-609. Index, pp. 611-19.

A text for a one-year course assuming knowledge of only high school algebra. Derivations presented in great detail and examples worked out in detail. Topics include binomial and Poisson probability distributions; estimation and hypothesis testing; Bayesian statistics; chi-square; analysis of variance; simple and multiple regression and correlation; index numbers and time series; and nonparametric tests. Chapters conclude with a large number of questions and problems.

Mendenhall, William. INTRODUCTION TO PROBABILITY AND STATISTICS. 4th ed., rev. North Scituate, Mass.: Duxbury Press, 1975. xiii, 460 p. Appendix I: Useful Statistical Tests and Confidence Intervals, pp. 401-5. Appendix II: Tables, pp. 406-43. Answers, pp. 444-56. Index, pp. 457-60.

A text for a one-year course requiring only a high school algebra background. Introduces statistical inference in the first chapter, with the introduction to every subsequent chapter explaining the role of the chapter in making inferences. Probability based on sample spaces and employed at the earliest opportunity in the problem of lot acceptance sampling and test of hypothesis. Other topics include random variables and probability distributions; estimation and hypothesis testing; linear regression and correlation; chi-square; experimental design, including noise-reducing designs; analysis of variance; and nonparametric tests. Exercises of graduated difficulty. The chapters conclude with references, supplementary exercises, and experiences with real data.

Mendenhall, William, and Reinmuth, James E. STATISTICS FOR MANAGEMENT AND ECONOMICS. 3d ed., rev. North Scituate, Mass.: Duxbury Press, 1978. x, 789 p. Appendix: Tables, pp. 705-43. Glossary, pp. 745-55. Answers, pp. 757-83. Index, pp. 785-89.

A text for a one-year course requiring knowledge of high school algebra. Includes few derivations. Emphasizes examples and exercises to illustrate concepts. All exercises coded to indicate specific areas of application (accounting, finance, marketing, production, etc.). Topics include events and probability; discrete and continuous random variables and their distributions; estimation and hypotheses testing; decision theory; simple and multiple regression and correlation; analysis of variance; time series and index numbers; forecasting, including exponential smoothing; autoregressive models, least squares sinusoidal models; survey sampling; chi-square; and nonparametric tests. Definitions, important words and concepts, graphs, examples, and solutions marked in orange for easy identification.

Merrill, William C., and Fox, Karl A. INTRODUCTION TO ECONOMIC STATISTICS. New York: Wiley, 1970. xiii, 658 p. Appendix I: Statistical Tables, pp. 568-92. Appendix II: Mathematical Appendix, pp. 593-652. Index, pp. 653-58.

A text for a one-year course in basic statistics or econometrics for students who have a good background in algebra and some familiarity with calculus and matrix algebra. Topics include rules of probability; random variables and their distributions; binomial, Poisson, chi-square, F, and t distributions; sampling and estimation; hypothesis testing; simple and multiple regression and correlation, including first differences, heteroscedasticity, and multicollinearity; time series and index numbers; and simultaneous equation models, including two-stage least squares. Matrix algebra used for multiple regression. Chapters conclude with exercises, arranged by sections, and selected references.

Meyers, Cecil H. ELEMENTARY BUSINESS AND ECONOMIC STATISTICS. 2d ed., rev. Belmont, Calif.: Wadsworth, 1970. viii, 664 p. Appendix A: Some Basic Numerical Considerations, 575-78. Appendix B: A Sampling Universe, pp. 579-80. Appendix C: Determining the Total Error in a Frequency Distribution, pp. 581-82. Appendix D: Logarithmic Straight-Line Trend Least Squares Method, pp. 583-86. Appendix E: Adjusting for Calendar Variation, pp. 587-88. Appendix F to L: Tables, pp. 589-624. List of Formulae Appearing Throughout the Book, pp. 625-39. Answers to Selected Problems, pp. 641-57. Index, pp. 658-64.

A comprehensive text for a one-semester course requiring a good high school algebra background. Emphasizes problem solving and decision making, with derivations omitted. Topics include set theory and probability; Bayes' formula; normal and binomial distributions; estimation and hypothesis testing; survey sampling; quality control; chi-square; index numbers and time series; and simple regression and correlation. Chapters conclude with exercises.

Miller, Irwin. A PRIMER ON STATISTICS FOR BUSINESS AND ECONOMICS. New York: Random House, 1968. x, 176 p. Bibliography, pp. 171-72. Index, pp. 173-76.

A nontechnical introduction to statistical methods for the layman employing simple numerical examples and a few formulas. Topics include averages; departures from average; taking a chance; decisions; and the numbers game.

Mills, Frederick C. STATISTICAL METHODS. 3d ed., rev. and enl. New York: Holt, Rinehart and Winston, 1955. xviii, 842 p. Appendix A, Statistical Data: The Raw Materials of Analysis; B, Note on Statistical Calculations; C, The Method of Least Squares as Applied to Certain Statistical Problems; D, Derivation of Formulae for Mean and Standard Deviation of the Binomial Distribution; E, Derivation of the Standard Error of the Arithmetic Mean; F, Illustrating the Measurement of Trend by a Modified Exponential Curve, a Gompertz Curve, and a Logistic Curve, pp. 703-63. The Greek Alphabet, p. 764. Appendix: Tables, pp. 765-819. List of References, pp. 821-30. Index, pp. 833-42.

A text for graduates and undergraduates, as well as a reference assuming a good background in algebra. Directed to the needs of users of statistics, with concepts explained and illustrated in great detail using examples from various fields of economics. Topics include probability rules; point and interval estimation; hypothesis testing; simple and multiple linear and nonlinear regression and correlation; partial correlation; rank correlation; time series and index numbers; chi-square and analysis of variance; and sampling and sample surveys. Chapters conclude with references.

Mills, Richard L. STATISTICS FOR APPLIED ECONOMICS AND BUSINESS. New York: McGraw-Hill, 1977. xvi, 618 p. Appendix A: Answers to Selected Exercises, pp. 543-65. Appendix B: Case Data, pp. 566-83. Appendix C: Tables, pp. 584-609. Bibliography, pp. 610-12. Index, pp. 613-18.

A text for a one-year course assuming knowledge of college algebra. Footnotes and starred sections provide hints as to how calculus may be used, with emphasis on understanding what a theorem or concept says rather than on proofs. Topics include probability and set theory; random variables and probability distributions; descriptive statistics; sampling and sampling distributions; estimation and hypothesis testing; chi-square and analysis of variance; nonparametric tests; simple and multiple regression and correlation; time series; decision theory; and an introduction to economic models. Chapters conclude with exercises and case questions.

Murdock, John, and Barnes, J.A. STATISTICS: PROBLEMS AND SOLUTIONS. New York: Wiley, 1973. xii, 225 p. No index.

A supplementary text for basic statistics and a reference for personnel in industry and commerce. Shows, through worked examples, some of the practical applications of simple statistical methods. Topics include probability; distributions, including hypergeometric, binomial, Poisson, and normal; relationships between distributions; distributions of linear functions of variables; central limit theorem; estimation and hypothesis testing; and linear regression and correlation. Chapters conclude with practical experiments.

Neiswanger, William Addison. ELEMENTARY STATISTICAL METHODS AS APPLIED TO BUSINESS AND ECONOMIC DATA. Rev. ed. New York: Macmillan, 1956. xx, 749 p. Appendixes, pp. 693-732. Index, pp. 733-49.

A text for a one-semester course requiring knowledge of only high school algebra. Emphasizes the meaning and interpretation of concepts, rather than the mechanics of computation and proofs. Topics include design of samples; estimation and hypothesis testing; index numbers; time series; business cycles; and simple and multiple regression and correlation. Appendixes consist of review of arithmetic, glossary of symbols, sampling variances for three types of sampling procedures, normal equations for fitting a second-degree parabola to data, and statistical tables. Chapters conclude with questions, problems, and references.

Neter, John; Wasserman, William; and Whitmore, G.A. APPLIED STATISTICS. Boston: Allyn and Bacon, 1978. xx, 743 p. Appendix A: Mathematical Review, pp. 683-90. Appendix B: Tables, pp. 691-712. Appendix C: Data Set, pp. 713-22. Answers to Selected Problems, pp. 723-35. Index, pp. 737-43.

A comprehensive text for a one-year course assuming knowledge of college algebra. Presents a balanced account of statistical concepts and applications to real-world problems. Mathematical derivations included if necessary for understanding, and each technique illustrated by one or more examples. Consists of the following eight parts: "Data"; "Probability"; "Sampling and Sampling Distributions"; "Estimation and Testing--I"; "Estimation and Testing--II"; "Linear Statistical Models"; "Bayesian Decision Making"; and "Time Series Analysis and Index Numbers." Computer printouts employed in several parts of the text.

______. FUNDAMENTAL STATISTICS FOR BUSINESS AND ECONOMICS. 4th abridged ed. Boston: Allyn and Bacon, 1973. xiii, 514 p. Appendix: Tables, pp. 477-98. Answers to Selected Problems, pp. 499-505. Index, pp. 507-14.

A text for a one-semester course and a reference for practitioners with a prerequisite of high school algebra. Detailed explanation of concepts always precedes the discussion of the statistical technique, and formulas and definitions are set out in a distinctive fashion for easy reference. Consists of the following six units: "Data Handling"; "Probability"; "Sampling and Sampling Distributions"; "Statistical Estimation"; "Statistical Decision-Making"; and "Regression and Correlation." Chapters conclude with references, questions, and problems.

Newton, Byron L. STATISTICS FOR BUSINESS. Chicago: Science Research Associates, 1973. ix, 553 p. Appendixes A to H: Tables, pp. 488-532. Solutions to Exercises, pp. 533-44. Index, pp. 545-53.

A text for a one-semester course for students with a high school algebra background. Examples, drawn mainly from business and industry, used to develop concepts, with mathematical models used only where necessary. Topics include sets and probability; normal curve and estimation of mean, proportion and standard deviation; tests of hypotheses; chi-square; analysis of variance; simple and multiple regression; index numbers and time series; and decision making. Chapters conclude with glossaries and exercises.

O'Hara, John B., and Clelland, Richard C. EFFECTIVE USE OF STATISTICS IN ACCOUNTING AND BUSINESS: ILLUSTRATIVE CASES. New York: Holt, Rinehart and Winston, 1964. vii, 231 p. No index.

Presents thirty-three cases covering a wide range of applications of statistical methods of interest to accountants. Each case followed by a series of questions related to the concepts. Cases grouped under the following ten sections: "Ratio Analysis"; "Index Numbers"; "Construction of Index Numbers"; "Lifo Method of Inventory Valuation"; "Averages and Measures of Dispersion"; "Compound Interest and Annuity Formulas"; "Regression and Correlation"; "Random Sampling and the Normal Distribution"; "More Complex Inventory Problems"; and "Problems in Production Control." Each section contains an unsolved case requiring creative thinking. Assumes knowledge of basic statistics.

Parket, I. Robert. STATISTICS FOR BUSINESS DECISION MAKING. New York: Random House, 1974. xiv, 434 p. Appendixes A to Q: Statistical Tables, 355-415. Appendix R: Review of Arithmetical and Algebraic Operations, pp. 416-22. Appendix S: Answers to Odd-Numbered Problems, pp. 423-28. Index, pp. 429-34.

A text for a one-semester course assuming knowledge of high school algebra. Emphasizes the types of problems that can be solved with each technique. Topics include decision theory; survey procedures, including cluster sampling; sets and probability; binomial, normal and Poisson probability distributions; estimation and hypotheses testing; one-way analysis of variance; index numbers and time series; linear regression and correlation; chi-square; and nonparametric tests. Chapters conclude with problems, notations, and references.

Parl, Boris. BASIC STATISTICS: A COLLEGE GUIDE. New York: Doubleday, 1967. xvi, 364 p. Appendix: Tables, pp. 337-54. Index, pp. 355-64.

A supplementary text for basic and intermediate statistics courses and a reference for practitioners in experimental science, finance, marketing, civil service, economics, and related fields. Assumes knowledge of college algebra. Emphasizes clarity, simplicity of presentation, and ease in locating specific statistical tools for application. Consists of the following eight sections: "Basic Concepts"; "Distribution and Dispersion"; "Sampling"; "Sampling Errors and Hypothesis Testing"; "Regression and Correlation Analysis"; "Time Series Analysis"; "Index Numbers"; and "New Trends." Topics include misuse of statistics; sampling distributions of normal, binomial, Poisson, and proportion; chi-square; analysis of variance; spurious correlation; and Bayesian statistics.

Parsons, Robert. STATISTICAL ANALYSIS: A DECISION-MAKING APPROACH. 2d ed., rev. New York: Harper & Row, 1978. xvi, 791 p. Appendixes: Tables, pp. 730-84. Index, pp. 785-91.

A text for a one-year course assuming knowledge of algebra. Provides a broad coverage of topics with a minimum of interdependence among chapters. Incorporates both classical and Bayesian approaches. The treatment of regression tied to the SPSS book of computer programs. Topics include probability calculus and Bayes' rule; discrete and continuous probability distributions; Bayesian approach to binomial sampling; classical and Bayesian interval estimation; tests of hypotheses; analysis of variance; decision theory; time series and index numbers; simple and multiple regression and correlation; and nonparametric tests.

Pazer, Harold L., and Swanson, Lloyd A. MODERN METHODS FOR STATISTICAL ANALYSIS. Scranton, Pa.: Intext Educational Publishers, 1972. ix, 483 p. Selected Bibliography, pp. 427-28. Tables, pp. 429-78. Index, pp. 479-83.

A text for an intermediate course assuming a prerequisite of basic statistics. Emphasizes integrating Bayesian and classical approaches to estimation and hypothesis testing. Topics include rules of probability; hypergeometric, Poisson, uniform, gamma, exponential, Erlang, normal, chi-square, and multivariate probability distributions; point estimators; hypotheses testing; three-way analysis of variance; factorial analysis; fixed-factor models; power curves; fixed-effects model; simple and multiple regression and correlation; analysis of covariance; and nonparametric tests. Includes suggestions for writing computer programs to work problems and do simulations. Chapters conclude with problems.

Pearlman, Richard. PROBLEMS IN STATISTICS FOR ECONOMICS AND BUSINESS STUDENTS. New York: Holt, Rinehart and Winston, 1963. xiii, 130 p. Answers, pp. 115-21. Tables, pp. 123-30. No index.

A collection of problems grouped into ten chapters according to the main topics usually treated in a basic statistics text. Each chapter begins with a sample problem, followed by the exercises, and concludes with a multiple-choice test. Includes answers for the problems and tests.

Perles, Benjamin, and Sullivan, Charles. FREUND AND WILLIAMS' MODERN BUSINESS STATISTICS. Rev. ed. Englewood Cliffs, N.J.: Prentice-Hall,

1969. xvii, 541 p. Appendix I: Pictorial Presentations, pp. 461-73. Appendix II: Quality Control, pp. 474-91. Appendix III: Calculations With Rounded Numbers, pp. 492-94. Appendix IV: The Use of Logarithms and Square Roots, pp. 495-98. Statistical Tables, pp. 499-523. Answers to Odd-Numbered Exercises, pp. 525-32. Index, pp. 533-41.

A text for a one-year course requiring knowledge of high school algebra. Includes examples and exercises based on actual experiments. Topics include descriptive statistics; probability; sampling distributions; estimation and hypothesis testing concerning two means and two proportions; chi-square; analysis of variance; nonparametric tests; simple regression and correlation; time series and index numbers; and statistical quality control. Sections conclude with exercises; chapters, with references.

Pfaffenberger, Roger C., and Patterson, James H. STATISTICAL METHODS FOR BUSINESS AND ECONOMICS. Irwin Series in Quantitative Analysis for Business. Homewood, Ill.: Irwin, 1977. xvii, 750 p. Appendix A: Statistical Tables, pp. 694-731. Answers to Selected Problems, pp. 733-44. Index, pp. 745-50.

A text for a one-year course for students with limited mathematics background. Develops the logic of statistics in a mathematically nonrigorous manner without derivations and proofs, with calculus used only occasionally to emphasize key points such as the connection between the summing process for discrete values and the integrating process for a continuum of values. FORTRAN computer programs available from the authors. Topics include sample spaces and probability; Bayes' theorem; random variables and their distributions; discrete and continuous probability distributions; inference concerning difference between two means and two proportions; analysis of variance; simple and multiple regression and correlation; revised probabilities; decision theory; index numbers and time series; forecasting, including exponential smoothing and autoregression approaches; and nonparametric tests. Chapters conclude with references and problems.

Richards, Larry E., and LaCava, Jerry J. BUSINESS STATISTICS: WHY AND WHEN. New York: McGraw-Hill, 1978. xiv, 466 p. Cases, pp. 385-410. Bibliography, pp. 411-12. Appendix: Tables, pp. 413-52. Selected Answers pp. 453-62. Index, pp. 463-66.

A text for a one-year course requiring limited mathematics. Introduces each statistical technique by describing a realistic business situation. Emphasizes identifying applications, with an attempt made to eliminate topics not necessary for basic statistics. For example, omits average deviation, Poisson, exponential, and rectangular distributions. Derivations kept to a minimum. Topics include index numbers; probability;

sampling; distributions; tests of hypotheses; analysis of variance; regression; nonparametric tests; and time series and forecasting.

Richmond, Samuel B. STATISTICAL ANALYSIS. 2d ed., rev. New York: Ronald Press, 1964. xv, 633 p. Glossary of Equations, pp. 511-61. Appendixes: Tables, pp. 565-624. Index, pp. 625-33.

A text for a one-year course for students with a minimum of mathematics background. Topics include sets and probability; Poisson and other distributions; Tchebycheff's inequality; inference; decision theory; chi-square; analysis of variance; sampling theory; forecasting techniques; time series and index numbers; and regression. Chapters conclude with glossaries of symbols and problems.

Roberts, Harry V. CONVERSATIONAL STATISTICS. Edited by Christine Doerr. University Business Series. Palo Alto, Calif.: Scientific Press, 1974. viii, 290 p. Appendix A: Applications, pp. 217-66. Appendix B: Computer Notes, pp. 267-76. Summary and Glossary, pp. 277-90. No Index.

A text for a one-semester course which represents a radical departure from traditional texts. Written in a question and answer script, with no reliance placed on mathematical ideas beyond those ordinarily covered in the first eight grades of school. Conversational aspect made possible by using interactive computer programs on Hewlett-Packard computers, with numerous printouts provided. Many key terms, such as arithmetic mean and probability, introduced as needed rather than developed in the traditional sequence. Topics include effective uses of statistics; observation and measurement; analysis of sequence;distributions; normal regression; inference; prior and posterior distributions; regression; autoregression; and time series.

Ryan, Thomas A.; Joiner, Brian L.; and Ryan, Barbara F. MINITAL STUDENT HANDBOOK. North Scituate, Mass.: Duxbury, 1976. ix, 341 p. Appendix A: Extended Examples, pp. 270-302. Appendix B: Preparing Data for Computer Analysis, pp. 320-7. Appendix C: Differences Between Interactive and Batch Computing, pp. 307-8. Appendix D: How Minitab Works, pp. 308-12. Appendix E: Other Features of Minitab, pp. 312-18. Appendix F: List of Commands, pp. 318-36. Index, pp. 337-41.

A handbook intended as a supplementary text for basic and intermediate statistics courses. Designed to be used with MINITAB (in FORTRAN IV), a computing system for doing statistical computations. Chapters designed independently and topics include introduction to minitab; simulation; binomial and Poisson distributions; normal distribution; tests concerning two population means; simple and multiple regression and correlation; transformations; two-way analysis of variance; chi-square and contingency tables; and nonparametric tests. Contains printouts of solutions.

Sanders, Donald H.; Murph, A. Franklin; and Eng, Robert J. STATISTICS: A FRESH APPROACH. New York: McGraw-Hill, 1976. xv, 367 p. Appendixes: Tables, pp. 343-62. Index, pp. 363-67.

A text for a one-semester course requiring college algebra. Emphasizes exploring statistical procedures and interpreting the results of statistical analyses. Consists of the following four parts: "Descriptive Statistics"; "Sampling in Theory and Practice"; "Coping with Change"; and "Beyond Statistics." Topics include binomial and normal probability distributions; sampling distributions of means and percentages; estimation and hypotheses testing; index numbers and time series; regression; chi-square; and an introduction to special procedures such as multiple regression, analysis of variance, and linear programming. Sections conclude with self-testing review questions; chapters, with summaries, terms and concepts, and answers to self-testing review questions.

Sasaki, Kyohei. STATISTICS FOR MODERN BUSINESS DECISION MAKING. Belmont, Calif.: Wadsworth, 1968. xiv, 562 p. Appendix: Matrix Algebra, pp. 477-85. Statistical Tables, pp. 487-538. Answers to Selected Problems, pp. 539-52. Index, pp. 553-62.

A text for a one-semester course in both classical and Bayesian statistics for graduates and undergraduates who have a college algebra background. Consists of the following four parts: "Probability and Classical Theory of Statistical Inference"; "Bayesian Decision Theory with Normal Sampling"; "Bayesian Decision Theory with Binomial Sampling"; and "Bayesian Decision Theory and Regression Analysis." Topics include random variables and their moments and distributions, including joint distributions; games and linear programming; analysis in the normal form; and estimation of regression coefficients with a priori information on the state of nature. Uses abstract models to introduce the reader to theoretical topics. Chapters conclude with problems and references.

Scalzo, Frank, and Hughes, Rowland. ELEMENTARY COMPUTER ASSISTED STATISTICS. New York: Van Nostrand Reinhold, 1976. xv, 345 p. Appendix A: Additional Basic Statements and Functions, pp. 267-74. Appendix B: Common BASIC Compiler Error Messages, pp. 275-76. Appendix C: A List of BASIC Program Statements, pp. 277-78. Appendix D: Statistical and Probability Formulas and Algorithms for Computations, pp. 279-88. Appendix E: Programming Projects, pp. 289-92. Appendix F: Tables of Statistics, pp. 293-309. Answers to Selected Problems, pp. 311-40. Index, pp. 341-45.

A text for a one-semester course which utilizes thirteen prepackaged computer programs in BASIC to solve problems. Topics (with programs) include sets; permutations and combinations; binomial theorem; elementary probability concepts; random variables and the normal distribution; interval estimation and hypothesis testing; chi-square; regression and correlation; and analysis of variance. Problems follow the presentation of important statistical concepts.

Schlaifer, Robert. INTRODUCTION TO STATISTICS FOR BUSINESS DECISIONS. New York: McGraw-Hill, 1961. x, 382 p. Index of Symbols, pp. 375-76. Subject Index, pp. 377-82.

A text for a one-semester course in classical and Bayesian statistics. Consists of the following four parts: "The Use of Probabilities Based Directly on Experience"; "Binomial Sampling"; "Introduction to the Normal Distribution"; and "Sampling of Measured Values." Topics include random variables and their distributions; incremental analysis; statistical decision rules in terms of expected loss; central limit theorem and large sample theory; expected loss with normal sampling; normal prior distributions; and the economics of two-action problems with linear profit or costs and normal distributions. Chapters conclude with problems.

______. PROBABILITY AND STATISTICS FOR BUSINESS DECISIONS: AN INTRODUCTION TO MANAGERIAL ECONOMICS UNDER UNCERTAINTY. New York: McGraw-Hill, 1959. xii, 732 p. Appendix: Continuous Prior Distributions for the Parameters of Bernoulli and Poisson Processes, pp. 670-78. Tables, pp. 680-710. Charts, pp. 711-18. Index of Symbols, pp. 719-21. Subject Index, pp. 723-32.

A text for a one-year course emphasizing both classical and Bayesian approaches. Consists of the following five parts: "The Use of Probabilities Based Directly on Experience"; "Simple Random Processes and Derived Probabilities"; "The Use of Information Obtained by Sampling"; "The Value of Additional Information"; and "Objectivist Statistics: Tests of Significance and Confidence Intervals." Presentation based on the theory of utility and subjective probability with the concepts developed directly from realistic problems faced by businessmen. Topics include inventory control; opportunity loss and cost of uncertainty; conditional and joint probabilities; normal approximation to empirical distributions; waiting lines; revised probabilities; sampling; normal prior distributions; preposterior analysis; two-action problems with linear costs; many-action problems with proportional losses; and sequential decision problems. Chapters conclude with problems.

Shao, Stephen P. ESSENTIALS OF BUSINESS STATISTICS. Columbus, Ohio: Charles E. Merrill, 1977. xi, 548 p. Appendix: Tables, pp. 479-531. Answers to Odd-Numbered Problems, pp. 532-39. Selected References, pp. 540-43. Index, pp. 544-48.

A text for a one-year course. Formulas derived intuitively and presented in their simplest form; mathematical proofs placed in footnotes. Consists of the following six parts: "Beginning Statistical Study"; "Probability and Probability Distributions"; "Estimation and Tests of Hypotheses"; "Time Series Analysis"; "Relationship Analysis"; and "Decision Theory and Techniques." Topics include chi-square; nonparametric tests; analysis of variance; nonlinear, multiple, partial, and rank correlation; Bayesian decision theory; statistical quality control; linear programming; game theory; and index numbers and time series. Chapters conclude with summaries and exercises.

______. STATISTICS FOR BUSINESS AND ECONOMICS. 3d ed., rev. Columbus, Ohio: Charles E. Merrill, 1976. xiii, 815 p. Appendix: Tables, pp. 745-92. Answers to Odd-Numbered Problems, pp. 793-803. Selected References, pp. 804-7. Index, pp. 808-15.

A text for a one-year course requiring a good high school algebra background. Consists of the following seven parts: "Beginning Statistical Study"; "Simple Statistical Analysis"; "Probability and Probability Distributions"; "Statistical Induction-Process and Application"; "Other Tests of Hypotheses and Decision Theory"; "Time Series Analysis"; and "Relationship Analysis." Topics include sets and probability; probability distributions; Tchebycheff's inequality; estimation and tests of hypotheses; quality control; chi-square; nonparametric tests; analysis of variance; Bayesian statistics; nonlinear regression; and rank correlation. Chapters conclude with formulas and exercises.

Shapiro, Jesse M., and Whitney, D. Ransom. ELEMENTARY ANALYSIS AND STATISTICS: MATHEMATICS FOR ADMINISTRATIVE, BEHAVIORAL, AND BIOLOGICAL SCIENCES. Merrill Mathematics Series. Columbus, Ohio: Charles E. Merrill, 1967. xiv, 704 p. Tables, pp. 637-57. Answers to Selected Odd-Numbered Problems, pp. 659-95. Index, pp. 697-704.

A text for a one-year course for use by mathematics departments. Covers differentiation and integration and the following statistical topics: discrete and continuous random variables and their distributions; properties of random variables; point estimation; interval estimation and hypothesis testing; and nonparametric tests. Calculus used in deriving moment-generating functions, expected value of random variables, and other concepts. Includes both formal and intuitive proofs. Sections conclude with problems.

Sielaff, Theodore, J., ed. STATISTICS IN ACTION: READINGS IN BUSINESS AND ECONOMICS. San Jose, Calif.: Lansford Press, 1963. vi, 251 p. No index.

Twenty-five reprints of articles grouped under the following headings: "Misuses and Abuses of Statistics" (1 article);

"Statistical Inference and Accounting" (5 articles); "Statistical Inference and Production Management" (5 articles); "Statistical Inference and Marketing" (2 articles); "Bayesian Statistics" (six articles); "Analysis of Time Series Data" (5 articles); and "The Occupation of Statisticians" (one article). Useful as a supplementary text for a course in basic statistics.

Sielaff, Theodore J., and Wang, P.S. PRACTICAL PROBLEMS IN BUSINESS AND ECONOMIC STATISTICS. San Francisco: Holden-Day, 1968. xvi, 272 p. Appendixes A to F, pp. 255-72. No index.

A programmed text for basic statistics divided into twenty-one units, including sources of data, frequency distributions, measures of central tendency, probability, Bayesian statistical decision making, sampling distributions, estimation, index numbers, regression and correlation, chi-square, and analysis of variance. Space provided on each page for answers to questions and problems. Includes examinations. The appendixes consist of statistical tables.

Spurr, William A., and Bonini, Charles P. STATISTICAL ANALYSIS FOR BUSINESS DECISIONS. Homewood, Ill.: Irwin, 1973. xii, 724 p. Appendix A: Glossary of Symbols, pp. 659-62. Appendix B: Logarithms, pp. 663-67. Appendixes C to P: Tables, pp. 668-709. Index, pp. 711-24.

A text for a one-year course with emphasis on practical applications rather than on theory and mathematical derivations. Topics include probability and probability distributions, including Poisson and exponential; decision theory; estimation and hypothesis testing, including the two-sample problem; chi-square and F statistics; sample survey methods; Bayes' theorem; Monte Carlo methods; simple and multiple regression and correlation; index numbers and time series; and seasonal and cyclical variations. Chapters conclude with problems.

Steel, Robert G.D., and Torrie, James H. INTRODUCTION TO STATISTICS. McGraw-Hill Series in Probability and Statistics. New York: McGraw-Hill, 1976. xiv, 382 p. Appendix A1: Greek Alphabet, pp. 340-41. Appendix A2: Symbols and Notation, pp. 342-43. Appendix B: Tables, pp. 345-54. References, pp. 355-58. Answers to Selected Problems, pp. 359-73. Index, pp. 375-82.

A text for a one-semester course assuming knowledge of high school algebra. Exercises which follow the sections include numerical problems and derivations. Topics include probability; sample spaces and random variables; hypothesis testing; nonparametric tests; analysis of variance; chi-square; and linear regression and correlation.

Stevenson, William J. BUSINESS STATISTICS: CONCEPTS AND APPLICATIONS. New York: Harper & Row, 1978. xviii, 518 p. Appendix: Tables, pp. 463-91. Answers, pp. 493-511. Index, pp. 513-18.

A text for a one-semester course with a prerequisite of only high school algebra. Avoids derivations and proofs entirely. Suitable for a self-paced approach as well as a lecture approach. Includes an abundance of worked out examples. Topics include events and probability; random variables; discrete and continuous probability distributions; sampling distributions; two-sample tests of means; analysis of variance; chi-square; tests for ranks and signs; simple and multiple regression; and index numbers and time series.

Stockton, John R., and Clark, Charles T. INTRODUCTION TO BUSINESS AND ECONOMIC STATISTICS. 5th rev. ed. Cincinnati, Ohio: South-Western, 1975. x, 595 p. Appendixes: Formulas and Tables, pp. 501-84. Index, pp. 585-95.

A text for a one-semester course with no derivations. Uses examples and the intuitive approach to present concepts. Emphasizes time series and index numbers with fairly complete coverage of regression and correlation. Other topics include probability and Bayes' theorem; probability distributions, including Poisson and hypergeometric; survey sampling; parametric tests of significance, including difference between two means; nonparametric tests; and quality control. Chapters conclude with study questions and problems. Important formulas and sentences set out in red.

Suits, Daniel B. STATISTICS: AN INTRODUCTION TO QUANTITATIVE ECONOMIC RESEARCH. Rand McNally Economics Series. Chicago: Rand McNally, 1963. xix, 260 p. Index, pp. 245-48. Appendixes A to F: Tables, pp. 250-60.

A text for a one-semester course with emphasis on multivariate functions. Topics include statistical and stochastic functions; analysis of variance; chi-square; time series and index numbers; simple linear and curvilinear regression; hypothesis testing; sampling distributions; and descriptive statistics. Chapters conclude with questions, problems, and references.

Summers, George W., and Peters, William S. BASIC STATISTICS IN BUSINESS AND ECONOMICS. Belmont, Calif.: Wadsworth, 1973. xii, 445 p. References, pp. 411-14. Appendix: Tables, pp. 415-40. Index, pp. 441-45.

A text for a one-semester course assuming knowledge of high school algebra, although familiarity with finite mathematics helpful. Mathematical derivations kept to a minimum with ease of reading, without sacrifice of rigor, a major goal. Regression taken up early, before probability and hypothesis testing. Topics include probability laws; sample spaces; random variables; Chebyshev's inequality; sampling distributions; Bayes' theorem; expected value of sample information; discrete and continuous probability distributions; hypothesis testing; two-way analysis of variance; multiple regression and correlation; nonparametric tests; sample survey methods; time series and index numbers; and decision theory. Chapters conclude with glossaries of equations.

Szulc, Stefan. STATISTICAL METHODS. Translation by J. Stadler and translation edited by H. Infeld and C.D.I. Forrester. New York: Pergamon, 1965. viii, 666 p. Appendix, pp. 607-60. Name Index, pp. 661-62. Subject Index, pp. 663-66.

Originally published in Polish. Covers much of the ground normally included in basic statistics. Consists of the following five parts: "The Organization and Technique of Statistical Research"; "Statistical Series"; "Relative Numbers, Composite Index Numbers, Elimination Tables"; "Correlation Analysis"; and "Introduction to Sampling." Appendix devoted to the smoothing of statistical series, integration methods, operations with approximate numbers, and statistical tables.

Tanur, Judith M., et al., eds. STATISTICS: A GUIDE TO BUSINESS AND ECONOMICS. Foreword by Frederick Mosteller. Holden-Day Series in Probability and Statistics. San Francisco: Holden-Day, 1976. xii, 132 p. Index, pp. 129-32.

A supplement for a course in basic statistics consisting of twelve heretofore unpublished contributions by different authors on real-life problems in business and economics. Topics include public finance policy; the plight of the whales; drug screening; consumer price index; census taking; subjective probability; and evaluation of a new product.

Thompson, Gerald E. STATISTICS FOR DECISIONS: AN ELEMENTARY INTRODUCTION. Little, Brown Series in Economics. Boston: Little, Brown, 1972. xii, 297 p. Index, pp. 291-97.

A text for a one-semester course in Bayesian statistics. Traditional procedures, such as confidence interval estimation and hypothesis testing examined and their relationship to Bayesian procedures explored. Topics include criteria for decisions; simple and compound events; conditional probability; random variables and their distributions; expected cost of uncertainty and opportunity loss; utility and decisions; binomial hypothesis testing and decision rules; prior probabilities; conditional opportunity losses; normal prior probabilities; sampling; confidence interval estimation from sample information; normal posterior probabilities; expected value of sample information; and simple regression. Chapters conclude with references and problems.

Tintner, Gerhard, and Millham, Charles B. MATHEMATICS AND STATISTICS FOR ECONOMISTS. 2d ed., rev. and enl. New York: Holt, Rinehart and Winston, 1970. xx, 485 p. Appendix A: Suggestions for Further Study, pp. 417-18. Appendix B: Answers to Selected Problems, pp. 419-53. Appendix C: Sources of Numerical Examples, pp. 454-55. Appendix D: Tables, pp. 456-70. Index of Names, pp. 471-72. Index of Mathematical and Statistical Terms, pp. 473-80. Index of Economic Terms, pp. 481-85.

A text for a one-semester or one-year course in mathematics and statistics for economic students who have knowledge of high school algebra and elementary economic theory. Consists of three parts: "Some Applications of Elementary Mathematics to Economics"; "Calculus"; and "Probability and Statistics." Style consists of definitions followed by several examples with exercises of additional examples and extensions of the concepts at the ends of the sections. Topics include sets; functions, graphs, systems of linear equations, logarithms, and progressions; determinants and matrixes; inequalities and linear programming; input-output analysis; linear difference equations with constant coefficients; functions and limits; differentiation; optimization involving several variables; integration; differential equations; calculus of variations; random variables; moments; sampling and hypothesis testing; goodness of fit; regression and correlation; and index numbers.

Wessel, Robert H.; Willett, Edward R.; and Simone, Albert J. STATISTICS AS APPLIED TO ECONOMICS AND BUSINESS. Rev. ed. New York: Holt, Rinehart and Winston, 1965. xvii, 446 p. Appendix A: Arithmetic and Algebraic Techniques, pp. 395-412. Appendix B: Tables, pp. 415-37. Index, pp. 438-46.

An early text for a one-year course in basic statistics for students who know only arithmetic. Consists of the following four parts: "Introduction"; "Descriptive Statistics"; "Statistical Inference"; and "Forecasting." Topics include probability; normal curve; sampling theory; tests for the difference between two means; binomial law; chi-square; statistical quality control; index numbers and time series; and cyclical movements. Chapters conclude with references and problems.

Wetherill, G. Barrie. ELEMENTARY STATISTICAL METHODS. London: Methuen, 1967. xi, 329 p. Miscellaneous Exercises, pp. 298-306. Appendix I: Notes on Desk Computation, pp. 307-13. Appendix II: Statistical Tables, pp. 314-20. References, pp. 321-24. Author Index, pp. 325-26. Subject Index, pp. 327-29.

A text for a one-semester course assuming a college algebra background. Uses calculus in a few places. Emphasizes logical reasoning. Topics include random variables and probability distributions; sampling distributions and statistical inference; single and two-sample problems; comparison of two

Poisson variates; comparison of observed and expected frequencies; simple and multiple regression; analysis of variance; and nonparametric tests. Examples and exercises follow discussion of the concepts.

Winn, Paul R., and Johnson, Ross H. BUSINESS STATISTICS. New York: Macmillan, 1978. xvii, 494 p. Appendixes: Tables, pp. 445-90. Index, pp. 491-94.

A text for a one-year course in business statistics for students who have knowledge of only high school algebra. Emphasizes conversational style with both realistic and actual business examples based on the authors' extensive business experience. Topics include laws of probability; normal, Bernoulli, and Poisson distributions; sampling distributions; sampling, including random and nonrandom; estimation and hypothesis testing; chi-square and analysis of variance; simple and multiple regression and correlation; nonparametric statistics; decision theory; and index numbers and time series. Chapter appendixes include derivations.

Wonnacott, Thomas H., and Wonnacott, Ronald J. INTRODUCTORY STATISTICS FOR BUSINESS AND ECONOMICS. 2d ed., rev. Wiley Series in Probability and Mathematical Statistics. New York: Wiley, 1977. xxii, 753 p. Glossary of Symbols, pp. xviii-xxii. Tables, pp. 701-24. Answers to Odd-Numbered Problems, pp. 725-44. Index, pp. 745-53.

A text for a one-year course assuming college algebra background. Uses calculus in a few places. Uses problems and examples, rather than abstract theory, to introduce new material. Stresses relationships between topics, such as estimation and hypothesis testing, with a high priority placed on regression and extensions. Includes many topics, such as revealed preference theory, normally excluded from basic texts. Topics include functions of two random variables; sampling theory; two-factor analysis of variance; estimation and hypothesis testing; nonparametric tests; maximum likelihood tests; Bayesian decision theory; time series and autocorrelation; covariance; and game theory. Examples and graphs are set out in pink.

Yamane, Taro. STATISTICS: AN INTRODUCTORY ANALYSIS. 3d ed., rev. and enl. New York: Harper & Row, 1973. xx, 1,130 p. Statistical Tables, pp. 1077-114. Index, pp. 1115-30.

A comprehensive text for a one-year course in basic statistics for students of business and economics who have knowledge of college algebra. Uses simple hypothetical examples to illustrate concepts. Topics include axioms of probability; random variables and expectation; normal curve; sampling distribution; estimation; maximum likelihood; sufficiency; testing hypotheses;

Bayes' decision rules; index numbers and time series; linear regression and correlation; Neyman-Pearson lemma; likelihood ratio; binomial distribution; Poisson; chi-square; analysis of variance; fixed effects and random effects; multiple linear regression; and decision theory. Topics in econometrics include autocorrelation, multicollinearity, and multivariate analysis.

Yule, G. Udny, and Kendall, Maurice G. AN INTRODUCTION TO THE THEORY OF STATISTICS. 14th ed., rev. and enl. New York: Harper & Row, 1968. xxiv, 701 p. Appendix: Tables, pp. 663-73. Answers to the Exercises, pp. 675-89. Index, pp. 691-701.

A text for a one-year course assuming a good college algebra background. Consists of twenty-six chapters and includes the following topics: theory of attributes; descriptive statistics; moments of distributions; univariate and bivariate regression and correlation; partial correlation; product-moment and rank correlation; curve fitting; sampling theory; large and small samples; chi-square; analysis of variance; practical problems of sampling; and time series. Practical research problems used for illustrations. Chapters conclude with exercises.

Zuwaylif, Fadil H. APPLIED BUSINESS STATISTICS. Reading, Mass.: Addison-Wesley, 1974. xiii, 399 p. Tables, pp. T-1 to T-35. Answers to Exercises, pp. A-1 to A-10. Index, pp. I-1 to I-6.

A text for a course in basic statistics for students with a high school algebra background. Features simplicity of exposition, extensive use of illustrative problems and exercises, and clear distinction between population and sample. Topics include population parameters, sets and probability, random samples, estimation and hypothesis testing, testing for the difference between two means and several means, Bayesian decision theory, linear regression and correlation, time series, and nonparametric tests. Sections conclude with exercises.

Chapter 3

BASIC STATISTICS—MISCELLANEOUS

Adler, Irving. PROBABILITY AND STATISTICS FOR EVERYMAN: HOW TO UNDERSTAND AND USE THE LAWS OF CHANCE WITH DIAGRAMS. New York: John Day, 1963. 256 p. Bibliography, p. 241. Answers to Exercises, pp. 243-54. Index, pp. 255-56.

> An elementary introduction to the concepts and uses of probability based on set theory; for the layman. Topics include sample spaces and events; probability rules; counting and computing, including the binomial coefficient; averages and derivations from it; normal distribution; statistical trials; and the relationship between subjective probability and statistical probability. Chapters conclude with exercises.

Aigner, Dennis J. PRINCIPLES OF STATISTICAL DECISION MAKING. Foreword by James L. McKenney. Macmillan Decision Series. New York: Macmillan, 1968. xii, 145 p. Tables, pp. 133-40. Index, pp. 141-45.

> A supplementary text, containing no problems but many simple derivations, for students in varied disciplines who know college algebra and calculus. Bridges the gap between classical and modern decision making. Begins with a Reader's Digest version of itself and proceeds to such topics as calculus of probability; conditional probability and independence; Bayes' rule; random variables and discrete and continuous distributions; moments of random variables; sampling distributions; classical hypothesis testing, including notion of a "best" test; decision errors; Bayesian decision making; and sample-size determination.

Aitchison, John. SOLVING PROBLEMS IN STATISTICS I. Solving Problems in Mathematics, vol. 3. London: Oliver & Boyd, 1968. viii, 168 p. No index.

> A supplementary text for a basic statistics course. Presents in a concise form the concepts of probability and statistics, illustrates the concepts with worked examples, and then challenges the student to test his understanding against worked

examples. Each section follows a pattern: explanatory text, worked examples, additional examples, and solutions. The mathematical skills include summation of series and simple integrations. The six chapter titles: "The Nature of Statistical Problems"; "Probabilistic Models for Random Experiments"; "Further Descriptions of Random Experiments"; "Some Important Probability Models"; "Sampling"; and "Estimation."

______. SOLVING PROBLEMS IN STATISTICS II. Solving Problems in Mathematics, vol. 7. Edinburgh: Oliver & Boyd, 1971. viii, 181 p. No index.

Follows the same style of presentation as SOLVING PROBLEMS IN STATISTICS I. Assumes knowledge of calculus. The five chapter titles: "Probability Descriptions of Dependence"; "Statistical Inference and Decision Making"; "The Statistical Analysis of Dependence"; "Tests of Association"; and "Sequential Analysis."

Alder, Henry L., and Roessler, Edward B. INTRODUCTION TO PROBABILITY AND STATISTICS. 6th rev. ed. A Series of Books in Mathematics. San Francisco: W.H. Freeman, 1977. xii, 426 p. Appendix, pp. 355-417. Index, pp. 419-26.

A text for a one-year course for students in a variety of fields who have had at least two years of high school algebra. Includes proofs based on high school algebra. Examples and exercises taken from a variety of fields. Topics include binomial and normal distributions; random sampling; hypothesis testing; nonparametric tests; regression and correlation; chi-square; index numbers and time series; and analysis of variance. Appendixes include references, tables, review exercises, and answers to problems. Chapters conclude with numerous exercises.

Alterman, Hyman. NUMBERS AT WORK: THE STORY AND SCIENCE OF STATISTICS. New York: Harcourt, Brace and World, 1966. 280 p. Answer Section, pp. 251-72. Index, pp. 273-80.

A nontechnical introduction to the role of statistics in everyday life for the layman, as well as students enrolled in basic statistics courses. The five chapter titles: "The Frequency Distribution and Its Uses"; "Averages"; "Probability"; "Sampling"; and "Computers and Automation."

Amos, Jimmy Ray; Brown, Foster Lloyd; and Mink, Oscar G. STATISTICAL CONCEPTS: A BASIC PROGRAM. New York: Harper & Row, 1965. ix, 125 p. Diagnostic Test and Alphabetical Index, pp. 107-20. Evaluation Data, pp. 121-25. No index.

A program consisting of 263 questions (with answers) on descriptive and inferential statistics, including analysis of variance.

Helps students in psychology, education, guidance, and similar fields in the behavioral sciences to gain a conceptual understanding of statistical procedures without having to attend class. Can be completed in about five hours.

Anderson, Theodore Wilbur, and Sclove, Stanley L. INTRODUCTORY STATISTICAL ANALYSIS. Boston: Houghton Mifflin, 1974. xv, 499 p. Appendixes. Tables, pp. 475-84. Answers to Selected Exercises, pp. 485-91. Index, pp. 492-99.

A text for a one-semester course for students in a variety of disciplines who have knowledge of high school algebra. Consists of the following four parts: "Introduction"; "Descriptive Statistics"; "Probability"; and "Statistical Inference." Uses the intuitive approach with graphs and numerical examples. Topics include organization of multivariate data; rules of probability and Bayes' theorem; sampling distribution of a sum; law of large numbers; and comparison of two sample means and two proportions. Chapters conclude with exercises, mathematical exercises, and references.

Arkin, Herbert, and Colton, Raymond R. STATISTICAL METHODS. 5th ed., rev. College Outline Series. New York: Barnes and Noble, 1970. viii, 344 p. List of Formulas, pp. 229-49. List of Symbols, pp. 250-53. Technical Appendixes, pp. 254-76. Tables, pp. 278-333. The Greek Alphabet, p. 334. Index, pp. 335-44.

A supplementary text for a basic statistics course for students in a variety of fields. Emphasizes applications, with derivations of important theorems provided in the technical appendixes. Topics include time series and least squares; simple and multiple regression and correlation; correlation of attributes; biserial correlation; normal curve; chi-square; sampling; analysis of variance; moments of a frequency distribution; collection of data; and statistical tables. Chapters conclude with references.

Bachi, Roberto. GRAPHICAL RATIONAL PATTERNS: A NEW APPROACH TO GRAPHICAL PRESENTATION OF STATISTICS. New York: Israel Universities Press, 1968. xvii, 262 p. Index, pp. 237-43. Colored Plates, pp. 246-62.

A monograph on statistical graphs in four parts: "Aims and Principles of the Graphic Methods Proposed"; "Examples of Graphical Rational Patterns (GRP) Representing Series Ordered According to One or More Linear Characteristics"; "Examples of GRP Representing Series Ordered According to One or More Circular or Qualitative Characteristics"; and "Examples of Maps Representing Geographical Statistical Series." Includes over 126 illustrative graphs depicting statistical data from a number of countries.

Barr, Donald Roy. FINITE STATISTICS. Topics in Contemporary Mathematics Series. Boston: Allyn & Bacon, 1967. viii, 193 p. Appendix: Tables, pp. 181-88. Bibliography, p. 189. Index, pp. 191-93.

A supplementary text for a basic statistics course for students who have knowledge of elementary set theory; knowledge of some probability also helpful. Treats both mathematical and philosophical concepts, and covers such topics as finite probability models; random variables; Chebyshev's inequality; law of large numbers; estimation and hypothesis testing, including the Neyman-Pearson lemma; quality control; and nonparametric tests. Sections conclude with exercises.

Bartholomew, David J., and Bassett, E.E. LET'S LOOK AT THE FIGURES: THE QUANTITATIVE APPROACH TO HUMAN AFFAIRS. Baltimore: Penguin Books, 1971. 319 p. Appendix 1: Table of Random Numbers, pp. 283-84. Appendix 2: Table of the Standardized Normal Distribution, pp. 285-86. Discussion of Exercises, pp. 286-302. Glossary of Standard Terms, pp. 303-5. References, p. 307. Bibliography, p. 309. Index, pp. 311-19.

Attempts to make quantitative methods interesting to the layman by using them in contexts which are both familiar and important. Consists of the following four parts: "Measurement"; "Prediction and Models"; "Sampling and Inference"; and "Time and Chance." Topics include uncertainty, variability, human variation, quantitative approach to elections, theory of committees, theory of games, opinion polls, methods of taking samples, and random processes. Applications taken from many fields, ranging from educational psychology to the weather.

Baum, Paul, and Scheuer, Ernest M. STATISTICS MADE RELEVANT: A CASEBOOK OF REAL LIFE EXAMPLES. New York: Wiley, 1976. xxii, 217 p. No index.

A supplementary text for a course in basic statistics. Contains forty-eight problems drawn mainly from news media covering a wide range of subjects and topics. Applications in automobile travel, civil service, communications, crime, draft, drugs, labor relations, medicine, sports, TV program ratings, weather, and traffic safety. Statistical tools taken from probability, descriptive statistics, inference, regression, and other areas.

Bevan, John Michael. INTRODUCTION TO STATISTICS. New York: Philosophical Library, 1968. vii, 220 p. Suggestions for Further Reading, p. 215. Tables, pp. 216-17. Index, pp. 218-20.

A nontechnical introduction to statistical methods for the serious layman. Consists of the following two parts: "Preparation" and "Into the Mathematician's Lair--Some of His Tools and Methods." Topics include descriptive statistics; probability; and significance tests and confidence intervals.

Bhattacharyya, Gouri K., and Johnson, Richard A. STATISTICAL CONCEPTS AND METHODS. Wiley Series in Probability and Mathematical Statistics. New York: Wiley, 1977. xv, 639 p. Appendix: Tables, pp. 587-624. Answers to Selected Odd-Numbered Exercises, pp. 625-29. Index, pp. 631-39.

A text for a one-year course in basic statistics for students in a variety of disciplines. Relies mainly on intuitive reasoning with those portions which involve either algebraic derivations or not so elementary concepts marked by asterisks. Mathematical exercises separated from others. Topics include sample spaces and probability; random variables and their distributions, including joint distributions of two random variables; distributions for counts (binomial, hypergeometric, geometric, and Poisson); normal distribution and random samples; central limit theorem; normal probability paper; point estimation; interval estimation and hypothesis testing; comparing two treatments; simple and multiple regression and correlation; analysis of categorized data; analysis of variance; factorial designs; nonparametric tests; and sample surveys. Chapters conclude with exercises.

Blackwell, David. BASIC STATISTICS. New York: McGraw-Hill, 1969. viii, 143 p. Answers, pp. 121-38. Appendix: Tables, pp. 139-40. Index, pp. 141-43.

A supplementary text for a basic statistics course for students in a variety of fields who know only arithmetic. Uses intuitive, informal, concise, decision-theoretic, and Bayesian approaches. Topics include probability; variables; densities; correlation; multiple and partial correlation; independence; binomial and normal approximation to binomial; inferences about proportions; independent proportions; and chi-square. Includes examples and problems.

Brodie, Morris Bernard. ON THINKING STATISTICALLY: A SHORT INTRODUCTION. New and rev. ed. New York: Crane, Russak & Co., 1972. 91 p. A Note on Further Reading, p. 86. Acknowledgments, pp. 87-88. Index, pp. 89-91.

A layman's introduction to statistics and an explanation of the assistance that a statistician can provide. The original edition written for managers, with revised edition designed for a wider audience in business, commerce, public service, and the professions. The six chapter titles: "Thinking Statistically"; "Collecting, Assessing, and Systematizing Data"; "Taking Examples"; "Analyzing Trends"; "Handling Complexity"; and "Using the Experts." Includes simple numerical examples. Assumes knowledge of only high school algebra.

Brookes, Bertram Claude, and Dick, W.F.I. INTRODUCTION TO STATISTICAL METHOD. 2d ed., rev. and enl. London: Heineman, 1969. xii, 332 p. Mathematical Appendix, pp. 276-308. Miscellaneous Exercises, pp. 309-19. Answers to Exercises in Part Two, pp. 320-22. Appendix: Tables and Charts, pp. 323-30. Index, pp. 331-32.

A text for a one-semester course in basic statistics for students in science, biology, physics, economics, and related areas. Topics include probability; binomial and Poisson distributions; normal; interval estimation and hypotheses testing; simple regression and correlation; chi-square; experimental design; Latin squares; and factorial designs. Some formulas derived, often with calculus. Examples utilize hypothetical data. Chapters conclude with general, algebraic, numerical, and mathematical exercises.

Burr, Irving W. APPLIED STATISTICAL METHODS. Operations Research and Industrial Engineering Series. New York: Academic Press, 1974. xix, 479 p. Appendix: Tables, pp. 429-59. Answers to Odd-Numbered Problems, pp. 461-68. Index, pp. 469-79.

A text for a one-semester course in basic statistics for students in a variety of disciplines and a self-study for researchers and line personnel in industry and government. Presentation of techniques accompanied by an extensive set of examples--many based on the author's experience in industry--with a liberal set of problems for assignment. Topics include sets, probability, and random variables; discrete and continuous probability distributions; sampling distributions; estimation and hypothesis testing; simple and multiple regression; analysis of variance, including two-factor problems; and chi-square. Presents both matrix and nonmatrix approaches to multiple regression. Chapters conclude with references and problems.

Burrington, Gillian A. HOW TO FIND OUT ABOUT STATISTICS. New York: Pergamon, 1972. ix, 153 p. Index, pp. 149-53.

Presents general information related to the study and application of statistical science for the purpose of directing the reader to the sources of information. Eleven chapter titles: "Careers for Statisticians"; "Education and Training for Careers in Statistics"; "Using Libraries"; "Statistical Associations"; "Textbooks"; "Periodicals"; "Bibliographies"; "General Statistical Serials and Compenda"; "Social Statistics"; "Economic Statistics"; and "National Statistics of Other Countries."

Cahen, Leonard S., and Hansen, Duncan N. APPLICATIONS AND PROBLEMS IN ELEMENTARY STATISTICS. Belmont, Calif.: Wadsworth, 1963. viii, 120 p. Appendixes: Tables, pp. 109-120. No index.

A supplementary text for a business statistics course in a

variety of fields. Provides practical applications and problems which emphasize the use of statistical concepts. Encourages the student to apply what he learns to other fields and related work. Each chapter concludes with true-false tests.

Campbell, Stephen Kent. FLAWS AND FALLACIES IN STATISTICAL THINKING. Englewood Cliffs, N.J.: Prentice-Hall, 1974. viii, 200 p. Index, pp. 197-200.

A nontechnical presentation of the fallacies in statistics (incorrect applications of statistical concepts). Useful as a supplement to basic statistics courses and as a self-study for the layman. Topics include basic measurement and definition problems, far-fetched estimates, cheating charts, ignoring dispersion, improper comparisons, faulty thinking about probability, faulty induction, and causal and casual relationships.

Carlborg, Frank W. INTRODUCTION TO STATISTICS. Glenview, Ill.: Scott, Foresman, 1968. viii, 293 p. Appendixes: Tables, pp. 277-86. Answers to Selected Exercises, pp. 287-90. Index, pp. 291-93.

A text for a one-semester course in intermediate statistics for students who know college algebra and some calculus. Surveys the statistical methods for multi-factor situations, specifically multiple regression and the analysis of variance. Includes a brief treatment of probability; estimation and hypothesis testing; and Bayes' theorem. Sections conclude with exercises; chapters, with readings and problems.

Carlson, Roger A. STATISTICS. Holden-Day Series in Probability and Statistics. San Francisco: Holden-Day, 1973. xiv, 393 p. Appendix, pp. 354-77. Bibliography, pp. 379-81. Solutions, pp. 383-90. Index, pp. 391-93.

A text for a one-semester course for a varied group of students who know only high school algebra. Emphasizes the rationale for using a formula or rule, rather than its application, and also the critical attitude toward the use of statistics. Topics include sets and probability, sampling, random variables and probability distributions, central limit theorem, law of large numbers, hypothesis testing and interval estimation, statistical inferences for the binomial distribution, Bayesian statistics, introduction to nonparametric statistics, and the analysis of variance. Most sections conclude with exercises. Most examples taken from the social sciences. Omits proofs.

Christensen, Howard B. STATISTICS BY STEPS. Boston: Houghton Mifflin, 1977. xviii, 670 p. Answers to Odd-Numbered Problems, pp. 641-43. Appendix: Tables, pp. 644-64. Index, pp. 665-70.

A self-study for a one-semester basic statistics course which is either a lecture course or an individualized self-paced course. Each unit consists of several lessons. Each lesson is composed of modules consisting of the following: title, task, definitions, discussion, simplified discussion examples, and practice problems. Topics include rules of probability; random variables and probability distributions; sampling distributions; estimation; categorical data, including chi-square; analysis of variance and randomized block designs; regression and correlation; and nonparametric tests. Examples and exercises taken from a wide variety of disciplines. Assumes knowledge of high school algebra.

Clark, Virginia A., and Tarter, Michael E. PREPARATION FOR BASIC STATISTICS: A PROGRAM FOR SELF-INSTRUCTION. New York: McGraw-Hill, 1968. x, 150 p. Table of Square Roots, pp. 143-48. Index, pp. 149-50.

A self-study which emphasizes the mathematical background required for an understanding of basic statistical concepts. Chapters begin with preview questions and end with review questions. Material in each chapter organized in small, graduated steps called frames. Each frame concludes with a question to test the reader's understanding. The first eight chapters include concepts such as equations, symbols, inequalities, square roots, etc., which might be introduced in an elementary algebra course, while the remaining five chapters deal with the application of algebra to statistical topics such as variance, histograms, and charts.

Connor, Lewis Roussez; and Morrell, A.J.H. STATISTICS IN THEORY AND PRACTICE WITH SPECIAL REFERENCE TO PUBLISHED STATISTICS. 5th ed., rev. London: Sir Isaac Pitman, 1964. x, 261 p. Appendix I: Automatic Data-Processing Equipment for Statistical Computation, pp. 247-52. Appendix II: Suggestions for Further Reading, pp. 253-54. Index, pp. 255-61.

Intended for students planning to take parts I and II of the Institute of Statisticians' examination in the United Kingdom or other elementary examinations in statistics, and for any others who require knowledge of the methods, sources, uses, and limitations of official statistics. Topics include time series and index numbers; regression and correlation; demographic statistics; and other statistics such as data on labor, production, internal trade, overseas trade, and national income.

Craddock, J.M. STATISTICS IN THE COMPUTER AGE. New York: Elsevier, 1969. x, 214 p. Suggestions for Further Reading, pp. 210-11. Epilogue, p. 212. Index, pp. 213-14.

A text for a one-semester course in basic statistics with emphasis on the use of computer programming in computations. Includes a pilot calculation designed to determine when a problem is worth putting on the computer. Topics include probability and randomness; statistical inference; binomial and Poisson, regression and correlation; chi-square; analysis of variance; use of random variables; and designing efficient filters. Use of computers illustrated in reference to analysis of time series and prediction.

Crovelli, Robert A. PRINCIPLES OF STATISTICS AND PROBABILITY. Boston: Prindle, Weber and Schmidt, 1973. xi, 307 p. References, p. 280. Appendix: Statistical Tables, pp. 281-88. Answers to Selected Exercises, pp. 289-301. Index, pp. 303-7.

A text for a one-semester course for students in a variety of disciplines who have a high school algebra background. Consists of the following two parts: "Descriptive Statistics" and "Statistical Inference and Probability." Topics include simple regression and correlation; sampling; set theory and probability; probability distributions; expected values; sampling distributions; and interval estimation and hypothesis testing for the difference between two means and two proportions. Examples conclude with exercises.

Daniel, Wayne W. INTRODUCTORY STATISTICS WITH APPLICATIONS. Boston: Houghton and Mifflin, 1977. xii, 475 p. Answers to Odd-Numbered Exercises, pp. 391-402. Appendix: Tables, pp. 403-70. Index, pp. 471-75.

A text for a one- or two-semester course in basic statistics for students in a variety of fields who have knowledge of arithmetic. Excludes derivations with each topic illustrated by at least one hypothetical but realistic example. Topics include sampling distributions; estimation and hypothesis testing; experimental design, including Latin square and completely randomized block designs; analysis of variance; chi-square; simple regression and correlation; and nonparametric statistics.

D'Arcy, J.A. CHANCE AND CHOICE. The General Studies Library. London: Thames and Hudson, 1968. 111 p. Answers to Questions, pp. 103-5. Suggestions for Further Reading, p. 107. Index, pp. 109-11.

A nontechnical presentation and application to everyday problems of a number of statistical concepts for the layman. Topics include frequency distributions and normal curves; price indexes; measurement of probability; theory of games; the probability tree; Markov chains; exponential curves; law of large numbers; and radioactive decay. Chapters conclude with exercises. No mathematical or statistical prerequisites.

David, Florence Nightingale, and Pearson, Egon Sharpe. ELEMENTARY STATISTICAL EXERCISES. New York: Columbia University Press, 1961. vii, 108 p. No index.

Part I consists of a collection of practical statistical exercises at the basic and intermediate levels grouped into forty-one sections largely independent of each other. Part II consists of examination questions in practical statistics; part III, contains answers to the exercises. Topics include histograms, moments of observed frequency distributions, Poisson's limit to the binomial, negative binomial, regression, chi-square, power of t and F tests, and the significance of the difference between two means and two variances. Useful to teachers of statistics who need data and exercises to illustrate theory, and for self-study. Chapters conclude with references.

Diamond, Solomon. THE WORLD OF PROBABILITY: STATISTICS IN SCIENCE. New York: Basic Books, 1964. ix, 193 p. Appendixes A to F, pp. 178-87. Name Index, pp. 189-90. Subject Index, pp. 191-93.

A nontechnical introduction to probability for the layman. Covers such topics as place of error, combination, scores, improbability, independence, cause, and the extent of reasonable doubt. Appendixes include sero sum of deviations, minimal sum of squares, variance law, variance of binomial and Poisson distributions, small samples, and best-fit regression line.

Dickinson, Gordon Cawood. STATISTICAL MAPPING AND THE PRESENTATION OF STATISTICS. London: Edward Arnold, 1963. 160 p. Appendix: List of Census Reports for Great Britain, 1801-1931, pp. 154-60. No Index.

A new approach to statistical presentation (statistical maps) based on the principles of cartography. Statistical illustrations include quantities distributed at a series of points; quantities contained within given areas; quantities distributed along a line; and non-quantitative maps. Other topics include general aspects of map design; worked examples; and sources of data. No mathematical or statistical prerequisites.

Dixon, Wilfrid Joseph, and Massey, Frank J., Jr. INTRODUCTION TO STATISTICAL ANALYSIS. 3d ed., rev. New York: McGraw-Hill, 1969. xiii, 638 p. General Comments, p. 427. References, pp. 439-43. List of Tables, pp. 445-585. Answers, pp. 587-630. Index, pp. 631-38.

A text for a one-year course in basic statistics for students in a variety of fields assuming a prerequisite of only arithmetic. Concepts of distribution, sample, and population introduced early in the text, with probability reserved for the final chapter. Topics include normal distribution, inference and tests of hypotheses; properties of estimators; analysis of variance; covariance; simple and multiple regression and correlation; chi-square; power function and operating characteristic curve; orthogonal contrasts; Latin squares; nonparametric tests; sequential analysis; and sensitivity experiments. Chapters conclude with glossaries, discussion questions, class exercises, and problems.

Downie, Norville Morgan, and Starry, Allan R. DESCRIPTIVE AND INFERENTIAL STATISTICS. New York: Harper & Row, 1977. ix, 362 p. Appendixes, pp. 269-344. Answers to Exercises, pp. 345-51. References, pp. 353. Index, pp. 355-62.

A text for a one-semester course for students in a variety of fields. Consists of four parts: "Descriptive Statistics"; "Inferential Statistics"; "Correlation and Regression"; and "Further Topics." Emphasizes the use of pocket calculators for solving problems, thus reducing the step-by-step cookbook orientation. One- and two-factor analysis of variance treated in some detail. Chapters conclude with exercises. Appendixes include reviews of arithmetic, tables, and lists of formulas.

Elzey, Freeman F. A FIRST READER IN STATISTICS. 2d ed. Monterey, Calif.: Brooks/Cole, 1974. viii, 79 p. Index, pp. 77-79.

An introduction to basic statistics with emphasis on the use of confidence intervals and comparisons among multiple samples using no derivations, computational formulas, or symbols. Useful to anyone desiring to understand statistical concepts without becoming involved with the actual applications of the techniques. Topics include organization and description of data; normal distributions; statistical inference; confidence intervals; comparisons among multiple samples; type I and II errors; one- and two-tailed tests; and analysis of variance.

______. A PROGRAMMED INTRODUCTION TO STATISTICS. 2d ed., rev. Belmont, Calif.: Brooks/Cole, 1971. xi, 385 p. Answers to Exercises, pp. 334-48. Formulas, pp. 349-57. Tables, pp. 359-78. Glossary, pp. 379-81. Index, pp. 383-85.

Organized into twenty-five sets, each set containing an introduction, a series of frames sequenced so that the required responses can be determined easily and compared with the correct response, and a series of exercises at the end. Formulas, tables, and glossaries presented near the end of the book. Fictitious data used for numerical examples. May be used for self study, supplementary test, or text for basic statistics courses.

Federer, Walter T. STATISTICS AND SOCIETY: DATA COLLECTION AND INTERPRETATION. Statistics: Texts and Monographs Series, vol. 3. New York: Marcel Dekker, 1973. ix, 399 p. Appendix: Examination Questions, pp. 359-94. Index, pp. 395-99.

A text for a one-semester course which presents the ideas, concepts, and philosophies associated with data with a minimum emphasis on methodology and mathematical theory. Emphasizes the relationship between sample and population and between statistics and parameter, and also probability of observations in the real world. Topics include data collection; principles of scientific investigations; surveys and survey designs; experimental design; summarization of data; probability; patterned variability; methodology; and statistical publications. Chapters conclude with references.

Fischer, Frederic E. FUNDAMENTAL STATISTICAL CONCEPTS. San Francisco: Canfield Press, 1973. x, 371 p. Bibliography, pp. 305-7. Appendix: Statistical Tables, pp. 309-33. Answers to Exercises, pp. 335-64. Index, pp. 365-71.

A text for a one-semester course in basic statistics for students in a variety of fields who have a high school algebra background. Consists of the following three parts: "Descriptive Statistics"; "Probability"; and "Statistical Inference." Definitions and theorems form the basic structure of the text, with some theorems proved algebraically and others intuitively. Topics include regression and correlation; events and probability; Bayes' theorem; discrete and continuous probability functions; tests concerning means, proportions, and variances; and nonparametric tests.

Freedman, David; Pisani, Robert; and Purves, Roger. STATISTICS. New York: W.W. Norton, 1978. xv, 593 p. A Review of Terms and Equations, pp. 509-13. Notes, pp. 514-33. Answers to Exercises, pp. 534-76. Tables, pp. 577-81. Index, pp. 583-93.

A text for a two-semester course in basic statistics for students in medicine and education who have had one year of high school algebra. Consists of the following eight parts: "Design of Experiments"; "Descriptive Statistics"; "Correlation and Regression"; "Probability"; "Chance Variability"; "Sampling"; "Chance Models"; and "Tests of Significance." Examples taken from education, medicine, urban policy, and economics. Emphasizes verbal description, charts, tables, and graphs, rather than formulas and derivations. Improper use of statistics covered.

Freund, John E. MODERN ELEMENTARY STATISTICS. 4th ed., rev. Englewood Cliffs, N.J.: Prentice-Hall, 1973. xii, 532 p. Statistical Tables, pp. 471-505. Answers to Odd-Numbered Exercises, pp. 507-23. Index, pp. 525-32.

A text for a one-year course for students in a variety of fields. Mathematical proofs and derivations keyed to the lowest level at which modern statistics can effectively be taught. Consists of the following three parts: "Descriptive Methods"; "Basic Theory"; and "Statistical Inference." Topics include rules of probability; probability distributions and sampling; inferences concerning means, standard deviations, and proportions; analysis of variance, including interaction; nonparametric tests; simple and multiple regression and correlation; and planning surveys and experiments. Sections conclude with exercises.

Fried, Robert. INTRODUCTION TO STATISTICS. Rev. ed. New York: Gardner, 1976. xv, 304 p. Appendix: Tables, pp. 263-97. Bibliography, pp. 298-302. Index, pp. 303-4.

A text for a one-semester course in basic statistics for undergraduates in varied disciplines who have a high school algebra background. Emphasizes verbal explanation, with numerous examples worked out in detail. Topics include probability; sampling distributions of $\bar{X}$ and t; estimation concerning a population mean and hypothesis testing concerning two means; analysis of variance; simple regression; biserial, tetrachoric, and rank-order correlations; chi-square; Mann-Whitney U-test; and trends in time-domain data distributions, including galvanic skin response, cardiac response, and analog measures. Chapters conclude with problems.

Garlington, Warren K., and Shimota, Helen E. STATISTICALLY SPEAKING. Springfield, Ill.: Charles C Thomas, 1964. xii, 110 p. Selected References, pp. 107-8. Symbols, p. 109. Index, p. 110.

Revised versions of a nontechnical ten-installment series which appeared in the journal NORTHWEST MEDICINE in 1962 for the layman as a consumer of research reports. Topics include the research report, distributions and averages, variability, the normal curve, correlations, sampling and probability, tests of significance, nonparametric tests, and statistical pitfalls.

Gemignani, Michael C. CALCULUS AND STATISTICS. Reading, Mass.: Addison-Wesley, 1970. xi, 353 p. Appendix: Tables, pp. 289-308. Answers to Selected Exercises, pp. 309-46. General Index, pp. 347-52. Index of Symbols, p. 353.

A text for a one-semester course in calculus and statistics for nonmathematics majors who have had analytic geometry and trigonometry. Presents a coordinated study of the interrelationship between calculus, probability, and statistics. Topics include functions and probability; Bayes' theorem; random variables and their distributions; derivatives and applications; sequences and series; integration and continuous random variables; moment-generating functions; chi-square; hypothesis testing; functions of several variables; linear regression and correlation. Sections conclude with exercises.

Goodman, Richard. MODERN STATISTICS. New York: Arc Books, 1964. 240 p. Appendix: Continuous Bivariate Distributions, pp. 228-38. Suggestions for Further Reading, pp. 239-40. No Index.

A supplementary text for a course in basic statistics and a self-study for students familiar with calculus. Topics include frequencies and probabilities; expectation; probability-generating functions; bivariate distributions; regression and correlation; polynomial regression; sampling theory; analysis of variance; and chi-square. Useful to anyone desiring an understanding of the mathematics involved in basic statistics. Chapters conclude with exercises, some of which involve simple numerical computations.

Goon, Atindra M.; Gupta, Milan K.; and Dasgupta, Bhagabat. FUNDAMENTALS OF STATISTICS. Vol. One. 3d ed., rev. Calcutta: World Press, 1968. xiv, 497 p. Appendix: Tables, pp. 479-94. Index, pp. 495-97.

A text for an undergraduate course in basic statistics for students who have knowledge of calculus. Emphasizes statistical theory and derivations. Consists of the following two parts: "Mathematical Preliminaries" and "General Statistical Methods." Topics include a review of numerical analysis; probability theory; univariate theoretical distributions; joint distribution of attributes; simple and multiple regression and correlation; sampling distributions; estimation and hypothesis testing, including chi-square; and nonparametric tests. Excludes practical applications. Chapters conclude with questions, exercises, and references.

______. FUNDAMENTALS OF STATISTICS. Vol. Two. Calcutta: World Press, 1968. xi, 380 p. Appendix A: Indian Official Statistics, pp. 351-65. Appendix B: Tables, pp. 366-76. Index, pp. 377-80.

Volume two comprises parts three and four as follows: "Analysis of Variance and Designs" and "Statistical Methods for Some Special Fields of Applications." Applications, which employ Indian data, include vital statistics; statistical methods in psychology and education; index numbers and time series; demand analysis; and statistical quality control. Chapters conclude with questions, exercises, and selected readings.

Gordon, Marshall, and Schaumberger, Norman. A FIRST COURSE IN STATISTICS. New York: Macmillan, 1978. ix, 214 p. Appendix A: Note on Summation Notation, pp. 195-96. Appendix B: Tables, pp. 197-209. Answers to Selected Problems, pp. 210-13. Index, p. 214.

A supplementary text for a course in basic statistics. Suitable also for general readership. Topics include organizing data; samples from populations; measures of central tendency and variability probability; nonparametric tests; and surveys. Chapters conclude with review of formulas and problems.

Gotkin, Lassar G., and Goldstein, Leo S. DESCRIPTIVE STATISTICS: A PROGRAMMED TEXTBOOK. Vol. 1. New York: Wiley, 1964. xiv, 255 p. No index.

A programmed text which consists of multiple-choice frames, providing an opportunity for students to make the correct choice using actual data and other supplementary information. Contains a fast track, enabling the student to jump ahead if desired. Consists of the following units; population and sample, variables, data arrangement, data presentation, measures of central tendency, and measures of dispersion.

______. DESCRIPTIVE STATISTICS: A PROGRAMMED TEXTBOOK. Vol. 2. New York: Wiley, 1965. xiv, 228 p. No index.

A continuation of volume 1 (above) containing the following units: the normal curve, correlation, and regression.

Gray, A. William, and Ulm, Otis M. ELEMENTARY PROBABILITY AND STATISTICS: WITH OPTIMAL COMPUTER APPLICATIONS. New York: Glencoe Press, 1973. xii, 272 p. Answers to Odd-Numbered Exercises, pp. 229-68. Index, pp. 269-72.

A text for a one-semester course in basic statistics for students in a variety of fields who have two years of high school algebra. Based on set theory and includes programming instruction in the BASIC language, as well as elementary programs for use in statistical computations. Topics include conditional probability and Bayes' theorem; discrete and continuous random variables and their distributions; sampling distributions; chi-square; interval estimation and hypothesis testing; and simple and multiple regression and correlation. Sections conclude with exercises.

Guenther, William C. CONCEPTS OF STATISTICAL INFERENCE. 2d ed., rev. and enl. New York: McGraw-Hill, 1973. xiv, 561 p. Appendix A: Some Additional Results, pp. 439-62. Appendix B: Tables and Graphs, pp. 463-534. Answers to Exercises, pp. 535-53. Index, pp. 555-61.

A text for a one-semester course in basic statistics for a varied audience assuming knowledge of only high school algebra. Minimum emphasis placed on algebraic derivations and computing, with examples and exercises at the ends of the sections taken from business, psychology, sociology, engineering, agriculture, education, quality control, the biological and biomedical sciences, and games of chance. Topics include probability and random variables, distributions; point estimation; interval estimation and hypothesis testing; one-way analysis of variance; regression and correlation (bivariate model); and nonparametric tests. Appendixes contain widely used mathematical results such as single and double summation; binomial expansion formulas; arithmetic operations; and statistical tables.

Haber, Audrey, and Runyon, Richard P. GENERAL STATISTICS. 3d ed. Addison-Wesley Series in Statistics. Reading, Mass.: Addison-Wesley, 1977. xvii, 462 p. References, pp. 242-43. Appendix I: Review of Basic Mathematics, pp. 344-52. Appendix II: Glossary of Symbols, pp. 353-58. Appendix III: Glossary of Terms, pp. 359-62. Appendix IV: List of Formulas, pp. 363-66. Appendix V: Tables, pp. 367-403. Answers to Selected Exercises, pp. 404-51. Index, pp. 452-62.

A text for a one-semester course in basic statistics for students from a variety of fields. Consists of the following three parts: "Descriptive Statistics"; "Parametric Tests of Significance"; and "Nonparametric Tests of Significance." Examples and exercises drawn from the literature with emphasis on the continuity of descriptive and inferential statistics. Formulas presented without derivation. Topics include regression and correlation; testing the significance between two population means; Sandler's A-statistic; analysis of variance; chi-square; binomial tests; and nonparametric tests. Chapters conclude with summaries and exercises.

Hadley, George F. ELEMENTARY STATISTICS. San Francisco: Holden-Day, 1969. xi, 457 p. Tables, pp. 441-54. Index, pp. 455-57.

A text for a one-semester course for students in the social and biological sciences, economics, and education. Includes examples from many fields and over 750 problems, arranged by sections at the ends of the chapters. Uses no calculus, although emphasizes the idea of mathematical models and their relation to the real world. Topics include finite probability and random variables; estimation and hypothesis testing; decision theory; Bayesian approach and prior and posterior probabilities; two-way analysis of variance; simple regression and correlation; and time series.

Hayslett, H.T. STATISTICS MADE SIMPLE. New York: Doubleday, 1968. 192 p. Some Notes about Desk Calculators, p. 178. List of Selected Symbols, p. 179. Tables, pp. 180-88. Answers to Exercises, pp. 189-90. Index, pp. 191-92.

A self-study in basic statistics for students with a high school algebra background. Includes derivations and emphasizes definitions of concepts and detailed procedures for conducting statistical tests, followed by detailed examples. Topics include measures of location and dispersion; probability; normal distribution; tests of hypothesis; correlation and regression; confidence limits; nonparametric tests; and analysis of variance. Chapters conclude with exercises.

Hodges, Joseph Lawson, and Lehmann, E.L. BASIC CONCEPTS OF PROBABILITY AND STATISTICS. Holden-Day Series in Probability and Statistics.

San Francisco: Holden-Day, 1969. xiii, 375 p. Tables, pp. 411-21. Selected Answers to Problems, pp. 423-30. Index, pp. 431-38. Example Index, pp. 439-41.

A text for a one-year course in probability and statistics for students in varied fields who know only high school algebra. Presents a careful treatment of the independence assumption in building probability models, and includes some proofs. Topics include events and probability; sampling; product models; conditional probability; law of large numbers; sequential stopping; random variables and their distributions; multivariate distributions; unbiased estimation; comparing two quantities or populations; estimating the effect of a treatment; estimation of variance; experimental design; stratified sampling; chi-square; nonparametric tests; and power of a test. Illustrations taken from genetics, criminology, economics, engineering, linguistics, agriculture, psychology, and sociology. Sections conclude with problems.

Hogge, James H. PROGRAMMING THE STATISTICAL LIBRARY. Philadelphia: Auerback, 1972. viii, 208 p. Appendix A: Listing of Subprograms, pp. 167-83. Appendix B: Peabody Computer Center User's Manual, pp. 185-202. Index, pp. 203-8.

Consists of instructions for creating statistical library routines from existing computing facilities and libraries with emphasis on efficient utilization of systems relatively limited in core memory. Topics include control cards for communication between the user and the library program; documentation with examples; programming the small computer, including methods for storing matrixes efficiently; use of the IBM 1130 disk for temporary and permanent files; use of IBM 1130 commercial subroutines package; standardization of inputs, outputs, documentation, and source deck; and case histories. Assumes knowledge of FORTRAN programming and basic statistics.

Hope, Keith. ELEMENTARY STATISTICS: A WORKBOOK. Commonwealth and International Library. New York: Pergamon, 1967. xii, 101 p. Appendix 1: Computational Hints, pp. 79-81. Appendix 2: Bibliography, pp. 82-83. Appendix 3: Answers to Problems, pp. 84-100. Appendix 4: Tables of 5% Points of the F Distribution, p. 101. No index.

A supplementary text for a basic statistics course containing worked examples in the following areas of parametric statistics: correlation, analysis of variance, matrixes, and factor analysis. Illustrate concepts with simple examples using a minimum of computations. Chapters contain problems for solution and detailed solutions.

Hultquist, Robert A. INTRODUCTION TO STATISTICS. International Series in Decision Processes. New York: Holt, Rinehart and Winston, 1969. xiii,

194 p. Appendix: Tables, pp. 159-83. Bibliography and References, pp. 187-88. Index, pp. 191-94.

A text for a one-semester course in basic statistics for students from a variety of disciplines who have knowledge of high school algebra. Topics include statistical inference based on one- and two-samples; linear regression and correlation; analysis of variance; and inference for n-way cross-classification designs.

Huntsberger, David V. ELEMENTS OF STATISTICAL INFERENCE. Boston: Allyn & Bacon, 1961. xi, 291 p. Appendix: Tables, pp. 249-83. Index, pp. 285-91.

A text for a one-semester course for students from a variety of disciplines who have knowledge of only college algebra. Topics include rules of probability; theoretical distributions of random variables; statistical inference from normal populations, including the two-sample problem; chi-square; simple regression and correlation; and one-way analysis of variance. Chapters conclude with problems, class sampling exercises, and references.

Johnson, Norman Lloyd, and Tetley, H. STATISTICS: AN INTERMEDIATE TEXT BOOK. Vol. I. 2d ed. London: Cambridge University Press, 1966. xii, 304 p. Appendix 1: Corrections for Grouping, pp. 271-76. Appendix 2: Stirling's Approximation to n!, pp. 276-79. Appendix 3: The Normal Curve as an Approximation to the Binomial Probabilities, pp. 279-81. Appendix 4: Values of the Ordinate and the Cumulative Distribution Function for the Normal Curve, pp. 282-83. Appendix 5: Generating Functions, pp. 283-90. Answers to the Exercises and Notes on the Solutions, pp. 291-97. Index, pp. 298-304.

Intended primarily for those studying for the statistical sections of the actuarial examinations. Rigor lies between elementary text and advanced text. Corresponds approximately to part I of the examination of the Institute of Actuaries in the United Kingdom. Includes practical acquaintance with the problems, theoretical studies, and application of theory to practical problems. Topics include presentation of observed data; probability theory; expected value; and random variables and probability distributions. Includes examples, exercises, and references.

_____. STATISTICS: AN INTERMEDIATE TEXT BOOK. Vol. II. London: Cambridge University Press, 1950. xi, 318 p. Appendix 5: Beta and Gamma Functions, pp. 255-60. Appendix 6: Multiple Integrals, pp. 260-69. Appendix 7: Tables of the Chi-Square Distribution, pp. 269-71. Appendix 8: Tables of the t Distribution, pp. 272-74. Appendix 9: Tables of the F Distribution, pp. 274-80. Answers to the Exercises and Notes on the Solutions, pp. 281-310. Index, pp. 311-18.

Corresponds to part II of the examinations of the Institute of Actuaries. Topics include calculus of distribution functions and its application to estimation and hypothesis testing; multinomial distributions with applications; most powerful tests; maximum likelihood estimates; stratified population and the analysis of variance; rank correlation; multiple and partial correlation; chi-square; and least squares. Derivations kept to a minimum. Assumes knowledge of calculus. Chapters conclude with exercises.

Johnson, Robert R. ELEMENTARY STATISTICS. North Scituate, Mass.: Duxbury Press, 1973. xvi, 480 p. Appendix: Tables, pp. 403-57. Answers to Selected Exercises, pp. 458-74. Answers to Chapter Quizzes, pp. 475-76. Index, pp. 477-80.

A text for a one-semester course in basic statistics for non-mathematics majors who have limited mathematics background. Motivates concepts by means of examples taken from the context of the student's personal experience. Chapters begin with summary of objectives and end with summary of content. Includes quizzes and vocabulary lists. Topics include events and probability; probability distributions; normal curve; sampling distributions; tests of hypotheses; chi-square; analysis of variance; simple regression and correlation; and nonparametric statistics. Chapters conclude with exercises, problems, and references.

Kalton, Graham. INTRODUCTION TO STATISTICAL IDEAS FOR SOCIAL SCIENTISTS. London: Chapman & Hall, 1966. v, 58 p. Bibliography, pp. 54-56. Index, pp. 57-58.

A monograph which emphasizes ideas, rather than computation. Style mathematical (with many symbols) based on a prerequisite of high school algebra. Useful as a supplementary text for a basic statistics course. Topics include summary statistics; sampling error; testing for the difference between two means; and association between variables and between an attribute and a variable.

Kearney, Patricia A. PROGRAMMED REVIEW OF FUNDAMENTAL MATHEMATICS FOR ELEMENTARY STATISTICS. Prentice-Hall Series in Educational Measurement, Research, and Statistics. Englewood Cliffs, N.J.: Prentice-Hall, 1970. x, 213 p. No index.

A self-instructional program designed to assist the student in remedying his mathematical deficiencies for studying basic statistics. Consists of four sections: "Fundamental Operations"; "Fractions"; "Exponents"; and "Equations." Pre-evaluation and post-evaluation tests in each section designed to fit the program to individual needs. Each question or problem in the pre-evaluation keyed to a set of frames within the program to which the student is directed when an item is missed.

Kimble, Gregory A. HOW TO USE (AND MISUSE) STATISTICS. Englewood Cliffs, N.J.: Prentice-Hall, 1978. xi, 290 p. Computational Appendix, pp. 221-53. End Notes, pp. 255-86. Index, pp. 287-90.

A nontechnical introduction to basic statistics with emphasis on an easy style of thought using an occasional formula. Useful to both laymen and students. Topics include pictures of data, frequency data, laws of chance, normal curve, sampling the universe, uses and misuses of correlation, and analysis of variance.

Korin, Basil P. INTRODUCTION TO STATISTICAL METHODS. Cambridge, Mass.: Winthrop, 1977. xvii, 426 p. Appendixes A to E, pp. 367-420. Index, pp. 421-26.

A text for a one-semester course in basic statistics for a general audience with a college algebra background. Emphasis on inference with numerical examples playing a key role. Topics include standardized variables and the normal distribution; linear regression; association between interval, ordinal, and nominal scales; probability and random variables; sampling distributions; interval estimation; tests of hypotheses for interval and ordinal scale variables; binomial, multinomial, and goodness of fit; multiple regression; and analysis of variance. Appendixes contain review of mathematics, linear transformations, tables, and answers. Chapters conclude with problems.

Kurtz, Thomas E. BASIC STATISTICS. Prentice-Hall Mathematics Series. Englewood Cliffs, N.J.: Prentice-Hall, 1963. xiii, 327 p. Appendix Tables, pp. 297-314. Answers to Exercises, pp. 315-21. Index, pp. 323-27.

A text for a one-semester course in probability and statistics for students who have had one semester of calculus and are familiar with elementary probability. Begins with a study of statistical inference, with emphasis on point and interval estimation rather than hypothesis testing. Takes up finite and discrete experiments based on the binomial, the Poisson, and the contingency table models, and includes nonparametric tests, such as the sign and rank-sum tests. Includes a thorough presentation of the linear model. Sections conclude with exercises; chapters, with references.

Langley, Russell. PRACTICAL STATISTICS, SIMPLY EXPLAINED. Rev. ed. Dover Books on Elementary and Intermediate Mathematics. New York: Dover Publications, 1970. ix, 399 p. Miscellaneous Questions, pp. 331-59. Answers, pp. 360-91. Tables of Squares and Square Roots, pp. 392-97. Guide to Significance Tests, pp. 398-99.

Presents statistical inference for the layman. All procedures illustrated with examples. Topics include laws of probability;

Poisson and normal probability distributions; simple random sampling; stratified random sampling; averages and scatter; harmonic and geometric means; logarithmic mean; designs of investigations, including paired comparisons, factorial designs, and sequential designs; and significance tests, including Z, t, Wilcoxon's sum of ranks; Wilcoxon's signed ranks test; Spearman's correlation coefficient; binomial test; Fisher's test; and runs for randomness.

Larsen, Richard J., and Stroup, Donna Fox. STATISTICS IN THE REAL WORLD: A BOOK OF EXAMPLES. New York: Macmillan, 1976. xxi, 245 p. List of Symbols, pp. xiii-xiv. List of Formulas, pp. xv-xxi. No index.

A collection of fifty examples based on recently published research in anthropology, psychology, medicine, sociology, economics, biology, literature, history, and law. Examples divided into the following six chapters that parallel the usual sequence of topics presented in a two-semester basic statistics course: "Characterizing Variability"; "One-Sample Problem"; "Two-Sample Problem"; "The Paired-Data Problem"; "The Correlation Problem"; and "Nonparametric Methods." Each example includes a nonstatistical introduction followed by a one-sentence statistical objective, a partial analysis of the data (for some examples a complete analysis), questions to assist the student in completing the analysis, and references.

Levine, Samuel, and Elzey, Freeman F. A PROGRAMMED INTRODUCTION TO RESEARCH. Belmont, Calif.: Wadsworth, 1968. x, 236 p. Index, pp. 235-36.

A programmed text for use as a supplement in a basic statistics course in the behavioral sciences. Consists primarily of a large number of completion-type problems with answers readily available. Topics include scientific methodology, variables and hypothesis, sampling techniques, control of extraneous variables, and use of statistics in research.

Levinson, Horace C. CHANCE, LUCK AND STATISTICS: THE SCIENCE OF CHANCE. Foreword by C.V. Newson. New York: Dover, 1963. xiii, 357 p. Appendix I, pp. 343-44. Appendix II, pp. 345-51. Index, pp. 353-57.

A nontechnical presentation of probability and statistics for the layman. Develops literacy in probability and statistics by analyzing step-by-step problems in games of chance with applications to problems of broad concern in government and business. Treatment flavored with a sense of humor. Consists of two parts: "Chance" and "Statistics." Topics include gamblers and scientists; fallacies; chance and speculation; poker changes; roulette; chance and statistics; statistics at work; and applications in advertising and business.

Li, Jerome C.R. STATISTICAL INFERENCE I. Ann Arbor, Mich.: Edward Brothers, 1964. xix, 658 p. Appendix: Tables, pp. 569-618. Solutions to Problems, pp. 619-34. Symbols and Abbreviations, pp. 635-45. Index to Theorems, p. 647. Index to Tables, pp. 648-50. Index to Figures, p. 651. Index to Subject Matter, pp. 652-58.

A nonmathematical exposition of the theory of statistics organized around a series of sampling experiments used for verifying the theorems; omits mathematical verification of theorems. Most frequently used examples refer to fertilizers, insecticides; teaching methods, and children's heights. Includes basic concept of statistical inference; normal, t, chi-square, and F distributions; analysis of variance; and nonparametric tests. Emphasizes relationships among the various methods and includes numerous cross references. Assumes knowledge of high school or college algebra. Chapters conclude with exercises and references.

______. STATISTICAL INFERENCE II. Ann Arbor, Mich.: Edward Brothers, 1964. xiv, 575 p. Solutions to Problems, pp. 541-52. Symbols and Abbreviations, pp. 553-60. Index to Tables, pp. 561-66. Index to Figures, p. 567. Index to Subject Matter, pp. 568-75.

Consists of the following five parts: "Matrix Algebra"; "Multiple and Curvilinear Regression"; "Fitting Constants"; "The Application of the Method of Regression to the Analysis of Variance and Covariance"; and "Experimental Designs." Useful as a text for courses of varied duration by students who have knowledge of only high school algebra. Derivations kept to a minimum. Topics include linear combinations of partial regression coefficients; distribution of adjusted means; transformed independent variables; randomized block; factorial experiment as a response surface; Latin squares; missing observations; analysis of variance in randomized blocks and in completely randomized experiments; fractional replication; split plot and incomplete block; simple linear regression; and the analysis of covariance. Chapters conclude with exercises and references.

Lindgren, Bernard William. BASIC IDEAS OF STATISTICS. New York: Macmillan, 1975. x, 352 p. Appendix: Tables, pp. 317-40. Answers, pp. 341-47. Index, pp. 349-52.

A text for a one-semester course in basic statistics for students in a variety of disciplines who have a high school algebra background. Some data used for illustrative purposes simulated by a computer, while other examples use both real and hypothetical data. Topics include linear transformations; parameters of discrete and continuous probability distributions; sampling distributions (empirical and theoretical); interval estimation and hypothesis testing; chi-square; simple and multiple regression; and nonparametric tests. Bayesian approach omitted and n, rather than n-1, used as divisor in defining the sample standard deviation. Sections conclude with problems.

Lindgren, Bernard William, and McElrath, G.W. INTRODUCTION TO PROBABILITY AND STATISTICS. 3d ed. New York: Macmillan, 1966. x, 305 p. List of Tables, pp. 267-89. Answers, pp. 290-98. Index, pp. 299-305.

A text for a one-semester course in statistics for students who have only a high school algebra background. Calculus used for the treatment of continuous probability distributions and moment-generating functions. Topics include probability models; discrete and continuous random variables and their distributions; sums of random variables; sampling; estimation and hypothesis testing; nonparametric statistics; least squares regression; and the analysis of variance. Omits such topics as sufficiency, multivariate distributions, and time series. Statistical inference treated from the point of view of the Neyman and Pearson theory. Power function plays a dominant role. Includes many worked examples. Chapters conclude with review problems.

McCollough, Celeste, and Van Atta, Loche. STATISTICAL CONCEPTS: A PROGRAM FOR SELF-INSTRUCTION. New York: McGraw-Hill, 1963. xv, 367 p. Appendix: Review of the Rectangular Coordinate System, pp. 337-45. References, p. 346. Answers to Problems, pp. 347-60. Completed Triangular Table, p. 361. Index, pp. 362-66. Special Answer Sheet, p. 367.

A text suitable for self-instruction as an introduction to a formal course, as a supplementary text during a basic course, or as a review following a formal course. Uses frames with portions of each frame to be completed by the student. Solutions located at right of frame. Topics include introduction to statistical inference; random sampling, expected frequency, and probability; computing probabilities; testing the null hypothesis; frequency distributions; chi-square; measures of central tendency and of dispersion; standard scores; normal curve and probability; significance tests; testing hypotheses about the mean (large and small samples); linear regression and correlation; and analysis of variance. Chapters conclude with review problems.

McGee, Victor E. PRINCIPLES OF STATISTICS. Century Psychology Series. New York: Appleton-Century-Crofts, 1971. x, 373 p. Appendixes, pp. 345-68. Index, pp. 369-73.

A text for a course in basic statistics for social science students who have a high school algebra background. Emphasizes practical applications and consists of the following two parts: "The Traditional Approach" and "The Bayesian Approach."

Topics include sampling distributions, including binomial and multinomial; one- and two-way analysis of variance; chi-square; simple regression; and Bayes' theorem. Sections conclude with exercises. Appendixes consist of statistical tables.

Mathematical Association of America. INTRODUCTORY STATISTICS WITHOUT CALCULUS: A REPORT OF THE PANEL ON STATISTICS. Berkeley, Calif.: Committee on the Undergraduate Program in Mathematics, 1972. xii, 63 p. Selected Bibliography, pp. 53-63. No index.

A report on the content of a one-semester introductory, terminal, statistics course for the physical sciences, economics, biology, and well prepared students in other social and life sciences who do not possess knowledge of calculus or linear algebra. A review of past and current approaches to basic statistics considered first, followed by recommended objectives and their implications, an outline of a conventional course, with alternative approaches, use of data sets and computers, the use of experiments, simulations, statistical data sources, and references. Useful to anyone involved in the preparation of outlines for introductory statistics.

______. PREPARATION FOR GRADUATE WORK IN STATISTICS: A REPORT OF THE PANEL ON STATISTICS. Berkeley, Calif.: Committee on the Undergraduate Program in Mathematics, 1971. vi, 14 p. No index.

A report on the content of a one-year undergraduate course in statistics for students who have had two years of calculus and also courses in linear algebra and mathematical analysis who desire to pursue graduate studies in statistics. Contains a recommended outline, and references to suitable textbooks and statistical data.

Meddis, Ray. A STATISTICAL HANDBOOK FOR NON-STATISTICIANS. New York: McGraw-Hill, 1975. viii, 162 p. Appendix A: Random Numbers, pp. 155-57. Appendix B: Bibliographical Notes, pp. 158-59. Index, pp. 160-62.

Strictly a reference comprising formulas, procedures, tables, and worked examples for use by beginning students in statistics. Includes summaries of statistical tests, procedures for carrying out each test, the assumptions of the test and the conclusions that can be drawn, and worked examples designed to show the similarities between tests.

Megeath, Joe D. HOW TO USE STATISTICS. San Francisco: Canfield Press, 1975. x, 310 p. Appendix: Statistical Tables, pp. 281-307. Index, pp. 308-10.

A basic statistics primer for students in a variety of fields who have no prior knowledge of the field and no more than a working knowledge of basic algebra. Excludes mathematics derivations and emphasizes intuitive understanding of concepts. Chapters begin with a set of objectives to alert the reader of the chapter's content, and end with a summary of information, equation, problems, and references. Consists of the following three parts: "How to Describe Data"; "How to Cope with Uncertainty"; and "How to Analyze Statistical Data." Topics include central tendencies and dispersion; probability distributions; expected values and payoff tables; sampling and sampling distributions; estimation; tests of hypothesis; chi-square; association analysis; and index numbers.

Mendenhall, William, and Ott, Lyman. UNDERSTANDING STATISTICS. 2d ed. North Scituate, Mass.: Duxbury, 1976. xi, 387 p. Appendix I: Useful Statistical Tests and Confidence Intervals, pp. 341-46. Appendix II: Statistical Tables, pp. 347-70. Glossary: Common Statistical Terms, pp. 371-75. Answers, pp. 376-83. Index, pp. 384-87.

A text for a one-semester course emphasizing the understanding of statistics, and not merely applications, for students who have knowledge of only arithmetic. Includes timely news clippings, cartoons, examples, and exercises to illustrate the uses of statistics in everyday living. Topics include probability distributions for discrete and continuous random variables; binomial experiment; normal distribution; estimation and hypotheses testing; linear models and correlation; design of experiments; testing a hypothesis concerning two population variances; analysis of variance; contingency tables; and lying with statistics. Chapters conclude with references.

Miller, Robert Bruce. STATISTICAL CONCEPTS AND APPLICATIONS: A NONMATHEMATICAL EXPLANATION. Chicago: Science Research Associates, 1968. 192 p. Glossary, pp. 182-91. Selected Bibliography, p. 192.

A self-study for the layman. Intended to impart concepts that sketch out the main ideas of statistics using the definition-note-example-application style, with exercises scattered throughout. Topics include general statistics; data; variability; averages; covariation; sampling; probability; measures of independence; enumerative statistics; and models.

Mode, Elmer B. ELEMENTS OF PROBABILITY AND STATISTICS. Englewood Cliffs, N.J.: Prentice-Hall, 1966. xii, 356 p. References, pp. 321-22. Mathematical Tables, pp. 323-40. Answers to Odd-Numbered Exercises, pp. 341-49. Index, pp. 351-56.

A text for a one-semester course in basic statistics for a mixed group of students who have had at least two years of high school algebra. Develops the basic concepts and rules of mathematical probability and applies them to practical problems in biology, education, economics, genetics, psychology, and sociology. Topics include sets; random variables; rules of probability, including Bayes' rule; miscellaneous probability problems, including the birthday problem; discrete and continuous probability distributions, including the normal curve; multinomial, chi-square, binomial, and hypergeometric distributions; bivariate binomial probability and discrete bivariate probability functions; statistical estimation and hypothesis testing; simple regression and correlation; and Markov chains. Includes simple derivations. Chapters conclude with exercises.

Mosteller, Frederick; Kruskal, William H.; Pieters, Richard S.; Rising, Gerald R.; and Link, Richard F. With the Assistance of Roger Carlson and Martha Zelinka, eds. STATISTICS BY EXAMPLE: DETECTING PATTERNS. Addison-Wesley Innovative Series. Reading, Mass.: Addison-Wesley, 1970. x, 166 p. Index, pp. 163-66.

Contains twelve real-life problems analyzed with the aid of several standard statistical tools including normal distribution, chi-square tests, and regression. Problems include predicting the outcome of the world series; how much does a 40-pound box of bananas weigh?; grocery shopping and the central limit theorem; the case of the vanishing women jurors; the acceleration of gravity; and calibration of an automobile speedometer. Includes examples, exercises, and answers.

______. STATISTICS BY EXAMPLE: FINDING MODELS. Addison-Wesley Innovative Series. Reading, Mass.: Addison-Wesley, 1973. xiv, 146 p. Index, pp. 143-46.

Contains twelve real-life problems on developing models as structures for data so that dependence from the models can be organized and new structures built. Examples use real data. Topics include estimating wild-life populations by the capture-recapture method; escape-avoidance experiment; the Poisson approximation for binomial probabilities; similarity of two poems; high-energy elementary particle physics experiments; remote geologic mapping; estimating population sizes; and how to buy a used telescope.

Mosteller, Frederick, and Rourke, Robert E.K. STURDY STATISTICS: NONPARAMETRICS AND ORDER STATISTICS. Reading, Mass.: Addison-Wesley, 1973. xv, 395 p. Appendixes I to VII, pp. 273-312. Glossary, pp. 369-70. References, pp. 371-72. Short Answers to Selected Odd-Numbered Exercises, pp. 373-82. Index, pp. 383-95.

A text for a one-semester course in nonparametric statistics for students in a variety of disciplines who have knowledge of high school algebra and one semester of basic statistics. Appendixes review statistical concepts needed in the exposition. Includes proofs and derivations if necessary, with emphasis on real-life examples followed by detailed solutions. Based on signs, counts, ranks, and order statistics, and includes the following topics: normal and non-normal data; application of binomial and multinomial, including sign test; ranking methods for two independent samples, including Mann-Whitney test; normal approximation Mann-Whitney test; Wilcoxon's signed rank test; rank correlation; Poisson; chi-square with application to counted data; Kruskal-Wallis statistic; Friedman index; probability distributions of order statistics; and point estimation of order statistics. Sections conclude with exercises.

O'Toole, Alphonsus Lawrence. ELEMENTARY PRACTICAL STATISTICS. New York: Macmillan, 1964. xiv, 416 p. Appendix, pp. 344-406. Index, pp. 407-16.

A text for a one-semester course for a varied group of students who have a high school algebra background. Topics include sampling; discrete and continuous random variables; testing a null hypothesis; binomial distribution; interval estimation and hypothesis testing; rank correlation and simple regression; linear prediction; and index numbers. Exercises, which follow the sections, include concepts in the mathematical theory of statistics and algebraic proofs. Appendix contains proofs and derivations, and additional techniques of analysis.

Ott, Lyman. AN INTRODUCTION TO STATISTICAL METHODS AND DATA ANALYSIS. North Scituate, Mass.: Duxbury Press, 1977. xi, 730 p. Glossary of Symbols and Key Words, p. 655. Appendix: Tables, pp. 657-704. Selected Answers, pp. 705-24. Index, pp. 725-30.

A text for a one-year course in basic statistics for students in a variety of fields who have a high school algebra background and a reference for research workers. Emphasizes the role of the computer with solutions to exercises illustrated by printouts from statistical packages and the SPSS. Starred exercises appropriate for computer solutions. Models used as a unifying theme for regression and analysis of variance. Topics include normal probability distribution; inference; simple and multiple regression; general linear model; experimental design, including completely randomized design and Latin square; chi-square; nonparametric tests; tests concerning variances; multiple comparisons; systems of coding; fixed, random, and mixed effects models; unbalanced designs; and analysis of covariance. Sections conclude with exercises; chapters, with references. Uses matrix algebra to develop regression models.

Peters, William Stanley, ed. READINGS IN APPLIED STATISTICS. Englewood Cliffs, N.J.: Prentice-Hall, 1969. viii, 376 p. No index.

Twenty-six reprints of articles previously published in journals and elsewhere, grouped under the following six headings:

"Dimensions of Statistics" (four articles); "Sources and Uses of Data" (three articles); "Control of Operations" (four articles); "Further Applications" (six articles); "Multivariate Analysis" (four articles); and "Econometrics and Time Series Problems" (five articles). Illustrates the versatility and scope of applied statistics. Useful as a supplement for graduate and undergraduate courses in business and economic statistics. Topics include the technical tools of statistics; simulation applied to industry; analysis of covariance; discriminant analysis; factor analysis; forecasting by exponentially weighted moving averages; and supply-demand models.

Peters, William Stanley, and Summers, George W. STATISTICAL ANALYSIS FOR BUSINESS DECISIONS. Prentice-Hall International Series in Management. Englewood Cliffs, N.J.: Prentice-Hall, 1968. xvi, 540 p. Glossary of Major Symbols, pp. 417-25. Appendix: Tables, pp. 427-531. Index, pp. 533-40.

A text for a one-semester course in basic statistics and probability for students with limited mathematics background. More advanced than most basic texts, providing a good background for courses in operations research, econometrics, simulation, and related courses. Emphasizes illustrative examples, use of small populations, simulation in the approach to sampling distributions, integration of analysis of variance and regression, and matrix methods where appropriate. Includes probability processes; Bayes' theorem; discrete and continuous random variables; chi-square; sampling distributions of means and variances; significance tests and decision procedures; probability distributions of a parameter; statistical inference for binomial and Poisson parameters; decision theory; correlation; and discriminant analysis. Sections conclude with problems; chapters, with references.

Phillips, John L., Jr. A STRUCTURAL APPROACH TO STATISTICAL THINKING. A Series of Books in Psychology. San Francisco: W.H. Freeman, 1973. xv, 124 p. Appendix I: Tests of Significance, pp. 104-9. Appendix II: List of Symbols, pp. 110-19. Notes, p. 119. Suggested Readings, p. 120. Index, pp. 121-24.

A supplemental text for basic statistics courses aimed at breaking the barrier that exists between students and the study of statistics. Relies on a thorough treatment of logical structures, rather than detailed numerical examples, and contains numerous cross references to topics. Topics include measures of central tendency and variations; measures of relationships; and interpreting individual measures, such as standard scores, precision of measurement, significance of a difference between two means, and testing of hypotheses, including chi-square and analysis of variance.

Råde, Lennart, ed. STATISTICS AT THE SCHOOL LEVEL: AN INTERPRETATION OF OFFICIAL STATISTICS. New York: Halsted Press, 1975. 242 p. List of Participants, pp. 241-42. No index.

Sixteen papers presented at the third round table meeting on the teaching of statistics organized by the International Statistical Institute under the auspices of UNESCO and held in Vienna from August 30 to Sept. 4, 1973. Topics include teaching official statistics; official statistics of population and production; computing and probability; a mobile-computer for schools' computing; and teaching probability and statistics in France, Austria, and Nigeria.

_____. THE TEACHING OF PROBABILITY AND STATISTICS. New York: Wiley-Interscience, 1970. 373 p. Bibliography, pp. 363-73. No index.

Nineteen papers on the teaching of probability and statistics at the pre-college level presented at the First International Comprehensive School Mathematics Program Conference held in Carbondale, Illinois, on March 18-27, 1969. Topics include combinatorics for school mathematics curricula; nonparametric statistics at the pre-college level; teaching probability in intermediate grades; probability and pre-calculus analysis; statistical examples for use in high schools; a multidisciplinary approach for teaching statistics and probability; a nonfrequentist view of probability and statistics; and experience in Australia, France, and Sweden.

Reichard, Robert S. THE NUMBERS GAME: USES AND ABUSES OF MANAGERIAL STATISTICS. New York: McGraw-Hill, 1972. xiv, 366 p. Supplementary Reading List, pp. 354-58. Index, pp. 359-66.

A nontechnical introduction to the uses of statistical tools and techniques for the layman and the manager who have little exposure to formal statistics and mathematics. Topics include use and misuse of averages; use of charts; construction and use of index numbers; advanced techniques such as regression and linear programming; advanced applications in quality control, inventory control, capital spending, and input-output analysis; the role of the computer; financial analysis; and break-even charts.

Rickmers, Albert D., and Todd, Hollis, N. STATISTICS: AN INTRODUCTION. New York: McGraw-Hill, 1967. xvi, 585 p. References, pp. 543-50. Appendix: Tables, pp. 552-78. Index, pp. 579-85.

A research-oriented text for a one-year course in basic statistics for undergraduates and graduates in science and engineering, and also students of medicine, biology, agriculture, physics, and chemistry who have a high school algebra background. Omits proofs and complex mathematics. Concepts introduced with examples familiar to the student. Topics include normal curve; tests of hypotheses and interval estimation; sample size for variables; chi-square; analysis of variance; components of variance; crossed and nested experiments; simple and multiple regression and correlation; experimental design; factorial experiments; confounding and fractional factorials; nonparametric statistics; acceptance sampling; Shewart control charts; and control charts based on moving average, moving range, and geometric moving average. Chapters conclude with problems, questions, and references.

Robbins, Herbert, and Ryzin, John Van. INTRODUCTION TO STATISTICS. Chicago: Science Research Associates, 1975. x, 427 p. Appendix: Statistical Tables, pp. 378-404. Short Answers to Odd-Numbered Problems, pp. 405-23. Index, pp. 424-27.

A text for a one-year course in basic statistics for students in a variety of fields who have knowledge of high school algebra. Emphasizes brevity and the logic of statistical inference from experimental data. Includes proofs and derivations. Topics include probability and Bayes' theorem; random variables; Chebyshev's inequality; law of large numbers; estimation and hypothesis testing; analysis of variance with interaction; simple regression and correlation; chi-square; contingency tables; multinomial distributions; and nonparametric tests. Sections conclude with problems.

Runyon, Richard P. WINNING WITH STATISTICS: A PAINLESS FIRST LOOK AT NUMBERS, RATIOS, PERCENTAGES, MEANS, AND INFERENCE. Reading, Mass.: Addison-Wesley, 1977. x, 210 p. Index, pp. 201-10.

A nontechnical exposition of basic statistical concepts for the layman written in an entertaining style using a few graphs and tables, but no formulas. Topics include two faces of statistics; bias; index numbers; means; standard deviations; probability; and inference. Useful to beginning students for self-study.

Savage, I. Richard. STATISTICS: UNCERTAINTY AND BEHAVIOR. Boston: Houghton-Mifflin, 1968. xiii, 344 p. References, pp. 328-31. Symbols, pp. 332-33. Index, pp. 335-44.

A text for a one-semester course in statistics for liberal arts students just beginning their mathematics education but who have the maturity gained in a one-year calculus course. Many topics ordinarily found in an introductory statistics book either omitted or treated lightly (for example, graphing and computing, and the t-test), but includes other topics, such as stochastic processes and prediction, not found in a basic text. Topics include probability and Bayes' theorem; random variables and expectation; states of nature; estimation, confidence, and tolerance intervals; nonparametric tests; decision theory; sequential analysis; least squares; likelihood ratios; mean square loss and normal probability functions; and central limit theorem. Chapters conclude with problems. Presentation rigorous from a symbolism viewpoint.

SCHOOL MATHEMATICS PROJECT. Further Mathematics V: Draft Edition. New York: Cambridge University Press, 1971. x, 133 p. Index, pp. 131-33.

A preliminary report on applications of probability theory designed to correct shortcomings in traditional school mathematics syllabuses. Assumes familiarity with the topics covered in the A-level syllabus for S.M.P. ADVANCED MATHEMATICS, Books 1-4. Topics include Markov chains, Poisson processes, goodness-of-fit, Student's t, correlation and regression, expectation algebra, and characteristic functions. Chapters conclude with exercises and answers.

Snedecor, George W., and Cochran, William G. STATISTICAL METHODS. 6th ed. Ames: Iowa State University Press, 1967. xiv, 593 p. Appendix: Tables, pp. 431-75. Author Index, pp. 577-80. Index to Numerical Examples, pp. 581-84. Subject Index, pp. 585-93.

A text for a one-year introductory course in basic statistics and a reference for research workers. Proof included if feasible or if necessary in order to understand the concepts. Examples mainly from biological investigations. Topics include confidence intervals; sampling distributions; comparisons of two samples; nonparametric methods; simple regression; correlation; sampling from the binomial distribution; chi-square; one- and two-way analysis of variance; factorial experiments; multiple regression, including curvilinear; and the design and analysis of sampling. Chapters conclude with references.

Spatz, Chris, and Johnston, James O. BASIC STATISTICS: TALES OF DISTRIBUTIONS. Brooks/Cole Series in Statistics. Monterey, Calif.: Brooks/Cole, 1976. xii, 380 p. References, pp. 280-82. Tables, pp. 283-311. Glossaries, pp. 312-24. Answers to Problems, pp. 325-76. Index, pp. 377-80.

A text for a one-semester course for students in a variety of fields. Written in a conversational style with most examples and problems reflecting situations that the student can readily understand and relate to. Includes detailed examples for each procedure, but avoids the strictly cookbook style of presentation. Topics include correlation and regression; normal curve and sampling; difference between two means; analysis of variance; factorial design; chi-square; and nonparametric tests. Chapters conclude with problems.

Spear, Mary Eleanor. PRACTICAL CHARTING TECHNIQUES. New York: McGraw-Hill, 1969. xxii, 394 p. Bibliography, pp. 369-71. Manufacturers and Suppliers of Visual Presentation Products, pp. 373-76. Index, pp. 377-94.

A manual which explains the principles of charting and illustrates standard methods and forms of graphic presentation using 276 graphs. Includes the following charts: line, bar, surface, column, Gantt, profiel, PERT, machine-record, and map.

Tanur, Judith M., et al., eds. STATISTICS: A GUIDE TO THE UNKNOWN. Foreword by Frederick Mosteller. Holden-Day Series in Probability and Statistics. San Francisco: Holden-Day, 1972. xxiii, 430 p. Essays Classified by Data Sources, pp. xvi-xvii. Essays Classified by Statistical Tools, pp. xviii-xxiii. Index, pp. 419-30.

A collection of forty-four essays, heretofore unpublished, on past accomplishments and current uses of statistics and probability for readers without any formal training in mathematics, probability, or statistics. Grouped under the following headings: "Man in His Biologic World" (ten essays); "Man in His Political World" (seven essays); "Man in His Social World" (twenty essays); "Man in His Physical World" (seven essays). Useful to parents and school children, school superintendents, principals, and teachers of mathematics. Also useful as a supplementary text for a basic statistics course.

Tippett, Leonard Henry Caleb. STATISTICS. Oxford Paperback University Series. 3d ed. New York: Oxford University Press, 1968. vi, 153 p. Notes on Books, pp. 148-49. Index, pp. 150-53.

A nontechnical introduction to basic statistical concepts for the layman. Contains examples on the misuse of statistical data as well as on its proper use. Topics include arranging and presenting the data; tables and diagrams; sampling; taking account of chance; statistical laws; statistical reasoning; and statistics in business affairs.

Townsend, Neal R., and Wheatley, Grayson H. DEVELOPING SKILLS IN STATISTICS. Boston: Allyn and Bacon, 1978. viii, 281 p. Appendix A: Summation Notation, pp. 231-34. Appendix B: Index Notation, pp. 235-43. Tables, pp. 245-68. Answers to Odd-Numbered Exercises, pp. 269-78. Index, pp. 279-81.

A text for a one-semester course for students in a variety of fields. Introduces each new concept with an example encountered by employees of the Oxford Truck Co. Includes detailed examples. Topics include binomial and normal distributions; sampling and the central limit theorem; regression; chi-square; and sign and rank-sum tests. Sections conclude with exercises.

Wallis, W. Allen, and Roberts, Harry V. THE NATURE OF STATISTICS. Glencoe, Ill.: Free Press, 1962. 218 p. Index, pp. 209-18.

A supplementary text for a basic statistics course which attempts to demonstrate the leveliness of statistics by the use of real examples from a wide variety of fields. Topics include effective uses of statistics; misuse of statistics; samples and populations; randomness; observation and measurement; kinds of statistical data; and how to read a table. No mathematical prerequisites. Mainly a revision of STATISTICS: A NEW APPROACH (see below).

______. STATISTICS: A NEW APPROACH. Glencoe, Ill.: Free Press, 1956. xxxviii, 646 p. Appendix: Tables, pp. 621-35. Index, pp. 637-46.

A text for a one-year course in basic statistics for students and layman. Virtually devoid of mathematics, with emphasis on ideas, principles, criteria, and methods rather than on techniques and details. Topics include uses of statistics; misuses of statistics; observation and measurement; averages and variability; association; randomness and probability; sampling distributions and the normal distribution; statistical trends and estimation concerning means and proportions; chi square; design of experiments; statistical quality control; simple regression and correlation; and time series. Chapters conclude with problems.

Walpole, Ronald E. ELEMENTARY STATISTICAL CONCEPTS. New York: Macmillan, 1976. viii, 231 p. References, pp. 209-10. Statistical Tables, pp. 211-18. Answers to Exercises, pp. 219-27. Index, pp. 229-31.

A text for a one-semester course in basic statistics for college freshmen who have limited mathematics background. Examples used as a substitute for proofs. Topics include sample spaces and probability; discrete and continuous random variables; estimation and hypothesis testing; simple regression and correlation; and chi-square. Chapters conclude with exercises. Graphs are set off in orange.

______. INTRODUCTION TO STATISTICS. 2d ed. New York: Macmillan, 1974. xiii, 340 p. References, pp. 301-2. Appendix: Statistical Tables, pp. 303-23. Answers to Exercises, pp. 325-34. Index, pp. 335-40.

A text for a one-semester course in basic statistics for students in varied disciplines who have knowledge of high school algebra. Emphasizes inference based on probability, and topics include sets and probability; random variables and expectation; discrete probability distributions; normal; sampling distributions; estimation and hypothesis testing; regression and correlation; nonparametric tests; and analysis of variance. Chapters conclude with exercises.

Williams, Frederick. REASONING WITH STATISTICS: SIMPLIFIED EXAMPLES IN COMMUNICATIONS RESEARCH. New York: Holt, Rinehart and Winston, 1968. ix, 182 p. Tables, pp. 167-75. Index, pp. 177-82.

A how-to-do-it handbook on statistics for students in various fields of communications who need to be knowledgeable readers of quantitative research but who lack the statistical background. Does not prepare the student to use statistical methods, but motivates him to undertake a more formal study of the subject later. Consists of the following three parts: "Basic Concepts"; "Assessing Differences"; and "Assessing Relationships." Topics include measurements and distributions, parameters, hypothesis testing, t-test, single- and multiple-factor analysis of variance, nonparametric tests, regression and correlation, prediction, and factor analysis. Knowledge of high school algebra is assumed. Chapters conclude with summaries and readings.

Wine, Russell Lowell. BEGINNING STATISTICS. Cambridge, Mass.: Winthrop, 1976. viii, 432 p. Annotated References and Bibliography, pp. 400-402. Statistical Tables, pp. 403-13. Answers to Even-Numbered Exercises, pp. 414-26. Index, pp. 427-32.

A text for a one-semester or two-quarter course in basic statistics for liberal arts students and others in the physical and social sciences. Uses the intuitive approach, accompanied by illustrations. Topics include discrete probability; random variables and their distributions; sampling distributions; estimation and hypothesis testing; chi-square; nonparametric tests; and linear regression and correlation. Sections conclude with exercises.

Wolf, Frank L. ELEMENTS OF PROBABILITY AND STATISTICS. 2d ed., rev. McGraw-Hill Series in Probability and Statistics. New York: McGraw-Hill, 1974. xiv, 450 p. Appendixes, pp. 361-422. Tables, pp. 425-45. Index, pp. 447-50.

A text for a one-semester course in basic statistics for students with a high school algebra background, with the starred sections suitable for the more advanced students familiar with calculus. Emphasizes the logical structure of statistics with the definition-theorem-proof style used freely. Topics include sets and probability; discrete and continuous probability distributions with application to estimation and hypothesis testing, nonparametric tests, and decision theory; random variables; chi-square and goodness of fit; F and t distributions; discrete and continuous marginal and conditional distributions; and bivariate normal distribution. Accessible to students in a variety of fields desiring a somewhat theoretical and abstract approach to basic statistics. Appendixes include notations, square roots, functions, inequalities and absolute values, graphs, basic limits, references to applications, answers to selected exercises, and statistical tables. Sections conclude with exercises.

Youden, William John. RISK, CHOICE AND PREDICTION: AN INTRODUCTION TO EXPERIMENTATION. Preface by Brian L. Joiner. North Scituate, Mass.: Duxbury, 1974. ix, 80 p. Appendix: Tables, pp. 79-80. No index.

A nontechnical exposition of the concepts and techniques of probability and statistics helpful in understanding the real world. Uses simple mathematics and helpful thinking to interpret experimental data. Topics include randomization; lotteries; penny-tossing experiments; experiments with cards and dice; Poisson's formula; and measuring the thickness of paper.

Zeisel, Hans. SAY IT WITH FIGURES. 5th ed., rev. Introduction by Paul F. Lazersfeld. New York: Harper & Row, 1968. xviii, 248 p. Index, pp. 241-48.

An introduction to social statistics for the layman in two parts: "The Presentation of Numbers" and "The Search for Causes." Topics include percent figures; tables of more than two dimensions; indexes; tools of causal analysis; cross-tabulations; and accounting schemes. Numerous examples are provided.

Zirkel, Gene, and Rosenfeld, Robert. BEGINNING STATISTICS. New York: McGraw-Hill, 1976. xiii, 320 p. Appendix A: Sample Data, pp. 243-46. Appendix B: Tables, pp. 247-65. Appendix C: Formulas, pp. 266-71. Appendix D: One-Tail Hypothesis Tests, pp. 272-78. Appendix E: Type II Errors, pp. 279-83. Appendix F: Bibliography, pp. 284-85. Appendix G: Selected Readings, pp. 286-93. Answers to Selected Assignments, pp. 294-316. Index, pp. 317-18. Symbols, pp. 319-20.

A work-text designed for classroom use where time is available to perform small statistical experiments. Little use made of formulas, with some examples couched in absurd situations for motivation. Uses computer programs to simulate experiments. Topics include sampling; probability; chi-square; testing proportions; two-sample experiments; averages and the central limit theorem; estimation and confidence intervals; correlation and prediction; and nonparametric tests. Chapters conclude with summaries and assignments.

Chapter 4

MATHEMATICAL STATISTICS

Adams, Joe Kennedy. BASIC STATISTICAL CONCEPTS. New York: McGraw-Hill, 1955. xvi, 304 p. References, pp. 213-14. Appendix A: Some Hints on How to Ask Questions of Mathematical Statisticians, pp. 215-18. Appendix B: Mathematical Appendix, pp. 219-54. Appendix C: Miscellaneous Tables, pp. 255-75. Appendix D: Tables of Sampling Distributions, pp. 277-88. Glossary, p. 289. Answers to Odd-Numbered Exercises, pp. 290-98. Index, pp. 299-304.

> An early text for a one-year course in mathematical statistics for students who have little or no training in calculus or statistics. Emphasizes developing an understanding of the language used in mathematical statistics, and applying theorems to empirical problems. Topics include sampling; inference; parameters and distributions; hypergeometic and binomial distributions; Poisson; discrete and continuous distributions; normal; chi-square; t and F distributions; bivariate distribution; analysis of variance; and nonparametric tests. Chapters conclude with exercises.

Ahmavaara, Yrjö, and Nordenstreng, Kaarle. TRANSFORMATION ANALYSIS OF STATISTICAL VARIABLES: AN INTRODUCTION OF GROUP-THEORETICAL IDEAS INTO MULTIVARIATE ANALYSIS. Transactions of the Westermarck Society, vol. xvii. Helsinki: Academic Bookstore, 1970. 103 p. References, pp. 102-3. No index.

> A monograph on transformation analysis in three parts: "The Theory of Transformation Analysis"; "The Technique of Transformation Analysis"; and "Examples of Applications." Presentation primarily verbal, but knowledge of mathematical statistics and matrix algebra helpful.

Aitken, Alexander C. STATISTICAL MATHEMATICS. 8th ed. University Mathematics Texts. New York: Interscience, 1957. vii, 153 p. Appendix, pp. 145-48. Index, pp. 149-53.

> An introduction to mathematical statistics for students who have knowledge of elementary differential and integral calculus.

Topics include probability, moments and their computation, probability distributions, least squares and regression, and the analysis of variance. Appendix includes a discussion of finite differences and factorial polynomials, finite sums, and other mathematical topics.

Albers, Willi. ASYMPTOTIC EXPANSIONS AND THE DEFICIENCY CONCEPT IN STATISTICS. Mathematics Centre Tracts 58. Amsterdam: Mathematisch Centrum, 1974. 144 p. Tables, pp. 218-39. References, pp. 140-42. Index, pp. 143-44.

Consists of the following six chapters: "Introduction"; "The Optimal Ratio of Sample Sizes for Comparing Two Distributions"; "Asymptotic Expansions for Nonparametric Test for the One Sample Problem"; "Deficiencies Between Various Tests for the One Sample Problem"; "Deficiencies of Some Related Estimators"; and "Finite Sample Computations." Assumes knowledge of mathematical statistics.

Alexander, Howard Wright. ELEMENTS OF MATHEMATICAL STATISTICS. Wiley Series in Probability and Mathematical Statistics. New York: Wiley, 1961. xi, 367 p. Appendix. Matrixes, pp. 327-36. Bibliography, pp. 337-38. Tables, pp. 339-49. Answers to Exercises, pp. 350-59. Index, pp. 361-67.

A text for an introductory course in probability and mathematical statistics for students who have completed one year of calculus. Approach measure-theoretic. Topics include descriptive statistics; continuous distributions, including gamma and beta; sampling distributions, including binomial and bivariate normal; multivariate, Poisson, Cauchy, Pearson's chi-square, and t; inference; regression and correlation; and analysis of variance. Includes proofs and examples. Sections conclude with exercise.

Anderson, R.L., and Bancroft, Theodore A[lfonso]. STATISTICAL THEORY IN RESEARCH. New York: McGraw-Hill, 1952. xix, 399 p. Appendix: Tables, pp. 379-87. Index, pp. 389-99.

A reference for research workers and a text for mathematical statistics courses requiring knowledge of calculus. Consists of two parts: "Basic Statistical Theory" and "Analysis of Experimental Models by Least Squares." Topics include probability; univariate parent population distributions and their properties; bivariate and multivariate distributions and their properties; derived sampling distributions and orthogonal linear functions; point estimation; maximum likelihood; estimation and tests of hypotheses; chi-square; regression and correlation; least squares for experimental design models; the analysis of design in complete blocks; the analysis of incomplete-block designs; factorial experiments; the analysis of covariance; analysis of data with both random and fixed effects (mixed models); and the recovery of interblock information in incomplete-block designs. Numerous examples provided. Chapters conclude with problems and references.

Antosik, Piotr; Mikusinski, Jan; and Sikorski, Roman. THEORY OF DISTRIBUTIONS: THE SEQUENTIAL APPROACH. Modern Analytic and Computational Methods in Science and Mathematics, no. 31. New York: American Elsvier, 1973. xiv, 273 p. Appendix, pp. 261-67. Bibliography, pp. 268-70. Index of Authors and Terminology, pp. 271-73.

An elementary introduction to distributions based on the sequential method in three parts: "Elementary Theory of Distributions of a Single Real Variable"; "Elementary Theory of Distributions of Several Real Variables"; and "Advanced Theory of Distribution." Topics include definitions; operations on distributions; local properties; convolutions and extension theorems; delta sequences and regular sequences; square integrable functions; inner product of functions; tempered distributions; periodic distributions; the Kothe spaces with applications; weak and strong convergence; and Hilbert and Fourier transforms with applications. Appendix includes mathematical derivations. The largest part of the book emphasizes rigor with proofs of theorems. Assumes knowledge of advanced calculus (or real analysis) and probability theory.

Bancroft, Theodore Alfonso. TOPICS IN INTERMEDIATE STATISTICAL METHODS. Vol. I. Ames: Iowa State University Press, 1968. xiii, 129 p. Appendix: Tables, pp. 115-24. Author index, pp. 125-26. Subject Index, pp. 127-29.

A collection of general intermediate statistical methods for graduate students in statistics in land-grant universities, and other graduate students in biology, agriculture, veterinary medicine, public health, behavioral and social sciences, and engineering. Methods include analysis of variance; two- and three-way classifications; extensions of exact and approximate methods to n-way classifications with unequal and disproportionate subclass numbers; analysis of covariance; orthogonal polynomials; and multiple comparison procedures. Useful as a supplementary text for courses in mathematical statistics. Chapters conclude with problems and references.

_____, ed. Assisted by S.A. Brown. STATISTICAL PAPERS IN HONOR OF GEORGE W. SNEDECOR. Foreword by W.R. Parks. Ames: Iowa State University Press, 1972. xvii, 328 p. No index.

Nineteen contributions by colleagues and friends of G.W. Snedecor covering such topics as linear multiple regression; sequential design of experiments; statistical decision processes; forecasting a tree crop by counts and measurements; history of statistics; statistical estimation of long-term population trends; and graphic and semigraphic displays.

Barnett, Victor David. COMPARATIVE STATISTICAL INFERENCE. Wiley Series in Probability and Mathematical Statistics. New York: Wiley, 1973. xv, 287 p. Bibliography, pp. 275-77. Subject and Author Index, pp. 279-87.

A text for a course in comparative statistical inference for graduates and undergraduates in mathematical statistics who have knowledge of calculus, linear algebra, and probability theory. Familiarity with specific methods of inference and decision theory also helpful. Surveys and contrasts the following three approaches to statistical inference and decision making: the estimation and hypothesis testing theories of Fisher, Neyman, Pearson, and others; Bayesian inferential procedures; and the decision theory approach originated by Wald. Excludes detailed mathematical proofs with a substantial amount of description accompanying the mathematical results. Concludes with a chapter on miscellaneous approaches, such as fiducial inference and likelihood inference, and an introduction to information theory. Chapters conclude with references.

Bechhoffer, Robert Eric; Kieffer, Jack; and Sobel, Milton. SEQUENTIAL IDENTIFICATION AND RANKING PROCEDURES WITH SPECIAL REFERENCE TO KOOPMAN-DARMOIS POPULATIONS. Statistical Research Monographs, Vol. III. Chicago: University of Chicago Press, 1968. 420 p. Bibliography, pp. 375-92. Glossary of Symbols, pp. 393-407. Index, pp. 409-20.

A monograph for research workers and practitioners on generalizations of Wald's sequential multiple decision procedures for ranking problems which arise naturally in research and development in industry, medicine, agriculture, and other areas where the experimenter must classify treatments as categories according to some criteria of goodness. Consists of the following three parts: "General Theory"; "Application to Ranking Koopman-Darmois Parameters with Special Reference to Normal Means: Unsolved Problems"; and "Monte Carlo Sampling."

BERKELEY SYMPOSIUM ON MATHEMATICAL STATISTICS AND PROBABILITY, THIRD PROCEEDINGS. Vol. I to V. Edited by Jerzy Neyman. Berkeley and Los Angeles: Univ. of California Press, 1956. Vol. I: CONTRIBUTIONS TO THE THEORY OF STATISTICS. viii, 208 p. Vol. II: PROBABILITY THEORY. viii, 246 p. Vol. III: ASTRONOMY AND PHYSICS. vii, 252 p. Vol. IV: BIOLOGY AND PROBLEMS OF HEALTH. ix, 179 p. Vol. V: ECONOMETRICS, INDUSTRIAL RESEARCH, AND PSYCHOMETRY. viii, 184 p. No index.

Sixty-three papers presented at the third symposium on mathematical statistics and probability held at the University of California, December 1954, and July and August, 1955, grouped in the following five volumes: vol. I (sixteen papers); vol. II (fifteen papers); vol. III (thirteen papers); vol. IV (nine papers); and vol. 5 (ten papers). Topics range from highly theoretical concepts in statistics and probability, including inadmissibility of estimators, asymptotic theory of estimation periodicity of random-valued functions, and stationary measures for Markov processes, to applied topics such as statistics of clusters of galaxies, epidemics in closed populations, and experimental design in industrial research. Contributors include eminent theoretical and applied statisticians from around the world. An invaluable reference on research results in both theory and application.

BERKELEY SYMPOSIUM ON MATHEMATICAL STATISTICS AND PROBABILITY, FOURTH PROCEEDINGS. Vol. I to IV. Edited by Jerzy Neyman. Berkeley and Los Angeles: University of California Press, 1961. Vol. I: THEORY OF STATISTICS. xii, 768 p. Vol. II: PROBABILITY THEORY. xvi, 634 p. Vol. III: ASTRONOMY, METEOROLOGY, AND PHYSICS. xi, 335 p. Vol. IV: CONTRIBUTIONS TO BIOLOGY, AND PROBLEMS OF MEDICINE. xii, 413 p. No index.

The 120 papers presented at the fourth symposium held at the Statistical Laboratory, University of California, June 20 to July 30, 1960, grouped in the following volumes: vol. I (forty-one papers); vol. II (thirty-five papers); vol. III (seventeen papers); vol. IV (twenty-seven papers). Topics include martingale system theory; asymptotic efficiency of a maximum likelihood estimator; Bayesian approach to rejection of outliers; two-sample tests based on order statistics; Brownian motion; random operator equations; Lebesgue measure of linear sets; theory of characteristic functions; recurrent random walk and logarithmic potential; problems in the theory of comets; stochastic description of precipitation; statistical problems of exploited fisheries populations; statistical uses of large computers; Latin square as a repeated measurements design; and stochastic processes in psychology.

BERKELEY SYMPOSIUM ON MATHEMATICAL STATISTICS AND PROBABILITY, FIFTH PROCEEDINGS. Vols. I to V. Edited by Lucien M. Le Cam and Jerzy Neyman. Berkeley and Los Angeles: University of California Press, 1967. Vol. I: THEORY OF STATISTICS. xvii, 666 p. Vol. II: Part I: THEORY OF PROBABILITY. xvi, 447 p. Vol. II: Part II: THEORY OF PROBABILITY. xvi, 483 p. Vol. III: PHYSICAL SCIENCES. xvi, 324 p. Vol. IV: BIOLOGY AND PROBLEMS OF HEALTH. xix, 934 p. Vol. V: WEATHER MODIFICATION. xix, 451 p. No Index.

The 191 papers presented at the fifth symposium held at the Statistical Laboratory, University of California, June 21 to July 18, 1965, and Dec. 27, 1965 to Jan. 7, 1966, grouped in the following five volumes: Vol. I (thirty-eight papers); vol. II (fifty-five papers); vol. III (seventeen papers); vol. IV (fifty-four papers); and vol. V (twenty-seven papers). Topics include information theory; nonparametric procedures; sequential procedures; probability on algebraic structures; distributions in functional spaces; stochastic processes and prediction; martingales; Markov processes; ergodic theory; astronomy; physics; spectral analysis; control processes; reliability; demography; ecology; epidemiology; genetics; chance mechanisms in living organisms; cellular phenomena; and decision theory in medical diagnosis.

BERKELEY SYMPOSIUM ON MATHEMATICAL STATISTICS AND PROBABILITY, SIXTH PROCEEDINGS. Vols. I to VI. Edited by Lucien M. Le Cam, Jerzy Neyman, and Elizabeth L. Scott. Berkeley and Los Angeles: University of California Press, 1972. Vol. I: THEORY OF STATISTICS. xvii, 599 p. Vol. II: PROBABILITY THEORY. xl, 757 p. Vol. III: PROBABILITY. xx, 711 p. Vol. IV: BIOLOGY AND HEALTH. xvi, 353 p. Vol. V: DARWIN NEO-DARWINIAN, AND NON-DARWINIAN EVOLUTION. xvi, 369 p. Vol. VI: EFFECTS OF POLLUTION ON HEALTH. xvii, 599 p. No index.

The 214 papers presented at the sixth symposium on mathematical statistics and probability held at the Statistical Laboratory, University of California, April 9-12, 1971, June 16-21, 1971, and July 19-22, 1971, grouped in the following six volumes: vol. I (thirty-nine papers); vol. II (thirty-three papers); vol. III (forty-two papers); vol. IV (twenty-five papers); vol. V (forty-one papers); and vol. VI (thirty-four papers). Topics include sequential analysis; asymptotic theory; regression; multivariate analysis; measure theory; inequalities; combinatorial analysis; ergodic theory; Gaussian processes; central limit theorem; passage problems; potential theory; functionals; point processes; information and control; branching processes; biostatistics; cellular phenomena and carcinogenesis; population studies and evolution; evolution theory; pollutants in food chains; ecological studies; and radiation and health controversy.

Berman, Simeon M. MATHEMATICAL STATISTICS: AN INTRODUCTION BASED ON THE NORMAL DISTRIBUTION. Scranton, Pa.: In text, 1971. xvi, 392 p. Appendix, pp. 371-88. Index, pp. 389-92.

A text for an introductory course in mathematical statistics for both undergraduates and graduates who have knowledge of differential and integral calculus. Presentation limited to the normal distribution, with probability based on the Rieman integral, rather than on the more general and more abstract Lebesgue integral. Following theorems proved: the sample mean is a uniformly minimum variance unbiased estimator of the population mean; the one-sided test on the mean of a normal population is uniformly most powerful; the two-sided test is uniformly most powerful unbiased; the t-test is uniformly most powerful invariant; and the conventional predictor of the next observation in linear regression is the best unbiased predictor. Method of sufficiency developed fully by using special properties of the normal sample space. Other topics include joint distributions; sequential testing; and analysis of variance. Omits Bayes' theory and minimax theory. Chapters end with sections showing how the results for the normal case can be extended to the general case, and also with examples. Sections conclude with exercises.

Bhattacharya, Rabindra Nath, and Rao, R. Ranga. NORMAL APPROXIMATION AND ASYMPTOTIC EXPANSIONS. Wiley Series in Probability and Mathematical Statistics. New York: Wiley, 1976. xiv, 274 p. List of symbols, pp. ix-xiv. Appendix A.1: Random Vectors and Independence, pp. 243-44. Appendix A.2: Functions of Bounded Variation and Distribution Functions, pp. 244-52. Appendix A.3: Absolutely Continuous, Singular, and Discrete Probability Measures, pp. 252-54. Appendix A.4: The Euler-Maclaurin Sum Formula for Functions of Several Variables, pp. 254-66. References, pp. 267-71. Index, pp. 273-74.

Presents various refinements of the classical limit theorems for independent random vectors. Includes the following five chapters: "Weak Convergence of Probability Measures and Uniformity Classes"; "Fourier Transforms and Expansions of Characteristic Functions"; "Bounds for Errors of Normal Approximation"; "Asymptotic Expansion-Nonlattice Distributions"; and "Asymptotic Expansions-Lattice Distributions." Assumes knowledge of real analysis, measure theory, and probability theory.

Bickel, Peter J., and Doksum, Kjell A. MATHEMATICAL STATISTICS: BASIC IDEAS AND SELECTED TOPICS. Holden-Day Series in Probability and Statistics. San Francisco: Holden-Day, 1977. xv, 493 p. Appendix: A Review of Basic Probability Theory, pp. 437-68. Tables, pp. 469-83. Acknowledgements and Sources for Tables and Figures, p. 484. Author Index, pp. 485-86. Subject Index, pp. 487-92. Notational Index, p. 493.

A text for a one-year course in mathematical statistics for students of mathematics, engineering, statistics, and physical sciences who have knowledge of linear and matrix algebra, advanced calculus, and probability theory. Includes a large number of problems of varying difficulty. Provides a careful development of the major results of mathematical statistics such as the Neyman-Pearson lemma, the Lehmann-Scheffe theorem, information inequality, and the Gauss-Markoff theorem. Heuristic discussions of the more advanced results such as the large sample theory of maximum likelihood estimates and the structure of both Bayes and admissible solutions in decision theory provided. Other topics include statistical models, including exponential families; sufficiency; uniformly minimum variance estimators; large sample theory; optimal tests and confidence intervals; likelihood ratio tests; regression and analysis of variance; simultaneous confidence intervals and multiple comparisons; analysis of discrete data; nonparametric tests; and decision theory. Chapters conclude with problems and complements, and references.

Bose, Purnendu Kumar, and Chaudhuri, S.B. ON SOME PROBLEMS ASSOCIATED WITH D^2-STATISTICS AND p-STATISTICS. Asia Monograph, 8. New York: Asia Publishing House, 1966. ix, 59 p. Tables, pp. 43-54. References, pp. 55-58. Index, p. 59.

> A monograph on recursion formulas and tables relating to the use of the D^2- and p-statistics. Provides methods of computing the incomplete probability integral of the multivariate distribution; construction of incomplete probability integral tables of the classical D^2-statistic and studentized D^2-statistic; construction of the incomplete probability integral tables of p-statistics; and application of D^2- and p-statistics.

Brunk, H.D. AN INTRODUCTION TO MATHEMATICAL STATISTICS. 2d ed., rev. A Blaisdell Book in Pure and Applied Mathematics. Waltham, Mass.: Blaisdell, 1965. 429 p. References, p. 372. Tables, pp. 373-407. Index, pp. 409-15. Answers, pp. 417-29.

> A text for a one-semester course in mathematical statistics. Controversial questions in probability avoided, and mathematical rigor de-emphasized. Topics include elementary and general probability spaces; conditional probability and Bayes' formula; discrete and continuous random variables; joint distributions; independence; the algebra of expectations; distributions; random sampling; law of large numbers; estimation, including maximum likelihood and Bayes' estimation; central limit theorem; confidence intervals and tests of hypotheses; decision theory; simple regression; chi-square; experimental design and analysis of variance; stratified and sequential sampling; statistical quality control; and distribution-free tests. Style of presentation primarily verbal. Sections conclude with problems.

Bulmer, M.G. PRINCIPLES OF STATISTICS. Cambridge: MIT Press, 1965. viii, 252 p. Statistical Tables, pp. 231-36. Answers to Exercises, pp. 237-40. Solutions to Problems, pp. 241-44. References, pp. 245-47. Index, pp. 248-52.

> Describes principles and concepts of statistics for mathematicians who require an elementary introduction and for the scientist who wishes an understanding of the theory of statistics. Chapters conclude with exercises and problems, both numerical and theoretical which serve to extend the exposition. Topics include laws of probability; random variables and probability distributions; moments of random variables; inference and tests of significance; point estimation; and regression and correlation.

Bury, Karl V. STATISTICAL MODELS IN APPLIED SCIENCE. Wiley Series in Probability and Mathematical Statistics. New York: Wiley, 1975. xvii, 625 p. Index, pp. 607-25.

> A self-contained treatment of most parts of mathematical statistics that find useful application in the applied sciences.

Suitable for a course in mathematical statistics for engineering and science students and a reference for researchers who have knowledge of calculus. Consists of three parts: "Statistical Analysis"; "Statistical Models"; and "Applications of Statistical Models." Topics include sets and probability; random variables and their distributions; order statistics; point estimation, including maximum likelihood; inference and hypothesis testing; nonparametric tests; normal, lognormal, gamma, beta, extreme value, Weibul, exponential, and Rayleigh models; applications to probabilistic designs, component reliability, system analysis, and material strength. Chapters conclude with notations and references.

Cox, David Roxbee. THE ANALYSIS OF BINARY DATA. London: Methuen, 1970. viii, 142 p. Appendix A: Further Results and Exercises, pp. 109-21. Appendix B: Bibliography and References, pp. 122-34. Author Index, pp. 135-37. Subject Index, pp. 138-42.

A monograph on the analysis of binary (or quantal) data, i.e., data in which an observation takes on one of two possible forms--success or failure. Develops the method of using linear logistic models for studying how the probability of success depends on explanatory variables and groupings of the material. Written mainly for statisticians, scientists, and technologists interested in applying statistical methods. Topics include empirical logistic transforms with application to factorial experiments; exact analysis for a single parameter; linear regression and combinations of regressions; maximum likelihood; and paired preferences. Assumes knowledge of mathematical statistics.

______. PROBLEMS AND SOLUTIONS IN THEORETICAL STATISTICS. New York: Wiley, 1978. vii, 193 p. References, pp. 176-84. Author Index, pp. 185-86. Subject Index, pp. 187-93.

Presents outline solutions and discussions of about 150 further results and exercises in THEORETICAL STATISTICS (see below). Includes statement of each problem and summary of main general ideas. Categories of problems include general concepts, significance tests; distribution-free and randomization tests; interval estimation; point estimation; asymptotic theory; Bayesian methods; and decision theory. Useful to teachers and graduate students for a review of statistical theory.

Cox, David Roxbee, and Hinkley, D.V. THEORETICAL STATISTICS. London: Chapman and Hall, 1974. xii, 511 p. Appendix 1: Determination of Probability Distributions, pp. 462-65. Appendix 2: Order Statistics, pp. 466-74. Appendix 3: Second-Order Regression for Arbitrary Random Variables, pp. 475-77. References, pp. 478-95. Author Index, pp. 496-98. Subject Index, pp. 499-511.

A text for a second or third course in theoretical statistics for students who are already familiar with elementary statistical techniques, elementary probability, and the theory of linear models. Omits numerical examples and detailed discussion of particularly advanced techniques and specific applications. Avoids the theorem-proof style, with examples playing a central role in the verbal discussions. Topics include sufficient statistics; composite null hypotheses; composite alternatives; multidimensional alternatives; nonparametric tests and randomization tests; point and interval estimation; asymptotic theory; Bayesian methods; and decision theory. Chapters conclude with bibliographies, notes, and exercises.

David, Florence Nightingale, ed. RESEARCH PAPERS IN STATISTICS, FESTSCHIFT FOR J. NEYMAN. New York: Wiley, 1966. vii, 468 p. No index.

Twenty-six heretofore unpublished contributions to mathematical statistics in honor of Jerzy Neyman (twenty-two in English and four in French) by eminent statisticians from around the world. Topics include epidemiological theory; procedures connected with the logistic qualitative response curve; Monte Carlo methods for the Monomer-Dimer problem; heteroscedasticity in the linear normal regression model; super-critical branching processes; statistical incidence of the masses and evolution of galaxies; generalized inverse for matrixes; asymptotic efficiency of estimates; jurimetrics; development in sampling theory; and random intersection of two graphs.

DeGroot, Morris H. OPTIMAL STATISTICAL DECISIONS. New York: McGraw-Hill, 1970. xvi, 489 p. References, pp. 447-64. Supplementary Bibliography, pp. 465-71. Name Index, pp. 475-79. Subject Index, pp. 481-89.

A text for a course in mathematical theory and methodology of optimal statistical decisions for students of engineering, economics, management, psychology, mathematics, and statistics who have a background in calculus and matrix algebra, with one year of mathematical statistics and probability. Complete proofs provided for nearly all theoretical results. Consists of four parts: "Survey of Probability Theory"; "Subjective Probability and Utility"; "Statistical Decision Problems"; and "Sequential Decisions." Topics include survey of probability theory; random variables; random vectors; univariate distributions and multivariate distributions, including Wishart and multivariate t; conditional likelihoods; convex and concave utility functions; Bayes' risk; prior and posterior distributions; estimation, testing hypotheses, and linear statistical models; one-way analysis of variance; sequential decision procedures; dynamic programming; optimal stopping rules; stopping rules for martingales; Markov processes; two-armed bandit problems; multidimensional control problems; search problems; and information theory. Chapters conclude with exercises with answers.

Deutsch, Ralph. ESTIMATION THEORY. Englewood Cliffs, N.J.: Prentice-Hall, 1965. xiv, 269 p. References, pp. 252-61. Index, pp. 263-69.

An introduction to both classical and modern techniques for estimating parameters from experimental data for those already familiar with mathematical statistics and noise theory. Matrix notation used throughout. Only formal and heuristic mathematics employed with theorems left for the referenced technical literature. Topics include optimal estimates, including minimum mean squared estimators; geometrical properties of optimal estimators; least squares; linear and nonlinear estimates; recursive estimators; moment and maximum likelihood estimators; estimation errors; least squares smoothing and prediction; differential equation techniques for filtering and prediction; and decision theory. Chapters conclude with problems dealing with applications and additional theorems and derivations.

Doornbus, R. SLIPPAGE TESTS. Mathematical Centre Tracts 15. Amsterdam: Mathematisch Centrum, 1966. vi, 97 p. Tables, pp. 85-89. References, pp. 90-94. Index, pp. 95-97.

Presents some landmarks in the study of the slippage problem, i.e., the problem of deciding whether one or more observations come from a different population than that generating the other observation. Three chapter titles: "Slippage Tests for One Outlier"; "Tests for More than One Outlier"; and "Optimum Properties and Efficiency."

Drygas, Hilmar. THE COORDINATE-FREE APPROACH TO GAUSS-MARKOV ESTIMATION. Lecture Notes in Operations-Research and Mathematical Systems, vol. 40. New York: Springer-Verlag, 1970. viii, 113 p. Bibliography, pp. 110-13. No index.

An exposition on the coordinate-free approach leading to proofs of Farka's theorem and the projection theorem. Latter theorem used to obtain the best linear unbiased estimators (BLUE) of a linear function of the expected value of a linear statistical model. Comparisons made with other estimation procedures and examples provided, including derivations of Aitken's formula and Schonfeld's formula, and step-wise regression. Knowledge of mathematical statistics and linear algebra assumed.

Durbin, J. DISTRIBUTION THEORY FOR TESTS BASED ON THE SAMPLE DISTRIBUTION FUNCTION. Regional Conference Series in Applied Mathematics, no. 9. Philadelphia: Society for Industrial and Applied Mathematics, 1973. vi, 64 p. References, pp. 59-64. No index.

Presents a coherent body of theory for the derivation of sampling distributions of a wide range of test statistics. Includes tests of Kolmogorov-Smirnov (finite-sample case), Cramér-von Mises, Kuiper, and Watson. Concludes with a section on tests following the estimation of parameters. Assumes knowledge of mathematical statistics.

Dym, H., and McKean, Henry P. GAUSSIAN PROCESSES, FUNCTION THEORY, AND THE INVERSE SPECTRAL PROBLEM. Probability and Mathematical Statistics: A Series of Monographs and Textbooks. New York: Academic Press, 1976. xi, 333 p. References, pp. 323-28. Index, pp. 329-33.

Deals with the relationship between the past and the future of a real, one-dimensional, stationary Gaussian process of mean zero, with special attention to predicting the future. Addressed primarily to a mathematical audience, but others who deal with the practical aspects of prediction, such as electrical engineers, will benefit. Assumes knowledge of complex variables, Fourier integrals, Hilbert space theory, abstract algebra, probability theory, and measure theory. Topics include review of function theory, Kolmogorov-Wiener prediction problem; Wiener's formula; filters and noise; rational spectral densities; type spaces; Okabe's formulas; strings and spectral functions; and spaces of integral functions. Exercises form an integral part of the text.

Edwards, Anthony William Fairbank. LIKELIHOOD: AN ACCOUNT OF THE STATISTICAL CONCEPT OF LIKELIHOOD AND ITS APPLICATION TO SCIENTIFIC INFERENCE. Cambridge: Cambridge University Press, 1972. xv, 235 p. Notes, pp. 213-17. References, pp. 219-24. Tables of Support Limits for t and Chi-Square, pp. 225-27. Index, pp. 229-35.

A critical review of statistical inference with reference to problems of population genetics for the scientist rather than the statistician. Topics include the likelihood concept; sufficient statistics; natural logarithm of the likelihood function; Bayes' theorem and inverse probability; maximum likelihood method; expected information and the distribution of estimates; support tests based on normal, chi-square, t, and F distributions; and miscellaneous topics, including least squares, experimental design, and fiducial probability. Assumes knowledge of probability calculus and elementary distribution theory.

Ehrenfeld, Sylvain, and Littauer, Sebastian B. INTRODUCTION TO STATISTICAL METHOD. McGraw-Hill Series in Probability and Statistics. New York: McGraw-Hill Series in Probability and Statistics. New York: McGraw-Hill, 1964. x, 533 p. Appendix: Tables, pp. 509-27. Index, pp. 529-33.

A text for a one-year course in probability and statistics for undergraduates who have a college algebra background. Provides a basis for advanced courses for mathematical statisticians. Topics include sample spaces and probability; distribution functions, including multivariate; moment-generating functions; statistical hypothesis tests; Neyman-Pearson approach; point and interval estimation; sampling and analysis of variance; linear regression; and statistical quality control. Chapters conclude with exercises.

Elderton, William Palin, and Johnson, Norman Lloyd. SYSTEMS OF FREQUENCY CURVES. Cambridge: Cambridge University Press, 1969. viii, 216 p. Appendix 1: Corrections for Moments, pp. 177-81. Appendix 2: β and Γ Functions, pp. 182-84. Appendix 3: The Equation to the Normal Surface, pp. 185-87. Appendix 4: The Integration of Some Expressions Connected with the Normal Curve of Error, pp. 188-92. Appendix 5: Other Methods of Fitting Curves, pp. 193-97. Appendix 6: Key to the Actuarial Terms and Symbols Used, pp. 198-200. Appendix 7: Abridged Reading, p. 201. Appendix 8: References and Bibliography, pp. 202-5. Appendix 9: Tables, pp. 206.13. Index, pp. 214-16.

> Presents a method of fitting curves to empirical data. Topics include method of moments for applying frequency curves to statistical examples; Pearson's system of frequency curves; curves represented by series expansion; translation systems; frequency surfaces; standard errors; and tests of goodness of fit. Knowledge of calculus and mathematical statistics necessary for some portions. Includes numerical examples.

Ferguson, Thomas S. MATHEMATICAL STATISTICS: A DECISION THEORETIC APPROACH. Probability and Mathematical Statistics: a Series of Monographs and Textbooks, vol. 1. New York: Academic Press, 1967. xi, 396 p. References, pp. 388-91. Subject Index, pp. 393-96.

> A text for a one-year graduate course in mathematical statistics for students who have knowledge of mathematical probability, mathematical analysis, Riemann integral, intermediate statistics, and matrix algebra. Presentation based on the theory of games as developed in Wald's theory of statistical decisions. Chapter titles: "Game Theory and Decision Theory"; "The Main Theorems of Decision Theory"; "Distributions and Sufficient Statistics"; "Invariant Statistical Decision Problems"; "Testing Hypotheses"; "Multiple Decision Problems"; and "Sequential Decision Problems." Sections conclude with problems.

Fisher, Ronald A. STATISTICAL METHODS AND SCIENTIFIC INFERENCE. 3d ed., rev. and enl. New York: Hafner, 1973. viii, 182 p. Index, pp. 181-82.

> A largely philosophical treatment of a number of methods of statistical inference. Topics include forms of quantitative inference, including the fiducial argument and mathematical likelihood; misapprehensions about tests of significance; examples of inference involving probability and likelihood; Bayesian prediction; inferences from likelihood; likelihood and information; simultaneous estimation; grouping of samples; and the use of ancillary information to recover information lost. Uses few formulas; knowledge of calculus helpful.

Fisz, Marek. PROBABILITY THEORY AND MATHEMATICAL STATISTICS. 3d ed. Translated by R. Bartoszynski. Wiley Series in Probability and Mathematical

Statistics. New York: Wiley, 1963. xvi, 677 p. Supplement, pp. 612-20. References, pp. 621-55. Statistical Tables, pp. 658-64. Author Index, pp. 665-69. Subject Index, pp. 671-77.

Originally published in Polish. A text for a one-year course in mathematical statistics for both graduates and undergraduates who have knowledge of calculus and linear algebra. Presentation mathematically rigorous, but intuitive approach and applications heavily stressed. Most theorems given with complete proofs. Topics include random variables; parameters of the distribution of a random variable; characteristic functions; probability distributions; limit theorems; Markov chains; stochastic processes; sample moments and their functions; order statistics; theory of runs; significance tests; theory of estimation; scheme of sampling; analysis of variance; hypothesis testing; and sequential analysis. Chapters conclude with problems and complements which vary in difficulty.

Fraser, Donald Alexander Stuart. STATISTICS: AN INTRODUCTION. Wiley Series in Probability and Mathematical Statistics. New York: Wiley, 1958. ix, 398 p. Appendix, pp. 387-94. Index, pp. 395-98.

A text for a one-year course in mathematical statistics for students with a background in calculus. Develops the subject without lengthy applications. Emphasizes probability distributions. Topics include discrete and continuous probability distributions, including bivariate and multivariate normal; generating functions; law of large numbers and the central limit theorem; estimation and hypothesis testing; regression analysis; factorial designs and analysis of variance; analysis of covariance; sequential sampling; and nonparametric tests. Chapters conclude with references and lengthy sets of problems. Appendix contains useful tables.

______. THE STRUCTURE OF INFERENCE. Wiley Series in Probability and Mathematical Statistics. New York: Wiley, 1968. x, 344 p. Answers to Selected Problems, pp. 331-39. Index, pp. 341-44.

A text which presents a unified theory of statistical inference, for a one-year course in mathematical statistics with a prerequisite of probability, vector analysis, and multiple differentiation and integration. Consists of three parts: "Foundations"; "Method of Analysis"; and "Extensions." Includes measurement and structural models, including regression and progression models, that have an error form not necessarily restricted to the normal or Gaussian error distribution; conditional analysis, such as marginal likelihood and transformed regression; marginal analysis, such as the measurement model on a sphere and multivariate models; local analysis, such as stochastically monotone model and linearized Poisson; inferences from likelihood and from frequencies; and precision and information with real- and vector-valued quantities. Chapters conclude with problems.

Freeman, Harold Adolph. INTRODUCTION TO STATISTICAL INFERENCE. Addison-Wesley Series in Statistics. Reading, Mass.: Addison-Wesley, 1963. xiv, 445 p. Discussion of and Answers to Problems, pp. 347-81. List of Selected Textbooks, pp. 382-83. List of Specialized Books, pp. 384. List of Books on Applications, pp. 385-86. Names Mentioned (Without References), p. 387. References, pp. 388-97. Appendix: Tables, pp. 398-432. Name Index, pp. 432-37. Subject Index, pp. 438-45.

A text for a one-year course in mathematical statistics for students who know calculus and matrix algebra. Consists of five parts: "Probability and Random Variables"; "Specific Probability Distributions"; "Sampling Theory"; "Statistical Inference"; and "An Application to Regression." About ninety homework problems, many calling for detailed derivations, provided at the ends of the chapters; few numerical examples provided. Topics include random variables and expectation; conditional expectation and prediction; several random variables; binomial, Poisson, hypergeometric, negative binomial, multinomial, uniform, Lapalce, Cauchy, and normal probability distributions; Gram-Charlier and Hermite polynomials; order statistics; Bayes' rule; point estimation; maximum likelihood; best linear unbiased estimation; Neyman-Pearson theorem; interval estimation; and hypothesis testing.

Freund, John E. MATHEMATICAL STATISTICS. 2d ed. Englewood Cliffs, N.J.: Prentice-Hall, 1971. xiii, 463 p. Appendix: Sums and Products, pp. 419-21. Statistical Tables, pp. 423-45. Answers to Odd-Numbered Exercises, pp. 446-56. Index, pp. 457-63.

A text for an introductory one-year course in mathematical statistics with a prerequisite of calculus. Topics include probability; distribution theory; limit theorems, with the treatment in the discrete case being more rigorous than in the continuous case; sampling distributions; point and interval estimation; methods of moments and maximum likelihood; the Neyman-Pearson lemma; tests of hypothesis concerning means and variances; nonparametric tests; regression and correlation; and analysis of variance. Provides short deviations with numerical examples. Sections conclude with exercises; chapters, with bibliographies.

Gani, Joseph Mark, ed. PERSPECTIVES IN PROBABILITY AND STATISTICS. New York: Academic Press, for the Applied Probability Trust, 1975. viii, 423 p. List of Contributors, pp. 417-18. Index, pp. 419-23.

Thirty heretofore unpublished contributions presented to Professor Maurice S. Bartlett on the occasion of his sixty-fifth birthday grouped under the following headings: "Historical Introduction" (one paper); "Probability Theory" (two papers); "Statistical Theory" (seven papers); "Mathematical Methods in Probability and Statistics" (two papers); "Stochastic Processes" (five papers);

"Statistical Inference on Stochastic Processes" (two papers); "Probability Models in the Physical Sciences" (four papers); "Probability Models in the Humanities" (two papers); and "Biomathematics and Epidemiology" (five papers). Assumes knowledge of mathematical statistics and linear algebra.

Gani, Joseph Mark; Sarkadi, K.; and Vincze, I. PROGRESS IN STATISTICS. 2 vols. Amsterdam: North Holland, 1975. 912 p. No index.

Eighty-one papers presented at the European meeting of statisticians held in Budapest between Aug. 31 and Sept. 5, 1972. Topics range from a highly theoretical probabilistic nature, through the applications of probability models in technology and biology, to the theory of estimation and hypothesis testing. Applications include experimental design, Monte Carlo methods, the statistical study of juries, and data analysis in archaeology.

Ghosh, Bhasker Kumar. SEQUENTIAL TESTS OF STATISTICAL HYPOTHESES. Reading, Mass.: Addison-Wesley, 1970. x, 454 p. Appendixes, pp. 427-38. Bibliography and Author Index, pp. 439-47. Subject Index, pp. 449-54.

A text and reference providing a systematic account of the mathematical theory of sequential analysis as applied to hypothesis testing requiring knowledge of calculus and classical methodology of statistical tests and estimation. Topics discussed in a framework of a family of cumulative distribution functions rather than in a family of probability measures on a given sigma-field of subsets. Topics include fixed-sample and sequential tests; sequential probability ratio tests; stochastic processes with a continuous time parameter; two-sample problems and Fraser-sufficiency, multiparameter families; analysis of variance; and nonparametric tests. Presentation rigorous with proofs of many theorems provided. Appendixes take up measures and subfields, statistics, sufficiency, and invariance; proof of Stein theorem and conditional independence; and transitivity in sequential procedures.

Godambe, V.P., and Sprott, D.A., eds. FOUNDATIONS OF STATISTICAL INFERENCE. Montreal: Holt, Rinehart & Winston of Canada, 1971. viii, 519 p. No index.

Twenty-eight papers presented at a symposium on foundations of statistical inference held at the University of Waterloo, Canada, March 31-April 9. The topics represent a wide range of disciplines, from abstract philosophy through pure mathematics to applied statistics, and include the logic of inference; informative inference; limiting properties of likelihood; the logical foundation of survey sampling; applications of statistical inference to physics; similarity and probability; measuring information and uncertainty; counter-example and likelihood; likelihood methods of prediction; the estimation of many parameters; and a comparison of frequentist and Bayesian approaches to inference with prior knowledge.

Gosset, William Sealy. "STUDENTS" COLLECTED PAPERS. Edited by E.S. Pearson and John Wishart. Foreword by Launce McMull. Cambridge: Cambridge University Press, 1942. xiv, 224 p. No index.

Contains all of the scientific papers published between 1907 and 1937 under the pseudonym "Student." They include twenty-one articles plus some letters and miscellaneous writings.

Govindarajuly, Z. SEQUENTIAL STATISTICAL PROCEDURES. Probability and Mathematical Statistics: A Series of Monographs and Textbooks, vol. 26. New York: Academic Press, 1975. xvi, 565 p. Appendix 1: Solution to Wald's Equation, pp. 513-14. Appendix 2: Differentiation of an Expectation, pp. 515-17. Appendix 3: On the Moments of a Random Variable, pp. 518-19. Appendix 4: The Normal Diffusion Process, pp. 520-26. Appendix 5: Large Sample Properties of Maximum Likelihood Estimates, pp. 527-29. Appendix 6: A Table of Standard Distributions, pp. 530-31. Appendix 7: A Useful Convergence Theorem of Cramér, pp. 532-33. Appendix 8: Backward Induction, pp. 534-36. References and Author Index, pp. 537-53. Subject Index, pp. 555-65.

A text for a one-semester course in sequential procedures. Assumes knowledge of mathematical statistics and advanced calculus. Brings together contributions heretofore scattered widely through the literature; self-contained with most proofs provided. Topics include finite termination of sequential probability ratio tests (SPRT); operating characteristic function; bounds for the expected sample size in a SPRT; truncated SPRT; asymptotic efficiency of SPRT; Bayes' sequential procedures; locally most powerful sequential tests; Cramér-Rao lower bound for the sequential case; sufficiency and completeness in the sequential case; sequential confidence intervals for the mean; symptotic theory of fixed-width sequential confidence intervals for the mean; and asymptotically optimal Bayes' sequential estimation. Presentation rigorous, consisting mainly of proofs of theorems followed by remarks and examples.

Gray, Henry L., and Schucany, W.R. THE GENERALIZED JACKNIFE STATISTICS. Statistics: Textbooks and Monographs. New York: Marcel Dekker, 1972. x, 308 p. Appendix, pp. 276-302. References, pp. 303-6. Index, pp. 307-8.

A monograph on the theory and application of the jacknife method for reducing bias in an estimator and for obtaining a measure of the variance of the resulting estimator. Useful to statisticians and practitioners. Chapter titles: "Reduction of

Bias by Jacknifing"; "Applications to Biased Estimators"; "Asymptotic Distributions"; "Jacknifing Stochastic Processes"; and "The $J^{(2)}$ Estimator." The appendix is devoted to proofs of important theorems.

Graybill, Franklin A. AN INTRODUCTION TO LINEAR STATISTICAL MODELS. Vol. I. McGraw-Hill Series in Probability and Statistics. New York: McGraw-Hill, 1961. xiv, 463 p. Appendix: Tables, pp. 421-59. Index, pp. 461-63.

A text for an introductory course in mathematical statistics for seniors and first-year graduate students who have knowledge of multivariate calculus and linear algebra, with one year of statistical theory. Also useful as a reference for practitioners who have limited training in mathematics. Most of the theorems proved in detail, with emphasis on the power of tests and on the width of confidence intervals. Topics include the multivariate normal distribution; distributions of quadratic forms; linear models; the general linear hypothesis of full rank; polynomial or curvilinear models; functional relational relationships; regression models; experimental design models; factorial models; incomplete block models; variance components; point and interval estimation; tests of hypotheses; covariance; and mixed models. Chapters conclude with problems on proofs, derivation, applications, and references.

Grenander, Ulf, ed. PROBABILITY AND STATISTICS: THE HARALD CRAMÉR VOLUME. Wiley Series in Probability and Mathematical Statistics. New York: Wiley, 1959. 434 p. No index.

Nineteen heretofore unpublished papers in mathematical statistics presented to Harald Cramér in honor of his sixty-fifth birthday. Topics include Markov chains; design of linear experiments; combinatorial methods in fluctuation theory; stable processes with independent increments; integral representations for transition probability matrices; nonlinear prediction; optimal asymptotic tests of composite statistical hypotheses; a survey of results in the collective theory of risks; an introduction to the measurement of spectra; and econometric model building.

Gumbel, Emil Julius. STATISTICS OF EXTREMES. New York: Columbia University Press, 1958. xx, 375 p. Bibliography, pp. 349-71. Index, pp. 373-75.

A reference for statisticians and statistically minded scientists and engineers. Emphasizes applications using graphical procedures rather than calculations. Topics include order statistics and their exceedances; exact distributions of extremes as functions of sample size; analytical study of extremes; the first asymptotic distributions (for distributions of the exponential type); the second asymptotic distribution obtained by several methods, including a logarithmic transformation of the first asymptotic distribution; the third asymptotic distribution; and asymptotic distributions of the range and midrange.

Guttman, Irwin. STATISTICAL TOLERANCE REGIONS: CLASSICAL AND BAYESIAN. Griffin's Statistical Monographs and Courses, no. 26. Darien, Conn.: Hafner, 1970. ix, 150 p. No index.

A monograph on the mathematical development of tolerance regions from both the classical (part I) and Bayesian (part II) viewpoints. Topics in part I include three types of tolerance regions: distribution-free, B-expectation, and B-content. Also includes a description of the "best" population and tolerance region. Part II includes two tolerance regions from a Bayesian viewpoint: B-expectation, and B-content. Also considers the problem of the "best" population. Assumes knowledge of mathematical statistics.

Haberman, Shelby J. THE ANALYSIS OF FREQUENCY DATA. Statistical Research Monographs, vol. IV. Chicago: University of Chicago Press, 1974. xii, 419 p. Appendix A: Basic Mathematical and Statistical Results Used in the Monograph, pp. 387-94. Appendix B: Procedures for Verification that Maximum-Likelihood Estimates Exist, pp. 395-404. Appendix C: Proof of Theorem 3.1, pp. 405-7. References, pp. 408-14. Index, pp. 415-19.

A rigorous general presentation of log-linear models (called linear manifolds) although the general reader may regard this monograph as an introduction to the analysis of counted data. Many proofs require knowledge of mathematical statistics. Topics include properties of log-linear models; numerical evaluation of maximum-likelihood estimates; asymptotic properties; complete factorial and social mobility tables; incomplete contingency tables; quantal-response models; and models for "flats" with applications to survey sampling. Useful to research workers, practitioners, and applied statisticians.

Hald, Anders. STATISTICAL THEORY WITH ENGINEERING APPLICATIONS. Wiley Series in Probability and Mathematical Statistics. New York: Wiley, 1952. xii, 783 p. Notation, p. 761. Index of Author References, pp. 763-65. Index of Symbols and Formulas, pp. 767-71. Index of Subjects, pp. 773-83.

Originally published in Danish in 1948. A comprehensive text and reference on the mathematical treatment of statistical methods in engineering requiring knowledge of differential and integral calculus. Topics include calculus of probability with applications to the binomial, multinomial, Pascal, and hypergeometric distributions; empirical distributions; one- and two-dimensional probability distributions; skew distributions; limit theorems, including law of large numbers and method of maximum likelihood; the distribution of the mean; chi-square; the distribution of the variance and the range; statistical quality control; variance ratio; one-, two-, and three-way analysis of variance; sample survey procedures; Latin squares; factorial experiments; simple and multiple regression and correlation; applications of the binomial distribution; Poisson distribution; and sequential analysis. Proofs of most of the results provided.

Hastings, Cecil, Jr., assisted by Jeanne T. Hayward and James P. Wong, Jr. APPROXIMATIONS FOR DIGITAL COMPUTERS. Princeton, N.J.: Princeton University Press, 1955. viii, 201 p. References for Part II, p. 201. No index.

A monograph on the best approximation in the sense of Chebyshev to univariate functional data by means of high-speed digital computers. Part I presents the collection of approximations, primarily by means of graphs, and part II contains approximately seventy approximating formulas, each with a carefully drawn error curve.

Heathcote, Christopher Robin. COMPLETE EXPONENTIAL CONVERGENCE AND SOME RELATED TOPICS. Methuen's Monographs on Applied Probability. London: Methuen, 1967. 41 p. References, pp. 38-40. Index, p. 41.

A review of research results on the rate at which convergence to the limit occurs for an exponential sequence of random variables. Useful to probabilists and statisticians.

Hemmerle, William J. STATISTICAL COMPUTATIONS ON A DIGITAL COMPUTER. A Blaisdell Book in Computer Science. Waltham, Mass.: Blaisdell, 1967. x, 230 p. Appendix A: Double Integrals, pp. 204-13. Appendix B: Problems in Regression and Analysis of Variance, pp. 214-26. Index, pp. 227-30.

A monograph, useful as a text on the scientific application of digital computers for students familiar with computer programming (FORTRAN), advanced calculus, and matrix algebra. Also useful to statisticians unfamiliar with numerical methods and numerical analysts unfamiliar with statistical theory. Topics include numerical methods of approximation, interpolation, and integration; Monte Carlo procedures; multiple-regression computations; computation and application of characteristic roots and vectors; and analysis of variance. Many theorems stated, but not proved. Chapters conclude with references.

Hengartner, Walker, and Theodorescu, R. CONCENTRATION FUNCTIONS. Probability and Mathematical Statistics. A Series of Monographs and Textbooks, vol. 20. New York: Academic Press, 1973. xii, 139 p. References, pp. 131-34. Author Index, p. 135. Subject Index, pp. 136-39.

A comprehensive treatment of topics on concentration functions, heretofore found scattered throughout the literature, for students who have a good background in probability theory. Includes applications in convergence problems. Useful as a text for a graduate course in special topics in probability theory, as a supplementary text in a graduate seminar course in probability, or as a reference for research workers in probability. Chapters conclude with complements and notes.

Hoel, Paul G. INTRODUCTION TO MATHEMATICAL STATISTICS. 4th ed., rev. Wiley Series in Probability and Mathematical Statistics. New York:

Wiley, 1971. xi, 409 p. Appendixes, pp. 359-72. Answers, pp. 373-80. Tables, pp. 381-404. Index, pp. 405-9.

A text for an introductory course in mathematical statistics using only elementary calculus. Includes elementary treatments of a wide range of techniques suitable for students in the physical sciences, engineering, and the social and life sciences, as well as in mathematics. Topics include probability and probability distributions, including joint discrete and continuous distributions, hypothesis testing and estimation; sampling theory of one variable; linear and nonlinear regression and correlation; theoretical frequency distributions for correlation and regression; chi-square and contingency tables; design of experiments; nonparametric tests; sequential analysis; and Bayes' theorem. Appendixes devoted to special mathematical results such as the Cramer-Rao inequality and the Jacobian. Chapters conclude with references, and problems varying in difficulty designed to illustrate the application of the theory. Proofs not emphasized.

Johnson, Norman Lloyd, and Kotz, Samuel. DISTRIBUTIONS IN STATISTICS: CONTINUOUS UNIVARIATE--I. New York: Houghton Mifflin, 1970. xiv, 300 p. Acknowledgements, pp. 297-98. Index, pp. 299-300.

Presents an account of the properties and uses of continuous univariate statistical distributions, but no development of statistical theory. Includes the following for each distribution: definitions, moments and properties, history, approximations and characterizations, estimation and estimators, applications and tables, related distributions, and references. Includes continuous (general), normal, lognormal, inverse Gaussian Wald), Cauchy, gamma, exponential, Pareto, Weibull, and extreme value distributions. Assumes knowledge of mathematical statistics.

_____. DISTRIBUTIONS IN STATISTICS: CONTINUOUS UNIVARIATE DISTRIBUTIONS--2. New York: Wiley, xiii, 306 p. Acknowledgements, pp. 303-4. Index, pp. 305-6.

A reference for those who wish to apply statistical methods and a supplement to graduate courses and seminars. Presents the properties and uses of statistical distributions, but no development of the theory. Deals with the following distributions: logistic, Laplace, Beta, uniform, F, t, noncentral chi-square; quadratic forms in normal variables, noncentral F, noncentral t, distributions of correlation coefficients. Kolmogorov-Smirnov, distance distributions, and life distributions. Assumes knowledge of mathematical statistics. Chapters conclude with references.

_____. DISTRIBUTIONS IN STATISTICS: CONTINUOUS MULTIVARIATE DISTRIBUTIONS. Wiley Series in Probability and Mathematical Statistics.

New York: Wiley, 1972. xiv, 333 p. Augmented Cumulative Index, pp. 309-21. Index, of References by Topics, pp. 322-28. Corrections for Volumes 1 to 3, pp. 329-31. Acknowledgements, pp. 332-33.

A reference on multivariate distributions for use in statistics courses and seminars. Includes the following for each distribution: historical remarks, properties, definitions, applications, estimation, specific types, and references. Includes multinormal; bivariate and trivariate normal; multivariate t; Wishart; distributions associated with the normal, including generalized beta, multinormal quadratic forms, latent roots of a Wishart matrix, and canonical correlations; multivariate beta and gamma; multivariate extreme value and exponential; Beta-Stacy; multivariate Pareto; Burr; logistic; and distributions classified by functional form.

_____. DISTRIBUTIONS IN STATISTICS: DISCRETE DISTRIBUTIONS. Houghton Mifflin Series in Statistics. New York: Houghton Mifflin, 1969. xvi, 328 p. Acknowledgements, pp. 325-26. Index, pp. 327-28.

A text and a source book on applied statistics for graduate courses and seminars for those who already have a sound background in statistical theory. Provides the following information on discrete probability distributions: definitions and properties, historical remarks, applications, approximating tables, estimation characteristics, truncations, related distributions, and references. Distributions include binomial, Poisson, negative binomial, hypergeometric, logarithmic, contagious, multivariate discrete, log-zero-Poisson, rectangular, zeta and Yule, hyper-Poisson and factorial, occupancy, matching, absorption, student's runs, distributions associated with queues, and distributions based on partial sums.

Kagan, Abram M.; Linnik, IUriĭ V.; and Rao, C. Radhakrishna. CHARACTERIZATION PROBLEMS IN MATHEMATICAL STATISTICS. Translated by B. Ramachandran. Wiley Series in Probability and Mathematical Statistics. New York: Wiley, 1973. xii, 499 p. Addendum A: Further Characterization of Probability Laws Through Properties of Linear Functions of Random Variables, pp. 467-78. Addendum B: Characterizations of Distributions Through Properties of Bayes Estimators, pp. 479-83. Bibliography, pp. 485-93. Author Index, pp. 495-96. Subject Index, pp. 497-99.

Originally published in Russian. An advanced text for graduate students and specialists in probability and mathematical statistics. Deals with the theory of characterization problems and their relationship to estimation theory, testing hypotheses, sequential analysis, and other topics. Topics include characterizations through stochastic properties of pairs of linear statistics of independent observations; independence of linear statistics; regression problems with linear and nonlinear statistics; characterizations of distributions through properties of admissibility and optimality of certain estimators and families of distributions admitting sufficient statistics; characterizations of random vectors with linear structure; and characterizations of sequential estimation plans. Presentation rigorous, consisting largely of proofs of theorems and lemmas, with some applications, and examples.

Keeping, E.S. INTRODUCTION TO STATISTICAL INFERENCE. New York: D. Van Nostrand, 1962. xi, 451 p. Appendix A: Mathematical Appendix, pp. 381-412. Appendix B: Tables, pp. 413-37. Answers to Problems, pp. 438-42. Index, pp. 443-51.

A text for a course in mathematical statistics for graduates and undergraduates who have knowledge of elementary differential and integral calculus. Proofs included where possible, with many mathematical details, such as gamma and beta functions, Stirling's approximation, Jacobians, matrix algebra, and Bernoulli numbers, placed in the appendixes. Begins with a heuristic treatment of the calculus of probability, followed by such topics as probability distributions; estimation and hypothesis testing; sampling procedures; analysis of variance; bivariate and multivariate problems; nonparametric tests; sequential sampling; and stochastic processes. Chapters conclude with problems.

Kendall, Maurice G. EXERCISES IN THEORETICAL STATISTICS: WITH ANSWERS AND HINTS ON SOLUTIONS. 2d ed. New York: Hafner, 1968. vii, 179 p. Answers and Hints on Solutions, pp. 123-79. No index.

A collection of 400 problems on theoretical statistics for use by graduate students and postgraduate students from sources such as examination papers and research journals. Problems arranged in five groups: "Distribution Theory" (100 problems); "Sampling Theory" (100 exercises); "Relationships" (75 problems); "Estimation and Inference" (75 problems); and "Time Series" (50 problems). Excludes exercises in quality control, experimental design, and other areas.

Kendall, Maurice G., and Stuart, Alan. THE ADVANCED THEORY OF STATISTICS. Vol. I. DISTRIBUTION THEORY. 2d ed. New York: Hafner, 1963. xii, 433 p. Appendix: Tables, pp. 397-409. References, pp. 410-18. Index, pp. 419-33.

Primarily a reference on the mathematical theory of statistics with a prerequisite of advanced calculus and mathematical statistics. Includes over 300 problems at the ends of the sections and chapters. Topics include frequency distributions; measure of location and dispersion; moments and cumulants; over one dozen discrete and continuous univariate distributions; calculus of probability; sampling errors and distributions; statistical inference; random sampling; approximations to sampling distributions; order statistics; multivariate normal distributions; quadratic forms; and distributions associated with the normal.

______. THE ADVANCED THEORY OF STATISTICS. Vol. 2. INFERENCE AND RELATIONSHIPS. New York: Hafner, ix, 676 p. Appendix: Tables, pp. 625-35. References, pp. 637-56. Index, pp. 657-76.

> Covers the theory of estimation and testing hypotheses; relationships; distribution-free tests; sequential analysis; fiducial intervals; composite hypotheses; likelihood ratio tests; general linear hypothesis; partial and multiple correlation; and categorized data. Assumes knowledge of linear algebra and real analysis. About 400 exercises given at the ends of the chapters and sections.

______. THE ADVANCED THEORY OF STATISTICS. Vol. 3. DESIGN AND ANALYSIS, AND TIME-SERIES. New York: Hafner, 1966. ix, 552 p. Appendix Tables, pp. 505-16. References, pp. 517-38. Index, pp. 539-52.

> Covers the analysis of variance; design of experiments; sample survey theory; multivariate analysis; and time series, including spectrum theory. Mathematical derivations extensive and knowledge of linear algebra and advanced calculus assumed. Chapters conclude with exercises with elaborations or extensions of the material covered. Few practical applications provided.

Kreyszig, Erwin. INTRODUCTORY MATHEMATICAL STATISTICS. New York: Wiley, 1970. xv, 470 p. Appendix 1: Additional Remarks and Proofs, pp. 394-402. Appendix 2: Answers to Odd-Numbered Problems, pp. 403-28. Appendix 3: References, pp. 429-34. Appendix 4: Tables, pp. 435-62. Index, pp. 463-70.

> A text for a one-semester course in mathematical statistics with a prerequisite of calculus. Consists of the following three parts: "Descriptive Statistics"; "Probability Theory"; and "Statistical Inference." Achieves a balance between theory and application, with most of data used in examples taken from actual experiments and observations. Includes over 1,000 problems from a number of fields.

Kruskal, William, ed. MATHEMATICAL SCIENCES AND SOCIAL SCIENCES. Behavioral and Social Science Survey. Mathematical Sciences Panel. Englewood Cliffs, N.J.: Prentice-Hall, 1970. viii, 83 p. No index.

> A panel report on the problems encountered in using mathematics, statistics, and computations in the behavioral and social sciences. Topics include two-choice experimental models for learning; the relevance of the mathematical sciences to the social sciences; the profession of social statistician; statistics, public policy, and data fallibility; data collection and data collectors; operations research; problems in computation; and teaching the mathematical sciences to social science students.

Krutchkoff, Richard G. PROBABILITY AND STATISTICAL INFERENCE. New York: Gordon and Breach, 1970. xiv, 291 p. Appendix A: Summary of Distributions and their Properties, pp. 250-66. Appendix B: Tables, pp. 267-80. Answers to Some Problems, pp. 281-87. Index, pp. 288-91.

A text for a one-semester course in probability and a one-semester course in statistical inference, or a one-year course in probability and statistical inference. Assumes knowledge of calculus. Topics include probability, including random variables and their distributions; the gamma and beta distributions; moment generating functions; multivariate distributions; distributions of functions of random variables; Markov's inequality; law of large numbers; convergence theorems; statistical inference, including sample moments, properties of estimators, uniformly minimum variance unbiased estimators, hypothesis testing, and confidence intervals. Sections conclude with exercises; chapters, with problems.

Larson, Harold J. INTRODUCTION TO PROBABILITY THEORY AND STATISTICAL INFERENCE. 2d ed. Wiley Series in Probability and Mathematical Statistics. New York: Wiley, 1974. xi, 430 p. References, pp. 387-88. Appendix: Tables, pp. 389-402. Answers to Exercises, pp. 403-24. Index, pp. 425-30.

A text for a course in mathematical statistics for students in varied disciplines who have had one year of calculus. Style somewhat rigorous from a notational viewpoint, with short derivations included. Includes numerous definitions and examples. Topics include probability axioms; sample spaces; random variables and distribution functions; moments and moment generating functions; standard distributions; jointly distributed random variables; law of large numbers; sampling; maximum likelihood and properties of point estimators; tests of hypotheses; composite hypotheses; contingency tables; Bayesian methods; and least squares and regression. Sections conclude with exercises.

______. INTRODUCTION TO THE THEORY OF STATISTICS. Wiley Series in Probability and Mathematical Statistics. New York: Wiley, 1973. x, 242 p. Appendix: Tables, pp. 223-28. References, p. 229. Answers to Even-Numbered Problems, pp. 231-37. Index, pp. 239-42.

A text for a one-semester course in statistical theory for students who have had a course in probability theory, a course in linear algebra, and calculus. Includes sixty-four examples and 350 exercises. Topics include probability; population and samples; estimation; confidence sets; Neyman-Pearson theory; tests of hypotheses; decision theory; least squares; experimental design; and nonparametric tests. Chapters conclude with exercises.

Lass, Harry, and Gottlieb, Peter. PROBABILITY AND STATISTICS. Reading, Mass.: Addison-Wesley, 1971. ix, 470 p. Appendix A: Mathematical Preliminaries, pp. 359-449. Appendix B: Tables, pp. 450-55. Answers to Selected Problems, pp. 456-65. Index, pp. 466-70.

A text for a one-year course in probability and statistics for students who possess knowledge of calculus. Each of the topics illustrated with several examples. Includes more than 200 problems designed to strengthen the student's intuitive understanding of the concepts. Topics include set theory and Boolean algebra; conbinatorial analysis; discrete and continuous probability distributions; statistical sampling; parametric point and interval estimation; order statistics; nonparametric methods; and hypothesis testing.

LaValle, Irving H. AN INTRODUCTION TO PROBABILITY, DECISION, AND INFERENCE. International Series in Decision Processes. New York: Holt, Rinehart & Winston, 1970. xvi, 767 p. Appendix. Tables, pp. 725-47. References, pp. 749-53. Index, pp. 755-67.

A Bayesian oriented text for a one-year course in probability and statistics for students in statistics, economics, engineering, and mathematics who have gone through an introductory course in differential and integral calculus and linear algebra. Consists of four parts: "Set Theory"; "Probability"; "Bayesian Decision Theory"; and "Statistical Inference." Topics include the distribution of several random variables; the k-variate normal and t distributions; the Wishart families; natural-conjugate distribution families; normal form analysis of decisions; multivariate point estimation with quadratic loss; a Bayesian interval estimation problem; confidence regions; generalized likelihood ratio tests; and sufficiency. Presentation somewhat rigorous in terms of notation. Chapters conclude with exercises.

Lehmann, Erich Leo. TESTING STATISTICAL HYPOTHESES. Wiley Series in Probability and Mathematical Statistics. New York: Wiley, 1959. xiii, 369 p. Appendix, pp. 348-56. Author Index, pp. 357-59. Subject Index, pp. 361-69.

A text for a course in decision theory which gives a systematic account of the Neyman-Pearson theory of hypothesis testing and of the closely related theory of confidence sets, together with their principle applications. Includes the standard one- and two-sample problems concerning normal, binomial, and Poisson distributions; some aspects of the analysis of variance and regression (linear hypothesis); certain multivariate and sequential problems; and an introduction to nonparametric tests. Presentation rigorous and includes many proofs of theorems. Assumes knowledge of measure theory. Chapters conclude with problems, many of them with outlines of solutions.

Lindgren, Bernard William. STATISTICAL THEORY. 3d ed., rev. New York: Macmillan, 1976. xiii, 614 p. References, pp. 569-70. Appendix: Tables, pp. 571-97. Answers to Problems, pp. 598-608. Index, pp. 609-14.

A text for a one-year course in the theory of statistics for students who have had one year of calculus, but no previous exposure to statistics. Multivariate calculus and linear algebra used in some of the sections. Topics include sample spaces; probability, including Cochran's independence concept; Bayes' theorem; random variables and their distributions; expectation; moments of distributions; generating functions; limit theorems; parametric families of distributions, including Poisson, normal, multinomial, and exponential families; sampling distributions; sufficient statistics; likelihood; criteria for point estimators; methods of moments and maximum likelihood; testing hypothesis, including uniformly most powerful tests; sequential tests; univariate normal inference; statistical decision theory; chi-square and analysis of variance; nonparametric tests; and regression and correlation. Sections conclude with problems.

Lindgren, Bernard William, and McElrath, G.W. INTRODUCTION TO PROBABILITY AND STATISTICS. 3d ed. New York: Macmillan, 1969. x, 305 p. List of Tables, pp. 267-89. Answers, pp. 290-98. Index, pp. 299-305.

A text for a one-semester course in probability and statistics for students who have knowledge of college algebra. Includes some calculus in the treatment of continuous probability, moment-generating functions, and some derivations. Emphasizes theoretical concepts and derivations, rather than methods and applications. Topics include discrete random variables; probability distributions; power function and acceptance sampling; continuous random variables; sampling and sampling statistics; confidence interval estimation for population means and proportions; control charts; maximum likelihood; Bayesian inference; posterior distributions; nonparametric procedures; regression; and analysis of variance. Sections conclude with problems.

Linnik, IUrii Vladimirovich. THE DISPERSION METHOD OF BINARY ADDITIVE PROBLEMS. Translated by S. Schur. Providence, R.I.: American Mathematical Society, 1963. x, 186 p. Bibliography, pp. 183-86. No index.

Originally published in Russian in 1961. Applies probability theory (concepts of dispersion, covariance, and the Chebyshev inequality) to the solution of a number of binary additive problems: divisor; problem of Hardy and Littlewood; problem of Titchmarch concerning divisors and primes; and application of the dispersion method to a generalization of a theorem of Kloosterman. Assumes knowledge of number theory and advanced probability theory.

_____. METHOD OF LEAST SQUARES AND PRINCIPLES OF THE THEORY OF OBSERVATIONS. Translated by Regina C. Elandt and N.L. Johnson. New York: Pergamon, 1961. xii, 360 p. Bibliography, pp. 352-55. Appendix, pp. 356-60. No index.

Originally published in Russian in 1958. Presents the theory (in matrix form) of the method of least squares with emphasis on the mathematical-statistical interpretation of the results obtained from applications. Topics include treatment of direct and indirect, unconditional and conditional measurements; estimation of linear forms in parameters from indirect observations (theorems of Neyman and David); reduction by means of correlates; examples of the analysis of observations in geodesy; estimation of results of direct and reverse bearings; parabolic interpretation by least squares; line of orthogonal regression and its application (investigations of A. Wald); and Cauchy's method of reduction of observations.

_____. STATISTICAL PROBLEMS WITH NUISANCE PARAMETERS. Translated by Scripta Technica, Inc. Translations of Mathematical Monographs, vol. 20. Providence, R.I.: American Mathematical Society, 1968. ix, 258 p. Appendix: Unsolved Questions, pp. 213-16. Supplement: "New Results in the Theory of Estimation and Testing Hypothesis for Problems with Nuisance Parameters," by A.M. Kagan and V.P. Palamodov, pp. 217-50. Bibliography, pp. 251-58. No index.

Originally published in Russian in 1966. A monograph on the theory of elimination of nuisance parameters in hypothesis testing and a theory of unbiased estimation, with emphasis on properties of tests and estimates and on the mathematical foundations for obtaining a test or unbiased estimate that is optimal. Topics include multiple Laplace transforms; properties and application of analytic sheaves with applications to the theory of exponential families; sufficient statistics for distributions in euclidean spaces; theory of similarity; similar tests and unbiased estimates in connection with the Behrens-Fisher problem and for incomplete exponential families; and problems with nuisance parameters. Concludes with a discussion of several unsolved problems that arise in analytical statistics.

_____, ed. ARTICLES ON MATHEMATICAL STATISTICS AND THE THEORY OF PROBABILITY. Translated by Lisa Rosenblatt. Proceedings of the Steklov Institute of Mathematics, no. 69. Providence, R.I.: American Mathematical Society, 1966. iv, 259 p. No index.

Eighteen papers presented at the Steklov Institute of Mathematics in the Academy of Sciences of the USSR in 1965. Topics include existence of independent partitions; sufficient systems; separating partitions; construction of optimal similar solutions of the Behrens-Fisher problem; Wald test with unequal samples, roundoff errors in multidimensional measurements;

distribution of observations by polynomial regression; theorems on decomposition of probability laws; and statistical problems in the interpretation of seismic data.

_____. STUDIES IN MATHEMATICAL STATISTICS. Translated by S. Kotz. Proceedings of the Steklov Institute of Mathematics, no. 104. Providence, R.I.: American Mathematical Society, 1971. iii, 260 p. No index.

Six papers presented at the Steklov Institute of Mathematics in the Academy of Sciences of the USSR in 1968 on such topics in mathematical statistics as the general linear hypothesis with unknown weights; estimation theory for families with location and scale parameters and for exponential families; limit properties of probability distributions; nonlinear filtering of Markov diffusion processes; families of transient densities in Markov chains admitting nontrivial sufficient statistics; and smoothing of observations with unknown weights by least squares.

_____. THEORETICAL PROBLEMS IN MATHEMATICAL STATISTICS. Proceedings of the Steklov Institute of Mathematics, no. 111 (1970). Providence, R.I.: American Mathematical Society, 1972. iv, 316 p. No index.

Thirteen papers presented at the Steklov Institute of Mathematics in the Academy of Sciences of the USSR in 1970. Problems include gamma distributions and partial sufficiency of polynomials; statistical and probabilistic problems on groups; estimation of parameters of a distribution from grouped samples; roundoff errors in measurements with a random shifting scale; gamma function and probabilistic limit theorems; the minimax character of the complex analog of the R^2 test; turnpike theorem for semi-Markov decision processes; completely regular multidimensional stationary processes with discrete time, optimal unbiased designs for regression experiments; and testing of hypothesis concerning parameters of normal correlation. Each paper translated by a different author.

Lippman, Steven A. ELEMENTS OF PROBABILITY AND STATISTICS. Series in Quantitative Methods for Decision-Making. New York: Holt, Rinehart and Winston, 1971. xvii, 330 p. Appendix: Preliminaries, pp. 290-303. References, pp. 304-5. Tables, pp. 306-15. Subject Index, pp. 319-25. Example Index, pp. 326-27. Symbol Index, pp. 328-29. Greek Alphabet, p. 330.

A text for a one-semester course in probability and statistics for graduate students in business, education, social sciences, and mathematics who have knowledge of one year of calculus. Emphasizes probability theory with numerous applications from business, physics, education, sociology, geography, and psychology. Includes proofs of theorems. Consists of two parts: "Probability" and "Statistical Inference." Topics include random invariables and expectation; hypothesis testing; Chebyshev inequality and the weak law of large numbers; power curves;

chi-square; estimation; properties of point estimators; linear regression; and nonparametric tests. Appendixes include sets, functions, and summation notation.

Lukacs, Eugene. CHARACTERISTIC FUNCTIONS. 2d ed. Griffin's Statistical Monographs and Courses, no. 5. London: Charles Griffin, 1970. 350 p. Appendixes, pp. 327-34. List of Examples of Characteristic Functions, pp. 335-36. References, pp. 337-43. Index, pp. 344-50.

A monograph on characteristic functions for their mathematical properties and not for their possible applications. Topics include properties and criteria for characteristic functions; factorization problems for characteristic functions; infinitely divisible characteristic functions; factorization of analytic characteristic functions; and mixtures of distribution functions and transformations of characteristic functions. Assumes knowledge of advanced calculus, mathematical analysis, and probability. Appendixes devoted to Schwarz's inequality, the notations O and e, Weierstrass's approximation theorem; order and type of entire function; Schwarz's reflection principle; and proofs of lemmas used in the presentation.

Mace, Arthur E. SAMPLE-SIZE DETERMINATION. New York: Reinhold, 1964. x, 226 p. References, pp. 190-92. Appendix: Tables, pp. 193-222. Index, pp. 223-26.

A manual designed to familiarize experimentalists with the kind of information required for sample-size determination, and to provide them with elementary procedures, formulas, and tables for choosing an economical sample size. Considers forty different types of objectives for a research experiment with formulas to determine the minimum number of observations necessary to achieve that objective. Includes tables to assist in the application of the formulas. Includes additional information on lot-acceptance sampling plans of the U.S. Department of Defense and on methods for constructing cost schedules for sample-size determination. Topics include objective of a sampling experiment; variability among observations; power-function approach; estimation problems; test of hypotheses; selection problems; sequential sampling; lot-acceptance sampling plans; and decision-function approach. Examples provided.

McLachlan, Gordon, ed. MEASURING FOR MANAGEMENT: QUANTITATIVE METHODS IN HEALTH SERVICE MANAGEMENT. New York: Oxford University Press, for the Nuffield Provincial Hospitals Trust, 1975. xii, 185 p. No index.

Eight essays based on research carried out by the Department of Mathematical Statistics and Operational Research and the Numerical Sciences Division of the Institute of Biometry and Community Medicine at Exeter University during the period from 1965 to 1975. Emphasizes applications in biology, medicine, and health care. Topics include monitoring the quality of health care; resource allocation in maternity care; public attitudes towards mental illness; family costs of maternity care; and work study as an aid to management. Papers descriptive and survey in nature; utilize measures from descriptive statistics.

Mardia, K.V. FAMILIES OF BIVARIATE DISTRIBUTIONS. Griffin's Statistical Monographs and Courses, no. 27. Darien, Conn.: Hafner, 1970. ix, 109 p. Appendix: List of Bivariate Distributions with their Relation to Families, pp. 96-99. References and Author Index, pp. 100-106. Subject Index, pp. 107-9.

A monograph which presents a systematic account of families of bivariate normal distributions for readers who are familiar with standard univariate distributions and mathematical statistics. Families grouped according to method of construction as follows: differential equation method, bivariate Edgeworth expansion, translation, dependence, regression, canonical representation, contingency-type distributions, and trivariate reduction. Includes an historical introduction to the subject and sixteen bivariate distributions which can be obtained by extending special features of well-known models, including bivariate Cauchy and student distributions.

_____. STATISTICS OF DIRECTIONAL DATA. Probability and Mathematical Statistics. A Series of Monographs and Courses, vol. 13. New York: Academic Press, 1972. xix, 357 p. Appendix 1: Bessel Functions, pp. 287-88. Appendix 2: Tables and Charts for the Circular Case (Abridged Titles), pp. 290-317. Appendix 3: Tables and Charts for the Spherical Case (Abridged Titles), pp. 320-30. Bibliography and Author Index, pp. 331-39. Subject Index, pp. 340-55. Index of Notation, pp. 356-57.

A systematic account of statistical theory and methodology for observations called directions (points on a circle in two dimensions or on a sphere of three dimensions). Includes the theory of each technique, as well as applications. Topics include descriptive statistics; characteristic functions; circular models; mixtures and multi-modal distributions; limit theorems and limit distributions; point estimates; tests for samples from von Mises populations; nonparametric tests; distributions on spheres; and inference problems on the sphere (single, two-, and multi-sample tests, etc.). Useful as a graduate text, reference, user's manual, and elementary methods text for those who have knowledge of undergraduate mathematical statistics.

Mathai, A.M., and Pederzoli, G. CHARACTERIZATION OF THE NORMAL PROBABILITY LAW. New York: Wiley, Halsted Press, 1977. x, 149 p. Bibliography, pp. 127-43. List of Symbols, pp. 144-45. Author Index, pp. 146-47. Subject Index, pp. 148-49.

A monograph on the properties of the normal probability law requiring knowledge of mathematical statistics, probability, and advanced calculus. Also useful as a text for a one-semester graduate course. Presentation semirigorous. Topics include: normal law from different hypotheses; characterizations through structural set-up exercises, independence of linear and quadratic forms; regression exercises, by solutions of functional equations, from Student's law, and functional equations; and characterizations of the multivariate normal law.

Mathai, A.M., and Saxena, R.K. GENERALIZED HYPERGEOMETRIC FUNCTIONS WITH APPLICATIONS IN STATISTICS AND PHYSICAL SCIENCES. New York: Springer-Verlag, 1973. vii, 314 p. Bibliography, pp. 261-305. Appendix: Orders of the Special Functions for Large and Small Values of the Argument, pp. 306-9. Index of Symbols, pp. 310-11. Author Index, pp. 312-13. Subject Index, p. 314.

A balanced treatment of theory and application of generalized hypergeometric functions with emphasis on Meyer's G-function and its application to prior and posterior distributions, characterizations of probability laws, sinusoidal signals in communication theory, conduction of heat and cooling, and dual integral equations. Includes formulas with outlines of proofs and references. Useful as a text or reference on special functions.

Matthes, Klaus; Kerstan, Johannes; and Mecke, Joseph. INFINITELY DIVISIBLE POINT PROCESSES. Wiley Series in Probability and Mathematical Statistics. New York: Wiley, 1978. xii, 532 p. References, pp. 516-29. Index, p. 530. Index of Notation, pp. 531-32.

A presentation of infinitely divisible point processes defined on Euclidean spaces R^s. Incorporates the Kallenberg method of backward clusters. Topics include canonical representation of infinitely divisible probability distributions; weak convergence of distributions; cluster fields; Campbell measures; stationary distributions; Cox distributions; the Palm measure; the Palm distribution, generalized Palm-Khinchin theorem; homogeneous cluster fields; and spatially homogeneous branching processes. Develops the theory of Campbell and Palm measures for stochastic point processes. Rigorous style, consisting of proposition-theorem-proof format.

Mendenhall, William, and Scheaffer, Richard L. MATHEMATICAL STATISTICS WITH APPLICATIONS. North Scituate, Mass.: Duxbury, 1973. xii, 652 p. Appendix I: Matrixes, pp. 563-83. Appendix II: Common Probability Distributions, Means, Variances, and Moment-Generating Functions, pp. 584-85. Appendix III: Tables, pp. 586-627. Answers to Exercises, pp. 628-47. Index, pp. 648-52.

A text for a one-year course in mathematical statistics for undergraduates in various disciplines who have one year of college calculus. Probability presented with a clear statement of the objectives of statistics and its role in scientific research. Emphasizes statistical inference and problems. Topics include discrete and continuous random variables and their distributions, including geometric Poisson, uniform, gamma, and beta; multivariate probability distributions; moment-generating functions; order statistics; limit theorems and convergence in probability and convergence in distribution; point estimates; confidence intervals; maximum likelihood estimation; method of moments; hypothesis testing, including Neyman-Pearson lemma; minimax and Bayes tests; linear models and estimation by least squares; design of experiments, including volume-increasing and noise-reducing designs; analysis of variance; chi-square; and nonparametric tests.

Miller, Rupert G. SIMULTANEOUS STATISTICAL INFERENCE. New York: McGraw-Hill, 1966. xv, 272 p. Appendix A: Strong Law for the Expected Error Rate, pp. 231-32. Appendix B: Tables, pp. 233-52. Bibliography, pp. 253-67. Author Index, pp. 268-69. Subject Index, pp. 270-72.

A monograph useful as a text or reference on simultaneous inference and a supplementary text for a course in analysis of variance. Includes a cookbook description of each procedure, followed by a rigorous development requiring knowledge of linear algebra and mathematical statistics. Topics include normal univariate techniques, including studentized range and maximum modulus; Bonferroni t; many-one t; least significant difference test; regression techniques, including surface confidence bands, prediction, discrimination, and tolerance intervals; nonparametric techniques, including k-sample sign and rank tests, many-one rank, Kruskal-Wallis rank, and Friedman rank; and multivariate techniques, including single population and k population, and multinomial techniques. Includes derivations, but no problems for assignment.

Mood, Alexander M.; Graybill, Franklin A.; and Boes, Duane C. INTRODUCTION TO THE THEORY OF STATISTICS. 3d ed., rev. New York: McGraw-Hill, 1974. xvi, 564 p. Appendix A: Mathematical Addendum, pp. 527-35. Appendix B: Tabular Summary of Parametric Families of Distributions, pp. 537-43. Appendix C: References and Related Reading, pp. 544-47. Appendix D: Tables, pp. 548-56. Index, pp. 557-64.

A text for a service-type course in mathematical statistics for students in a variety of disciplines who have gone through a one-year course in calculus. No previous knowledge of statistics assumed. An attempt made to impart a "feel" for the theory. Topics include axiomatic probability, including random variables and univariate, joint, and conditional distributions; stochastic independence; moment-generating functions; laws of large numbers; order statistics; parametric point and interval estimation; tests of hypotheses, including composite hypotheses; linear models; and nonparametric tests. Examples used to illustrate concepts. Each chapter concludes with a lengthy problem set.

Myers, Buddy L., and Enrick, Norbert L. STATISTICAL FUNCTIONS: A SOURCE OF PRACTICAL DERIVATIONS BASED ON ELEMENTARY MATHEMATICS. Kent, Ohio: Kent University Press, 1970. ix, 174 p. Bibliography, p. 150. Appendix A: Differentiation Formulas, pp. 152-53. Appendix B: Integration Formulas, pp. 154-55. Appendix C: Fundamental Trigonometric Relations, pp. 156-58. Appendix D: Selected Topics from Algebra, pp. 159-63. Appendix E: Problems, pp. 164-71. Index, pp. 173-74.

A collection of derivations of the principal statistical functions and formulas in a methodical, detailed, and gap-free manner for those who have a background in algebra and basic statistics. Formulas treated in terms of their origin, statistical theory, applications, and limitations. Formulas discussed in the following chapter titles: "Summations"; "Probability"; "Expected Value"; "Some Applications of Expected Values"; "Probability Distributions"; "Moments of a Distribution"; "Maximum Likelihood Functions"; "Analysis of Variance"; "Linear Regression, Correlation"; and "Series, Transformations, and Additional Functions."

Nahi, Nasser E. ESTIMATION THEORY AND APPLICATIONS. New York: Wiley, 1969. xv, 280 p. Appendix A, pp. 273-75. Index, pp. 277-80.

An introduction to the theory of estimation with emphasis on recursive methods for use as a text for graduate students in engineering, mathematics, physics, or related areas, and as a reference for engineers. Topics include Fourier transforms and spectral density; calculus of variations; modeling of stochastic processes; linear estimators and their recursive (Kalman) formulations; nonlinear estimation; signals of known form in the presence of noise; and estimation by means of the Cramér-Rao lower bound for the variance of an estimate. Chapters conclude with problems and selected readings. Appendix includes a solution to a constrained maximization problem using Pontryagin's maximum principle.

Nalimov, Vasiliĭ Vasil'evich. THE APPLICATION OF MATHEMATICAL STATISTICS TO CHEMICAL ANALYSIS. Translated by Prasenjit Basu. English translation edited by M. Williams. Addison-Wesley Series in Avanced Chemistry. Reading, Mass.: Addison-Wesley, 1963. ix, 294 p. Bibliography, pp. 236-51. Appendix: Tables, pp. 252-90. Index, pp. 291-94.

A handbook on the application of mathematical statistics to chemical analysis for use by engineer-physicists and chemists working in analytical laboratories. Includes numerical examples, and emphasizes physical interpretation of statistical investigations. Assumes knowledge of mathematical statistics and probability. Topics include errors in chemical analysis; random variables and their characteristics; normal distributions; Poisson and binomial distributions; sequential analysis; nonparametric statistics; comparison of several variables; analysis of variance; regression and correlation; and design of experiments.

Neyman, Jerzy. A SELECTION OF EARLY STATISTICAL PAPERS OF J. NEYMAN. Berkeley and Los Angeles: University of California Press, 1967. viii, 429 p. Appendix: Bibliography of Scientific Papers of J. Neyman, pp. 424-29. No index.

A collection of reprints of thirty-eight articles by Jerzy Neyman published in various journals from 1923 to 1949. Articles representative of Neyman's scientific activity including applications in agriculture and biology.

Neyman, Jerzy, and Pearson, E.S. JOINT STATISTICAL PAPERS. Foreword by L.H.C. Tippett. Berkeley and Los Angeles: University of California Press, 1967. viii, 299 p. No index.

Reprints of ten papers published jointly by the authors during the period 1928-1938 in the journals BIOMETRIKA, PHILOSOPHICAL TRANSACTIONS OF THE ROYAL SOCIETY, PROCEEDINGS OF THE CAMBRIDGE PHILOSOPHICAL SOCIETY, BULLETIN OF THE ACADEMY OF POLITICAL SCIENCE, and STATISTICAL RESEARCH MEMOIRS. Topics include problems of two and k samples; chi-square; the problem of the most efficient tests of statistical hypotheses; and sufficient statistics and uniformly most powerful tests of statistical hypotheses.

Odeh, Robert E., and Fox, Martin. SAMPLE SIZE CHOICE: CHARTS FOR EXPERIMENTS WITH LINEAR MODELS. Statistics: Textbooks and Monographs, vol. 14. New York: Marcel Dekker, 1975. vii, 190 p. References, pp. 59-62. Tables, pp. 65-79. Charts, pp. 83-188. Index, pp. 189-90.

The developments of charts and tables enabling one to find the required sample size for a given level of significance and power when testing statistical models involving linear models using the F and t statistics. Numerical data for the charts and tables computed on an IBM 370/145 computer. Part I includes the general linear hypothesis; survey of the literature; and the use of the tables and charts for the following models: one-way layout, two-way layout, randomized blocks, simple and quadratic regression, multivariate t tests, and fixed alpha on a sphere. Part II presents tables for the upper percentage points of the F, chi-square, and t distributions. Part III contains the charts.

Olkin, Ingram; Ghurye, Sudhish G.; Hoeffding, Wassily; Madow, William G.; and Mann, Henry B., eds. CONTRIBUTIONS TO PROBABILITY AND STATISTICS: ESSAYS IN HONOR OF HAROLD HOTELLING. Stanford Studies in Mathematics and Statistics, III. Stanford, Calif.: Stanford University Press, 1960. x, 517 p. Bibliography of Harold Hotelling, pp. 25-32. No index.

> Forty-two heretofore unpublished contributions grouped into two headings: "An Appreciation" (four papers) and "Contributions to Probability and Statistics" (thirty-eight papers). Topics include design of experiments; sequential probability ratio tests; two- and k-sample rank tests; robust tests for equality of variances; infinitesimal renewal processes; sampling from contaminated distributions; stochastic models of ecology and epidemiology; characterizations of some location and scale parameter families of parameters; and a bivariate Chebyshev inequality for symmetric convex polygons.

Patil, Ganapati P.; Kotz, S.; and Ord, J.K., eds. A MODERN COURSE ON STATISTICAL DISTRIBUTIONS IN SCIENTIFIC WORK. Vol. 1: MODELS AND STRUCTURES. NATO Advanced Study Institute Series. Boston: D. Reidel, 1975. xx, 424 p. Subject Index, pp. 419-24.

> Thirty-three papers presented at the NATO Advanced Study Institute held at the University of Calgary, Calgary, Alberta, Canada, July 29-August 10, 1974. Papers grouped under the following headings: "Inaugural Address" (one paper); "Power Series and Related Families" (six papers); "Recent Trends in Univariate Models" (six papers); "Moment-Related Problems" (three papers); "Limit Distributions" (three papers); "Multivariate Concepts and Models" (four papers); "Certain Multivariate Distributions" (five papers); and "Sampling Distributions and Transformations" (five papers).

_____. A MODERN COURSE ON STATISTICAL DISTRIBUTIONS IN SCIENTIFIC WORK. Vol. 2: MODEL BUILDING AND MODEL SELECTION. NATO Advanced Study Institute Series. Boston: D. Reidel, 1975. xvii, 399 p. Subject Index, pp. 397-99.

> Twenty-seven papers presented at the NATO Advanced Study Institute held at the University of Calgary, Calgary, Alberta, Canada, July 29-August 10, 1974, grouped under the following headings: "Modelling and Simulation" (five papers); "Model Identification and Discrimination" (six papers); "Models in the Social Sciences and Management" (four papers); "Models in the Physical and Biomedical Sciences" (eight papers); and "Models in the Environmental Sciences" (four papers). Concludes with a course outline on statistical distributions by the editors.

_____. A MODERN COURSE ON STATISTICAL DISTRIBUTIONS IN SCIENTIFIC WORK. Vol. 3: CHARACTERIZATIONS AND APPLICATIONS. NATO Advanced Study Institute Series. Boston: D. Reidel, 1975. xviii, 436 p. Subject Index, pp. 433-36.

Thirty-seven papers presented at the NATO Advanced Study Institute held at the University at Calgary, Alberta, Canada, July 29-August 10, 1974. Papers grouped under the following headings: "Linnik Memorial Inaugural Lecture" (one paper); "Mathematical Tools for Characterization Problems" (three papers); "Characterizations Using Order Statistics" (eight papers); "Characterizations by Other Statistical Properties" (six papers); "Characterizations on Spaces and Processes" (four papers); "Characterization Problems for Damaged Observations" (four papers); "Characterizations Using Entropy Measures and Related Problems" (four papers); "Characterizations for Discrete Distributions and Families" (three papers); and "Characterizations for Continuous Distributions and Families" (four papers).

Pearson, Egon Sharpe. THE SELECTED PAPERS OF E.S. PEARSON. Foreword by L.H.C. Tippett. Berkeley and Los Angeles: University of California Press, 1966. viii, 327 p. Appendix: Bibliography of Scientific Papers, etc., by E.D. Pearson, pp. 324-27. No index.

A selection of Professor Pearson's own papers, and a few written in collaboration with other authors, originally published in BIOMETRIKA, JOURNAL OF THE ROYAL STATISTICAL SOCIETY, and ANNALS OF MATHEMATICAL STATISTICS. Issued by the BIOMETRIKA trustees to celebrate his thirty years as editor.

Pearson, Egon Sharpe, and Kendall, M.G., eds. STUDIES IN THE HISTORY OF STATISTICS AND PROBABILITY. New York: Hafner, 1970. xi, 481 p. Appendix: Summary of Contents of Karl Pearson's Lectures on the History of Statistics in the 17th and 18th Centuries, pp. 479-81. No index.

Twenty-eight reprints of articles originally published in BIOMETRIKA during the period 1906-1968, and one article, "The Neyman-Pearson Story: 1926-34. Historical Sidelights on an Episode in Anglo-Polish Collaboration," taken from FESTSCHRIFT FOR J. NEYMAN, by E.D. Pearson (Wiley: 1966). The articles represent studies involving much research effort and employ no higher mathematics; some use no formulas at all. Topics include medical statistics to Farr; Wm. S. Gossett, 1876-1937; history of correlation; history of the graphic representation of data; reflections on continuity in the development of mathematical statistics; G.U. Yule; history of probability; and a note on playing cards.

Peters, Charles C., and Van Voorhis, Walter R. STATISTICAL PROCEDURES AND THEIR MATHEMATICAL BASIS. New York: McGraw-Hill, 1940. xiii, 516 p. Appendix: Tables, pp. 481-510. Index, pp. 511-16.

Presents the mathematical origins of the most widely used statistical formulas in terms that persons with comparatively little mathematics knowledge can follow. Topics include formulas for descriptive statistics; rectilinear correlation; percentile, ranges, and proportions; multiple-factor analysis; normal probability curve; correlation ratio; analysis of variance; chi-square; curve fitting; and controlled experimentation. Intended to bridge the gap between elementary formulas and original contributions. Derivations short and often intuitive. Includes verbal description and examples. Chapters conclude with exercises and references.

Plackett, R.L. AN INTRODUCTION TO THE THEORY OF STATISTICS. University Mathematics Texts. Edinburgh, Scot.: Oliver & Boyd, 1971. viii, 204 p. Bibliography, pp. 199-200. Subject Index, pp. 201-4.

A text for a first course in mathematical statistics for students of mathematics who have knowledge of calculus, linear algebra, and elementary complex variables. Complete proofs given for nearly all results. Exercises at the end of each chapter consist of extensions of the text material. Topics include discrete and continuous probability distributions; moments of random variables; calculus of distributions; statistical inference; normal samples; linear statistical models; asymptotic distributions; and analysis of frequencies. Assumes knowledge of calculus.

Puri, Madam Lal, ed. STATISTICAL INFERENCE AND RELATED TOPICS. Vol. 2. New York: Academic Press, 1975. xii, 352 p. No index.

Fifteen papers presented at the Summer Institute on Statistical Inference for Stochastic Processes, Bloomington, Indiana, July 31-August 9, 1975. Topics include asymptotically complete classes, Monte Carlo of two-dimensional Brownian sheets, a Bernstein polynomial approach to density function estimation, parametric and nonparametric sequential subset selection procedures, asymptotic properties of maximum probability estimates in the IID case, inference in a distribution related to a 2x2 Markov Chain, and record values in Markov sequences.

Quenouille, M.H. THE FUNDAMENTALS OF STATISTICAL REASONING. Griffin's Statistical Monographs, no. 3. New York: Hafner, 1965. 169 p. Name Index, pp. 165-66. Subject Index, pp. 166-69.

A monograph presenting the concepts and ideas which form the basis of statistics with few proofs and practical applications. Consists of three parts: "Basic Concepts"; "Deductive Methods"; and "Testing of Hypotheses." Topics include probability theorems; probability distributions; characteristic functions; derived distributions; central limit concepts; moments of derived statistics; properties of point estimators, with applications to design of experiments and inverse sampling; testing of hypotheses, including comparison of proportions and sequential tests; maximum likelihood; fiducial limits and distributions; Fisher-Behrens distribution tests; variance components; power functions;

minimax principle; and likelihood ratio tests. Chapters conclude with references and tables of 1,000 standardized random deviates from certain non-normal distributions.

Ractliffe, J.F. ELEMENTS OF MATHEMATICAL STATISTICS. 2d ed. Oxford Mathematical Handbooks. New York: Oxford University Press, 1967. x, 224 p. Miscellaneous Test Papers, pp. 202-11. Appendix of Tables, pp. 213-22. Index, pp. 223-24.

A text for a one-semester course in mathematical statistics for students of science and engineering who have knowledge of elementary calculus. Topics include descriptive statistics; rules of probability; binomial, Poisson, and normal distributions; statistical quality control; tests of hypotheses concerning a mean and differences between two means; analysis of variance; rank correlation; chi-square; regression and correlation; and moment-generating functions. Emphasizes illustrative examples rather than formal proofs. Sections conclude with exercises on application.

Rahman, N.A. A COURSE IN THEORETICAL STATISTICS. London: Charles Griffin, 1967. xv, 542 p. Appendix: Tables, pp. 515-25. Index, pp. 526-42.

A text for a one-year course in mathematical statistics for students of mathematics who have knowledge of calculus (A-level syllabuses in England). Also serves as an introduction to the statistics profession. Consists of three parts: "Mathematical Introduction"; "Statistical Mathematics and Probability"; and "Statistical Inference." Topics include gamma and beta functions; discrete and continuous probability distributions; stochastic difference equations with applications; test of significance in binomial sampling; sampling, including stratified random sampling; methods of estimation (lease squares, maximum likelihood, moments); large-sample tests of significance in continuous populations; exact tests of significance and the analysis of variance, including F, chi-square, and t; regression and correlation; and applications of the chi-square distribution. Includes a large number of solved examples and a limited number of unsolved problems.

Rao, C. Radharkrishna. LINEAR STATISTICAL INFERENCE AND ITS APPLICATION. 2d ed., rev. Wiley Series in Probability and Mathematical Statistics. New York: Wiley, 1973. xx, 625 p. Publications of the Authors, pp. 605-13. Author Index, pp. 615-17. Subject Index, pp. 618-25.

A text for a graduate course in statistical inference for students who have a background in vector spaces and line algebra, and the calculus of probability. Topics include the theory of least squares and analysis of variance, including analysis of covariance; Gauss-Markov model; variance components model and biased estimation in linear models; criteria and methods of estimation, including minimum variance unbiased estimation; Fisher's information measure; Bayes' theorem; minimax principle; method of moments; maximum likelihood and method of scoring; large sample theory and methods including chi-square; contingency tables, order statistics, transformations of statistics, and standard errors of moments and related statistics; theory of statistical inference, including tests of hypotheses and confidence interval estimation; sequential analysis; problem of identification; nonparametric tests; and multivariate analysis, including multivariate normal, Wishart, analysis of dispersion, discriminatory analysis, canonical and factor analysis, and the Gram-Schmidt basis. Chapters conclude with problems and references.

______, ed., in Collaboration with D.B. Lahiri, K.R. Nair, P. Pant, and S.S. Shrikhande. CONTRIBUTIONS TO STATISTICS. Foreword by C.D. Deshmukh. New York: Pergamon, 1963. 528 p. No index.

Thirty-three heretofore unpublished papers presented to Professor P.C. Mahalanobis on his seventieth birthday in June 1963. Topics include combinatorial properties of partially balanced designs and association schemes; lattice sampling by means of Lahiri's sampling schemes; von Mises functionals and maximum likelihood estimation; partially balanced asymmetrical factorial designs; multi-subject sample survey systems; fitting asymptotic regression curves with different asymptotes; asymptotic expansions for the distribution of maximum likelihood estimates; international aspects of quality control; criteria of estimation in large samples; discrimination of Gaussian processes; hierarchial and p-block multiresponse designs; field cost for the collection of household consumption data; and fixed interval analysis and fractile analysis.

Rao, S.K. STATISTICAL INFERENCE AND MEASUREMENT OF STRUCTURAL CHANGES IN AN ECONOMY. Foreword by C.N. Vakil. University of Bombay Publications. Economic Series no. 7. New York: Oxford University, 1964. xvi, 345 p. Appendixes: Tables for Easy Construction of Periodograms of Time Series, pp. 295-31. Bibliography, pp. 333-39. Index, pp. 341-45.

A monograph on selected topics in mathematical statistics for students who are acquainted with calculus and probability theory. Topics include relative frequencies in sampling, theoretical frequency distributions, correlation and regression, sampling errors, the Lexis theory, and the Gram-Charlier Series. Chapters conclude with references.

Rietz, Henry Lewis. MATHEMATICAL STATISTICS. Carus Mathematical Monographs, no. 3. La Salle, Ill.: Open Court Publishing, for the Mathematical Association of America, 1927. xi, 181 p. Notes, pp. 173-77. Index, pp. 178-81.

A monograph on selected topics in mathematical statistics for students who are acquainted with elementary differential and integral calculus, and probability theory. Emphasizes applications and includes such topics as relative frequencies in simple sampling; theoretical frequency distributions; correlation and regression; sampling errors; the Lexis theory; and the Gram-Charlier Series. Chapters conclude with references.

Rivlin, Theodore J. THE CHEBYSHEV POLYNOMIALS. New York: Wiley, Interscience, 1974. vi, 186 p. References, pp. 177-81. Glossary of Symbols, pp. 183-84. Index, pp. 185-86.

A monograph which presents a survey of the most important properties of the Chebyshev polynomials, and which illustrates applications in interpolation theory, orthogonal polynomials, approximation theory, numerical integrations, and ergodic theory. Includes the expansion of a function in a series of Chebyshev polynomials and more than 200 exercises of varying degrees of difficulty.

Roach, Stanley Alex. THE THEORY OF RANDOM CLUMPING. London: Methuen, 1968. vii, 94 p. References, pp. 91-92. Index, pp. 93-94.

A monograph on the theory of random clumping, beginning with the simplest one-dimensional model and examining the progressive stages leading to the more complex two-dimensional models. Includes numerous examples of applications in astronomy, particle physics, and bacterial counting. Assumes knowledge of calculus and probability theory.

Rustagi, Jagdish S. VARIATIONAL METHODS IN STATISTICS. Mathematics in Science and Engineering, vol. 121. New York: Academic Press, 1976. xii, 236 p. Index, pp. 233-36.

An exposition of calculus of variations and its modern generalizations with applications to statistical problems. Assumes knowledge of advanced calculus and linear algebra. Includes Pontryagin's maximum principle; Bellman's dynamic programming; linear and nonlinear moments with variational techniques for their solution; optimal design for regression experiments, including designs using splines; theory of optimal control, including controlled Markov chains; the Wiener process and stopping problems; and miscellaneous applications of variational methods such as reliability, bio-assay, stochastic programming, and the relationship between mathematical programming and statistics. Useful as a text for a course in optimizing in statistics and as a supplementary text for courses in statistics, mathematics, and operations research.

_____, ed. OPTIMIZING METHODS IN STATISTICS. New York: Academic Press, 1971. xvi, 488 p. Participants, pp. 481-88.

Twenty-six papers presented at a symposium on optimizing methods held at Ohio State University on June 14-16, 1971. Includes the following sessions: variational methods, regression, optimum seeking methods, mathematical programming, stochastic processes, optimum design of experiments, optimum spacings and order statistics, and problems and applications. Topics include optimization problems in simulation, isotonic approximation, variational methods in adaptive filtering, necessary conditions for a local optimum without prior constraint qualification, chance-constrained programming, and tests of homogeneity against ordered alternatives.

Sadowski, Wiestaw. STATISTICS FOR ECONOMISTS. Translated by J. Stadler. New York: Pergamon, 1968. vii, 323 p. Bibliography, pp. 295-96. Appendix: Tables, pp. 297-319. Index, pp. 321-23.

Originally published in Polish in 1965. An elementary exposition of mathematical statistics based on lectures given at the Central School of Planning and Statistics in Warsaw. Mainly for economists interested in econometrics. Assumes knowledge of basic statistics, calculus, and probability theory. Presentation intermediate between a recipe book, with statistical procedures given without proof, and a rigorous, mathematically oriented text. Topics include probability theory; sampling distributions; moment-generating functions; estimation, including maximum likelihood; tests of significance; nonparametric statistics; most powerful tests; likelihood ratio tests; multidimensional populations; and sequential analysis.

Sarkadi, Károly, and Vincze, I., eds. STUDIES IN MATHEMATICAL STATISTICS: THEORY AND APPLICATIONS. Budapest: Hungarian Academy of Sciences, 1968. 210 p. No index.

Twenty-five papers presented at an international symposium on mathematical statistics held in Budapest in 1964. Papers dealt with theoretical problems in mathematical statistics, reliability, quality control, and life testing.

Savage, Leonard J. THE FOUNDATIONS OF STATISTICAL INFERENCE: A DISCUSSION. London: Methuen, 1962. 112 p. References, pp. 104-8. Name Index, p. 109. Subject Index, pp. 110-12.

A monograph based on papers presented at the Joint Statistics Seminar of Birkbeck and Imperial Colleges on July 27 and 28, 1959, in London with applications of subjective probability to statistics. Consists of three parts: an expanded version of L.R. Savage's opening lecture on subjective probability; five short contributions by M.S. Bartlett, G.A. Barnard, D.R. Cox, E.S. Pearson, and C.A.B. Smith; and a discussion of the issues raised by Savage.

Scarborough, James Blaine, and Wagner, R.W. FUNDAMENTALS OF STATISTICS. New York: Ginn & Co., 1948. vii, 146 p. Appendix A: Probability, pp. 109-28. Appendix B: Tables, pp. 129-35. Appendix C: Books Recommended for Collateral Reading, p. 136. Answers to Problems, pp. 137-41. Index, pp. 143-46.

> A brief introduction to mathematical statistics for students who understand elementary calculus. Curve fitting, time series, and small sample distributions omitted. Topics include probability functions; Tchebycheff's inequality; normal curve; and random variables.

Schaafsma, W. HYPOTHESIS TESTING PROBLEMS WITH THE ALTERNATIVE RESTRICTED BY A NUMBER OF INEQUALITIES. Groningen, The Netherlands: P. Noordhoff N.V., 1966. x, 134 p. References, p. 134. No index.

> A monograph on methods of deriving decision procedures (tests), as solutions of clearly stated optimum problems, for certain classes of hypotheses with alternatives defined by a number of inequalities. Both the Neyman-Pearson formulation and decision-theoretical formulations considered. Applications include testing homogeneity against trends, testing additivity of effects against positive interaction, and testing independence against positive dependence or against positive correlation. Assumes knowledge of mathematical statistics.

Schmetterer, Leopold. INTRODUCTION TO MATHEMATICAL STATISTICS. 2d ed. Translated by Kenneth Wickwire. New York: Springer-Verlag, 1974. viii, 502 p. Appendix, pp. 476-82. Bibliography, pp. 483-97. Name and Subject Index, pp. 498-502.

> Originally published in German in 1966. A text and reference for a course in mathematical statistics with a prerequisite of calculus. Topics include probability; sampling theory; hypothesis testing; theory of confidence sets; regression; multidimensional normal distributions; and nonparametric tests. Treatment rigorous, consisting of proofs of theorems, followed by brief descriptions.

SELECTED STATISTICAL PAPERS 1. Mathematical Centre Tracts 26. Amsterdam: Mathematisch Centrum, 1968. 95 p. No index.

> Eight papers presented at the European Meeting on statistics, econometrics, and management science held in Amsterdam in 1968. Topics include renewal processes invariant under translations; tests for ordered alternatives under interior slippage; the development concept of statistical decision theory; effects of errors of measurement on multiple regression; recent developments in the theory of Markov chains; and sequential search.

Shchigolev, Boris Mikailovich. MATHEMATICAL ANALYSIS OF OBSERVATIONS. Translated by Scripta Technica, Inc. New York: Elsevier, 1965. xv, 350 p. Bibliography, pp. 336-37. Appendix, pp. 338-42. Index, pp. 343-50.

Originally published in Russian in 1960. A text for students in applied mathematics and physics, as well as other branches of science and technology who have a good background in calculus. Consists of five parts: "Operations with Approximate Numbers"; "Point Interpolation"; "Probability Theory"; "Fundamentals of the Theory of Random Measurement Errors"; and "Analysis of Statistical Material." Topics include error in functions of several variables; point interpolation; Newton's, Stirling's and Bessel's formulas; random variables; law of large numbers; joint probability; and regression and correlation. Derivations kept simple and some theorems proved. Numerical examples included.

Shiriaev, Al'bert Nikolaevich. STATISTICAL SEQUENTIAL ANALYSIS: OPTIMAL STOPPING RULES. Translated by Lisa and Judah Rosenblatt. Translations of the Mathematical Monographs, vol. 38. Providence, R.I.: American Mathematical Society, 1973. iv, 174 p. Notes, pp. 168-70. Bibliography, pp. 171-74. No index.

Originally published in Russian in 1969. An exposition of the theory of optimal stopping rules in sequential analysis with applications to problems of mathematical statistics. Topics include probability concepts; derivations in the theory of Martingale and Markov processes; the problem of existence; and ways of constructing optimal Markov times for the discrete and continuous cases. Assumes knowledge of measure theory and stochastic processes.

Silvey, Samuel David. STATISTICAL INFERENCE. Library of University Mathematics. Baltimore: Penguin Books, 1970. 192 p. Appendix A: Some Matrix Results, pp. 177-79. Appendix B: The Linear Hypothesis, pp. 180-88. References, pp. 189-90. Index, pp. 191-92.

A monograph on statistical inference which concentrates on a relatively small number of techniques, illustrating them with simple examples and avoiding detailed derivations. Assumes knowledge of probability theory, linear algebra, calculus of several variables; and some measure theory. Topics include minimum variance unbiased estimation; method of least squares; maximum likelihood; confidence sets; hypothesis testing; likelihood ratio tests, sequential tests; nonparametric methods; Bayesian approach; and decision theory. Omits models of specific situations, and uses no real data.

Steffense, John Frederick. INTERPOLATION. 2d ed. New York: Chelsa, 1950. ix, 248 p. Appendix: On Differential Coefficients of Arbitrary Order, pp. 321-42. Index, pp. 243-48.

A text on interpolation methods with emphasis on formulas with workable remainder-terms. Assumes knowledge of differential and integral calculus. Many numerical examples provided. Topics include divided difference; interpolation formulas; factorial coefficients; numerical differentiation; inverse interpolation; summation; repeated summation; Laplace's and Gauss's summation formulas; Bernoulli's polynomials; Euler's summation formula; Lubbock's and Woolhouse's formula; numerical integration of differential equations; calculus of symbols, interpolation with several variables; and mechanical cubature.

Stout, William F. ALMOST SURE CONVERGENCE. Probability and Mathematical Statistics: A Series of Monographs and Textbooks. New York: Academic Press, 1974. x, 381 p. References, pp. 367-74. Index, pp. 375-81.

A text for a course on almost sure behavior for students familiar with real analysis and measure theory. Presents a systematic and unified treatment of almost sure convergence; almost sure convergence of partial sums, almost sure stability of partial sums, almost sure stability of weighted partial sums, and recurrence of partial sums. Topics omitted include almost everywhere convergence of Fourier series and the pointwise ergodic theory of operators in L_p spaces. Includes examples.

Stuart, Alan, and Kendall, Maurice G., eds. STATISTICAL PAPERS OF GEORGE UDNY YULE. New York: Hafner, 1971. viii, 447 p. Bibliography, pp. 445-47. No index.

Twelve reprints of articles by George Udny Yule grouped under the following headings: "The Notation and Theory of Association and Correlation" (four papers); "Epidemiology" (four papers); and "Time Series" (four papers).

Tarter, Michael E., ed. COMPUTER SCIENCE AND STATISTICS. North Hollywood, Calif.: Western Periodicals, 1972. viii, 173 p. Participants, pp. 170-73. No index.

Twenty-six papers presented at the sixth annual symposium on the interface held at the University of California, Berkeley, October 16-17, 1972. Conference designed to facilitate the design and improvement of computer systems and software by the use of statistics; to facilitate the implementation of statistical methods by making the most efficient use of computation machinery; and to enhance the combined uses of statistics and computation as adjuncts to the basic and applied sciences. Papers grouped under the following six headings: "Large-Scale Computer-Oriented Statistical Mathematics" (one paper); "Consultation and Education" (four papers); "Graphics" (six papers); "Numerical Analysis" (four papers); "Management and Decision Sciences" (five papers); and "Storage and Retrieval Problems for Medical Information" (six papers).

Taylor, Lester D. PROBABILITY AND MATHEMATICAL STATISTICS. New York: Hafner, 1974. xiv, 346 p. Appendix 1: The Algebra of the Subsets of a Set, pp. 313-17. Appendix 2: Binomial and Multinomial Theorems, pp. 318-23. Appendix 3: Characteristic Functions of Related Theorems, pp. 324-27. Appendix 4: Green's Theorem and Other Results from Advanced Calculus, pp. 328-32. Appendix 5: Real Symmetric, Positive Definite, and Idempotent Matrices, pp. 333-38. Appendix 6: The Liendeberg-Levy Central Limit Theorem, pp. 339-42. Index, pp. 343-46.

A text for an introductory course in probability and mathematical statistics for students who have knowledge of advanced calculus and linear algebra. Includes a wide-ranging list of examples and problems from economics, psychology, sociology, physics, engineering, biology, and medicine. Topics include random variables in n dimensions and their distributions; change of variables; convolution; multivariate normal distribution; distribution associated with the normal; maximum likelihood estimation; interval estimation and hypothesis testing; least squares; order statistics; and Bayesian inference. Includes exercises for assignment. Chapters conclude with reference.

Tschuprov, Aleksandr Aleksandrovich. PRINCIPLES OF THE MATHEMATICAL THEORY OF CORRELATION. Translated by M. Kantorowitsch. London: William Hodge, 1939, x, 194 p. Appendix, pp. 159-82. Notes and Bibliography, pp. 183-94. No index.

Originally published in Russian. Presents a logical foundation of the theory of correlation between two variables with emphasis on the role of probability theory. Applications excluded. Topics include a priori joint frequency-distribution; empirical material and coefficients; estimate of a priori coefficients; stochastic supposition of measurements; and object and value of correlation measurement. Appendix contains the derivations of mathematical formulas and equations used in the presentation.

Urbanik, K. LECTURES ON PREDICTION THEORY. Lecture Notes in Mathematics, vol. 44. Prepared for Publication by J. Rosenmuller. New York: Springer-Verlag, 1967. 50 p. No index.

A report on the mathematics of prediction consisting of such topics as positive definitive sequences; Herglotz theorem; vector valued measures; spectral decomposition and ergodic theorem; series representation; Wald decomposition; the Szego-Krein-Kolmogorov theorem; and predictors for completely undetermined sequences. Concludes with a mathematical presentation of the general prediction problem and the interpolation problem. Assumes knowledge of functional analysis and real analysis.

Von Mises, Richard. MATHEMATICAL THEORY OF PROBABILITY AND STATISTICS. Preface by H. Geiringer. New York: Academic Press, 1964. xiv, 694 p. Selected References, pp. 669. Tables, pp. 670-85. Index, pp. 687-94.

A text on the mathematical theory of probability and statistics with a prerequisite of real analysis and abstract algebra. Emphasizes the frequency theory of probability. Topics include random variables and their distributions and moments, including distributions of more than one dimension; Bernoulli's theorem; Markov chains; laws of large numbers; characteristic functions; asymptotic distribution of the sum of random variables; central limit theorem and Lindeberg's and Liapounoff's conditions; compound Poisson distribution; Bayes' theorem and limit theorems for Bayes' problem; multivariate normal distribution and various other distributions related to the normal; inference and estimation, including Neyman-Pearson method; regression and correlation; and introduction to the theory of statistical functions. Includes problems and references.

Waerden, Bartel Leendert van der. MATHEMATICAL STATISTICS. Foreword to the English edition by B.L. van der Waerden. Translated by Virginia Thompson and Ellen Sherman. New York: Springer-Verlag, 1969. xi, 367 p. Tables, pp. 339-58. Examples Arranged According to Subject Matter, pp. 359-60. Author and Subject Index, pp. 361-67.

Originally published in German in 1965. A text for a course in mathematical statistics. Topics include probability; random variables and their distributions; multiple integrals; beta and gamma functions; orthogonal transformation; quadratic forms; empirical determination of distribution functions; Fourier integrals and limit theorems; Gauss theory of errors and Student's t distribution; least squares; estimation of unknown constants; maximum likelihood and minimum chi-square; response curves; hypothesis testing; analysis of variance; most powerful tests; order statistics; and correlation. Proofs of difficult theorems omitted. Assumes knowledge of the theory of functions and of the Lebesque theory of integration. Important topics, such as sequential analysis, decision theory, and stochastic processes omitted.

Wald, Abraham. SELECTED PAPERS IN STATISTICS AND PROBABILITY. Edited for the Institute of Mathematical Statistics, Committee on the Wald Memorial Volume. T.W. Anderson, Chairman. New York: McGraw-Hill, 1955. ix, 702 p. Name Index, pp. 697-98. Subject Index, pp. 699-702.

A collection of most of the published research of A. Wald, except for books under his authorship. Also includes an essay, "The Life of Abraham Wald," and a discussion of his published works divided into the following sections: "Statistical Decision Function Theory and Sequential Analysis"; "Probability"; "Nonparametric Inference"; "Theory of Testing Hypotheses and Estimation"; "Analysis of Variance," and "Other Topics."

______. SEQUENTIAL ANALYSIS. Wiley Series in Probability and Mathematical Statistics. New York: Wiley, 1947. xii, 212 p. Appendix, pp. 157-207. Index, pp. 209-12.

A monograph on sequential analysis for students whose mathematical background does not go beyond college algebra and a first course in calculus. Knowledge of mathematical statistics helpful, but not necessary. Rigorous mathematical derivations contained in the appendix. Topics include sequential probability ratio test; sequential tests of simple and composite hypotheses against a set of alternatives; tests of the mean of a binomial distribution; difference between means of two distributions; that the mean of a normal distribution with known standard deviation falls short of a given value; and that the standard deviation of a normal distribution does not exceed a given value; the choice of a hypothesis from a set of mutually exclusive hypotheses; and sequential estimation.

Wasan, M.T. PARAMETRIC ESTIMATION. McGraw-Hill Series in Probability and Statistics. New York: McGraw-Hill, 1970. xiv, 256 p. Index, pp. 247-56.

A text for a one-year course on estimation theory for students who have knowledge of mathematical statistics and probability. Presentation rigorous with proofs of theorems and illustrative algebraic examples provided. Restricted to the univariate density case, and includes such topics as least squares and its application to problems of spacing in order statistics; completeness, including strongly complete families of probability measures; sufficiency; convex functions; unbiased estimation, including modal unbiasedness; lower bound of the variance of an estimate; maximum likelihood; Rao-Blackwell theorem; admissible and minimax estimation; and empirical Bayes methods. Omits such topics as confidence sets, fiducial inference, nonparametric estimation, estimation of parameters of multivariate densities, and estimation for stochastic processes. Includes examples. Chapters conclude with problems and references.

Weatherburn, Charles Ernest. A FIRST COURSE IN MATHEMATICAL STATISTICS. 2d ed. New York: Cambridge University Press, 1962. xv, 277 p. Literature for Reference, pp. 263-72. Index, pp. 273-77.

A text for a course in mathematical statistics for students from many disciplines who have knowledge of integral calculus. Emphasizes explaining the principles, deriving formulas, and discussing the validity of the results with numerous examples. Topics include properties of distributions and some standard distributions; regression and correlation; sampling theory; standard errors of statistics; beta and gamma distributions; chi-square with applications; tests of significance; variance ratio; Fisher's transformation of the correlation coefficient;

analysis of variance and covariance; multivariate distributions; and partial and multiple correlations. Chapters conclude with examples and references.

Wetherill, G. Barrie. SEQUENTIAL METHODS IN STATISTICS. 2d ed. Monographs on Applied Probability and Statistics. New York: Wiley, Halsted Press, 1975. x, 232 p. Appendix: The Normal Diffusion Process, pp. 213-14. References, pp. 215-27. Author Index, pp. 228-30. Subject Index, pp. 231-32.

A monograph on sequential analysis with emphasis on methods useful for practical applications. Proofs omitted except where needed for extensions or generalizations. Chapters conclude with problems, some of the research type. Topics include sequential probability ratio tests; sequential tests between three hypotheses; application of Cox's theorem; composite hypothesis; Wald's theory of weight functions; asymptotic tests; decision theory; sequential estimation of points on regression functions and of points on quantal response curves; double sampling; and selection procedures. Assumes knowledge of mathematical statistics.

Whitney, D. Ransom. ELEMENTS OF MATHEMATICAL STATISTICS. New York: Henry Holt, 1959. ix, 148 p. Tables, pp. 121-44. Bibliography, pp. 145-46. Index, pp. 147-48.

A text for a one-semester course in mathematical statistics for undergraduates who have completed a course in calculus through multiple integration. Topics include descriptive statistics; combinatorial probability and distribution functions; goodness-of-fit tests; methods of moments and maximum likelihood; confidence interval estimation; hypothesis testing against single and multiple alternatives; tests concerning the Poisson distribution; simple regression; and comparison of means and variances of two normal populations. Chapters conclude with problems and references.

Whittaker, Edmund, and Robinson, G. THE CALCULUS OF OBSERVATIONS. 4th ed. New York: Cambridge University Press, 1944. xvi, 397 p. Answers, pp. 385-88. Index of Names, pp. 389-91. General Index, pp. 393-97.

A treatise on mathematical problems which arise in dealing with numerical data with emphasis on analytical methods. Topics include interpolation with equal and unequal intervals of the argument; central-difference formulas; determinants and linear equations; numerical solution of algebraic and transcendental equations; numerical integration and summation; normal frequency distributions; method of least squares; Fourier analysis; smoothing of data; correlation; search for periodicities; numerical solution of differential equations; and the Rayleigh-Ritz method for minimum problems. Useful to workers in many fields:

astronomers, meteorologists, physicists, engineers, actuaries, biometricians, and statisticians. Chapters conclude with exercises and references.

Wilks, Samuel Stanley. COLLECTED PAPERS: CONTRIBUTIONS TO MATHEMATICAL STATISTICS. Edited by T.W. Anderson. Wiley Series in Probability and Mathematical Statistics. New York: Wiley, xxxii, 693 p. Samuel Stanley Wilks, 1906-1964, pp. vii-xxvi. No index.

A collection of all published articles (forty-eight articles) of S.S. Wilks arranged according to year of publication and a listing of his other publications such as reviews, discussions, and books.

______. MATHEMATICAL STATISTICS. Wiley Series in Probability and Mathematical Statistics. New York: Wiley, 1962. xvi, 644 p. References and Author Index, pp. 603-21. Subject Index, pp. 623-44.

A text for a course in mathematical statistics for students with a good undergraduate background in mathematics. Fairly comprehensive with emphasis on theory with verbal discussions kept to a minimum. Topics include k-dimensional random variables, their moments, and their distributions; sequences of random variables; characteristic functions and generating functions; discrete and continuous distributions; sampling theory; asymptotic sampling theory for large samples; linear statistical estimation; nonparametric tests; parametric estimation and hypothesis testing; sequential analysis; decision theory; time series; and multivariate statistical theory. Chapters conclude with problems.

Zacks, Shelemyahu. THE THEORY OF STATISTICAL INFERENCE. Wiley Series in Probability and Mathematical Statistics. New York: Wiley, 1971. xiii, 609 p. Commonly Used Abbreviations, p. xiii. References, pp. 583-601. Index, pp. 603-9.

An advanced text on statistical inference for graduate students and researchers in mathematical statistics who are proficient in probability and the theory of statistical distribution functions, and who have some knowledge of advanced stochastic processes; knowledge of advanced calculus, real variables, and functional analysis also helpful. Topics include sufficient statistics; unbiased estimation; the efficiency of estimators under quadratic loss; maximum likelihood estimation; Bayes' and minimax estimation; equivariant estimators; admissibility of estimators; testing statistical hypotheses; and confidence and tolerance intervals. Chapters conclude with problems and references. Presentation rigorous with proofs of theorems included.

Chapter 5

PROBABILITY AND STOCHASTIC PROCESSES

Aitchison, John, and Brown, J.A.C. THE LOGNORMAL DISTRIBUTION: WITH SPECIAL REFERENCE TO ITS USES IN ECONOMICS. University of Cambridge Department of Applied Economics Monograph 5. New York: Cambridge University Press, 1957. xviii, 176 p. References, pp. 146-53. Appendix A: Tables of Functions, pp. 154-65. Appendix B: The Results of Applying the Different Methods of Estimation to the 65 Artificial Samples, pp. 166-74. Index, pp. 175-76.

An exposition of the properties, examples, and applications of the lognormal probability distribution with special reference to its use in analyzing economic data. Topics include history; properties and genesis of the lognormal; artificial lognormal samples and tests of lognormality; estimation of parameters in two-, three-, and four-parameter distributions; lognormal distribution and profit analysis; comparison of lognormal populations; and examples and applications in biology, abundance of species, household size, astronomy, ages at first marriage, distribution of incomes, and consumer behavior. Assumes knowledge of elementary mathematical statistics.

Ash, Robert B. BASIC PROBABILITY THEORY. New York: Wiley, 1970. xii, 337 p. Tables, pp. 286-88. A Brief Bibliography, p. 289. Solutions to Problems, pp. 290-332. Index, pp. 333-37.

A text for a one-semester course in probability for graduates and undergraduates in mathematics, engineering, and physics who have knowledge of calculus. Measure theoretic concepts, although suggested in appropriate places, largely undeveloped. Topics include random variables and their distributions; moments of random variables; characteristic functions; infinite sequences of random variables; Markov chains; and an introduction to statistical inference. Presentation consists of theorem-proof-example-remark sequence. Sections conclude with problems.

______. REAL ANALYSIS AND PROBABILITY. Probability and Mathematical Statistics: A Series of Monography and Courses, vol. 11. New York: Academic

Press, 1972. xv, 476 p. Appendix: On General Topology, pp. 369-408. Bibliography, p. 409. · Solutions to Problems, pp. 411-67. Subject Index, pp. 469-76.

A text for a graduate course in modern probability for students who have had advanced calculus, and mathematical analysis. Includes reviews of measure theory, functional analysis, and topology. Topics include outline of an undergraduate course in probability from a measure-theoretic viewpoint; conditional probability and expectation; laws of large numbers; martingale theory; and the one-dimensional central limit theorem emphasizing the role of Prokhorov's weak compactness theorem. Presentation rigorous consisting of proofs of theorems, with exercises at the ends of the sections devoted to additional derivations.

Ash, Robert B., and Gardner, Melvin F. TOPICS IN STOCHASTIC PROCESSES. Probability and Mathematical Statistics: A Series of Monographs and Textbooks, vol. 27. New York: Academic Press, 1975. viii, 321 p. Appendix 1: Some Results from Complex Analysis, pp. 234-41. Appendix 2: Fourier Transforms on the Real Line, pp. 242-47. References, pp. 248-49. Solutions to Problems, pp. 250-318. Index, pp. 319-21.

A text for a course in stochastic processes for students who have a good background in measure-theoretic probability, strong law of large numbers, central limit theorem, and the basic properties of martingale sequences. Topics selective and include L^2 stochastic processes; prediction theory; ergodic theory with applications to real analysis, Markov chains, and information theory; sample function behavior of continuous parameter processes; the Ito integral and stochastic differential equations; martingales; one-dimensional Brownian motion; spectral theory; and the Shannon-McMillan theorem. Sections conclude with problems.

Barr, Donald Roy, and Zehna, Peter W. PROBABILITY. Belmont, Calif.: Wadsworth, 1971. xi, 414 p. Appendix: Tables, pp. 360-89. Solutions to Selected Exercises, pp. 391-405. References, p. 407. Index, pp. 409-14.

A text for a one-semester course in probability for undergraduate mathematics majors who have knowledge of advanced calculus and matrix algebra. Emphasizes the mathematical structure of probability theory, with applications from a variety of experimental situations. Topics include Kolmogorov axioms; conditional probability and Bayes' theorem; discrete probability models; random variables and their distributions; moments of random variables; conditional expectation; functions of random variables; multivariate normal distributions; sampling and asymptotic distribution, including order statistics; and stochastic processes. Sections conclude with both theoretical and practical exercises. Useful preparation for the study of mathematical statistics.

Bass, Jean. ELEMENTS OF PROBABILITY THEORY. Foreword to the English edition by E.W. Barankin. Translated by W. McKay. Translation edited by A. Jeffrey. New York: Academic Press, 1966. xiv, 249 p. Tables, pp. 219-24. Exercises, pp. 225-42. Bibliography, pp. 243-46. Index, pp. 247-49.

A text, originally published in French in 1962, for a one-semester course in probability and statistics for undergraduates in mathematics, engineering, and physics who have knowledge of linear algebra, multiple integrals, Fourier integrals, and complex variables. Develops a broad grounding in probability theory, followed by an exposition of stochastic processes (random functions), and the most commonly employed statistical methods. Verbal explanation extensive. Detailed illustrative examples provided.

Bates, Grace Elizabeth. PROBABILITY. Addison-Wesley Series in Mathematics. Reading, Mass.: Addison-Wesley, 1965. v, 58 p. References for Further Reading, p. 42. Appendix 1: Some Counting Principles, pp. 43-48. Appendix 2: Multiplication of Matrices, pp. 48-56. Index, pp. 57-58.

A short introduction to probability theory for finite sample spaces with applications in statistical decision theory of industrial sampling, medical studies, and Markov processes. Topics include probability measures; combination of events; conditional probability and independent events; probability trees; and the binomial distribution. Useful as a supplementary text in a probability course.

Bauer, Heinz. PROBABILITY THEORY AND ELEMENTS OF MEASURE THEORY. Translated by Lisa Rosenblatt. International Series in Decision Processes. New York: Holt, Rinehart & Winston, 1968. xiii, 427 p. Appendix: Continuous Mappings into the Circle, pp. 407-11. Bibliography, pp. 413-15. Index, pp. 419-27.

A text for a two-semester course in classical probability for students who have knowledge of advanced calculus and mathematical analysis. Measure theory used only to the extent necessary to deal with problems in probability. Consists of four parts: "Measure and Integration Theory"; "Probability Theory"; "Continuation of Measure and Integration Theory"; and "Further Development of Probability Theory." Topics include law of large numbers; measures on topological spaces; Fourier analysis; infinitely divisible distributions; conditional expectation; martingales; and stochastic processes. Emphasizes proofs of theorems. Sections conclude with problems.

Beck, Anatole, ed. PROBABILITY IN BANACH SPACES. Lecture Notes in Mathematics, vol. 526. New York: Springer-Verlag, 1976. vi, 290 p. No index.

Twenty-five papers presented at the first international conference on probability in Banach spaces held in Oberwolfach, West Germany, July 20-26, 1975. Topics include cancellation in Banach spaces; vector-valued martingales; functional central limit theorem in Banach spaces; the law of the iterated logarithm for Banach space valued random variables; distribution theory on Banach spaces; laws of large numbers on Banach spaces; and asymptotic behavior of martingales in Banach spaces.

Beckmann, Petr. ELEMENTS OF APPLIED PROBABILITY THEORY. Harbrace Series in Electrical Engineering. New York: Harcourt, Brace & World, 1968. vi, 189 p. Further Reading, pp. 181-84. Index, pp. 185-89.

An extract from the author's PROBABILITY IN COMMUNICATION ENGINEERING (Harcourt, Brace & World, 1967) containing only those parts of interest to engineers, physicists, and others going through a first course in probability. Assumes knowledge of calculus, but no previous knowledge of probability. Topics include conditional probability; theorem on total probability and Bayes' theorem; continuous random variables; characteristic functions and central limit theorem; random processes, including Markov chains; and queueing theory. Sections conclude with problems.

Behara, M; Krickeberg, K; and Wolfowitz, J., eds. PROBABILITY AND INFORMATION THEORY. Lecture Notes in Mathematics, no. 89. New York: Springer-Verlag, 1969. v, 256 p. No index.

Seventeen papers presented at an international symposium held at McMaster University, Canada, April 4-5, 1968. Topics include Boolean algebraic methods in Markov chains; maximums of partial sums; statistical mechanics; continuity of Markov processes; optimum rate of transmitting information; mixing in topological spaces; almost sure convergent constructions of weakly convergent processes; and maximum probability estimators with a general loss function.

______. PROBABILITY AND INFORMATION II. Lecture Notes in Mathematics, 296. New York: Springer-Verlag, 1973. 223 p. No index.

Nine papers presented at seminars sponsored jointly by McMaster University and the University of Montreal since 1968. Topics include uniform flows in cascade graphs; moments of point processes; additive and nonadditive entropies of finite measurable partitions; groups with Chu duality; and invariance of decision functions under Lie groups I.

Berman, Simeon M. THE ELEMENTS OF PROBABILITY. Reading, Mass.: Addison-Wesley, 1969. xiii, 224 p. Tables, pp. 200-205. Answers to Odd-Numbered Exercises, pp. 207-17. Index, pp. 221-24.

A text for a one-semester course in the axiomatic theory and application of probability requiring only a good high school algebra background. Use of symbolic notation minimized and one half of book devoted to the single model of tossing a coin n times. Topics include law of large numbers for coin tossing; normal approximation to the binomial; runs and the random walk; random variables for coin tossing; empirical frequencies; the geometric, Poisson, and normal distributions; sums and products of random variables; conditional probability; Markov chains; and application of the random walk to sequential testing. Chapters conclude with application exercises, questions about structures of proofs, and theoretical extensions and verifications.

Bharucha-Reid, Albert T., ed. PROBABILISTIC METHODS IN APPLIED MATHEMATICS. Vol. 3. New York: Academic Press, 1973. x, 346 p. Author Index, pp. 337-41. Subject Index, pp. 342-46.

The following five heretofore unpublished articles on the role of probability theory in applied mathematics: "Statistically Well-Set Cauchy Problems," by G. Birkhoff, J. Bona, and J. Kampe de Feriet; "Wave Propagation in Random Anistropic Media," by D. Dence and J.E. Spence; "Stochastic Processes in Heat and Mass Transport," by V.A. Lo Dato; "Potential Theory for Markov Chains," by R. Syski; and "One Some Stochastic Differential Games," by C.P. Tsokos and Wm. G. Nichols.

Billingsley, Patrick. CONVERGENCE OF PROBABILITY MEASURES. New York: Wiley, 1968. xii, 253 p. Appendix I: Metric Spaces, pp. 215-21. Appendix II: Miscellany, p. 222-32. Appendix III: Theoretical Complements, pp. 233-42. Bibliography, pp. 243-47. Summary of Notation, pp. 248-49. Index, pp. 251-53.

Presents methods of weak convergence of probability functions in metric spaces with applications to the space of continuous functions on the unit interval and the space of functions with discontinuities of the first kind. Other topics include derivations of a variety of limit theorems, including theorems characterizing Brownian motion, and diffusion processes. Assumes knowledge of measure theory. Chapters conclude with problems.

Birnbaum, Zygmunt William. INTRODUCTION TO PROBABILITY AND MATHEMATICAL STATISTICS. New York: Harper & Bros., 1962. viii, 325 p. Appendix A: Some Elementary Concepts of the Theory of Sets, pp. 305-9. Appendix B: The Inequalities of Schwarz and Cauchy, pp. 310-11. Tables, pp. 315-19. Index, pp. 321-25.

A text for a course in probability and mathematical statistics for students who know calculus and matrix algebra. Emphasizes careful formulation of assumptions and derivations. Topics include discrete and continuous n-dimensional random variables; transformations of random variables; mathematical expectation; characteristic function; regression and correlation; estimation; sampling of normal random variables; tests of hypotheses; chi-square; and nonparametric statistics. Omits the theory of random variables based on Stieltjes integrals. Includes examples. Chapters conclude with exercises. Useful mainly to mathematicians.

Bizley, Michael Terence Lewis. PROBABILITY: AN INTERMEDIATE TEXTBOOK. New York: Cambridge University Press, 1957. viii, 230 p. Appendix I: Well-Known Definitions and Theories of Probability, pp. 220-24. Appendix II: Tables, p. 225. Answers to Exercises, pp. 226-28. Index, pp. 229-30.

A text for a course in probability for actuarial students who have a working knowledge of calculus. Presents the calculus of probability nonrigorously using hypothetical examples and problems for illustrations. Topics include rules of combination of probability; theorems of Waring and Bayes; repeated trials; expectation; runs; and continuous random variables.

Blanc-Lapierre, André, and Fortet, R. THEORY OF RANDOM FUNCTIONS. Vol. I. Translated by J. Gani. New York: Gordon and Breach, 1965. xxi, 443 p. Mathematical Appendix, pp. 377-432. Bibliography, pp. 433-43. No index.

Contains the first seven chapters of a two-volume series on the theory of random functions with applications in physics originally published in French in 1953. Topics include axioms, basic concepts, and theorems of probability; multi-dimensional random variables; convergence of random variables; stochastic continuity, integrability, and differentiability of a random function; additive processes and functions with independent random increments; random functions derived from Poisson processes; Markov processes; permanent discontinuous and permanent continuous Markov chains; and additive functionals of a Markov process. Emphasizes mathematical rigor with almost all theorems proved and many illustrated with examples.

______. THEORY OF RANDOM FUNCTIONS. Vol. II. Translated by J. Gani. New York: Gordon and Breach, 1968. xx, 324 p. Bibliography, pp. 309-19. Cumulative Index, pp. 321-24.

A continuation of volume I treating such topics as harmonic analysis of random functions; energy properties of second order random functions; problems connected with harmonic analysis; second order stationary random functions; normal random functions; an application; random noise in communication theory; and random functions and the statistical theory of turbulence (by J. Kampe de Feriet). Useful as a text for a one-year course in random function theory and as a reference.

Bochner, Salomon. HARMONIC ANALYSIS AND THE THEORY OF PROBABILITY. California Monographs in Mathematical Sciences. Berkeley: University of California Press, 1960. viii, 176 p. Notes and References, pp. 168-72. General Index, pp. 173-76.

A tract on the relationship between Fourier analysis of finitely and infinitely many variables and probability theory. Topics include Fourier expansions; closure properties of Fourier transforms; Laplace and Mellin transforms; stochastic processes and characteristic functionals; and expansion of stochastic processes in series and integrals. Emphasizes rigor, knowledge of mathematical analysis assumed.

Borel, Émile Félix Édouard Justin. ELEMENTS OF THE THEORY OF PROBABILITY. Translated by J.E. Freund. Englewood Cliffs, N.J.: Prentice-Hall, 1965. xii, 179 p. Appendix One: Psychological Games and the Imitation of Chance, pp. 155-64. Appendix Two: Objective and Subjective Probabilities, pp. 165-73. Appendix Three: The Petersburg Paradox, pp. 174-77. Appendix Four: Table, p. 178. Index, p. 179.

A monograph, originally published in French in 1950, on both the mathematical and philosophical nature of probability as well as on some controversial issues, such as objective and subjective aspects. Consists of three parts: "Discrete Probabilities"; "Continuous Probabilities"; and "Probabilities of Causes." Topics include counting procedures; rules of probability; Stirling's formulas and other approximating formulas; law of large numbers; geometrical probability; arbitrary probability functions with applications to the kinetic theory of gases; law of Laplace-Gauss; choice in continuum; discrete and continuous probability distributions; with applications to births, mortality, urn models, and other problems. Includes fifty-one examples analyzed in detail. Assumes knowledge of multivariate calculus.

______. PROBABILITIES AND LIFE. Translated by Maurice Baudin. New York: Dover, 1962. vi, 87 p. Appendix One: On Recurrence of Figures in Winning Lottery Numbers, pp. 64-72. Appendix Two: On Poisson's Formula, pp. 73-74. Appendix Three: On Mortality Tables and the Statistics Relative to Causes of Death, pp. 75-83. Index, pp. 85-87.

A monograph, originally published in French in 1943, on the application of probability to problems of concern to the layman. Topics include probabilities and the general opinion; probabilities concerning life and death; negligible probabilities; events of small probability; the Poisson law; and applications to disease, accidents, and heredity.

Bose, R.C.; Chakravarti, I.M.; Mahalanobis, P.C.; Rao, C.R.; and Smith, K.J.C. ESSAYS IN PROBABILITY AND STATISTICS. University of North Carolina Monograph Series in Probability and Statistics. Chapel Hill: University of North Carolina Press, 1970. xviii, 750 p. No index.

Thirty-nine heretofore unpublished essays by eminent statisticians dedicated to the memory of the late Professor Samarendra Nath Roy. Topics include conditional test levels in large samples; generalized discriminant functions; estimating multinomial response relations; multivariate multiple comparisons; dependence in joint distributions; gammaization of the variance ratio; computation of the probability integral of the non-central chi-square; embedding for Hadamard matrices; fractional factorial designs; and Tchebycheff-type inequalities for matrix valued random variables.

Breiman, Leo. PROBABILITY AND STOCHASTIC PROCESSES: WITH A VIEW TOWARD APPLICATIONS. Boston: Houghton Mifflin, 1969. xii, 324 p. Table of the Cumulative Distribution Function for the Normal N(O,1) Distribution, p. 320. Index, pp. 321-24.

An applications-oriented text for undergraduate and graduate courses in probability for engineers and physical scientists. Proofs omitted unless necessary to understand applications of theorems. Topics include random variables and their distributions; conditional probability; Markov chains; continuous time Markov processes; independence of random vectors; multivariate normal distributions; and stationary time series. Sections conclude with problems.

Bunt, Lucas N.H., and Barton, Alan. PROBABILITY AND HYPOTHESIS TESTING. London: George G. Harrap, 1967. vi, 207 p. Answers, pp. 194-205. Index, pp. 206-7.

A text for a course in probability and hypothesis testing for students in nonmathematical fields who have an algebra background, and also for mathematics students who desire an introduction to probability before taking up advanced topics. Topics selected and treated in depth with the more rigorous sections marked with asterisks. Topics include descriptive statistics; permutations and combinations; rules of probability; binomial distribution; hypothesis testing; and the normal curve, including law of large numbers. Sections conclude with exercises from varied fields.

Burrill, Claude W. MEASURE, INTEGRATION, AND PROBABILITY. New York: McGraw-Hill, 1972. xiv, 464 p. Bibliography, pp. 455-56. Index, pp. 457-64.

A text for a one-year graduate course in measure and integration, including a measure-theoretic treatment of probability. Also useful for a one-semester course in measure and integration, or a one-semester course in probability. Includes numerous examples and exercises, some accompanied by elaborate suggestions for solution. Topics include metric spaces; measure and measurable functions; integration; differentiation; types of convergence; Hilbert spaces; characteristic functions; almost sure convergence; central limit theorem; martingales; and stochastic processes. Emphasizes mathematical rigor with proofs of theorems included.

Chapman, Douglas G., and Schaufele, Ronald A. ELEMENTARY PROBABILITY MODELS AND STATISTICAL INFERENCE. Waltham, Mass.: Xerox College Publishing, 1970. xix, 358 p. Appendix One: Summarization of Data, pp. 313-21. Appendix Two: Tables, pp. 322-38. References, p. 339. Answers to Selected Problems, pp. 341-53. Index, pp. 355-58.

A text for a one-semester course in basic statistics for non-mathematics majors in the natural and social sciences who have a high school algebra background. Topics include discrete random variables and their distributions, including one chapter devoted to the binomial; point estimation and hypothesis testing for the binomial; random sampling and descriptive statistics; expectation and variance for discrete and continuous distributions; normal and Poisson approximation to the binomial; point estimation and hypothesis testing for the normal; confidence intervals; joint probability; regression and correlation; chi-square; and nonparametric tests. Chapters conclude with problems and experiments.

Chow, Yuan-Shih; Robbins, Herbert; and Siegmund, David. GREAT EXPECTATIONS: THE THEORY OF OPTIMAL STOPPING. New York: Houghton Mifflin, 1971. xii, 141 p. Bibliographical Notes, pp. 130-32. Bibliography, pp. 133-38. List of Symbols, p. 139. Index, p. 141.

A monograph on the mathematical foundations of the theory of optimal stopping in discrete times together with examples. Assumes knowledge of measure-theoretic probability, including conditional expectation. Topics include martingales and Wald's lemma with application to the sequential probability ratio test; general theory of optimal stopping with applications to martingale theory; and the Markov and independent case. Chapters conclude with problems on proofs and derivations.

Chung, Kai Lai. A COURSE IN PROBABILITY THEORY. 2d ed. Probability and Mathematical Statistics. A Series of Monographs and Textbooks, vol. 21. New York: Academic Press, 1974. xii, 365 p. General Bibliography, pp. 358-60. Index, pp. 361-65.

A text for a one-year course in probability for graduate and advanced undergraduates in mathematics. Topics include measure theory; random variables and their moments; modes of convergence and uniform integrability; strong and weak laws of large numbers; characteristic functions with applications; central limit theorem; infinite divisibility; random walk; conditioning; Markov property; and martingales. Chapters conclude with exercises and bibliographical notes.

______. ELEMENTARY PROBABILITY THEORY WITH STOCHASTIC PROCESSES. Undergraduate Texts in Mathematics. New York: Springer-Verlag, 1974. x, 325 p. General References, pp. 306-7. Answers to Problems, pp. 309-21. Index, pp. 323-25.

A text for a two-quarter course in probability for students of mathematical sciences and engineering who have a working knowledge of calculus, although discrete distributions can be followed without calculus. Development based on set theory and covers such topics as discrete and continuous random variables; Borel fields and general random variables; conditioning and independence with applications to sequential sampling; mean, variance, and transforms; Poisson and normal distributions; Stirling's formula and De Moivre-Laplace's theorem; random walks and Markov chains with applications to Brownian motion and branching processes; Markov chains; and martingales. Emphasizes rigor, with theorems, corollaries, and propositions proved and illustrated. Chapters conclude with problems.

Ciesielski, Ž.; Urbanik, K.; and Woyczynski, W.A. PROBABILITY-WINTER SCHOOL. New York: Springer-Verlag, 1975. 283 p. No index.

Fifteen papers presented at the Fourth Winter School on Probability held January 9-19, 1975, in Karpacz, Poland, under sponsorship of Wroclaw University and the Polish Academy of Sciences. Includes survey, expository, and research contributions. Topics include noncommutative probability theory, random fields, and probabilities on linear spaces.

Cinlar, Erhan. INTRODUCTION TO STOCHASTIC PROCESSES. Englewood Cliffs, N.J.: Prentice-Hall, 1975. x, 402 p. Appendix: Non-Negative Matrices, pp. 364-81. References, pp. 383-85. Answers to Selected Exercises, pp. 387-92. Index of Notation, pp. 393-94. Subject Index, pp. 395-402.

A text for a course in stochastic processes for students in a variety of fields who have knowledge of calculus but no measure theory. Topics developed in depth with numerical examples worked out in detail. Presentation uses matrix algebra and recursive methods rather than transform methods. Topics include random variables and probability; expectations and independence; Bernoulli processes and sums of independent random variables; Poisson processes; Markov chains; limiting behavior and application of Markov chains; optimal stopping of Markov chains; renewal theory; and a limit theorem on the ratio of additive functionals of Markov processes. Chapters conclude with exercises.

Clarke, A. Bruce, and Disney, Ralph L. PROBABILITY AND RANDOM PROCESSES FOR ENGINEERS AND SCIENTISTS. New York: Wiley, 1970. xv, 346 p. Bibliography, pp. 338-39. Index, pp. 341-46.

A text for a one-year course in probability for undergraduates in engineering, the physical and social sciences, and management who have knowledge of the rudiments of calculus. Topics include sample spaces; combinatorial probability; random variables and random sequences; expectation and Bernoulli, binomial, geometric, Poisson, uniform, negative exponential, gamma, normal, and Cauchy distributions; two-state Markov sequences; discrete parameter Markov processes; eigenvalues and eigenvectors; nonirreducible or noninfinite Markov chains; continuous parameter Markov chains; limiting distribution of continuous parameter Markov processes; and queueing theory. Proofs not emphasized; examples provided. Chapters conclude with exercises.

Clarke, Lionel Edward. RANDOM VARIABLES. Longman Mathematical Texts. New York: Longman, 1975. ix, 185 p. Appendix A: Lebesgue Theory, pp. 154-58. Appendix B: The Extension Theorem, pp. 159-64. Appendix C: The Rieman-Stieltjes Integral, pp. 165-76. Appendix D: The Strong Law of Large Numbers, pp. 177-82. Further Reading on Probability, pp. 183-84. Index, p. 185.

An introduction to advanced probability for third-year college students of mathematics with emphasis on mathematical rigor. Topics include probability spaces; random variables; probability distributions; independence and characteristic functions; proofs of the main limit theorems for independent and identically distributed random variables; weak and strong laws of large numbers; and the central limit theorem. Chapters conclude with exercises.

Coleman, Rodney. STOCHASTIC PROCESSES. Problem Solvers 14. London: George Allen & Unwin, 1974. vi, 93 p. Recommendations for Further Reading, p. 91. Index, pp. 92-93.

A collection of problems with solutions grouped in the following eight chapters: "What is a Stochastic Process?"; "Results from Probability Theory"; "The Random Walk"; "Markov Chains"; "The Poisson Process"; "Markov Chains with Continuous Time Parameters"; "Non-Markov Processes in Continuous Time with Discrete State Space"; and "Diffusion Processes."

CONTRIBUTIONS TO ERGODIC THEORY AND PROBABILITY. Lecture Notes in Mathematics 160. New York: Springer-Verlag, 1970. viii, 279 p. No index.

Nineteen papers presented at the First Midwest Conference on Ergodic Theory held at Ohio State University, March 27-30, 1970. Emphasizes continuous flows in R^2 and orbit diagrams of such flows. Topics include existence of invariant measures in ergodic theory; approximation and spectral multiplicity; ergodic theory; ergodic measure preserving transformations on an infinite measure space; super-mean-valued functions on semipolar sets; liftings and derivation bases; weak ratio convergence of measures in infinite measure spaces; embedding Bernoulli shifts in flows; the Ambrose-Kakutani theorem and the Poisson process; generalized martingales; and local ergodic theorems for N-parameter semigroups of operators.

Cox, David Roxbee, and Lewis, P.A.W. THE STATISTICAL ANALYSIS OF SERIES OF EVENTS. New York: Wiley, 1966. viii, 285 p. Appendix I: Some Sets of Data, pp. 251-57. Appendix II: Asymptotic Significance Points for Some Distribution-Free Statistics, p. 258. Appendix III: Exercises and Further Results, pp. 259-67. Appendix IV: References, pp. 268-76. Author Index, pp. 277-78. Subject Index, pp. 279-85.

A monograph on point events occurring in a continuum, space, or time. Consists of description of the main methods, surveys of the problems in mathematical statistics that stem from such data, and applications in theoretical statistics. Events in questions consist of running time of machines; failures, breakdown or replacement of equipment; faults in a fabric; plants of a particular species distributed over an area, etc. Topics include the Poisson process; analysis of trends; stationary point processes; estimation of second-order properties of stationary processes; renewal processes; superposition of processes; and comparison of rates of occurrence.

Cox, Richard T. THE ALGEBRA OF PROBABLE INFERENCE. Baltimore: Johns Hopkins University Press, 1961. x, 114 p. Notes, pp. 99-108. Index, pp. 109-14.

First chapter derives the axioms of probability using Boolean algebra; the second chapter deals with entropy; and the third chapter examines the relationship between expectation and experience.

Cramér, Harald. THE ELEMENTS OF PROBABILITY THEORY AND SOME OF ITS APPLICATIONS. Wiley Series in Probability and Mathematical Statistics. New York: Wiley, 1955. 281 p. Appendix, pp. 263-64. References, p. 265. Solutions to Problems, pp. 266-72. Tables, pp. 273-78. Index, pp. 279-81.

An elementary treatise on the mathematical theory of probability with emphasis on the theory of random variables and their distributions. Includes applications to modern statistics with illustrative examples. Sections conclude with problems and complements. Assumes knowledge of analytic geometry, calculus, and algebra.

______. RANDOM VARIABLES AND PROBABILITY DISTRIBUTIONS. 3d ed., rev. Cambridge Tracts in Mathematics and Mathematical Physics, no. 36.

Cambridge: Cambridge University Press, 1970. viii, 118 p. Bibliography, pp. 115-17. Some Recent Works on Mathematical Probability, p. 118. No index.

Develops the axiomatic foundations of probability without applications in three parts: "Principles"; "Distributions in R_1 "; and "Distributions in R_2." Theory confined largely to problems connected with the central limit theorem for sums of independent random variables and some of its generalizations and modifications.

Cristescu, Romulus, and Marinescu, Gheorghe. APPLICATIONS OF THE THEORY OF DISTRIBUTIONS. Translated by Silviu Tjeleman. New York: Wiley, 1973. 227 p. References, pp. 226-27. No index.

Originally published in Romanian in 1966. Emphasizes applications for use by mathematicians, physicists, and engineers. Topics include Banach and Hilbert spaces; convolution of distributions; families of distributions; Fourier transforms; differential equations and integral equations; partial differential equations; and applications of distributions to electrical circuits, optics, random variables; stochastic processes, linear dynamic systems, and prediction. Some results given without proofs. Assumes knowledge of linear algebra, measure theory, and the theory of integrals of complex valued functions.

Davenport, Wilbur B., Jr. PROBABILITY AND RANDOM PROCESSES: AN INTRODUCTION FOR APPLIED SCIENTISTS AND ENGINEERS. New York: McGraw-Hill, 1970. xvii. 542 p. Bibliography, pp. 527-31. Index, pp. 533-42.

An applications-oriented text for a one-year course in probability and random processes for engineering students who have knowledge of calculus and Fourier analysis. Topics include sample points and sample spaces; probability; random variables, random vectors, and functions of random variables; properties and moments of random variables; estimators, including minimum-variance; prediction; random processes, including binomial and sine wave processes; linear transformations; spectral analysis; sums of independent random variables; and Poisson and Gaussian processes. Sections conclude with exercises, and chapters conclude references.

David, Florence Nightingale, and Barton, D.E. COMBINATORIAL CHANCE. Griffin's Statistical Monographs and Courses, no. 9. New York: Hafner, 1962. ix, 356 p. Glossary of Notation and Usage, pp. 347-51. Index, pp. 353-56.

Develops combinatorial theory for use by statisticians. Topics and applications include probability and moment-generating functions; expectation; limiting distributions and their properties;

distribution theory of runs; derangements and matching; multiple runs both in line and ring; multivariate moments and cumulants; runs of order; ranking tests on the random sequence; variants of the matching problem; combinatorial extreme-value distributions; occupancy; generalized Bernoulli numbers; approximations to differences of zero and to differences of reciprocal powers of unity; symmetric functions and polykays; and non-central distributions. Assumes knowledge of one year of calculus. Chapters conclude with references.

de Finetti, Bruno. THEORY OF PROBABILITY: A CRITICAL INTRODUCTORY TREATMENT. Vol. I. Foreword by D.V. Lindley. Translated by Antonio Machi and Adrian Smith. Wiley Series in Probability and Mathematical Statistics. New York: Wiley, 1974. xix, 300 p. Index, pp. 299-300.

Originally published in Italian in 1970. Deals critically with the various approaches to probability, emphasizing the idea that probability is a description of one's uncertainty about the real world. Contains few formulas and derivations. Chapter titles: "Introduction"; "Concerning Certainty and Uncertainty"; "Prevision and Probability"; "Conditional Prevision and Probability"; "The Evaluation of Probabilities"; and "Distributions." Topics include logical and arithmetic operations; digressions on decisions and utilities; zero probabilities; linear dependence; the continuity property; likelihood; stochastic dependence and independence; partitions into equally probable events; and limits of distributions. Useful to a wide audience, including philosophers, as supplementary reading. Knowledge of intermediate probability theory helpful.

_____. THEORY OF PROBABILITY: A CRITICAL INTRODUCTORY TREATMENT. Vol. II. Foreword by D.V. Lindley. Translated by Antonio Machi and Adrian Smith. Wiley Series in Probability and Mathematical Statistics. New York: Wiley, 1975. xviii, 375 p. Appendix, pp. 256-72. Index, pp. 373-75.

Originally published in Italian in 1970. Examines critically several prevailing views of probability and concludes that probability is always subjective. Frequency concept of probability replaced by idea of exchangeability. Presents a view of statistics based on a single concept of uncertainty. Topics include random processes with independent increments; law of large numbers; central limit theorem; Wiener-Levy process; stable distributions; ruin and ballot problem; Markov processes; inductive reasoning; mathematical statistics, including likelihood principle and Bayes' theorem; and statistical inference. Suitable for graduate seminars and for a mixed group of readers, including mathematicians and operation research workers.

De Haan, L. ON REGULAR VARIATION AND ITS APPLICATION TO THE WEAK CONVERGENCE OF SAMPLE EXTREMES. Mathematical Centre Tracts 32.

Amsterdam: Mathematisch Centrum, 1970. 124 p. References, pp. 123-24. No index.

A monograph on the extensions of the theory of regular variation for use in extreme value theory. Chapter titles: "Regular Variation and Related Concepts" and "Extreme Value Theory."

Derman, Cyrus; Gleser, Leon J.; and Olkin, Ingram. A GUIDE TO PROBABILITY THEORY AND APPLICATION. International Series in Decision Processes. New York: Holt, Rinehart and Winston, 1973. xvi, 750 p. Bibliography, pp. 663-70. Tables, pp. 671-716. Answers, pp. 717-42. Name Index, pp. 743-44. Subject Index, pp. 745-50.

An extensive elementary treatment of probability with emphasis on the needs and interests of research workers in the social and environmental sciences, and professionals in medicine, law, and business. Topics include random variables and their moments; a number of discrete and continuous probability distributions; multivariate distributions; weighted sums of random variables; and Markov chains, including first passage times, recurrent states, and long-run probabilities. Useful as a text for a one-year course with a prerequisite of college algebra. Chapters conclude with notes and references.

Deutsch, Ralph. NONLINEAR TRANSFORMATIONS OF RANDOM PROCESSES. Prentice-Hall International Series in Applied Mathematics. Englewood Cliffs, N.J.: Prentice-Hall, 1962. xi, 157 p. Appendix: Notes on Hypergeometric Functions, pp. 139-46. References, pp. 147-53. Index, pp. 155-57.

A reference on the theory and application (in communication and control) of nonlinear transformations of random processes assuming a prerequisite of statistical theory, probability, and noise theory. Includes following techniques for closed form solutions for statistical properties of the transformation process: envelopes and pre-envelopes; characteristic functions; correlation functions; multiplication and power law; and modulation and detection. Also includes techniques based on series representations, and differential and integral equations suitable for Markov processes. Concludes with a chapter on sampling and quantizing of a random process.

Drake, Alvin W. FUNDAMENTALS OF APPLIED PROBABILITY THEORY. McGraw-Hill Series in Probability and Statistics. New York: McGraw-Hill, 1967. xv, 283 p. Appendix 1: Further Reading, pp. 265-70. Appendix 2: Common PDF's, PMF's and Their Means, Variances, and Transforms, pp. 271-76. Index, pp. 277-83.

A text for a one-semester course in applied probability for a varied group of students who have at least one year of calculus. Emphasizes sample space representation of probabilistic processes and the need for explicit modeling of nondeterministic processes.

Topics include sample spaces and probability; random variables and their distributions; transforms and some applications to sums of independent random variables; probabilistic processes, including Poisson, Bernoulli, and renewal; discrete-state Markov processes; limit theorems; and an introduction to statistics, including estimation and hypothesis testing. Detailed examples often solved in separate sections. Chapters conclude with problems from a variety of fields.

Draper, Norman Richard, and Lawrence, Willard E. PROBABILITY: AN INTRODUCTORY COURSE. Chicago: Markham, 1970. xi, 231 p. Answers to Exercises, pp. 218-26. Index, pp. 227-31.

A monograph on probability for students with only a high shcool algebra background suitable as a supplementary text and a self-study. Topics include sets; sample spaces; Bayes' theorem; random variables and their distributions and moments; joint probability simple correlation and regression; law of large numbers; discrete Markov processes and random walks; and decision making using expectations. Includes proofs of theorems and illustrative examples. Sections conclude with exercises.

Dubes, Richard C. THE THEORY OF APPLIED PROBABILITY. Information Theory Series. Englewood Cliffs, N.J.: Prentice-Hall, 1968. xv, 506 p. List of References, pp. 471-74. Appendix 1: Tables, pp. 475-87. Appendix 2: Definitions of Limits, pp. 488-90. Appendix 3: Impulse Functions, pp. 491-96. Index, pp. 497-506.

A text for a course in probability for graduates and undergraduates in communication, control, cybernetics, and applied sciences who have knowledge of calculus. Includes extensive example and problem sets. Topics include random variables in one- and n-dimensions; expectation and characteristic functions; functions of random variables; sequences of random variables; including laws of large numbers and convergence in distribution; stochastic processes; harmonic analysis for nonrandom functions; harmonic analysis for stochastic processes; and n-dimensional Gaussian stochastic processes. Emphasizes proofs of theorems. Chapters conclude with problems.

Dudewicz, Edward John. INTRODUCTION TO STATISTICS AND PROBABILITY. New York: Holt, Rinehart and Winston, 1976. xii, 512 p. Statistical Tables, pp. 435-68. Selected References, pp. 469-70. Answers to Selected Problems, pp. 471-80. Glossary of Symbols, pp. 481-90. Author Index, pp. 491-94. Subject Index, pp. 495-512.

A text for a one-year course in mathematical statistics and probability for graduates and undergraduates in the mathematical sciences and related fields who have had at least a two-semester course in calculus. Knowledge of matrix algebra, set theory, and topology also helpful. Intended to fill the gap between theoretical and practical texts. Topics include naive set theory and probability; discrete and continuous random variables and their moments; multivariate distributions; Chebyshev and Markov inequalities; central limit theorem; laws of large numbers; point estimation; maximum likelihood estimation; asymptotic normality; Cramer-Rao inequality; tests of hypotheses; interval estimation; ranking and selection procedures; decision theory; nonparametric statistical inference; and regression.

Dwass, Meyer. FIRST STEPS IN PROBABILITY. New York: McGraw-Hill, 1967. xii, 282 p. Appendix A: Counting Methods and Series, pp. 252-72. Appendix B: Functions, pp. 273-75. Index, pp. 277-82.

A text for a one-semester course in probability for mathematics students requiring only elementary algebra. Constructs a mathematical model for chance experiments, including those based on cards, dice, coins, balls, etc. Topics include sample space; probability measures; random variables; expected value; frequency distributions for one and several random variables; law of large numbers; regression and correlation; central limit theorem; simple random walk; and a number of specific probability distributions. Exercises interspersed throughout the text. Chapters conclude with supplementary problems.

______. PROBABILITY: THEORY AND APPLICATIONS. New York: Benjamin, 1970. xvi, 413 p. Bibliography, pp. 405-8. Index, pp. 409-13.

A text for a one-semester undergraduate course in probability for students of mathematics who have had about two years of calculus, including multiple integration. Also useful for undergraduates and graduates in the natural and social sciences, engineering, and business. Topics include combinatorics; random variables; conditional probability and independence; generating functions discrete and continuous probability distributions; density functions; sums and products of random variables; limit laws; and stochastic processes. Chapters conclude with summaries, exercises, and notes.

______. PROBABILITY AND STATISTICS: AN UNDERGRADUATE COURSE. New York: Benjamin, 1970. xvii, 635 p. Bibliography, pp. 623-28. Index, pp. 629-35.

A text for a one-year course in probability and statistics for undergraduates and graduates in mathematics, social science, natural science, engineering, and business who have had at least one and one-half years of calculus. Topics include random variables; combinatoric problems; conditional probability and independence; generating functions; special discrete and continuous distributions; integrating density functions; sums of products of random variables; limit laws; stochastic processes, including random walk, Markov chains, and Poisson processes; estimation and testing hypothesis, including Neyman-Pearson theorem; sufficient statistics; dichotomous populations; linear models; analysis of variance; and nonparametric tests. Emphasizes derivations, both in text and in problems at ends of the chapters.

Dym, H., and McKean, H.P. FOURIER SERIES AND INTEGRALS. Probability and Mathematical Statistics. A Series of Monographs and Textbooks, vol. 14. New York: Academic Press, 1972. x, 295 p. Additional Reading, p. 282. Bibliography, pp. 283-87. Index, pp. 289-95.

A mathematical account of Fourier integrals on the circle and on the line, on finite commutative groups, and on a few important noncommutative groups. Omits purely technical aspects such as pointwise convergence of Fourier series of wild functions. Emphasizes the power and flexibility of Fourier's basic series and integrals, and applications include the isoperimetric problem, heat flow, wave motion, random walks, Poisson summation formula, central limit theorem, Heisenberg's inequality, Minkowski's theorem; Spitzer's identity, polynomial approximation, distribution of primes, and representations of the rotation group. Assumes knowledge of advanced calculus and complex function theory.

Eisen, Martin M. INTRODUCTION TO MATHEMATICAL PROBABILITY THEORY. Englewood Cliffs, N.J.: Prentice-Hall, 1969. xxi, 535 p. Index, pp. 525-35.

A text for a one-semester course in probability theory for graduates and undergraduates who have had a course in advanced calculus or measure theory. Topics include probability theory of discrete spaces; measure theory and integration, with applications to probability spaces; laws of large numbers; and classical limit theorems with examples. Emphasizes mathematical rigor, with theorems proved in detail. Sections conclude with exercises on additional derivations and on applications.

Ephremides, Anthony, ed. RANDOM PROCESSES II: POISSON AND JUMP-POINT PROCESSES. Benchmark Papers in Electrical Engineering and Computer Science. New York: Wiley, 1975. xii, 352 p. Selected Bibliography, pp. 343-44. Author Citation Index, pp. 345-47. Subject Index, pp. 349-52.

Fourteen papers previously published in journals and elsewhere on the theory of point and jump processes with emphasis on application to estimation, detection, filtering, and control. Grouped under four headings: "Poisson Models in Communication" (five papers); "Statistical Analysis and Applications of Noise" (three papers); "General Point Processes" (four papers); and "Martingale Representation" (two papers).

Ephremides, Anthony, and Thomas, John B., eds. RANDOM PROCESSES: MULTIPLICITY THEORY AND CANONICAL DECOMPOSITIONS. Benchmark Papers in Electrical Engineering and Computer Science. New York: Wiley, 1973. xi, 393 p. Author Citation Index, pp. 387-89. Subject Index, pp. 391-93.

Twenty papers previously published in journals and elsewhere in engineering and mathematical fields on random processes. Topics include linear least squares smoothing and prediction theory; analytic random processes; canonical representations of Gaussian processes and their applications; the structure of purely nondeterministic stochastic processes; linear filtering and prediction theory; multiplicity and representation theory of purely nondeterministic stochastic processes; stochastic processes as curves in Hilbert space; multivariate wide-sense Markov processes; nonsingular detection and likelihood ratio for random signals in white Gaussian noise; and canonical Hida-Cramér representation for random processes.

Epstein, Richard A. THE THEORY OF GAMBLING AND STATISTICAL LOGIC. New York: Academic Press, 1967. xvi, 491 p. Epilogue, pp. 431-33. Appendix: Tables, pp. 435-79. Author Index, pp. 481-84. Subject Index, pp. 485-91.

A unified and fairly complete mathematical theory of gambling heretofore found only in widely scattered sources. Topics include review of the theory; coins, wheels, and addments; coups and games with dice; the play of the cards; blackjack; contract bridge; weighted statistical logic and statistical games; and games of pure skill and competitive computers. Concludes with a chapter on fallacies and sophistries. Assumes knowledge of calculus and set theory.

Erdös, Paul, and Spencer, Joel. PROBABILISTIC METHODS IN COMBINATORICS. Probability and Mathematical Statistics: A Series of Monographs and Textbooks. New York: Academic Press, 1974. 106 p. References, pp. 103-6. No index.

A monograph on the probabilistic method for proving theorems in combinatorics. Includes Ramsey's and Van der Waerden's theorems; tournaments; Zarankiewicz's problem and bipartite Ramsey theorems; asymmetric graphs; imbalance problems; and a coin-weighing problem. Chapters conclude with exercises which vary in difficulty. Assumes knowledge of advanced probability.

Ewart, Park J.; Ford, James S.; and Lin, Chi-Yuan. PROBABILITY FOR STATISTICAL DECISION MAKING. Prentice-Hall International Series in Management. Englewood Cliffs, N.J.: Prentice-Hall, 1974. xiv, 385 p. Appendix I: Summaries, pp. 319-25. Appendix II: Tables, pp. 327-68. Answers to Selected Problems, pp. 369-78. Index, pp. 379-85.

A text for a one-semester course in probability theory for students who have knowledge of the rudiments of calculus, and a supplementary text for statistics courses. Topics include combinatorial analysis; sets and sample spaces; events; Bayes' theorem; random variables; discrete and continuous probability distributions; probability approximations; Chebyshev's inequality; decision criteria; value of information; and utility. Examples and problems demonstrate the application of probability.

Exton, Harold. MULTIPLE HYPERGEOMETRIC FUNCTIONS AND APPLICATIONS. Foreword by L.J. Slater. New York: Wiley, 1976. 312 p. Appendix A: Formulas Relayed to Multiple Hypergeometric Functions, pp. 284-92. Appendix B: Two Useful Computer Programs, pp. 293-95. Bibliography, pp. 296-304. Index of Applications, p. 305. Index of Symbols, pp. 306-8. Subject Index, pp. 309-12.

A comprehensive treatment of multiple hypergeometric functions--a generalization of the hypergeometric function of one variable. Includes both the theory and applications to statistics, engineering, celestral mechanics, asymptotic theory, operations research, telecommunications engineering, and heat conduction theory. Statistical applications include univariate distributions (beta and gamma functions); multivariate normal; Bayesian inference; and genetics. Appendix contains two computer programs for evaluating Lauricella functions. Useful to mathematicians, statisticians, engineers, and physicists.

Fehr, Howard Franklin; Bunt, Lucas N.H.; and Grossman, George. AN INTRODUCTION TO SETS, PROBABILITY AND HYPOTHESIS TESTING. Boston: Heath, 1964. x, 230 p. Appendix A: A Boolean Algebra of Sets, pp. 207-10. Appendix B: On Venn Diagrams, pp. 211-13. Appendix C: The Birthday Problem, pp. 214-17. Appendix D: The Multinomial Distribution, pp. 218-21. Tables, pp. 222-26. Index of Symbols, p. 227. Index, pp. 228-30.

A text for a one-semester course in introductory probability and statistics for students in their last year of secondary school and first year of college. Development based on sample spaces and set theory, with applications to hypothesis testing. Sections conclude with exercises carefully selected from science, psychology, and opinion pools. Assumes knowledge of high school algebra.

Feinsilver, Philip J. SPECIAL FUNCTIONS, PROBABILITY SEMIGROUPS, AND HAMILTONIAN FLOWS. Lecture Notes in Mathematics 696. New York: Springer-Verlag, 1978. vi, 112 p. Bibliography, pp. 109-12. No index.

A monograph on limiting distributions for sums of independent random variables in three parts: "Probabilistic Aspects"; "Analytical and Probabilistic Basis"; and "Extensions." Shows that many functions (in particular, many functions in physics) are limiting cases of the model of sequential independent coin flips. Discusses the relationships among five standard processes: exponential, symmetric, Bernoulli, Poisson, and Brownian motion. Provides a basis for the study of multiple stochastic integrals, and processes other than Brownian motion. Provides a method for analyzing systematically fairly general functionals of general probabilistic and quantum processes.

Feller, William. AN INTRODUCTION TO PROBABILITY THEORY AND ITS APPLICATIONS. Vol. II. 2d rev. ed. New York: Wiley, 1971. xxiv, 669 p. Abbreviations and Conventions, p. xv. Answers to Problems, pp. 651-54. Some books on Cognate Subjects, pp. 655-56. Index, pp. 657-69.

Useful as a text for a graduate course in probability and for independent study, and as a reference. Topics include probability densities and distributions; limit theorems; infinitely divisible distributions and semi-groups; the Laplace transform and its application; characteristic functions; applications of Fourier methods to random walks; and harmonic analysis. Chapter VI contains definitions and examples and serves as an introduction to the remaining thirteen chapters. Assumes knowledge of linear algebra, advanced calculus, intermediate probability theory, and abstract algebra.

Fellner, William. PROBABILITY AND PROFIT: A STUDY OF ECONOMIC BEHAVIOR ALONG BAYESIAN LINES. Books in the Irwin Series in Economics. Homewood, Ill.: Irwin, 1965. x, 239 p. Bibliographical Commentaries, pp. 210-33. Index, pp. 235-39.

An introduction to the study of subjective probability, utility, and profit based on the Bayesian approach. Topics include postulates underlying modern theories of utility and probability; economic theories of profit and rent; applications to simple and complex judgements, profit maximization, and average cost pricing; joint maximization and reformulated Cournot results in oligopoly; and liquidity versus risky returns. Assumes knowledge of probability theory.

Fine, Terrence L. THEORIES OF PROBABILITY: AN EXAMINATION OF FOUNDATIONS. New York: Academic Press, 1973. xii, 263 p. Author Index, pp. 253-55. Subject Index, pp. 256-63.

A presentation of the various theories of probability classified according to the following dimensions: domain of application, form of probability statements, relations between probability statements, procedures for measuring initial probability statements, and purpose of the theory. Theories include axiomatic comparative; Kolmogorov's calculus; usual relative frequency; Von Mises' relative frequency; Reichenbach-Salmon relative frequency; Solomanoff's complexity-based theory; Laplace's classical theory; Jaynes' classical theory; Koopman's comparative logical theory; Carnap's logical theory; and de Finetti subjective personalistic theory. Assumes knowledge of intermediate probability theory. Chapters conclude with references.

Fischer, Frederic E. BASIC CONCEPTS OF PROBABILITY: A PROGRAMMED APPROACH. Boston: Allyn & Bacon, 1969. vi, 218 p. Review Problems, pp. 210-14. Answers to Review Problems, pp. 215-16. Bibliography, p. 217. Index, p. 218.

A supplementary text for students majoring in any field except mathematics who wish to take statistics later. Consists of individual frames containing one or more blanks indicating the omission of one or more words (or symbols). Divided into eleven units: "Notation"; "Concept of Probability"; "Chance Experiments"; "Sample Spaces and Events"; "The Classical Definition of Probability"; "Counting Techniques"; "Probability of Compound Events"; "The Addition Law"; "The Multiplication Law"; "Mutually Exclusive and Independent Events"; "The Binomial Probability Distribution"; and "The Hypergeometric Probability Distribution."

Fraleigh, John B. PROBABILITY AND CALCULUS: A BRIEF INTRODUCTION. Addison-Wesley Series in Mathematics. Reading, Mass.: Addison-Wesley, 1969. vi, 250 p. Answers to Odd-Numbered Exercises, pp. 232-46. Index, pp. 247-50.

A text for a one-semester course in probability and calculus for mathematics students who have knowledge of high school algebra and geometry. Topics include set theory; probability, including random walks and the central limit theorem; real analytic geometry; functions; differential calculus; and integral calculus. Theorems proved and concepts illustrated with examples. Sections conclude with exercises; chapters, with references.

Fraser, Donald Alexander Stuart. PROBABILITY AND STATISTICS: THEORY AND APPLICATIONS. North Scituate, Mass.: Duxbury, 1976. xii, 623 p. Appendix I: Supplementary Material, pp. 511-98. Appendix II: Tables, pp. 599-604. Answers, pp. 605-14. Index, pp. 615-23.

A text for a one-year course in probability and statistics for students who have had one year of calculus, some multiple integration, and linear algebra. Likelihood function emphasized, with conditional probability given special and detailed treatment. Topics include probability; location and scaling of a distribution; moment-generating and characteristic functions; limiting distributions and limiting functions; law of large numbers; unbiased estimation; composite hypotheses; location and scale models; information inequality for unbiased estimators; regression; and design of experiments, including two-factor designs. Sections conclude with exercises and problems.

Freiberger, W., and Grenander, U. A SHORT COURSE IN COMPUTATIONAL PROBABILITY AND STATISTICS. Applied Mathematical Sciences, vol. 6. New York: Springer-Verlag, 1971. xii, 156 p. References, pp. 151-52. Index, pp. 153-56.

A monograph on computational aspects of probability and statistics using APL for students who have had courses in basic statistics, calculus, and linear algebra. Includes computer programs to perform numerous plottings and simulations for illustrating concepts and models. Topics include randomness, including random number generators; Monte Carlo simulations; limit theorems and the insurance model; stochastic processes, including Markov chains; growth models; random phase model; renewal processes; decision problems; a search problem; analysis of variance; Bayesian estimators; regression analysis of time series; and the fast Fourier transform. Useful to a mixed group, including those in mathematics, computer science, operations research, and economics.

Friday, Frank A. THE ELEMENTS OF PROBABILITY AND SAMPLING. Foreword by P.W.S. Andrews. New York: Barnes & Noble, 1967. xvii, 130 p. Bibliography, p. 128. Index, pp. 129-30.

Presents sampling and probability in a step-by-step reasoning process leading to solutions of problems of chance by means of combinations, permutations, and the normal curve and confidence limits without recourse to rigorous mathematical theory. Topics include addition and multiplication laws; finding the unknown; the normal curve; limits of confidence; meaning of probability and randomness; equally likelihood; and measurement by sample in which samples of different sizes are used to illustrate changes in the variance of the sample mean. Assumes knowledge of high school algebra.

Friedman, Avner. STOCHASTIC DIFFERENTIAL EQUATIONS AND APPLICATIONS. Vol. I. Probability and Mathematical Statistics: A Series of Monographs and Textbooks, vol. 28. New York: Academic Press, 1975. xiii, 231 p. Bibliographical Remarks, pp. 224-25. References, pp. 226-28. Index, pp. 229-31.

Develops the basic theory of stochastic differential equations based on probability assuming a prerequisite of conditional expectation, independence, and the Borel-Cantelli lemma. Chapter titles: "Stochastic Processes"; "Markov Processes"; "Brownian Motion"; "The Stochastic Integral"; "Stochastic Differential Equations"; "Elliptic and Parabolic Partial Differential Equations and their Relations to Stochastic Differential Equations"; "The Cameron-Martin-Girsanov Theorem"; "Asymptotic Estimates for Solutions"; and "Recurrent and Translent Solutions." Rigor emphasized.

_____. STOCHASTIC DIFFERENTIAL EQUATIONS AND APPLICATIONS. Vol. 2. Probability and Mathematical Statistics: A Series of Monographs and Textbooks, vol. 28. New York: Academic Press, 1976. xiii, 528 p. Bibliographic Remarks, pp. 520-22. References, pp. 523-26. Index, pp. 527-28.

Presents the following applications of the theory of stochastic differential equations: behavior of the sample paths of solutions of stochastic differential equations; applications to partial differential equations (Dirichlet problem for degenerate elliptic equations, singular perturbations, and degenerate parabolic equations); stopping times; stochastic games; and stochastic differential games. Chapters conclude with problems.

Gala, Basil E. THE COMPUTATION OF PROBABILITY WITH BASIC. San Francisco: Holden-Day, 1977. x, 179 p. Appendix A: Binomial and Poisson Tables, pp. 159-61. Appendix B: How to Run Your Program: Batch Processing, p. 162. Appendix C: How to Run Your Program: Time Sharing, pp. 163-64. Appendix D: Elementary BASIC Reference Manual, pp. 165-70. Appendix E: Extended BASIC Statements, pp. 171-75. Index, pp. 177-79.

A text for an undergraduate course in business and technical schools. Combines discrete probability and BASIC. Topics include probability and the BASIC language; sets, events, and probabilities; counting and combinatorial probability; random variables and empirical distributions; and the binomial and Poisson distributions. Traditional approaches to probability, such as coin tossing and dice throwing omitted. Sections conclude with programming exercises, and answers.

Gangolli, R.A., and Ylvisaker, Donald. DISCRETE PROBABILITY. Foreword by Salomon Bochner and W.G. Lister. Harbrace College Mathematics Series. New York: Harcourt, Brace & World, 1967. xii, 223 p. Appendix, pp. 205-19. Index, pp. 221-23.

A text for a first course in discrete probability, with calculus used primarily in the proof of the weak law of large numbers for sequences of independent and identically distributed random variables and for some of the problems. Useful to students of business, biological science, social sciences, and engineering as background for a course in statistical methodology. Topics include sample spaces, axioms of probability, conditional probability and independence, random variables, independent trials, expectation, sums of independent random variables, and random variables with a countable number of values. Sections conclude with exercises.

Gemignani, Michael C. FINITE PROBABILITY. Reading, Mass.: Addison-Wesley, 1970. iv, 122 p. Appendix: Finite Induction, pp. 110-11. Answers to Selected Problems, pp. 112-20. Index, pp. 121-22.

A supplementary text for courses in basic and intermediate

statistics and probability requiring only a high school algebra background. Includes set-theoretic development of the theory of probability for finite sample spaces with emphasis on motivation of the concepts as well as proofs of theorems and corollaries. Topics include review of set theory; relative frequencies; probability measures; selection with and without replacement; Bayes' theorem; random variables and expected values; and hypergeometric and rectangular distributions. Sections conclude with exercises.

Getoor, Ronald K. MARKOV PROCESSES: RAY PROCESSES AND RIGHT PROCESSES. Lecture Notes in Mathematics, vol. 440. New York: Springer-Verlag, 1975. v, 118 p. Bibliography, pp. 113-14. Index, of Notation, pp. 115-16. Subject Index, pp. 117-18.

Develops the basic properties of Ray processes and applies them to right processes. Useful to mathematicians and others familiar with the general theory of processes and, in particular, Markov processes.

Gillies, Douglas Angus. AN OBJECTIVE THEORY OF PROBABILITY. London: Methuen, 1973. x, 250 p. Appendix: Explanation of Technical Terminology, pp. 227-38. References, pp. 239-43. Index to Appendix, p. 245. General Index, pp. 247-50.

Presents a philosophical theory of probability based on the views of von Mises (an objective view) as opposed to subjective. Consists of three parts: "The Special Sciences in General"; "The Axiomatic Superstructure"; and "A Falsifying Rule for Probability Statements." Includes critical viewpoints of probability using few formulas.

Giri, Narayan C. INTRODUCTION TO PROBABILITY AND STATISTICS (IN TWO PARTS). PART I: PROBABILITY. Statistics Textbooks and Monographs, vol. 7. New York: Marcel Dekker, 1974. viii, 260 p. Appendix A: Vectors and Matrices, pp. 213-46. Appendix B: Statistical Tables, pp. 247-55. Index, pp. 257-60.

A text for a one-year course in probability for undergraduates in mathematics who possess a thorough knowledge of calculus and who have a special interest in statistics. Topics include classical and axiomatic definitions of probability; Bayes' theorem; random variables, probability distributions, and characteristic functions; stochastic convergence and limit theorems; and univariate, multivariate, and sampling distributions. Includes examples and exercises designed to make the mathematical treatment more understandable.

______. INTRODUCTION TO PROBABILITY AND STATISTICS (IN TWO PARTS). PART II: STATISTICS. Statistics Textbooks and Monographs, vol. 7. New

York: Marcel Dekker, 1975. viii, 314 p. Appendix A: Vectors and Matrices, pp. 251-97. Appendix B: Statistical Tables, pp. 299-310. Index, pp. 311-14.

A text for a one-year course in mathematical statistics for students who possess a thorough knowledge of calculus. Topics include order statistics and related distributions; parametric point estimation; statistical inference and tests of hypotheses; sequential analysis; nonparametric tests; and the general linear hypothesis and analysis of variance. Chapters conclude with bibliographies.

Gmurman, Vladimir Efimovich. FUNDAMENTALS OF PROBABILITY THEORY AND MATHEMATICAL STATISTICS. Translated by Scripta Technica, Inc. New York: Elsevier, 1968. vii, 249 p. Appendixes: Tables, pp. 236-44. Index, pp. 245-49.

Originally published in Russian. Consists of three parts: "Random Events"; "Random Variables"; and "The Elements of Mathematical Statistics." Includes proofs of elementary theorems using calculus. Topics include rules of probability; discrete and continuous random variables and their properties; law of large numbers; rules of combination of several random variables; sampling and distributions of parameters; computational methods of sample statistics; and introduction to statistical quality control. Chapters conclude with problems.

Gnedenko, Boris V. THE THEORY OF PROBABILITY. Translated by B.D. Seckler. New York: Chelsea, 1962. 529 p. Tables, pp. 485-500. Bibliography, pp. 501-9. Index, pp. 513-20. Answers to the Exercises, pp. 523-29.

Foundations of the mathematical theory of probability, originally published in Russian. Topics include various definitions of probability; sequences of independent trials; Markov chains; and the generalization of the DeMoivre-Laplace theorem to a sequence of chain-dependent trials; random variables and distribution functions and moments; the weak and strong laws of large numbers; characteristic functions; classical limit theorems; the theory of infinitely divisible distribution laws; the theory of stochastic processes; queueing theory; and statistical estimation and hypothesis testing. Assumes knowledge of calculus of several variables; and some mathematical analysis and matrix algebra. Chapters conclude with exercises devoted to applications, derivations, and additional proofs.

Gnedenko, Boris V., and Kolmogorov, A.N. LIMIT DISTRIBUTIONS FOR SUMS OF INDEPENDENT RANDOM VARIABLES. Translated, annotated, and revised by K.L. Chung. Addison-Wesley Series in Statistics. Reading, Mass.: Addison-Wesley, 1968. ix, 293 p. Appendix I: Notes on Chapter 1, by J.L. Doob, pp. 245-51. Appendix II: Notes on Paragraph 32, pp. 252-55. Appendix III: A General Weak Limit Theorem for Independent Distributions, by P.L. Hsu, pp. 256-83. Bibliography, pp. 285-89. Index, pp. 291-93.

Originally published in Russian in 1949. Useful as a reference, text, or supplementary text for advanced courses in probability. Consists of three parts: "Introduction"; "General Limit Theorems"; and "Identically Distributed Summands." Topics include random variables and their distributions; characteristic functions; infinitely divisible distributions; limit theorems for sums of independent summands and cumulative sums; convergence to normal, Poisson, and unitary distributions; and local limit theorems for lattice distributions. Presentation rigorous, with proofs of theorems provided.

Godwin, Herbert James. INEQUALITIES ON DISTRIBUTION FUNCTIONS. Griffin's Statistical Monographs and Courses, no. 16. New York: Hafner, 1964. 96 p. Exercises, pp. 89-93. Bibliography, pp. 94-96. No index.

A monograph dealing with the bounds which may be placed on the probability of random variables taking values belonging to some given set. Distributions include univariate, multivariate, and sums of variables.

Goldberg, Samuel. PROBABILITY: AN INTRODUCTION. Prentice-Hall Mathematics Series. Englewood Cliffs, N.J.: Prentice-Hall, 1960. xiv, 322 p. Answers to Odd-Numbered Problems, pp. 295-315. Index, pp. 317-22.

A text for a one-semester course in probability for students who have only a high school algebra background. Topics include sets and probability; Bayes' formula; counting techniques; random variables and their moments; joint probability; covariance and correlation; testing hypotheses; binomial distribution; and decision making under uncertainty. Emphasizes proofs and derivations, supplemented by illustrative examples. Sections conclude with problems; chapters, with references.

Goldman, Malcolm. INTRODUCTION TO PROBABILITY AND STATISTICS. New York: Harcourt, Brace & World, 1970. xv, 546 p. References, pp. 511-12. Appendix: Tables, pp. 513-25. Answers to Selected Exercises, pp. 527-40. Index, pp. 541-46.

A text for a one-year course for undergraduates in a variety of fields who have knowledge of calculus through multiple integrals, power series, and elementary differential equations. Topics include combinatorial and geometric probability; random variables; expectation; limit theorems; characteristic functions; stochastic processes; estimation; hypothesis testing; and mathematical models. Included under stochastic processes are such topics as first passage walks, arcsine law, potential-theoretic approach to recurrence of multidimensional simple random walks, and transformations of Gaussian processes. Proofs of key theorems provided; exercises and examples, representing a wide range of difficulty, are included.

Good, Irving John. THE ESTIMATION OF PROBABILITIES: AN ESSAY ON MODERN BAYESIAN METHODS OF PROBABILITY. Foreword by J.A. Stratton. Research Monographs, no. 30. Cambridge, Mass.: MIT Press, 1965. xii, 109 p. Appendix A: The Incompatibility of Fiducial and Bayesian Inference, pp. 81-83. Appendix B: Hausdorff Summation as a Monte Carlo Process, p. 84. Appendix C: Folded Contingency Tables, pp. 85-86. Appendix D: A Minimax Property of Singular Values of a Matrix, pp. 87-89. Appendix E: Learning from Experience in the Treatment of Contingency Tables, pp. 90-95. References, pp. 97-102. Index, pp. 103-9.

Review of Bayesian methods of estimating probabilities from small samples, with implications for tests of significance for multinomial samples and for contingency tables. Assumes knowledge of calculus and mathematical statistics. Emphasizes mathematical rigor accompanied by verbal descriptions.

Gray, James R. PROBABILITY. University Mathematical Texts. London: Oliver & Boyd, 1967. viii, 267 p. Answers to Exercises, pp. 263-64. Index, pp. 265-67.

A text for an introductory course in probability for undergraduates who have knowledge of calculus. Emphasizes the set-theoretic approach and considers such topics as generating functions; discrete and continuous random variables; occupancy problems; runs and matching; recurrence relations for probabilities; recurrent events and renewal processes; and Markov chains and queues. Proofs of theorems omitted, and derivations relatively short and simple. Chapters conclude with problems on the theory and its extensions.

Grenander, Ulf. PROBABILITIES ON ALGEBRAIC STRUCTURES. New York: Wiley, 1963. 218 p. Outlook, pp. 183-85. Notes, pp. 186-210. Bibliography, pp. 211-16. Index, pp. 217-18.

A monograph on the calculus of probability on algebraic structure, such as topological semi-groups and groups, topological vector spaces, and algebras. Based on probability measures that have a separable Hausdorff space. Emphasizes concrete results that can be used and that lead to solutions that can be determined analytically and numerically. Assumes knowledge of advanced probability, measure theory, functional analysis, and topology. Topics include historical background; stochastic semi-groups; stochastic Lie groups; probabilities on a Banach space; normal distribution in a Hilbert space; Fourier analysis in a stochastic Banach space; stochastic operators and random equations; and stochastic Schwartz distributions.

Guenther, William C. CONCEPTS OF PROBABILITY. New York: McGraw-Hill, 1968. xi, 384 p. Appendix A: Some Mathematical Results, pp. 330-48. Appendix B: Tables, pp. 349-67. Answers to Exercises, pp. 368-79. Index, pp. 381-84.

A text for a one-year course in probability for students with a college algebra background. Limited primarily to discrete probability with emphasis on derivations and applications. Topics include calculation of probabilities; survey sampling; Markov chains; expectation; continuous random variables and large-sample approximations; and estimation and hypothesis testing. Includes tables for computing probabilities. Balance achieved between examples and verbal discussion. Sections conclude with exercises consisting of both algebraic and numerical types.

Hadley, George F. INTRODUCTION TO PROBABILITY AND STATISTICAL DECISION THEORY. Holden-Day Series in Industrial Engineering and Management Science. San Francisco: Holden-Day, 1967. x, 580 p. Tables, pp. 571-76. Index, pp. 577-80.

A text for a one-year course in probability and statistics for students in engineering and the physical and social sciences. Topics include event sets containing a finite number of events; discrete random variables and their moments; theory of utility; single stage and sequential decision problems; Bayes' strategies; conditional probability models and joint distributions; continuous random variables; use of prior probabilities in decision problems with examples in oil producer wells, radio and textile manufacturing, and a tomatoe soup company's problem; classical statistical inference; stochastic processes; and multistage inventory problems. Sections conclude with examples; chapters, with references. Problems grouped according to the sections of the chapter.

Harding, E.F., and Kendall, D.G. STOCHASTIC GEOMETRY: A TRIBUTE TO THE MEMORY OF ROLLO DAVIDSON. Wiley Series in Probability and Mathematical Statistics. New York: Wiley, 1974. xiii, 400 p. Author Index, pp. 385-87. Subject Index, pp. 388-400.

Twenty-four contributions consisting of all of Davidson's published and most of his unpublished work on stochastic line processes, and a number of heretofore unpublished contributions to stochastic geometry, including the theory of random sets and the theory of random processes. Contributions grouped under the following seven headings: "Introduction" (one contribution); "General Theory" (eight contributions); "Special Problems" (seven contributions); "Stochastic Tree-Structures" (two contributions); "Navigation in the Presence of an Uncertainty" (two contributions). Topics include exchangeable point processes; invariance properties of the correlation measure of line processes; moments of point-processes; mean values and curvature; Poisson process; the elimination of edge effects in planar sampling; and the Fitzwilliam street problem.

Harris, Bernard. THEORY OF PROBABILITY. Reading, Mass.: Addison-Wesley, 1966. ix, 294 p. Appendix I: A Summary of the Algebra of Sets, pp. 251-55. Appendix 2: The Riemann-Stieltjes Integral, pp. 256-62. Appendix 3: Characteristic Functions, pp. 263-69. Appendix 4: Tables, pp. 270-82. References, pp. 283-86. Index, pp. 287-94.

A text for a first course in probability theory for undergraduates and graduates who have had a good course in calculus. Development begins with the Kolmogorov axioms, followed by the cumulative distribution function. Other topics include Rieman-Stieltjes integrals for moments and expected values; characteristic functions; random experiments, with emphasis on the empirical cumulative distribution function; distribution theory; and limit theorems. Proofs of theorems and illustrative examples included. Chapters conclude with exercises stressing applications.

Hastings, N.A.J., and Peacock, J.B. STATISTICAL DISTRIBUTIONS: A HANDBOOK FOR STUDENTS AN D PRACTITIONERS. New York: Wiley, 1975. xiii, 130 p. Bibliography, p. 130. No index.

Presents certain information related to twenty-five distributions, including diagrams of their shapes and other general properties. A consistent system of nomenclature used throughout. Fills the need for rapid access to information not readily available elsewhere. Distributions considered include normal, Poisson, binomial, lognormal, beta and gamma, chi-square, Cauchy, Erlang, exponential, extreme value; Weibull, hypergeometric; rectangular, power, multinomial, and F.

Haugen, Edward B. PROBABILISTIC APPROACHES TO DESIGN. New York: Wiley, 1968. 323 p. References, pp. 315-16. Index, pp. 317-23.

A text for a course in engineering design for students who have knowledge of calculus. Consists of two parts: "Foundation" and "Applications." Topics include probability; discrete and continuous random variables and their distributions; point estimation; distribution functions; method of partial derivatives; special correlation combinations; laws of combinations; Monte Carlo methods; reliability; numerical methods; and applications in mechanics, simple beams, cantilever beams, column design, torsion, and electromechanical devices. Chapters conclude with problems.

Hausner, Melvin. ELEMENTARY PROBABILITY THEORY. Harper's Series in Modern Mathematics. New York: Harper & Row, 1971. viii, 310 p. Appendixes: Tables, pp. 276-85. Answers to Selected Odd-Numbered Exercises, pp. 290-303. Index, pp. 307-10.

A text for a one-semester, precalculus introduction to probability theory for mathematics students. Emphasizes mathematical rigor while still maintaining motivation. Topics include finite probability spaces; combinatorics; set theory; independence and conditional probability; random variables; Chebyshev's theorem; law of large numbers; binomial distribution; normal density and the normal approximation to the binomial; and standard deviation. Numerous applications included. Includes exercises which deal with simple applications.

Heathcore, Christopher Robin. PROBABILITY: ELEMENTS OF THE MATHEMATICAL THEORY. New York: Wiley, Interscience, 1971. xii, 267 p. Answers to Selected Exercises, pp. 257-62. Index, pp. 263-67.

A text for an undergraduate course in probability theory for students who have had a one year course in calculus and real variables. Emphasizes both theory and applications. Some theorems presented without proofs. Topics include probability spaces and random variables; real variable theory; several random variables; weak convergence; almost sure convergence; and Markov processes. Sections conclude with exercises.

Hines, William W., and Montgomery, Douglas C. PROBABILITY AND STATISTICS IN ENGINEERING AND MANAGEMENT SCIENCE. New York: Ronald Press, 1972. xii, 509 p. References, pp. 465-68. Appendix: Tables, pp. 471-503. Index, pp. 505-9.

A text for an introductory course in probability and statistics for students in engineering, management science, and operations research who have knowledge of calculus, linear algebra, and matrices. Emphasizes development of formal statistical background required for model formulation and analysis. Over 250 examples and 500 exercises included. Topics include one-dimensional random variables; functions of one random variable and expectation; higher-dimensional random variables; discrete distributions, including geometric, pascal, multinomial, hypergeometric, Poisson, and binomial; continuous distributions; including exponential, gamma, Weibull, and uniform; sampling and descriptive statistics; principle of statistical inference, including Neyman-Pearson lemma, likelihood ratio tests; tests of hypothesis, and estimation; analysis of variance; regression analysis; design of experiments; control and reliability; and statistical decision theory.

Hodges, Joseph Lawson, Jr., and Lehman, E.L. ELEMENTS OF FINITE PROBABILITY. Holden-Day Series in Probability and Statistics. San Francisco: Holden-Day, 1965. vi, 230 p. Tables, pp. 216-21. Index, pp. 223-27. Example Index, pp. 229-30.

A text for a one-semester course in finite probability at the precalculus level for a varied group of students who have knowledge of only high school algebra. Style consists of problem-definition-example sequence. Sections conclude with up to one dozen problems each. Topics include probability models; sampling; product models; conditional probability; random variables; special distributions, including hypergeometric, Poisson, uniform, and normal; and multivariate distributions.

Hoel, Paul G.; Port, Sidney C.; and Stone, Charles J. INTRODUCTION TO PROBABILITY THEORY. Boston: Houghton Mifflin, 1971. xi, 258 p. Answers to Exercises, pp. 239-50. Table I, pp. 252-53. Index, pp. 255-58.

A text for a one-semester course in probability at the senior level with a prerequisite of elementary calculus and multiple integration. Designed to provide adequate preparation for either a course in statistics or further study in probability and stochastic processes. Topics include probability spaces; combinatorial analysis; discrete and continuous random variables and their moments; jointly distributed random variables; central limit theorem; moment-generating functions and characteristic functions; and random walks and Poisson processes. Many theorems proved and illustrated with examples. Chapters conclude with exercises, some of which extend the ideas developed in the text.

Hogben, Lancelot. STATISTICAL THEORY: THE RELATIONSHIP OF PROBABILITY, CREDIBILITY AND ERROR: AN EXAMINATION OF THE CONTEMPORARY CRISIS IN STATISTICAL THEORY FROM A BEHAVIOURIST VIEWPOINT. New York: W.W. Norton, 1971. 510 p. Appendix I: Central Limit Theorem, pp. 477-79. Appendix II: The Umpire Bonus Model, pp. 480-84. Appendix III: Determinant Notation, pp. 485-86. Appendix IV: Significance as Interpreted by the School of R.A. Fisher, pp. 487-506. Index, pp. 507-10.

A critical examination of four modern statistical methods: calculus of error, as propounded by Legendre, Laplace, and Gauss; calculus of aggregates, including the kinetic theory of gases and the genetical theory of population; calculus of exploration (regression and factor analysis); and calculus of judgements (inference and hypothesis testing). Emphasizes the growing gap between statistical theory and reality using only a few formulas.

Hogg, Robert V., and Tanis, Elliot A. PROBABILITY AND STATISTICAL INFERENCE. New York: Macmillan, 1977. ix, 450 p. References, pp. 415-16. Appendix: Tables, pp. 417-33. Answers to Selected Exercises, pp. 435-46. Index, pp. 447-50.

A text for a one-year course in probability and statistics for mathematics students who have had one year of calculus. Style consists of definition-derivation-example sequence, with several numerical and algebraic examples often used to illustrate a single concept. Computer printouts for some examples included. Topics include conditional probability and Bayes' formula; random variables and their distributions; moment-generating functions; empirical distribution; continuous probability distributions; sums of independent random variables; nonparametric tests; parametric tests of hypotheses; multivariate distributions; chi-square; two-factor analysis of variance; comparisons of several distributions; transformations of random variables; best critical regions; likelihood ratio tests; sufficient statistics; decision theory; order statistics; and maximum likelihood estimation. Sections conclude with exercises.

Hoyt, John P. A BRIEF INTRODUCTION TO PROBABILITY THEORY. Scranton, Pa.: International Textbook, 1967. viii, 151 p. Answers to Exercises, pp. 143-48. Index, pp. 149-51.

A self-study and supplementary text for anyone who has completed a course in calculus. Emphasizes random variables (Bernoulli, binomial, Poisson, and normal). Probability distributions obtained by means of probability-generating functions (discrete case) and moment-generating functions (continuous case). Proofs kept simple or omitted. Concludes with two chapters on statistics for illustrating applications of probability theory to decision making.

Hymans, Saul H. PROBABILITY THEORY WITH APPLICATIONS TO ECONOMETRICS AND DECISION-MAKING. Prentice-Hall International Series in Management. Englewood Cliffs, N.J.: Prentice-Hall, 1967. xvii, 333 p. Appendix, pp. 311-27. Index, pp. 329-33.

A text for a one-semester course in quantitative methods for students of economics and business who have only a high school algebra background. Topics include set theory; random variables and their distributions; binomial; converging binomial distribution; classical estimation theory; simple regression; Bayesian analysis; and inventories. Proofs omitted and detailed examples provided. Chapters conclude with exercises.

Isaacson, Dean L., and Madsen, Richard W. MARKOV CHAINS THEORY AND APPLICATIONS. Wiley Series in Probability and Mathematical Statistics. New York: Wiley, 1976. x, 256 p. References, pp. 249-51. Index, pp. 253-56.

A text for a one-semester graduate or undergraduate course in Markov chains for students in a variety of disciplines who have knowledge of advanced calculus, elementary probability theory, and linear algebra. Important results illustrated by examples and exercises. Emphasizes discrete Markov chains with an entire chapter devoted to applications in various fields. Topics include Markov property and transition matrices; the classical and algebraic approaches to Markov chains, including renewal theory, absorption times, absorption probabilities, and ratio limit theorems; nonstationary Markov chains and the ergodic coefficient, including weak, strong, and C-strong ergodicity; analysis of Markov chains on computers; and continuous-time Markov chains, including the transition function and birth and death processes.

Jansson, Birger. RANDOM NUMBER GENERATORS. Stockholm: Almqvist and Wiksell, 1966. 205 p. Bibliography, pp. 195-205. No index.

A monograph on the history and development of random number generators. Topics include random number generators from rectangular distributions (dice-like methods, tables of random numbers, physical devices, arithmetic procedures, and digits of transcendental numbers); methods for generating sequences of numbers (Fibonacci multiplicative, mixed congruential, and middle-square); samples produced by generators and descriptions of statistical tests used for studying random number generators; theorems, variances, and serial correlation coefficients for different lags within sequences of numbers generated by the mixed and the multiplicative congruential generators; distributions of sequences of deterministic numbers reduced modulo, joint distribution multiplicative and mixed congruential generators, runs up and down, pseudo-random sequences considered as permutations, and pseudo-random numbers from various non-rectangular distributions such as exponential, univariate, bivariate normal, and multivariate normal. Includes numerical results of number generators. Assumes knowledge of number theory and mathematical statistics.

Jeffreys, Harold. THEORY OF PROBABILITY. 3d ed. International Series of Monographs on Physics. Oxford, Engl.: Clarendon Press, 1961. x, 447 p. Appendix A: Mathematical Theorems, pp. 425-31. Appendix B: Tables of K, pp. 432-41. Index, pp. 443-47.

An exposition of methods of drawing inferences from observational data based on theoretical probability distributions for experimental work in physics. Topics include rules of probability; distributions, including Poisson, normal, rectangular, chi-square, parabolic, negative binomial and binomial; prior probabilities; characteristic functions; limit theorems, including central limit theorem; estimation of parameters, including least squares and the Pitman-Koopman theorem concerning the existence of sufficient statistics; maximum likelihood, orthogonal parameters, smoothing of observed data, and rank correlation; significance test; one parameter, and various complications in the two-parameter case; and frequency definitions and direct methods. Presentation assumes knowledge of advanced calculus and provides derivations with considerable descriptive and intuitive justifications, as well as examples from physics.

Jelinek, Frederick. PROBABILISTIC INFORMATION THEORY. DISCRETE AND MEMORYLESS MODELS. McGraw-Hill Series in Systems Science. New York: McGraw-Hill, 1968. xiv, 609 p. List of Symbols, pp. xiii-xiv. Appendix A: Variable-Length Encoding of Fixed-Rate Sources, pp. 451-89. Appendix B: The Strong Converse and Systematic Construction of Good Codes, pp. 490-509. Appendix C: Inequalities Useful in Probability of Error Estimation, pp. 510-18. Appendix D: Constrained Optimization of Concave Function, pp. 519-29. Appendix E: Lower Bounds for Sequential Decoding, pp. 530-47. Appendix F: Buffer Overflow and the Probability of Deficient Sequential Decoding of Finite-Constraint-Length Codes, pp. 548-65. Appendix G: Tables of Functions, pp. 566-76. Bibliography, pp. 577-87. Index of Definitions, Tables, Figures, Lemmas, and Theorems, pp. 589-93. Name Index, pp. 595-98. Subject Index, pp. 599-609.

A text for a one-semester course in information theory for graduates who have knowledge of probability theory and calculus. Topics include transmission of information; digital sources and their encoding; the entropy functions and some applications of its properties to coding; moment-generating functions and performance bounds for source block codes; transmission of messages through discrete memoryless channels; upper and lower bounds to probability of decoding errors; systematic codes; sequential decoding; and transmission of information within an allowed distortion tolerance. Appendixes devoted to advanced topics based on Shannon's approach. Chapters conclude with problems and complements.

Johnson, Leonard G. THEORY AND TECHNIQUE OF VARIATION RESEARCH. New York: Elsevier, 1964. vii, 105 p. References, p. 101. Subject Index, pp. 102-5. Appendix: Tables (attached).

Presents variational research for statistics with emphasis on the graphical approach using probability paper. Useful to industrial personnel who have limited formal training in statistics. Topics include confidence limits for cumulative distribution functions; comparing two samples; multivariate analysis; including main effects and interactions and random balance experimentation; graphical variational research, including graphical portrayal of interaction in analysis of variance; prediction equations; summational algebra with applications to curve fitting; order statistics in variational research; and the theory of incomplete tests. Chapters conclude with exercises.

Johnson, Norman L., and Kotz, Samuel. URN MODELS AND THEIR APPLICATION: AN APPROACH TO MODERN DISCRETE PROBABILITY THEORY. New York: Wiley, 1977. xiii, 402 p. Author Index, pp. 387-91. Subject Index, pp. 393-400. Urn Models Index, pp. 401-2.

A text for a one-semester course in probability theory and for probability seminars for students who have knowledge of college algebra and a working knowledge of calculus. Demonstrates that many results in probability can be derived from simple urn models. Topics include special distributions via urn models; occupancy and related problems; urn models with stochastic replacement; applications to genetics, capture-recapture models, learning processes, and computer theory; and limit distributions for urn models. Sections conclude with exercises.

Johnston, John B.; Price, G. Bailey; and Van Vleck, Fred S. SETS, FUNCTIONS, AND PROBABILITY. Addison-Wesley Series in Behavioral Sciences: Quantitative Methods. Reading, Mass.: Addison-Wesley, 1968. viii, 376 p. Answers to Selected Problems, pp. 341-62. Index, pp. 365-76.

A text for an introductory course in finite probability theory and applications for students in the biological, management, and social sciences who have knowledge of only high school algebra. Topics include review of sets, functions, and counting methods; probability spaces, applications to urn models, acceptance sampling, zoological sample census, cell occupancy problems, and matching problems; conditional probability and independence, with applications to genetics; random variables and their distributions and moments; the bakery chain problem; and learning models. Few theorems proved. Sections conclude with exercises; chapters, with biographical notes and biographies.

Kac, Mark. STATISTICAL INDEPENDENCE IN PROBABILITY, ANALYSIS AND NUMBER THEORY. Carus Mathematical Monographs, no. 12. New York: Wiley, for the Mathematical Association of America, 1959. xiv, 93 p. No index.

A mongraphy dealing with the notion of statistical independence, with a concluding chapter on the application of ergodic theory to continued fractions. Assumes knowledge of Lebesgue theory of measure and integration, elementary theory of Fourier integrals, and rudiments of number theory. Complicated proofs omitted. Topics include Vieta's formula, coin tossing experiments, laws of large numbers, convergence and divergence of series with random signs, DeMoivre's law, the normal law in number theory, the Euler ϕ - Function, and the Riesz-Fischer theorem. Includes problems. Chapters conclude with bibliographies.

Kahane, Jean Pierre. SOME RANDOM SERIES OF FUNCTIONS. Heath Mathematics Monographs. Lexington, Mass.: Heath, 1968. viii, 184 p. Notes, pp. 175-79. Bibliography, pp. 180-82. Index, pp. 183-84.

A monograph for research workers on the application of Fourier methods to the study of stochastic processes such as Gaussian stationary processes, Brownian motion, random intervals on the circle, and random point-masses on the circle. Assumes knowledge of probability, Banach spaces, Hilbert spaces, and Fourier series. Limited to stochastic series of randomly independent functions.

Kalinin, Velentin Mikhaĭlovich, and Shalaevskii, O.V. INVESTIGATIONS IN CLASSICAL PROBLEMS OF PROBABILITY THEORY AND MATHEMATICAL STATISTICS. Part I. Seminars in Mathematics, vol. 13. New York: Consultants Bureau, 1971. viii, 141 p. No index.

Three contributions which describe some of the work being carried out at the Laboratory for Statistical Methods of the V.A. Steklov Mathematical Institute in Leningrad: "Special Functions and the Limit Properties of Probability Distributions I," by V.M. Kalinin; "Minimax Character of Hotelling's T^2 Test. I," by O.V. Shalaevskii; and "Minimax Character of the R^2 Test. I," by O.V. Shalaevskii.

Karlin, Sameul, and Studden, William J. TCHEBYCHEFF SYSTEMS: WITH APPLICATIONS IN ANALYSIS AND STATISTICS. Pure and Applied Mathematics. A Series of Texts and Monographs, vol. XV. New York: Wiley, 1966. xviii, 586 p. Bibliography, pp. 566-78. Author Index, pp. 579-81. Subject Index, pp. 583-86.

A research monograph on the theory of the Tchebycheff system (T-system). Topics include moment spaces induced by T-systems and their duals; the Markov-Krein theorem; classical moment spaces; moment spaces for T-systems defined on discrete sets; moment spaces generated by restricted measures; the Markoff-Bernstein inequality; problems of best interpolating systems, maximization of moment determinants, and applications to optimum experimental designs; generalized Tchebycheff inequalities; multivariate Tchebycheff inequalities; and Tchebycheff-type inequalities for sums of random variables and nonlinear problems.

Kawata, Tatsuo. FOURIER ANALYSIS IN PROBABILITY THEORY. Probability and Mathematical Statistics. A Series of Monographs and Textbooks, vol. 15. New York: Academic Press, 1972. xii, 668 p. References, pp. 642-60. Index, pp. 661-68.

A text for a graduate course in probability for students who have knowledge of complex function theory, measure theory, and probability theory. Uses results from Fourier series, Fourier transforms, Laplace transforms, and related topics in the analytic theory of probability. Other topics include characteristic functions of probability distributions; convergence of distribution functions in terms of characteristic functions; and series of independent random variables. Emphasizes the measure-theoretic approach requiring knowledge of advanced calculus and real analysis. Chapters conclude with notes.

Keilson, Julian. GREEN'S FUNCTION METHODS IN PROBABILITY THEORY. Griffin's Statistical Monographs and Courses, no. 17. New York: Hafner, 1965. viii, 220 p. Bibliography, pp. 199-204. Supplementary Notes, pp. 205-17. Index, pp. 218-20.

Presents the theory and application of Markov processes which are homogeneous in space and time and the family of related inhomogeneous Markov processes induced by boundaries. Assumes knowledge of probability theory, stochastic processes, and complex variables. Topics include homogeneous Markov processes on the lattice and continuum for discrete and continuous time; structure of associated ergodic Green's functions of potential theory; conjugate transformation and asymptotic behavior in space and time; the passage problem for homogeneous skip-free processes; bounded processes and Green's theorem; ergodic distribution; ruin problems and extremes; and processes with representation of finite dimension. Applications discussed in detail.

Kempthorne, Oscar, and Folks, Leroy. PROBABILITY, STATISTICS, AND DATA ANALYSIS. Ames: Iowa State University Press, 1971. xvii, 555 p. Appendix: Tables, pp. 513-30. Bibliography, pp. 531-43. Index, pp. 545-55.

An applications-oriented text for a one-year course in statistics for students in mathematics, physical sciences, and engineering who have knowledge of calculus. Also suitable preparation for specialized courses in sample surveys, design of experiments, econometrics, psychometrics, and statistical theory. Topics include discrete probability; nature of real populations; commonly occurring probability distributions; distribution of functions of random variables; distribution of sample statistics; stochastic processes, including Markov and Poisson; chi-square; parametric models and likelihood; decision making; and simple regression and analysis of variance. Chapters conclude with problems.

Kendall, Maurice G., and Moran, P.A.P. GEOMETRICAL PROBABILITY. Griffin's Statistical Monographs and Courses, no. 10. New York: Hafner, 1963. 125 p. Bibliography, pp. 119-24. Index, p. 125.

A monograph on the theory and application of geometrical probability useful to scientists of all kinds. Consists of the following five chapters: "Distributions of Geometrical Elements"; "Distributions of Points in Euclidean Space"; "Random Lines in a Plane and in Space"; "Random Planes and Random Rotations"; and "Problems of Coverage." Applications include astronomy, physics, biology, crystallography, petrography, sampling theory, and silviculture. Assumes knowledge of multivariate calculus.

Kerrich, J.E. AN EXPERIMENTAL INTRODUCTION TO THE THEORY OF PROBABILITY. Copenhagen: E. Munksgaard, 1946. 98 p. No index.

Presents physical results of mathematical probability as a prerequisite to the study of probability based on the axioms. Presents estimates of 10,000 spins of an ordinary coin and 5,000 drawings of two balls from an urn containing two red and two green balls. Includes the problem of estimation of the numerical value of a probability, the limits within which p lies for a binomial distribution, and approximations to the binomial distribution. Assumes knowledge of high school algebra.

Khazanie, Ramakant. BASIC PROBABILITY: THEORY AND APPLICATIONS. Pacific Palisades, Calif.: Goodyear, 1976. xi, 516 p. References, p. 491. Solutions to Selected Problems, pp. 493-506. Tables, pp. 507-12. Index, pp. 513-16.

A text for a one-year course in probability for mathematics students who have a background in calculus through multiple integration and power series. Provides an excellent background for further study of statistics, operations research, and communications theory. Topics include sample space and events; sigma fields, including the Borel field; rules of probability; conditional probability and independent events; discrete and continuous random variables; functions of a random variable; expectation and variance; joint and marginal distributions; conditional distribution and independent random variables; functions of several random variables; generating functions; and limit theorems. Numerous examples and exercises included.

King, James R. PROBABILITY CHARTS FOR DECISION MAKING. New York: Industrial Press, 1971. xiv, 290 p. Appendix, pp. 273-81. Bibliography, pp. 283-84. Index, pp. 285-90.

An exposition on probability plotting as a graphical method for data analysis for use as a reference in conjunction with a conventional statistics course. Includes the following probability distributions: uniform, normal, logarithmic, extreme value, Weibull, reciprocal functions, gamma, chi-square, and binomial. Choice of probability paper also considered. Includes brief mathematical results and numerous illustrations of graphs.

King, William R. PROBABILITY FOR MANAGEMENT DECISIONS. Wiley Series in Management and Administration. New York: Wiley, 1968. xix, 372 p. Appendix: Sets, pp. 357-67. Index, pp. 369-72.

A text for a one-semester course in probability for students who have knowledge of elementary calculus. Topics include discrete sample spaces and definitions of probability; probabilities and decision analysis; assessing probabilities for management decisions; conditional probability and independence; discrete and continuous random variables in management decision; probability functions for several variables; expectations and variability; empirical and theoretical probability distributions; Bayesian analysis; and stochastic process analysis, including Markov and queueing analysis. Chapters conclude with references and exercises.

Kuo, Hui-Hsiung. GAUSSIAN MEASURES IN BANACH SPACES. Lecture Notes in Mathematics, no. 463. New York: Springer-Verlag, 1975. vi, 224 p. References, pp. 218-22. Index, pp. 223-24.

A monograph on the applications of measure theory in Banach spaces with emphasis on the Wiener space. Topics include Borel measures in a Hilbert space; Wiener measure and Wiener integral in C[0,1]; Kakutan's theorem on infinite product measures; equivalence of Gaussian measures in Hilbert space; equivalence and transformation formulas for abstract Wiener measures; and potential theory. Assumes knowledge of real analysis and measure theory. Presentation rigorous with theorems, examples, and exercises.

Kyburg, Henry E., Jr. PROBABILITY AND THE LOGIC OF RATIONAL BELIEF. Middleton, Conn.: Wesleyan University Press, 1961. viii, 346 p. Appendix I: Possible Ramifications, pp. 325-32. Appendix II: Bibliography, pp. 334-46. No index.

Develops a mathematically formal analogue of the intuitive concept of rational belief in three parts: "Problem"; "Theory"; and "Practice." Topics include review of various concepts of probability; object language; metalanguage; rational matrices and statistical statements; rational inheritance; rational inference; probability and betting quotients; induction; and statistical inference. Assumes knowledge of set theory and mathematical logic.

______ PROBABILITY THEORY. Englewood Cliffs, N.J.: Prentice-Hall, 1969. x, 294 p. Appendix: Tables, pp. 285-90. Index, pp. 291-94.

A text for a one-semester course in probability and statistics for students of science and engineering who have knowledge of calculus. Develops the set-theoretic approach to probability, followed by the measure-theoretic approach. Topics include distribution of several random variables; limit theorems; conditional distributions and correlation; point and interval estimation; and Bayes' decision theory. Chapters conclude with exercises.

Kyburg, Henry E.[Jr.], and Nagel, Ernest, eds. INDUCTION: SOME CURRENT ISSUES. Middletown, Conn.: Wesleyan University Press, 1963. xxi, 220 p. Index, pp. 218-20.

Nine papers presented at a conference on induction held at Wesleyan University, June 12-17, 1961. Topics include statistical and inductive probabilities; induction, prediction, and decision making in cybernetic systems; motivation of inductive behavior; temporally asymmetric principles; and the role of values in scientific inference.

Kyburg, Henry E., Jr., and Smokler, Howard E., eds. STUDIES IN SUBJECTIVE PROBABILITY. New York: Wiley, 1964. vii, 203 p. Selected Bibliography, pp. 189-97. Index, pp. 199-203.

Six classical contributions on subjective probability previously published in journals during the period 1888-1961 together with a bibliography of the most important works in the field.

Lamperti, John. PROBABILITY: A SURVEY OF THE MATHEMATICAL THEORY. Mathematics Monograph Series. New York: W.A. Benjamin, 1966. x, 150 p. Bibliography, pp. 144-47. Index, pp. 148-50.

Developes classical probability based on measure theory. Topics include probability spaces; random variables and expectations; the construction of random variables; laws of large numbers; the law of the iterated logarithm; central limit theorem; symmetric stable laws; infinitely divisible laws; recurrence and stochastic processes; Brownian motion; Markov processes; and Kolmogorov's equations. Theorems either proved or stated without proof and illustrated with examples. Problems deal with the applications of the theorems.

_____. STOCHASTIC PROCESSES: A SURVEY OF THE MATHEMATICAL THEORY. Applied Mathematical Sciences 23. New York: Springer-Verlag, 1977. xviii, 266 p. Appendix 1: Existence of Random Processes with Given Finite-Dimensional Distributions, pp. 250-54. Appendix 2: Review of Conditional Probability, pp. 255-59. Bibliography, pp. 260-61. Index, pp. 262-66.

A monograph on stochastic processes in two parts: "Stationary Processes" and "Markov Processes." Topics include Wald decomposition for linear prediction; ergodic theorems; strong law of large numbers; strong Markov processes; properties of path functions; spectral representation; spectral decomposition; continuous parameter submartingales; Brownian motion; the Dirichlet problem; Yille-Yosida theorem; and measure preserving transformations. Assumes knowledge of real analysis and measure theory.

Lancaster, Henry Oliver. THE CHI-SQUARED DISTRIBUTION. Wiley Series in Probability and Mathematical Statistics. New York: Wiley, 1969. xiv, 356 p. Bibliography, pp. 283-335. Index to the Bibliography, pp. 337-50. Subject Index, pp. 351-56.

An exposition of the history, theory, and application of the Pearson chi-square distribution. Topics include chi-square distribution theory; discrete distributions; orthogonality; the multinomial distribution; canonical or standard form for probability distributions; non-central chi-square; goodness of fit in the multinomial distribution; problems of inference; normal correlation; and two-way contingency tables. Presentation rigorous with proofs of theorems provided. Assumes knowledge of mathematical statistics and linear algebra. Chapters conclude with exercises and complements.

Lebeder, Vsevolod Leonidovich. RANDOM PROCESSES IN ELECTRICAL AND MECHANICAL SYSTEMS. Translated by J. Flancreich and M. Segal. Moscow: State Publishing House of Physical and Mathematical Literature, 1958. vi, 122 p. Bibliography, pp. 119-22. No index.

A monograph on the theory of electrical and mechanical systems with lumped constants under a statistically characterized external force. Topics include concepts in the theory of random functions and their linear transformations; methods of analysis of random processes in linear systems with lumped constants using stochastic differential equations and the method of impulse characteristics; applications to Brownian motion, electric fluctuations, thermal movement of a galvanometer, and transmission of telegraph signals and fluctuation of noise through a low-pass filter; and theory of inertialess nonlinear systems under random action with applications. Assumes knowledge of probability theory and calculus.

Lempers, Fred B. POSTERIOR PROBABILITIES OF ALTERNATIVE LINEAR MODELS: SOME THEORETICAL CONSIDERATIONS AND EMPIRICAL EXPERIMENTS. Foreword by T. Kloek. Rotterdam, The Netherlands: Rotterdam University Press, 1971. vi, 110 p. Bibliography, pp. 103-7. Index, pp. 109-10.

Takes up the problems involved in applying probability to discriminate between alternative linear models. Posterior probabilities derived for natural-conjugate prior distributions and uniform prior distributions and applied to sets of linear models differing only in the assumptions about the distributions and different explanatory variables. Also includes experiments with alternative model specifications. Assumes knowledge of calculus, linear algebra, probability, mathematical statistics, and Bayesian statistics.

Lewis, Theodore Gyle. DISTRIBUTION SAMPLING FOR COMPUTER SIMULATION. Lexington, Mass.: Heath, Lexington Books, 1975. xvi, 150 p. Appendixes for Generators, pp. 111-24. Appendixes for Tests, pp. 125-46. Index, pp. 147-50.

Presents distribution sampling in two parts: "Pseudorandom Numbers" and "Nonuniform Distribution Sampling." Provides a definitive summary of mathematical theory to date, with emphasis on computer science aspects. Includes many computer programs for IBM 360. Topics include pseudorandom sequences in n-space; generalized algorithm for feedback shift registers; empirical testing of pseudorandom number generators; reversion and rejection techniques in nonuniform sampling distributions; and conditional bit sampling.

Lindley, D.V. INTRODUCTION TO PROBABILITY AND STATISTICS: FROM A BAYESIAN VIEWPOINT. PART I. PROBABILITY. New York: Cambridge University Press, 1965. xi, 259 p. Bibliography, pp. 249-51. Subject Index, pp. 253-57. Index of Notations, pp. 258-59.

A text for a course in probability for students of mathematics who have courses in calculus and linear algebra. Includes rigorous proofs, but no data analysis. Topics include axioms of probability and elementary deductions from them; random variables in one and higher dimensions; stochastic processes; queueing theory; renewal theory; and Markov chains. Style consists of definition, proofs, examples, and discussions.

_____. INTRODUCTION TO PROBABILITY AND STATISTICS FROM A BAYESIAN VIEWPOINT. PART 2. INFERENCE. New York: Cambridge University Press, 1965. xiii, 292 p. Appendix: Two-Sided Tests for the Chi-Square Distribution, pp. 282-84. Bibliography, pp. 285-86. Subject Index, pp. 287-91. Index of Notation, p. 292.

A text for mathematics students who have knowledge of calculus and linear algebra. Includes some proofs with the intuitive approach; examples also stressed. Topics include inference problems for the normal distribution; use of Bayes' theorem to modify prior beliefs into posterior beliefs; inference for several normal distributions (two-sample and several-sample problems and the analysis of variance); inferences for distributions besides the normal (Poisson, chi-square); maximum likelihood; and least squares, particularly tests and estimation for linear hypotheses. Chapters conclude with problems.

Loeve, Michael. PROBABILITY THEORY. 3d ed. University Series in Higher Mathematics. New York: Van Nostrand, 1963. xvi, 685 p. Bibliography, pp. 657-64. Index, pp. 665-85.

A text and reference for graduate students who have a good background in calculus. Consists of the following five parts: "Notions of Measure Theory"; "General Concepts and Tools of Probability Theory"; "Independence"; "Dependence"; and "Elements of Random Analysis." A three-chapter introduction useful as a text for an undergraduate course in probability. Emphasizes rigor with proofs and non-numerical applications.

_____. PROBABILITY THEORY I. 4th rev. ed. Graduate Texts in Mathematics, 45. New York: Springer-Verlag, 1977. xvii, 425 p. Bibliography, pp. 407-12. Index, pp. 413-25.

A text for a graduate course and a reference for research workers in probability and statistics who have a good calculus background. Consists of three parts: "Notions of Measure Theory"; "General Concepts and Tools of Probability Theory"; and "Independence." Presentation follows theorem-proof format.

Topics include set theory; topological spaces; additive set functions; construction of measures; measurable functions and integration; continuous random variables and their distributions; distribution functions; convergence of probabilities on metric spaces; characteristic functions with applications; rules of probability; sums of independent random variables and their convergence and stability; exponential bounds and normed sums; central limit theorem; independent identically distributed summands; and random walks. Chapters conclude with complements and details.

Lucas, John Randolph. THE CONCEPTS OF PROBABILITY. New York: Oxford University Press, 1970. x, 220 p. Appendix I: Alternative Proof of Bernoulli's Theorem, pp. 209-12. Appendix II: Summary of Theories of Probabilities, pp. 213-15. Index, pp. 217-20.

A largely philosophical treatment of probability theory and its application to statistical inference based on Bernoulli's theorem and including no more complicated distribution than the normal one. Topics include the measurement of probability; conditional probabilities, singular propositions; equiprobability and randomness; inverse arguments; continuity and density; biological probabilities and imperfect information; and objective probability. Useful to mathematicians and others interested in philosophical issues arising in probability and statistics.

Luxemburg, W.A.J., ed. APPLICATIONS OF MODEL THEORY TO ALGEBRA, ANALYSIS, AND PROBABILITY. New York: Holt, Rinehart and Winston, 1969. vii, 307 p. No index.

Nineteen papers presented at an international symposium held at the California Institute of Technology, May 23-26, 1967, under sponsorship of the Office of Naval Research. Topics include a general theory of monads; a set-theoretical characterization of enlargements; nonstandard analysis of almost periodic functions; nonstandard measure theory; nonstandard proofs of invariance principles in probability theory; infinite quantifiers and continuous games; and nonstandard analysis in topological algebra.

McCord, James R. III, and Moroney, Richard M., Jr. INTRODUCTION TO PROBABILITY THEORY. New York: Macmillan, 1965. xvi, 232 p. Bibliography, pp. 212-13. Tables of the Normal Distribution, pp. 214-15. Answers to Exercises, pp. 217-26. Index, pp. 227-32.

A text for a one-semester course for undergraduates and a reference for engineers and scientists with a prerequisite of calculus. Emphasizes the axiomatic approach first presented by A.N. Kolmogorov. Some results stated without proof and others with only heuristic justification. About 300 exercises given at the ends of the chapters ranging from pure mathematics to rigorous applications. Topics include axiomatic probability; construction of probability spaces; conditional probability and independence; random variables and their distributions, including Poisson, gamma, beta, and rectangular; expectation; joint distribution; sums of random variables; law of large numbers; and central limit theorem.

McFadden, James Alfred. PHYSICAL CONCEPTS OF PROBABILITY. New York: Van Nostrand Reinhold, 1971. viii, 224 p. Appendix: Probability by Digital Computer, pp. 215-22. Index, pp. 223-24.

A text for a one-semester course in probability for undergraduates and graduates in engineering who have had two semesters of calculus. Uses only elementary mathematics, and develops probability by means of physical ideas. Topics include events; random variables and their distributions; Chebyshev's inequality; normal distribution; correlation and dependence; stochastic processes; conditional probability; and expectation. Chapters conclude with problems.

McKean, Henry P., Jr. STOCHASTIC INTEGRALS. Probability and Mathematical Statistics. A Series of Monographs and Textbooks, vol. 6. New York: Academic Press, 1969. xii, 140 p. List of Notations, pp. xi-xiii. References, pp. 133-38. Subject Index, pp. 139-40.

A monograph on differential and integral calculus based upon the Brownian motion for use by mathematicians. Chapter titles are: "Brownian Motion"; "Stochastic Integrals and Differentials"; "Stochastic Integral Equations ($d \leq 1$)"; and "Stochastic Integral Equations ($d \geq 2$)." Assumes knowledge of mathematical physics, conditional probabilities and expectations, the Borel-Cantelli lemmas, and Brownian motion. Emphasizes rigor with proofs of theorems and lemmas included.

Maksoudian, Y. Leon. PROBABILITY AND STATISTICS WITH APPLICATIONS. Scranton, Pa.: International Textbook, 1969. xi, 416 p. Bibliography, pp. 379-80. Appendix: Tables, pp. 381-409. Principal Notations and Abbreviations, pp. 411-12. Index, pp. 413-16.

A text for a one-year course in probability and statistics for students in engineering, science, and mathematics who have knowledge of calculus. Topics include discrete and continuous probability functions; moments of functions; multivariate or joint probability functions; descriptive statistics; sampling distributions; interval estimation; hypothesis testing; regression and correlation; design of experiments; and analysis of variance; Latin and Graeco-Latin squares; and factorial designs. Sections conclude with problems.

Maruyama, G., and Prokhorov, Yu. V., eds. PROCEEDINGS OF THE SECOND JAPAN-USSR SYMPOSIUM ON PROBABILITY THEORY. New York: Springer-Verlag, 1973. vi, 550 p. No index.

Forty papers presented at the second Japan-USSR Symposium held at Tokyo, Japan, August 2-9, 1972. All papers printed in English and topics include statistical problems in quantum physics; convergence theorems for random processes; Markov processes by symmetric forms; optimal coding in white Gaussian channels with feedback; ergodicity of the dynamical system of a particle on a domain with irregular walls; white noise and infinite dimensional orthogonal groups; moment inequalities and identities for stochastic integrals; concentration functions of sums of independent random variables; branching Markov processes with derivatives; and extensions of measures.

______. PROCEEDINGS OF THE THIRD JAPAN-USSR SYMPOSIUM ON PROBABILITY THEORY. Lecture Notes in Mathematics, no. 550. New York: Springer-Verlag, 1976. vi, 722 p. No index.

Forty-six papers presented at the third Japan-USSR symposium on probability held in Tashkent, USSR, Aug. 27-Sept. 2, 1975. Papers printed in English and include such topics as renewal approach to Markov processes; limit theorems for linear combinations of order statistics; expectation semigroup of a cascade process and a limit theorem; Hilbert space methods in classical problems of mathematical statistics; central limit theories for subadditive processes; multiple branching with immigration; statistics of stochastic processes with jumps; optimal stopping of controlled diffusion processes; second order asymptotic efficiencies of estimators; diffusion processes by means of Poisson point processes of Brownian extensions; nonanticipating solutions of stochastic equations; stationary linear processes with Markovian property; and additive arithmetic functions and Brownian motion.

Mason, J. David, ed. STOCHASTIC DIFFERENTIAL EQUATIONS AND APPLICATIONS. New York: Academic Press, 1977. ix, 253 p. No index.

Eleven papers presented at a conference held in Park City, Utah, February 17-20, 1976, under sponsorship of the Office of Naval Research and the University of Utah. Topics include limit theorems for random evolutions having nonergodic driving processes; ergodic theorem for the diffusion on a manifold of negative curvature; diffusion on the line and additive functionals of Brownian motion; diffusion approximations in population genetics; fluctuation phenomena in underwater sound propagation; and optimal stopping and quasi-variational inequalities.

Matheron, Georges. RANDOM SETS AND INTEGRAL GEOMETRY. Foreword by G.S. Watson. New York: Wiley, 1975. xxiii, 261 p. Notation, pp. xxi-xxiii. Bibliography, pp. 254-56. Index, pp. 257-61.

Develops the mathematical theory of geometrical probability based on the theory of random sets. Topics include definitions and general properties of random closed sets in a locally compact and separable set; relationship between random closed sets in Euclidean space and integral geometry where convexity plays an essential role; and mappings valued in closed and compact sets. Useful in the application of computers and mathematics to data analysis. Emphasizes rigor. Assumes knowledge of algebraic topology and probability.

Medgyessy, Pál. DECOMPOSITION OF SUPERPOSITIONS OF DENSITY FUNCTIONS AND DISCRETE DISTRIBUTIONS. New York: Wiley, 1977. 308 p. References, pp. 267-88. Chronological Bibliography to the Problems of Decomposition, pp. 289-94. Author Index, pp. 295-98. Subject Index, pp. 299-306. Index of Unsolved Problems, p. 306. Index of Notations, pp. 307-8.

A unified treatment of numerical methods of decomposition of superpositions consisting of the following five chapters: "Introduction"; "Some Mathematical Tools"; "Decomposition of Superpositions, I: Decomposition of Superpositions of Density Functions"; "Decomposition of Superpositions, II: Decompositions of Superpositions of Discrete Distributions"; and "Appendix: Numerical Methods that can be Applied in Carrying out Decomposition Methods." Assumes knowledge of mathematical probability and elementary numerical analysis. Includes applications to the following functions: normal, lognormal, beta, exponential, gamma, stable, Cauchy, and Voight. Style rigorous, consisting of proofs of theorems, derivations, and examples.

Melsa, James L., and Sage, Andrew P. AN INTRODUCTION TO PROBABILITY AND STOCHASTIC PROCESSES. Prentice-Hall Information and System Sciences Series. Englewood Cliffs, N.J.: Prentice-Hall, 1973. xii, 403 p. Appendix A: Operational Mathematics and the Laplace Transform, pp. 372-82. Appendix B: System Representation by State Variables, pp. 383-98. Index, pp. 399-403.

A text for a one-semester course in probability and stochastic processes for graduates and undergraduates who have some experience with system analysis, including state-variable and Laplace-Transform concepts. Introduces concepts in probability and statistics needed in system analysis, control, and communication. Topics include random variables and functions of random variables; spectral density; orthogonal representation; linear system response to stochastic processes; Gaussian processes; and Markov processes with stochastic differential equations. Numerous examples provided, and detailed applications included. Chapters conclude with references and problems.

Meshalkin, L.D. COLLECTIONS OF PROBLEMS IN PROBABILITY THEORY. Translated and edited by L.F. Boron and B.A. Haworth. Leyden, Holland: Noordhoff International, 1973. x, 148 p. Appendix, pp. 117-24. Answers, pp. 125-43. Suggested Reading, p. 145. Index, pp. 147-48.

A collection of 500 problems for university students in physics and mathematics originally published in Russian in 1963. Useful as a supplement in probability courses. Chapter titles: "Fundamental Concepts"; "Random Variables and Their Properties"; "Basic Limit Theorems"; "Characteristic and Generating Functions"; "Application of Measure Theory"; "Infinitely Divisible Distributions"; "Normal Law"; "Multidimensional Distributions"; and "Markov Chains." Problems represent a wide range of difficulty and include proofs of theorems.

Meyer, Paul L. INTRODUCTORY PROBABILITY AND STATISTICAL APPLICATIONS. 2d ed., rev. Addison-Wesley Series in Statistics. Reading, Mass.: Addison-Wesley, 1970. xiv, 367 p. References pp. 338-39. Appendix: Tables, pp. 341-55. Answers to Selected Problems, pp. 357-62. Index, pp. 363-67.

A text for a one-semester course in probability theory for students in engineering and the natural sciences who have gone through one year of calculus. Mathematics concise but not detailed, and some proofs included with intuitive views provided. Topics include finite sample spaces; conditional probability and independence; one-dimensional random variables; functions of random variables; two- and higher-dimensional random variables; moments of random variables; Chebyshev's inequality; Poisson and other discrete random variables; continuous random variables, including gamma and bivariate normal; moment-generating functions; sums of random variables; sampling distributions; and estimation and hypothesis testing. Chapters conclude with problems.

Miller, Kenneth S. MULTIDIMENSIONAL GAUSSIAN DISTRIBUTIONS. SIAM Series in Applied Mathematics. New York: Wiley, 1964. viii, 129 p. Appendix 1: Identities Involving Special Functions, pp. 113-16. Appendix 2: Multiple Integrals, pp. 117-20. Bibliography, pp. 121-24. Index, pp. 125-29.

Presents the basic facts concerning multidimensional Gaussian distributions using matrix algebra and linear vector spaces. Restricted to properties that depend on the full generality of a nondiagonal covariance matrix and does not consider problems where the n-dimensional distribution is a product of n one-dimensional distributions. Topics include joint normal distributions and theorems concerning Gaussian variates and linear combinations of Gaussian variates; Rayleigh distributions; multidimensional singular Gaussian distributions; and applications to Gaussian random noise in the following problems: estimating signal parameters in the presence of additive and multiplicative noise, and the statistics of the output noise resulting from the passage of a Gaussian process through a linear filter. Presentation rigorous with proofs of theorems and derivations provided.

______. MULTIVARIATE DISTRIBUTIONS. Huntington, New York: Krieger, 1975. viii, 167 p. Appendix 1: Identitied Involving Special Functions, pp. 147-52. Appendix 2: Multiple Integrals, pp. 153-57. Bibliography, pp. 159-62. Index, pp. 163-67.

Presents the theory of multidimensional Gaussian distributions based on the full generality of a nondiagonal covariance matrix, omitting problems where the n-dimensional distribution is the product of n one-dimensional distributions. Assumes knowledge of linear algebra, advanced calculus, and probability theory. Topics include a review of quadratic forms; matrices; covariance matrix; generalized spherical coordinates; integrals of quadratic forms; joint normal distribution and linear combinations of Gaussian variates; Rayeigh distributions; regression function, linear least squares, and multidimensional singular Gaussian distributions; and applications to Gaussian random noise. Presentation rigorous, consisting largely of proofs of theorems.

Milton, Roy C. RANK ORDER PROBABILITIES: TWO-SAMPLE NORMAL SHIFT ALTERNATIVES. Foreword by I.R. Savage. Wiley Series in Probability and Mathematical Statistics. New York: Wiley, 1970. xvi, 302 p. References, pp. 67-69. Tables, pp. 275-300. Index, pp. 301-2.

A monograph on the evaluation of probabilities of rank orders for the case of two samples differing in means only. Parameter limited to the ratio of the difference of the two means divided by the common standard deviation. Topics include methods of constructing the tables; accuracy of tables; illustrations of the use of the tables; power function of standard nonparametric tests; sequential probability ratio procedures based on rank data; problems of multiple selection; and asymptotic formulas of Hodges and Lehmann with numerical results.

Mode, Charles J. MULTIPLE BRANCHING PROCESSES: THEORY AND APPLICATIONS. Modern Analytic and Computational Methods in Science and Engineering: A Group of Monographs and Textbooks, vol. 34. New York: Elsevier, 1971. xx, 330 p. References, pp. 318-24. Author Index, pp. 325-26. Subject Index, pp. 327-30.

A mathematical exposition of the theory of multiple branching processes as a field of applied probability. Assumes knowledge of mathematical analysis and advanced probability. Emphasizes theoretical developments, with few applications provided. Topics include the multitype Galton-Watson process, including the positively regular and nonpositively regular cases; generalized multitype age-dependent branching processes; general stochastic population processes; and Markov branching processes with discrete time and continuous time parameters.

Molenaar, W. APPROXIMATIONS TO THE POISSON, BINOMIAL AND HYPERGEOMETRIC DISTRIBUTION FUNCTIONS. Mathematisch Centre Tracts, 31. Amsterdam: Mathematisch Centrum, 1970. 160 p. References, pp. 155-59. List of Symbols, p. 160. No index.

Provides guidelines for the choice of an approximation to discrete distribution functions. Includes asymptotic and numerical properties of previously published approximations and additional ones. Topics include normal approximation to the Poisson; normal and Poisson approximation to the binomial; and normal, Poisson and binomial approximations to the hypergeometric distribution.

Moran, Patrick Alfred Pierce. AN INTRODUCTION TO PROBABILITY THEORY. New York: Oxford University Press, 1968. vi, 542 p. Bibliography, pp. 505-32. Author Index, pp. 533-37. Subject Index, pp. 538-42.

Presents probability theory in an abstract manner for describing complicated phenomena in the natural sciences. Includes measure theory for treating infinite sums and sequences and for preparation of advanced texts based on measure theory. Topics include sets and probability; Tchebychev's inequality; Stirling's formula; occupancy problems; martingales; distributions in contingency tables; Markov processes, including Ehrenfest's model, the gambler's ruin problem, finite birth processes, the Borel-Tanner process, and simple queues; measurable functions; random variables and their moments; characteristic functions; the Cramér-Wold theorem; special continuous distributions, including rectangular, distributions dependent on the normal, multivariate normal, logarithmic normal, gamma, F, t, and distribution on a circle; sequences and sums, including almost sure convergence, theorems of Tauberian type, Kolmogorov inequalities; laws of large numbers, law of the iterated logarithm, and identically distributed variates; Brownian motion; and random walks. Designed as a text for graduates and undergraduates, although numerical examples lacking. Chapters conclude with exercises involving proofs of theorems.

Munroe, Marshall E. THEORY OF PROBABILITY. New York: McGraw-Hill, 1951. viii, 213 p. Index, pp. 211-13.

A text for a course in the mathematics of probability for undergraduates and graduates who have had one year of calculus. Presentation based on the Lebesgue-Stieltjes integral with the discrete and continuous cases of random variables treated simultaneously. Topics include joint distributions, Bernoulli trials and random walks; moments of random variables; limit theorems; central limit theorems; Poisson distributions; and laws of large numbers. Chapters conclude with references and problems.

Neuts, Marcel F. PROBABILITY. Boston: Allyn and Bacon, 1973. xii, 555 p. Appendixes, pp. 394-546. Index, pp. 547-55.

A text for a course in probability for a mixed group of students in economics, management science, etc., who have knowledge of calculus. Contains some 630 problems at the ends of the chapters with detailed solutions for 50 problems. Topics include sample spaces, events, and probability; combinatorial and geometric probability; conditional probability; random variables and functions of random variables; probability distributions, including multivariate densities; types of convergence and limit theorems; strong and weak laws of large numbers; renewal theory; and finite Markov chains. Derivations extensive with numerical examples confined to problems. Appendixes consist of the history of probability, theorems from analysis, detailed solutions to problems, and tables.

Neveu, Jacques. DISCRETE-PARAMETER MARTINGALES. Translated by T.P. Speed. North-Holland Mathematical Library. New York: Elsevier, 1975. viii, 236 p. Appendix: On the Use of Young's Functions in the Theory of Martingales, pp. 210-21. References, pp. 222-34. Index of Terminology and Notation, pp. 235-36.

Originally published in French in 1972. Useful as a text for a course in discrete-parameter martingales for students familiar with integration and probability. Topics include conditional expectation; convergence and stopping theorems, with applications to measure theory and Markov chains; martingales with directed index sets; vector-valued martingales; reversed martingales; Snell's problem; Doob's decomposition of submartingales with applications to square-integrable martingales; Doob's decomposition of positive supermartingales; and applications to random walks, sequential statistical analysis, and stochastic games. Chapters conclude with exercises.

______. MATHEMATICAL FOUNDATIONS OF THE CALCULUS OF PROBABILITY. Foreword by R. Fortet. Translated by A. Feinstein. Holden-Day Series in Probability and Statistics. San Francisco: Holden-Day, 1965. 223 p. Bibliography, pp. 215-19. Index, pp. 221-23.

Originally published in French in 1964. A text for a graduate course in probability for students familiar with the theory of measure and integration, calculus of probability topology, metric spaces, and the theory of Hilbert and Banach spaces. Topics include probability spaces; integration of random variables on topological spaces; product spaces and random functions;

conditional expectations and martingales; ergodic theory; and Markov processes. Sections conclude with complements and problems.

Ney, Peter, ed. ADVANCES IN PROBABILITY AND RELATED TOPICS. Vol. I. New York: Marcel Dekker, 1971. xiii, 215 p. No index.

The first of a series of volumes reporting current research on probability and related issues. Consists of the following heretofore unpublished titles: "Random Walks and Discrete Subgroups of Lie Groups," by H. Furstenburg; "The Technique of Using Random M Measures and Random Sets in Harmonic Analysis," by J.P. Kahane; "Recent Developments in the Theory of Finite Toeplitz Operators," by I.I. Hirschman, Jr.; and "Matching Theory, An Introduction," by Gian-Carlo Rota and L.H. Harper. Papers emphasize mathematical rigor.

_____. ADVANCES IN PROBABILITY AND RELATED TOPICS. Vol. II. New York: Marcel Dekker, 1970. ix, 248 p. Author Index, pp. 241-42. Subject Index, pp. 243-48.

Consists of the following five heretofore unpublished contributions: "Ergodic Properties of Operators in Lebesgue Space," by M.A. Akcoglu and R.V. Chacon; "The Role of Reproducing Kernel Hilbert Spaces in the Study of Gaussian Processes," by G. Kallianpur; "The Sums of Iterates of a Positive Operator," by D. Ornstein; "Boundary Decomposition of Locally-Hunt Processes," by A.O. Pittenger; and "Some New Stochastic Integrals and Stieltjes Integrals. Part I. Analogues of Hardy-Littlewood Classes," by L.C. Young.

Ney, Peter, and Port, Sidney, eds. ADVANCES IN PROBABILITY AND RELATED TOPICS. Vol. III. New York: Marcel Dekker, 1974. viii, 410 p. Author Index, pp. 397-401. Subject Index, pp. 403-10.

Consists of the following heretofore unpublished contributions: "Multiplicative Operator Functionals and Their Asymptotic Properties," by Mark A. Pinsky; "Some New Stochastic Integrals and Stieltjes Integrals, Part II. Nigh-Martingales," by L.C. Young; "Aspects of Random Measures and Point Processes," by Peter Jagers; and "Sample Functions of Stochastic Processes with Stationary, Independent Increments," by Bert Fristedt.

Niemi, Richard G., and Weisberg, Herbert F., eds. PROBABILITY MODELS OF COLLECTIVE DECISION MAKING. Merrill Political Science Series. Columbus, Ohio: Charles E. Merrill, 1972. x, 413 p. Bibliography, pp. 396-406. Name Index, pp. 407-10. Subject Index, pp. 411-13.

Sixteen contributions on models of collective decision making grouped under the following four headings: "Constitutional Design" (four contributions); "Coalition Formation" (four contributions); "The Paradox of Voting" (four contributions); and "Spatial Modeling of Competition" (four contributions). Knowledge of calculus and basic statistics helpful. Topics include independent voter model based on binomial theorem; positional preference; majority rule model; cost-benefit analysis of coalition formation in voting bodies; effects of group size on collective decision making; theory of formation of opinion coalitions; cyclical majorities in congressional voting; probability analysis of voting blocks; mathematical treatment of electoral competition under uncertainty; spatial strategies for sequential elections; and spatial competition under constrained choice.

Niven, Ivan. MATHEMATICS OF CHOICE: HOW TO COUNT WITHOUT COUNTING. New Mathematical Library. New York: Random House, 1965. xi, 202 p. Miscellaneous Problems, pp. 153-59. Answers and Solutions, pp. 160-97. Bibliography, p. 199. Index, pp. 201-2.

A monograph on combinatorial analysis containing numerous problems and requiring only algebra as a prerequisite. Topics include combinations and binomial coefficients; the inclusion-exclusion principle; probability; partitions of an integer; generating polynomials; configuration problems; mathematical induction; and nonassociative products.

Oberhettinger, Fritz. FOURIER TRANSFORMS OF DISTRIBUTIONS AND THEIR INVERSES: A COLLECTION OF TABLES. Probability and Mathematical Statistics: A Series of Textbooks and Monographs, vol. 16. New York: Academic Press, 1973. ix, 167 p. Appendix: Distribution Functions and Their Fourier Transforms Found in the Statistical Literature, pp. 153-61. List of Abbreviations, Symbols, and Notations, pp. 162-67.

A collection of integrals of the Fourier transform type (including their inverses) involving the class of functions which are non-negative and integrable over the interval $(-\infty, +\infty)$, with emphasis on probability densities. Consists of two parts: "Tables of Fourier Transforms" and "Tables of the Inverse Transforms." Functions include even functions, functions which vanish identically for negative values of the argument, and functions not belonging to either of these classes. Appendix includes lists of univariate and multivariate density functions, and univariate discrete distributions, as well as the Fourier transforms of these functions. Results collected from widely scattered sources.

Padgett, W.J., and Taylor, R[obert]. L. LAWS OF LARGE NUMBERS FOR NORMED LINEAR SPACES AND CERTAIN FRÉCHET SPACES. New York: Springer-Verlag, 1973. vi, 111 p. Bibliography, pp. 104-11. No index.

A unified presentation of the weak and strong laws of large numbers for random elements in linear topological spaces. Assumes knowledge of basic probability theory. Topics include laws of large numbers for random variables and separable Hilbert spaces; strong and weak laws of large numbers for normed linear spaces; laws of large numbers for Frechet spaces; and applications in stochastic processes and decision theory. Useful to probabilists.

Parratt, Lyman G. PROBABILITY AND EXPERIMENTAL ERRORS IN SCIENCE: AN ELEMENTARY SURVEY. New York: Wiley, 1961. xv, 255 p. Glossary, pp. 241-47. Index, pp. 249-55.

A text for a one-semester undergraduate course in probability with emphasis on the experimental definition of probability, rather than the classical definition. Topics include maximum likelihood; rules for the propagation of errors, curve fitting; applications of least-squares; consistency tests; analysis of variance; correlation; Poisson probability model with applications; and tests of statistical hypotheses. Derivations kept to a minimum. Numerous problems included at ends of sections and chapters.

Parthasarathy, K.R. PROBABILITY MEASURES ON METRIC SPACES. Probability and Mathematical Statistics. A Series of Monographs and Textbooks. New York: Academic Press, 1967. xi, 276 p. Bibliographical Notes, pp. 268-69. Bibliography, pp. 270-72. List of Symbols, p. 273. Author Index, p. 275-76.

A monograph on the general theory of probability measures in abstract metric spaces, complete separable metric spaces, locally compact Abelian groups, Hilbert spaces, and the spaces of continuous functions and functions with discontinuities of the first kind only. Emphasizes mathematical rigor, with lemmas and theorems proved. Promotes the Indian school of probabilists.

Parthasarathy, K.R., and Schmidt, K. POSITIVE DEFINITE KERNELS, CONTINUOUS TENSOR PRODUCTS, AND CENTRAL LIMIT THEOREMS OF PROBABILITY THEORY. Lecture Notes in Mathematics, 272. New York: Springer-Verlag, 1972. vi, 107 p. References, pp. 105-7. No index.

Studies the connection between continuous tensor products and the theory of infinitely divisible distributions of probability theory in terms of positive definite kernels with invariance properties under a group action. Consists of three parts: "Positive Definite Kernels and Continuous Tensor Products"; "Limit Theorems for Uniformly Infinitesimal Families of Positive Definite Kernels"; and "The Analysis of Cocycles of First Order on Some Special Groups."

Parzen, Emanuel. MODERN PROBABILITY THEORY AND ITS APPLICATION. Wiley Series in Probability and Mathematical Statistics. New York: Wiley, 1960. xv, 464 p. Tables, pp. 441-45. Answers to Odd-Numbered Exercises, pp. 447-57. 459-64.

A text for a one-semester course in probability for students with diverse interests and backgrounds who have a good working knowledge of calculus. Contains more than 160 examples, 120 theoretical exercises which serve to extend the theory, and 480 nontheoretical exercises which serve to illustrate the theory. Topics include independence and dependence; random variables and their probability distributions and moments; conditional probability and expectation; expectations of jointly distributed random variables; limit theorems and the role of characteristic functions; derivations of the law of large numbers and the central limit theorem; and applications to birth and death processes, reliability, Brownian motion, and inventories.

Patil, Ganapati P., ed. CLASSICAL AND CONTAGIOUS DISCRETE DISTRIBUTIONS. New York: Pergamon, 1965. xiv, 552 p. No index.

Forty papers presented at the international symposium on classical and contagious discrete distributions held at McGill University, Montreal, August 15-20, 1963. Also includes a bibliography on classical and contagious distributions. Papers grouped under the following eleven headings: "Inaugural Session" (three papers); "Certain Stochastic Systems" (three papers); "Structural Properties" (three papers); "Limit Distributions" (three papers); "Unified Models and Inference" (six papers); "Some Classical Distributions" (four papers); "Contagious Distributions" (six papers); "Inference Mixtures of Distributions" (three papers); "Certain Distributions in Biological Sciences" (three papers); "Finite Populations" (two papers); and "General Topics" (four papers). Topics include incomplete and absolute moments of some discrete distributions; normal approximations to the classical discrete distributions; estimation of parameters of hyper-Poisson and generalized Poisson distribution; sequential estimation of a binomial distribution; analysis of contagious data through behavioristic models; mixtures of discrete distributions; and distribution of the product in random samples from a finite population.

Paz, Azaria. INTRODUCTION TO PROBABILISTIC AUTOMATA. Computer Science and Applied Mathematics. A Series in Monographs and Textbooks. New York: Academic Press, 1971. xxv, 228 p. Notation, pp. xv-xvii. References, pp. 199-208. Answers and Hints to Selected Exercises, pp. 209-22. Author Index, pp. 223-25. Subject Index, pp. 226-28.

A monograph on automata theory for students who have knowledge of finite automata theory, linear algebra, and elementary probability theory. Chapter titles: "Stochastic Sequential

Machines"; "Markov Chains"; "Events, Languages, and Acceptors"; and "Applications and Generalizations." Emphasizes rigor with proofs of theorems and a large number of exercises included. Applications in information theory, reliability, learning theory, pattern recognition, and control systems.

Pfeiffer, Paul E. CONCEPTS OF PROBABILITY THEORY. McGraw-Hill Series in Probability and Statistics. New York: McGraw-Hill, 1965. xiii, 399 p. Appendix A: Some Elements of Combinatorial Analysis, pp. 359-61. Appendix B: Some Topics in Set Theory, pp. 362-69. Appendix C: Measurability of Functions, pp. 370-71. Appendix D: Proofs of Some Theorems, pp. 372-75. Appendix E: Integrals of Complex-Valued Random Variables, pp. 376-77. Appendix F: Summary of Properties and Key Theorems, pp. 378-89. Bibliography, pp. 390-92. Index, pp. 393-99.

A text for an undergraduate course in probability for students in science and engineering who have knowledge of calculus. Provides a firm theoretical foundation for applications in decision theory, reliability theory, dynamic programming, game theory, coding and information theory, and communications and control in the presence of noise. Topics include events and probability; random variables and their distributions; functions of random variables; limit theorems; Lebesgue-Stieltjes integral; mathematical expectation; probability and information; moment-generating functions; laws of large numbers; central limit theorem; Markov chains; distributions functions for random processes; correlation and covariance; stationary random processes; and Gaussian random processes. Proofs included. Chapters conclude with references and lengthy sets of problems.

Pfeiffer, Paul E., and Schum, David A. INTRODUCTION TO APPLIED PROBABILITY. New York: Academic Press, 1973. xiii, 403 p. Appendix A: Numerical Tables, pp. 374-79. Appendix B: Some Mathematical Aids, pp. 381-85. Selected References, pp. 387-88. Selected Answers and Hints, pp. 389-93. Index of Symbols and Abbreviations, pp. 395-96. Index, pp. 397-403.

A text for an introductory course in applied probability for students in the behavioral, biological, and physical sciences, as well as computer science and operations research. Emphasizes concepts and the interpretation of basic mathematical patterns, events determined by random variables, combinations of events, conditional probability, independence, and conditional independence. Consists of five parts: "Introduction"; "Basic Probability Model"; "Random Variables"; "Mathematical Expectation"; and "Sequences of Random Variables." Other topics include occupancy problem; set theory; joint probability; functions of random variables; correlation and covariance; and Markov chains. Chapters conclude with problems.

Pinsky, Mark A., ed. PROBABILISTIC METHODS IN DIFFERENTIAL EQUATIONS. Lecture Notes in Mathematics, vol. 451. New York: Springer-Verlag, 1974. viii, 162 p. No index.

Fourteen papers presented at a conference on stochastic differential equations held at the University of Victoria, British Columbia, August 19-20, 1974. Papers emphasize mathematical rigor and include such topics as stochastic parallel displacement; stochastic differentials and quasi-standard random variables; random evolutions; application of branching random fields to genetics; relativistic Brownian motion; and dual multiplicative operator functionals.

Preston, Christopher J. RANDOM FIELDS. Lecture Notes in Mathematics, 534. New York: Springer-Verlag, 1976. 200 p. References, pp. 192-97. Index, pp. 198-200.

A monograph on the properties of classical equilibrium states from statistical mechanics defined in terms of conditional probabilities. Assumes knowledge of measure theory, conditional expectation, martingale convergence theory, and probability kernels. Topics include existence of the Gibbs states; invariant specifications; lattice models; continuous models; and attractive specification.

Puri, Madam Lal, ed. STOCHASTIC PROCESSES AND RELATED TOPICS. Vol. 1. Foreword by L. Le Cam. New York: Academic Press, 1975. xiii, 315 p. No index.

Fourteen papers presented at the Summer Research Institute on statistical inference for stochastic processes held in Bloomington, Indiana, July 31-August 9, 1975. Topics include local and global properties in the theory of asymptotic normality of experiments; some dimension results for processes with independent increments; conditional limit theorems for random walks; stochastic iteration of stable processes; the ergodic behavior of a class of real transformations; random fields generated by quantum fields; and a survey of abstract Wiener spaces.

Rahman, N.A. EXERCISES IN PROBABILITY AND STATISTICS FOR MATHEMATICS UNDERGRADUATES. WITH ANSWERS AND HINTS ON SOLUTIONS. Foreword by M.G. Kendall. New York: Hafner, 1967. xi, 307 p. No index.

Over 400 exercises for use in a first course for mathematics students classified into the following four chapters: "Discrete Probability and Random Variables"; "Continuous Random Variables"; "Estimation, Tests of Significance, and Inference"; and "Characteristic Functions." Topics include difference equations and generating functions; joint and simple derived distributions of random variables; bivariate correlation and regression; and sampling distributions.

Renyi, Alfréd. PROBABILITY THEORY. Preface by Pal Revesz. Translated by L. Vekerdi. North-Holland Series in Applied Mathematics and Mechanics, vol. 10. New York: Elsevier, 1970. 666 p. Tables, pp. 617-37. Remarks and Bibliographical Notes, pp. 638-43. References, pp. 645-60. Author and Subject Index, pp. 661-66.

Originally published in Hungarian. A text for a graduate course in probability for students who have knowledge of calculus and elementary probability theory. Consists of proofs of many theorems supplemented by a fair amount of verbal description. Topics include discrete random variables; general theory of random variables; convolution of distributions; Kolmogorov probability spaces; characteristic functions; laws of large numbers; limit theorems of probability theory; and an introduction to information theory. Chapters conclude with exercises which extend to text results with hints provided.

Revesz, Pal. THE LAWS OF LARGE NUMBERS. Probability and Mathematical Statistics. A Series of Monographs and Textbooks, vol. 4. New York: Academic Press, 1968. 176 p. References, pp. 169-73. Author Index, pp. 175-76.

A general survey of the results and the most important methods of proof concerning the relationships between the axiomatic definition of probability and the relative frequency concept by means of the following three laws of large numbers: stochastic convergence, mean convergence, and convergence in probability. Topics include summary of definitions and theorems; general theorems of the laws of large numbers; laws of large numbers of different classes of stochastic processes; laws not related to any concrete class of stochastic processes; random values taking values in an abstract space; and application of the results to number theory, statistics, and information theory. Assumes familiarity with probability theory, stochastic processes, measure theory, ergodic theory, and functional analysis.

______, ed. LIMIT THEOREMS OF PROBABILITY THEORY. Amsterdam: North-Holland, 1975. 420 p. No index.

Twenty-five papers presented at the colloquium on limit theorems of probability and statistics organized by the Bolyai Janos Mathematical Society and held in Keszthely June 24-29, 1974. Includes the following sessions: invariance principle; limit properties of order statistics; limit theorems in stochastic approximation; limit theorems of independent random variables and martingales; limit theorems for dependent random variables; and limit theorems of abstract valued random variables. Knowledge of higher mathematics, including normed linear spaces and topology, assumed.

Robinson, Enders A. AN INTRODUCTION TO INFINITELY MANY VARIATES.

Griffin's Statistical Monographs and Courses, no. 6. New York: Hafner, 1959. 132 p. Exercises, pp. 111-25. References, pp. 126-28. Index, pp. 129-32.

A concise presentation of probability theory, limit theorems, and stationary stochastic processes involving an infinite number of random variables. Topics include metric spaces; measure spaces; central limit theorem; convergence in metric spaces; regression analysis of a finite number of random variables to an infinite number of stationary stochastic processes; Hilbert space; linear operators; and spectral representation. Useful as a supplementary text with knowledge of measure theory and integration helpful but not necessary.

Rohatgi, V.K. AN INTRODUCTION TO PROBABILITY THEORY AND MATHEMATICAL STATISTICS. Wiley Series in Probability and Mathematical Statistics. New York: Wiley, 1976. xiv, 684 p. References, pp. 641-47. Tables, pp. 648-67. Glossary of Some Frequently Used Symbols and Abbreviations, pp. 668-69. Author Index, pp. 671-73. Subject Index, pp. 675-84.

A mathematically oriented text for a one-year course in mathematical statistics for seniors and beginning graduate students in mathematics, engineering, and physics, who have knowledge of set theory, linear algebra, and advanced calculus. Contains 550 problems at the ends of the sections, 350 examples, 200 remarks, and 150 references. Proofs of central limit theorem and strong law of large numbers included. Topics include random variables and their distributions; moments and moment-generating functions; random vectors limit theorems; sample moments and their distributions; theory of point estimation; Neyman-Pearson lemma; confidence estimation; general linear hypothesis; nonparametric statistical inference; and sequential statistical inference.

Rosenblatt, Murray. RANDOM PROCESSES. 2d ed. Graduate Texts in Mathematics, 17. New York: Springer-Verlag, 1973. x, 229 p. References, pp. 221-26. Index, pp. 227-28.

A text for a graduate course in the theory of random processes for students in mathematics and statistics who have had courses in advanced calculus and matrix algebra. Limited to the discrete case, although measure theoretic tools required for continuous cases included without proofs with intuitive discussions and by comparison with the discrete cases. Emphasizes intuitive understanding of concepts. Topics include discrete and continuous Markov chains; probability spaces with an infinite number of sample points; stationary processes; ergodic theory; Brownian motion; weakly stationary processes and random harmonic analysis; martingales; zero-one law; and uniform mixing conditions and narrow band-pass filtering. Chapters conclude with problems and notes.

Ross, Sheldon M. APPLIED PROBABILITY MODELS WITH OPTIMIZATION APPLICATIONS. Holden-Day Series in Management Science. San Francisco: Holden-Day, 1970. x, 198 p. Appendixes, pp. 192-94. Index, pp. 195-98.

A text for a one-semester course for students with an intermediate probability background. Proofs based on probability, rather than on analysis. Topics include Poisson process; renewal theory; Markov chains; semi-Markov, Markov renewal, and regenerative processes; Markov decision processes; semi-Markov decision processes; inventory theory; and Brownian motion. Appendixes include contraction mappings, and a counter example for which there is an optimal nonstationary policy better than every stationary policy. Chapters conclude with problems and references.

_____. INTRODUCTION TO PROBABILITY MODELS. Probability and Mathematical Statistics. A Series of Monographs and Textbooks, vol. 10. New York: Academic Press, 1972. xiii, 272 p. Answers and Solutions to Selected Problems, pp. 244-67. Index, pp. 269-72.

A text for a one-year course in probability or stochastic processes for students who have knowledge of calculus and matrix algebra. Approach heuristic and nonrigorous rather than measure theoretic. Topics include conditional probability and conditional expectations; Markov chains; Poisson processes and exponential distributions with applications to birth and death models and queueing; renewal theory; reliability theory; and statistical estimation, including Bayes' estimation. Consists of definition, discussion, example style, with derivations included in the solutions to examples. Applications represent engineering, management science, physical and social sciences, and operations research.

Roussas, George G. CONTIGUITY OF PROBABILITY MEASURES: SOME APPLICATIONS IN STATISTICS. Cambridge Tracts in Mathematics and Mathematical Physics, vol. 63. New York: Cambridge University Press, 1972. xiii, 248 p. Appendix, pp. 199-239. Bibliography, pp. 240-45. Index, pp. 246-48.

A monograph on the mathematical theory of contiguity treating such topics as asymptotic expansion and asymptotic distribution of likelihood functions; approximation of a family of probability measures by an exponential family; asymptotic efficiency of estimates; and multiparameter asymptotically optimal tests. Assumes knowledge of mathematical statistics. Appendixes include proofs of theorems. Chapters conclude with exercises.

Rozanov, I͡Uriĭ Anatol'evich. INFINITE-DIMENSIONAL GAUSSIAN DISTRIBUTIONS. Translated by G. Biriuk. Proceedings of the Steklov Institute of Mathematics, no. 108. Providence, R.I.: American Mathematical Society, 1971. iv, 161 p. Bibliography, pp. 157-61. No index.

A monograph, originally published in Russian, on the equivalence of Gaussian probability distributions in various infinite-dimensional Gaussian distribution). Topics include definition of Gaussian probability measures in various linear spaces; equivalence of Gaussian distributions in Hilbert spaces; construction of the best unbiased estimates for an unknown mean value and the correlation function of an arbitrary Gaussian distribution; structure of conditional mathematical expectations of various functionals of a Gaussian random process; and structure of linear measurable functionals and transformations in an arbitrary linear space with Gaussian measures. Includes proofs, and knowledge of measure theory and functional analysis assumes.

_____. INNOVATION PROCESSES. Translation edited by A.V. Balakrishnan. Scripta Series in Mathematics. New York: Wiley, Halsted Press, 1977. vii, 136 p. Subject Index, pp. 135-36.

Originally published in Russian. Deals with the construction of innovation processes based on the following concepts of Gaussian processes: regularity and multiplicity (including the infinite dimensional case); Wold decomposition and factorization; and equivalence and orthogonality. Four chapters titles: "Innovation Processes and Canonical Representations"; "Regular Processes"; "Regular Stationary Processes"; and "Equivalent Random Processes." Assumes knowledge of advanced stochastic processes and probability theory. Useful to both pure and applied mathematicians.

_____. INTRODUCTORY PROBABILITY THEORY. Translated and edited by R.A. Silverman. Selected Russian Publications in the Mathematical Sciences. Englewood Cliffs, N.J.: Prentice-Hall, 1969. ix, 148 p. Appendix 1: Information Theory, pp. 115-20. Appendix 2: Game Theory, pp. 121-26. Appendix 3: Branching Processes, pp. 127-35. Appendix 4: Problems in Optimal Control, pp. 136-42. Index, pp. 145-48.

Originally published in Russian. Consists of an introduction to modern probability with emphasis on discrete models and prerequisites of calculus and mathematical analysis. Topics include sets and events; random variables and the binomial, Poisson, and normal distributions; weak and strong laws of large numbers; Markov chains; and continuous Markov processes. Includes 150 problems. Useful as a text for a one-semester course.

Scheaffer, Richard L., and Mendenhall, William. INTRODUCTION TO PROBABILITY: THEORY AND APPLICATIONS. North Scituate, Mass.: Duxbury, 1975. x, 289 p. Appendix I: Common Probability Distributions, Means, Variances, and Moment Generating Functions, pp. 265-66. Appendix II: Tables, pp. 267-79. Answers to Exercises, pp. 281-85. Index, pp. 287-89.

A text for a one-semester course in probability for undergraduates in mathematics and related disciplines who have knowledge of calculus. Emphasizes connectivity of topics and applications in examples, exercises, and statistical inference. Topics include set theory; Bayes' rule; random variables; discrete and continuous distributions; multivariate probability distributions; functions of random variables; hypothesis testing; and minimas and Bayes' decisions. Chapters conclude with references and problems.

Schwartz, Laurent. RADON MEASURES ON ARBITRARY TOPOLOGICAL SPACES AND CYLINDRICAL MEASURES. Tata Institute of Fundamental Research Studies in Mathematics. New York: Oxford University Press, 1973. 393 p. Appendix: Complements on Narrow Convergence, pp. 369-89. Terminological Index to Part II, pp. 390-91. References, pp. 392-93. No index.

Part I devoted to the study of Radon measures on arbitrary (Housdorff) topological spaces and properties relative to Polish, Lusin, and Luslin spaces. Part II considers cylindrical probabilities and radonifying maps.

Skorokhod, Anatoliĭ Vladimirovich. STUDIES IN THE THEORY OF RANDOM PROCESSES. Translated by Scripta Technica, Inc. Adiwes International Series in Mathematics. Reading, Mass.: Addison-Wesley, 1965. viii, 199 p. Supplementary Remarks, pp. 186-89. Bibliography, pp. 190-97. Index, pp. 198-99.

Originally published in Russian in 1961. Devoted to the development of probabilistic methods in stochastic differential equations and limit theorems for Markov processes. Topics include review of martingales, Markov processes, and processes with independent increments; stochastic integrals with respect to Brownian motion, a martingale, and random measures; existence and uniqueness of the solution to stochastic equations; differential equations defining the distributions of Markov processes; one-dimensional diffusion processes; transition from a Markov chain to a Markov process with continuous time; and limit theorems for sums of independent random variables. Emphasizes mathematical rigor, with proofs of theorems provided. Assumes knowledge of the theory of random processes.

Smart, William Marshall. COMBINATION OF OBSERVATIONS. New York: Cambridge University Press, 1958. xiv, 253 p. Appendixes: Tables, pp. 246-50. Index, pp. 251-53.

A study of frequency distributions encountered in the experimental sciences and the treatment of observations and measures in which the incidence of errors is present. Topics include frequency distributions; least squares; probability and the normal law; measures of precision for weighted observations; equations in several unknowns; theoretical frequency distributions, including their representation by trigonometric series and the

Gram-Charlier series; corrections of statistics, including Sheppard's correction; Eddington's solution of the integral equation; application of Fourier transforms; correlation; contingency tables; and normal bivariate and trivariate distributions. Presentation consists of derivations with simple numerical illustrations. Assumes knowledge of calculus, including multiple integrals.

Sobol, I.M. THE MONTE CARLO METHOD. Translated by Robert Messer, John Stone, and Peter Fortini. Popular Lectures in Mathematics. Chicago: University of Chicago Press, 1974. viii, 67 p. Appendix: Tables, p. 65. Bibliography, p. 67. No index.

Originally published in Russian in 1967. A monograph on the Monte Carlo method for individuals in all disciplines. Presents a number of problems solvable by the Monte Carlo method. Consists of two parts: "Simulating Random Variables" and "Examples of the Applications of the Monte Carlo Method." Applications include simulating a mass supply system; calculating the quality and reliability of products; simulating the penetration of neutrons through a block; evaluating definite integral; and proofs of certain propositions. Assumes knowledge of calculus, basic statistics and probability theory.

Spanier, Jerome, and Gelbard, Ely M. MONTE CARLO PRINCIPLES AND NEUTRON TRANSPORT PROBLEMS. Addison-Wesley Series in Computer Science and Information Processing. Reading, Mass.: Addison-Wesley, 1969. xiv, 234 p. Author Index, pp. 227-28. Subject Index, pp. 229-34.

Presents the general mathematical principles of Monte Carlo techniques with emphasis on the use of variance reducing devices to improve the information content in Monte Carlo samples and the methods of superposition and reciprocity, with applications to neutron transport problems. Assumes knowledge of the standard mathematical skills of engineering, familiarity with the transport equation, and reactor theory. Topics include discrete and continuous random walk processes; track length estimators; random number generators; estimators for integral equations; standard variance reduction techniques; superposition and reciprocity in one-energy problems; computation of thermal neutron fluxes; and the superposition principle in resonance escape computations.

Staël, Von Holstein, and Carl-Avel, S. ASSESSMENT AND EVALUATION OF SUBJECTIVE PROBABILITY DISTRIBUTIONS. Stockholm: Economic Research Institute, Stockholm School of Economics, 1970. x, 225 p. Appendix 1: A Family of Strictly Proper Scoring Rules Which Are Sensitive to Distance, pp. 195-201. Appendix 2: A Geometrical Representation of Certain Concepts, pp. 202-3. Appendix 3: Concave Scoring Rules, pp. 204-6. Appendix 4: Devices Used in the Two Die Experiments, pp. 207-9. Frequently Used Symbols, pp. 210-11. References, pp. 212-19. Author Index, pp. 220-21. Subject Index, pp. 222-25.

Presents procedures for assessing and revising subjective probability distributions in three parts: "Assessment and Evaluation of Subjective Probability Distributions"; "Four Experiments with Assessment of Subjective Probability Distributions"; and "An Introduction to Bayesian Decision Theory with Emphasis on Economic Applications." Includes both theory and applications. Designed to determine if individuals improve their performance with the help of feedback.

Steindl, Josef. RANDOM PROCESSES AND THE GROWTH OF FIRMS: A STUDY OF THE PARETO LAW. New York: Hafner, 1965. 249 p. Appendix A: Brief Guide to the Study of Random Processes, pp. 147-86. Appendix B: Empirical Data, pp. 187-246. Index, pp. 247-49.

A monograph on the stochastic laws governing the size distribution of firms. Both time series and cross-section data for various years and for various countries (United States, Sweden, Germany) used to derive Pareto and Gibrat distributions for firm size. Assumes knowledge of intermediate probability.

Suppes, Patrick. A PROBABILISTIC THEORY OF CAUSALITY. Acta Philosophica Fennica, Fasc. XXIV. Amsterdam: North-Holland, 1970. 130 p. Appendix on Probability, pp. 96-120. References, pp. 121-24. Index of Names, pp. 125-26. Index of Subjects, pp. 127-30.

A monograph which develops the concept of causality in terms of probability with applications to philosophical problems that arise in discussions of causality. Topics include causal relations among events (prima facia, spurious, direct, supplementary, sufficient, and negative causes); qualitative theory of causal relations; causal relations among quantitative properties; and general philosophical issues.

Sveshnikov, Aram Arutiunovich. PROBLEMS IN PROBABILITY THEORY: MATHEMATICAL STATISTICS AND THEORY OF RANDOM FUNCTIONS. Foreword by B.R. Belbaum. Translated by Scripta Technica, Inc. Saunders Mathematics Books. Philadelphia: W.B. Saunders, 1968. ix, 481 p. Answers and Solutions, pp. 375-470. Sources of Tables Referred to in the Text, pp. 471-73. Bibliography, pp. 475-77. Index, pp. 479-81.

Originally published in Russian. Consists of a broad and deep cross-section of problems (with solutions) ranging from the simplest combinatorial problems in finite sample spaces through information theory, limit theorems, and the use of moments. Chapter titles: "Random Events"; "Random Variables"; "Systems of Random Variables"; "Numerical Characteristics and Distribution Laws of Functions of Random Variables"; "Entropy and Information"; "The Limit Theorems"; "The Correlation Theory of Random Functions"; "Markov Processes"; and "Methods of Data Processing." Useful as a reference and supplementary text in a wide variety of courses in probability and statistics.

SYMPOSIUM ON PROBABILITY METHODS IN ANALYSIS. Lecture Notes in Mathematics, no. 31. New York: Springer-Verlag, 1967. iv, 329 p. No index.

Twenty-eight papers presented at a symposium held at Loutraki, Greece, in 1966 under the sponsorship of the NATO Scientific Affairs Division. Papers written in French, German, and English consider such topics as axiomatic potential theory; martingale convergence theorem; a theory of patterns; invariant and noninvariant measures; renewal sequences and their arithmetic; Fourier transforms in infinitely many dimensions; spectral analysis; analytical methods in probability theory; sums of Markov-chains on finite semigroups; superefficiency; and explicit Martin Boundary conditions. Assumes knowledge of advanced mathematics and mathematical statistics.

Taylor, Robert L. STOCHASTIC CONVERGENCE OF WEIGHTED SUMS OF RANDOM ELEMENTS IN LINEAR SPACES. Lecture Notes in Mathematics, 672. New York: Springer-Verlag, 1978. vii, 216 p. Bibliography, pp. 202-11. Subject Index, pp. 212-16.

A monograph for probabilistics, statisticians, and mathematicians involved in research concerning convergence theory, stochastic processes, and ergodic theory. Assumes a good background in probability theory. Topics include random elements in linear spaces; laws of large numbers, uncorrelation, and convergence of weighted sums of random variables; laws of large numbers in normed linear spaces; randomly weighted sums; and applications in stochastic processes, decision theory, quality control, and estimation.

Thomas, John B. AN INTRODUCTION TO APPLIED PROBABILITY AND RANDOM PROCESSES. New York: Wiley, 1971. x, 338 p. Appendixes, pp. 299-317. References, pp. 319-20. Tables, pp. 321-26. Answers to Problems, pp. 327-30. Index, pp. 331-38.

A text for a two-semester course in probability and/or random processes for engineering students who have knowledge of engineering calculus. Emphasizes both rigorous and intuitive proofs with numerous examples provided. Topics include axiomatic foundation of probability; fields, Borel fields, and infinite samples spaces; discrete and continuous random variables; expectation and moments; characteristic functions; the Bienoyme-Chebyshev theorem; multivariate normal distribution; transformation of random variables; sequences of random variables; linear filtering of stationary processes; infinitely divisible distributions; processes with independent increments; random walk; and the Wiener-Levy process. Chapters conclude with problems. Appendixes include review of essential mathematics topics.

Thomasian, Aram J. THE STRUCTURE OF PROBABILITY THEORY WITH APPLICATIONS. McGraw-Hill Series in Probability and Statistics. New York: McGraw-Hill, 1969. xvii, 746 p. Appendix 1: Several Frequently Used Formulas, pp. 629-30. Appendix 2: The Supremum, pp. 630-33. Appendix 3: Summability, pp. 634-37. Summaries, pp. 639-725. Selected Answers and Solutions, pp. 727-40. Index, pp. 741-46.

First half suitable for a one-semester course in probability, while second half for a course in stochastic processes. Presentation somewhat abstract, with knowledge of calculus required for some portions. Intuitive explanations separated from formal proofs. Topics include combinatorics; countability in sets; absolutely convergent series; independent events and experiments; discrete and continuous probability densities; law of large numbers; random variables; central limit theorem; conditional expectations and branching processes; distribution functions; multivariate normed densities and characteristic functions; method of truncation; stochastic processes; Poisson processes; and the Wiener process. Sections conclude with exercises.

Thorp, Edward O. ELEMENTARY PROBABILITY. New York: Wiley, 1966. x, 152 p. References, p. 127. Solutions to Exercises, pp. 129-46. Index, pp. 147-52.

A text for a one-semester course in probability for students who have had about two years of calculus. Includes proofs of simple theorems and examples. Topics include set theory and Bayes' rule; random variables and their distributions; absolutely convergent series; geometric and exponential power series; continuous probability and Borel sets; integration; normal approximation to the binomial; and probability and measure. Emphasizes conceptual development of probability. Also useful to those in economics, psychology, and biology. Sections conclude with suggested readings and exercises involving proofs, derivations, applications, and problems.

Tjur, Tue. ON THE MATHEMATICAL FOUNDATIONS OF PROBABILITY. Lecture Notes, 1. Copenhagen: Institute of Mathematical Statistics, University of Copenhagen, 1972. viii, 183 p. Literature, pp. 171-74. Some Remarks on Notation, pp. 175-76. List of Some Symbols and Standard Notation, pp. 177-79. Index, pp. 180-83.

Applies measure theory to probability theory in three parts: "Discussion of the Foundation"; "Introduction to Probability"; and "Stochastic Processes." Concludes that a relevant theory of probability can be formulated by using Radon measures. Topics include finite case axioms; infinite case; Kolmogorov's axioms; probability on a compact space; measures on compact spaces; positive and transition operators with measures; product measures; family of finite dimensional distributions; integration;

almost continuous mappings and linear operators; Hilbert space; conditional distributions; convergence in probability; predictability; stopping times; and Markov processes.

Tsokos, Chris P. PROBABILITY DISTRIBUTIONS: AN INTRODUCTION TO PROBABILITY THEORY WITH APPLICATIONS. Belmont, Calif.: Wadsworth, 1972. x, 657 p. Tables, pp. 585-633. Answers, pp. 635-53. Index, pp. 655-57.

A text for an introductory course in probability for students in varied fields who have knowledge of calculus. Emphasizes distribution theory with each new concept, theorem, definition, and corollary followed by one or more examples. Topics include one- and n-dimensional discrete and continuous random variables and their distributions; functions of a random variable; expected values, moments, moment-generating and characteristic functions; two random variables; sequence of random variables; limit theorems, including DeMoivre-Laplace theorem and the weak and strong laws of large numbers; and finite Markov chains. Chapters conclude with exercises.

Tsokos, Chris P., and Padgett, W.J. RANDOM INTEGRAL EQUATIONS WITH APPLICATIONS TO LIFE SCIENCES AND ENGINEERING. New York: Academic Press, 1974. x, 278 p. Bibliography, pp. 260-73. Index, pp. 275-78.

A fairly complete development of nonlinear stochastic integral equations of the Volterra and Fredholm type, including the problems of existence, uniqueness, stability, and approximation of random solutions of the equations. Integral equations of the Ito-Doob type also investigated. Applications made to telephone traffic theory, heredity, turbulence theory, population growth, stochastic control systems, physiological models, communicable diseases, and stochastic integrodifferential systems. Useful for a graduate course on modern integral equations with emphasis on probabilistic modeling of various problems in life science and engineering. Also useful as a reference.

_____. RANDOM INTEGRAL EQUATIONS WITH APPLICATIONS TO STOCHASTIC SYSTEMS. Lecture Notes in Mathematics, no. 233. New York: Springer-Verlag, 1971. vii, 174 p. References, pp. 166-74. No index.

A monograph which presents the theory of existence and uniqueness of random solutions of the most general random Volterra and Fredholm equations with applications to the theory of stochastic differential systems. Useful to mathematicians, probabilists, and engineers who are working in systems theory or who are merely interested in the theory of random equations.

Van Zwet, W.R. CONVEX TRANSFORMATIONS OF RANDOM VARIABLES. Mathematical Centre Tracts, 7. Amsterdam: Mathematisch Centrum, 1964. viii, 116 p. References, pp. 113-16. No index.

A rigorous study of the behavior of real-valued, nondecreasing convex functions of random variables. Topics include Jensen's inequality and moment inequalities; order statistics and asymptotic expressions for their expectations and central moments needed to establish characterization theorems; converse theorems that characterize weak orderings in terms of large sample inequalities; symmetric inverse beta distributions and small sample inequalities; and applications to hypothesis testing. Includes examples.

Vervaat, Wim. SUCCESS EPOCHS IN BERNOULLI TRIALS (WITH APPLICATIONS IN NUMBER THEORY). Mathematical Tracts, 42. Amsterdam: Mathematisch Centrum, 1972. ii, 166 p. Appendix, pp. 152-55. References, pp. 156-60. Author Index, pp. 161-62. Index of Definitions, pp. 163-64. List of Symbols, pp. 165-66.

A revised version of the author's thesis submitted to the University of Amsterdam. Concerned with the development of limit theorems for success epochs in Bernoulli trials with applications to the derivation of probabilistic limit theorems for special classes of series expansions of the real numbers in the unit interval. Emphasizes mathematical rigor, with probability theory, real analysis, and topology necessary for comprehension. Appendixes devoted to additional theorems.

Wadsworth, George P., and Bryan, Joseph G. APPLICATIONS OF PROBABILITY AND RANDOM VARIABLES. 2d ed., rev. and enl. McGraw-Hill Series in Probability and Statistics. New York: McGraw-Hill, 1974. xv, 448 p. Index, pp. 443-48.

An applied text for a one-semester course in probability with a prerequisite of calculus, and a reference for scientists, engineers, and operations research workers. Topics include discrete and continuous random variables and their distribution, including hypergeometric, geometric, Pascal, gamma, beta, and Poisson; joint distributions; derived distributions, including probability transformation and distributions of functions of two or more independent variates; expectation, including probability of extreme values, multivariate functions, covariance and correlation; generating functions; Markov processes and waiting lines; Bayesian approach to estimation; and application of probability in statistical inference. Consists of definitions, brief derivations, and verbal discussions, followed by examples with additional derivations. Chapters conclude with appendixes devoted to additional derivations and proofs and problems.

_____. INTRODUCTION TO PROBABILITY AND RANDOM VARIABLES. McGraw-Hill Series in Probability and Statistics. New York: McGraw-Hill, 1960. vii, 292 p. Index, pp. 287-92.

A text for a one-semester course in probability for undergraduates who have knowledge of calculus, and a self-study for engineers and research workers. Statistical concepts derived from direct applications in probability, and topics include tests of significance, confidence limits, and sampling distributions. Probability topics include rules of probability, discrete and continuous random variables, joint and derived distributions, probability of extreme values, covariance and correlation, and multivariate moment generating functions. Includes numerous examples, set out in fine print, with chapters concluding with exercises.

Wasan, M.T. STOCHASTIC APPROXIMATION. Cambridge Tracts in Mathematics and Mathematical Physics, no. 58. Cambridge: Cambridge University Press, 1969. x, 202 p. Appendix 1: Iterative Techniques of Numerical Analysis, pp. 150-54. Appendix 2: Limit Theorems, pp. 155-74. Appendix 3: Inequalities, pp. 175-94. Bibliography, pp. 195-99. Index, pp. 201-2.

A text for a course in stochastic approximation for students of mathematics, computer science, and mathematical statistics, and a reference for research workers in science, engineering, statistics, and related fields. Assumes knowledge of numerical analysis, probability theory, and inequalities. Proofs of theorems detailed. Methods include Robbins-Monroe; Kiefer-Wolfowitz; multivariate approximation method of asymptotic normality, including methods of moments and characteristic functions; and up-and-down method. Chapters conclude with problems. Applications include filtering problems, adaptive control, regression, reliability, quantal response, estimation, and pharmacology.

Weaver, Warren. LADY LUCK: THE THEORY OF PROBABILITY. Garden City, N.Y.: Doubleday, 1963. 392 p. Index, pp. 378-92.

An elementary treatment of probability for the layman and high school students. Topics include introduction to mathematical probability; rules of probability; expectation; binomial experiments; law of large numbers; distribution functions and probabilities; rare events, coincidences, and surprising occurrences; probability and statistics; gambling; and birthday problem.

Weiss, Lionel, and Wolfowitz, Jacob. MAXIMUM PROBABILITY ESTIMATORS AND RELATED TOPICS. Lecture Notes in Mathematics, vol. 424. New York: Springer-Verlag, 1975. 106 p. Appendix, pp. 93-104. References, pp. 105-6. No index.

A self-contained introduction to the method and theory of maximum probability estimators for graduate students working by themselves or in a seminar. Method gives asymptotically efficient estimators for almost all statistical problems of theoretical or practical interest, and the appendix contains a number of nontechnical examples. Assumes knowledge of mathematical statistics.

Whitmore, G.A., and Findlay, M.C., eds. STOCHASTIC DOMINANCE. Lexington, Mass.: Lexington Books, 1978. xiv, 401 p. Bibliography, pp. 373-93. Index, pp. 395-98. List of Contributors, p. 399. About the Authors, p. 401.

A reference-text on stochastic dominance consisting of eight contributions originally presented at a symposium held at McGill University April 1, 1974. Useful to students and scholars in finance, economics, and other areas of the social sciences concerned with decision-theoretic methodology as a supplementary text for graduate courses and seminars. Topics include computational aspects of portfolio; empirical studies in portfolio analysis; applications of stochastic dominance to capital markets and economic theory; and convex stochastic dominance.

Whittle, Peter. PROBABILITY. Penguin Education Library of University Mathematics. Baltimore: Penguin, 1970. 239 p. Index, pp. 235-39.

An introductory text on the theory and application of probability using the axiomatic approach with set theory introduced as needed. Assumes knowledge of calculus, matrix algebra, mathematical analysis, and probability generating functions. Topics include expectation; simple probability processes, such as the binomial, normal, and Poisson; Markov processes; convergence of random processes, including laws of large numbers and martingale convergence; and applications to optimization, quantum mechanics, information theory, and statistical mechanics. Emphasizes proofs of theorems, with no numerical examples. Sections conclude with exercises.

Woodroofe, Michael. PROBABILITY WITH APPLICATIONS. New York: McGraw-Hill, 1975. x, 372 p. Appendix A: Set Theory, pp. 346-47. Appendix B: Integration, pp. 348-52. Appendix C: Tables, pp. 353-55. Appendix D: References, pp. 356-57. Appendix E: Answers to Selected Problems, pp. 358-64. Index, pp. 365-72.

A text for a course in probability for graduates and undergraduates in mathematics, engineering, mathematical psychology, and econometrics, and a reference for those whose formal training in probability does not go beyond the introductory level. Topics include axiomatic probability; conditional probability and independence; binomial and related probabilities; random variables and vectors; distribution theory; expectation; limit theorems; random walks; and martingales. Also include applications to scientific and statistical problems. Chapters conclude with problems.

Wright, Fred B., ed. ERGODIC THEORY. New York: Academic Press, 1963. xi, 316 p. Author Index, pp. 315-16.

Nineteen mathematically oriented papers presented at a symposium on ergodic theory held at Tulane University, October 23-27, 1961. Topics include asymptotic convergence theorems; convergence of operator averages; and irreversible minimal set; finite invariant measures for temporally homogeneous Markov processes; ergodic decomposition of the Kolmogorov-Sinai invariant; an adjoint ergodic theorem; a random ergodic theorem and its application in the theory of Markov chains; and Abelian ergodic theorems in locally convex space.

Wrighton, R.F. ELEMENTARY PRINCIPLES OF PROBABILITY AND INFORMATION. New York: Academic Press, 1973. viii, 91 p. Index, pp. 89-91.

A unified approach to probability and information theory with special reference to the biological sciences. Emphasizes the intuitive approach to highly mathematical topics using only a few formulas and derivations. Assumes knowledge of elementary probability. Consists of the following chapters: "Classical Random-Event Probability"; "Information and Information Potential"; "Communication in the Presence of Noise"; "Inverse Problems in Probability"; "Random Sampling Theory"; "Statistical Experimentation"; and "Information Potential."

Yaglom, A.M. AN INTRODUCTION TO THE THEORY OF STATIONARY RANDOM FUNCTIONS. Translated by R.A. Silverman. Rev. English ed. Englewood Cliffs, N.J.: Prentice-Hall, 1962. xiii, 235 p. Appendix I: Generalized Random Processes, pp. 207-13. Appendix II: Some Recent Developments, pp. 214-16. Bibliography, pp. 217-23. Supplementary Bibliography, pp. 224-25. Name Index, pp. 227-29. Subject Index, pp. 231-35.

A monograph, originally published in Russian in 1952, on a mathematically rigorous treatment of extrapolating and filtering stationary random functions (both sequences and processes). Emphasizes the simpliest case where the spectral density is a rational function. Assumes knowledge of probability theory, complex function theory, and the geometry of Hilbert spaces. Useful to mathematicians, physicists, and engineers who deal with random functions.

Yakowitz, Sidney J. COMPUTATIONAL PROBABILITY AND SIMULATION. Reading, Mass.: Addison-Wesley, 1977. xxii, 240 p. Index, pp. 235-40.

Employs random generator routines of digital computers to simulate experiments based on probability models. Provides insights into theorems, such as the central limit theorem, and probability laws, such as the laws of large numbers. Topics include theory and limitations of pseudo-random number generators;

methods for generating independent observations of a random variable with a given probability distribution; simulation of die throwing; exponentially distributed observations, bivariate random variables, and random vectors; gaming and random walks; gambler's ruin with extensions to inventory control; limiting processes for random walks and stationary Gaussian time series; simulation of Brownian motion; and integration and solution of differential equations. Useful as a supplement to a course in probability for graduates and undergraduates. Chapters conclude with exercises and references.

Yaspan, Arthur. ESSENTIALS OF PROBABILITY. Boston: Prindle, Weber and Schmidt, 1968. viii, 200 p. Appendix: Tables, pp. 181-97. Index, pp. 199-200.

An exposition of the main features of ordinary probability for use as a text for a one-semester course for students who have had two years of college mathematics. Emphasizes methodology rather than applications. Presentation begins with simple counting techniques, proceeding to random variables, and ending with limit theorems, with examples and problems provided.

Yeh, Jui-Ching. STOCHASTIC PROCESSES AND THE WIENER INTEGRAL. Pure and Applied Mathematics. A Series of Monographs and Courses. New York: Marcel Dekker, 1973. viii, 551 p. Appendix: A Synopsis of Probability Theory, pp. 521-37. Bibliography, pp. 539-41. Addenda, pp. 543-46. Index, pp. 547-51.

A theoretical introduction to stochastic processes, Brownian motion, Gaussian processes, Wiener measures, and Wiener integrals. Topics include how a stochastic process on an arbitrary probability space induces a probability measure on the space of all real numbers; martingale convergence and closing theorems; existence proof of additive processes; Brownian motion as an additive process; stochastic integral of stepwise stochastic process with respect to a continuous Brownian motion process as a random variable; Hajek's proof of the Feldman-Hajek dichotomy that two Gaussian measures on a function space are either equivalent or singular; and the Cameron-Martin translation theorem of Wiener integrals. Assumes knowledge of measure theory and stochastic processes.

Zehna, Peter W. FINITE PROBABILITY. Topics in Contemporary Mathematics. Boston: Allyn & Bacon, 1969. x, 193 p. Bibliography, p. 161. Solutions to Exercises, pp. 163-87. Index, pp. 189-93.

A text for a course in mathematical probability based on finite sample spaces. Topics include events and sample spaces; probability spaces; conditional probability and independence;

compound experiments; random variables and probability distributions, including joint and multivariate distributions; and expectation. Emphasizes motivation of each axiom, definition, and theorem, with clear distinction between the theoretical structure of probability models and their applications and interpolation. Most sections conclude with exercises on applications.

Zubrzycki, Stefan. LECTURES IN PROBABILITY THEORY AND MATHEMATICAL STATISTICS. Translated by R. Bartoszynski. Modern Analytic and Computational Methods in Science and Mathematics. New York: Elsevier, 1972. xi, 321 p. References, p. 315. Index, pp. 317-21.

Originally published in Polish in 1970. Presents the present state of the measure-theoretic approach to probability. Topics include events and probability; distributions on the real line and in multidimensional euclidean spaces; conditional probability and stochastic independence of events; classical limit theorems; random variables and their properties; laws of large numbers; central limit theorem; most powerful and uniformly most powerful tests of hypotheses; Bayesian estimates; maximum likelihood estimators; and minimax estimators. Consists of definition, theorem, proof, and example style, with few numerical examples. Some sections conclude with problems on proofs and applications of theorems.

Chapter 6

TIME SERIES AND FORECASTING

Aitchison, John, and Dunsmore, I.R. STATISTICAL PREDICTION ANALYSIS. New York: Cambridge University Press, 1975. xi, 273 p. Appendix I: Notation for Standard Distributions, pp. 249-57. Appendix II: Classification of Prediction Problems, p. 258. Bibliography, pp. 259-65. Author Index, pp. 267-68. Subject Index, pp. 269-72. Example and Problem Index, p. 273.

An attempt to present statistical prediction (any form of statistical analysis with consideration given to what may happen in future experiments) within a unified framework and notation. Development considered from both a frequentist and a Bayesian viewpoint. Topics include predictive distribution, including regression models; decisive prediction, including point and set prediction; information prediction, including Bayesian information prediction; mean coverage tolerance prediction and guaranteed coverage tolerance prediction for binomial, Poisson, gamma, normal, multinomial, and the two-parameter exponential cases; distribution-free prediction; sampling inspection; regulation and optimization; calibration; diagnosis, and treatment allocation. Applications in the areas of medical prognosis, antibiotic assay, and machine tool replacement. Assumes knowledge of mathematical statistics.

Allen, Ray George Douglas. INDEX NUMBERS IN THEORY AND PRACTICE. Chicago: Aldine, 1975. x, 278 p. Bibliography, pp. 270-74. Index, pp. 275-78.

A simple comprehensive test on the construction and use of index numbers for use in basic statistics courses, and a reference for practitioners. Topics include the theory of the two-year case (year O and year 1) problem, including Laspeyres, Paasche, and Fisher indices; runs of index numbers; chain index numbers; and applications to commodity prices, retail prices, inequality of incomes, international comparison of real income, industrial production, and so on.

American Management Association. SALES FORECASTING: USES, TECHNIQUES, AND TRENDS. Special Report, no. 16. New York: 1956. 159 p. Appendix: Survey of Sales Forecasting Practices, by Lydia Strong, pp. 141-59. No index.

Thirteen nontechnical papers on sales forecasting presented at a conference held April 30-May 1, 1958, in Chicago, grouped under the following two headings: "Methods and Materials" (ten papers) and "Company Experience" (three papers). Topics include objectives of sales forecasting, increasing forecast accuracy, evaluating basic data, use of mathematics, presentation of forecast information, new product forecasting, short- medium- and long-range forecasts, and forecasting experiences at Corning Glass Works and Dodge Manufacturing Corp.

Anderson, Oliver D. TIME SERIES ANALYSIS AND FORECASTING: THE BOX JENKINS APPROACH. Boston: Butterworths, 1976. vi, 182 p. Appendix I: Collection of Time Series, pp. 159-66. Appendix II: Identification Programs, pp. 167-72. Appendix III: Inequality Proof, pp. 173-74. References, pp. 175-78. Index, pp. 179-82.

A self-contained presentation of the Box-Jenkins approach to forecasting time series. Includes properties of a flexible class of stable linear statistical models; the Box-Jenkins iterative cycle of identification, estimation, and verification, with applications in forecasting; and recent work on the Box-Jenkins approach. Useful to students and research workers in mathematics and in the social and physical sciences and related disciplines. Access to a digital computer helpful. Other topics include autoregressive, moving average, and mixed processes; identification; estimation; verification; seasonal models; and autoaggregation.

Armitage, Peter H.; Smith, Cyril; and Alper, Paul. DECISION MODELS FOR EDUCATIONAL PLANNING. Foreword by C.A. Moser and P. Redfern. London: Allen Lane, 1969. viii, 124 p. References, pp. 121-22. Index, pp. 123-24.

A monograph dealing with the development of two Markov process models designed to forecast the number of students in primary, secondary, and university education in the United Kingdom as well as the flows of students to these systems. Projects stocks (of students) in each year from 1965 to 1974, using 1964 stocks as the base year, assuming linear trends in the transition probabilities. Useful to anyone interested in education planning, and to researchers working in the areas of model building for education planning. Assumes knowledge of stochastic processes, but those without this knowledge can benefit from the analysis of simulation results.

Ascher, William. FORECASTING: AN APPRAISAL FOR POLICY-MAKERS AND PLANNERS. Foreword by Harold D. Lasswell. Baltimore: Johns Hopkins University Press, 1978. xiii, 239 p. Notes, pp. 215-28. Index, pp. 229-39.

A nontechnical appraisal of a number of forecasting results, as well as methods, in population, energy, transportation, technology, and economics. Based on an analysis of hundreds of forecasts. Emphasizes the presentation of errors of forecasts on graphs (for example, errors of five-, ten-, and twenty-year U.S. population forecasts; errors of ten-year petroleum consumption; and errors of ten-year domestic airline revenue-passenger miles forecasts). Useful to policymakers and planners.

Ash, J.C.K., and Smyth, D.J. FORECASTING THE UNITED KINGDOM ECONOMY. Lexington: D.C. Heath, 1973. xv, 267 p. Index, pp. 265-67.

Analyzes the accuracy of some 3,000 short-run forecasts (one quarter to one year ahead) of the major aggregates in the British economy made by the Treasury, the National Institute of Economics and Social Research, the Organization for European Cooperation and Social Research, the London Business School, and private economists during the 1960s and early 1970s. Includes procedures used to assess forecasting accuracy, and comparisons with forecasts made for other countries.

Balakrishna, S. TECHNIQUES OF DEMAND FORECASTING FOR INDUSTRIAL PRODUCTS. New Delhi: Sundar Publishers, 1968. iv, 233 p. Tables, pp. 111-79. Appendixes A to J, pp. 181-233. No index.

Applies four methods of forecasting industrial products in India-trend method, regression technique, historical and geographical analysis (country comparison), and end-use method. Includes the following categories of products for which forecasts are made: basic goods (coal, oil, cement, etc.), capital goods and machinery, and consumer products. Useful to planners, research organization, consulting firms, and students and teachers.

Banerjee, Kali S. COST OF LIVING INDEX NUMBERS: PRACTICE, PRECISION, AND THEORY. Statistics: Textbooks and Monographs, vol. 11. New York: Marcel Dekker, 1975. xi, 179 p. Appendixes A to F, pp. 125-70. References, pp. 171-75. Index, pp. 177-79.

A reference for professionals engaged in the construction and maintenance of cost of living index numbers in government, business, and industrial organizations, at national or international levels, and a supplementary text for statistics courses in colleges and universities. Includes the construction of cost of living index numbers utilizing the Paspeyre and Paasche formulas, the concept of the true index, unbiased estimation of index numbers, the development of formulas for calculating sampling errors, and procedures of constructing index numbers over geographical areas. Appendixes deal with special topics and derivations, including Divisia's differential derivation of the index, derivation of an index of a discontinued series, precision in constructing cost of living index numbers, Thiel's best linear and Kloek and De Wit's best linear average unbiased index numbers. Assumes knowledge of only basic statistics.

Baron, Raphael Raymond V. ANALYSIS OF SEASONALITY AND TRENDS IN STATISTICAL SERIES: METHODOLOGY AND APPLICATIONS IN ISRAEL. Vol. I. METHODOLOGY, CAUSES AND EFFECTS OF SEASONALITY. Technical Publication, no. 39. Jerusalem: Central Bureau of Statistics, 1973. xix, 261 p. Selected Bibliography on Time Series Analysis, pp. 229-57. Index to Principal Terminology, pp. 259-61.

A reference on methods of decomposing time series, with detailed analyses of 250 demographic and economic series in the Israel economy. Describes the use of seasonally adjusted data in current problems and month-to-month changes in trends with applications of projections of seasonality and trends in the preparation of short- and medium-term forecasts. Other topics include causes of seasonality, economic consequences of seasonality, and a new measure for the effect of seasonal demand--"The Maximal Annual Utilization Factor Constrained by Seasonality"--with emphasis on hotel services.

Battersby, Albert. SALES FORECASTING. London: Cassell and Co., 1968. xii, 144 p. Appendix: Logarithms, pp. 103-17. Solutions to Exercises, pp. 119-38. References, p. 139. Index, pp. 141-44.

A nonmathematical presentation of some of the simpler and more widely used methods of forecasting for sales managers. Topics include moving averages; weighted moving averages; regression analysis; seasonal effects; reordering levels; and market saturation, including exponential growth and Pearl's law. Includes simple numerical examples. Assumes knowledge of basic statistics.

Blohm, Hans, and Steinbuch, Karl, eds. TECHNOLOGICAL FORECASTING IN PRACTICE. Translated by Frederick Crowley and Christine Crowley. Westmead, Engl.: Saxon House (also Lexington: Lexington Books), 1973. viii, 177 p. Selected Bibliography, p. 173. Index, pp. 175-77.

Originally published in German as TECHNISCHE PROGNOSEN IN DER PRAXIS in 1972 in cooperation with the Research Group for Technological Forecasting in Karlsrube. Consists of twenty nontechnical, heretofore unpublished papers on technological forecasting arranged under the following three headings: "Methods" (five papers); "Examples" (six papers); and "Problems" (nine papers). Emphasizes the use of charts, graphs and tables, rather than mathematical formulas. Topics include the Delphi and other methods of forecasting; examples in passenger transport, computer industry, and energy; and problems of product planning, technology, policy, political planning, and the integration of technological prediction into management systems by improvement of forecasting analysis.

Bloomfield, Peter. FOURIER ANALYSIS OF TIME SERIES: AN INTRODUCTION. Wiley Series in Probability and Mathematical Statistics. New York: Wiley, 1976. xiii, 258 p. References, pp. 247-50. Index, pp. 251-58.

A supplementary text for a course in time series analysis and a reference for practitioners who use time series. Methods introduced in the context of specific sets of data, with knowledge of introductory statistics and some acquaintance with Fourier analysis and calculus helpful. Topics include harmonic analysis: least squares regression on a simusoid or sinusoids; harmonic analysis; the discrete Fourier transform, periodgram analysis; complex demodulation; and spectrum analysis. Exercises at the ends of the sections include algebraic questions involving discrete Fourier analysis, questions on theory, and problems dealing with the analysis of data. Includes FORTRAN programs.

Bolt, Gordon J. MARKET AND SALES FORECASTING--A TOTAL APPROACH. Marketing Text Series. New York: Wiley, 1972. 359 p. References, pp. 349-53. Index, pp. 355-59.

A reference for executives in small- and medium-sized companies and marketing researchers, forecasters, and management trainees in large organizations. Brings together all approaches to forecasting (statistical, behavioral, subjective, etc.) in terms of an overall framework and philosophy. Consists of the following two parts: "The Forecasting Environment" (two chapters) and "The Market and Sales Forecasting Plan" (nine chapters). Topics include product life cycle; the market and a sales forecasting plan; collection of data for forecasting; measurement of change; objective and subjective methods of forecasting; sales forecasting for a new product; the application of the forecast; and controlling forecasting. Provides simple numerical examples based on simple statistics.

Box, George E.P., and Jenkins, Gwilym M. TIME SERIES ANALYSIS: FORECASTING AND CONTROL. Rev. ed. Holden-Day Series in Time Series Analysis. San Francisco: Holden-Day, 1976. xxi, 575 p. Collection of Tables and Charts, pp. 517-37. References, pp. 538-43. Index, pp. 545-55. Exercises and Problems, pp. 557-75.

A text for a graduate course in time series analysis and a reference for applied research workers. Consists of the following four parts: "Stochastic Models and Their Forecasting";

"Stochastic Model Building"; "Transfer Function Model Building"; and "Design of Discrete Control Schemes." Topics include autocorrelation functions and spectrum; spectral properties of stationary models; linear stationary models, including moving average processes and mixed autoregressive; linear nonstationary processes; minimum square forecasting; model identification and estimation; model diagnostic checking; seasonal models; identification, fitting, and checking of transfer function models; and design of feedforward and feedback control systems. Assumes knowledge of stochastic processes, mathematical statistics, probability, and linear algebra.

Bratt, Elmer Clark. BUSINESS FORECASTING. New York: McGraw-Hill, 1958. vii, 366 p. Bibliography, pp. 349-57. Index, pp. 359-66.

Outlines the major areas of business forecasting including growth of total industry and individual industries, short-term movements of total industry and individual industries, and company sales and commodity prices. Includes two chapters describing economic indicators. Relies mainly on the graphic method utilizing real life data provided by the U.S. Census, National Bureau of Economics Research, and other groups.

Bright, James R., ed. TECHNOLOGICAL FORECASTING FOR INDUSTRY AND GOVERNMENT: METHODS AND APPLICATIONS. Englewood Cliffs, N.J.: Prentice-Hall, 1968. xxi, 484 p. Appendix 1: Technological Forecasting Bibliography (partially annotated) by Marvin J. Cetron, pp. 451-63. Appendix 2: Bibliography of Appraisal Techniques for Research Development, and Technological Planning by Marvin J. Cetron, pp. 464-74. Index, pp. 475-84.

Twenty-three papers presented at the first annual technology and management conference held in Lake Placid, New York, in May 1967, grouped under the following five parts: "Lessons from the Past" (two papers); "Techniques of Technological Forecasting" (seven papers); "Integrating Technological and Environmental Forecasting" (four papers); "Applying Technological Forecasting" (seven papers); and "Organizing the Technological Forecasting Effort" (three papers). Topics include trend extrapolation; measuring uncertainty in forecasting; Delphi method; multiple contingency concept of long-range technological forecasting; application of forecasts for research and development programming; and U.S. Army long-range technological forecasting. No mathematical or statistical prerequisites.

Brillinger, David R. TIME SERIES: DATA ANALYSIS AND THEORY. International Series in Decision Processes. New York: Holt, Rinehart and Winston, 1975. xii, 500 p. Proofs of Theorems, pp. 392-460. References, pp. 461-87. Notation Index, pp. 488-89. Author Index, pp. 490-95. Subject Index, pp. 496-500.

A text for a graduate course in time series analysis and a reference for researchers interested in frequency analysis who have knowledge of linear algebra, mathematical statistics, advanced calculus, and probability theory. Statistical techniques based on functions of discrete Fourier transforms and of the observed values of time series. Definitions, procedures, techniques, and statistics based on simple extensions of existing multiple regression and multivariate analysis techniques. Topics include analytic properties of Fourier transforms and complex matrices; stochastic properties of finite Fourier transforms; estimation of power spectra; linear time invariant relations between a stochastic series and several deterministic series; estimating the second-order spectra of vector-valued series; linear time invariant relation between two vector valued stochastic series; principal components in the frequency domain; and the canonical analysis of time series. Chapters conclude with exercises.

Brown, Robert Goodell. STATISTICAL FORECASTING FOR INVENTORY CONTROL. New York: McGraw-Hill, 1959. xvii, 232 p. Appendix A: Monte Carlo Simulations, pp. 163-85. Appendix B: Z-Transforms for Discrete Variables, pp. 186-96. Appendix C: The Lognormal Distribution, pp. 197-216. Appendix D: Bibliography, pp. 217-23. Glossary, pp. 225-27. Index, pp. 229-32.

A nontechnical reference for industrial and system engineers and production managers on inventory control systems, including examples and practical suggestions for adapting such systems to specific needs. Assumes knowledge of only high school algebra. Topics include exponential smoothing; noise; autocorrelation functions; safety factors; cyclic patterns; order points; Monte Carlo simulation; Z-transforms for discrete variables; and lognormal distributions.

Butler, William F., and Kavesh, Robert A., eds. HOW BUSINESS ECONOMISTS FORECAST. Englewood Cliffs, N.J.: Prentice-Hall, 1966. xiv, 540 p. No index.

Twenty-six unpublished essays on the techniques and problems of forecasting in business, government, and academic institutions grouped under the following five headings: "Major Approaches to Business Forecasting" (five essays); "Forecasting the Gross National Product" (seven essays); "Industrial and Sales Forecasting" (eight essays); "Financial Forecasting" (three essays); and "Using and Evaluating Forecasts" (three essays). Topics include leading indicators; diffusion indexes; short-term forecasting of the gross national product, business inventories, and domestic capital spending; forecasting the automobile market, steel, fuels, energy, and appliances; forecasting of monetary policy, profits, and the stock market; and the use of economic forecasts in management decision.

Butler, William F.; Kavesh, Robert A.; and Platt, Robert B., eds. METHODS AND TECHNIQUES OF BUSINESS FORECASTING. Englewood Cliffs, N.J.: Prentice-Hall, 1974. xv, 635 p. No index.

Thirty-two chapters on methods and techniques of forecasting written by thirty-nine authors grouped under the following six headings: "The Forecasters Kit of Tools" (five chapters); "Major Approaches to Business Forecasting" (four chapters); "Aggregate Forecasting in Practice" (ten chapters); "Industry and Sales Forecasting" (four chapters); "Financial Forecasting" (four chapters); and "The Accuracy of Forecasts and Their Uses by Business and Government" (five chapters). Topics include econometric methods; indicators; surveys; federal, state, and local budgets; sources of data; input-output forecasting; judgement forecasting; forecasting defense outlays,plant and equipment, housing, and inventories; regional and urban forecasting; forecasting in the auto and steel industries; forecasting corporate profits and monetary policy; and statistical measures of forecast accuracy.

Cetron, Marvin J. TECHNOLOGICAL FORECASTING: A PRACTICAL APPROACH. Foreword by Ralph C. Lenz, Jr. New York: Gordon and Breach, for the Technology Forecasting Institute, 1969. xxvi, 345 p. Appendixes, pp. 219-96. Bibliographies, pp. 297-340. Author Index, pp. 341-42. Subject Index, pp. 343-45.

A nonmathematical presentation of the most significant, practical aspects of technological forecasting and the role of such forecasts in decision making. Useful to a varied group, including students and managers. Topics include conceptual framework; forecasting in the department of defense and other government agencies; forecasting methodologies; problems and pitfalls; and survey of quantitative methods. Appendixes include a case study, critical appraisal of exploratory and informative forecasting, and organizations involved in forecasting.

Chambers, John Carlton; Mullick, Satinder K.; and Smith, Donald D. AN EXECUTIVE'S GUIDE TO FORECASTING. New York: Wiley, Interscience, 1974. xii, 308 p. Appendix A: Bibliography for Forecasting and Market Research Techniques, pp. 292-96. Appendix B: Market Research Statistical Techniques, pp. 297-303. Index, pp. 304-8.

Presents the various techniques of forecasting for the manager and others who have had little formal training in forecasting. Topics include quantitative methods; time series analysis and projection; causal models; pre-product and product stages and rapid growth of product stages; steady-state and phase-out stages; and forecasting of inventories and innovations.

Chatfield, Christopher. THE ANALYSIS OF TIME SERIES: THEORY AND PRACTICE. New York: Wiley, 1975. xiv, 263 p. Appendix I: The Fourier,

Laplace, and Z-Transforms, pp. 233-37. Appendix II: The Dirac Delta Function, pp. 238-39. Appendix III: Covariance, pp. 240-41. References, pp. 242-51. Answers to Exercises, pp. 252-57. Author Index, pp. 258-60. Subject Index, pp. 261-63.

A text for undergraduate and graduate courses, and a self-study for students who have knowledge of basic probability and elementary statistical inference. Bridges the gap between theory and application, with mathematical derivations kept to a minimum. Topics include procedures for analyzing trends, including filtering and differencing; probability models for time series, including random walk and autoregressive processes; estimation of the time domain, including the Box-Jenkins seasonal model; univariate and multivariate forecasting procedures; stationary processes in the frequency domain; spectral analysis; bivariate processes, and linear systems. Chapters conclude with exercises.

Chisholm, Michael; Frey, Allan E.; and Haggett, Peter, eds. REGIONAL FORECASTING. Foreword by C. Pittman. London: Butterworths, for the Colston Research Society, 1970. x, 467 p. No index.

Twenty-three papers presented at the twenty-second symposium of the Colston Research Society on April 6-10, 1970, grouped under the following six headings: "Preface" (one paper); "Statistical Methods" (five papers); "Forecasting and Behavior of Physical Systems" (three papers); "Forecasting for Socio-Economic Systems" (six papers); "Applications in the United Kingdom" (seven papers); and "Discussion" (one paper). Topics include space-time moving-average forecasting; regression approach; time series analysis; weather forecasting; forecasting in earth sciences; structural taxonomy of spatial hierarchies; redistribution of real income in an urban system; population forecasts; land values and urban growth; application of input-output models; and forecasting freight traffic in Great Britain.

Choucri, Nazle, and Robinson, Thomas W., eds. FORECASTING IN INTERNATIONAL RELATIONS: THEORY, METHODS, PROBLEMS, PROSPECTS. San Francisco: Freeman, 1978. xii, 468 p. Bibliography, pp. 427-53. Index, pp. 455-68.

Twenty-eight heretofore unpublished contributions on forecasting applied to international relations grouped under the following five headings: "Introduction" (two contributions); "Forecasting in International Relations: Requirements of Theory" (four contributions); "Forecasting Methodologies: Applications to International Relations" (eleven contributions); "The Time Perspective in International Relations" (four contributions); and "Policy Analysis and International Relations Forecasting" (seven contributions). Topics include Bayesian decision analysis; process models; use of econometric analysis; system dynamics forecasting; computer simulation; short- and long-range forecasting; problem-oriented forecasting; forecasting in the USSR; and use of expert opinion.

Cicchetti, Charles J. FORECASTING RECREATION IN THE UNITED STATES: AN ECONOMIC REVIEW OF METHODS AND APPLICATIONS TO PLAN FOR THE REQUIRED ENVIRONMENTAL RESOURCE. Lexington, Mass.: Lexington Books, 1973. xx, 200 p. Notes, pp. 193-96. Bibliography, pp. 193-96. Index, pp. 197-200.

A monograph which reviews three main types of analytical economic models for use in recreation planning; site-specific recreation area models, site-specific user models, and population-specific models. Includes population-specific models, and reduced form models for estimating the number of swimmers and swimming days for 1980 and 2000 in Onondago County, New York. Provides empirical results for 1965, 1980, and 2000 of estimating twenty-four different recreation activities on national and regional levels using reduced form models and data based on the 1965 national recreation survey. Includes forecasts of participation in outdoor recreation in the United States using reduced form models under varying assumptions about future conditions. Assumes knowledge of econometrics.

Clark, John J., ed. THE MANAGEMENT OF FORECASTING. New York: St. John's University Press, 1969. xi, 424 p. Footnotes, pp. 401-24. No index.

Thirteen heretofore unpublished contributions on forecasting arranged under the following four headings: "The Management of Forecasting" (two contributions); "Methodology of Forecasting" (five contributions); "Sales Forecasting" (four contributions); and "Accuracy in Sales Forecasting" (two contributions). Topics include business cycle indicators; econometric models; input-output analysis; consumer surveys in forecasting; advertising and sales promotion as a predictor variable; and criteria for evaluating short-term sales forecasts. Most of the contributions do not require formal training in mathematics.

Copulsky, William. PRACTICAL SALES FORECASTING. New York: American Management Association, 1970. 109 p. No index.

A nontechnical introduction to sales forecasting. Describes briefly a number of numerical techniques, including trend and cycle, linear regression, cross-section analysis, economic indicators for an economy, and economic models. Concludes with an example of simple model forecasting. No mathematical prerequisites.

Coutie, G.A.; Davies, O.L.; Hossell, C.H.; Millar, D.W.G.P.; and Morrell, A.J.H. SHORT-TERM FORECASTING. Mathematical and Statistical Techniques for Industry, Monograph no. 2. London: Oliver & Boyd, for Imperial Chemical Industries Limited, 1964. viii, 36 p. Appendix A: Seasonal Variations, pp. 26-27. Appendix B: Derivation of Control Limits, pp. 28-32. Appendix C:

Computer Programs, pp. 33-34. Appendix D: Simplification of the Use of Control Limits when Forecasts and Control are Operated by a Computer, pp. 25-26. No index.

Presents a mathematical method for forecasting sales for periods of up to six months called the Holt method. Based entirely on the previous history of demand for a product, and utilizes moving averages and seasonal variations techniques with special consideration given to errors of forecasts. Computer programs available.

Crawford, C.M. SALES FORECASTING: METHODS OF SELECTED FIRMS. Bulletin Series, no. 78. Urbana: Bureau of Economics and Business Research, University of Illinois, 1955. 72 p. Appendix: Description of Firms Interviewed, pp. 67-68. Bibliography, pp. 69-72. No index.

An analysis of sales forecasting techniques used in twenty selected business firms, including the place of sales forecasting in the organization of the firm, types of sales forecasts and uses to which they are put, and methods of checking and verifying forecasts. Presentation primarily verbal with no formulas or numerical illustration.

Crowe, Walter R. INDEX NUMBERS: THEORY AND APPLICATIONS. London: MacDonald and Evans, 1965. Bibliography, pp. 355-60. Index, pp. 361-68.

Presents the basic theories of index numbers together with examples from both British and American experiences. Written for the nonmathematical student with no previous knowledge of statistics. Includes a weighted index formula subject to time and factor reversal tests, and the circular test. Chapters conclude with questions and exercises.

Dauten, Carl A. BUSINESS CYCLES AND FORECASTING. 2d ed. Cincinnati, Ohio: South-Western, 1961. x, 566 p. Index, pp. 557-66.

A text for a course in business cycle forecasting in eight parts: "Introduction"; "Causal Factors in the Cyclical Process"; "Measurement of Economic Fluctuations"; "Statistical Record of Business Fluctuations"; "Historical Record of Business Fluctuations"; "Forecasting Economic Activity"; "Forecasting Sales"; and "Proposals for Achieving Economic Growth and Stability." Presentation descriptive, with many tables and charts, but no formulas. Assumes knowledge of intermediate economic theory and one semester of basic statistics.

Davis, Harold Thayer. THE ANALYSIS OF ECONOMIC TIME SERIES. Foreword by Alfred Cowles. Reissued ed. San Antonio, Tex.: The Principia Press of Trinity University, 1963. xiv, 620 p. Table 1: Values of the Walker Probability Function, P_w, pp. 583-600. Table 2: Values of the Fisher Probability Function, O_f, pp. 601-5. Index of Names, pp. 609-12. Index of Subjects, pp. 613-20.

Originally published in 1941 as Monograph 6 of the Cowles Foundation. Considers in detail the analysis and mathematical interpretation of economic time series beginning with a history of the problem and then taking up such topics as the techniques of harmonic analysis and serial correlation analysis, random series theory, degrees of freedom in time series, periodogram analysis, business cycles, wealth and income, the dynamics of trends from the point of view of the question of exchange, and forecasting economic time series. Based on the relation of economic time series to economic theory, and includes numerous detailed calculations based on real data. Assumes knowledge of economic theory, differential and integral calculus, differential equations, probability theory, and elementary mathematical statistics.

Ferber, Robert. THE RAILROAD SHIPPERS' FORECASTS. Studies in Business Expectations and Planning. Preface by Franco Modigliani. Urbana: University of Illinois, 1953. 140 p. Appendix: Tables, pp. 138-40. No index.

A monograph on the results of one part of a three-year research project of an empirical investigation of the influence of expectations on economic activity. Analyzes shippers' forecasts of carloadings for various commodities from the points of view of accuracy and the factors controlling the formation of expectations. Uses data on quarterly forecasts of shipments by rail from 1927 to 1950 as reported by a large sample of shippers representing most of the industries that are important users of railroad facilities.

Fisher, Franklin M. A PRIORI INFORMATION AND TIME SERIES ANALYSIS: ESSAYS IN ECONOMIC THEORY AND MEASUREMENT. Contributions to Economic Analysis, vol. XXVI. Amsterdam: North Holland, 1962. xii, 168 p. Appendix A: Theorem on Identification, pp. 115-54. Appendix B: Data Used in Chapter 4, p. 155. Appendix C: Data Used in Chapter 5, pp. 156-57. Bibliography, pp. 161-65. Index, pp. 166-68.

Develops a model of economic behavior over time which includes: (1) the role which outside information plays in the analysis of economic time series; (2) the effect on consumer behavior of exogenous shocks and parameter shifts; and (3) the importance of abnormal events in a world of uncertainty. Model tested using data of the United Kingdom wheat market, 1967-1914; the demand for aluminum ingot in the United States, 1925-1940; and the demand for railroad passenger transportation between Boston and New York. Models single-equation using first differences in logarithmic as well as nonlogarithmic forms, including lagged values. Estimated by ordinary least squares.

Fisher, Irving. THE MAKING OF INDEX NUMBERS: A STUDY OF THEIR VARIETIES, TESTS, AND RELIABILITY. 3d ed., rev. Reprints of Economic

Classics. New York: Augustus M. Kelley, 1967. xxxiii, 538 p. Appendixes, pp. 371-531. Index, pp. 533-38.

A reprint of the original edition first published by Houghton Mifflin in 1927. Develops and illustrates six types of index numbers, including the simple arithmetic average of relative prices, and tests them under various rules, such as the reversal and circular rules. Appendixes include notes, the influence of weighting, history of index numbers, list of formulas for index numbers, numerical data, examples, and reference.

FORECASTING ON A SCIENTIFIC BASIS. Foreword by H.O.A. Wold. Lisboa, Portugal: Centro de Economia E. Financas, 1967. x, 409 p. List of participants, pp. 403-9. No index.

Five contributions summarizing the proceedings of an International Summer Institute held in Curia, Portugal, September 1966, sponsored by the NATO Science Committee and the Gulbenkim Foundation: "Forecasting and Scientific Method," by H.O.A. Wold; "Microeconomic Analysis for Prediction of National Accounts," by Guy H. Orcutt; "Realizability and Minimum-Delay Aspects of Multichannel Models," by Enders A. Robinson; "Applied Econometric Forecasting and Policy Analysis," by Daniel B. Suits; and "Macroeconomic Forecasting," by Pieter de Wolff.

Fuller, Wayne A. INTRODUCTION TO STATISTICAL TIME SERIES. Wiley Series in Probability and Mathematical Statistics. New York: Wiley, 1976. ix, 470 p. Bibliography, pp. 452-61. Index, pp. 463-70.

A text for a graduate course in time series for students of economics and statistics who have taken a graduate course in statistical theory and one in regression analysis. Follows the theorem-proof format. Includes homework problems at the ends of the chapters. Topics include moving average and autoregressive processes; Fourier analysis; spectral theory; estimation of the mean and autocorrelation; the periodogram; estimation for autoregressive and moving average time series; and regression, trend, and seasonality. Chapters conclude with references.

Gilchrist, Warren. STATISTICAL FORECASTING. Wiley, Interscience, 1976. xiv, 308 p. Appendix A: Some Terminology and Definitions for Stochastic Processes, pp. 293-97. Appendix B: Proof that Conditional Expectation Gives Minimum Mean Square Error Forecasts, pp. 298-300. Appendix C: Two-way Exponential Smoothing, p. 301. Appendix D: A Technical Note on Discounted Least Squares, pp. 302-3. Index, pp. 305-8.

A systematic account of the method of statistical forecasting in common use in three parts: "Preliminaries"; "Forecasting for Some Basic Models"; and "The Forecasting Process." The models include constant mean model; linear trend; regression, stochastic, seasonal, growth curves, probabilities, and multivariate. Each forecasting method developed and illustrated by examples in such a way that the reader may then be able to use it himself. Assumes knowledge of intermediate statistics and calculus. Other topics include forecasting criteria, adaptive methods, comparison of methods, forecast control, and two-stage forecasting. Chapters conclude with references.

Glass, Gene V.; Willson, Victor L.; and Gottman, John M. DESIGN AND ANALYSIS OF TIME-SERIES EXPERIMENTS. Boulder, Colo.: Associated University Press, 1975. xi, 241 p. Appendix A: Spectral Analysis of Time-series, pp. 205-16. Appendix B: Data Lists, pp. 217-20. Appendix C: Linear Model and Least-Squares Theory, pp. 221-26. References, pp. 227-34. Subject Index, pp. 235-38. Author Index, pp. 239-41.

A monograph on certain methodological developments in time series experimental design. Offers an opportunity to evaluate intervention affects with control by the traditional simultaneous comparative design approach in which the effects of intervention, such as might arise in social organizations, are not taken into account. Topics include variations on the basic time-series experimental design; intervention effects; sources of invalidity in time-series experiments; mathematical model of time-series, including autoregressive and first order moving average models; estimating and testing intervention effects in six commonly encountered time-series models (two stationary processes and four nonstationary processes); concomitant variation in time-series experiments; and special topics. Assumes knowledge of time-series analysis and econometric methods.

Granger, C.W.J. In association with M. Hatanaka. SPECTRAL ANALYSIS OF ECONOMIC TIME SERIES. Foreword by O. Morgenstern. Princeton Studies in Mathematical Economics, no. 1. Princeton, N.J.: Princeton University Press, 1964. xviii, 299 p. Index, pp. 297-99.

A description and application of Fourier methods of analyzing stationary and nonstationary time series by breaking them up into components of different oscillatory frequencies. Topics include spectral and cross-spectral analysis of economic data, processes involving feedback, series with spectrum changing over time, and demodulation. Concludes with two chapters applying the methods to the study of business cycle indicators and the accelerator principle. Useful to graduate students in econometrics.

Granger, C.W.J., and Newbold, Paul. FORECASTING ECONOMIC TIME SERIES. Economic Theory and Mathematical Economic Series. New York: Academic Press, 1977. xii, 333 p. References, pp. 318-25. Author Index, pp. 327-29. Subject Index, pp. 330-33.

A monograph which presents a number of forecasting techniques which emphasize methods applicable to economic data. Contrasts two approaches to the analysis of economic data by two groups: time series analysts and econometricians. Topics include autoregressive models; Wold's decomposition; models for seasonal time series; spectral analysis; linear time series models; optimal forecasts for particular models; frequency-domain approach; forecasting with misspecified models; Box-Jenkins and exponential smoothing methods; stepwise autoregression; forecasting from regression models, including simultaneous equation models; multiple series models; combination and evaluation of forecasts; nonlinear models of forecasts; and nonstationary processes. Assumes knowledge of mathematical statistics, linear algebra, and time series analysis.

Greenberg, Michael R.; Krueckeberg, Donald A.; and Mautner, Richard. LONG-RANGE POPULATION PROJECTIONS FOR MINOR CIVIL DIVISIONS: COMPUTER PROGRAMS AND USER'S MANUAL. New Brunswick, N.J.: Center for Urban Policy Research, Rutgers University, 1973. viii, 126 p. Bibliography, pp. 125-26. No index.

A monograph which presents three classes of programmed models that project the populations of minor civil divisions (MCD) up to fifty years. Each model constrained by county projections which are, in turn, constrained by state and national projections. Techniques developed for application to nuclear power plant siting studies, but directly transferrable to many other applications, such as studies of sewage collection systems, water supply, land use, and market areas.

Gregg, James Vincent; Hossell, C.H.; and Richardson, J.T. MATHEMATICAL TREND CURVES: AN AID TO FORECASTING. Mathematical and Statistical Techniques for Industry. Monograph no. 1. London: Oliver & Boyd, for Imperial Chemical Industries Limited, 1964. viii, 99 p. Appendix 1: Alternative Methods for Estimating the Slopes, p. 42. Appendix 2: Gome Functions for the Fitting of Modified Exponentials, p. 43. Appendix 3: The Slope Characteristics, pp. 44-46. Appendix 4: The General Modified Exponential, pp. 47-50. Appendix 5: Mathematical Basis for Fitting Modified Exponentials, pp. 51-57. Appendix 6: Computer Programs Available from Imperial Chemical Industries Limited, p. 58. Tables and Graphs, pp. 60-99. No index.

Illustrates the use of mathematical trend curves for forecasting demand in fields as diverse as sales, usage of natural resources and raw materials, and labor requirements. Curves include straight line and parabola, simplified modified exponential, simple exponential and log parabola, Gompertz, and logistic. Derives confidence limits for mean values and individual values. Includes the mathematical basis for each method and numerical illustrations.

Grenander, Ulf, and Rosenblatt, Murray. STATISTICAL ANALYSIS OF STATIONARY TIME SERIES. Wiley Series in Probability and Mathematical Statistics. New York: Wiley, 1957. 300 p. Problems, pp. 278-87. Appendix on Complex Variable Theory, pp. 288-93. Bibliography, pp. 294-98. Index, pp. 299-300.

A reference for researchers on time series who have knowledge of mathematical statistics and who are familiar with some of the theory of stochastic processes. Emphasizes rigorous proofs of theorems. Topics include representations of stationary stochastic processes; filtering of stationary processes; statistical analysis of parametric models; estimation and application of the spectrum; distribution of spectrum estimates; linear estimation; the asymptotic distribution of an integral of a spectrograph estimate; prefiltering of a time series; and the zeros and maxima of stationary stochastic processes. Examples chosen from the physical sciences. Provides few problems which supplement and extend the theory.

Hannan, Edward James. MULTIPLE TIME SERIES. Wiley Series in Probability and Mathematical Statistics. New York: Wiley, 1970. xi, 536 p. Mathematical Appendix, pp. 496-518. Bibliography, pp. 519-27. Table of Notations, pp. 529-30. Index, pp. 531-36.

A text for a course in time series analysis for students who have knowledge of functional analysis, mathematical statistics, and Fourier methods. Consists of two parts: "Basic Theory" and "Inference." Includes fairly complete treatments of the underlying probability theory for second-order stationary processes, and the theory of prediction, interpolation, signal extraction, and smoothing of time series. Presents formulas but does not usually discuss computational details, and omits computer programs. With few exceptions, excludes numerical examples. Includes difficult and technical proofs in chapter appendixes and in starred sections.

______. TIME SERIES ANALYSIS. Science Paperbacks. New York: Barnes and Noble, 1960. viii, 152 p. Appendix: The Spectral Representation of x(t), pp. 139-42. Bibliography, pp. 143-47. Index, pp. 149-52.

A monograph on univariate analysis of time series using a stochastic model consisting of a time dependent mean plus a stationary component. Assumes knowledge of mathematical statistics. Chapter titles: "The Spectral Theory of Discrete Stochastic Processes"; "Estimation of the Correlogram and of the Parameters of Finite Parameter Schemes"; "Estimation of the Spectral Density and Distribution Functions"; "Hypothesis Testing and Confidence Intervals"; and "Processes Containing a Deterministic Component."

Harris, Bernard, ed. SPECTRAL ANALYSIS OF TIME SERIES. Publication no. 18 of the Mathematics Research Center, United States Army, University of Wisconsin. New York: Wiley, 1967. x, 319 p. Index, p. 313-19.

Ten papers presented at a seminar held at the University of Wisconsin, October 3-5, 1966, on the theory of recent developments in spectral analysis of time series. Topics include calculations of numerical spectrum analysis; quartic statistics in spectral analysis; cross-spectral method; estimation of coherency, computation, and interpretation of the k-th order spectra; models of signal plus white noise; and models for forecasting seasonal and nonseasonal time series. Assumes knowledge of mathematical statistics and spectral analysis.

Hartley, Philip B. SHORT-RANGE BUSINESS FORECASTING: A STUDY OF METHODS USED BY A SAMPLE NUMBER OF BUSINESSES IN KANSAS CITY, MISSOURI, AND WICHITA, KANSAS. Lawrence, Kans.: Center for Research in Business, University of Kansas, 1962. vi, 78 p. Appendixes, pp. 63-73. Bibliography, pp. 75-78. No index.

Based on a mail questionnaire survey of thirty small firms. Describes the forecasting methods used by small businesses. Reviews various forecasting procedures, the results of other studies designed to evaluate forecasting procedures, and the results of the Kansas City-Wichita survey. The appendixes present the questionnaire used and a summary of the response from the survey.

Hasting, Delbert C. THE PLACE OF FORECASTING IN BASIC PLANNING FOR SMALL BUSINESS. Foreword by John E. Horne. Minneapolis: University of Minnesota, 1961. viii, 60 p. Appendix: Pertinent Parts of Interviewer's Schedules, pp. 53-54. Bibliography, pp. 55-60.

A study based on a survey of forecasting activities of 106 small business firms in Minnesota. Attempts to define the role of forecasting by small firms and make suggestions for the proper use of short- and long-term forecasting small firms.

Jenkins, Gwilyn, and Watts, Donald G. SPECTRAL ANALYSIS AND ITS APPLICATIONS. Holden-Day Series in Time Series Analysis. San Francisco: Holden-Day, 1968. xviii, 525 p. Index, pp. 515-23. Author Index, pp. 524-25.

A text for a graduate course for engineers and a handbook on the application of spectral analysis to practical time series problems. Topics include stationary, autocorrelation, and moving average-autoregressive processes; methods for estimating autocorrelation functions and parameters in linear processes; spectrum analysis; simulated and practical examples of spectral estimation, including the window closing method; cross correlation function and cross spectrum; estimation of cross spectra;

estimation of frequency response functions; and spectral analysis of a vector of several time series. Assumes knowledge of the usual engineering mathematics, including linear algebra. Also useful to mathematicians, statisticians, economists, physicists, and biologists.

Jiler, Harry, ed. GUIDE TO COMMODITY PRICE FORECASTING. New York: Commodity Research Bureau, 1965. 275 p. No index.

Twenty-four articles reprinted from COMMODITY YEAR BOOKS either in their original or revised and updated forms on commodity price forecasting. Concerned with techniques of forecasting and applications to forecasting price of agricultural products.

Kendall, Maurice George. CONTRIBUTIONS TO THE THEORY OF OSCILLATORY TIME-SERIES. National Institute of Economic and Social Research. Occasional Paper IX. New York: Cambridge University Press, 1946. 76 p. Appendix: Tables for Harmonic Analysis, pp. 67-76. No index.

Applies the following techniques in the analysis of time series containing autoregressive errors: periodogram, method of counting intervals, variate-difference method, and the correlogram.

______. TIME-SERIES. London: Charles Griffin, 1973. ix, 197 p. References, pp. 167-70. Appendix A: Weights for Fitting Polynomial Trends, pp. 171-92. Appendix B1: Significance Points of the Durbin-Watson Statistics d_L and d_U: 1 per cent, p. 193. Appendix B2: Significance Points of the Durbin-Watson Statistic d_L and d_U: 5 per cent, p. 194. Index, pp. 195-97.

Presents the basic ideas and techniques of time series analysis with as little mathematics as possible. Topics include tests of randomness, methods of removing trends from time series, seasonality, stationary series, problems in sampling serial correlation and correlogram, spectrum analysis, forecasting by autoprojective methods, multivariate series, forecasting from lagged relationships, and regression and autocorrelated residuals. Includes numerical examples. Assumes knowledge of basic statistics, linear algebra, and calculus. Chapters conclude with notes.

Koopmans, Lambert Herman. THE SPECTRAL ANALYSIS OF TIME SERIES. Probability and Mathematical Statistics: A Series of Monographs and Textbooks, no. 22. New York: Academic Press, 1974. xiv, 366 p. References, pp. 354-58. Index, pp. 359-66.

An introduction to the techniques and theory of the frequency domain (spectral) analysis of time series. Useful as a text or for individual reading by a diverse and varied audience. Mathematical prerequisites include calculus, linear algebra, complex variables through power series, and the calculus of probability. The topics include the univariate case, discrete-time models, linear filters, multivariate models, digital filters, real-time filtering, the distribution theory of spectral estimates, properties of spectral estimates, and applications.

Linstone, Harold A., and Sahal, Devendra, eds. TECHNOLOGICAL SUBSTITUTION: FORECASTING TECHNIQUES AND APPLICATIONS. New York: Elsevier, 1976. xv, 288 p. Selected Bibliography, pp. 277-81. Index, pp. 283-88.

Sixteen articles, thirteen originally published in TECHNOLOGICAL FORECASTING AND SOCIAL CHANGE, dealing with various aspects of technological substitution grouped under the following six parts: "Basic Models" (three articles); "Determinants of Substitution Rate" (four articles); "Economic Analysis" (three articles); "Applications to Energy Production" (three articles); "Diffusion Processes" (one article); and "The Future" (two articles). Topics include system dynamic modeling for forecasting multilevel technological substitution; the normal distribution as a model of technological substitution; innovation in commercial aircraft jet engine market; international diffusion of new technology; explicit technological substitution in long-range input-output models; an econometric analysis of the substitution of mechanical corn pickers by field shelling technology; and step-wise growth of electrical generator size.

Linstone, Harold A., and Turoff, Murray, eds. THE DELPHI METHOD: TECHNIQUES AND APPLICATIONS. Foreword by Olaf Helmer. Reading, Mass.: Addison-Wesley, 1975. xx, 620 p. No index.

Twenty-eight heretofore unpublished papers on the Delphi technique and four reprints of articles from TECHNOLOGICAL FORECASTING AND SOCIAL CHANGE arranged in the following six sections: "Philosophy" (eleven papers); "Evaluation" (five papers); "Cross-Impact Analysis" (four papers); "Specialized Techniques" (five papers); "Computers and the Future of Delphi" (six papers); and "Eight Basic Pitfalls: A Checklist" (one paper). Topics include a Delphi evaluation of agreement between organizations; Delphi research in the corporate environment; a Delphi forecasting study of plastics and competing materials by 1985; a Delphi on the future of the steel and ferroalloy industries; the performance of forecasting groups in computer dialogue and face-to-face discussion; a Delphi study of factors affecting the quality of life; a Delphi-based paradigm for normative system-building; group communication through electronic media; and a theory of group estimation.

Lippitt, Vernon G. STATISTICAL SALES FORECASTING. Foreword by Donald P. Jones. New York: Financial Executives Research Foundation, 1969. vii, 347 p. Appendixes A to G, pp. 255-340. Index, pp. 341-47.

A reference for managers and specialists on analytical techniques in sales forecasting with the following aims: (1) assembling and adjusting data; (2) mathematical extrapolation of trends and cycles; (3) correlation with business indication; (4) relating company sales to causal variables; and (5) simulating the outcome of the effect of various influences on the expected sales volume for a product. Topics include long-term sales forecasting; forecasting new product sales; time series analysis; indicators (illustrated with NBER research); general additive model; regression model; and simulation model. Appendixes include case studies of forecasting, including curve fitting for Eastman Kodak sales and sales forecasting of household durables.

McKinley, David H.; Lee, Murray G.; Duffy, Helene; and McGee, L. Randolph. FORECASTING BUSINESS CONDITIONS. Foreword by D.C. Miller. New York: American Bankers Assoc., 1969. vi, 122 p. Appendixes, pp. 118-22. No index.

Presents in outline form what bankers and businessmen should know about the nature of business fluctuations and the forecasting of short-run business trends. Consists of the following three parts: "Fluctuations in Our National Income"; "Forecasting by the Use of the National Income Accounts"; and "The Indicators Approach to Forecasting." Topics include description of cycles; circular flow of income; causes of cycles; forecasting of inventories; construction and equipment, residential construction, and consumer goods and services; and economic barometers. Appendixes devoted to an 1884 business forecast, meaning of seasonal adjustment, and selected readings.

Makridakis, Spyros, and Wheelwright, Steven C. INTERACTIVE FORECASTING. Vol. 1. Foreword by Robert L. McLaughlin. University Business Series. Palo Alto, Calif.: Scientific Press, 1974. 314 p. Appendix A: Cases for Interactive Forecasting, pp. 225-314. No index.

Describes an interactive time-sharing system for forecasting by twenty-two techniques for use by students and practitioners. Includes computer programs available from the author in BASIC and FORTRAN for those who do not have access to timesharing BASIC. Provides an overview of each technique and a description of how to use the representative computer program. Techniques include autocorrelation; moving average; several exponential smoothing techniques; trend analysis; classical decomposition; adaptive filtering; Box-Jenkins; regression; and harmonic smoothing. Other topics include choosing a forecasting method, preparing the final forecast, and business cases useful in teaching forecasting in marketing, production, finance and general management.

Martino, Joseph Paul. TECHNOLOGICAL FORECASTING FOR DECISION MAKING. Policy Sciences Book Series. New York: Elsevier, 1972. xvii, 750 p. Appendix 1: Regression Analysis of Time Series, pp. 661-702. Appendix 2: Statistical Tables, pp. 703-11. Appendix 3: Historical Data Tables, pp. 712-39. Index, pp. 741-50.

An advanced treatment of technological forecasting for the practicing scientist or engineer. Presents the following information for a number of important techniques; the rationale behind the technique; where appropriate; description, including mathematical derivations; and one or more historical examples. Techniques include Delphi; forecasting by analogy; growth curves; trend extrapolation; analytical models; breakthrough; normative; combining forecasts; research and development; product development; test and evaluation; technological forecasting in government and social decisions; evaluating forecasts as decision information; and the future of technological forecasting. Knowledge of calculus, differential equations, and basic statistics helpful. Chapters conclude with references and problems.

______, ed. AN INTRODUCTION TO TECHNOLOGICAL FORECASTING. Futurist Library, vol. 1. New York: Gordon and Breach, 1972. x, 108 p. No index.

Eleven nontechnical and descriptive contributions in the relatively new field of technical forecasting. Topics include methods of forecasting, forecasting technology in space exploration and military operations, how to plot a breakthrough, and industrial implications of technological forecasting.

Maunder, W.F., ed. BIBLIOGRAPHY OF INDEX NUMBERS: AN INTERNATIONAL TEAMS PROJECT. Rev. ed. Introduction to the First Edition by R.G.D. Allen. London: The Athlone Press, 1970. xxvii, 215 p. No index.

Contains 2,600 references to articles, books, monographs, and pamphlets on index numbers published up to 1967 including a few available in 1968. Listings generated by computer with an intensive effort made to secure a full international coverage including entries relating to Russian and East European literature. The parts of the book: "Chronological Index," "Subject Index," "Author Index," and "List of Journals Scrutinised." Excludes annotations.

Merkies, A.H.Q.M. SELECTION OF MODELS BY FORECASTING INTERVALS. Translated by M. von Holten-de Wolff. Boston: D. Reidel, 1973. viii, 136 p. Appendix A, pp. 130-32. Bibliography, pp. 133-36. No index.

Originally published in Dutch. Presents procedures for choosing the linear model with the smallest 95 percent forecasting interval for micro-economic forecasts. Topics include a statement of forecasting as a selection problem; the criterion for selection; the set of admitted models and the procedures in which the selection is carried out; and examples of forecasts of export surplus of the Netherlands for one year in advance, two years in advance, and forecasts of the gross national product. Assumes knowledge of calculus, mathematical statistics, and econometrics.

Milne, Thomas E. BUSINESS FORECASTING: A MANAGERIAL APPROACH. London Business School Series. New York: Longman, 1975. xiv, 204 p. Appendix, pp. 191-92. Further Reading, pp. 193-96. Index, pp. 197-204.

A practical approach to business forecasting. Topics include the type of forecasts that managers need to make; forecasting on different levels, such as the firm and the industry, with comments on input-output analysis as a forecasting tool; forecasting based on mathematical trends, including a simple regression model; analysis of time series, including seasonal index; simple models, including additive and multiplicative; economic forecasts, including business cycles; surveys as a basis for forecasting; using forecasts for decision making, including the break-even chart, decision trees, and Monte Carlo simulations; and the specification of forecasts. Assumes knowledge of high school algebra. Chapters conclude with references.

Mincer, Jacob, ed. ECONOMIC FORECASTS AND EXPECTATIONS: ANALYSIS OF FORECASTING BEHAVIOR AND PERFORMANCE. Studies in Business Cycles, 19. New York: Columbia University Press, for the NBER, 1969. xix, 251 p. Index, pp. 243-51.

The fourth in the series of research reports of the National Bureau's study of short-term forecasting. Consists of a collection of five essays as follows: "The Evaluation of Economic Forecasts," by J. Mincer and V. Zarnowitz; "Data Errors and Forecasting Accuracy," by R. Cole; "Models of Adaptive Forecasting," by J. Mincer; "Expectations in the Term Structure of Interest Rates," by S. Diller; and "Consumer Anticipations and Models of Durable Goods Demand," by F.T. Juster. Includes methodological frameworks for the statistical analysis of forecasting data, empirical applications and related research in expectational economics, and an analysis of predictive performance of intentions or plans to buy consumer durables as expressed in periodic consumer anticipation surveys.

Mitchell, Wesley C. THE MAKING AND USING OF INDEX NUMBERS. Reprints of the Economic Classics. New York: Augustus M. Kelley, 1965. 114 p. No index.

Originally published in 1915 as part of Bulletin 173 of the Bureau of Labor Statistics on wholesale price index numbers in the United States and foreign countries. Revised in 1921 as

Bulletin 284. Topics include history of index numbers, characteristics of price fluctuations, methods used in constructing index numbers, and a comparison of leading index numbers in the United States for the years 1890 to 1918. While the methods presented here are largely obsolete, this reprint is in continued demand, particularly in colleges and universities, for historical reasons.

Morrison, Norman. INTRODUCTION TO SEQUENTIAL SMOOTHING AND PREDICTION. New York: McGraw-Hill, 1969. xvii, 645 p. Appendix I: Properties of the Discrete Legendre Polynomials, pp. 623-27. Appendix II: Proof of Equations (13.3.8), pp. 628-32. Index, pp. 633-45.

An introduction to sequential smoothing and prediction of numerical data for students who have had a course in linear algebra and a course in probability of statistics. Consists of the following four parts: "Background"; "Fixed-Memory Filtering"; "Expanding-Memory Filtering"; and "Fading-Memory Filtering." Covers the fields of polynomial estimators with generalizations and extensions to state estimation of deterministic processes governed by arbitrary differential equations. Omits detailed numerical examples.

Mudgett, Bruce D. INDEX NUMBERS. Wiley Series in Probability and Mathematical Statistics. New York: Wiley, 1951. x, 135 p. Bibliographical References Cited in Text, pp. 130-31. Index, pp. 133-35.

Presents and evaluates methods of constructing index numbers in two parts: "The Measurement of Price and Quality Change"; and "Current Construction Methods and Their Shortcomings." Topics include the meaning of price and quantity change, the problem of measurement, formulas for binary comparisons, errors in the basic data of index numbers, long-distance and series comparisons, and wholesale and consumer price indexes of the U.S. Department of Labor.

Nelson, Charles R. APPLIED TIME SERIES ANALYSIS FOR MANAGERIAL FORECASTING. San Francisco: Holden-Day, 1973. xiv, 231 p. Appendix: Computer Programs for Identification, Estimation, and Forecasting, pp. 222-25. Index, pp. 227-31.

A text for a course in forecasting for graduate students in business, economics, management science, and industrial engineering. Presents recent developments in applied time series, particularly those due to Box and Jenkins, with emphasis on the use of backshift algebra and first-hand data analysis. Topics include forecasting methods including structural and econometric models; models for stationary time series, including moving-average and first-second and higher-order autoregressive processes; models for nonstationary time series, including difference-equation and random shock forms of the integrated autoregressive-moving-average process (ARIMA); identification and estimation of ARIMA models; forecasting ARIMA processes; and models for seasonal time series. Concludes with a forecast evaluation of the Federal Reserve-MIT-Penn model of the U.S. economy. Knowledge of calculus helpful for comprehension. Chapters conclude with exercises and references. Appendix contains a brief description of three computer programs for identification, estimation, and forecasting in FORTRAN IV for the IBM 360.

Otnes, Robert K., and Enochson, Loren. DIGITAL TIME SERIES ANALYSIS. Wiley Series in Probability and Mathematical Statistics. New York: Wiley, Interscience, 1972. x, 467 p. Appendix A: Glossary of Abbreviations and Symbols, pp. 445-49. Appendix B: Miscellaneous Numerical Expressions, pp. 451-53. Appendix C: References, pp. 455-60. Index, pp. 461-67.

A text for a graduate course in time series analysis for students in engineering and related fields, and a reference for individuals actively engaged in digital data analysis in the fields of vibration, acoustics, medicine, seismology, communication, and oceanography. Topics include preprocessing of data; recursive digital filtering; Fourier series and Fourier transform computations; computing power spectral density; correlation functions and Black-Tukey spectrum computations; power and cross spectra from fast Fourier transforms; filter methods for the power spectral density; transfer functions and coherence function computations; probability density function computations; and nonstationary data analysis. Concludes with a chapter on plots of frequency response functions obtained by computer programs.

Owen, Donald B., ed. THE SEARCH FOR OIL: SOME STATISTICAL METHODS AND TECHNIQUES. Statistics: Textbooks and Monographs, vol. 13. New York: Marcel Dekker, 1975. vii, 196 p. Index, pp. 191-96.

Nine papers presented at two symposiums held at Southern Methodist University in 1973. Topics include cross probability bounds for nonstationary Gaussian processes; multivariate prediction and spline functions; nonparametric classification rules; pattern classification by attributes; the role of canonical variables in discriminant analysis; selecting a pattern recognition algorithm; and autoregressive, maximum entropy, and G-spectral estimation. Assumes knowledge of time series analysis, mathematical statistics, and spectral analysis.

Parzen, Emanuel. TIME SERIES ANALYSIS PAPERS. Holden-Day Series in Time Series Analysis. San Francisco: Holden-Day, 1967. xv, 565 p. No index.

Nineteen reprints of articles on time series by the author; one reprint published jointly by the author and Norman Shiren; and one reprint of the article "General Considerations in the Analysis of Spectra," by G.M. Jenkins. Topics include central limit theorem for multilinear stochastic processes; consistent estimates of the spectrum of a stationary time series; spectral analysis with missing observations and amplitude modulation; probability density functionals and reproducing kernel Hilbert spaces; and models for the probability of fatigue failure of a structure.

Pyke, Ronald. TIME SERIES AND STOCHASTIC PROCESSES: CONVEXITY AND COMBINATORICS. Montreal: Canadian Mathematical Congress, 1970. xiv, 279 p. Open Problems, pp. 265-67. Index of Open Problems, p. 269. Subject Index, pp. 271-75. Appendix: List of Canadian Mathematical Congress's Biennial Seminars, 1947-1969, pp. 277-79.

Dedicated to the memory of Alfred Renyi. Consists of fifteen papers presented at the Twelfth Biennial Seminar of the Canadian Mathematical Congress held at the University of British Columbia, Vancouver, British Columbia Aug. 11-27, 1969. Grouped under the following headings: "Time Series and Stationary Processes" (six papers); "Markov Processes" (three papers); "Applications of Probability" (three papers); and "Convexity and Combinatorics" (three papers). Topics include efficient estimators in spectral analysis; central limit theorem for stationary Markov sequences; dual processes and potential theory; regularity of excessive functions; applications of probability to biology; combinatorial properties of convex sets; and centrally symmetric polytopes.

Quenouille, M.H. THE ANALYSIS OF MULTIPLE TIME-SERIES. Griffin's Statistical Monographs and Courses, no. 1. London: Charles Griffin, 1957. 105 p. List of Symbols, pp. 103-4. References, p. 105. No index.

A monograph on the theory of multiple time series. Topics include forms by which series may be represented; determination of the moving-average process from knowledge of the covariance structure; practical complications including serially correlated error terms; estimation of the parameters of schemes by which series may be represented, including Markov schemes for one variable and for several variables; significance and goodness-of-fit tests; and U.S. hog series and a practical example. Assumes knowledge of matrix algebra and mathematical statistics.

Rayner, J.N. AN INTRODUCTION TO SPECTRAL ANALYSIS. Monographs in Spatial Environmental Systems Analysis. New York: Academic Press, 1971. x, 174 p. References, pp. 129-42. Appendix A: List and Definition of Symbols, pp. 144-52. Appendix B: Partial Classification of References, pp. 153-57. Answers to Exercises, pp. 158-68. Reference Index, pp. 169-70. Subject Index, pp. 171-74.

A monograph on the application of spectral analysis to the two-dimensional study of the circulation of the atmosphere (as an illustration of nonperiodic data). Omits mathematical proofs, but knowledge of one year of basic statistics and the rudiments of differential and integral calculus assumed. Topics include Fourier analysis and Fourier integrals; filtering; spectral analysis of nonperiodic functions; cross spectral analysis; and two-dimensional analysis, including spectral analysis in two dimensions; and cross-spectral analysis in two dimensions. Most examples and exercises taken from meteorology, geology, and related areas.

Reichard, Robert S. PRACTICAL TECHNIQUES OF SALES FORECASTING. New York: McGraw-Hill, 1966. xii, 272 p. Glossary-Dictionary Terms Commonly Used in Sales Forecasting, pp. 255-62. Supplementary Reading List, pp. 263-66. Index, pp. 267-72.

A nontechnical reference on the role of sales forecasting in business. Topics include basic problems in forecasting; sales-forecasting surveys; forecast uses; economic and industry forecasts; company sales forecasts; determining length and scope of forecasts; data collection; time series; correlation; stepwise regression; model building; operations research; the use of surveys; the role of the computer; forecasting new products; and evaluation of accuracy of forecasts.

Robinson, Enders A. MULTICHANNEL TIME SERIES ANALYSIS WITH DIGITAL COMPUTER PROGRAMS. Holden-Day Series in Time Series Analysis. San Francisco: Holden-Day, 1967. xxiii, 298 p. Appendix 1: Relationship to Mathematical Operator Theory, pp. 270-74. Appendix 2: Glossary of Subroutines, pp. 275-78. Appendix 3: Program Revisions, pp. 279-91. Index, pp. 293-98.

A monograph on digital processing of time series data using FORTRAN IV subroutines to make explicit the computational steps in various operations on time series. Presents methods useful in the analysis of geophysical time series recorded in the seismic exploration for oil. Methods include single-channel and multichannel digital filtering and spectral analysis; multichannel prediction and signal enhancement; computer program to find marine seismogram from reflection coefficients; subroutines for inverting matrix polynomials; factoring matrix polynomials into binomial factors; and computer programs for performing Fourier transformations. Assumes knowledge of FORTRAN.

Rosenblatt, Murray. PROCEEDINGS OF THE SYMPOSIUM ON TIME SERIES ANALYSIS. The SIAM Series in Applied Mathematics. New York: Wiley, 1963. xiv, 497 p. No index.

Twenty papers presented at the symposium on time series analysis held at Brown University in 1962 under the joint sponsorship of Brown University and the Office of Naval Research. Grouped under the following eight headings: "Regression Analysis" (three papers); "Zeros of Processes and Related Questions" (three papers); "Meteorological Problems" (four papers); "Structural Problems" (four papers); "Spectral Analysis" (four papers); "Structural Problems" (four papers); "Signal Detection" (three papers); and "Estimation and Prediction" (three papers). Topics include distribution of zeros for first passage time problems; estimation of spectra; regression analysis with stationary residuals; tests of hypothesis; and applications in geophysics, meteorology, oceanography, engineering, economics, and biology.

Rozeboom, William W. FOUNDATIONS OF THE THEORY OF PREDICTION. Dorsey Series in Psychology. Homewood, Ill.: Dorsey, 1966. viii, 628 p. Appendix A: The Normal Distribution, pp. 571-73. Appendix B: Matrix Derivations, pp. 574-602. References, pp. 603-6. Glossary, pp. 607-15. Name Index, pp. 617-18. Subject Index, pp. 619-28.

A text and a handbook for a course in prediction theory for students of psychology who have a high school algebra background. Consists of two parts: "The Statistics of Prediction" and "Test Theory: The Assessment of Predictors." Topics include descriptive statistics; regression; factor analysis; centroids and variance structure; reliability; and the variance structure of composite tests. Concludes with a chapter summarizing certain theorems from statistical sampling theory.

Sanderson, Fred H. METHODS OF CROP FORECASTING. Cambridge, Mass.: Harvard University Press, 1954. xiv, 259 p. Index, pp. 255-59.

Critically examines crop forecasting methodology located in a large and scattered literature. Consists of the following four parts: "The Statistical Tools"; "Estimating and Forecasting Acreage"; "Forecasting Crop Yields: Observing the Crop"; and "Forecasting Crop Yields: Observing the Crop's Environment." Topics include design of sample surveys, use of correlation and regression; subjective methods of estimating and forecasting acreage; usefulness and limitations of crop condition reports; application of sampling to measurements of the growing crop; testing weather-crop hypothesis; and the analysis of weather-crop relationship by means of regression integrals. Assumes knowledge of basic statistics. Chapters conclude with references.

Sartorius, Lester C., and Mohn, N. Carroll. SALES FORECASTING MODELS: A DIAGNOSTIC APPROACH. Research Monograph, no. 69. Atlanta: Georgia State University, School of Business Administration, 1976. xi, 620 p. Appendixes: Tables, pp. 611-19. Acknowledgements for Appendixes, p. 620. No index.

A text for course in forecasting for graduates and undergraduates who have knowledge of basic statistics, and a guide to forecasting methods for businessmen. Consists of the following seven parts: "Introduction and Overview"; "Time Series Analysis"; "Exponential Smoothing and Adaptive Forecasting"; "Regression Causal Models"; "Other Causal Models"; "Appraising, Testing, and Monitoring Sales Forecasts"; and "Conclusions." Topics include seasonal analysis of time series; exponential smoothing of cyclical data; selecting the smoothing constant; stepwise multiple regression; input-output analysis; spectral analysis; Box-Jenkins; and judgement forecasting methods. Uses real company cases and data. Chapters conclude with references.

Scott, Claudia Devita. FORECASTING LOCAL GOVERNMENT SPENDING. Foreword by William Gorham. Prepared in Cooperation with the Municipal Finance Officers Association of the United States and Canada. Washington, D.C.: Urban Institute, 1972. xvi, 142 p. Appendix A: Review of Literature on the Budgetary Process, pp. 109-16. Appendix B: Supplementary Materials and Analysis, pp. 117-35. Bibliography, pp. 137-42. No index.

Develops a model for forecasting public expenditures for use in the city of New Haven which takes into account unions, personnel and non-personnel expenditures. Uses single-equation regression models to forecast current and capital expenditures for the following nine categories of public expenditures; education, library, police, fire, health, welfare, public works, parks and recreation, and administration. Independent variables include population, salary, and services. Uses annual data for 1960-70. Assumes knowledge of basic statistics.

Silk, Leonard A., and Curley, M. Louise. A PRIMER ON BUSINESS FORECASTING: WITH A GUIDE TO SOURCES OF BUSINESS DATA. New York: Random House, 1970. xiv, 144 p. Index, pp. 137-44.

A guide on business forecasting divided into three parts: "Methods of Business Forecasting"; "Data for Business Forecasting"; and "Index of Sources of Materials." Topics include description of deterministic, symptomatic, and systematic techniques; description of data on national income, population, and labor force, investment and construction, production and trade, commodity prices, and finance; and sources of data on a variety of series. No mathematical or statistical prerequisites.

Spencer, Milton H.; Clark, Colin G.; and Hoguet, Peter W. BUSINESS AND ECONOMIC FORECASTING: AN ECONOMETRIC APPROACH. Irwin Series in Economics. Homewood, Ill.: Irwin, 1961. xii, 412 p. Classified Bibliography, pp. 398-403. Index, pp. 407-12.

A text for a course in business forecasting for students, consultants, and professional researchers. Emphasizes both principles and techniques. Consists of the following three parts: "Forecasting Methods, Materials, and Tools"; "Forecasting by Sectors"; and "Forecasting the Total Economy." The tools discussed include naive methods, barometric techniques, opinion polling, business indicators, econometrics, and correlation. Applications to a variety of goods in the following sectors: prices, consumers' nondurable goods, consumers' durable goods, capital goods, and construction materials. Includes aggregate models such as the Klein-Goldberger and Econometric Institute models.

Stekler, Herman O. ECONOMIC FORECASTING. New Directions in Management and Economics. New York: Praeger, 1970. xii, 182 p. Appendix to Chapter 2: A Priori Information, Models and Forecasting, pp. 155-61. Appendix A to Chapter 2: Regression Estimates of Inventory Equations, pp. 162-72. Appendix B to Chapter 3: Inventory Anticipation Data, pp. 173-79. Index, pp. 181-82.

Presents quantitative techniques and empirical results useful for evaluating and improving quantitative economic forecasts. Emphasizes the use of econometric models, although judgemental techniques also considered, and on the accuracy of forecasts. Models include Klein quarterly, OBE, Wharton, Suits, Fromm, Liu and Friend, and Taubman. Other topics include data revisions, the selection of economic data, and the federal budget as a short-term forecasting tool.

Surrey, M.J.C. THE ANALYSIS AND FORECASTING OF THE BRITISH ECONOMY. National Institute of Economic and Social Research. Occasional Papers, no. 25. New York: Cambridge University Press, 1971. xii, 107 p. Conventions and Symbols, pp. xi-xii. Appendix I: Measuring National Product, pp. 96-97. Appendix II: Parameters of the Model, pp. 98-99. Appendix III: The Computer Programme for Solving the Model, pp. 100-104. Index, pp. 105-7.

A short general account of the institute's model of the British economy, including details of the component parts of the short-term forecasting process. Produces a consistent set of quarterly estimates for the recent past and the immediate future of the principal components of national income, such as consumption, investment, exports, and imports.

TECHNIQUES OF ECONOMIC FORECASTING: AN ACCOUNT OF THE METHODS OF SHORT-TERM ECONOMIC FORECASTING USED BY THE GOVERNMENTS OF CANADA, FRANCE, THE NETHERLANDS, SWEDEN, THE UNITED KINGDOM, AND THE UNITED STATES. With an introduction by C.W. McMahon. Foreword by Thorkil Kristensen. Paris: Organization for Economic Co-operation and Development, 1965. 173 p. Bibliography, pp. 169-73. No index.

An account of aggregate forecasting methods used in six countries. Topics include first-, second-, and third-stage forecasting in France with input-output analysis; short-term planning in the Netherlands using econometric models; short-term forecasting in Sweden using econometric models; short-term forecasting of domestic activity and balance of payments in the United Kingdom; short-term forecasting by the President's Council of Economic Advisors; and short-term forecasting in the Federal Service in Canada. Presentation largely descriptive with a limited number of graphs and tables used for illustrations.

Wendt, Paul F., ed. FORECASTING TRANSPORTATION IMPACTS UPON LAND USE. Studies in Applied Regional Sciences, vol. 2. The Netherlands, Leiden: Stenfert Kroese B.V., 1976. xi, 145 p. No index.

Seven heretofore unpublished contributions on land use models for the Georgia Transportation Planning Land Use Model Project. Topics include the Georgia macroeconometric model of 125 equations (82 stochastic and 43 identities); growth and change in the Georgia regional economies; a Delphi approach to land use forecasting; land suitability and land use analysis; and interaction of transportation and land use.

Wheelwright, Steven C., and Makridakis, Spyros. FORECASTING METHODS FOR MANAGEMENT. 2d ed. Wiley Series on Systems and Controls for Financial Management. New York: Wiley, 1977. xv, 266 p. Index, pp. 261-66.

Presents a wide range of forecasting methods that can be used by managers and guidelines that describe the forecasting function in the organization. Topics include adaptive filtering; regression and correlation; decomposition method of time series forecasting; Box-Jenkins; input-output tables; and inventory-control theory. The remainder of the book considers data acquisition, forecasts based on subjective methods, qualitative approaches; and organizing and implementing a corporate forecasting function. Chapters conclude with references. No mathematics prerequisites necessary. Includes numerical examples and graphs.

Whittle, Peter. PREDICTION AND REGULATION BY LINEAR LEAST-SQUARES METHODS. Applied Mathematics Series. London: English Universities Press, 1963. x, 147 p. References, pp. 142-43. Index, pp. 145-47.

Presents prediction of a random process at a level intermediate between prediction as a topic in probability and as a technique in the fields of communication and control. Topics include linear least-squares prediction and estimation; stationary and related processes, including multivariate processes and canonical factorization of the spectral density function; pure prediction in continuous time and prediction of one series from another; methods of inverting a covariance matrix and minimisation of more general quadratic for forms; projections on the finite, semi-infinite, and infinite samples; and regulation. Assumes knowledge of real analysis, linear algebra, and probability theory. Includes derivations and non-numerical examples, but no problems.

Wiener, Norbert. EXTRAPOLATION, INTERPRETATION, AND SMOOTHING OF STATIONARY TIME SERIES: WITH ENGINEERING APPLICATIONS. Cambridge: MIT Press, 1949. x, 163 p. Appendix A: Table of the Laguerre Functions, pp. 124-28. Appendix B: The Wiener RMS (root mean square) Error Criteria in Filter Design and Prediction by Norman Levinson, pp. 129-48. Appendix C: A Heuristic Exposition of Wiener's Mathematical Theory of Prediction and Filtering by Norman Wiener, pp. 150-60. Index, pp. 161-63.

Attempts to unite the theory and practice of time series in statistics and communications engineering. Consists largely of proofs and derivations, with examples, and assumes knowledge of Fourier methods, harmonic analysis, and the calculus of probability. Topics include linear predictors and filters for single and multiple, discrete and continuous time series.

Wold, Herman O.A. A STUDY IN THE ANALYSIS OF STATIONARY TIME SERIES. 2d ed. With an appendix by Peter Whittle. Stockholm: Almqvist and Wicksell, 1954. viii, 236 p. Appendix 1: Notes to the Second Edition, pp. 191-95. Appendix 2: Some Recent Contributions to the Theory of Stationary Processes, pp. 196-228. List of References, pp. 229-33. Index, pp. 234-36.

A monograph on the theory and application of discrete stationary processes. Excludes problems of evolutive time series. Topics include a survey of hypotheses and methods for the analysis of time series; the theory of discrete stationary random processes, including linear autoregression; analysis of the discrete stationary process; stochastic difference equations; stationary processes with finite dispersion and with no singular component; the process of moving average; applications to linear programming, linear autocorrelation, and moving averages. Assumes knowledge of Fourier series, calculus, and probability theory.

______, ed. BIBLIOGRAPHY ON TIME SERIES AND STOCHASTIC PROCESSES: AN INTERNATIONAL TEAM PROJECT. Cambridge: MIT Press, 1965. xv, 516 p. No index.

Each entry annotated by a code which gives the following six types of information: type of process, scientific nature of the entry, group of problems, presence of empirical applications, field of application, and language. Includes the following for each entry: author, year of publication, title, location, and review reference. Begins with a graphic introduction to three types of stochastic processes: sums of independent variables, stationary processes, and Markov chains. Bibliography divided into the following three periods: up to 1930, 1930-1950, and 1951-1959.

Wolfe, Harry Deane. BUSINESS FORECASTING METHODS. New York: Holt, Rinehart and Winston, 1966. ix, 225 p. Index, pp. 219-25.

A combination handbook and methods book that demonstrates to the reader how to make short-term, cyclical, and long-range business forecasts. Acquaints the reader with four aspects of forecasting: obtaining adequate and accurate data, preparing the data for use, applying more than one different forecasting method to the data, and applying sound judgement and intuition to the forecasts. Includes applications to forecasts of the economy, industry market potentials, and company sales. Assumes knowledge of economic theory and basic statistics.

Young, Michael, ed. FORECASTIN G AND THE SOCIAL SCIENCES. London: Heinemann, 1968. ix, 166 p. No index.

Eight heretofore unpublished papers on forecasting from a social science viewpoint drawn from various disciplines--economics, geography, political science, psychology, sociology, and town planning. Topics include consumption in the year 2000, future research needs of transport planners, land use, the spread of towns into the country, social security research, and forecasting in the electricity supply industry. An introductory paper, "Forecasting and the Social Sciences," by the editor, is also included.

Chapter 7
REGRESSION

Albert, Arthur E. REGRESSION AND THE MOORE-PENROSE PSEUDOINVERSE. Mathematics in Science and Engineering, vol. 94. New York: Academic Press, 1972. xiii, 180 p. References, pp. 173-76. Index, pp. 177-78.

> A monograph-textbook suitable for a two-quarter course in regression for students who have knowledge of mathematical statistics and linear algebra. Consists of two parts: "The General Theory and Computational Methods" and "Statistical Applications." Topics include review of real linear spaces; geometrical and analytic properties of the Moore-Penrose pseudoinverse; pseudoinverse of partitioned matrices and sums and products of matrices; computational methods (Gram-Schmidt method of Rust, Burrus, and Schneeburger; Gauss-Jordan elimination method of Ben-Israel, Werson, and Noble; gradient projection method of Pyle; and Cayley-Hamilton method of Decell, Ben Israel, and Charnes); constrained least squares, penalty functions, and BLUE's recursive computation of least squares estimators; and nonnegative definite matrices, conditional expectation, and Kalman filtering. Rigorous style consisting of theorems and proofs, with few numerical examples. Exercises scattered throughout the book include extensions of the subject matter.

Albert, Arthur E., and Gardner, Leland A., Jr. STOCHASTIC APPROXIMATION AND NONLINEAR REGRESSION. Research Monograph, no. 24. Cambridge, Mass.: MIT Press, 1967. xv, 204 p. Appendix: Lemmas 1 through 8, pp. 189-99. References, pp. 200-201. Index, pp. 203-4.

> A monograph on curve fitting in the presence of noise from both statistical and computation viewpoints. Consists of two parts: "The Scalar Parameter Case" and "The Vector Parameter Case." Development based on "differential correction" type estimators defined recursively so that the parameter estimate reflects data arriving in temporal succession. Monograph relates large-sample statistical behavior of such estimates (consistency, rate of convergence, asymptotic efficiency, and large-sample distribution theory) to the properties of the re-

gression function and the choice of smoothing vectors. Applications include estimating the initial state of a linear system via noisy nonlinear observations; estimating the parameters of a time invariant linear system; elliptical trajectory parameter estimation; and estimating input amplitude through an unknown saturating amplifier. Assumes knowledge of mathematical statistics and linear algebra.

Andrews, Frank M.; Morgan, James N.; Sonquist, John A.; and Klein, Laura. MULTIPLE CLASSIFICATION: A REPORT ON A COMPUTER PROGRAM FOR MULTIPLE REGRESSION USING CATEGORICAL PREDICTORS. 2d ed., rev. Ann Arbor: Survey Research Center, Institute for Social Research, University of Michigan, 1973. xi, 104 p. Appendix A: Set-Up Instructions, pp. 57-64. Appendix B: Reading the Printout and Presenting Results, pp. 65-72. Appendix C: MCA Macro Flow Chart, pp. 73-78. Appendix D: Sample Output, pp. 79-98. Appendix E: Obtaining the Program and Adopting it to Other Systems, pp. 99-100. Bibliography, pp. 101-2. Index, pp. 103-4.

A monograph on multiple classification analysis (MCA) in two parts: "A Non-Technical Description of Multiple Classification Analysis" and "A Statistical Description of the Programs." Compiled in FORTRAN IV and 360 ASSEMBLER for IBM 360 computers. Investigates the interrelationships between several predictor variables and a dependent variable within the context of an additive model. Includes problems appropriate for MCA; description of MCA; limitations; additive model; and relation of MCA to traditional analysis of variance and multiple regression. Dependent variable measured on an interval scale, while predictors on nominal, ordinal, or interval scale.

Bard, Yonathan. NONLINEAR PARAMETER ESTIMATION. New York: Academic Press, 1973. x, 341 p. Appendix A: Matrix Analysis, pp. 296-309. Appendix B: Probability, pp. 310-12. Appendix C: The Rao-Crámer Theorem, pp. 313-15. Appendix D: Generating a Sample from a Given Multivariate Normal Distribution, pp. 316-17. Appendix E: The Gauss-Markov Theorem, pp. 318-19. Appendix F: A Convergence Theorem for Gradient Methods, pp. 320-22. Appendix G: Some Estimation Programs, pp. 323-24. References, pp. 325-32. Author Index, pp. 333-36. Subject Index, pp. 337-41.

A text for a practical course in data analysis for scientists and engineers. Concerned with fitting mathematical models to numerical data, primarily by least squares, and includes techniques for formulation problems, computational methods, conclusions based on the estimates of the parameters, models in the form of differential equations, and the planning of experiments. Includes review of statistical concepts. Appendixes devoted to proofs of theorems. Assumes knowledge of linear algebra and probability theory. Chapters conclude with problems.

Barford, N.C. EXPERIMENTAL MEASUREMENTS: PRECISION, ERROR AND TRUTH. Reading, Mass.: Addison-Wesley, 1967. xi, 143 p. Appendix 1: The Gaussian or Normal Distribution, p. 131. Appendix 2: The Integral Gaussian Probability, p. 132. Appendix 3: The Poisson Distribution Function, pp. 133-35. Appendix 4: Hypothesis Test, pp. 136-39. Further Reading, p. 140. Index, pp. 141-43.

> Presents an approach to the analysis of errors using data derived from actual laboratory experiments. Gaussian and Poisson distributions developed and used to simulate errors and statistical fluctuations for testing against experimental data. Chapter titles: "Introduction"; "Interpretation of Results"; "Least Squares"; "Causes of Error"; "Elementary Theory of Errors"; and "Likelihood, Confidence, and Truth." Assumes knowledge of only high school algebra. Chapters conclude with problems.

Barlow, Richard E.; Bartholomew, D.J.; Bremner, J.M.; and Brunk, H.D. STATISTICAL INFERENCE UNDER ORDER RESTRICTIONS: THE THEORY AND APPLICATION OF ISOTONIC REGRESSION. Wiley Series in Probability and Mathematical Statistics. New York: Wiley, 1972. xii, 388 p. Appendix: Tables, pp. 359-63. Bibliography and Author Index, pp. 365-77. Subject Index, pp. 379-88.

> A text for a course in regression analysis with emphasis on isotonic functions (rather than, for example, linear functions). Topics include isotonic regression; estimation under order restrictions; testing the equality of ordered means using likelihood ratio tests, tests based on contrasts among the means, distribution-free tests, ordered tests for non-normal distributions, and one-sided tests for the multivariate normal mean; estimation of distributions; isotonic tests for goodness of fit; and conditional expectation given a 6-lattice. Approach measure-theoretic with knowledge of measure theory necessary. Use of numerical examples limited. Chapters conclude with complements on historical development and references.

Bjerhammar, Arne. THEORY OF ERRORS AND GENERALIZED MATRIX INVERSES. New York: Elsevier, 1973. xii, 420 p. Appendix 1: General Definitions and Computational Rules for Matrix Calculations, pp. 369-99. Appendix 2: Tables, pp. 400-406. References, pp. 407-14. Index, pp. 415-20.

> English edition of the Swedish text FELTEORI by the author, published in 1955. Useful as a text for an intermediate statistics course. Topics include probability theory, hypothesis testing and interval estimation; least squares; analysis of variance; advanced analysis of distributions; correlation analysis; and numerical methods. Matrix algebra reviewed in Appendix 1.

Boullion, Thomas L., and Odell, Patrick L., eds. THEORY AND APPLICATION OF GENERALIZED INVERSES OF MATRICES. Texas Technical College Mathematics Series, no. 4. Lubbock: Texas Technical College, 1968. iii, 315 p. No index.

Fifteen papers presented at a symposium on generalized inverses of matrices defined on a complex number field held in Lubbock, Texas, in March 1968. Topics include inverses of rank invariant powers of a matrix; characteristic vectors for rectangular matrices; specification problems in regression; maximal subgroups of the semigroup of m x n complex matrices; application of generalized inverses in nonlinear analysis; partial isometries and generalized inverses; generalized inverse epsilon-algorithm for matrices; computing generalized characteristic vectors and values for a rectangular matrix; p-q generalized inverse; and a bibliography on generalized matrix inverses.

Boyce, David E.; Farhi, A.; and Weischedel, R. OPTIMAL SUBSET SELECTION, MULTIPLE REGRESSION, INTERDEPENDENCE AND OPTIMAL NETWORK ALGORITHMS. Lecture Notes in Economics and Mathematical Systems. New York: Springer-Verlag, 1974. xiv, 187 p. Bibliography, pp. 183-84. Index, pp. 185-87.

Presents computer programs and experimental results for solving three optimal subset selection problems; optimal regression analysis; interdependence analysis; and optimal network analysis. First two problems result from the Beale, Kendall, Mann tree search algorithm, and the third generalizes this tree search algorithm. Each algorithm includes an introduction, description, examples and case studies, strategy for using the computer programs, program user's manual description of input cards and output, and programmers' manual description of subroutines. Useful to anyone interested in stepwise regression.

Chatterjee, Samprit, and Price, Bertram. REGRESSION ANALYSIS BY EXAMPLE. Wiley Series in Probability and Mathematical Statistics. New York: Wiley, 1977. xiv, 228 p. Statistical Tables, pp. 218-24. Index, pp. 225-28.

A text for a course in applied regression analysis, data analysis, econometrics, and related subjects for students with diverse backgrounds who have knowledge of basic statistics and matrix algebra. Emphasizes analysis of data, rather than formulas, hypothesis testing or confidence interval estimation. Concepts and techniques developed with aid of examples, with reliance placed on graphic representation using both real and hypothetical data. Topics include analysis of residuals and effects of outliers in simple regression; detection and correction of model violations in simple regression through transformations of variables; removal of heteroscedasticity; weighted least squares; assumptions about explanatory variables; qualitative variables as regressors; dummy variables; stability of regression parameters over time; two-stage estimation; logistic model; autocorrelation and its removal; multicollinearity; principal components in detection of multicollinearity; ridge regression; removing dependence among the explanatory variables; and stepwise regression and other methods for selecting independent variables.

Cohen, Jacob, and Cohen, Patricia. APPLIED MULTIPLE REGRESSION/CORRELATION ANALYSIS FOR THE BEHAVIORAL SCIENCES. New York: Wiley, Halsted Press, 1975. xvii, 490 p. Appendixes, pp. 449-68. Appendix Tables, pp. 469-80. References, pp. 481-83. Author Index, pp. 485-86. Subject Index, pp. 487-90.

A nonmathematical, applied text for students in the behavioral and social sciences who have had one semester of basic statistics, and a manual for research workers. Consists of three parts: "Basics"; "The Representation of Information in Independent Variables"; and "Applications." Topics include bivariate correlation and regression; multiple regression and correlation; multicollinearity; power analysis; sets of independent variables; nominal and qualitative scales; quantitative scales; missing data; interactions; analysis of covariance; repeated measurement and matched subjects designs; and canonical analysis. Appendixes devoted to formulas, calculator solutions to multiple regression problems, and computer analysis of multiple regression.

Daniel, Cuthbert, and Wood, Fred S. With the Assistance of John W. Gorman. FITTING EQUATIONS TO DATA: COMPUTER ANALYSIS OF MULTIFACTOR DATA FOR SCIENTISTS AND ENGINEERS. New York: Wiley, 1971. xiv, 342 p. Glossary, pp. 264-77. User's Manual, pp. 278-333. Bibliography, pp. 335-37. Index, pp. 339-42.

Presents procedures, mainly by examples, of fitting equations to unbalanced data where little or no attention is given to the requirements of statistical design of experiments. Recognizes the strengths and limitations of data, tests the assumptions of least squares, and selects appropriate forms of the variables. Topics include fitting equations with one-, two-, and three-independent variables; selection of independent variables; selection of variables in nested data; and nonlinear least squares. Includes two computer programs in FORTRAN, one for linear and one for nonlinear least-squares curve fitting.

Draper, Norman Richard, and Smith, Harry. APPLIED REGRESSION ANALYSIS. Wiley Series in Probability and Mathematical Statistics. New York: Wiley, 1966. ix, 407 p. Percentage Points of the t-Distribution, p. 305. Percentage Points of the F-Distribution, pp. 306-7. Bibliography, pp. 309-16. Answers to Exercises, pp. 317-45. Appendix A, pp. 347-64. Appendix B, pp. 365-402. Index, pp. 403-7.

A text for a standard, basic one-semester course in multiple regression with emphasis on practical applications and with many theoretical results stated without proof. Computer printouts included in portions of the book. Topics include simple regression; matrix approach to regression; analysis of residuals; selection procedures in various types of regression programs, including backward elimination, forward selection, stepwise regression, and stagwise regression; the planning of large regression studies; analysis of variance, including two-way classification; and introduction to nonlinear regression. Assumes knowledge of basic statistics. Chapters conclude with exercises.

Dunn, Olive Jean, and Clark, Virginia A. APPLIED STATISTICS: ANALYSIS OF VARIANCE AND REGRESSION. Wiley Series in Probability and Mathematical Statistics. New York: Wiley, 1974. 387 p. Appendix: Tables, pp. 355-81. Index, pp. 383-87.

A text for a one-semester course in the analysis of variance, regression, and covariance for students who have had a one-year course in basic statistics. Examples based on random experiments simulated by computer programs from normally distributed populations. Topics include descriptive statistics; inference from a single sample and samples from two populations; one-, two-, and three-way analysis of variance; factorial designs; simple and multiple linear regression and correlation; polynomial regression; analysis of covariance; and data screening. Chapters conclude with summaries, references, and problems.

Edwards, Allen Louis. AN INTRODUCTION TO LINEAR REGRESSION AND CORRELATION. A Series of Books in Psychology. San Francisco: W.H. Freeman, 1976. xv, 213 p. Answers to Exercises, pp. 171-76. Appendix: Tables, pp. 177-210. Index, pp. 211-13.

A supplementary text for a course in basic and intermediate statistics for students in the behavioral sciences. Includes both the similarities and differences between correlation and regression. Topics include simple regression; nonlinear relationships that can be transformed into linear relationships; correlation coefficient; correlation and regression with standardized variables; factors influencing the magnitude of the correlation coefficient; phi coefficient, point biserial, and rank order coefficient; test of significance for correlation and regression coefficients; coefficients of orthogonal polynomials; analysis of variance for a simple repeated measure design; and multiple correlation and regression. Chapters conclude with exercises. Assumes knowledge of basic statistics and college algebra.

Ezekiel, Mordecai, and Fox, Karl A. METHODS OF CORRELATION AND REGRESSION ANALYSIS: LINEAR AND CURVILINEAR. 3d ed., rev. and enl. New York: Wiley, 1959. xv, 548 p. Appendix 1: Glossary and Important Equations, pp. 479-88. Appendix 2: Methods of Computation, pp. 489-530. Appendix 3: Technical Notes, pp. 531-35. Author Index, pp. 537-41. Subject Index, pp. 543-48.

An exposition of standard statistical methods used in studying the relation between variables. Emphasizes applications, largely from agriculture. Includes the following sections: "Introductory Concepts"; "Simple Regression, Linear and Curvilinear"; "Multiple Linear Regression"; "Multiple Curvilinear Regression"; "Significance of Correlation and Regression Results"; "Miscellaneous Special Regression Methods"; and "Uses and Philosophy of Correlation and Regression." Useful as a supplementary text and reference. Chapters conclude with references.

Goldberger, Arthur S. TOPICS IN REGRESSION ANALYSIS. Macmillan Series in Economics. New York: Macmillan, 1968. x, 144 p. Bibliography, pp. 137-39. Index, pp. 141-44.

Based on a course of eight lectures presented at the Center of Planning and Economic Research, Athens, Greece, in 1966, for research workers. Topics include partial gross regression coefficients for the two- and k-regressor cases; coefficients of determination; precision of estimation; stochastic specification for the one-, two-, and k-regressor cases; functional forms; and multicollinearity. Useful to anyone interested in applied regression. Assumes knowledge of regression analysis, statistical inference, and matrix algebra. Fairly rigorous with few numerical examples.

Haitovsky, Yoel. REGRESSION ESTIMATION FROM GROUPED OBSERVATIONS. Griffin's Statistical Monographs and Courses, no. 33. New York: Hafner, 1973. x, 94 p. Appendixes, pp. 77-90. References, pp. 91-92. Index, pp. 93-94.

A monograph which develops regression techniques for the analysis of grouped data such as that presented in published form or in coded form in contrast to the original observations. Topics include regression from cross-classified observations; unbiased regression from one-way classification tables; regression from differently grouped observations; and regression from midpoints of grouped observations-bias and loss of efficiency. Includes simple numerical exercises. Appendixes devoted to statistical tables and proofs and derivations. Assumes knowledge of linear algebra, regression analysis, and mathematical statistics.

Hellwig, Zdzistaw. LINEAR REGRESSION AND ITS APPLICATION TO ECONOMICS. Translated by J. Stadler. Translation edited by H. Infeld. New York: Macmillan, 1963. xii, 238 p. Appendix: Proofs of Theorems and Statistical Data Used in the Book, pp. 213-22. List of Symbols, pp. 223-28. Tables, pp. 229-34. Bibliography, pp. 235-38. No index.

> A reference for scientists in economics, agriculture, and technical colleges, and for graduates of economic and technical colleges employed in different branches of the economy who use statistical methods in studying relationships between phenomena. Topics include two-dimensional random variables; simple regression and correlation; estimating linear regression parameters; testing hypotheses concerning regression; transformation of curvilinear into linear regression; and the regression line and the trend. Assumes knowledge of mathematical statistics. Emphasizes intuitive and computational aspects rather than derivations.

Heward, James H., and Steele, Peter M. BUSINESS CONTROL THROUGH MULTIPLE REGRESSION: A TECHNIQUE FOR THE NUMERATE MANAGER. Gower Press Special Studies. London: Gower Press, 1972. 116 p. Appendix 1: Some Commercial Enterprises Offering Multiple Regression Analysis Facilities, pp. 97-99. Appendix 2: F Distribution Table, pp. 100-101. Appendix 3: Explanation of Stepwise Regression Program Output Shown in Figure 4:2, pp. 102-5. Appendix 4: Multiple Regression Analysis Worksheets, pp. 106-12. Index, pp. 113-16.

> A guide for managers in the use of multiple regression analysis (MRA) as a tool for solving business problems. Emphasizes industrial applications, rather than derivations. Includes the following chapter titles: "Definition and Uses of MRA"; "Using MRA in Business"; "The Dependent Variable"; "Computer Analysis"; "The Statistical Method"; "Having Confidence in the Results"; and "Making Use of the MRA Equation."

Kelly, Francis J.; Beggs, Donald L.; and McNeil, Keith A. With Tony Eichelberger, and Judy Lyon. RESEARCH DESIGN IN THE BEHAVIORAL SCIENCES: MULTIPLE REGRESSION APPROACH. Carbondale: Southern Illinois University Press, 1969. xiii, 353 p. Appendix A: Answer Section, pp. 299-321. Appendix B: FORTRAN Programs, pp. 323-47. References, pp. 348-50. Index, pp. 351-53.

> Develops a multiple regression model for the behavioral scientist with emphasis on the use of FORTRAN programs for computations. Regression presented as a general case of the analysis of variance. Topics include review of vector notation; traditional analysis of variance; computer program LINEAR for regression analysis; nonlinear regression; use of co-variables and co-variance; relation of linear regression to other multivariate methods, such as discriminant analysis and canonical analysis; and a continuous predictor variable combined with

categorical data. Knowledge of matrix algebra and computer programming helpful. Derivations kept to a minimum. Useful as a supplementary text and as a reference. Chapters conclude with problems.

Kerlinger, Fred N., and Pedhazur, Elazar J. MULTIPLE REGRESSION IN BEHAVIORAL RESEARCH. New York: Holt, Rinehart and Winston, 1973. x, 534 p. Appendix A: Matrix Algebra in Multiple Regression Analysis, pp. 452-66. Appendix B: The Use of the Computer in Data Analysis, pp. 467-76. Appendix C: MULR: Multiple Regression Program, pp. 477-511. Appendix D: The 5 and 1 Percent Points for the Distribution of F, pp. 512-15. References, pp. 517-26. Author Index, pp. 527-29. Subject Index, pp. 530-34.

A text for a one-semester course in intermediate statistics or research design for students in the behavioral sciences who have had a course in basic statistics. Consists of five parts: "Foundations of Multiple Regression Analysis"; "The Regression Analysis of Experimental and Nonexperimental Data"; "Multiple Regression and Multivariate Analysis"; "Research Applications"; and "Scientific Research and Multiple Regression Analysis." Topics include dummy variables; categorical variables; analysis of covariance; discriminant analysis; factor analysis; canonical correlation; factorial design; and analysis of variance. Chapters conclude with study suggestions and problems for solution by computer programs.

Kleinbaum, David G., and Kupper, Lawrence L. APPLIED REGRESSION ANALYSIS AND OTHER MULTIVARIABLE MODELS. North Scituate, Mass.: Duxbury, 1978. xiv, 556 p. References, pp. 486-90. Appendix A: Tables, pp. 491-507. Appendix B: Matrices and Their Relationship to Regression Analysis, pp. 508-20. Appendix C: Solutions to Exercises, pp. 521-52. Index, pp. 553-56.

A text for an intermediate course in basic statistics for students in the health, biological, social,and behavioral sciences who plan to undertake applied research. Emphasizes the intuitive logic and assumptions underlying the statistical techniques with proofs of secondary importance. Topics include linear regression; analysis of variance; comparing two straight line regression models; polynomial regression; multiple regression and correlation; hypothesis testing in multiple regression; dummy variables in regression; analysis of covariance; selecting the best regression equation; residual analysis; weighted least squares; two-way analysis of variance; factorial analysis; discriminant analysis; and analysis of categorical data. Chapters conclude with problems.

Lange, Franz Heinrich. CORRELATION TECHNIQUES: FOUNDATIONS AND APPLICATIONS OF CORRELATION ANALYSIS IN MODERN COMMUNICATIONS, MEASUREMENT AND CONTROL. Translated by P.B. Johns. Princeton, N.J.: D. Van Nostrand, 1967. 464 p. References, pp. 427-54. Index, pp. 455-64.

A text, originally published in German in 1962, for students in radio measurement and control engineering who have knowledge of advanced calculus and probability theory. Topics include spectral representation of the auto-correlation function; probability; direct and indirect correlation measurement methods; auto-correlation function as a parameter in telecommunications and as means of investigating communications transmission systems; and correlation detector as a signal receiver. Derivations minimized, with much use made of charts and graphs. Includes references to works which have found no practical applications.

Lawson, Charles L., and Hanson, Richard J. SOLVING LEAST SQUARES PROBLEMS. Prentice-Hall Series in Automatic Computation. Englewood Cliffs, N.J.: Prentice-Hall, 1974. xii, 340 p. Appendix A: Basic Linear Algebra Including Projections, pp. 233-39. Appendix B: Proof of Global Quadratic Convergence of the QR Algorithm, pp. 240-47. Appendix C: Description and Use of FORTRAN Codes for Solving Least Squares Problems, pp. 248-311. Bibliography, pp. 312-26. Index, pp. 327-40.

A text and reference on numerical methods for obtaining linear least squares solutions under a variety of circumstances and assumptions for students and researchers in a variety of fields. Assumes knowledge of linear algebra. Emphasizes rigor, with proofs, development of algorithms for computing, and numerical examples provided. Topics include orthogonal decomposition; perturbation theorems for singular values; perturbation bounds for the pseudoinverse; solution for overidentified, exactly determined, and underdetermined full rank problems; computation of covariance matrix; computing errors for Householder transformations; computing errors for least squares problems; computation of the singular value decomposition and the solution of least squares; least squares by direct elimination; least squares with linear equality and linear inequality constraints; examples of methods of analysing least squares problems; and Cholesky decomposition and Gram-Schmidt orthogonalization. Chapters conclude with exercises.

Lee, T.C.; Judge, G.G.; and Zellner, A. ESTIMATING THE PARAMETERS OF THE MARKOV PROBABILITY MODEL FROM AGGREGATE TIME SERIES DATA. Contributions to Economic Analysis, vol. 65. Amsterdam: North Holland, 1970. 254 p. Appendix A: The Generalized Inverse Method, pp. 163-82. Appendix B: The General Linear Probability Model, pp. 183-90. Appendix C: Estimation of Variance Transition Probabilities, pp. 191-97. Appendix D: The FORTRAN Programming of Classical and Bayesian Transition Probability Estimators, pp. 199-241. References, pp. 243-49. Author Index, pp. 250-52. Subject Index, pp. 253-54.

A reference and supplementary text on estimating transition probabilities from time series data generated by a stationary first order Markov process. Also includes estimation of transition probabilities with nonconstant time and with the use of proportion data. Estimation methods include weighted inequality restricted least squares; generalized least squares; Bayesian and minimum absolute deviation estimators; minimum chi-square; and maximum likelihood. Assumes knowledge of linear algebra, mathematical statistics, and econometric methods.

Lewis, Truman Orvile, and Odell, P.L. ESTIMATION IN LINEAR MODELS. Englewood Cliffs, N.J.: Prentice-Hall, 1971. xi, 193 p. References, pp. 177-90. Index, pp. 191-93.

A monograph for scientists and engineers who have knowledge of calculus and linear algebra. Emphasizes definitions and theorems, and includes such topics as least squares and minimum variance estimators of nonrandom and random parameters using discrete random samples; best linear unbiased estimation, using continuous data; linear estimation with constraints; estimating a stochastic process in a dynamic model using continuous data; best estimators using an estimated covariance matrix; selecting an optimal design matrix; matrix lower bound; and least squares estimation in a nonlinear model. Chapters conclude with numerical examples and exercises.

Liebelt, Paul B. AN INTRODUCTION TO OPTIMAL ESTIMATION. Reading, Mass.: Addison-Wesley, 1967. xii, 273 p. Bibliography, pp. 255-56. Appendix, pp. 257-63. Answers, pp. 264-67. Index, pp. 269-73.

A text for students in applied mathematics, engineering, and the physical and social sciences who have knowledge of matrix algebra and some familiarity with variational calculus, harmonic analysis, the Laplace transform, and advanced topics in probability. Gauss-Markoff theorem provides the basis for estimation of parameters. Topics include linear and nonlinear systems; probability; random dynamical systems; linear estimation theory (weighted least squares, polynomial forms, Kalman estimates, and orbit determination); filtering; smoothing; and prediction. Includes derivations and examples from communication and control theory. Sections conclude with exercises. Appendix includes transition matrices from constant coefficient equations.

Lutjohann, Harry. LINEAR AGGREGATION IN LINEAR REGRESSION. Stockholm: University of Stockholm, Institute of Statistics, 1974. 208 p. References, pp. 201-6. Index, pp. 207-8.

A monograph on linear aggregation in the context of linear regression. Topics include generalization of the concept of consistency to micro and macro relations consisting of linear statistical models; a review of least-squares theory; two types of linear aggregation in dimensions of the regression variables and two types in dimensions of the observations; and development of formal analysis of linear aggregation and its application to five types of aggregation. Includes macro parameters and macro relations of Theil's linear aggregation. Assumes knowledge of linear algebra and regression.

Lyle, Philip. REGRESSION ANALYSIS OF PRODUCTION COSTS AND FACTORY OPERATIONS. 2d ed., rev. London: Oliver & Boyd, 1946. xii, 204 p. Appendix I, pp. 119-60, Appendix II, pp. 161-73. Bibliography, p. 174. Summary of Equations, pp. 175-82. Figures, pp. 183-97. Glossary, pp. 198-202. Index, pp. 203-4.

A monograph on the application of simple and quadratic regression for estimating total cost as a function of output with illustrations from sugar refining. Useful as a review of early work in applied regression analysis.

McNeil, Keith A.; Kelly, Francis J.; and McNeil, Judy T. TESTING RESEARCH HYPOTHESES USING MULTIPLE LINEAR REGRESSION. Carbondale: Southern Illinois University Press, 1975. xii, 578 p. Appendixes, pp. 489-569. References, pp. 571-78. Name Index, pp. 579-80. Subject Index, pp. 581-87.

A monograph on the use of multiple linear regression for testing research hypotheses. Emphasizes formulating research hypotheses and the use of vectors, rather than matrices, in formal presentation. Also employs graphs and brief numerical examples for illustrative purposes. Topics include vector operations; linear models; research control of possible confounding variables; dichotomous variables in regression; nonlinear relations; detection of change; and strategy of research. Appendixes include a computer program; a note on the relationship between analysis of variance, multiple correlation, analysis of covariance; and multiple linear regression; and abstracts of multiple linear regression viewpoints.

Mendel, Jerry M. DISCRETE TECHNIQUES OF PARAMETER ESTIMATION. Control Theory: A Series of Monographs and Textbooks, vol. 1. New York: Marcel Dekker, 1973. xiv, 385 p. Appendix A: Representations of Abstract Digital Systems, pp. 320-24. Appendix B: Discrete-Time Representations of Continuous-Time Systems, pp. 325-39. Appendix C: Parameter Transformation Matrices, pp. 340-50. Appendix D: Lyapunov's Main Stability Theorem: Statement and Proof, pp. 351-56. Appendix E: Some Facts About Conditional Expectations, pp. 357-60. Appendix F: Venter's Theorem, pp. 361-66. Appendix G: Upper Bound for $\|\tilde{\theta}(k+\ell)\|^2$ pp. 367-73. Author Index, pp. 375-77. Subject Index, pp. 379-85.

Presents the following four estimation techniques from a unified point of view: generalized least squares (weighted least squares); unbiased minimum-variance (best linear unbiased estimation); deterministic gradient; and stochastic gradient (a special case of stochastic approximation). Unification based on equation error method, using classical batch processing estimation algorithms and sequential estimation algorithms. Includes estimating constant parameters with perfect or noisy measurements with extensions to estimation of time-varying parameters. Applications include curve fitting, estimating coefficients in a superposition summation, estimating coefficients for a high performance adaptive aerospace control system; and estimating coefficients in a finite-difference equation. Assumes knowledge of probability and random variables; stochastic process; linear differential equations; and the theory of linear systems. Chapters conclude with problems.

Mitropol'skii, Aristarkh Konstantinovich. CORRELATION EQUATIONS FOR STATISTICAL COMPUTATIONS. Translated by E.S. Speigelthol. New York: Consultants Bureau, 1966. viii, 103 p. Appendix: Moments and Statistical Tables, pp. 72-102. Literature Cited, p. 103. No index.

Originally published in Russian. Presents methods for computing the following correlation equations: first-, second-, and third-order ordinary correlation equations for large and small samples by Chebyshev's and least squares methods; computations by Chebyshev numbers and the method of sums; computations of a nonpolynomial type, including power, exponential, logarithmic, and periodic; Chebyshev's method for setting up multiple correlation equations; and the establishment of equations of distribution surfaces. Topics illustrated by examples from the analysis of mechanical properties of steel, wood, and other materials. Assumes knowledge of the moments of random variables.

Mosteller, Frederick, and Tukey, John W. DATA ANALYSIS AN D REGRESSION: A SECON D COURSE IN STATISTICS. Addison-Wesley Series in Behavioral Science: Quantitative Methods. Reading, Mass.: Addison-Wesley, 1977. xviii, 588 p. Appendix: Details about the Need to Re-express, pp. 449-66. Problems, pp. 467-50. Data Exhibits for Problems, pp. 551-77. Index, pp. 579-88.

A text for a second course in statistics for students of the social sciences who have had one year of basic statistics. Emphasizes philosophical attitudes and approaches needed for effective data analysis, and techniques to put these attitudes to work. Attitudes include the importance of display and the value of graphs in revealing relationships; iterated calculation; robustness and resistance; what regression coefficients can and can't do; importance of residuals; and role of indications. Topics include kinds of distributions; indication and indicators; straightening curves and plots; the practice of regression; hunting out the real uncertainty; direct assessment; cross-validation; two- and more-way tables; standardization for comparison; regression for fitting; techniques for fitting lines, including ordinary least squares and weighted least squares; and guided regression. Problems and projects grouped at the end of book and organized by section.

Neter, John, and Wasserman, William. APPLIED LINEAR STATISTICAL METHODS: REGRESSION, ANALYSIS OF VARIANCE, AND EXPERIMENTAL DESIGN. Homewood, Ill.: Irwin, 1974. xvii, 842 p. Appendix Tables, pp. 803-34. Index, pp. 835-42.

A text for a two-semester course in regression, analysis of variance, or experimental design for students in management and the social sciences. Strikes a balance between theory and application with extensive use made of computer capabilities for performing computations. Topics include polynomial regression; indicator variables; multicollinearity; autocorrelation; how to search for the best set of independent variables, including stepwise regression; single-factor and two-factor analysis of variance with regression approaches; random effects model; three-factor studies; analysis of covariance for randomized designs; and Latin square designs. Assumes knowledge of basic statistics. Chapters conclude with problems and references.

Plackett, R.L. PRINCIPLES OF REGRESSION ANALYSIS. New York: Oxford University Press, 1960. ix, 173 p. Author Index, pp. 167-68. Subject Index, pp. 169-73.

An exposition of the algebraic theory and numerical methods associated with least squares for mathematicians familiar with statistical theory, matrices, complex variables, and group theory. Emphasizes assumptions and properties of estimates and tests. Topics include quadratic forms in normal variables; least squares; linear hypotheses; polynomial regression; stationary processes; autoregressive sequences; stationary processes; autoregressive sequences; symmetrical factorial experiments; and permutation distributions and tests. Numerical methods provided in terms of layouts for desk calculators. Chapters conclude with exercises and references.

Salzman, Lawrence. COMPUTERIZED ECONOMIC ANALYSIS. New York: McGraw-Hill, 1968. xiii, 253 p. Appendix, pp. 197-249. Index, pp. 251-53.

A collection of FORTRAN routines for use in elementary economic analysis. Each chapter includes a specific technique and includes the following: (1) representative computer output and analysis; (2) specific computer programs which generated the output; (3) statistical concepts; and (4) economic concepts. Emphasizes minimum use of key punching and control cards by use of a data bank. Topics include seasonal adjustment of economic time series; adjustment for trading-day variations; smoothing of series; polynomial curve fitting; exponential curve fitting; multiple regression; and stepwise regression. Appendix includes versions of several programs using less storage capacity than that needed by large computers (IBM 1401, for example). Useful to anyone interested in computer applications and statistics.

Seber, George Arthur Frederick. THE LINEAR HYPOTHESES: A GENERAL THEORY. Griffin's Statistical Monographs and Courses, no. 19. London: Griffin, 1965. viii, 115 p. Appendixes, pp. 101-3. References, pp. 104-11. Index, pp. 113-15.

A rigorous development of the linear hypothesis in a vector space framework rather than a geometrical framework. Assumes knowledge of matrix algebra and vector spaces. Topics include least squares estimation; hypothesis testing; properties of the F test; testing several hypotheses; modified hypotheses; missing observations; multivariate linear hypotheses; nonlinear normal models; and large sample theory for nonlinear hypotheses. Appendixes devoted to properties of positive definite matrices and matrix differentiation. Chapters conclude with additional references.

______. LINEAR REGRESSION ANALYSIS. New York: Wiley, 1977. xvii, 465 p. Appendix A: Some Matrix Algebra, pp. 383-93. Appendix B: Orthogonal Projections, pp. 394-97. Appendix C: Normal Probability Paper, pp. 398-401. Appendix D: Percentage Points of the Bonferroni t-Statistic, pp. 402-3. Appendix E: Distribution of the Largest Absolute Value of k Student t Variates, pp. 404-10. Appendix F: Working-Hotelling Confidence Bands for Finite Intervals, pp. 411-12. Outline Solutions to Exercises, pp. 413-32. References, pp. 433-57. Index, pp. 459-65.

A theoretically oriented text for a course in regression analysis for students who have knowledge of matrix algebra, straight-line regression, and analysis of variance. Includes an account of computational methods and algorithms. Topics include expectation and covariance operators for vectors of random variables; multivariate normal distribution; quadratic forms; generalized least squares; method of Lagrange multipliers; orthogonal projections biased estimators, and nonnegative and robust estimation; hypothesis testing; confidence intervals and regions; models with random regressors; regressor variables measured with error; straight line regression through the origin; weighted least squares; comparing straight lines; two-phase linear regression; random regressor variables; polynomial regression; two-way analysis of variance; analysis of covariance and missing observations; computational techniques for fitting a specified regression; choosing the "best" regression; stepwise regression; and factor and principal component analysis. Sections conclude with exercises and chapters conclude with review exercises.

Smillie, K.W. AN INTRODUCTION TO REGRESSION AND CORRELATION. New York: Academic Press, 1966. x, 168 p. Appendix 1: Some Notes on Matrix Algebra, pp. 123-33. Appendix 2: The Gauss-Jordan Method of Solving the Normal Equations, pp. 134-48. Appendix 3: Input Format for Regression Program, pp. 149-52. Appendix 4: FORTRAN IV Regression Programs, pp. 153-61. Bibliography, pp. 162-64. Index, pp. 165-68.

A text for a one-semester course in regression and correlation for students who have access to a computer and who have had basic statistics. Topics include simple linear regression; correlation between two variables; the general linear regression model; nonlinear regression; errors in variables; autocorrelation; weighted regression; and the programming of regression calculations. Appendix contains computer programs in FORTRAN IV.

Sonquist, John A., and Morgan, James N. THE DETECTION OF INTERACTION EFFECTS: A REPORT ON A COMPUTER PROGRAM FOR THE SELECTION OF OPTIMAL COMBINATIONS OF EXPLANATORY VARIABLES. Monograph no. 35. Ann Arbor: Survey Research Center, Institute for Social Research, University of Michigan, 1964. xi, 296 p. Appendixes, pp. 141-296. No index.

Describes a computer program for the IBM 7090 useful for studying the interrelationships among a set of thirty-seven variables. With one of the variables as dependent, program selects the optimal set of independent variables for predicting values of the dependent variable using analysis of variance. Formulas, examples, research strategy, and unsolved problems included. Appendixes devoted to references, formulas, derivations, algorithms, computer printouts, suggestions for use of programs, and problems encountered in analysing survey data.

Sprent, Peter. MODELS IN REGRESSION AND RELATED TOPICS. London: Methuen, 1969. x, 173 p. References, pp. 161-66. Author Index, pp. 167-68. Subject Index, pp. 169-73.

A survey of regression and related topics in curve and surface fitting in the presence of random variation for students of mathematical statistics and research workers who need guidance in the choice of models for a particular problem. Assumes knowledge of matrix algebra and basic statistics. Topics include simple linear regression and correlation; maximum likelihood estimators with unknown variances; multiple linear and nonlinear regression and correlation; canonical analysis; application of regression to inverse estimation; comparison of regression equations, concurrent lines, two phase regression, analysis of covariance; and linear transformation of the independent variables; law-like relationships in practice; the probit regression line; Berkson's model with controlled variables; and nonlinear models. Computational details omitted. Chapters conclude with exercises of varying difficulty.

Swamy, P.A.V.B. STATISTICAL INFERENCE IN RANDOM COEFFICIENT REGRESSION MODELS. Lecture Notes in Operations Research and Mathematical Systems, vol. 55. New York: Springer-Verlag, 1971. vii, 209 p. Bibliography, pp. 204-9. No index.

Presents a unified treatment of the theory of estimating an economic relationship from time series and cross-section data from regression analysis with some or all of the coefficients varying randomly. Applications include investment models and consumption functions. Assumes knowledge of matrix algebra, quadratic forms, and statistical estimation theory.

Ward, Joe H., and Jennings, Earl. INTRODUCTION TO LINEAR MODELS. Englewood Cliffs, N.J.: Prentice-Hall, 1973. xviii, 333 p. Bibliography, pp. 282-83. Appendix A: Computation of Least-Squares Coefficients, pp. 284-88. Appendix B: Assumptions Underlying the Use of the F Value as a Decision Rule, pp. 289-95. Appendix C: An Iterative Technique for Computing Least-Squares Coefficients, pp. 296-305. Appendix D: Model Recognition, pp. 306-16. Appendix E: Program Model, pp. 317-27. Index, pp. 329-33.

A monograph on the application of the general linear model in research in two major categories: Model Development and Computing Procedures. Models include one-attribute model with least squares estimates; one-attribute model with two categories and with multiple categories; linear dependence; independence and equivalent models; one-attribute model with ordered categories; two-attribute model with multiple categories; two-attribute model with one attribute ordered and with both attributed ordered; application of one- and two-attribute problems; and application to problems involving several attributes. Assumes knowledge of basic statistics and matrix algebra. Chapters conclude with exercises. Omits detailed discussion of confidence intervals, proofs of theorems, matrices, properties of estimators, probability, and distribution theory.

Wesolowsky, George O. MULTIPLE REGRESSION AND ANALYSIS OF VARIANCE: AN INTRODUCTION FOR COMPUTER USERS IN MANAGEMENT AND ECONOMICS. New York: Wiley, 1976. xi, 292 p. Appendix A: Mathematical Notes, pp. 247-70. Appendix B: Matrices, pp. 271-77. Appendix C: Tables, pp. 278-87. Index, pp. 289-92.

A text for a course in multiple regression for students in a variety of disciplines who have had one semester of basic statistics and who have access to computer programs in multiple regression. Emphasizes interpretation of the results of regression rather than theory. Topics include review of statistical concepts; linear regression; dummy variables; stepwise regression; heteroscedasticity; multicollinearity; autocorrelation; analysis of variance and covariance; and Latin square designs. Chapters conclude with exercises and references. Also useful as a reference in marketing, finance, geography as well as economics and business.

Williams, Evan James. REGRESSION ANALYSIS. Wiley Series in Probability and Mathematical Statistics. New York: Wiley, 1959. ix, 214 p. References, pp. 209-11. Index, pp. 212-14.

A reference for research workers in the experimental sciences. Presentation based on problems that arise in practice, especially in biology. Includes the origins of a statistical problem and range of problems for a given technique. Topics include linear, multiple, and polynomial regression; regression equations requiring iterative calculations; choice among regression formulas; estimation from regression equations; analysis of covariance; treatment of heterogeneous data; simultaneous regression equations; discriminant functions; and functional relations. Numerous examples used to illustrate concepts.

Wiseman, Stephen. CORRELATION METHODS. Statistical Guides in Educational Research, no. 1. Manchester, Engl.: Manchester University Press, 1966. vi, 44 p. No index.

A guide to simple computational methods for the following correlations: product-moment, rank, correlation by centroids, correlation ratio, biserial, point biserial, phi-biserial, phi-coefficient, tetrachoric, and multiple correlation. Assumptions and limitations in the use of the methods considered. Numerous examples provided.

Wolberg, John R. PREDICTION ANALYSIS. New York: D. Van Nostrand, 1967. xi, 291 p. Index, pp. 289-91.

A reference for scientists and engineers interested in experimental work who have knowledge of calculus. Develops techniques of statistical analysis with applications to several classes of experiments. Emphasizes least squares with computer applications. Chapters conclude with problems and computer projects. Functions include polynomial, exponential, sine series, and Gaussian.

Young, Hugh D. STATISTICAL TREATMENT OF EXPERIMENTAL DATA. New York: McGraw-Hill, 1962. xv, 172 p. Appendixes A to D, pp. 139-59. Tables, pp. 160-64. Bibliography, p. 165. Answers to Problems, pp. 166-68. Index, pp. 169-72.

A text for a short four to six weeks course in the analysis of experimental data for engineers and scientists who have knowledge of calculus and one year of physics. Topics include errors; probability distributions, including binomial, Poisson, and normal; chi-square; least squares; and correlation. Mathematical developments intuitive rather than rigorous. Chapters conclude with problems on applications. Appendixes devoted to formulas, derivations of means and variances, derivation of Gauss distribution, and evaluation of normal error integral.

Chapter 8

MULTIVARIATE ANALYSIS

Aaker, David A., ed. MULTIVARIATE ANALYSIS IN MARKETING: THEORY AND APPLICATION. Belmont, Calif.: Wadsworth, 1971. ix, 358 p. References, p. 351. Index, pp. 353-58.

A supplementary text for courses in marketing, models, and intermediate statistics for students who have had basic statistics, and a reference for research workers. Consists of thirty reprints of articles grouped under the following headings: "Regression Analysis" (five articles); "Simultaneous-Equation Regression Analysis" (four articles); "Discriminant Analysis" (three articles); "Canonical Analysis" (two articles); "Experimental Design" (four articles); "Factor Analysis" (five articles); "Multidimensional Scaling" (four articles); and "Cluster Analysis" (three articles). Articles treat both theory and applications and include such topics as transformations; comparison of single and simultaneous equation techniques; recursive model of communication process; discriminant analysis of audience characteristics; factorial design in a pricing experiment; covariance analysis; factor analysis of qualitative attributes of coffee; similarity and preference mapping; and visual clustering using principal components analysis.

Adcock, C.J. FACTORIAL ANALYSIS FOR NON-MATHEMATICIANS. Carlton, Victoria, Australia: Melbourne University Press, 1954. 88 p. Appendix: Basing Factors on Correlation Clusters. Formulas for Correlation Matrix, pp. 85-87. Further Reading, p. 88.

A nonmathematical exposition of factor analysis relying primarily on graphs and numerical examples. Topics include correlation, factors, principle of rotation, simple structure, combining centroid and group analysis, and the role of factor analysis.

Amick, Daniel J., and Walberg, Herbert J., eds. INTRODUCTORY MULTIVARIATE ANALYSIS FOR EDUCATIONAL, PSYCHOLOGICAL, AND SOCIAL RESEARCH. Foreword by R. Ferber. Berkeley, Calif.: McCutchan, 1975. xiv, 301 p. Appendix A: Available Computer Packages by D.J. Amick, pp. 285-87. Appendix B: Four Tables, pp. 289-97. Index, pp. 299-301.

Ten contributions by different authors presented at a workshop on multivariate methods held at the Survey Research Laboratory of the University of Illinois in 1973. Useful as a reference on applied multivariate techniques for anyone having knowledge of basic statistics. Topics include regression analysis, path analysis, analysis of variance, discriminant analysis, canonical analysis; classification analysis, and reduction of a large set of variables to a more compact and meaningful set using factor analysis.

Anderberg, Michael Rex. CLUSTER ANALYSIS FOR APPLICATIONS. Probability and Mathematical Statistics. A Series of Monographs and Textbooks, 19. New York: Academic Press, 1973. xiii, 359 p. Appendixes, pp. 216-346. References, pp. 347-53. Index, pp. 355-59.

A text for a course in cluster analysis for the life sciences, behavioral and social sciences, earth sciences, medicine, policy sciences, and engineering. Consists of a synthesis of the literature, and assumes knowledge of computer programming and basic statistics. Topics include conceptual problems in cluster analysis, measures of association, hierarchical and nonhierarchical clustering; and strategies for using cluster analysis. Appendixes devoted to computer programs for cluster analysis.

Anderson, Theodore Wilbur. AN INTRODUCTION TO MULTIVARIATE STATISTICAL ANALYSIS. Wiley Series in Probability and Mathematical Statistics. New York: Wiley, 1958. xii, 374 p. Appendix 1: Matrix Theory, pp. 333-51. Appendix 2: Bibliography, pp. 352-68. Index, pp. 369-74.

A text for a one-year course in multivariate statistics and a reference for statisticians. Topics include multivariate normal distribution; estimation of mean vector and covariance matrix; correlation coefficients; generalized T^2 statistic; classification of observations; generalized variance; analysis of variance; testing independence of sets of variates; testing hypothesis of equality of covariance matrices and equality of mean vectors and covariance matrices; principal components; canonical correlation and canonical variables; distribution of characteristic roots and vectors; noncentral Wishart distribution; factor analysis; stochastic equations; and time series analysis. Assumes knowledge of the theory of univariate statistics and matrix algebra. Derivations rigorous with proofs of theorems provided and few examples included. Chapters conclude with references and problems.

Anderson, Theodore Wilbur; Das Gupta, Somesh; and Styan, George P.H. A BIBLIOGRAPHY OF MULTIVARIATE STATISTICAL ANALYSIS. New York: Wiley, Halsted Press, 1972. x, 642 p. No index.

A bibliography divided into the following three parts: an annotated listing of 213 books published in 1970 or earlier on multivariate statistical analysis and related topics, including psychometrics and econometrics; an annotated listing of 819 journals and other collections containing research papers; and 6,093 research papers, reprints, translations, and amendments arranged alphabetically by author published in 1966 or earlier. Includes subject matter code for topics of interest and an index of authors.

Anderson, Virgil L., and McLean, Robert A. DESIGN OF EXPERIMENTS: A REALISTIC APPROACH. Statistics: Textbooks and Monographs, vol. 5. New York: Marcel Dekker, 1974. xvii, 418 p. Appendixes, pp. 388-412. Author Index, pp. 413-14. Subject Index, pp. 415-18.

A text for an introductory course in experimental design for students in varied fields who have a high school algebra background and knowledge of basic statistics. Emphasizes the interpretation and usefulness of the results of multivariate analysis. Topics include one- and two-way classification; randomized designs; randomized complete block designs; nested (hierarchical) and nest factorial designs; split plot designs; Latin square designs; 2^n factorial experiments (complete and incomplete blocks); fractional factorial experiments for two-leveled factors; three-level factorial experiments; mixed factorial experiments and other incomplete block designs; and response surface exploration. Sections conclude with problems, and chapters conclude with references. Appendixes devoted to statistical tables and derivations.

Andrews, Frank M., and Messenger, Robert C. MULTIVARIATE NOMINAL SCALE ANALYSIS: A REPORT ON A NEW ANALYSIS TECHNIQUE AND A COMPUTER PROGRAM. Ann Arbor: Survey Research Center, University of Michigan, 1973. vi, 108 p. Bibliography, pp. 82-84. Appendix A: Set Up Instructions, pp. 85-93. Appendix B: MNA Macro Flow Chart, pp. 94-96. Appendix C: Sample Output, pp. 97-106. Appendix D: Obtaining the Program and Adapting it to Other Systems, pp. 107-8. No index.

A monograph on the use of computer programs for analyzing attribute data (nominally scaled data). Methods provide for the analysis of one dependent variable and two or more independent variables for various levels of measurement-nominal, ordinal, and interval. Includes the mathematical description of the program and comparisons with other techniques of multivariate analysis of attribute data. Appendixes devoted to instructions for using the computer program.

Andrews, Harry C. INTRODUCTION TO MATHEMATICAL TECHNIQUES IN PATTERN RECOGNITION. New York: Wiley, 1972. xiii, 242 p. Appendix A: Multidimensional Rotations in Feature Selection, pp. 211-23. Appendix B: A Rate Distortion Criteria for Feature Selection, pp. 225-34. Author Index, pp. 235-38. Subject Index, pp. 239-42.

A text for an introductory course in mathematical pattern recognition for students in computer science, mathematics, and engineering who have knowledge of vector spaces and higher dimensional geometry, probability theory, and calculus. Includes the following six chapters: "Mathematical Pattern Recognition"; "Feature Selection"; "Distribution Free Classification"; "Statistical Classification"; "Nonsupervised Learning"; and "Sequential Learning." Chapters conclude with extensive bibliographies and problems, some requiring computer selections.

Atchley, William R., and Bryant, Edwin H., eds. MULTIVARIATE STATISTICAL METHODS: AMONG-GROUPS COVARIATION. Benchmark Papers in Systematic and Evolutionary Biology, 1. New York: Wiley, Halsted Press, 1975. xv, 464 p. Author Citation Index, pp. 455-60. Subject Index, pp. 461-64.

Twenty-seven reprints of articles grouped under the following five headings: "Introduction" (one article); "Multivariate Analysis of Variance" (six articles); "Discriminant Analysis" (nine articles); "Cluster Analysis" (nine articles); and "Nonmetric Scaling" (two articles). Emphasizes applications in biology. Topics include generalization of student's ratio; geographical variation in European Rana; multiple measurements in taxonomic problems; multivariate geographical variation in the wolf; multivariate methods in plant ecology; adoptive hierarchical clustering schemes; distance analysis in biology; and an empirical comparison of three ordination techniques in numerical taxonomy.

Baird, John C., and Noma, Elliot. FUNDAMENTALS OF SCALING AND PSYCHOPHYSICS. Wiley Series in Behavior. New York: Wiley, 1978. xi, 287 p. Index, pp. 277-87.

A reference and supplementary text on scaling and mathematical psychology with emphasis on theory, experimental procedures, and data analysis. Traces the historical development of the field, from Fechner's and Steven's methods of measurement and scaling of sensating and response to current models of multidimensional scaling, cluster analysis, and information theory. Knowledge of college algebra and basic statistics helpful. Includes few derivations. Chapters conclude with references.

Banerjee, Kali S. WEIGHING DESIGNS. FOR CHEMISTRY, MEDICINE, ECONOMICS, OPERATIONS RESEARCH, STATISTICS. Statistics: Textbooks and Monographs, vol. 12. New York: Marcel Dekker, 1975. xv, 141 p. Exercises, pp. 91-98. Appendix A: The General Linear Hypothesis Model and the Method of Least Squares, pp. 99-107. Appendix B: Weighing Designs Illustrated, pp. 109-23. Appendix C: A List of Weighing Designs, pp. 125-31. References, pp. 133-38. Index, pp. 139-41.

A reference for research workers in all applied fields on weighing designs in which the measure of a combination is expressed as a linear combination of the separate measures with numerically equal coefficients. Includes the following chapters: "Formulation of the Weighing Problems"; "Chemical Balance Problem"; "Spring Balance Problem"; and "Miscellaneous Issues Concerning the Weighing Problem." Appendixes designed to meet the needs of researchers in fields other than statistics.

Banks, Seymour. EXPERIMENTATION IN MARKETING. New York: McGraw-Hill, 1965. xiii, 275 p. Appendix: Tables, pp. 253-62. Consolidated Bibliography, pp. 263-69. Index, pp. 271-75.

Illustrates the use of standard statistical techniques, statistical decision theory, and Bayesian statistics in experimentation in marketing and advertising. Includes situations which lend themselves to experimentation and a large numbers of actual experiments. Topics include completely randomized designs; randomized block designs; Latin square designs; the double change-over design; factorial designs; balanced incomplete block designs; fitting models to experimental data; and planning the size of experiments. Useful as a reference for administrators and technicians.

Becker, Peter W. RECOGNITION OF PATTERNS USING THE FREQUENCIES OF OCCURRENCE OF BINARY WORDS. 2d rev. ed. New York: Springer-Verlag, 1974. xiv, 215 p. Glossary of Symbols, pp. xi-xiv. Bibliography, pp. 203-15. No index.

Presents a new method for the design of pattern recognition in which a nonexhaustive, iterative procedure generates effective pattern attributes from existing, less effective attributes. Each pattern first reduced to a binary sequence by a suitable coding method. Each sequence then described in a statistical sense by the observed frequency of occurrence of certain selected binary words, with the categorization of patterns performed on the basis of the observed values.

Bennett, Spencer, and Bowers, David. AN INTRODUCTION TO MULTIVARIATE TECHNIQUES FOR THE SOCIAL AND BEHAVIORAL SCIENCES. New York: Wiley, 1976. xii, 156 p. References, pp. 151-52. Index, pp. 153-56.

A text for an introductory course in multivariate statistics for students in the behavioral sciences who have had basic statistics. Extensive use made of numerical examples, with use of matrix algebra, proofs, and derivations minimized. Topics include centroid method of factor analysis; rotation of factors; principal factor analysis; multiple groups; multidimensional scaling; discriminant analysis; and analysis of qualitative data. Omits multiple regression, multivariate analysis of variance, and canonical correlation.

Bijnen, E.J. CLUSTER ANALYSIS: SURVEY AND EVALUATION OF TECHNIQUES. Translated by C.E. Brand-Maher. Foreword by Ph. C. Stouthard. Tilburg Studies in Sociology, no. 1. Groningen, The Netherlands: Tilburg University Press, 1973. xi, 112 p. Conclusion, pp. 100-102. Bibliography, pp. 103-12. No index.

> A survey of a number of techniques of cluster analysis useful in the social sciences, medicine, and biology. Topics include indexes of Zubin, Rogers, and Jaccard; G-index of Holley and Guilford; methods developed for forming clusters of variables, including the method of Weiss, Spilerman, and Gengeielli; methods of forming clusters for objects, including theorems of Sawrey, Bonner, Hyärinen, and Mattson; methods for the construction of the types following McQuitty; and application in the 1963 Dutch parliamentary election in twenty-five towns. Assumes knowledge of basic statistics.

Bishop, Yvonne M.M.; Fienberg, Stephen E.; and Holland, Paul W. With the Collaboration of Richard J. Light and Frederick Mosteller. DISCRETE MULTIVARIATE ANALYSIS: THEORY AND PRACTICE. Cambridge, Mass.: MIT Press, 1975. x, 557 p. References, pp. 531-42. Index to Data Sets, pp. 543-46. Author Index, pp. 547-50. Subject Index, pp. 551-57.

> A text for undergraduates and graduates in biology, medicine, and the social sciences and a reference for practitioners. One computer program performs most of the calculations described. Topics include log-linear model and its use in analyzing contingency tables; structural models for counted data; maximum likelihood estimates for complete and incomplete tables; estimating the size of a closed population; models for measuring change; analysis of square tables; symmetry and marginal homogeneity; estimation and testing in cross-classifications; measures of association and agreement; pseudo-estimates of cell probabilities; and asymptotic methods. Assumes knowledge of linear algebra and basic statistics, with knowledge of mathematical statistics helpful.

Blackith, R.E., and Reyment, R.A. MULTIVARIATE MORPHOMETRICS. New York: Academic Press, 1971. x, 412 p. Glossary, pp. 347-64. Bibliography and Author Index, pp. 365-91. Subject Index, pp. 392-412.

> A text on morphometrics (quantitative study of animals and plants). Includes application of multivariate statistical techniques to biology, sociology, and geology with a prerequisite of basic statistics. Topics include mathematical and biological framework of morphometrics; discriminant analysis; canonical correlation; nonlinear taxonomy; measurement of environmental variation; multivariate studies in ecology; phytosociological studies; quantitative comparisons of faunal elements; genetical aspects of morphometrics; numerical taxonomy; cluster analysis; graph theory and dendrograms; trend-surface analyses of trans-

formation grids; and applications of morphometrics in paleontology. Derivations omitted, with reliance placed on graphs, numerical examples, and computer printouts.

Bock, Richard Darrell. MULTIVARIATE STATISTICAL METHODS IN BEHAVIORAL RESEARCH. McGraw-Hill Series in Psychology. New York: McGraw-Hill, 1975. xiii, 623 p. Appendix A: A Table of the Generalized F Statistic, pp. 560-83. Appendix B: Orthogonal Polynomials to n - 10, pp. 584-88. References, pp. 589-605. Name Index, pp. 607-11. Subject Index, pp. 613-23.

A text for an advanced course in behavioral statistics for students who have had one year of basic statistics. Assumes knowledge of calculus and matrix algebra. Emphasizes theory and interpretation, with computer programs used for computation. Topics include multivariate normal distribution; multivariate least-squares estimation; linear models for designed experiments; linear models for nonexperimental analysis; analysis of repeated measurements; and multivariate analysis of qualitative data. Examples and applications provided.

Bolch, Ben W., and Huang, Cliff J. MULTIVARIATE STATISTICAL METHODS FOR BUSINESS AND ECONOMICS. Prentice-Hall International Series in Management. Englewood Cliffs, N.J.: Prentice-Hall, 1974. xiv, 329 p. Appendix: Tables, pp. 305-15. Bibliography, pp. 316-21. Index, pp. 323-29.

A text for a one-semester course in multivariate analysis for students in economics and business who have already taken one year of basic statistics and one year of calculus. FORTRAN programs discussed in chapter appendixes. Emphasizes regression rather than experimental design. Topics include matrix algebra; univariate and multivariate normal density functions; tests concerning means; linear regression and correlation; analysis of variance and covariance; nonlinear regression; discriminant, principal components, and canonical analyses; and spectral analysis. Derivations and numerical illustrations included. Chapters conclude with questions and problems.

Brownlee, K.A. INDUSTRIAL EXPERIMENTATION. 3d ed. Foreword by R.C. Bowden. Brooklyn: Chemical Rubber Co., 1949. 194 p. Appendix: Tables, pp. 181-90. Bibliography, pp. 191-92. Index, pp. 197-94.

A monograph intended as a guide to both the planning and interpretation of industrial experiments. Emphasizes tests of significance to attain reliability from experimental data and the use of statistical design to attain maximum precision with minimum of expenditures. Illustrates each statistical method with examples taken from the Royal Ordnance Factories in the United Kingdom. Topics include comparison of variances; chi-square; Poisson distribution; analysis of variance; quality control; simple and multiple correlation; Latin and completely orthogonal squares; balanced incomplete blocks; confounding; and the fractional replication of factorial experiments. Assumes knowledge of introductory research methods.

Bryant, Edwin H., and Atchley, William R., eds. MULTIVARIATE STATISTICAL METHODS: WITHIN-GROUP COVARIATION. Vol. two. Benchmark Papers in Systematic and Evolutionary Biology, 2. New York: Wiley, Halsted Press, 1975. xv, 436 p. Author Citation Index, pp. 429-32. Index, pp. 433-36.

Twenty-four reprints of articles in quantitative methodology in biology grouped under the following four headings: "Introduction" (one article); "Principal Component Analysis" (five articles); "Factor Analysis" (twelve articles); and "Multivariate Regression and Correlation" (six articles). Topics include size and shape variation in the painted turtle; estimation and tests of significance in factor analysis; rotation for simple loadings; factor analysis in morphometric traits of the house mouse; canonical correlation and its relationships and canonical trend surfaces.

Budd, Richard W.; Thorp, Robert K.; and Donohew, Lewis. CONTENT ANALYSIS OF COMMUNICATIONS. Foreword by Malcolm S. MacLean, Jr. New York: Macmillan, 1967. xi, 147 p. Bibliography, pp. 100-142. Index, pp. 143-47.

A monograph on the application of content analysis in communication with examples from mass media. Emphasizes the verbal style, with knowledge of basic statistics helpful for understanding certain portions. Topics include hypothesis formulation; sampling; measurement; categories; direction; problem of reliability and validity; statistical tests for measuring the relationship between variables; and use of the computer. Useful to people in journalism, political science, speech, psychology, sociology, and broadcasting.

Cacoullos, Theophilus, ed. DISCRIMINANT ANALYSIS AND APPLICATIONS. New York: Academic Press, 1973. xviii, 434 p. A Bibliography of Discriminant Analysis by T.Cacoullos and George P.H. Styan, pp. 375-434. No index.

Nineteen papers presented at the NATO Advanced Study Institute on discriminant analysis held in Kifissia, Athens, Greece, June 8-20, 1972. Topics include logistic discriminant analysis with medical applications; graphical techniques for high dimensional data; methods and applications of equal-mean discrimination; computer graphical analysis and discrimination; discriminant problems about Gaussian processes; multiple group discriminant problems; simulation experiments with multiple group linear and quadratic discriminant analysis; quasi-linear discrimination; the discriminant function in systematic biology; and operating characteristics of linear discriminant functions. Assumes knowledge of mathematical statistics for most papers.

Campbell, Donald Thomas, and Stanley, Julian C. EXPERIMENTAL AND QUASI-EXPERIMENTAL DESIGNS FOR RESEARCH. Chicago: Rand McNally, 1963. ix, 84 p. References, pp. 71-76. Some Supplementary References, p. 77. Name Index, pp. 79-81. Subject Index, pp. 83-84.

A monograph on experimental design for research in education, and the social sciences using few formulas. Topics include pre-experimental designs (one-shot, one-group, pretest-posttest, and static group comparison); true experimental design (pretest-posttest control group, Solomon design, and posttest-only control group design); factorial designs; quasi-experimental designs (time-series experiment, multiple time-series, and regression discontinuity analysis); and correlation. Useful as a supplementary text for a course in experimental design in education.

Carney, Thomas F. CONTENT ANALYSIS: A TECHNIQUE FOR SYSTEMATIC INFERENCE FROM COMMUNICATIONS. Winnipeg, Manitoba: University of Manitoba Press, 1972. xx, 343 p. Appendix: Applying Content Analysis of Synopsizing, Abstracting, and Reviewing, pp. 309-21. Bibliography, pp. 323-32.

A nonmathematical survey of content analysis--a method designed to improve the quality of the inferences made from communications (verbal, written, or even pictorial). Useful to anyone desiring to be objective and systematic in searching for evidence. Points out the details of analyzing a text systematically and objectively using multivariate analysis. Some applications of multivariate analysis included. No prerequisites.

Cattell, Raymond B. REAL BASE TRUE ZERO FACTOR ANALYSIS. Multivariate Behavioral Research Monographs, no. 72-1. University Park: Society of Multivariate Experimental Psychology, Department of Psychology, Pennsylvania State University, 1972. 162 p. References, pp. 127-29. Appendixes, pp. 130-55. Glossary of Definitions, pp. 156-61. Glossary of Regarding Notation, pp. 161-62. No index.

A monograph on factor analysis covering such topics as factor potency; law of constancy of factor effect; multi-situation-multi-demo design; general principles seeking equal interval and true zero scales; approaches to true zero through relational simplex; and combining covariance and true zero calculations in staggered on set real base factoring. Appendixes devoted to additional comments, mathematical derivations, applications, and estimation of factor scores.

______, ed. HANDBOOK OF MULTIVARIATE EXPERIMENTAL PSYCHOLOGY. Chicago: Rand McNally, 1966. xxxi, 959 p. Bibliography, pp. 878-937. Author Index, pp. 939-47. Subject Index, pp. 948-59.

Thirty heretofore unpublished contributions on multivariate experiments in psychology for use as a handbook for graduate students and researchers. Both theory and applications included. Topics include experimental design in relation to theory; the data box; the essentials of multivariate analysis; regression; discriminant analysis, and a standard notation for basic statistics; factor analysis; analysis of variance; factor-analytic experimental design patterns of change; canonical factor models; game theory; man-machine interaction; order analysis of correlation matrices; interaction and nonlinearity in multivariate experiments; learning theory; personality theory; biological correlates of mental processes; multivariate experiment in behavioral genetics; multivariate analysis of the behavior and structure of groups and organizations; and cultural design in education, industrial and military personnel, and clinical psychology. Assumes knowledge of basic statistics.

Cattell, Raymond B., and Jaspers, Joseph. A GENERAL PLASMODE (NO. 30-10-5-2) FOR FACTOR ANALYTIC EXERCISES AND RESEARCH. Multivariate Behavioral Research Monographs, no. 67-3. University Park: Society of Multivariate Experimental Psychology, Department of Psychology, Pennsylvania State University, 1967. iv, 211 p. References, pp. 56-57. Appendixes, pp. 58-211. No index.

Presents methods for constructing a plasmode (a set of numerical values fitting a mathematico-theoretical model). Topics include the nature, requirements, and uses of an analytic plasmode; generating a plasmode; introducing errors; recovery of the first, second, and third order analytic structure in the three plasmodes I, T, and E; and introducing outcomes. Appendixes contain numerical data for the plasmode.

Chakrabarti, Mukunda Chandra. MATHEMATICS OF DESIGN AND ANALYSIS OF EXPERIMENTS. New York: Asia Publishing House, 1962. vii, 121 p. List of References, pp. 119-20. Index, p. 121.

A supplementary text for a graduate course in experimental design based on lectures by the author at Maharja Sayajirao University of Baroda, India, from 1954 to 1956. Consists of the following chapter titles: "Theory of Linear Estimation"; "General Structure of Analysis of Designs"; "Standards Designs"; "Applications of Galois Fields and Finite Geometry in the Construction of Designs"; and "Selected Topics in Design of Experiments." Assumes knowledge of abstract algebra and mathematical statistics. Chapters conclude with problems on derivations and proofs of theorems.

Chen, Chi-hau. STATISTICAL PATTERN RECOGNITION. Rochelle Park, N.J.: Hayden, 1973. xvi, 236 p. Appendix A: Derivation of Fisher Discriminant Function, pp. 225-26. Appendix B: Convergence of the Supervised Estimation-Process, p. 226. Appendix C: Identifiability of Finite Mixtures, pp. 226-27. Appendix D: Similarity Matrix Method, pp. 227-28. Appendix E: List of Iris Data Set, pp. 228-29. Index, pp. 231-36.

Attempts to organize the results of statistical pattern recognition into a coherent logical framework useful to students and researchers. Topics include linear and nonlinear classification theories; representation of patterns; feature selection and extraction; supervised and unsupervised Bayesian parameter estimations; recursive algorithms using stochastic approximation; sequential pattern recognition systems; nonparametric methods and compound decision theory; recognition systems with finite memory and feedback; contextual analysis in pattern recognition; and application of nonparametric methods in communication theory. Chapters conclude with problems; some on computer recognition experiments. Emphasizes intuitive interpretation, with detailed derivations minimized. Assumes knowledge of mathematical statistics, mathematical analysis, and statistical decision theory. Chapters conclude with references.

Chew, Vector, ed. EXPERIMENTAL DESIGNS IN INDUSTRY. Foreword by Gertrude M. Fox. Wiley Series in Probability and Mathematical Statistics. New York: Wiley, 1958. xi, 268 p. References, pp. 253-68. No index.

Nine papers presented at a symposium on experimental design held at North Carolina State College Nov. 5-9, 1950, under sponsorship of the Office of Scientific Research. Papers grouped under the following two headings: "Review of Experimental Designs Useful in Industrial Research" (four papers) and "Industrial Experiences with Experimental Designs" (five papers). Topics include simple and multiple regression; review of experimental designs; complete factorials, fractional factorials, and confounding; experimental designs for exploring response surfaces; incomplete block designs; fractional factorials with applications in a food research laboratory; and design in ordnance experimentation. Emphasizes verbal explanation and numerical examples.

Child, Dennis. THE ESSENTIALS OF FACTOR ANALYSIS. New York: Holt, Rinehart and Winston, 1973. viii, 107 p. Appendix A: Finding Factor Loadings Using Sample Summation Methods, pp. 89-94. Appendix B: Significance Levels for Pearson Product-Moment Correlation Coefficients, pp. 95-96. Appendix C: Significance Levels of Factor Loadings Using the Burt-Banks Formula, pp. 97-100. Suggested Further Reading, pp. 101-2. Index, pp. 103-7.

An elementary introduction to factor analysis for students, teachers, and researchers who require sufficient knowledge of factor analysis to read books and research papers. Also preparation for advanced reading in factor analysis. Topics include a geometrical approach to factor analysis; the language and interpretation of factor analysis; the rotation of factors; and applications to human ability, personality, Osgood's semantic differential, medicine, and public health.

Clifford, A.A. MULTIVARIATE ERROR ANALYSIS. A HANDBOOK OF ERROR PROPAGATION AND CALCULATION IN MANY-PARAMETER SYSTEMS. New York: Wiley, Halsted Press, 1973. ix, 112 p. Appendix A: Bibliography, p. 83. Appendix B: Computer Procedures, pp. 84-110. Index, pp. 111-12.

A handbook for scientists on the techniques of multivariate error analysis with emphasis on describing the procedures for a given case. Least squares given only brief treatment. Topics include review of variance and covariance; error propagation from two observables to two parameters and from several observations to the same number of parameters; and errors in two parameters obtained from several observables and in several parameters obtained from many observables. Assumes knowledge of mathematical statistics and regression analysis. Computer programs in Appendix B, written in ALGOL and FORTRAN, useful in carrying out error analysis.

Cochran, William Gemmell, and Cox, Gertrude M. EXPERIMENTAL DESIGN. 2d ed., rev. Wiley Series in Probability and Mathematical Statistics. New York: Wiley, 1957. xiv, 617 p. Selected Bibliography, p. 597. List of Author References, pp. 599-601. Index, pp. 603-11. Tables, pp. 613-17.

A comprehensive treatment of the design of experiments requiring knowledge of the analysis of variance for students, teachers, and research workers. Topics include completely randomized, randomized block, and Latin square designs; factorial experiments; confounding; factorial experiments with confounding; response surfaces; incomplete block designs; lattice designs; balanced and partially balanced incomplete block designs; lattice squares; incomplete Latin squares; and random permutations of 9 and 16 numbers. Chapters conclude with references.

Comrey, Andrew Laurence. A FIRST COURSE IN FACTOR ANALYSIS. New York: Academic Press, 1973. xii, 316 p. References, pp. 306-9. Index, pp. 311-16.

A text for a beginning course in factor analysis for students who have knowledge of matrix algebra and basic statistics. Topics include the factor analytic model; factor extraction by the centroid method; principal factor and minimum residual methods of factor extraction; orthogonal hand rotations; oblique hand rotations; planning the standard design factor analysis; alternative designs in factor analysis; interpretation and application of factor analysis; and development of the Comrey personality scales. Concludes with twelve FORTRAN computer programs developed by the author to execute various kinds of computations.

Connor, William Stokes, and Young, Shirley. FRACTIONAL FACTORIAL DESIGNS FOR EXPERIMENTS WITH FACTORS AT TWO AND THREE LEVELS.

Applied Mathematics Series, 58. Washington, D.C.: Superintendent of Documents, National Bureau of Standards, 1961. v, 65 p. No index.

Contains fractional factorial designs for use in experiments with m factors at two levels and n factors at three levels. Designs provide for estimation of grand mean, all main effects, and all two-factor interaction effects. Designs constructed for each of 39 pairs (m,n) from $m+n=5$ through $m+n=10$ $(m,n \neq 0)$, each design designated by 2^m3^n. Includes description of the mathematical model, method of testing hypotheses and construction confidence intervals, and worked examples. Six designs for which interaction effects between factors at three levels also included.

Connor, William Stokes, and Zelen, Marvin. FRACTIONAL FACTORIAL EXPERIMENTAL DESIGNS FOR FACTORS AT THREE LEVELS. Applied Mathematics Series, no. 54. Washington, D.C.: Superintendent of Documents, National Bureau of Standards, 1959. v, 37 p. No index.

A monograph containing a collection of fractional factorial designs for factors at three levels. Includes fractional replicates for the fractions 1/3, 1/9, 1/27, 1/81, 1/243 for n ranging from 4 to 10 factors. Treatment combinations grouped into blocks designated r.n.k (3.4.9 indicating 1/3 replicate of a 3^4 factorial design having three blocks of nine units each).

Cooley, William W., and Lohnes, Paul R. MULTIVARIATE DATA ANALYSIS. New York: Wiley, 1971. x, 364 p. Appendix A: Statistical Tables, pp. 341-44. Appendix B: Talent Data, pp. 345-57. Appendix C: Rectangles Data, pp. 358-60. Index, pp. 361-64.

A text for a graduate course in multivariate analysis for students in education and the social sciences who have knowledge of one year of basic statistics. Matrix algebra and other mathematical concepts introduced as needed. FORTRAN programs included. Consists of three parts: "Introduction"; "Studies of a Single Population"; and "Multiple Population Studies." Topics include principal components; factor analysis canonical correlation; multiple partial correlation; discriminant analysis; analysis of variance; covariance analysis; and factorial discriminant analysis. Chapters conclude with exercises.

______. MULTIVARIATE PROCEDURES FOR THE BEHAVIORAL SCIENCES. New York: Wiley, 1962. x, 211 p. Index, pp. 209-11.

A supplementary text for a course in multivariate analysis. Includes procedures with examples, flow charts for programming the procedure on any digital computer, and a listing of FORTRAN programs. Procedures include multiple and canonical correlation; multivariate analysis of variance and covariance;

multiple-discriminant analysis; classification procedures; and factor analysis. Concludes with a chapter on subroutines for matrix inversion and methods for extracting latent roots and vectors. Assumes knowledge of basic statistics. Chapters conclude with references.

Cooper, Brian Edward. STATISTICS FOR EXPERIMENTALISTS. New York: Pergamon, 1969. viii, 336 p. Hints and Answers to Problems, pp. 297-309. References, pp. 311-12. Tables Section, pp. 313-30. Index, pp. 331-36.

A reference for the experimental scientist who understands calculus and basic statistics. Topics arranged according to experiment rather than to sequence found in statistical theory. Topics include probability; random variables and their distributions; estimators and estimation, including least squares and maximum likelihood; analysis of variance, including two-way factorial experiments; balanced incomplete randomized block designs; analysis of covariance; correlation and curve fitting; Poisson process and counting problems; and nonparametric tests. Based on the author's experience at the Atomic Energy Research Establishment at Harwell, United Kingdom. Chapters conclude with questions.

Coult, Allan D., and Habenstein, Robert W. CROSS-TABULATION OF MURDOCK'S WORLD ETHNOGRAPHIC SAMPLE. Columbia: University of Missouri Press, 1965. lxxi, 549 p. Alphabetical Key to Tribes, pp. xxxviii-xlv. Alphabetical List of Tables, pp. xlvi-lxix. References, lxxi. Tables, pp. 1-528. List of IBM Codes, pp. 529-49. No index.

A reference handbook containing a complete set of all two-dimensional cross-tabulations of Murdock's world ethnographic sample in 528 tables accompanied by paired tables showing the level of significance and phi correlation coefficient of association for the relationship between each pair of variables.

Cox, David Roxbee. PLANNING OF EXPERIMENTS. Wiley Series in Probability and Mathematical Statistics. New York: Wiley, 1958. vii, 308 p. General Bibliography, pp. 292-300. Author Index, pp. 301-2. Subject Index, pp. 303-8.

A reference and self-study on statistical aspects of experimental design requiring no special prerequisites. Verbal discussion in terms of examples drawn from many fields of application. First nine chapters include general concepts and key designs such as randomized blocks and Latin squares. Chapters ten to fourteen include advanced topics such as incomplete block designs, fractional replication, and confounding; cross-over designs; and trend-free systematic designs.

Cronbach, Lee J.; Gleser, Goldine C.; Nanda, Harinder; and Rajaratnam, Nageswari. THE DEPENDABILITY OF BEHAVIORAL MEASUREMENTS: THEORY OF GENERALIZABILITY FOR SCORES AND PROFILES. New York: Wiley, 1972. xix, 410 p. Appendix: Proof Regarding Covariance Components, pp. 394-95. Bibliography, pp. 396-405. Index, pp. 407-10.

A text for a course in behavioral measurements for students of education and psychology who have had a course in basic statistics. Topics include experimental designs and estimates of variance components; inference from D-study data regarding the universe score μ_p ; universe with fixed facets; analyses of crossed designs; analyses of partially nested designs; multifacet correlational analysis; multivariate generalizability theory; and multivariate estimation of universe scores. Chapters conclude with exercises and answers.

Cuppens, Roger. DECOMPOSITION OF MULTIVARIATE PROBABILITY. Probability and Mathematical Statistics. A Series of Monographs and Textbooks, vol. 29. New York: Academic Press, 1975. xv, 244 p. Appendix A: Some Results of Function Theory, pp. 205-16. Appendix B: Exponentials of Polynomials and Functions, pp. 217-35. References, pp. 236-42. Index, pp. 243-44.

A report on the theory of multivariate characteristics functions. Topics include review of measure and integration; Fourier-Stieltjes transforms of finite signed measures; multivariate characteristic functions with extensions of the Paley-Wiener theorem on entire functions of the exponential and square-integrable type; theory of infinitely divisible probabilities and the classical results of Hincin; decompositions of analytic characteristic functions; and description of the class of n-variate probabilities without decomposable factors; and the problem of $\mathcal{L}$-decomposition of multivariate characteristic functions. Applications of characteristic functions omitted.

Daniel, Cuthbert. APPLICATIONS OF STATISTICS TO INDUSTRIAL EXPERIMENTATIONS. Wiley Series in Probability and Mathematical Statistics. New York: Wiley, 1976. xvi, 294 p. Bibliography and Index of Authors, pp. 289-92. Index, pp. 293-94.

A reference for research workers engaged in confirmation experiments in industry who have knowledge of basic statistics. Develops subject by example, rather than derivations. Includes the following experiments: simple comparison experiments; two factors, each at two levels; unreplicated three-factor, two-level experiments; unreplicated four-factor, two-level experiments; three five-factor, two-level unreplicated experiments; two-way layouts; blocking factorial experiments; factorial replication; incomplete factorials; sequences of fractional replicates; trend-robust plans; and nested designs.

David, Herbert Aron. THE METHOD OF PAIRED COMPARISONS. Griffin's Statistical Monographs and Courses, no. 12. London: Charles Griffin, 1969. 124 p. References, pp. 104-9. Appendix: Tables, pp. 110-22. Index, pp. 123-24.

A monograph on the method of paired comparisons with emphasis on simple, widely applicable procedures resting on a minimum of assumptions. Presentation written from a statistical viewpoint, avoiding detailed terms from other fields. Topics include probability models; combinatorial linear models, including Bradley-Terry model; designs, including linked paired comparisons; selection of the best object, including knock-out and other tournaments; Scheffe's procedure; and Guttman's procedure. Assumes knowledge of basic statistics. Chapters conclude with exercises. Useful as a supplementary test and reference.

Davies, Owen L., ed. THE DESIGN AND ANALYSIS OF INDUSTRIAL EXPERIMENTS. New York: Hafner, 1967. xiv, 637 p. Glossary of Technical Terms, pp. 579-92. Tables of Statistical Functions, pp. 593-628. General Index, pp. 629-36. Index of Proper Names, p. 637.

A reference for research workers in the chemical industry who have limited knowledge of mathematical statistics. Each new principle illustrated by one or more practical examples. Topics include sequential tests of significance; randomized block and Latin squares; incomplete randomized block designs; factorial experiments with factors at more than two levels; confounding in factorial design; fractional factorial experiments; and the determination of optimum conditions, such as minimization of cost.

Day, Ralph L., and Parsons, Leonard J., eds. MARKETING MODELS: QUANTITATIVE APPLICATIONS. Scranton, Pa.: Intext, 1971. ix, 693 p. Index, pp. 689-93.

Thirty-four reprints of articles on applications of marketing models grouped under the following nine headings: "Deterministic Optimization Models" (four articles); "Stochastic Process Models" (six articles); "Discriminant and Canonical Analysis" (three articles); "Bayesian Decision Theory" (four articles); "Experimental Designs" (three articles); "Regression Analysis" (three articles); "Factor and Cluster Analysis" (five articles); "Heuristic Problem Solving" (four articles); and "Simulation" (two articles). Knowledge of intermediate statistics, calculus, operations research, and stochastic processes helpful for some articles. Topics include use of linear programming in media selection; consumer brand choice as a learning process; sales planning and control using absorbing Markov chains; testing brand-switching models; Bayesian classification procedures in analyzing customer characteristics;

simultaneous equation regression analysis of sales and advertising; demand structure for branded consumer products; numerical taxonomy in marketing analysis; and simulating market processes.

Dayton, Chauncey Mitchell. THE DESIGN OF EDUCATIONAL EXPERIMENTS. New York: McGraw-Hill, 1970. xiv, 441 p. Appendix A: Some Basic Principles of Matrix Algebra, pp. 353-73. Appendix B: Tables, pp. 375-428. References, pp. 429-31. Index, pp. 433-41.

An exposition of advanced statistical procedures for students in education with emphasis on designs widely used in education with worked examples. Topics include completely randomized designs; factorial designs; incomplete factorial designs; randomized block designs; nested designs; repeated measures designs; and analysis of covariance. Includes general design characteristics and the theory underlying the design, and numerical examples based on hypothetical data. Assumes knowledge of basic statistics.

Delbeke, L. CONSTRUCTION OF PREFERENCE SPACES: AN INVESTIGATION INTO THE APPLICABILITY OF MULTIDIMENSIONAL SCALING MODELS. Louvain-Leuven, Belgium: University of Louvain, 1968. vi, 180 p. References, pp. 109-14. Tables, pp. 115-46. Figures, pp. 147-80. No index.

A monograph on the construction of a model designed to measure how much each stimulus is preferred over another stimulus. Models include Coombs' unfolding technique; Tucker's vector model for paired comparisons; Messick's individual differences model for multidimensional scaling; Torgerson's and Ekman's model for multidimensional scaling; nonparametric multidimensional models; and the axiomatic method of measurement. Includes an experiment on paired comparison based preferences between different types of families. Assumes knowledge of linear algebra and basic statistics.

Dempster, Arthur P. ELEMENTS OF CONTINUOUS MULTIVARIATE ANALYSIS. Addison-Wesley Series in Behavioral Sciences: Quantitative Methods. Reading, Mass.: Addison-Wesley, 1969. xii, 388 p. Bibliography, pp. 375-81. Index, pp. 383-88.

A text for a rigorous course in mathematical multivariate analysis for students who have knowledge of linear algebra and real analysis. Topics include review of vector space theory and statistical analysis; multiple regression and correlation; principal component analysis; canonical correlation analysis; theory of two or more samples of individuals; randomized experiments; multivariate normal sampling theory; sampling distributions; and role of contemporary theories of statistical inference. Includes numerical examples. Chapters conclude with exercises on mathematical derivations.

Denenberg, Victor H. STATISTICS AND EXPERIMENTAL DESIGN FOR BEHAVIORAL AND BIOLOGICAL RESEARCHERS: AN INTRODUCTION. New York: Wiley, 1976. viii, 344 p. Appendix, pp. 297-324. Answers to Problems, pp. 325-34. Glossary, pp. 335-40. References, p. 341. Index, pp. 342-44.

A reference for use in experimental research with animals. Concepts and procedures introduced by means of illustrations drawn from experimental research. Topics include descriptive statistics; inferences about population parameters; normal curve; t distribution; comparing means of an experimental and control group; analysis of variance, including nested designs; randomized blocks; factorial experiments; regression; chi-square; and order statistics for ranked data. Chapters conclude with summaries of definitions and problems.

DuBois, Philip Hunter. MULTIVARIATE CORRELATION ANALYSIS. New York: Hafner, 1957. xv, 202 p. Appendix A: Table of R as a Function of the Partial Variance, pp. 171-72. Appendix B: Table of the Partial Standard Deviation, pp. 173-79. Appendix C: The Multivariate Analysis Chart, pp. 181-85. Glossary, pp. 187-96. Index of Names, p. 197. Index of Subjects, pp. 199-202.

A reference for courses in multivariate analysis and for practitioners in the social sciences. Topics include formulation of multiple and partial correlation that relates the formula methods of Yule to the matrix methods in common use; a matrix method of multivariate correlational analysis in which every element has statistical meaning; a procedure for finding multiple R by removing from the variance of the criterion the variance associated with the predictor variable; a method of computing higher-order partial correlations; simple procedure for partial correlation of any order and for combining the correlation of residuals with multiple R; and implications of multivariate analysis for social science research. Emphasizes computational techniques with illustrations. Factor analysis included in two of the fifteen sections of the book.

Duda, Richard O., and Hart, Peter E. PATTERN CLASSIFICATION AND SCENE ANALYSIS. New York: Wiley, 1973. xvii, 482 p. Author Index, pp. 467-71. Subject Index, pp. 472-82.

A text for a one-year course in pattern recognition for students with a mathematical background comparable to first-year students in computer science, electrical engineering or statistics. Consists of two parts: "Pattern Classification" and "Scene Analysis." Topics include parameter estimation and supervised learning; nonparametric techniques; linear discriminant functions; unsupervised learning and clustering; representation and initial simplifications; description of line and shape; perspective transformations; projective invariants; and descriptive methods in scene analysis. Includes numerous charts and graphs. Chapters conclude with references and problems.

Duran, Benjamin S., and Odell, Patrick L. CLUSTER ANALYSIS: A SURVEY. Lecture Notes in Economics and Mathematical Systems, 100. New York: Springer-Verlag, 1974. vi, 137 p. References, pp. 110-37. No index.

A survey of cluster analysis in seven chapters: "The Cluster Problem and Preliminary Ideas"; "Clustering by Complete Enumeration"; "Mathematical Programming and Cluster Analysis"; "Similarity Matrix Representations"; "Clustering Based on Density Estimation"; "Applications"; and "Historical Comments." Applications include remote sensing data and Fisher's Iris data.

Edwards, Allen Louis. EXPERIMENTAL DESIGN IN PSYCHOLOGICAL RESEARCH. 4th ed. New York: Holt, Rinehart and Winston, 1972. 488 p. References, pp. 403-7. Answers to Selected Problems, pp. 408-18. Appendix: Tables, pp. 419-72. Name Index, pp. 473-76. Subject Index, pp. 477-88.

A text for a one-semester course in experimental design for students of psychology who have had courses in basic statistics and college algebra. Includes proofs of theorems and examples based on both hypothetical and real data. Topics include sampling from binomial populations; chi-square; t test for means; heterogeneity of variance; analysis of variance for a randomized block design; multiple comparison of means and sums; factorial experiments; randomized block; Latin square; analysis of covariance; and least squares. Chapters conclude with questions and problems.

______. TECHNIQUES OF ATTITUDE SCALE CONSTRUCTION. Century Psychology Series. New York: Appleton-Century-Crofts, 1957. xiii, 256 p. Appendix: Tables, pp. 246-51. Index of Names, pp. 252-53. Index of Subjects, pp. 254-56.

Presents techniques for the construction of attitude scales for those who wish to develop their own attitude scales. Topics include paired comparisons; equal-appearing intervals; successive intervals; summated ratings; scale-discrimination; scalogram analysis; and the improvement of cumulative scales. Includes numerical examples.

Enslein, Kurt; Ralston, Anthony; and Wilf, Herbert S., eds. STATISTICAL METHODS FOR DIGITAL COMPUTERS. Vol. III of MATHEMATICAL METHODS FOR DIGITAL COMPUTERS. New York: Wiley, 1977. viii, 454 p. Appendix: Subroutines, pp. 440-43. Author Index, pp. 445-47. Subject Index, pp. 449-54.

Fifteen contributions to multivariate statistical computations using computer programming (FORTRAN) grouped under the following headings: "Introduction" (two contributions); "Regression and Discriminant Analysis" (four contributions); "Principal Components and Factor Analysis" (four contributions); "Cluster Analysis and Pattern Recognition" (three contributions); and "Time Series" (two contributions). Topics include Monte Carlo methods; stepwise regression; stepwise discriminant analysis; factor analysis by least squares and maximum likelihood methods; Minres method of factor analysis; unique rotation in factor analysis; analysis of variance and covariance; multidimensional scaling; hierarchial classificatory methods; relative perception of similarities and differences in complex and real data; Fourier transform and its application to time series analysis; and time series forecasting. Assumes knowledge of basic statistics. Useful as a text in statistics and computer science courses, and as a reference for a varied group, including computer programmers and applied mathematicians.

Everitt, B.S. THE ANALYSIS OF CONTINGENCY TABLES. Foreword by A.E. Maxwell. New York: Wiley, Halsted Press, 1977. x, 128 p. Appendix A: Percentage Points of the Chi-Square Distribution, pp. 118-19. Appendix B: Computer Programs, pp. 120-21. Bibliography, pp. 122-25. Index, pp. 126-28.

A reference for researchers in psychiatry, the social sciences, psychology, and a supplementary text for students taking courses in medical and applied statistics. Concerned with the analysis of frequency data in the form of cross-classification or contingency tables. Topics include rxc tables, multidimensional tables; log-linear models for contingency tables; square contingency tables; tables with a priori zeros; and quasi-independence in tables. Emphasizes verbal explanation using numerical examples, rather than mathematical developments.

Everitt, Brian. CLUSTER ANALYSIS. An SSRC Review of Current Research. London: Heinemann, for SSRC, 1974. vi, 122 p. Appendix A: Some Technical Terms Defined, pp. 98-99. Appendix B: Availability of Programs, pp. 99-101. Appendix C: Assignment Techniques, pp. 101-7. Appendix D: Concrete Examples, pp. 107-9. Appendix E: Bibliography, pp. 110-22. No index.

A monograph on cluster analysis (methods of grouping individuals), often referred to as Q-analysis, typology, grouping, clumping, classification, numerical taxonomy, and pattern recognition. Topics include review of clustering techniques; problems of cluster analysis; an empirical investigation of methods of cluster analysis; and applications and guidelines. Assumes knowledge of basic statistics.

Farrell, Roger H. TECHNIQUES OF MULTIVARIATE CALCULATION. Lecture Notes in Mathematics, vol. 520. New York: Springer-Verlag, 1976. x, 337 p. References, pp. 328-37. No index.

A monograph on methods of multivariate calculation (calculation of density functions) heretofore found only in articles. Assumes knowledge of complex variables, measure theory, theory of analytic manifolds, and canonical forms. Techniques include transform; noncentral Wishart density function problems; examples using differential forms; examples of maximal invariants; and random variable techniques. Concludes with zonal polynomials for the evaluation of multivariate integrals.

Federer, Walter T. EXPERIMENTAL DESIGN: THEORY AND APPLICATION. New York: Macmillan, 1965. xix, 591 p. Literature Cited, pp. 523-38. Index, pp. 539-44. Problems, pp. 546-91.

A comprehensive coverage of the mathematical theory of the design and analysis of experiments requiring knowledge of calculus and matrix algebra. Topics include analysis of designs with missing observations; the analyses of variations from standard designs; components of various analyses; covariance analyses; confounding in factorial experiments; incomplete block designs. Extensive use made of numerical examples. Assumes knowledge of intermediate statistical analysis. Useful as a text in several types of courses, including one on variance component analysis.

Federer, Walter T., and Balaam, Leslie N. BIBLIOGRAPHY ON EXPERIMENT AND TREATMENT DESIGN PRE-1968. New York: Hafner, 1973. vi, 769 p. References, p. 769. No index.

Eighty-seven hundred different literature citations on the philosophy, layout, conduct, and statistical analysis of experimental investigations. Emphasizes the construction and use of experiment and treatment designs and their associated statistical analyses. Bibliography divided into the following sub-bibliographies: "The Pre-1950 Bibliography with Some Comments on Associated Developments"; "Bibliography for Experiment Design"; "Bibliography for Treatment Design"; "Bibliography on Topics Related to Experiment and Treatment Design"; and "Books on Experiment and Treatment Design." Second, third, and fourth bibliographies include listings from 1950 to 1967. Classification techniques for each bibliography explained and listing of reference numbers by classification provided.

Fedorov, Valeriĭ Vadimovich. THEORY OF OPTIMAL EXPERIMENTS. Translated and edited by W.J. Studden and E.M. Klimko. Probability and Mathematical Statistics: A Series of Monographs and Textbooks, no. 12. New York: Academic Press, 1972. xi, 292 p. References, pp. 285-88. Subject Index, pp. 289-92.

A monograph suitable as a reference on the problem of optimal allocation of resources in conducting experiments (the optimal design of experiments) based on regression for use by a broad circle of researchers and technologists in physics, biology, chemistry, metallurgy, etc. Based on concepts of mathematical statistics. Fairly rigorous, with few numerical examples provided. Topics include loss function for regression experiments; polynomials and trigonometric regression; response surface; linear-optimal designs; quadratic loss; D-optimal designs; sequential methods of designing experiments; design of experiments in the case of simultaneous observations of several random quantities; likelihood ratio; and criteria of optimality.

Fienberg, Stephen E. AN ANALYSIS OF CROSS-CLASSIFIED CATEGORICAL DATA. Cambridge, Mass.: MIT Press, 1977. x, 151 p. Appendix I: Statistical Terminology, pp. 129-30. Appendix II: Basic Estimation Results for Loglinear Models, pp. 131-34. Appendix III: Percentage Points of Chi-Square Distribution, p. 135. References, pp. 137-46. Author Index, pp. 147-48. Subject Index, pp. 149-51.

A monograph on cross-classified categorical data using loglinear models for use by nonstatisticians familiar with analyses of two-dimensional contingency tables, regression analysis, and analysis of variance models. Includes two-, three-, four-, and higher-dimensional contingency tables; fixed margins and logit models; recursive and nonrecursive systems of logit models; and incomplete two- and several-dimensional contingency tables. Examples and applications taken from biology, sociology, medicine, and education.

Finn, Jeremy D. A GENERAL MODEL FOR MULTIVARIATE ANALYSIS. International Series in Decision Processes. New York: Holt, Rinehart and Winston, 1974. xvi, 423 p. Appendix A: Answers to Matrix Algebra Exercises (Section 2.7), pp. 394-96. Appendix B: Program User's Guide, pp. 397-408. Appendix C: Input-Output Listings, Computer Printout C.1 - C.166, p. 409 plus pp. C-1 to C-166 (Separately Numbered). References, pp. 410-13. Index, pp. 417-23.

A text and reference for users and potential users of multivariate statistical techniques who have had one year of applied statistical methods and some familiarity with the algebra of matrices. Describes five sample problems for use throughout the text as the appropriate analysis is encountered. Includes linear estimation and hypothesis testing for the following univariate and multivariate problems; multiple correlation and regression; canonical correlation; principal components; analysis of variance, with equal or unequal subclass frequencies; analysis of covariance; discriminant analysis; and step-down analysis. Appendix includes computer input-output listings for the five problems together with a brief version of the MULTIVARIANCE user's manual.

Fisher, Ronald A. THE DESIGN OF EXPERIMENTS. 5th ed. New York: Hafner, 1949. xi, 242 p. Index, pp. 241-42.

Presents the following experimental designs successfully used in applications: an agricultural experiment in randomized blocks; the Latin square; the factorial design; confounding; and precision of concomitant measurements.

_____. STATISTICAL METHODS FOR RESEARCH WORKERS. 14th ed., rev. and enl. Preface by E.A. Cornish. Edinburgh, Scot.: Oliver and Boyd, 1970. xiii, 362 p. Sources Used for Data and Methods, pp. 340-44. Bibliography, pp. 345-58. Index, pp. 359-62.

A reference for research workers, especially biologists, on methods of applying statistical tests to numerical data accumulated in laboratories or available in the literature. Tests based primarily on chi-square, t, and Z distributions and include such topics as tests of goodness of fit, independence, and homogeneity; tests of significance of means, difference of means, and regression coefficients; the correlation coefficient; intraclass correlation and the analysis of variance; and the principle of statistical estimation. Numerical example exemplify the variety of applications and methods. Primarily of historical interest.

Friedrich, Douglas. A PRIMER FOR DEVELOPMENTAL METHODOLOGY. Minneapolis, Minn.: Burgess, 1972. v, 122 p. References, pp. 109-17. Subject Index, pp. 119-20. Name Index, pp. 121-22.

An introduction to model and methodological advancements in the area of human development for students interested in the classical experimental approach to exploring behavior. Topics include classical development designs; multivariate data collection designs; cohort-sequential; time-sequential; and cross-sequential designs.

Fu, King S. SEQUENTIAL METHODS IN PATTERN RECOGNITION AND MACHINE LEARNING. Mathematics in Science and Engineering, vol. 52. New York: Academic Press, 1968. xi, 227 p. Appendix A: Introduction to Sequential Analysis, pp. 171-80. Appendix B: Optimal Properties of Generalized Karhunen-Loeve Expansion, pp. 181-84. Appendix C: Properties of the Modified SPRT, pp. 185-90. Appendix D: Enumeration of Some Combinations of the k_i's and Derivation of Formulas for the Reduction of Tables Required in the Computation of Risk Functions, pp. 191-95. Appendix E: Computations Required for the Feature Ordering and Pattern Classification Experiments Using Dynamic Programming, pp. 196-200. Appendix F: Stochastic Approximation: A Brief Survey, pp. 201-13. Appendix G: The Method of Potential Functions of Reproducing Kernels, pp. 214-22. Author Index, pp. 223-25. Subject Index, pp. 226-27.

A monograph on problems of pattern recognition and learning

by use of sequential methods in statistical decision theory. Useful as a reference for system engineers and computer scientists and a supplementary text for courses in pattern recognition and adaptive learning. Assumes knowledge of calculus and introductory mathematical statistics. Topics include information-theoretic and Karhunen-Loeve expansion approaches to feature selection and ordering; modified sequential probability ratio tests for the discrete and continuous cases; finite sequential recognition using dynamic programming; nonparametric procedures in sequential pattern recognition; Bayesian learning in sequential pattern recognition; and learning in sequential systems using stochastic approximation.

Fukunaga, Keinosuke. INTRODUCTION TO STATISTICAL PATTERN RECOGNITION. Electrical Science Series. New York: Academic Press, 1972. xiii, 369 p. References, pp. 355-61. Index, pp. 363-69.

A text for a graduate course in statistical pattern recognition and a reference with a prerequisite of probability theory, calculus, and linear algebra. Based on statistical decision theory with applications to engineering problems, such as waveform analysis. Topics include random vectors and their properties; linear classifiers; parameter estimation; Bayes' estimation; estimation of density functions; linear mapping for one distribution and multidistributions, and nonlinear mapping. Chapters conclude with computer projects and problems.

Geer, Johannes Petrus van de. INTRODUCTION TO MULTIVARIATE ANALYSIS FOR SOCIAL SCIENCES. San Francisco: W.H. Freeman, 1971. xi, 293 p. Appendix: An Iterative Solution for Eigenvalues and Eigenvectors, pp. 273-76. Answers to Selected Exercises, pp. 277-83. References, pp. 285-87. Index, pp. 289-93.

A text for a course in applied multivariate analysis for graduate students in the behavioral and social sciences who have had courses in basic statistics and calculus. Consists of two parts: "Introduction to Matrix Algebra" and "Techniques of Multivariate Analysis." Omits statistical theory and analysis of variance, and emphasizes similarities between multivariate techniques. Topics include simple regression and correlation; multiple and partial correlation; path analysis; factor analysis; canonical correlation; variates of factor analysis; nonrecursive linear models requiring two-stage least squares and limited-information solutions; factors and structural equations; and discriminant analysis.

Gerber, George; Holsti, Ole R.; Krippendorff, Klaus; Paisley, Wm. J.; and Stone, Philip J., eds. THE ANALYSIS OF COMMUNICATION CONTENT: DEVELOPMENTS OF SCIENTIFIC THEORIES AND COMPUTER TECHNIQUES.

New York: Wiley, 1969. xix, 597 p. Appendix: Education in Content Analysis: A Survey by F. Earle Barcus, pp. 539-54. Bibliography, pp. 555-78. Index, pp. 579-97.

A reference on content analysis for researchers in any field. Consists of four parts: "Theories and Analytical Constructs"; "Aspects of Inference from Content Data"; "The Recording and Notation of Data"; and "Computer Techniques in Content Analysis and Computational Linguistics." Presentation verbal with no tables, charts, or formulas. Emphasizes content analysis as a specialized research activity in the study of communications.

Gibbons, Jean Dickinson; Olkin, Ingram; and Sobel, Milton. SELECTING AND ORDERING POPULATIONS: A NEW STATISTICAL METHODOLOGY. Wiley Series in Probability and Mathematical Statistics. New York: Wiley, 1977. xxi, 569 p. Appendix: Tables, pp. 395-542. Bibliography, pp. 543-52. References for Applications, pp. 553-56. Index for Data and Examples, pp. 557-59. Name Index, pp. 561-63. Subject Index, pp. 565-69.

A reference or handbook on ordering and selection procedures for applied statisticians. Applications described in nonmathematical terminology and can be understood by anyone with knowledge of basic statistics. Topics include selecting the one best population for normal, binomial (or Bernoulli), and multinomial distributions; nonparametric procedures; selection procedures for a design with paired comparisons; selecting the normal distribution with the best regression value; selecting the t best out of k populations; complete ordering of k populations; selecting the best gamma population; and selection procedures for multivariate normal distributions. Useful to students and research workers in education, engineering, business, and the behavioral, social, and physical sciences. Chapters conclude with problems.

Giri, Narayan C. MULTIVARIATE STATISTICAL INFERENCE. Probability and Mathematical Statistics. A Series of Monographs and Textbooks. New York: Academic Press, 1977. xvi, 319 p. Author Index, pp. 313-15. Subject Index, pp. 316-19.

A text for a one-year course in multivariate analysis for students of mathematics and statistics who have knowledge of mathematical statistics and applied multivariate analysis. Includes examples based on real data. Topics include groups and Jacobians of transformations; invariance; regression; maximum likelihood estimation of multivariate normal distribution; multivariate sampling distributions; Wishart distribution; Hotelling's T^2; tests of hypotheses about mean vectors; admissibility of estimators; discriminant analysis; multivariate covariance models; principal components; general linear hypothesis;

canonical analysis; and time series. Presentation rigorous with proofs included. Chapters conclude with references.

Goldstein, Matthew, and Dillon, William R. DISCRETE DISCRIMINANT ANALYSIS. Wiley Series in Probability and Mathematical Statistics. New York: Wiley, 1978. x, 186 p. References, pp. 179-82. Index, pp. 183-86.

A monograph devoted to a comprehensive treatment of the theory and application of discriminant analysis for students in a variety of fields who have a sound background in probability and statistics. Topics include the linear discriminant function; discrete classification models; error rates and the problem of bias; the variable-selection problem; methods for comparing experiments; and sampling experiments. Concludes with six computer programs in FORTRAN. Numerous examples included.

Gorden, Raymond L. UNIDIMENSIONAL SCALING OF SOCIAL VARIABLES: CONCEPTS AND PROCEDURE. New York: Macmillan, 1977. xii, 175 p. Appendix A: Blank Forms and Data, pp. 156-62. Appendix B: Solutions to Laboratory Problems, pp. 163-68. Bibliography, pp. 169-71. Index, pp. 173-75.

An extensive presentation of strategies and techniques of discovering, selecting, and construction attitude items at three levels: selection of content themes; construction of facet types; and construction of response forms. Appendix A includes forms for use in the scalogram-sheet method for testing and diagnosing unidimensionality for samples (from 10 to 30) necessary for the laboratory problems at the ends of the chapters. Topics include scaling theory; Guttman scale; designing and administering the scale; scalogram analysis; purifying the scale; and interpreting and presenting scales. Intended for the layman.

Gorsuch, Richard L. FACTOR ANALYSIS. Saunders Books in Psychology. Philadelphia: W.B. Saunders, 1974. xv, 370 p. Appendix A: Data for Examples, pp. 337-38. Appendix B: Developing a Library of Factor-Analytic Computer Programs, pp. 339-45. References, pp. 347-59. Author Index, pp. 361-64. Subject Index, pp. 365-70.

A text for a graduate course in factor analysis and a reference for research workers. Emphasizes factor analysis as a tool in research, and derivations kept to a minimum. Topics include basic factor models; matrix algebra and factor analysis; diagonal and multiple-group analysis; principal factor solutions; maximum likelihood and other solutions; determining the number of factors; rotation and interpretation of factors; higher-order factors; factor scales; data transformations and indices of association; two- and three-mode factor analysis; and the replication and invariance of factors. Assumes knowledge of algebra, multiple correlation, and tests of significance. Numerical examples provided, but no problems included.

Green, Paul E., and Carmone, Frank J. MULTIDIMENSIONAL SCALING AND RELATED TECHNIQUES IN MARKETING ANALYSIS. Foreword by Robert D. Buzzell. Boston: Allyn and Bacon, 1970. xv, 203 p. Appendix A: Capsule Description of Computer Programs, pp. 141-60. Appendix B: Bibliography on Multidimensional Scaling and Related Methods, pp. 161-95. Index, pp. 197-203.

A monograph on multidimensional scaling for applications in marketing. Methods computer oriented with mathematical details de-emphasized. Topics include measurement theory and overview of scaling applications; classification of data; analysis of similarities data; analysis of preference data; reduced space analysis; and cluster analysis.

Green, Paul E., and Rao, Vithala R. APPLIED MULTIDIMENSIONAL SCALING: A COMPARISON OF APPROACHES AND ALGORITHMS. Editors' Series in Marketing. New York: Holt, Rinehart and Winston, 1972. xviii, 292 p. Appendix A: Questionnaire and Basic Data of Study, pp. 152-80. Appendix B: Details of the Program Used, pp. 181-218. Appendix C: Supporting Material for Chapter Discussions, pp. 219-72. References, pp. 273-84. Index, pp. 285-92.

A reference for the practitioner and a text for a graduate course in marketing and behavioral research. Includes a large variety of techniques and a small data bank consisting of responses by forty-two subjects to questions about relative similarities, attribute ratings, and preference rankings for fifteen breakfast food items. Computer algorithms for data analysis provided. Topics include aggregate and disaggregate level analyses of dissimilarities data; internal and external analyses of preference data; and potential areas of research. Assumes knowledge of basic statistics.

Green, Paul E., and Wind, Yoran. MULTIVARIATE DECISIONS IN MARKETING: A MEASUREMENT APPROACH. Editor's Series in Marketing. Editor's foreword by Philip Kotler. Hinsdale, Ill.: Dryden, 1973. xvii, 396 p. Appendix A: Questionnaires and Supporting Tables, pp. 249-98. Appendix B: Models and Algorithms for Multidimensional Scaling, Conjoint Measurement, and Related Techniques, by J. Douglas Carroll, pp. 299-372. References, pp. 373-87. Index, pp. 389-96.

A problem-oriented reference for use as a supplementary text in graduate course in marketing research or behavioral science with a prerequisite of scaling and multivariate statistics. Consists of four parts: Concepts; Methods; Applications; and Conclusions. Concerned with the application of multidimensional scaling and conjoint measurement to multiattribute problems.

Includes computer programs for the analysis of real data. Topics include analysis of dissimilarities data and of preference data in multiattribute decisions; consumer evaluation of retail discount cards and restaurant menus; image congruence of occupational and behavioral stereotypes; and future research.

Guenther, William C. ANALYSIS OF VARIANCE. Englewood Cliffs, N.J.: Prentice-Hall, 1964. viii, 199 p. Appendix: Tables, pp. 168-95. Index, pp. 197-99.

A text for an elementary course in analysis of variance for students who have a background in basic statistics and college algebra. Topics include one-way classification, including Tukey's method of multiple comparisons; fixed-effects model for randomized blocks, including Tukey's test for nonadditivity; fixed-effects model for Latin squares; factorial experiments (including three-factor completely randomized experiments); and analysis of covariance. Examples and exercises included.

Guertin, Wilson H., and Bailey, John P., Jr. INTRODUCTION TO MODERN FACTOR ANALYSIS. Ann Arbor, Mich.: Edwards Brothers, 1970. xiv, 472 p. Appendix: Transformation of Oblique Reference to Primary Factor Matrices, pp. 315-24. Computer Source Program Listings, pp. 325-436. Answers to Problem Exercises, pp. 437-40. Bibliography, pp. 441-50. List of Figures, pp. 451-52. List of Tables, pp. 453-58. Author Index, pp. 459-60. Subject Index, pp. 461-72.

A text and reference for a course in factor analysis for students with limited training in mathematics. Relies on the verbal style, with a wide variety of contexts for understanding terms. Includes over one hundred pages of computer printouts for factor analysis problems in FORTRAN. Topics include review of matrix algebra and geometry; major methods in factor analysis; meaning of factors; principle of rotation; computer rotation procedures; principal diagonal; sampling; prediction and inferential statistics; instrument development; three-dimensional score matrix; profiles, patterns, and prediction; Q-analysis; and computer procedures. Chapters conclude with summaries.

Gulliksen, Harold, and Messick, Samuel, eds. PSYCHOLOGICAL SCALING: THEORY AND APPLICATIONS. New York: Wiley, 1960. xvi, 211 p. Bibliography, pp. 187-97. Name Index, pp. 199-201. Subject Index, pp. 203-11.

Fourteen papers presented at a conference on psychological scaling held at Princeton University in May 1958, grouped under the following five headings: "Scaling Properties" (four papers); "Psychological Scaling" (two papers); "Test Theory and Psychological Scaling" (two papers); "Choice and the Measurement of Utility" (three papers); and "Multivariate

Scaling Models" (three papers). Topics include method of successive intervals; quantitative judgement scales; ratio scales, partition scales and confusion scales; latent structure analysis and test theory; measurement of utility and subjective probability; intra-individual and inter-individual multidimensionality; and empirical consequences of a choice axiom.

Gupta, R.P., ed. APPLIED STATISTICS. New York: Elsevier, 1975. x, 416 p. No index.

Twenty-eight papers presented at a conference on applied statistics held at Dalhousee University May 2-4, 1974. Topics include statistical models and medical reality; split plot; unbiased and invariant estimators for regression parameters based on ordered observations; a Bayesian approach to some problems involving the detection of spuriosity; quantifying teaching quality and variations in grading standards; cluster analysis; the reduced form model; trimmed means when spurious observations are present; spherical and hyperspherical structures; estimation of finite distribution mixtures; analysis of fish count data obtained using a digital echo counting system; axial and bimodal data on a sphere; testing for equality of means in two gamma distributions; and time series analysis and econometric model construction.

Harman, Harry H. MODERN FACTOR ANALYSIS. 3d ed., rev. Chicago: University of Chicago Press, 1976. xx, 487 p. Statistical Tables, pp. 441-45. Bibliography, pp. 447-74. Author Index, pp. 475-77. Subject Index, pp. 478-85. Problem Index, pp. 486-87.

A text and reference on the use of factor analysis in the analysis and interpretation of multivariate data. Consists of five parts: "Foundations of Factor Analysis"; "Direct Factor Analysis Methods"; "Derived Factor Solutions"; "Factor Measurements"; and "Problems and Exercises." Topics include matrix and geometric concepts; principal factor and maximum likelihood direct factor methods; orthogonal and oblique multiple-factor solutions; congruent and prescribed factor solutions; measurement of principal components; and estimation by regression, theoretical models, minimizing unique factors, and ideal variables. Assumes knowledge of basic statistics for psychology and matrix algebra. Includes detailed computing procedures and numerical illustrations.

Harris, Richard J. A PRIMER OF MULTIVARIATE STATISTICS. New York: Academic Press, 1975. xiv, 332 p. Digression 1: Finding Maxima and Minima of Polynomials, pp. 241-44. Digression 2: Matrix Algebra, pp. 245-60. Digression 3: Solution of Cubic Equations, pp. 261-65. Digression 4: Use of Canned Computer Programs, pp. 267-92. Appendix A: Statistical Tables, pp. 293-310. Appendix B: FORTRAN IV Program Listings, pp. 312-16. References, pp. 317-22. Index, pp. 323-32.

A text for a one- or two-semester course in multivariate analysis for students in sociology, psychology, anthropology, and other social sciences who have had at least an introductory course in statistics. Emphasizes heuristic descriptions of techniques, with examples for illustrating the mathematical results. Topics include multiple regression; tests on one or two mean vectors; multivariate analysis of variance; canonical correlation; principal component analysis; and factor analysis. Assumes knowledge of matrix algebra and calculus.

Hicks, Charles R. FUNDAMENTAL CONCEPTS IN THE DESIGN OF EXPERIMENTS. New York: Holt, Rinehart and Winston, 1965. x, 293 p. Statistical Tables, pp. 265-78. Answers to Odd-Numbered Problems, pp. 279-90. Index, pp. 291-93.

A text and reference on experimental design for those engaged in experimental work who have a good background in statistical inference and basic calculus. Emphasizes design, analysis and distinction among experiments. Topics includes single factor experiments with no restrictions on randomization and with randomized block designs; Latin and other squares; factorial experiments; fixed, random, and mixed models; nested and nested-factorial experiments; experiments of two or more factors--restrictions on randomization; factorial experiment-split-plot design; factorial experiment-confounding in blocks; and covariance analysis; and response surface experimentation. Derivations kept to a minimum. Chapters conclude with problems.

Hildebrand, David K.; Laing, James D.; and Rosenthal, Howard. PREDICTION ANALYSIS OF CROSS CLASSIFICATIONS. Wiley Series in Probability and Mathematical Statistics. New York: Wiley, 1977. xv, 311 p. References, pp. 294-99. Author Index, pp. 301-2. Subject Index, pp. 303-11.

A unified approach to prediction based on analysis of cross-classified data. Develops a formal language for using data to predict one variable from one or more other variables using cross-classifications of real data from sociology, political science, and game theory. Topics include prediction from nominal and ordinal data; linear models; measuring prediction success in the 2x2 table and the RxC table; differential weighting of prediction errors; prediction analysis of actuarial propositions; bivariate prediction analysis for pairs of events; and statistical inference in multivariate analysis. Useful as a reference and text in sociology, psychology, and political science courses.

Hope, Keith. METHODS OF MULTIVARIATE ANALYSIS WITH HANDBOOK OF MULTIVARIATE METHODS PROGRAMMED IN ATLAS AUTOCODE. New York: Gordon and Breach, 1969. 288 p. Index, pp. 162-65. Handbook of Multivariate Methods Programmed in Atlas Autocode, pp. 166-288.

A supplementary text and a reference for research workers illustrating the application of parametric multivariate techniques with examples from psychology, economics, sociology, and biology. Derivations and proofs omitted. Includes analysis of variance, factorial designs; principal components; multiple regression; discriminant function analysis; imposition of structure; and analysis of covariance. Computer programs for the analysis of multivariate data includes a general description of what the programs do and how to use them, a printout of an actual data tape, and the output resulting from the data tape. Matrix algebra reviewed in chapter 1.

Horst, Paul. FACTOR ANALYSIS OF DATA MATRICES. New York: Holt, Rinehart and Winston, 1965. xix, 730 p. Bibliography, pp. 596-98. Appendix: FORTRAN II Computer Programs, pp. 599-718. Index, pp. 719-30.

A text and reference for graduates and undergraduates in any science (social, biological, or physical) who have knowledge of basic statistics and matrix algebra. Consists of six parts: "Introductory Background"; "Matrix Factoring Methods--A"; "Matrix Factoring Methods--B"; "Categories, Origin, and Scale"; "Transformation Problems and Methods"; and "Special Problems." Appendix contains FORTRAN II programs for most of the methods. Topics include centroid method; grouping methods; basic structure successive factor methods; simultaneous basic structure methods; order reduction methods; Jacobi-type solutions; solutions from incomplete covariance matrices; categorical variations in factor analysis; image analysis; analytical rotations; direct varimax solutions; factor score matrices; prediction; and multiple set factor analysis. Proofs of theorems provided.

Huitson, Alan. THE ANALYSIS OF VARIANCE. Griffin's Statistical Monographs and Courses, no. 18. London: Griffin, 1966. 83 p. References, pp. 80-81. Index, p. 83.

A monograph on the algebraic development of the analysis of variance and the assumptions involved in its application. Differentiate between use of interaction mean square and the error mean square when carrying out a variance ratio test. Topics include one- and two-way classifications; nested classifications; randomized and balanced incomplete blocks; split-plot designs; Latin squares; analysis of covariance; two-level experiments, including confounding; and applications to linear regression.

Jeffers, John Norman Richard. EXPERIMENTAL DESIGN AND ANALYSIS IN FOREST RESEARCH. Foreword by H. van Vloten and J. MacDonald. Stockholm: Almqvist & Wiksell, 1960. 172 p. Appendix I: Working Sheets for the Analysis of Experiments, pp. 153-62. Appendix II: References, pp. 163-64.

Appendix III: Shortened Forms of Statistical Tables, pp. 165-68. Appendix IV: Glossary of Statistical Terms, pp. 169-72. No index.

Explains, by example, important statistical designs used in forest research, including when and why they are used. Topics include randomized block, Latin square, factorial split-plot, and incomplete block designs; transformations from distributions other than the normal; chi-square; methods of sampling; regression and correlation; and analysis of variance. Assumes knowledge of basic statistics.

John, Peter William Meredith. STATISTICAL DESIGN AND ANALYSIS OF EXPERIMENTS. New York: Macmillan, 1971. xii, 356 p. Appendix: Matrices and Quadratic Forms, pp. 329-37. Bibliography, pp. 339-50. Index, pp. 351-56.

A mathematically oriented, graduate-level text for a one-year course for mathematics students with examples from engineering and agricultural experiments. Assumes knowledge of linear algebra and mathematical statistics. Topics include linear models and quadratic forms; one- and two-factor experiments; experiments with several factors; Latin square designs; confounding in factors with two or three levels; fractions of 2^n factorial designs; fractional factorials with more than two levels; response surfaces; incomplete block designs; partially balanced incomplete block designs; balanced incomplete block designs; and partially balanced designs. Chapters conclude with exercises.

Johnson, Norman L., and Leone, Fred C. STATISTICS AND EXPERIMENTAL DESIGN IN ENGINEERING AND THE PHYSICAL SCIENCES. Vol. I. 2d ed. Wiley Series in Probability and Mathematical Statistics. New York: Wiley, 1976. xiv, 601 p. Appendix: Tables, pp. 498-551. Solutions to Selected Exercises, pp. 552-92. Index, pp. 593-601.

A text for a one-year course in applied statistics for students of engineering and the physical sciences who have knowledge of engineering mathematics, including calculus. Mathematical rigor occasionaly used. Topics include empirical distributions and descriptive measures; Chebyshev's inequality; moment-generating functions; probability theory; discrete and continuous distributions; order statistics; hypothesis testing and interval estimation; ratio tests and uniformly most powerful tests; nonparametric tests; control charts; decision theory; ancillary quantities; and regression and correlation. Chapters conclude with references and problems of varying difficulty and applications to serve a mixed audience.

______. STATISTICS AND EXPERIMENTAL DESIGN IN ENGINEERING AND THE PHYSICAL SCIENCES. Vol. II. Wiley Series in Probability and Mathematical Statistics. New York: Wiley, 1964. ix, 399 p. Selected Bibliography of Statistical Tables and Periodical Publications, pp. 372-78. Solutions of Selected Exercises, pp. 379-92. Index, pp. 393-99.

A continuation of volume I. Topics include analysis of variance; sequential analysis; multivariate analysis; and sample structures. Chapters conclude with references and problems.

Kabe, D.G., and Gupta, R.P., eds. MULTIVARIATE STATISTICAL INFERENCE. New York: Elsevier, 1973. x, 258 p. No index.

Eighteen papers presented at a seminar on multivariate statistical analysis held at Dalhousie University, Halifax, Nova Scotia, March 23-25, 1972. Emphasizes application methodology, rather than theory, and treats such topics as alternatives to least squares in regression; multiple birth discrimination; differential representation of a bivariate stochastic process; unbiased tests for the equality of K covariance matrices; Rao's generalized U statistic; testing and estimation for structures circularly symmetric in blocks; nonparametric procedures in multivariate analysis; and a sequential solution of Wilcoxon types for a slippage problem.

Kempthorne, Oscar. THE DESIGN AND ANALYSIS OF EXPERIMENTS. Wiley Series in Probability and Mathematical Statistics. New York: Wiley, 1952. 631 p. Appendix: Tables, pp. 610-28. Index, pp. 629-31.

A text for a course in the design of experiments for a heterogeneous group of students who are familiar with basic statistics. Attention given to experiments in which two or more treatments are compared with preassigned replication. Topics include least squares; multiple regression and the analysis of variance; multiple classification; randomized blocks; Latin squares; plot design; experiments involving several factors; 2^n factorial experiments; p^n factorial experiments; fractional replication; quasifactorial and incomplete block designs; lattice designs; rectangular lattices; balanced incomplete block designs; experiments with infinite populations and groups of experiments; and treatments applied in sequence. Includes examples but no practical applications. Chapters conclude with references.

Kendall, Maurice George. A COURSE IN MULTIVARIATE ANALYSIS. Griffin's Statistical Monographs and Courses, no. 2. New York: Hafner, 1961. 185 p. References, pp. 171-79. Exercises, pp. 180-85. No index.

A text for a short course in multivariate analysis with emphasis on applications for students who have knowledge of matrix algebra, geometry and beta functions, and statistical theory up to regression and correlation and tests of significance. Topics include component and factor analysis; functional relationships; canonical relationships; tests on homogeneity; discriminatory analysis; problems of sampling; and the history of multivariate analysis. Proofs of theorems omitted, with mathematical results usually stated without detailed derivations. Includes examples in agriculture, education, economics, politics, biometrics, sociology, and physics.

_____. MULTIVARIATE ANALYSIS. London: Charles Griffin, 1975. viii, 210 p. Appendix: A Note on Multivariate Scaling, pp. 197-98. References, pp. 199-205. Name Index, pp. 207-8. Subject Index, pp. 209-10.

A reference for practitioners which recognizes the role of the computer in solving problems. Topics include principal components; classification and clustering; factor analysis; canonical correlations; distribution theory; regression analysis; functional relationships; tests of hypotheses; discrimination; and categorized multivariate data. Emphasizes numerical examples. Assumes knowledge of mathematical statistics. Chapters conclude with notes.

_____. RANK CORRELATION METHODS. 3d ed., rev. New York: Hafner, 1962. vi, 199 p. References, pp. 167-71. Appendix: Tables, pp. 173-97. Index, pp. 198-99.

An account of the ranking techniques used in psychology, education, and economics. Topics include theory of rank correlation; tied ranks; partial rank correlation; relationship between ranks and variate values; and paired comparisons. Two chapters devoted to each topic: one describing results, applications, and basic ideas; and another on mathematical derivations. No calculus or matrix algebra used. Chapters conclude with references.

Keppel, Geoffrey. DESIGN AND ANALYSIS: A RESEARCHER'S HANDBOOK. Prentice-Hall Series in Experimental Psychology. Englewood Cliffs, N.J.: Prentice-Hall, 1973. xiii, 658 p. Appendix A: Orthogonality of Sources of Variance, pp. 567-79. Appendix B: Calculation of Orthogonal Polynomial Coefficients, pp. 581-89. Appendix C: Statistical Tables, pp. 591-611. Appendix D: Answers to Problems and Exercises, pp. 613-43. References, pp. 645-49. Author Index, pp. 650-51. Subject Index, pp. 652-58.

A problem-oriented handbook for research workers who have knowledge of one year of basic statistics. Also useful as a text for a one-semester course in experimental design. Consists of the following seven parts: "Introduction"; "Single-Factor Experiments"; "Factorial Experiments with Two Factors"; "Higher-Order Factor Case: Interaction and the Basic Analysis"; "Designs with Repeated Measures"; "Designs Intended to Describe Error Variance"; and "Sensitivity of Experimental Designs and Controversial Topics."

Kerlinger, Fred N. FOUNDATIONS OF BEHAVIORAL RESEARCH. 2d ed. New York: Holt, Rinehart, and Winston, 1973. xx, 741 p. Appendix A: The Research Report, pp. 694-700. Appendix B: Historical and Methodological Research, pp. 701-4. Appendix C: The Computer and Behavioral Research, pp. 705-11. Appendix D: Random Numbers and Statistics, pp. 712-18. Author Index, pp. 719-21. Subject Index, pp. 723-41.

> A text for a graduate course in behavioral research for students who have a background in psychology, statistics, and measurement. Consists of the following eight parts: "The Language and Approach of Science"; "Sets, Relations, and Variance"; "Probability, Randomness, and Sampling"; "Analysis of Variance"; "Types of Research"; "Measurement"; "Methods of Observation and Data Collection"; and "Multiple Regression and Factor Analysis." Emphasizes psychological and educational problems and examples. Chapters conclude with exercises.

Kimmel, H.D. EXPERIMENTAL PRINCIPLES AND DESIGN IN PSYCHOLOGY. New York: Ronald Press, 1970. vi, 280 p. References, pp. 263-66. Appendix: Statistical Tables, pp. 267-75. Index, pp. 277-80.

> A text for a one-semester advanced course in experimental psychology. Topics include the logical and methodological aspects of experimentation in psychology; use of statistical inference in planning data collection and analysis; and experimental designs, including factorial experiments; the blocking principle; and deliberate and inadvertent confounding. Includes few numerical examples.

Kirk, Roger E. EXPERIMENTAL DESIGN: PROCEDURES FOR THE BEHAVIORAL SCIENCES. Belmont, Calif.: Wadsworth, Brooks-Cole, 1968. xii, 577 p. Appendix A: Rules of Summation, pp. 505-8. Appendix B: Rules of Expectation, pp. 509-12. Appendix C: Orthogonal Coefficients for Unequal Intervals and Unequal n's, pp. 513-17. Appendix D: Tables, pp. 519-70. Index, pp. 571-77.

> A text for a two-semester graduate course in experimental design and a reference for students who have taken courses in college algebra and basic statistical inference. Each experimental design introduced by a research problem and computational example. Topics include basic assumptions in analysis of variance; multiple comparison tests; completely randomized designs; randomized block designs; Latin square and related designs; completely randomized, hierarchal, and randomized block factorial designs; split-plot design (factorial design with block-interaction confounding); factorial designs with block-interaction confounding; fractional factorial designs; incomplete block designs; analysis of covariance; and nonparametric analysis of multigroup experiments. Chapters conclude with references.

Klepikov, N.P., and Sokolov, S.N. ANALYSIS AND PLANNING OF EXPERIMENTS BY THE METHOD OF MAXIMUM LIKELIHOOD. New York: Pergamon, 1962. x, 127 p. Appendix I: Some Information on Distributions of Probabilities, pp. 100-110. Appendix II: Properties of Estimates, pp. 111-17. Notation Index, pp. 118-21. References, p. 122. Table of Quantiles of the V^2-Distribution, pp. 123-27.

> A manual for physicists on the treatment and analysis of experimental data with emphasis on the determination of the number of parameters necessary for the description of a curve and the errors in regression analysis and confluence analysis.

Krishnaiah, Paruchuri R., ed. MULTIVARIATE ANALYSIS. New York: Academic Press, 1966. xix, 592 p. No index.

> Thirty papers presented at an international symposium held in Dayton, Ohio, June 14-19, 1965, grouped under the following eight headings: "Nonparametric Methods" (three papers); "Multivariate Analysis of Variance and Related Topics" (five papers); "Classification" (three papers); "Distribution Theory" (three papers); "Optimum Properties of Test Procedures" (two papers); "Estimation and Prediction" (six papers); "Ranking and Selection Procedures" (three papers); and "Applications" (five papers). Topics include nonparametric tests for the multivariate several sample location problem; a k-sample regression model with covariance; power of the likelihood-ratio test; predictive discrimination; a multiple Behrens-Fisher distribution; noncentral multivariate beta distribution; fully invariant proper Bayes' tests; multidimensional information inequalities and prediction; estimation of principal components; clustering procedures; multivariate response in comparative experiments; and parametric representation of nonlinear data structures. Assumes knowledge of mathematical statistics, multivariate variance analysis, probability theory, and processes. Useful to applied statisticians and mathematicians.

______. MULTIVARIATE ANALYSIS--II. New York: Academic Press, 1969. xx, 696 p. No index.

> Thirty-six papers presented at the second international symposium on multivariate analysis held at the Wright State University, Dayton, Ohio, June 17-22, 1968, grouped under the following seven headings: "Nonparametric Methods" (three papers); "Multivariate Analysis of Variance and Related Topics" (six papers); "Distribution Theory" (six papers); "Characteristic Functions and Characterization Problems" (three papers); "Time Series and Stochastic Processes" (seven papers); "Decision Procedures" (four papers); and "Econometrics, Principal Components, Reliability, and Applications" (seven papers). Topics include robust nonparametric estimation in some multivariate linear models; statistical inference for covariance matrices with linear

structure; intersection tests in multivariate analysis; tests of equality of latent roots of the covariance matrix; approximate confidence regions for constraint parameters; canonical analysis of stochastic approximation; structure and estimation of general interdependent systems; and optimality of principal components.

_____. MULTIVARIATE ANALYSIS--III. New York: Academic Press, 1973. xvii, 410 p. No index.

Twenty-seven papers presented at the third international symposium on multivariate analysis held at Wright State University, Dayton, Ohio, June 12-14, 1972, grouped under the following five headings: "Time Series and Stochastic Processes" (six papers); "Distribution Theory and Inference" (six papers); "Characteristic Functions and Characterizations" (four papers); "Design and Analysis of Experiments" (five papers); and "Classification, Modelling, and Reliability" (six papers). Topics include concepts of consistency in spectral estimation for multivariate time series; abstract martingales and ergodic theory; innovation and non-anticipative processes; aspects of the multinomial logit model; inference and redundant parameters; a characterization of the multivariate geometric distribution; max-min designs in the analysis of variance; optimal designs for fitting biased multiresponse surfaces; correlation and affinity in Gaussian cases; and nonlinear iterative partial least squares.

Kshirsagar, Anant M. MULTIVARIATE ANALYSIS. Statistics: Textbooks and Monographs, vol. 2. New York: Marcel Dekker, 1972. xiv, 534 p. Exercises, pp. 469-519. References for Exercises, pp. 520-24. Appendix: Jacobians of Certain Transformations, p. 525. Errata, p. 526. Author Index, pp. 527-30. Subject Index, pp. 531-34.

A text for an advanced two-semester course in multivariate analysis for students who have knowledge of linear algebra, quadratic forms, and univariate analysis of variance and covariance. Restricted to derivations of theoretical results, with no numerical examples provided. Topics include multivariate normal distribution; Wishart distribution; distribution associated with regression; Hotelling's T^2 and its application; discriminant analysis; canonical variables and canonical correlations; Wilks's criterion; multivariate analysis of variance and discrimination in the cases of several groups; likelihood ratio tests; and principal components. Chapters conclude with references.

Lachenbruch, Peter A. DISCRIMINANT ANALYSIS. New York: Hafner, 1975. ix, 128 p. Bibliography, pp. 96-126. Index, pp. 127-28.

A monograph on applied discriminant analysis for those who

wish a brief summary of the field and who have knowledge of basic statistics and matrix algebra. Topics include evaluation of discriminant functions; robustness of the linear discriminant function; nonparametric methods; multiple-group problems; sequential discrimination; logistic discrimination; constrained discrimination; and Bayesian methods. References include works of engineers in the areas of character recognition and pattern recognition.

Lawley, D.N., and Maxwell, A.E. FACTOR ANALYSIS AS A STATISTICAL METHOD. 2d ed. New York: Elsevier, 1971. viii, 153 p. Appendix I: Matrix Algebra, pp. 121-37. Appendix II: Some Methods of Minimizing Functions, pp. 138-46. References, pp. 147-49. Index, pp. 151-53.

Presents the statistical theory of factor analysis with illustrative examples for use by research workers. Topics include principal component analysis; maximum likelihood estimation in unrestricted and restricted factor models; factor transformation and interpretation; estimation of factor scores; and identifying factors in different populations. Assumes knowledge of mathematical statistics and matrix algebra.

Lawlis, G. Frank, and Chatfield, Douglas. MULTIVARIATE APPROACHES FOR THE BEHAVIORAL SCIENCES: A BRIEF TEXT. Lubbock: Texas Tech University, 1974. 453 p. No index.

A text for an introductory course in multivariate analysis for students lacking extensive mathematical background. Useful as a primer for more advanced works in the field. Topics include bivariate approaches (product moment, eta, point-serial, biserial, correlations; and phi, tetrachoric, partial, and semipartial coefficients); multivariate correlation, including stepwise regression and canonical correlation; factor analysis; and applications of multivariate statistics to factor analysis, changes or difference scores, and discriminant analysis. Examples and charts used freely, and matrix algebra taken up as needed.

Lazarsfeld, Paul F., and Henry, Neil W. LATENT STRUCTURE ANALYSIS. New York: Houghton Mifflin, 1968. ix, 294 p. Appendix A: Matrix Algebra, pp. 264-72. Appendix B: Large Sample Distribution Theory for Estimates of the Parameters of a Latent Class Model by T.W. Anderson, pp. 273-87. Bibliography, pp. 288-92. Index, pp. 293-94.

A mathematical treatment of latent structure analysis for use as a text and reference. Topics include basic concepts; general latent class models; estimation of parameters by minimum chi-square, maximum likelihood, and partitioning methods; the problem of ordered classes; latent structure models with continuous latent space; latent profile model; latent class models for repeated behavior; and latent Markov chain models. Assumes knowledge of matrix algebra.

Lee, Wayne. EXPERIMENTAL DESIGN AND ANALYSIS. A Series of Books in Psychology. San Francisco: W.H. Freeman, 1975. xvi, 353 p. Appendix A: Statistical Tables, pp. 316-32. Appendix B: Power Charts, pp. 334-39. Summary of Notation, pp. 341-43. Design Index, pp. 344-46. Index, pp. 347-53.

A text for a course in multifactor experimental design and analysis of variance for students in the behavioral sciences who have knowledge of basic statistics. Emphasizes designs having factors related by crossings and nesting, including kinds of factors entering into designs, methods for symbolizing designs, classification of designs, and a comparison of purposes and relative merits of classes. Topics include score models (one-, two-, and three-factor designs, nested designs, etc.); analysis of variance of scores; expected mean squares and significance tests; Latin square designs; analysis of covariance; power considerations; missing scores and transformation of scores; and trend analysis.

Li, Ching Chun. INTRODUCTION TO EXPERIMENTAL STATISTICS. McGraw-Hill Series in Probability and Statistics. New York: Hafner, 1964. xii, 460 p. References, pp. 453-55. Index, pp. 457-60.

A text for a nonmathematical course in experimental statistics and a reference for researchers. Consists of three parts: "Basic Mechanics and Theory"; "Experimental Designs"; and "Some Related Topics." Topics include linear models and least squares estimates; variance-ratio test; regression; orthogonal contrasts; analysis of variance; randomized experiments and blocks; Latin square; factors at three levels; simple confounding systems; split-plot designs; balanced incomplete blocks; symmetrical pairs; multiple comparisons; and unequal group variances. Chapters conclude with exercises designed to review the text material and provide experience with computations.

Lindman, Harold R. ANALYSIS OF VARIANCE IN COMPLEX EXPERIMENTAL DESIGNS. San Francisco: W.H. Freeman, 1974. x, 352 p. Appendix: Tables, pp. 313-29. List of Symbols, pp. 330-34. Bibliography, pp. 335-41. Index, pp. 343-52.

An applied text for a graduate course for students who have had a noncalculus course in basic statistics. Emphasizes planned comparisons and combinations of planned comparisons with a bias toward Bayesian statistics. Topics include one- and two-way analysis of variance; random effects; higher-way designs; nested designs; one-way designs with quantitative factors; trend analysis in multiplifactor designs; and multifactor designs with random numerical factors. Chapters conclude with exericses.

Magnussan, David. TEST THEORY. Translated by Hunter Mabon. Reading, Mass.: Addison-Wesley, 1966. x, 270 p. Answers, pp. 249-59. Appendix, pp. 260-61. Index of Notation, pp. 263-65. Author Index, pp. 266-67. Subject Index, pp. 268-70.

Originally published in Swedish in 1961. Presents a theoretical and statistically coherent introduction to the theory of measurement of individual differences, methods for applications to dependability problems, and models for using differential psychology data in test construction, diagnosis, counseling, selection, and classification. Assumes knowledge of descriptive statistics. Topics include the sample item and its variance; correlation and prediction; covariance; reliability; difference scores; validity; prediction and its dependability; factor theory; guessing; and scales and transformations. Chapters conclude with references.

Mandel, John. THE STATISTICAL ANALYSIS OF EXPERIMENTAL DATA. New York: Wiley, 1964. xi, 410 p. Appendix, pp. 391-402. Index, pp. 403-10.

An analysis of the problems that confront the physical scientist in the analysis of experimental data. Topics include the nature of measurement; random variables and expected values; normal distribution; central limit theorem; law of propagation of errors; control charts; order statistics; extreme-value theory; precision and accuracy of measurements; method of least squares; analysis of variance; general linear hypothesis; principles of sampling; fitting of curves and surfaces; fitting of straight lines; evaluation of measuring processes, including interlaboratory studies of test methods; and between-laboratory variability; and comparison of methods of measurement. Examples based on real data. Fairly rigorous style employed. Chapter conclude with references.

Maranell, Gary M., ed. SCALING: A SOURCEBOOK FOR BEHAVIORAL SCIENTISTS. Methodological Perspectives. Chicago: Aldine, 1974. xix, 436 p. Selected Bibliography, pp. 407-17. Appendix: Tables, pp. 419-22. Index, pp. 429-36.

A sourcebook on scaling methods for students interested in scaling. Methods and topics grouped under the following six headings: "Measurement and Scaling"; "Thurstonian Methods"; "Scalogram Analysis"; "Summated Rating Methods"; "Unfolding Theory"; and "Related Material." Topics include paired comparison; equal-appearing intervals; successive intervals; Guttman scales; attitude scales; cumulative scales; unfolding theory; and rank order categories. Mathematically within the reach of everyone willing to read with some care.

Maxwell, Albert Ernest. ANALYSING QUALITATIVE DATA. Methuen's Monographs on Applied Probability and Statistics. New York: Wiley, 1961. 163 p. Index, pp. 161-63.

A reference and supplementary text on the statistical techniques available for the analysis of qualitative data with examples largely from psychology. Chi-square technique applied to 2x2 and 3x3 contingency tables, multiple classification categories, 2xN contingency tables, with partitioning of the degrees of freedom, testing for trends in contingency tables, comparing results from different investigations, 2^n contingency tables, and tests of goodness of fit. Other techniques include rank correlation; sign tests; Cox's cumulative score test; classification procedures based on Bayes' theorem and decision theory; and item analysis and the construction of attitude scales. Concepts explained intuitively and illustrated with examples. Assumes knowledge of basic statistics. Chapters conclude with references.

______. EXPERIMENTAL DESIGN IN PSYCHOLOGY AND THE MEDICAL SCIENCES. New York: Wiley, 1958. 147 p. Appendixes: Tables, pp. 138-42. Bibliography, pp. 142-43. Index, pp. 145-47.

An introduction to experimental design in psychology and the medical sciences using a minimum of mathematical terminology for use by students and researchers who have had a course in basic statistics. Each design introduced by means of a practical example with real data. Designs include randomized block; Latin and Graeco-Latin squares; factorial, balanced incomplete blocks, linear regression, and product-moment correlation; analysis of covariance; and systematic designs. Emphasizes details of calculations. Concludes with a chapter on evaluating the relative efficiency of the different designs.

______. MULTIVARIATE ANALYSIS IN BEHAVIORAL RESEARCH. Wiley Series in Probability and Mathematical Statistics. New York: Wiley, 1977. ix, 164 p. References, pp. 153-57. Index, pp. 159-64.

An introduction to classical multivariate analysis requiring knowledge of matrix algebra. Topics include historical background, review of matrices and determinants, principal component; factor; multiple linear regression; canonical correlations; discriminant function analysis; contingency tables; analysis of variances; and cluster analysis. Numerical examples included.

Meisel, William S. COMPUTER-ORIENTED APPROACHES TO PATTERN RECOGNITION. Mathematics in Science and Engineering. A Series of Monographs and Textbooks, vol. 83. New York: Academic Press, 1972. xii, 250 p. Appendix A: A Set of Orthogonal Polynomials, pp. 228-29. Appendix B: Efficient Representation and Approximation of Multivariate Functions, pp. 230-46. Index, pp. 247-50.

A text for a one-semester course in pattern recognition for undergraduates and graduates who have knowledge of probability theory and linear algebra. Also useful as a reference for courses in operations research, computer science, and biomedical engineering. Emphasizes computer-oriented methods. Topics include statistical formulation and parametric methods; optimization techniques, including linear programming; linear discriminant functions with extensions; indirect and direct approximation of probability densities; cluster analysis and unsupervised learning; measures of quality; sequential feature selection; linguistic analysis of patterns; and nonstationary pattern recognition. Chapters conclude with exercises and references.

Mendenhall, William. INTRODUCTION TO LINEAR MODELS AND THE DESIGN AND ANALYSIS OF EXPERIMENTS. Belmont, Calif.: Wadsworth, 1968. xiv, 465 p. Appendix I: A Glossary of Symbols, pp. 408-9. Appendix II: Useful Statistical Tests and Confidence Intervals, pp. 410-16. Appendix III: Tables, pp. 417-46. Answers, pp. 447-62. Index, pp. 463-65.

A text for a course in experimental design for students in engineering, and the social and biological sciences who have knowledge of basic statistics, and a reference for research workers. Matrix algebra taken up as needed. Topics include simple and multiple regression; noise-reducing experimental designs (randomized block and Latin square); volume-increasing designs (factorial experiments); analysis of variance; fractional experiments and incomplete block designs; completely random models; and mixed models. Least squares and sums of squares approaches contrasted, with advantages of each method pointed out. Chapters conclude with problems and references.

Montgomery, Douglas C. DESIGN AND ANALYSIS OF EXPERIMENTS. New York: Wiley, 1976. 418 p. Bibliography, pp. 387-91. Appendix: Tables, pp. 392-414. Index, pp. 415-18.

A text for a one-year course in experimental design for graduates and undergraduates in a variety of disciplines, including engineering, physical sciences, mathematics, biology, and the social sciences, who have had a course in basic statistics. Knowledge of calculus helpful, but not necessary. Balance maintained between derivations and descriptive illustrations. Topics include review of statistical estimation and hypothesis testing; experiments with a single factor, including fixed and random effects models; randomized blocks, Latin squares, and incomplete block designs; factorial experiments, including 2^k and 3^k factorial designs; confounding; fractional replication; nested or hierarchial designs; multifactor experiments with randomization restrictions; regression analysis; response surface methodology; and analysis of covariance. Chapters conclude with problems.

Morgan, James N., and Messenger, Robert C. THAID: A SEQUENTIAL ANALYSIS PROGRAM FOR THE ANALYSIS OF NOMINAL SCALE DEPENDENT VARIABLES. Ann Arbor: Survey Research Center, Institute for Social Research, University of Michigan, 1973. vi, 92 p. Bibliography, p. 46. Appendix A: Set-up Instructions, pp. 47-53. Appendix B: Macro Flow Chart, pp. 54-56. Appendix C: Sample Output, pp. 57-90. Appendix D: Obtaining the Programs and Adapting it to Other Systems, pp. 91-92. No index.

> A monograph which presents the THAID computer algorithm in FORTRAN for the analysis of categorical data (nominal or ordinal). Model in THAID predictive and provides users with a subset of predictors (40 or less) and possible interactions for a given dependent variable. Includes a linear least squares regression model.

Morrison, Donald F. MULTIVARIATE STATISTICAL METHODS. 2d rev. ed. McGraw-Hill Series in Probability and Statistics. New York: McGraw-Hill, 1976. xv, 415 p. References, pp. 346-62. Appendix: Tables and Charts, pp. 363-402. Name Index, pp. 404-6. Subject Index, pp. 407-15.

> A reference on multivariate techniques in the design and analysis of experimental data for the life and behavioral sciences, and a text for a course in multivariate methods for undergraduates and graduates who have knowledge of basic statistics and calculus, including partial differentiation. Topics include a review of univariate statistical concepts and matrix algebra; standard results on the multinomial distribution; correlation analysis; tests of hypotheses on means; multivariate analysis of variance; classification by the linear discriminant function; inferences from covariance matrices; principal components; and factor analysis. Based on the Roy union-intersection principle. Includes illustrative examples. Chapters conclude with exercises, notes, and references.

Mulaik, Stanley A. THE FOUNDATIONS OF FACTOR ANALYSIS. McGraw-Hill Series in Psychology. New York: McGraw-Hill, 1972. xvi, 354 p. Bibliography, pp. 429-36. Name Index, pp. 437-41. Subject Index, pp. 443-53.

> A text for a graduate course in the mathematical theory of factor analysis for graduates and undergraduates who have knowledge of differential calculus. Emphasizes algebraic methods, rather than statistical methods, the key concept being random variables treated as a vector in a unitary space with scalar product of vectors a defined operation. Topics include multiple and partial correlation; fundamental equations of factor analysis; methods of factor extraction; common-factor analysis; graphed rotation; orthogonal analytic rotation; oblique analytic rotation; procrustean transformations; factor scores; factorial invariances; confirmatory factor analysis; and factor analysis

in multivariate analysis. Most derivations based on matrix algebra and accompanied by considerable verbal description and explanation.

Myers, Jerome L. FUNDAMENTALS OF EXPERIMENTAL DESIGN. 2d ed. Boston: Allyn and Bacon, 1972. xii, 465 p. Answers to Exercises, pp. 404-26. Appendix Tables, pp. 427-58. Index, pp. 459-65.

A text for a one-semester course in experimental design or analysis of variance for students in the behavioral sciences who have a high school algebra background and who have had one semester of basic statistics covering bivariate regression, correlation, and statistical inference. Emphasizes applications rather than mathematical theory. Topics include completely randomized multi-factor designs; designs using a concomitant variable; repeated measurement designs; mixed designs (between- and within-variability); hierarched designs; Latin square designs; expected mean squares; analysis of covariance; and analysis of qualitative variables. Chapter conclude with exercises and references.

Myers, Raymond H. RESPONSE SURFACE METHODOLOGY. Boston: Allyn and Bacon, 1971. x, 246 p. Appendix A: pp. 219-25. Appendix B, pp. 226-31. Appendix C: Tables, pp. 232-43. Index, pp. 245-46.

Presents both the theory and application of response surface methodology for those with a background in matrix algebra, elementary experimental design, and least squares. Consists of two parts: "Analysis" and "Design." Includes techniques for analyzing experimental information in a first or second order response model, layouts for fitting first and second order models, and examples from actual industrial problems. Chapters conclude with exercises and references. Appendixes devoted to certain mathematical results.

Namboodiri, N. Krishnan; Carter, Lewis F.; and Blalock, Hubert M., Jr. APPLIED MULTIVARIATE ANALYSIS AND EXPERIMENTAL DESIGN. New York: McGraw-Hill, 1975. xvi, 688 p. Appendix A: Program CARTROCK, pp. 613-20. Appendix B: Simulated Data Set, pp. 621-26. Appendix C: Matrices, pp. 627-52. Appendix D: Tables, pp. 653-60. Appendix E: References, pp. 661-69. Name Index, pp. 671-73. Subject Index, pp. 674-88.

A text for a course in multivariate analysis for graduate students in sociology, political science, and secondarily for social scientists in other fields. Consists of four parts: Multiple Regression and Related Techniques; Experimental Design; Simultaneous-Equation Models; and Models Involving Measurement Errors. Topics include one- and two-way analysis of variance; multiple regression; analysis of covariance; random-effects model; interclass correlation; randomized block designs; Latin squares; 2^n factorial experiments; fractional replications; recursive models and one-way causation; nonrecursive models and reciprocal causation; and random and nonrandom measurement errors. Assumes exposure to analysis of variance and multiple regression. Chapters conclude with exercises.

Ogawa, Junjiro. STATISTICAL THEORY OF THE ANALYSIS OF EXPERIMENTAL DESIGN. Statistics: Textbooks and Monographs, vol. 8. New York: Marcel Dekker, 1974. vi, 465 p. Bibliography, pp. 447-61. Index, pp. 463-65.

A text for a graduate course on the mathematical theory of experimental design based on linear models and normal distributions. Design construction not covered. Topics include analysis of variance; design of experiments; factorial design; theory of block designs--intrablock and interblock designs; and randomization of partially balanced incomplete block designs. Assumes knowledge of linear algebra, real analysis, and statistical inference. Chapters conclude with references.

O'Muircheartaigh, Colm A., and Payne, Clive, eds. THE ANALYSIS OF SURVEY DATA. Vol. I. EXPLORING DATA STRUCTURES. New York: Wiley, 1977. xiv, 273 p. Index, pp. 259-73.

A practical and up-to-date guide on the processing and analysis of survey data for survey practitioners in academia, government, and industry with emphasis on multivariate techniques. Detailed derivations included in sections marked with asterisks. Recognizes new techniques in data analysis, increased formal training of social scientists, and use of computers in research. Each chapter written by a different author. Topics include preparation and processing of survey data; cluster analysis; principal component and factor analysis; latent structure analysis; multidimensional scaling; attitude scale construction; and binary segmentation (the automatic interaction detector and related techniques for exploring data structures). Chapters conclude with references.

_____. THE ANALYSIS OF SURVEY DATA. Vol. 2. MODEL FITTING. New York: Wiley, 1977. xvi, 255 p. Author Index, pp. 241-45. Subject Index, pp. 247-55.

Deals with model fitting and testing procedures in multivariate analysis of data. Includes general linear model with extensions; path analysis; log-linear model for contingency tables; analysis of data arising from stochastic processes in discrete and continuous time; effect of complex sample design on the correlation coefficient in multivariate analysis; and sources, identification, and effect of response errors and their impact on inferences from survey data. Chapters conclude with references.

Overall, John Ernest, and Klett, C. James. APPLIED MULTIVARIATE ANALYSIS. McGraw-Hill Series in Psychology. New York: McGraw-Hill, 1972. xxii, 500 p. Appendix: Tables, pp. 469-91. Index, pp. 493-500.

A text for a course in applied multivariate analysis for graduate students in the social and behavioral sciences who have knowledge of basic statistics and matrix algebra, and a reference for research workers. Consists of five parts: "Preliminary Considerations"; "Two Factor Analysis and Related Methodology"; "Discrimination of Groups"; "Classification Among Groups"; and "Multiple Regression and Analysis of Variance." Topics include review of matrix concepts; principal-components analysis; principal-axis factor analysis; orthogonal powered vector factor analysis; oblique primary- and reference factor analysis; multiple discriminant analysis; normal-probability-density model for classification among several groups; use of canonical variates for classification; simple profile analysis for classification; and pattern-probability model for classification using qualitative data.

Patrick, Edward A. FUNDAMENTALS OF PATTERN RECOGNITION. Prentice-Hall Information and System Science Series. Englewood Cliffs, N.J.: Prentice-Hall, 1972. xxiv, 504 p. Index, pp. 491-500. Author Index, pp. 501-4.

A text on theoretical and practical procedures for classifying patterns from their measurements. Patterns include diseases, brain cells, blood cells, cancer cells, chromosomes, crops, clouds, etc. Topics include properties of estimators, including maximum likelihood estimators; Bayes' decision rules for use in pattern recognition; supervised Bayes' estimation, including adaptive threshold elements; unsupervised Bayes' estimation; feature selection and feature extraction; and pattern recognition through statistical verification of a priori problem knowledge. Assumes knowledge of linear algebra and mathematical statistics. Chapters conclude with references and problems.

Peng, Kan Chen. THE DESIGN AND ANALYSIS OF SCIENTIFIC EXPERIMENTS: AN INTRODUCTION WITH SOME EMPHASIS ON COMPUTATION. Reading, Mass.: Addison-Wesley, 1967. ix, 252 p. General References, p. 217. Appendix I: A Computer Program for the Analysis of Common Factorial Experiments, pp. 219-30. Appendix II: A Computer Program for the Analysis of Latin Square and Graeco-Latin Square Experiments, pp. 231-36. Appendix III: A Computer Program for the Analysis of Fractional Factorial Experiments with Factors at Two Levels, pp. 237-47. Index, pp. 249-52.

An introduction to the design and analysis of experiments for statisticians, computer programmers, and researchers who have a background in calculus, matrix algebra, and one-year of statistics. Topics include noncentral chi-square and F tests; methods of multiple comparisons; two-way analysis of variance; three-way and multiway arrangements; orthogonal contrasts and orthogonal polynomials; nested experiments; fixed, random, and mixed models; randomized-blocks, Latin-square, and split-plot designs; fractional factorial designs and confounding; response surface designs; analysis of covariance; and nonfactorial experiments. Chapters conclude with references.

Plackett, R.L. THE ANALYSIS OF CATEGORICAL DATA. Griffin's Statistical Monographs and Courses, no. 35. London: Griffin, 1974. viii, 159 p. Exercises, pp. 115-39. References, pp. 140-50. Author Index, pp. 151-53. Subject Index, pp. 155-57. Experimental Index, p. 159.

A reference on the analysis of categorical data for students taking advanced courses in statistics, teachers, and research workers who have a good grasp of statistical inference. Includes some proofs in outline form. Describes concepts, develops statistical methods, illustrates applications, and suggests questions for further study. Topics include single, two-, and three-way classification; models and methods; matching; and multivariate data. Problems designed to extend the concepts.

Pool, Ithiel de Sola, ed. TRENDS IN CONTENT ANALYSIS. Urbana: University of Illinois Press, 1959. vi, 244 p. Selected Bibliography, pp. 235-40. Name Index, pp. 241-43. Subject Index, p. 244.

Seven papers presented at a workshop on content analysis sponsored by the committee on linguistics and psychology of the SSRC held at the University of Illinois in Monticello during the winter of 1955. Uses the verbal style and explores content analysis in the following fields: biography and history; folkloristics; and linguistics. Topics include quantitative and qualitative approaches; representational model; research methods; and trends.

Press, S. James. APPLIED MULTIVARIATE ANALYSIS. Series in Quantitative Methods for Decision-Making. New York: Holt, Rinehart and Winston, 1972. xxii, 521 p. Appendix A: Computer Programs for Multivariate Models, pp. 423-55. Appendix B: Tables, pp. 458-80. Appendix C: Bibliography, pp. 483-509. Index, pp. 511-12.

A text for a graduate course in applied multivariate analysis for students in the social sciences and statistics who have knowledge of linear algebra and elementary mathematical statistics. Consists of two parts: "Foundations" and "Models." Topics include continuous multivariate distributions; multivariate central limit theorem; asymptotic distribution of a function of a random matrix; asymptotic posterior distributions; the Wishart and related distributions; multivariate statistics in the normal distribution; regression and analysis of variance; principal components; factor analysis and latent structure analysis; canonical correlations; stable portfolio analysis; classification and discrimination models; and multidimensional scaling and clustering.

Excludes multivariate time series and spectral analysis; simultaneous equation systems; path analysis; nonparametric multivariate analysis; multivariate random coefficient models; and problems involving discrete multivariate distributions. Chapters conclude with exercises.

Rabinowicz, Ernest. AN INTRODUCTION TO EXPERIMENTATION. Addison-Wesley Series in Mechanics and Thermodynamics. Reading, Mass.: Addison-Wesley, 1970. viii, 124 p. Index, pp. 123-24.

A text for a short course in physical measurement and analysis for students in engineering and a reference for practitioners in industry. Emphasizes interpretation of measurements and their errors, and an evaluation of conditions under which formulas or distributions do not apply. Includes the following chapters: "A Qualitative Evaluation of Experiments"; "Evaluation of Functional Relationships"; and "The Technical Report." Topics include instruments for taking measurements; probability distributions; regression and correlation; autocorrelation; design of experiments to reduce errors; and internal estimation of error. Assumes knowledge of calculus.

Raghavarao, Damaraju. CONSTRUCTION AND COMBINATORIAL PROBLEMS IN DESIGN OF EXPERIMENTS. Wiley Series in Probability and Mathematical Statistics. New York: Wiley, 1971. xviii, 386 p. Appendix A: Mathematics for Statisticians, pp. 337-60. Appendix B: Statistics for Mathematicians, pp. 361-70. Miscellaneous Exercises, pp. 371-77. Index, pp. 379-86.

A text for a course in the combinatorial theory of the design of experiments and a reference for statisticians and mathematicians doing research. Topics include complete sets of mutually orthogonal Latin squares; orthogonal arrays; pairwise balanced designs and mutually orthogonal Latin squares; general properties of incomplete block designs; balanced incomplete block designs; system of distinct representatives and Youden squares; tactical configurations and doubly balanced designs; partially balanced incomplete block designs; symmetrical unequal block arrangements with two unequal block sizes; nonexistence of incomplete block designs; confounding in symmetrical factorial experiments; fractional replication; rotatable designs; and weighing designs. Also presents the necessary and sufficient conditions for the existence of designs using the Hasse-Minkowski invariant concept. Chapters contain references.

Reynolds, Henry T. THE ANALYSIS OF CROSS-CLASSIFICATIONS. New York: Free Press, 1977. xiv, 236 p. Appendix A: Vectors and Matrices, pp. 214-17. Appendix B: Distribution of Chi-Square, pp. 218-19. Appendix C: Data Sources, p. 220. References, pp. 221-30. Index, pp. 231-36.

An intuitive, nonrigorous description of techniques for analyzing cross-classifications and ways of displaying and studying nominal and ordinal variables. Emphasizes computational aspects, interpretation, and practical strengths and weaknesses of the methods. Accessible to anyone having knowledge of basic statistics. Topics include analysis of two-way tables; measures of association for nominal and ordinal data; multivariate analysis of cross-classifications; log-linear models; estimation and partitioning log-linear models; and regression analysis of cross-classification.

Romney, A. Kimball; Shepard, Roger N.; and Nerlove, Sara Beth, eds. MULTIDIMENSIONAL SCALING: THEORY AND APPLICATIONS IN THE BEHAVIORAL SCIENCES. Vol. II. APPLICATIONS. New York: Seminar Press, 1972. xvi, 323 p. Author Index, pp. 315-18. Subject Index, pp. 319-23.

Ten papers presented at an advanced seminar on theoretical and methodological developments in multidimensional scaling held at the University of California at Irvine in June 1969. Topics include semantic dimensions of occupational names; individual variations in cognitive structures; structural representations of perceived personality trait relationships; consistence among judgements of adjective combinations; marketing research applications of nonmetric scaling methods; structural approach to predicting patterns of electoral substitution; and applications of multidimensional scaling to social sciences problems.

Roscoe, John T. FUNDAMENTAL RESEARCH STATISTICS FOR THE BEHAVIORAL SCIENCES. 2d ed. International Series in Decision Processes. New York: Holt, Rinehart and Winston, 1975. xvii, 483 p. Appendix: Tables, pp. 409-70. Answers to Selected Exercises, pp. 471-78. Index, pp. 479-83.

A text for a one-year course in research statistics for students in the behavioral sciences who have a background in elementary algebra. Consists of forty-six chapters and includes such topics as standard scores; Pearson product-moment correlation and other correlations such as Spearman and Kendall Tau rank correlation and the Goodman-Kruskal gamma coefficient; prediction including regression equations; probability, sampling, interval estimation, and hypothesis testing; experimental design; two-sample problem; nonparametric tests; chi-square and contingency tables; analysis of variance and covariance; and multiple regression. Emphasizes selection of the most appropriate analysis for a given research problem. Every procedure illustrated with a practical example. Chapters conclude with exercises and references.

Roskam, Edward Elias Charles Iben. METRIC ANALYSIS OF ORDINAL DATA IN PSYCHOLOGY: MODELS AND NUMERICAL METHODS FOR METRIC ANALYSIS OF CONJOINT ORDINAL DATA IN PSYCHOLOGY. Voorschoten, The Netherlands: V.A.N., 1968. 163 p. Appendix, pp. 139-52. Summary, pp. 153-56. References, pp. 159-63. No index.

Presents four models for analyzing nonnumerical information based on Kruskal's method originally devised for multidimensional scaling of rank-ordered dissimilarities: distance, linear, compensatory distance, and additive. Includes extensions to three models in which elements enter from more than two different sets. Appendix includes formulas for the application of Kruskal's method to given models.

Roy, S.N.; Gnanadesikan, R.; and Srivastava, J.N. ANALYSIS AND DESIGN OF CERTAIN QUANTITATIVE MULTIRESPONSE EXPERIMENTS. With an Appendix on Computer Algorithms and Programs, by E.B. Fowlkes II, and Elisa T. Lee. New York: Pergamon, 1971. x, 304 p. Bibliography, pp. 146-50. Appendix A: Some Specific Matrix Results, pp. 151-56. Appendix B: Tables and/or Charts Associated with the Procedures, pp. 157-215. Appendix C: I, Computer Programs for Multivariate Analysis; II, Computer Programs for Interval Comparisons, pp. 216-99. Author Index, pp. 301-2. Subject Index, pp. 303-4.

A monograph on multiresponse analysis of variance based on the authors' research in the area. Based on the same factor setup as in classical analysis of variance. Presents both formal and informal techniques for the analysis and design of multiresponse experiments. Topics include linear models; point estimation of location parameters; testing of the linear hypothesis; properties of the test procedures; confidence bounds; graphical methods and interval comparisons; incomplete multiresponse designs; and construction of multiresponse designs. Chapters conclude with references.

Royce, Joseph R. MULTIVARIATE ANALYSIS AND PSYCHOLOGICAL THEORY. New York: Academic Press, 1973. xvi, 567 p. Author Index, pp. 541-52. Subject Index, pp. 553-67.

Fourteen papers presented at the third Banff Conference on theoretical psychology held at the Banff School of Fine Arts, Banff, Canada, September 27-October 2, 1971, and an introduction by the editor. Papers grouped under the following two headings: "Methodological, Pre-theoretical and Metatheoretical Issues" (eight papers) and "Toward a Comprehensive, Multivariate, Psychological Theory" (six papers). Topics include linear regression equations as behavioral models, multivariate approaches to the study of cognitive style; multiple factor ability measures; multi-factor theory of individuality; causal theories of personality; multidimensional theory of depression; and psychological structures of peer group forces in delinquency. Verbal style employed, and little statistics used.

Rulon, Phillip J.; Tiedeman, David V.; Tatsuoka, Maurice M.; and Langmuir, Charles R. MULTIVARIATE STATISTICS FOR PERSONNEL CLASSIFICATION. New York: Wiley, 1967. xi, 406 p. Appendix A: Contour Ellipses for a

Large Sample of Airmen, pp. 367-95. Appendix B: Rosters of Passenger Agents, Mechanics, Operations Control Agents, pp. 396-403. References, pp. 404-6. No index.

An exposition of the problem of personnel classification in terms of probability theory. Principles of geometry, matrix algebra, and topology introduced as needed. Consists of five parts: "Personnel Classification and the Job Psychograph"; "The Geometry of the Psychological Profile"; "Regions of the Test Space"; "The Problem of Reducing Dimensionality"; and "Statistical Procedures and Personnel Procedures." Topics include the one-, two-, and three-variable cases; the general case; factor analysis; discriminant analysis; regression analysis; and joint probability of membership and success in a group. Includes illustrations, but omits analyses of sampling error and tests of significance. Includes simple derivations, but no proofs.

Rummel, Rudolph J. APPLIED FACTOR ANALYSIS. Evanston: Northwestern University Press, 1970. xxii, 617 p. Tables of Notation, pp. xxi-xxii. Bibliography, pp. 568-600. Name Index, pp. 601-7. Subject Index, pp. 609-17.

A supplementary text for a course in factor analysis for social science students and a manual for research workers. Primarily descriptive, and includes five parts: "Orientation"; "Structures, Matrices, and Design of Factor Analysis"; "Preparing the Data"; "The Analysis"; and "The Results." Includes few computational procedures and no problems.

Scheffé, Henry. THE ANALYSIS OF VARIANCE. Wiley Series in Probability and Mathematical Statistics. New York: Wiley, 1959. xvi, 477 p. Appendixes, pp. 371-423. Statistical Tables, pp. 424-55. Author Index and Bibliography, pp. 457-65. Subject Index, pp. 467-77.

A text for a one-semester or two-quarter course for graduates and undergraduates who are familiar with calculus and matrix algebra, and also a second course in statistics covering probability, confidence intervals, and power of tests. Derivations algebraic with vector and matrix algebra the main tools. Includes the following models: fixed effects, and independent observations of equal variance, including one-, two-, and three- and higher-way layouts, incomplete layouts, and analysis of covariance; random-effects models; mixed models (both fixed and random effects); and randomization models. Also includes 117 problems, thirty-eight of which utilize real data. Omitted topics include multivariate generalizations of univariate theory; sequential methods; nonparametric theory; confounding, fractional replication, and response-surface exploration; and some complicated designs. Appendixes devoted to treatments of ellipsoids and their planes of support, noncentral chi-square, F and t statistics, multivariate normal distribution, and Cochran's theorem.

Sebestyen, George S. DECISION-MAKING PROCESSES IN PATTERN RECOGNITION. ACM Monographs Series. New York: Macmillan, 1962. viii, 162 p. Bibliography, pp. 152-59. Index, pp. 161-62.

Shows how decision-theoretic methods can be applied to pattern recognition problems. Pattern recognition presented as the two-fold problem of learning the common properties of a set of n-dimensional vectors of samples of a given class, and of recognizing a new vector as a possible member of the class by noting the properties common to both vector. Includes linear, nonlinear approximate, and adaptive techniques of classification. Applications include the assignment of numerical values to subjective measurements, selection of computational procedures, recognition of voiced and unvoiced speech sounds, and automatic recognition of spoken numericals.

Shepard, Roger N.; Romney, A. Kimball; and Nerlove, Sara Beth, eds. MULTIDIMENSIONAL SCALING: THEORY AND APPLICATIONS IN THE BEHAVIORAL SCIENCES. Vol. I: THEORY. New York: Seminar Press, 1972. xvi, 261 p. Author Index, pp. 251-54. Subject Index, pp. 255-61.

Nine papers presented at an advanced seminar on recent theoretical and methodological developments in multidimensional scaling and on applications in a wide range of social and behavioral science fields. Topics include taxonomy of some principal types of data; survey of the Guttman-Lingoes nonmetric program series; polynomial conjoint analysis algorithms; individual differences and multidimensional scaling; nonmetric multidimensional techniques for summated ratings; linear transformations of multivariate data to reveal clustering; information distance for discrete structures; and structural measures and the method of sorting.

Solomon, Herbert, ed. STUDIES IN ITEM ANALYSIS AND PREDICTION. Stanford Mathematical Studies in the Social Sciences, VI. Stanford, Calif.: Stanford University Press, 1961. xiii, 310 p. No index.

Thirteen heretofore unpublished contributions on item analysis and test design and six reprints of articles previously published grouped under the following three headings: "Item Selection: Multivariate Normal Structure" (seven articles); "Item Selection: Several Non-parametric Situations" (seven articles); and "The Classification Statistic and Its Distribution" (five articles). Topics include the algebra of dichotomous systems; joint distribution of responses to n dichotomous items; decision theory approach to item selection; empirical Bayes' approach; the W-classification statistic; and a nonparametric solution for the k-sample slippage problem.

Sonquist, John A. MULTIVARIATE MODEL BUILDING: THE VALIDATION OF A SEARCH STRATEGY. Ann Arbor: University of Michigan, Survey Research

Center, Institute for Social Research, 1970. xiii, 244 p. Appendix A: The AID Algorithm Description and Flow Charts, pp. 221-30. Appendix B: Partial Bibliography of Research Reports and Citations Referring to AID of MCA, pp. 231-34. References, pp. 235-44. No index.

> A monograph on sequential data-analysis procedures in inductive sociological research with emphasis on a computer program AID. Program applies one-way analysis of variance to a sample of subgroups of independent variables using the interactive mode of computer usage.

Sonquist, John A.; Baker, Elizabeth L.; and Morgan, James N. SEARCHING FOR STRUCTURE (ALIAS-AID-III): AN APPROACH TO ANALYSIS OF SUBSTANTIAL BODIES OF MICRO-DATA AND DOCUMENTATION FOR A COMPUTER PROGRAM. (SUCCESSOR TO THE AUTOMATIC INTERACTION DETECTOR PROGRAM). Ann Arbor: University of Michigan, Survey Research Center, Institute for Social Research, 1971. x, 287 p. Appendix I: References, pp. 165-66. Appendix II: Set Up Instructions, pp. 167-79. Appendix III: Coding Forms for Set Up, pp. 181-92. Appendix IV: Program Documentation, pp. 193-201. Examples of Output, pp. 203-87. No index.

> A reference and user documentation for the computer program, the Automatic Interaction Detector. Program simulates procedures of a good researcher in searching for the best set of independent variables for a given dependent variable. Procedure based on regression analysis. Program divides data into subgroups and measures the effect of each predictor on each subgroup. Large data sets can be accommodated.

Srivastava, Jagdish N. A SURVEY OF STATISTICAL DESIGN AND LINEAR MODELS. New York: Elsevier, 1975. viii, 699 p. Author Index, pp. 691-99.

> Forty-two papers presented at an international symposium held at Colorado State University March 19-23, 1973. Papers surveyed the following fields: optimal designs; sequential designs; search problems; factorial and incomplete blocks; designs for stochastic processes; sampling; general linear models; randomization theory; variance analysis; designs for model building; and applications to biology, clinical trials, genetics, econometrics, computer simulation, weather modification, industry, etc. Assumes knowledge of experimental design, mathematical statistics, and matrix algebra.

Stanley, Julian C., ed. IMPROVING EXPERIMENTAL DESIGN AND STATISTICAL ANALYSIS. Chicago: Rand McNally, 1967. ix, 308 p. References, pp. 292-301. Author Index, pp. 303-5. Subject Index, pp. 307-8.

> Five papers by two mathematical statisticians, George E.P. Box and Ingram Olkin, and three educational research methodologists, Frank B. Baker, Leslie D. McLean, and Julian C.

Stanley, on experimental design presented at the seventh annual Phi Delta Kappa symposium on educational research held at the University of Wisconsin in 1965. Topics include Bayesian approach to problems in data analysis; incomplete designs in behavioral research; experimental design in large-scale research; correlations; and administrative experimentation, institutional records, and nonreactive measures.

Sterling, Theodor D., and Pollack, Seymour V. INTRODUCTION TO STATISTICAL DATA PROCESSING. Prentice-Hall Series in Automatic Computation. Englewood Cliffs, N.J.: Prentice-Hall, 1968. xvii, 663 p. Appendix A: Review of Fundamental Mathematical Manipulations, pp. 569-627. Appendix B: Some Commonly Used Statistical Tables, pp. 629-48. Answers to Problems, pp. 649-52. Index, pp. 653-63.

A text for a one-year course in statistical data processing for students in biology, botany, medicine, and the social sciences who are somewhat familiar with computer programming. Emphasizes example problems, with practice problems at the ends of the chapters, and flow charts and computer programs. Topics include computing hardware and software; organization and collection of data; descriptive statistics; statistical hypothesis testing; linear and nonlinear regression; automatic search techniques; analysis of variance; Latin squares; covariance analysis; and the man-machine Combo, the intellectual robot.

Stone, Philip J.; Dunphy, Dexter C.; Smith, Marshall S.; and Ogilvie, Daniel M. THE GENERAL INQUIRER: A COMPUTER APPROACH TO CONTENT ANALYSIS. Cambridge, Mass.: MIT Press, 1966. xx, 651 p. Topics Index, pp. 639-44. Name Index, pp. 645-51.

A reference and introduction to content analysis for both the layman and professional with no previous experience with computer applications but with some knowledge of basic statistics. Emphasizes content analysis research, and includes applications in a variety of social science areas, small groups, personality, clinical psychology, social psychology, cross-cultural studies, and product image. Presentation verbal, with few charts, graphs, and tables.

Subrahmaniam, Kocherlakota, and Subrahmaniam, Kathleen. MULTIVARIATF ANALYSIS: A SELECTED AND ABSTRACTED BIBLIOGRAPHY, 1957-1972. Statistics: Textbooks and Monographs, vol. 4. New York: Marcel Dekker, 1973. xiii, 265 p. Subject Index, pp. 253-65.

Abstracts of 1,189 articles dealing with multivariate normal and related distributions arranged alphabetically by author. Includes list of journals where articles originally appeared, and a subject index.

Sullins, Walter L. MATRIX ALGEBRA FOR STATISTICAL APPLICATIONS. Danville, Ill.: Interstate, 1973. viii, 108 p. Exercises, pp. 97-103. References, pp. 105-6. Index, pp. 107-8.

> A supplementary text in statistics courses, a self-study, or a text for short course in applied matrix algebra for advanced students and researchers in the behavioral sciences, biology, and the physical sciences. Emphasizes applications of matrix algebra in multiple regression, factor analysis, discriminant analysis, multivariate analysis of variance; and canonical analysis. Development intuitive, with rigorous proofs included only when necessary to understand applications. Assumes knowledge of algebra and basic statistics.

Tatsuoka, Maurice M. MULTIVARIATE ANALYSIS: TECHNIQUES FOR EDUCATIONAL AND PSYCHOLOGICAL RESEARCH. New York: Wiley, 1971. xvi, 310 p. Appendix, pp. 243-300. References, pp. 301-4. Index, pp. 305-10.

> A text for an advanced graduate course for students in education and psychology who have had a graduate course in applied statistics and who have knowledge of linear algebra. Topics include analysis of covariance with more than one covariate; multivariate significance tests of group differences; discriminant analysis and canonical correlation; multivariate analysis of variance for factorial experiments; and applications to classification problems. Chapters conclude with exercises involving simple applications and statistical derivations.

Thorndike, Robert M. CORRELATION PROCEDURES FOR RESEARCH. New York: Gardner, 1978. xi, 340 p. References, pp. 331-37. Index, pp. 338-40.

> A reference on correlation procedures in multivariate analysis for users of multivariate techniques in the behavioral sciences. Style intuitive and geometrical, rather than mathematical, with formulas given without derivations. Consists of three parts: "Bivariate Relationships"; "External Factor Analysis"; and "Internal Factor Analysis." Topics include least squares; product moment correlation; multivariate correlation; canonical analysis; discriminant analysis; cluster analysis; and factor analysis, including cross-validation.

Thurstone, Louis Leon. THE MEASUREMENT OF VALUES. Chicago: University of Chicago Press, 1959. viii, 322 p. No index.

> Twenty-seven contributions by the author, a few heretofore unpublished, on the general topic of learning, test theory, factor analysis, psychophysics, and applications in the behavioral sciences. Useful as a supplement to courses in basic statistics in psychology.

______. MULTIPLE-FACTOR ANALYSIS: A DEVELOPMENT AND EXPANSION OF THE VECTORS OF MIND. Chicago: University of Chicago Press, 1947. xix, 535 p. Index, pp. 517-35.

A summary of the work done at the Psychometric Laboratory at the University of Chicago during the past decade. Topics include the factor problem; geometrical models, including the factorial structure; spherical models; the centroid method of factoring; configuration and factor analysis; rotation of axis; the method of extended vectors; the special case of unit work; the unknown communalities; oblique structure; factorial invariance; second-order factors; the effects of selection; and the principal axes. Assumes knowledge of matrix algebra and basic statistics.

______. THE VECTORS OF MIND. University of Chicago Science Series. Chicago: University of Chicago Press, 1935. xv, 266 p. Appendix I: Outline of Calculations for the Centroid Method with Unknown Diagonals, pp. 232-50. Appendix II: A Method of Finding the Roots of a Polynomial, pp. 251-52. Appendix III: A Method of Determining the Square Root on the Calculating Machine, p. 253. Index, pp. 255-66.

Presents the factor problem in psychology based on the assumption that a test score can be expressed as a linear function of a number of factors. Topics include the fundamental factor theorem, the centroid method, the principle axes primary traits, isolation of primary factors, the positive manifold, orthogonal transformation; and the appraisal of abilities. Assumes knowledge of analytic geometry and calculus.

Thurstone, Louis Leon, and Chave, E.J. THE MEASUREMENT OF ATTITUDE: A PSYCHOLOGICAL METHOD AND SOME EXPERIMENTS WITH A SCALE FOR MEASURING ATTITUDE TOWARD THE CHURCH. Chicago: University of Chicago Press, 1929. xii, 97 p. Index, p. 97.

A monograph which outlines and tests experiments for measuring attitudes toward the church using the method of equal-appearing intervals. Based on 130 statements about the church by 300 persons.

Timm, Neil H. MULTIVARIATE ANALYSIS WITH APPLICATIONS IN EDUCATION AND PSYCHOLOGY. Brooks/Cole Series in Statistics. Monterey, Calif.: Brooks/Cole, 1975. xi, 689 p. References, pp. 571-82. Tables, pp. 583-666. Partial Solutions to Selected Exercises, pp. 667-85. Index, pp. 687-89.

A text for a two- or three-semester course in multivariate analysis for students who have been exposed to univariate analysis of variance and regression analysis, and a reference for researchers. Consists of six chapters: "Fundamentals of Vector and Matrix Algebra"; "Multivariate Sampling Theory"; "One- and Two-Sample Tests on Means and the General Linear

Model"; "Multivariate Regression and Canonical Correlation Analysis"; "Multivariate Analysis of Variance and Covariance Analysis"; and "Principal-Component Analysis." Computations require a standard computer program. Models presented in matrix algebra form. Topics include growth-curve analysis; extended linear model; analysis of heterogeneous data; partial and bi-partial canonical correlation analysis; the Behren-Fisher problem; and analysis of nonorthogonal designs. Assumes knowledge of calculus. Sections conclude with exercises.

Torgerson, Warren S. THEORY AND METHODS OF SCALING. Foreword by Harold Gulliksen. New York: Wiley, 1960. xiii, 460 p. Appendix: Tables, pp. 426-28. Bibliography, pp. 429-51. Index, pp. 453-60.

A monograph on the procedures for constructing scales for the measurement of psychological attributes for readers who have taken differential and integral calculus, basic statistics, including regression, and matrix algebra. Includes the following methods: scaling, subjective estimates; fractionation, equisection, and differential sensitivity. Topics include Thurstone's judgement scaling model, law of comparative judgement, law of categorical data, multidimensional scaling, deterministic and probabilistic models for categorical data, and models for comparative response data.

Tou, Julius T., and Gonzales, Rafael C. PATTERN RECOGNITION PRINCIPLES. Applied Mathematics and Computation, no. 7. Reading, Mass.: Addison-Wesley, 1974. xxii, 377 p. Notation, pp. xix-xxii. Bibliography, pp. 363-71. Index, pp. 372-77.

A text for a course in pattern recognition and a reference for engineers, scientists, and students involved in data analysis and information processing who have knowledge of computer programming, statistics, matrix theory, and mathematical analysis. Emphasizes development of results from basic concepts, with numerous examples. Topics include linear and generalized decision functions; multivariate functions; orthogonal systems of functions; pattern classification by distance functions; pattern classification by likelihood functions; the deterministic and statistical approaches to trainable pattern classifiers; pattern preprocessing and feature selection; and syntactic pattern recognition. Chapters conclude with references and problems.

Tracy, Derrick S., ed. SYMMETRIC FUNCTIONS IN STATISTICS. Windsor, Canada: University of Windsor, 1971. 224 p. No index.

Twelve papers presented at a symposium on symmetric functions in statistics held at the University of Windsor, Canada, on March 13, 1971. Symposium dedicated to Professor Paul S. Dwyer on the occasion of his retirement from the university.

Topics include cumulant component analysis; bias of the estimate of correlation for a finite universe; ordered partitions and unbiased estimates of central moments; symmetry in nonparametric statistics; classes of optimal incomplete designs of analysis of variance settings; and a test for uniformity of a circular distribution based on a density estimator.

Tryon, Robert C. IDENTIFICATION OF SOCIAL AREAS BY CLUSTER ANALYSIS: A GENERAL METHOD WITH AN APPLICATION TO THE SAN FRANCISCO BAY AREA. University of California Publications in Psychology, vol. 8, no. 1. Berkeley: University of California Press, 1955. viii, 99 p. Appendix A: Definitions of the 33 Demographic Variables, pp. 85-86. Appendix B: Finding Variables with Congruent Correlation Profiles, pp. 87-88. Appendix C: Tests of Fit of the General Variations Described by the Cluster, pp. 89-92. Appendix D: Dimension Analysis by the Key Cluster Method, pp. 93-97. Bibliography, pp. 98-99. No index.

A monograph on a method of cluster analysis for isolated subcultural groups in the San Francisco Bay area in 1940. Includes 33 demographic and economic characteristics for 243 census tracts of people. Cluster analysis of these 243 census tracts reveal eight relatively homogeneous social areas. Assumes knowledge of basic statistics.

Tryon, Robert C., and Bailey, Daniel E. CLUSTER ANALYSIS. Foreword by Charles Wrigley. New York: McGraw-Hill, 1970. xviii, 347 p. References, pp. 339-41. Index, pp. 343-47.

A text for both undergraduates and graduate courses and a guide for researchers. Consists of a theoretical and applied description of cluster analysis as conceived by the late Robert C. Tryon over the span of more than thirty years with emphasis on logic and application, rather than on mathematics. Includes a computer program in FORTRAN designed to perform basic computations in cluster analysis. Topics include generality of individual differences; conceptually defined groupings of variables vs. empirical clusters; communalities of the variables; key-cluster factoring; cluster structure of demographic characteristics and voting attitudes; domain-sampling theory of structures; the cluster correlation matrix; object cluster analysis; comparative cluster analysis of variables, individuals and groups; unrestricted cluster and factor analyses; and user's manual of the BC TRY computer system.

Uhr, Leonard. PATTERN RECOGNITION, LEARNING, AND THOUGHT: COMPUTER-PROGRAMMED MODELS OF HIGHER MENTAL PROCESSES. Englewood Cliffs, N.J.: Prentice-Hall, 1973. xxi, 506 p. Appendix: Easey-1: An English-Like Program Language, pp. 446-56. Bibliography, pp. 457-82. Glossary, pp. 483-88. Index, pp. 489-506.

Presents and examines structured learning systems by means of computer programs. Compares a variety of programs for recognizing patterns such as letters of the alphabet, spoken speech, simple line drawings of objects, proving theorems, playing games, and solving problems. Topics include perceptual learning; template recognition; dissection of patterns into their primitive pieces; recognition of configurations over variations; networks for the assessment of contours and curves; flexible, hierarchical pattern recognizers; scene analysis; ill-formed problems, creativity, and conversation; generation of new characterizers; question asking; learning to generate better operators; and explicit learning. Assumes knowledge of FORTRAN.

Ullmann, Julian Richard. PATTERN RECOGNITION TECHNIQUES. New York: Crane, Russak, 1973. x, 412 p. References, pp. 374-403. Index, pp. 405-12.

An informal introduction to the techniques of automatic pattern recognition for engineers, computer scientists, and biologists who have no specialist knowledge of the subject. Uses elementary concepts from statistics, switching theory, Fourier theory, graph theory, linguistics, and optics. Topics include mask matching, preprocessing for character recognition; linear and piecewise linear techniques; method of potentials; polynomial discriminant and n-tuple methods; Boolean and sequential decision making; features; contextual, linguistic, and array techniques; coefficient analysis; and learning.

Vajda, Steven. THE MATHEMATICS OF EXPERIMENTAL DESIGN, INCOMPLETE BLOCK DESIGNS, AND LATIN SQUARES. Griffin's Statistical Monographs and Courses, no. 23. New York: Hafner, 1967. viii, 110 p. Solutions to Exercises, pp. 91-99. Bibliography, pp. 100-108. Index, pp. 109-10.

Presents the mathematical description and construction of experimental designs developed for agriculture and other statistical experiments. Excludes practical applications. Topics include balanced incomplete block designs; Latin squares and orthogonal arrays; partially balanced incomplete block designs; and partially balanced incomplete block designs with two associate classes. Includes exercises. Assumes knowledge of linear and abstract and mathematical statistics.

Watanabe, Satosi, ed. FRONTIERS OF PATTERN RECOGNITION. New York: Academic Press, 1972. xi, 602 p. Author Index, pp. 591-96. Subject Index, pp. 597-602.

Twenty-nine papers in English presented at the international conference on frontiers of pattern recognition held at the University of Hawaii, Honolulu, January 18-20, 1971, and attended by participants from eleven countries. Topics include techniques for recognizing patterns in pictures; a survey of results in grammatical inference; boundary detection of radiographic image by a threshold method; syntactic pattern recognition and stochastic languages; computer identification of bacteria by colony morphology; experiments with an on-line picture language; a basic study on human face recognition; cluster analysis; on the computation of shape; pattern recognition and group theory; bounds on the complexity of grammars; learning algorithms of pattern recognition in nonstationary conditions; and least-mean-square approach to pattern classification. Most papers assume knowledge of mathematical statistics and advanced mathematics.

______. METHODOLOGIES OF PATTERN RECOGNITION. New York: Academic Press, 1969. xi, 578 p. Name Index, pp. 559-67. Subject Index, pp. 569-78.

Twenty-nine papers presented at an international conference on methodologies of pattern recognition co-sponsored by the University of Hawaii and the Air Force Office of Scientific Research and held in Honolulu January 24-26, 1968. Emphasizes the role of philosophy in pattern recognition, rather than mathematical derivations and experimental data. Topics include implications of interactive graphic computers for pattern recognition; statistical analysis as a tool for making patterns from data; nonsupervised learning in statistical pattern recognition; parallel computations in pattern recognition; automatic classification of fingerprints; network properties for pattern recognition; goal-directed pattern recognition; evaluation of the statistical classifier; adaptive system of pattern recognition; pattern recognition as an inductive process; and invariant recognition of geometric shapes.

Winer, B.J. STATISTICAL PRINCIPLES IN EXPERIMENTAL DESIGN. 2d ed. New York: McGraw-Hill, 1971. xv, 907 p. Appendix A: Random Variables, pp. 813-47. Appendix B: Topics Closely Related to the Analysis of Variance, pp. 848-59. Appendix C: Tables, pp. 860-87. Content References, pp. 888-92. References to Experiments, pp. 893-95. Index, pp. 897-907.

A text and a comprehensive reference source on statistical principles underlying experimental design with emphasis on those designs likely to prove useful in research in the behavioral and social sciences. Assumes knowledge of statistical inference and college algebra. Emphasizes the logic and principles underlying concepts rather than mathematical details and proofs. Includes one entire chapter devoted to illustrative examples and computational procedures of factorial experiments. Other topics include linear models; multifactor experiments having repeated measures on the same element; factorial experiments in which some of the interactions are confounded; Latin square and related measures; and analysis of covariance. Most illustrative material taken from agriculture.

Yates, Frank. EXPERIMENTAL DESIGN: SELECTED PAPERS. Foreword by Wm. G. Cochran, D.J. Finney, and M.J.R. Healy. London: Griffin, 1970. xi, 296 p. Bibliography, pp. 287-93. Index, pp. 295-96.

Twelve reprints of articles on experimental design published by the author during the period 1933-1966 in various journals, including the JOURNAL OF AGRICULTURAL SCIENCE. Topics include the formation of Latin squares for use in field experiments; analysis of groups of experiments; incomplete randomized blocks; the recovery of inter-block information in balanced incomplete block designs; and principles governing the amount of experimentation in development work.

Young, Tzay Y., and Calvert, Thomas W. CLASSIFICATION, ESTIMATION AND PATTERN RECOGNITION. New York: Elsevier, 1974. xiv, 366 p. References, pp. 351-54. Author Index, pp. 355-59. Subject Index, pp. 361-66.

A text for a one-year course in pattern recognition based on knowledge of matrix algebra and mathematical probability and statistics. First six chapters include material normally considered as pattern recognition theory with emphasis on the statistical approach and with some nonstatistical approaches such as perception. Remaining two chapters deal with applications: one on the computer processing of electrocardiograms and the other on image analysis and character recognition. Topics include classification of Gaussian patterns; sequential classification; parameter estimation; Cramér-Rao inequality; machine learning; linear discriminant functions and clustering; stochastic approximation; and feature extraction theory. Chapters conclude with problems and references.

Chapter 9
ENGINEERING

Action, Forman S. ANALYSIS OF STRAIGHT-LINE DATA. New York: Dover, 1959. xiii, 267 p. References, pp. 232-33. Additional Bibliography, pp. 234-39. Appendix, pp. 240-61. Index, pp. 263-67.

> A reference for engineers and physical scientists on the analysis of straight-line data using primarily least squares and analysis of variance. Other topics include curve fitting by polynomials, the rejection of unwanted data, and use of transformations. Each subject introduced with data from a real world experiment.

Baird, David Carr. EXPERIMENTATION: AN INTRODUCTION TO MEASUREMENT THEORY AND EXPERIMENTAL DESIGN. Englewood Cliffs, N.J.: Prentice-Hall, 1962. x, 198 p. Appendix 1: The Statistics of the Gaussian or Normal Distribution, pp. 177-85. Appendix 2: Least Squares Fit to Straight Lines, pp. 186-88. Bibliography, pp. 189-91. Problem Solutions, pp. 192-95. Index, pp. 196-98.

> A text and reference on the analysis of measurements obtained from laboratory experiments for use by scientists and engineers with emphasis on error calculation and analysis. Mathematical derivations kept to a minimum. Topics include nature of measurements; uncertainties; standard deviations; experiment planning and evaluation; and the scientific report. Chapters conclude with problems.

Bartee, Edwin M. STATISTICAL METHODS IN ENGINEERING EXPERIMENTS. Columbus, Ohio: Charles E. Merrill, 1966. xviii, 206 p. Appendixes, pp. 161-98. Bibliography, pp. 200-201. Index, pp. 202-6.

> A text for introductory statistics for engineering students who have knowledge of calculus. Includes probability, distributions, and sampling; simple and multiple regression; interpretation of probability, means, and variances; and estimation and hypothesis testing. Concludes with a chapter on analysis of variance. Appendixes include combinatorial analysis, joint continuous frequency functions, data sets for exercises, FORTRAN programs, and tables. Chapters conclude with exercises.

Beck, James V., and Arnold, Kenneth J. PARAMETER ESTIMATION IN ENGINEERING AND SCIENCES. New York: Wiley, 1977. xix, 501 p. Appendix A: Identifiability Condition, pp. 481-87. Appendix B: Estimators and Covariance for Various Estimation Methods for the Linear Model $\eta = XB$, pp. 488-89. Appendix C: List of Symbols, pp. 490-92. Appendix D: Some Estimation Programs, pp. 493-94. Index, pp. 495-501.

> A text for an undergraduate or graduate course in statistics for engineering students who have already had a course in basic statistics. Includes detailed treatment of the assumptions in estimation. Topics include a survey of parameter estimation; probability; random variables and their distributions; expectation; law of large numbers; central limit theorem; point estimation; maximum likelihood estimators; confidence limits; least squares; Gauss-Markov and Monte Carlo methods of estimation; linear multiple regression using matrix algebra; maximum a posteriori (map) estimation; analysis of variance about the sample mean and about the regression line; minimization of sums of squares in nonlinear models; and design of optimal experiments. Chapters conclude with references.

Bellman, Richard Ernest, ed. STOCHASTIC PROCESSES IN MATHEMATICAL PHYSICS AND ENGINEERING. Proceedings of Symposia in Applied Mathematics, vol. XVI. Providence, R.I.: American Mathematical Society, 1964. 318 p. Author Index, pp. 303-6. Subject Index, pp. 307-18.

> Fifteen papers presented at a symposium in applied mathematics in New York in 1963 with emphasis on the descriptive and decision aspects of stochastic processes. Topics include the use of ordinary and partial differential equations in models of wave propagation and scattering theory; Reynolds operators; stochastic transformations and functional equations; random walks on lattices; statistical spectral analysis; stability in single detection problems; construction of a class of stationary Markov processes; Markovian processes; Markovian sequential decision processes; and application of truncated hierarchy techniques.

Benjamin, Jack R., and Cornell, C. Allen. PROBABILITY, STATISTICS, AND DECISION FOR CIVIL ENGINEERS. New York: McGraw-Hill, 1970. xiv, 684 p. Appendix A: Tables, pp. 653-69. Appendix B: Derivation of the Asymptotic Extreme-Value Distribution, pp. 670-72. Name Index, pp. 673-75. Subject Index, pp. 677-84.

> A text for basic statistics for students of civil engineering and a reference for practitioners and researchers. Emphasizes concepts and illustrations with problems taken solely from civil engineering. Topics include probability, random variables, moments of random variables; discrete and continuous univariate and multivariate probability models; hypothesis testing; and Bayesian decision theory. Each of the six chapters concludes

with references and problems. Assumes knowledge of differential and integral calculus.

Bethea, Robert M.; Duran, Benjamin S.; and Boullion, Thomas L. STATISTICAL METHODS FOR ENGINEERS AND SCIENTISTS. Statistics: Textbooks and Monographs, vol. 15. New York: Marcel Dekker, 1975. xxi, 583 p. Appendix A: Matrix Algebra, pp. 482-89. Appendix B: Answers to Selected Problems, pp. 490-502. Appendix C: Tables of Statistical Functions, pp. 503-57. Subject Index, pp. 559-83.

A text for a one-year course in introductory statistics for undergraduates in engineering and the physical sciences. Examples oriented toward chemical engineering and chemistry. Topics include probability; theoretical distributions; descriptive statistics; expected values and moments; inference and hypothesis testing concerning means, proportions, variances, and differences between two proportions and two variances; analysis of variance; simple and multiple regression and correlation; orthogonal polynomials in polynomial regression; and experimental design, including Latin squares and factorial designs. Chapters conclude with problems.

Blackman, Ralph Beebe. LINEAR DATA-SMOOTHING AND PREDICTION IN THEORY AND PRACTICE. Foreword by S. Darling. Addison-Wesley Series in Electrical Engineering. Reading, Mass.: Addison-Wesley, 1965. xiii, 182 p. References, pp. 165-70. Some Additional Literature, p. 168. Appendix, pp. 171-78. Index, pp. 179-82.

Based on the author's twenty-four years of participation in projects which involved data-smoothing and prediction and on lectures at the Flight Simulation Laboratory of the White Sands Proving Ground, New Mexico. Emphasizes practical techniques, and topics include polynomial methods; discrete and continuous optimization schemes; discrete weighing sequences optimized for bandlimited white noise; discrete smoothing by cascaded simple averagings; variable smoothing schemes; and measurement of power spectra. Includes a chapter on practical analog approximations and their realization with RC networks and high-gain amplifiers. Derivations extensive with results illustrated with simple numerical examples and graphs. Assumes knowledge of advanced calculus and mathematical statistics. Appendixes include Laning and Battin method for solving ordinary linear differential equations, network configurations, noise power integrals, and algebraic power sums.

Blanchard, Benjamin S. LOGISTICS ENGINEERING AND MANAGEMENT. Foreword by Carl L. Henn. Prentice-Hall International Series in Industrial and Systems Engineering. Englewood Cliffs, N.J.: Prentice-Hall, 1974. xvi, 399 p. Appendix A: Cost Analysis Data, pp. 316-43. Appendix B: Maintenance Analysis Data, pp. 344-67. Appendix C: Logistic Support Models, pp. 368-75. Appendix D: System Design Review Checklist, pp. 376-89. Appendix E: Normal Distribution Tables, pp. 390-93. Index, pp. 395-99.

A text for a course in logistics for graduates and undergraduates and a reference for practicing engineers. Topics include cost effectiveness; system effectiveness; reliability and maintainability; applications of statistical techniques in logistics; the system and equipment life-cycle; and total management overview. Assumes knowledge of basic statistics.

Bogdanoff, John L., and Kozin, Frank, eds. PROCEEDINGS OF THE FIRST SYMPOSIUM ON ENGINEERING APPLICATIONS OF RANDOM FUNCTION THEORY AND PROBABILITY. New York: Wiley, 1963. x, 421 p. No index.

Ten papers presented at a symposium on engineering applications of random function theory and probability held at Purdue University in 1960. Papers include latest contributions in stochastic analysis and stochastic models which have application in engineering. Topics include application of random functions to noise in radio receivers; information theory; aerodynamic noise; traffic on an open road; Wiener filtering theory; and random process in communication engineering.

Bolotin, Vladimir Vasil'evich. STATISTICAL METHODS IN STRUCTURAL MECHANICS. Translated by S. Aroni. Holden-Day Series in Mathematical Physics. San Francisco: Holden-Day, 1969. xix, 240 p. Bibliography, pp. 223-34. Author Index, pp. 235-37. Subject Index, pp. 238-40.

Originally published in Russian in 1967, a monograph on the application of probability and mathematical statistics to structural mechanics and strength. Proofs of theorems omitted or only suggested by hints. Topics include review of probability and mathematical statistics; the reliability of structures and the statistical nature of the safety factor; statistical theories of brittle and fatigue fracture; stability of structures in the presence of random disturbances; vibrations of elastic systems subjected to random forces; damage accumulation in structures under random loadings; and statistical theory of seismic stability of structures.

Bowker, Albert H., and Lieberman, Gerald L. ENGINEERING STATISTICS. 2d ed., rev. Englewood Cliffs, N.J.: Prentice-Hall, 1972. xviii, 641 p. Appendix: Tables, pp. 600-617. Answers to Selected Problems, pp. 618-22. Index, pp. 623-41.

A text for a one-semester course in basic statistics for students in engineering and the physical sciences who have knowledge of calculus. Presents statistics as a science rather than an art, with each technique illustrated by fully worked examples. Topics include descriptive statistics; random variables and their distributions; decision theory, including posterior analysis; tests of hypothesis about a single parameter, including operating characteristic curves; tests of hypothesis about two parameters; nonparametric tests; interval estimation; simple regression; two-way analysis of variance with n observations per cell; statistical quality control; sampling inspection by attributes; and lot-by-lot sampling inspection by variables.

Brewer, John Michael; Pesce, A.J.; and Ashworth, R.B. EXPERIMENTAL TECHNIQUES IN BIOCHEMISTRY. Prentice-Hall Foundations of Modern Chemistry Series. Englewood Cliffs, N.J.: Prentice-Hall, 1974. x, 374 p. Appendixes, pp. 313-66. Index, pp. 367-74.

A reference for a graduate student techniques laboratory course in biochemistry. Describes techniques in more detail than that found in most laboratory manuals. Topics include statistical analysis of Gaussian measurements and description and analysis of the following procedures: immunochemistry, electrophoresis, ultracentrifugation, absorption and flourescence, and radioactivity and counting. Descriptions mainly verbal with equations used for concise summaries. Chapters conclude with references and the appendixes contain statistical tables, chemical formulas and procedures, properties of various chemicals, and computer programs for statistical and chemical analysis.

Bridgeman, Percy Williams. DIMENSIONAL ANALYSIS. New Haven, Conn.: Yale University Press, 1931. vi, 113 p. Problems, pp. 107-9. Appendix, pp. 110-11. Index, pp. 112-13.

An exposition of the principles underlying the method of dimensional analysis with many examples chosen to emphasize points most commonly misunderstood such as the nature of dimensional formulas, the proper number of fundamental units, and the nature of dimensional constants. Provides certain information about the relations which hold between measurable quantities associated with various phenomena. Topics include dimensional formulas, use of dimensional formulas in changing units, dimensional constants and the number of fundamental units, and application of dimensional analysis to engineering and physics. Chapters conclude with references.

Brownlee, K.A. STATISTICAL THEORY AND METHODOLOGY IN SCIENCE AND ENGINEERING. 2d ed., rev. Wiley Series in Probability and Mathematical Statistics. New York: Wiley, 1965. xvi, 590 p. Appendix, pp. 558-78. Partial Answers to Selected Exercises, pp. 579-84. Index, pp. 585-90.

A text for a one-year course in statistical methods for students in engineering who have had at least one year of calculus. Topics include statistical inference; probability; distributions;

chi-square and contingency tables; queueing theory; tests of randomness; statistical control charts; nonparametric tests; analysis of variance; simple and multiple regression--partially hierarchical situations; and experimental design. Presentation rigorous mathematically although proofs of theorems omitted with most of the applications given in the problems at the ends of the chapters. Chapters also conclude with references. The appendix contains statistical tables.

Burrows, Walter Herbert. GRAPHICAL TECHNIQUES FOR ENGINEERING COMPUTATIONS. New York: Chemical Rubber Co., 1965. xiii, 435 p. Appendix: Tables, pp. 419-32. Index, pp. 433-35.

A reference on graphical methods in the field of computation with applications to a broad spectrum of scientific and engineering formulas. Topics include scales, graph paper, calculating with scales and graph paper, graphs, nomography and their construction, hyperbolic coordinates; three-dimensional nomographs, and nomographs from graphs and tables.

Chapanis, Alphonse Robert Everysta. RESEARCH TECHNIQUES IN HUMAN ENGINEERING. Baltimore: Johns Hopkins University Press, 1959. xii, 316 p. Bibliography, pp. 303-9. Index, pp. 311-16.

A reference on applied human engineering with emphasis on the principles of human experimentation useful in the study of men and machines. Includes numerous examples of both good and bad studies. Topics include method of direct observation; including sampling and micromotion techniques; methods for the study of accidents and near accidents; statistical methods used in analyzing data; design of experiments; special problems in experimenting with people; psychophysical methods; and articulation test methods. Practical examples taken from radar, aircraft, and earplugs.

Chatfield, Christopher. STATISTICS FOR TECHNOLOGY. Baltimore: Penguin Books, 1970. 359 p. Appendix A: The Relationship Between the Normal, Chi-Square, t- and F- Distributions, pp. 332-34. Appendix B: Statistical Tables, pp. 335-45. Further Reading, pp. 346-48. Answers to Exercises, pp. 349-52. Author Index, p. 353. Subject Index, pp. 355-59.

A text for a one-semester course in basic statistics for students of engineering and applied science who have knowledge of calculus and the ability to manipulate algebraic formulas. Consists of the following three parts: "Introduction"; "Theory"; and "Applications." Examples make up a large portion of the text. Topics include probability; discrete and continuous probability distributions; random variables and expectation; point estimators and their properties; hypothesis testing concerning two means; chi-square; nonparametric tests; simple and multiple regression and correlation; two-way analysis of variance; factorial experiments; quality control; life testing and failure rates; Latin squares; and balanced incomplete block designs. Chapters conclude with references and exercises.

Chayes, Felix. RATIO CORRELATION: A MANUAL FOR STUDENTS OF PETROLOGY AND GEOCHEMISTRY. Chicago: University of Chicago Press, 1971. viii, 99 p. References, pp. 97-99. No index.

A supplementary text for a course in correlation analysis for students of petrology and geochemistry (and a self-study) who have knowledge of basic statistics and matrix algebra, and a good background in petrography. Topics include simple ratio correlations; part-whole and common-element correlations; correlations between proportions; testing the significance of an observed correlation between proportions; the effect of ratio formation on regression; the remaining-space transformation; and Harker and related variation diagrams. Sections conclude with exercises.

Davies, Owen L., and Goldsmith, Peter L., eds. STATISTICAL METHODS IN RESEARCH AND PRODUCTION: WITH SPECIAL REFERENCE TO THE CHEMICAL INDUSTRY. 4th ed., rev. New York: Hafner, for Imperial Chemical Industries Limited, 1972. xiii, 478 p. Statistical and Mathematical Symbols, pp. 423-30. Tables and Charts of Statistical Functions, pp. 431-71. Index, pp. 473-78.

A problem-oriented text for a course in basic statistics for students of physics, chemistry, and engineering who have knowledge of calculus, and a supplementary text for courses in mathematical statistics. Contributors include eight research workers for Imperial Chemical Industries, with examples representing real problems met in practice. Topics include descriptive statistics; inference and hypothesis testing concerning means and comparison of two means; analysis of variance; simple and multiple regression and correlation; chi-square and contingency tables; control charts; sampling; and simulation. Considerable verbal discussion follows the derivations.

Derman, Cyrus, and Klein, Morton. PROBABILITY AND STATISTICAL INFERENCE FOR ENGINEERS: A FIRST COURSE. New York: Oxford University Press, 1959. xii, 144 p. No index.

An early text for a one-semester course in probability theory and statistical inference for engineering students who have had differential and integral calculus. Emphasizes brief derivations and applications. Topics include sample spaces; random variables; probability distributions and their moments; joint distributions; conditional probability and independence; independent random variables; law of large numbers; central limit theorem; decisions with known and unknown distributions; decision rules; principles of choice; tests of hypotheses; and confidence interval estimation.

Douglas, John F. AN INTRODUCTION TO DIMENSIONAL ANALYSIS FOR ENGINEERS. London: Pitman and Sons, 1969. viii, 134 p. Appendix 1: Dimensions of Mechanical Quantities, p. 114. Appendix 2: Dimensionless Parameters, pp. 115-29. Appendix 3: Interconversion of British and SI Units, pp. 130-32. Index, pp. 133-34.

A simple guide to engineering applications of dimensional analysis with illustrations from all branches of mechanics, thermodynamics, and electrical engineering. Considers both dimensions (measurable properties) and units (terms in which properties can be measured). Topics include application of dimensional reasoning; construction of relationships by dimensional analysis; dimensional analysis by the group method; dimensionless groups; and application to scale model testing. Knowledge of calculus assumed.

Duckworth, Walter Eric. STATISTICAL TECHNIQUES IN TECHNOLOGICAL RESEARCH: AN AID TO RESEARCH PRODUCTIVITY. London: Methuen, 1968. xv, 303 p. Answers to Exercises, pp. 241-97. Index, pp. 300-303.

Deals with the use of statistical techniques in cost control and productivity improvement for industrial scientists and research managers with minimal mathematics background. Topics include a review of descriptive statistics; classical tests of significance; factorial design of experiments and the analysis of variance; fractional factorial experiments; analysis of Latin squares; balanced incomplete blocks; chi-square; tests based on rank; and statistical quality control. Derivations kept to a minimum with examples taken from production and control and consist of such problems as tests concerned with tensile strength of steel and with the number of defective items in a lot. Statistical tables dispersed throughout the book. Chapters conclude with references and exercises.

Eadie, W.T.; Dryard, D.; James, F.E.; Ross, M.; and Sadoulet, B. STATISTICAL METHODS IN EXPERIMENTAL PHYSICS. Amsterdam: North-Holland, 1971. xii, 296 p. Bibliography, pp. 288-91. Subject Index, pp. 292-96.

A reference on statistical methods in physics with many results stated without proof. Also useful as a text on statistical methods for students of physics. Provides few numerical examples. Topics include probability and random variables; characteristic functions; laws of large numbers; discrete and continuous probability distributions; real life distributions; information; sufficient statistics; decision theory; point estimation; maximum likelihood; least squares; nonparametric statistics; likelihood function; interval estimation and tests of hypotheses; and chi-square.

Eckschlager, Karel. ERRORS, MEASUREMENT AND RESULTS IN CHEMICAL ANALYSIS. Translated by Ota Sofr. Translation edited by R.A. Chalmers.

Van Nostrand Series in Analytical Chemistry. New York: Van Nostrand, 1969. 155 p. Literature, pp. 149-51. Index, pp. 153-55.

Originally published in Czechoslovakia in 1961. Presents the theory and application of measurement errors in chemical processes for the purpose of evaluating the reliability of analytical results. Presentation based on the methods of mathematical statistics, and includes such topics as a survey of errors of chemical analysis; measurements used in chemical analysis; specific errors, including emission spectrography; photometric determination; flame photometry and atomic absorption photometry, electroanalytical determinations, polarographic analysis, and extraction methods; application of mathematical statistics, including tests of hypotheses, and graphical and numerical methods.

Eisenschitz, R. STATISTICAL THEORY OF IRREVERSIBLE PROCESSES. Oxford Library of the Physical Sciences. New York: Oxford University Press, 1958. viii, 84 p. References and Notes, pp. 80-83. Index, p. 84.

Concerned with the micro-physical interpretation of the properties of matter in bulk using molecular dynamics and probability theory. Topics include classical equilibrium theory; irreversability and Tokker-Planck equation; viscosity and thermal conductivity of liquids; statistical quantum mechanics; Brownian movement; stochastic processes; and probability. Knowledge of engineering mathematics assumed.

Focken, C.M. DIMENSIONAL METHODS AND THEIR APPLICATIONS. Foreword by H. Dingle. London: Edward Arnold, 1953. viii, 224 p. Bibliography, p. 219. Index, pp. 220-24.

A monograph dealing with the critical appraisal of the present state of dimensional analysis. Useful to teachers and students of physics, engineering, and allied subjects. Topics include units and magnitudes; uses of dimensional analysis; formulas and equations, including Buckingham's method; dimensions of various physical magnitudes; and physical and engineering applications of dimensional methods.

Fry, Thornton C. PROBABILITY AND ITS ENGINEERING USES. 2d ed., rev. Bell Telephone Laboratories Series. New York: D. Van Nostrand, 1965. xv, 462 p. Appendixes I to IX: Tables, pp. 413-56. Index of Notation, p. 457. Index, pp. 459-62.

A text for a course in probability. Based on lectures presented at the Bell Telephone Laboratories and later at MIT in its Department of Electrical Engineering. Presentation nonrigorous with calculus used in only a few places. Topics include probability; permutations, combinations, and rules of probability; Bernoulli's theorem and Stirling's formula; Bayes' theorem; derivation of a distribution function for the velocities of gas molecules; averages, including expectation and covariance; St. Petersburg paradox; distribution functions most frequently used in engineering; matrix methods and Markov processes; and probability theory applied to congestion. Sections conclude with problems; chapters, with answers to problems.

Gibra, Isaac N. PROBABILITY AND STATISTICAL INFERENCE FOR SCIENTISTS AND ENGINEERS. Englewood Cliffs, N.J.: Prentice-Hall, 1973. xii, 596 p. Appendix: Tables, pp. 550-84. Answers, pp. 585-91. Index, pp. 592-96.

A text for a one-year course in probability and statistics (or a one-semester course in each topic) for engineering students who possess knowledge of algebra and calculus. Less mathematical than most engineering statistics texts. Contains detailed solutions to numerous examples of varying difficulty. Topics include probability and random variables; expectation; moment-generating functions; approximately twenty common distribution functions; order statistics; significance tests; hypothesis tests for single and two parameters; nonparametric tests; analysis of variance; regression and correlation; chi-square; statistical quality control; acceptance sampling; and queueing theory. Chapters conclude with problems and references.

Gould, Leonard A. CHEMICAL PROCESS CONTROL: THEORY AND APPLICATIONS. Reading, Mass.: Addison-Wesley, 1969. xiii, 370 p. Appendix A: Roots of a Transcendental Equation, pp. 335-42. Appendix B: Short Table of Integrals, pp. 343-44. Appendix C: Static Characteristics for Flow Control, pp. 345-49. Bibliography, pp. 351-64. Index, pp. 365-70.

A text for a one-semester course in process control for students who have knowledge of control engineering. Attempts to bridge the gap between theory and application with emphasis on the physical process and the art of engineering approximation. Topics include partial differential equation models of flow processes; theory of flow regulation; applications in flow, pressure, liquid levels, heat transfer, and mass transfer; modal analysis of distributed systems; and design and performance of chemical reactors. Useful to individuals of diverse backgrounds, including students of industrial management. Chapters conclude with problems.

Grant, Eugene L.; Ireson, W. Grant; and Leavenworth, Richard S. PRINCIPLES OF ENGINEERING ECONOMY. 6th ed. New York: Ronald, 1976. vi, 624 p. Appendix A: Continuous Compounding of Interest and the Uniform Flow Convention, pp. 531-41. Appendix B: The Analysis of Prospective Cash Flow Series That Have Two or More Reversals of Sign, pp. 543-62. Appendix C: The Reinvestment Fallacy in Project Evaluation, pp. 563-71. Appendix D: Compound Interest Tables, pp. 573-611. Appendix E: Selected References, pp. 613-17. Index, pp. 619-24.

A text for a course in engineering economy for engineering students as well as students in economics, finance, and management, and a reference for engineers, management personnel, government officials, and others. Consists of three parts: "Some Basic Concepts in Engineering Economy"; "Judging the Attractiveness of Proposed Investments"; and "Techniques for Economy Studies." Topics include interest formulas; equivalent uniform cash flow; benefit-cost ratio; depreciation; sensitivity analysis in economy studies; probability and expected value; replacement; income tax consequences of investment decisions; and multiple alternatives. Chapters conclude with problems. Assumes knowledge of high school algebra.

Gray, Henry L., and Odell, Patrick L. PROBABILITY FOR PRACTICING ENGINEERS. Professional Engineering Career Development Series. New York: Barnes and Noble, 1970. xi, 217 p. References and Selected Readings, pp. 201-2. Appendix: Tables, pp. 203-12. Symbols, pp. 213-14. Index, pp. 215-17.

A reference for practicing engineers which describes how probability can be of value in illustrating physical phenomena. Includes proofs of theorems only when necessary. Important concepts set off as definitions. Topics include discrete and continuous random variables and their distributions; moments of random variables; limit theorems; moment generating functions; laws of large numbers; multivariate and continuous probability distributions; eighteen specific probability distributions with properties; minimum variance estimators; interval estimators; stochastic processes; linear estimation of stochastic processes; and white noise. Knowledge of calculus assumed.

Guest, Philip George. NUMERICAL METHODS OF CURVE FITTING. New York: Cambridge University Press, 1961. xiv, 422 p. Bibliography, pp. 410-17. Index, pp. 418-22.

A reference for students in physics, statisticians, and biologists on methods of treating series of observations with examples from the physical sciences. Consists of the following three parts: "General Theory for a Single Variable"; "Simple Regression Theory"; and "Polynomials and Other Curves." Topics include normal and chi-square distributions; tests of significance; discrete probability distributions; Gauss-Doolittle method for estimating polynomial coefficients; orthogonal polynomials; analysis of variance; functions which are not polynomials; multiple regression and functional relationship problems in several variables. Assumes knowledge of calculus and matrix algebra. Numerical problems designed for a desk calculator. Chapters conclude with notes and references.

Guttman, Irwin; Wilks, S.S.; and Hunter, J. Stuart. INTRODUCTORY ENGINEERING STATISTICS. 2d ed. New York: Wiley, 1971. xix, 549 p. Appendixes, pp. 471-516. Charts, pp. 517-20. References, pp. 521-22. Answers to Selected Problems, pp. 523-42. Index, pp. 543-49.

A text for a one-year course in applied statistics for undergraduate engineering students who have knowledge of calculus. Presentation fairly rigorous with proofs included, and examples set off in small print. Topics include probability and random variables; discrete and continuous distributions; acceptance sampling based on sample means and sample variances; moment generating functions; maximum likelihood estimators; Bayesian approach to estimation of population parameters; hypotheses testing; sequential testing; control charts; chi-square; order statistics; nonparametric tests; regression analysis; and experimental design. The appendixes contain proofs of theorems, derivations, and tables.

Haan, Charles T. STATISTICAL METHODS IN HYDROLOGY. Ames: Iowa State University Press, 1977. xv, 378 p. Appendixes A to E, pp. 313-51. Bibliography, pp. 353-65. Index, pp. 367-78.

A reference on the use of statistical tools in hydrologic problems for hydrologists and engineers who have had no prior knowledge of statistics, although knowledge of calculus and familiarity with matrix algebra is assumed. Topics include basic concepts of probability and random variables; discrete and continuous probability distributions; probability plotting and frequency analysis; confidence intervals and hypothesis testing; simple and multiple regression and correlation; principal component analysis; canonical correlation; analysis of hydrological series; and Markov chain models. Appendixes contain proofs, statistical tables, matrix algebra, and data for use in problem solving.

Hahn, Gerald J., and Shapiro, Samuel S. STATISTICAL MODELS IN ENGINEERING. Wiley Series on Systems Engineering and Analysis. New York: Wiley, 1967. xviii, 355 p. Tables, pp. 309-35. Categorized Bibliography, pp. 337-45. Index, pp. 347-55.

A reference for practicing engineers and a supplementary text for an introductory statistics course for engineers who possess knowledge of undergraduate engineering mathematics. Based on the author's experience consulting with electrical, mechanical, chemical, industrial and reliability engineers in widely divergent product areas in the General Electric Company and other organizations. Shows the engineer responsible for a product who performance is subject to chance fluctuations how to choose a statistical model and how to use the model in the evaluation of practical problems. Models include normal, exponential, gamma, beta, Weibull, log-normal, Gauchy,

Rayleigh, Poisson, multinomial, hypergeometric, Pascal, negative-binomial, and uniform. Empirical distributions include the Johnson and Pearson families of distributions. Chapters conclude with references.

Hájek, Jaroslav, and Dupač, Václav. PROBABILITY IN SCIENCE AND ENGINEERING. Translated by Michal Basch and Jaroslav Hajek. New York: Academic Press, 1967. 120 p. Index, pp. 119-20.

Originally published in Czechoslovak. Takes up selected probability concepts and applications for the layman and secondary school graduates using no higher mathematics. Employs mainly verbal, numerical, and graphical techniques. Topics include events and probability; random variables, expectation, and variance; distribution laws of random variables, including hypergeometric, Poisson, and normal; law of large numbers; information theory; games; estimation and hypothesis testing concerning means and variances; applications in medical research; sample surveys; and Monte Carlo simulation.

Hamilton, Walter Clark. STATISTICS IN PHYSICAL SCIENCE: ESTIMATION, HYPOTHESIS TESTING, AND LEAST SQUARES. New York: Ronald, 1964. xi, 230 p. Appendix: Tables, pp. 205-22. Bibliography, pp. 223-25. Index, pp. 227-30.

A text consisting of a comprehensive treatment of least squares, linear hypothesis testing, and multivariate analysis for use by laboratory scientists in chemistry. Excludes proofs. Topics include probability, random variables, and their moments; statistical estimation and hypothesis testing; estimation of parameters from univariate populations using the normal distribution, t, chi-square, and F statistics; least squares, error distribution of quadratic forms, and general linear hypothesis; nonlinear least squares; optimal experimental design; and applications of least squares. Assumes knowledge of calculus and some linear algebra. Chapters conclude with exercises.

Haviland, Robert P. ENGINEERING RELIABILITY AND LONG LIFE DESIGN. New York: D. Van Nostrand Reinhold, 1964. vii, 205 p. Bibliography, pp. 197-98. Solutions to Problems, p. 199. Index, pp. 201-5.

Presents concepts and techniques essential to the attainment of engineering solutions to reliability problems with emphasis on graphic methods, rather than mathematical methods. Based on probability models and includes such topics as strength, load, and failure in simple objects; failure predictions in an eventful life; strength and life of similar, nonsimilar, and complex objects; safety factor and the risk of failure; and measurement and control of strengths, deterioration, and loads. Assumes knowledge of the rudiments of calculus. Chapters conclude with problems. Useful to individuals with diverse interests and backgrounds.

Hoffman, W.C., ed. STATISTICAL METHODS IN RADIO WAVE PROPAGATION. New York: Pergamon, 1960. xiii, 334 p. No index.

Twenty-three papers presented at a symposium held at the University of California, Los Angeles, June 18-20, 1958, grouped under the following headings: "Statistical Theory and Methodology" (ten papers); "Radio Propagation Phenomenology" (eleven papers); and "Instrumentation for Processing Radio Propagation Data" (two papers). Brings together the two widely separated disciplines of modern statistical theory and propagation of radio waves, Gives only brief treatment to many topics such as the design of experiments and the analysis of variance. Topics include theory of fading phenomena; seaclutter spectra; propagation of random radiation in free space; multidimensional prediction problem; statistical methods in radio wave propagation; auto-correlated fading signals; antenna tolerance theory; transhorizon measurement techniques; application of lognormal distribution to atmospheric studies; diversity statistics in scatter propagation; and statistical analysis equipment for propagation research. Knowledge of stochastic processes and mathematical statistics, as well as radio wave theory, assumed.

Hovanessian, Shahen A. COMPUTATIONAL MATHEMATICS IN ENGINEERING. Boston: Lexington Books, 1976. xvii, 251 p. Answers to Problems, pp. 231-46. Index, pp. 247-51.

A text for graduates and undergraduates in engineering and related fields and a reference for practicing engineers. Includes numerical evaluation of matrices and simultaneous equations; calculation of finite differences; numerical solutions of differential equations; probability theory; least squares methods; Kalman filtering; Fourier series and transforms; linear programming; quadratic programming; nonlinear programming; and computation of characteristics values and vectors. Chapters conclude with references.

Huntley, H.E. DIMENSIONAL ANALYSIS. New York: Dover, 1967. 158 p. Appendix: Tables of Dimensional Formulas, pp. 149-51. Bibliography, p. 153. Index, pp. 155-58.

A monograph on dimensional analysis for undergraduates in physics. Useful as a supplementary text for a short course. Topics include method of dimensions; historical outline; examples; vector lengths; motion of bodies in fluids; and thermal and electrical quantities. Avoids rigorous proofs.

Isaacson, E. de St. Q., and Isaacson, M. de St. Q. DIMENSIONAL METHODS IN ENGINEERING AND PHYSICS: REFERENCE, SETS AND THE POSSIBILITIES OF THEIR EXTENSION. New York: Halsted, 1975. xvi, 220 p. Appendix 1: Dimensions of Physical Quantities, pp. 203-6. Appendix 2: Miscellaneous Problems and Points for Discussion, pp. 207-12. References and Bibliography, pp. 213-15. Index, pp. 217-20.

A reference for students and professional workers in engineering and physics. Results used without proofs, and use of mathematics kept to a minimum. Develops the Buckingham pi-theorem from semi-intuitive appeals to physical principles, with a rigorous treatment contained in the appendix. Topics include units of measurement and physical dimensions; dimensional homogeneity of physical equations; calculation of dimensional products; extensions to the set of reference dimensions; dimensions of thermal, fluid mechanics, and electric and magnetic quantities; reduction of undetermined functions; model laws and similarity; restrictions on the method of dimensional analysis; and application to cosmology.

Jupp, Edmund W. AN INTRODUCTION TO DIMENSIONAL METHOD. London: Cleaver-Hume, 1962. 89 p. Index, pp. 87-89.

A brief monograph on an introduction to dimensional analysis and its application in physics and engineering. Topics include units of measurement; system of units; dimensional homogeneity; similarity; and dimensionless groups. Most examples deal with problems in mechanics, and center around quantities of length, mass, and time. Thermal and electrical quantities introduced whenever appropriate. Strikes a balance between a restricted treatment of the subject and the exhaustive presentation of the specialized literature.

Kennedy, John B., and Neville, Adam M. BASIC STATISTICAL METHODS FOR ENGINEERS AND SCIENTISTS. 2d ed. New York: Dun-Donnelley, 1976. xvi, 490 p. Appendix A: Bessel's Correction, pp. 434-35. Appendix B: Derivation of $Pr = \frac{e^{-\mu}\mu^r}{r!}$ from the Poisson Process, pp. 436-38. Appendix C: Mean and Standard Deviation of Terms of Expansion of $(1/2+1/2)^{2n}$, pp. 439-41. Appendix D: Evaluation of $\int_{-\infty}^{+\infty} e^{-x^2/2}\,dx$ pp. 442-44. Appendix E: Relation Between t and r, pp. 445-46. Appendix F: Proof that the Regression Plane Contains the Centroid Point, pp. 447. Tables, pp. 448-70. Answers to Problems, pp. 471-79. Index, pp. 480-90.

A text for a one- or two-semester course in statistics for engineers and scientists who do not wish a detailed treatment of the underlying mathematical theory. Also suitable for the engineer who wants to teach himself the basic statistical methods, as well as for those dealing with a specific problem requiring statistical treatment. Topics include descriptive statistics; probability and expectation; sampling; binomial distribution; Poisson distribution; normal curve; interval estimation and hypothesis testing; the F test; regression; analysis of variance; distribution of extremes; tolerance and control charts; and design of experiments. Includes illustrative problem in both the text and at the end of each chapter. Chapters also conclude with problems.

Kirkpatrick, Elwood G. INTRODUCTORY STATISTICS AND PROBABILITY FOR ENGINEERING, SCIENCE, AND TECHNOLOGY. Prentice-Hall International Series in Industrial and Systems Engineering. Englewood Cliffs, N.J.: Prentice-Hall, 1974. xiv, 446 p. Appendixes A to I: Tables, pp. 395-435. Index, pp. 439-46.

A text for a course in basic statistics for undergraduates in engineering who have knowledge of calculus. Topics include elementary probability; discrete and continuous random variables and their distributions; characteristics functions; hypothesis testing and estimation; operating characteristic curve; statistical quality control; simple and multiple regression and correlation; analysis of variance; and Latin square designs. Strikes a balance between theory and application. Chapters conclude with references and problems. Emphasizes the combinatorial approach to probability.

Kneafsey, James T. TRANSPORTATION ECONOMIC ANALYSIS. Lexington, Mass.: Lexington Books, 1975. xxvii, 418 p. Appendix A: Glossary of Transportation Terms, pp. 403-10. Index, pp. 411-18.

A text for a graduate course in transportation economics for students of economics, engineering, geography, urban planning, and related disciplines. Consists of the following six parts: "Microeconomic Theory and Transportation"; "The Domestic Transportation Industries"; "The Urban Passenger Sector"; "The Intercity Passenger Sector"; "The Commodity (Freight) Sector"; "Microeconomics and Econometric Applications to Transportation." Topics inclued forecasting methods, including causal methods and time series projections; regulation of transportation; airline, motor trucking, and railroad industries; Amtrak; data sources for the analysis of commodity flows; modeling in commodity transportation; transportation and logistics; estimates of cost functions in railroad transportation; production function analysis; economies of scale in railroads and motor trucking; and a brief introduction to cost-benefit analysis, simulation, and linear programming models of transportation systems. Some chapters conclude with bibliographies.

Lambe, Cyril Gerard. ELEMENTS OF STATISTICS. 2d ed., rev. and enl. London: Longmans, Green & Co., 1968. viii, 138 p. References for Further Reading, p. 126. Tables, pp. 127-32. Answers to Examples, pp. 133-35. Index, pp. 137-38.

A text for a course in basic statistics for engineering students who know calculus. Includes proofs as an aid to the logical development of the subject. Topics include descriptive statistics; permutations, combination, and rules of probability; binomial, Poisson, and normal probability distributions; simple and multiple regression and correlation; the theory of errors; quality control; sampling inspection techniques; significance tests for means and comparison of means; and chi-square. Chapters conclude with references and exercises.

Langhaar, Henry L. DIMENSIONAL ANALYSIS AND THE THEORY OF MODELS. New York: Wiley, 1951. xi, 166 p. Answers to Problems, pp. 157-62. Index, pp. 163-66.

An early systematic and thorough treatment of the principles of dimensional analysis (the general form of equations that describe natural phenomena). Includes rigorous development of the theory of dimensional analysis, with proofs of theorems, and the following applications in engineering: similarity and model testing, problems of stress and strain; fluid mechanics; theory of heat; electromagnetic theory; and differential equations involving rivers and estuaries. Assumes knowledge of algebra, and engineering and physics found in the first three years of an engineering curriculum. Chapters conclude with problems.

Lenard, Andrew, ed. STATISTICAL MECHANICS AND MATHEMATICAL PROBLEMS. Lecture Notes in Physics. New York: Springer-Verlag, 1973. viii, 246 p. No index.

Five papers presented at the Recontres in Mathematics and Statistics held in Seattle during the summer of 1971 under sponsorship of the Battelle Memorial Institute. Topics include entropy and equilibrium states in classical statistical mechanics; the Coulomb stability theorem; the thermodynamic limit for Coulomb systems; and states and automorphisms of operation algebras, standard representations and the Kubo-Martin-Schwinger boundary conditions.

Levins, Alexander Sander. GRAPHICAL METHODS IN RESEARCH. New York: Wiley, 1965. viii, 217 p. Appendixes 1 to 8, pp. 119-213. Index, pp. 215-17.

A reference for researchers and students of engineering in two parts: "Graphical Methods in Research" and "Use of Nomography in Research Projects." Topics include graphical calculus; theory and application of nomography; transformation of cartesian charts to alignment charts; validation of families of experimental data curves for which implicit relations exist, graphical solutions of a nonlinear problem; and employment of the vector polar method in solving propulsion dynamics problems. Examples include problems in the fields of microwave optics, gas dynamics, aircraft runway deflectors, ballistics, radiology, food technology, zoology, stress analysis and hydraulics. Appendixes include tables, material on graphical determination of centroids and moments of inertia of areas, summary of nomographic type forms, and useful nomographs.

Lifson, Melvin W. DECISION AND RISK ANALYSIS FOR PRACTICING ENGINEERS. Barnes and Noble Professional Engineering Career Development Series. Boston: Cahners, 1972. xiii, 274 p. Appendix I: Review of Basic Probability Concepts, pp. 215-60. Appendix II: Measurement, pp. 261-64. Appendix III: Flow of Value in Time, pp. 265-70. Index, pp. 271-74.

A reference for engineers on a decision methodology which adapts decision theory, utility theory, and Bayesian statistics to the needs of system decision makers. Assumes knowledge of elementary calculus and probability. Concludes with a chapter on three applications: planning an environment data collection system; expansion of the New York City water-supply system, and a medical diagnosis treatment problem.

Mack, Cornelius. ESSENTIALS OF STATISTICS FOR SCIENTISTS AND TECHNOLOGISTS. New York: Plenum Press, 1967. vii, 174 p. Appendix, pp. 151-57. Answers, pp. 158-69. Index, pp. 171-74.

A text which presents the essentials of statistics for students with a background in calculus. Some proofs outlined or given in full to illustrate derivations. Emphasizes tests and methods most useful to a scientist or technologist. Topics include random variables and probability distributions; estimation and hypothesis testing; chi-square; least squares regression and correlation; nonparametric tests; sampling techniques; and quality control. Concludes with a chapter on applications. The appendix contains statistical tables.

Mackie, Raymond Keith; Shepherd, T.M.; and Vincent, C.A. MATHEMATICAL METHODS FOR CHEMISTS. New York: Wiley, 1972. v, 154 p. Appendix A: Basic Equations, pp. 119-24. Appendix B: Derivatives, p. 125. Appendix C: Standard Integrals, pp. 126-27. Appendix D: Laplace Transforms, p. 128. Appendix E: Solution of Polynomial Equations, pp. 129-32. Tables, pp. 133-51. Index, pp. 152-54.

A reference on mathematics for chemists and a source book on definitions with emphasis on the mathematics of relationships between physical quantities. Topics include functions and operators; differential and integral calculus; differential equations; coordinate systems; complex numbers; vector analysis; determinants and matrices; expansion of functions; statistical methods; and graphical methods. Style consists of definition-explanation-example format with some mathematical derivations in the examples portion.

Marlow, W.H., ed. MODERN TRENDS IN LOGISTICS RESEARCH. Cambridge: MIT Press, 1976. xvi, 461 p. Name Index, pp. 437-48. Subject Index, pp. 449-61.

Sixteen papers presented at a Logistics Research Conference held at George Washington University in 1974 grouped under the following four headings: "Issues and Problems in Logistics" (four papers); "Information Processes and Systems Design" (two papers); "Probabilistic and Statistical Models" (four papers); and "Production, Scheduling and Facility Layout" (three papers); and "Mathematical Programming" (three papers). Topics include logistic research in army and weapons research; organization of information for logistic decision making; computer-based logistic support systems; econometric production functions; branch-and-bound techniques; inventory control; repair models; parametric programming for transportation problems; and integer programming in logistics.

Martin, Brian Robert Charles. STATISTICS FOR PHYSICISTS. New York: Academic Press, 1971. xiii, 209 p. Appendix A: Miscellaneous Mathematics, pp. 148-52. Appendix B: Orthogonal Polynomials, pp. 153-55. Appendix C: Optimization of Functions of Several Variables, pp. 156-67. Appendix D: Statistical Tables, pp. 168-201. Bibliography, pp. 203-4. Index, pp. 205-9.

A brief, but systematic, guide to statistical techniques commonly used in physics for use by working physicists, as well as students at both graduate and undergraduate levels. Topics include calculus of probabilities; univariate and multivariate theoretical distributions with examples; distributions associated with the normal; maximum likelihood estimation; least-squares; minimum chi-square; minimum variance; Bayes' estimators; method of moments; confidence intervals and regions; and hypothesis testing.

Massey, B.S. UNITS, DIMENSIONAL ANALYSIS, AND PHYSICAL SIMILARITY. New York: Van Nostrand Reinhold, 1971. viii, 140 p. Appendix 1: Symbols, Dimensional Formulas and Units for Physical Quantities, pp. 123-27. Appendix 2: Approximate Values of Some Physical Constants and Common Properties, pp. 128-29. Appendix 3: Some Other Units Used in Scientific Work, pp. 130-31. Further Reading, p. 133. List of Symbols, pp. 134-35. Index, pp. 137-40.

A monograph on dimensional analysis in the physical sciences and engineering. Topics include Newton's definitions of laws of motion; units of mechanics, thermodynamics, and electricity; conversion factors; physical algebra and dimensional formulas; and geometric, kinematic, and dynamic similarity.

Merriam, Daniel F., ed. MATHEMATICAL MODELS OF SEDIMENTARY PROCESSES: AN INTERNATIONAL SYMPOSIUM. Computer Applications in the Earth Sciences. New York: Plenum, 1972. xi, 271 p. Index, pp. 269-71.

Thirteen papers presented at a symposium held at the VIII International Sedimentological Congress in Heidelberg, West Germany, on August 31, 1971. Knowledge of calculus, differential equations, mathematical statistics, and probability necessary for following the derivations in some papers. Topics include optimization criteria for mathematical models used in sedimentology; mathematical models for hydrologic processes; Monte Carlo simulation of some blysch deposits from East Carpathians; areal variations and statistical correlation; models for solution rates of different-sized particles in liquids; and the semi-Markov process as a general sedimentation model.

_____. QUANTITATIVE TECHNIQUES FOR THE ANALYSIS OF SEDIMENTS: AN INTERNATIONAL SYMPOSIUM. Computer and Geology. New York: Pergamon, 1976. xii, 174 p. Index, pp. 173-74.

Thirteen papers presented at a symposium held at the IX International Sedimentological Congress in Nice, France, on July 8, 1975. Papers largely verbal and descriptive with charts and graphs and few formulas. Topics include trend analysis of sedimentary thickness data; quantitative methods of comparing lithological succession data; statistical recognition of terrestrial and marine sediments in the lower Cretaceous of Portugal; sedimentary environmental analysis of Long Island Sound; simulation techniques of matching and its stability; mathematical modeling of sediment accumulation in prograding deltaic systems; multidimensional scaling of sedimentary rock descriptors; and identification of discontinuities from areally distributed data.

Meyer, Stuart L. DATA ANALYSIS FOR SCIENTISTS AND ENGINEERS. New York: Wiley, 1975. xiv, 513 p. Appendixes, pp. 401-98. Guide for Further Reading and Bibliography, pp. 499-504. Index, pp. 505-13.

Primarily a self-study and reference for engineering students who have knowledge of the rudiments of calculus, and also a reference for practicing scientists and engineers. Consists of five parts: "Introduction to Scientific Measurement"; "Introduction to Graphical Techniques and Curve Fitting"; "Probability"; "Some Probability Distributions and Application"; and "Statistical Inference." Useful as a supplement in courses containing laboratory sessions where data is gathered and analyzed. Worked examples may be followed with the aid of a pocket calculator. Appendixes devoted to a review of mathematics and statistical tables.

Miller, Irwin, and Freund, John E. PROBABILITY AND STATISTICS FOR ENGINEERS. Prentice-Hall Mathematics Series. Englewood Cliffs, N.J.: Prentice-Hall, 1965. x, 432 p. Bibliography, pp. 383-85. Statistical Tables, pp. 387-415. Answers to Odd-Numbered Exercises, pp. 417-28. Index, pp. 429-32.

A text for one-year course in probability and statistics for students of engineering and the physical sciences who have one year of calculus. Topics include sets and probability; probability distributions; descriptive statistics; inferences concerning means, variances and proportions; nonparametric tests;

simple and multiple regression and correlation; analysis of variance; factorial experimentation; statistical quality control; and applications to reliability and life testing. Many sections conclude with one dozen or more exercises. Derivations kept to a minimum, with emphasis on verbal description, graphs, and examples.

Neyman, Jerzy. A FIRST COURSE IN PROBABILITY AND STATISTICS. New York: Henry Holt, 1950. ix, 350 p. Appendix: Tables of the Normal Integral, pp. 345-47. Index of Names, p. 348. Index of Terms, pp. 349-50.

A text for a one-semester course in statistics for engineering students and others who are interested in taking a course in mathematical statistics later on. Topics include probability theorems and counting techniques; probabilistic problems in genetics; random variables and their distributions; theorem of Laplace; statistical hypotheses and their tests. Emphasizes statistical hypotheses. Chapters conclude with problems and exercises.

Oi, Walter Y., and Hurter, Arthur P., Jr. ECONOMICS OF PRIVATE TRUCK TRANSPORTATION. Dubuque, Iowa: Wm. C. Brown, for the Transportation Center at Northwestern University, 1965. xvii, 365 p. Index, pp. 359-65.

Studies why some shippers choose to provide their own transportation rather than use independent private motor trucking firms. Uses cross-section classification, supplemented with analysis of variance, to explain the incidence of private motor trucking in the United States using data from published courses and a survey of shippers conducted in 1962 by the Transportation Center, as well as other surveys. Concludes that private motor transport is cheapest for relatively short hauls, particularly with inter-plant back hauls. Regression analysis emphasized to study the relationship between rail freight rates and weight of shipment, distance shipped, and unit value of commodity in order to study the degree of rate discrimination using cross section (firm) data for 1950, 1956, and 1959 for over 250 commodity groups. Useful to anyone involved with transport policy.

Ostle, Berhard, and Mensing, Richard W. STATISTICS IN RESEARCH: BASIC CONCEPTS AND TECHNIQUES FOR RESEARCH WORKERS. 2d ed., rev. Ames: Iowa State University Press, 1975. xiv, 596 p. Appendixes, pp. 520-81. Index, pp. 583-96.

A text for a course in intermediate statistics, or an integrated course in probability and statistics, for students in engineering and the physical sciences, and a reference for research workers. Attention given to the assumptions underlying techniques and when and where to use the techniques, and also to the use of computers and packaged programs especially for regression and analysis of variance. Other topics include sampling distributions, including multinomial and geometric; estimation and hypothesis testing for difference between two means and two proportions; sequential tests; chi-square; simple and multiple regression and correlation; biserial and tetrachoric correlation; correlations of sums and differences; completely randomized and randomized complete block designs; split plot designs; Latin and Graeco-Latin squares; response surface techniques; analysis of covariance; distribution-free methods; and statistical quality control and reliability. Chapters conclude with problems and references. Appendixes devoted to further derivations and statistical tables.

Pankhurst, R.C. DIMENSIONAL ANALYSIS AND SCALE FACTORS. London: Chapman and Hall, for the Institute of Physics and the Physical Society, 1964. 151 p. Appendixes 1 to 5, pp. 129-38. References, p. 139. Bibliography, pp. 140-42. Index, pp. 143-51.

A monograph on the principles and practices of dimensional analysis with emphasis on physical significance of the dimensionless parameters and their derivations by indicial equations rather than by rigorous mathematics. Topics include units and dimensions in mechanics; dimensionless products and quantities; scale factors in fluid dynamics; heat transfer; combustion; elasticity; and electromagnetic phenomena. Appendixes devoted to tables and named dimensional products. Useful to anyone interested in dimensional anaylsis.

Paradine, C.G., and Rivett, B.H.P. STATISTICAL METHODS FOR TECHNOLOGISTS. 2d ed., rev. General Engineering Series. London: English Universities Press, 1962. viii, 288 p. Tables, pp. 271-79. Answers to the Examples, pp. 280-85. Index, pp. 287-88.

A reference for research workers on statistical theory with emphasis on mathematical derivations. Knowledge of calculus assumed. Omits use of generating functions. Topics include descriptive statistics; probability and probability distributions; sums of squares of normal variates; statistical quality control; sampling inspection schemes; theory of errors; method of least squares; correlation; analysis of variance; principle of maximum likelihood; probit analysis; and applications. Sections conclude with exercises and chapters conclude with examples requiring short calculations.

Roberts, Sanford M. DYNAMIC PROGRAMMING IN CHEMICAL ENGINEERING AND PROCESS CONTROL. Mathematics in Science and Engineering: A Series of Monographs and Textbooks, vol. 12. New York: Academic Press, 1964. xiii, 457 p. Author Index, pp. 451-52. Subject Index, pp. 453-57.

A text for a course in dynamic programming for students of

chemical engineering and practitioners in engineering. Includes typical problems with computational techniques and numerical solutions. Topics include equipment replacement, calculus of variations and its relation to dynamic programming, role of dynamic programming in overcoming the deficiencies of calculus of variations, control problems from the viewpoint of dynamic programming, and applications of this technique to chemical engineering and inventories. Conclude with a chapter on the application of dynamic programming to stochastic processes and adaptive processes. Assumes knowledge of calculus of variations. Derivations fairly extensive.

Seinfeld, John H., and Lapidus, Leon. MATHEMATICAL METHODS IN CHEMICAL ENGINEERING. Vol. 3. PROCESS MODELING, ESTIMATION, AND IDENTIFICATION. Englewood Cliffs, N.J.: Prentice-Hall, 1974. xiii, 545 p. Index, pp. 539-45.

A self-contained, comprehensive treatment of the mathematical techniques of process modeling for use as a text for a one-year course. Emphasizes two methods of process modeling: (1) probability theory and stochastic processes and (2) parameter estimation and system identification. Topics include types of process models; the Laplace transform; stochastic mathematical models; parameter estimation; and process identification in linear and nonlinear systems. Assumes knowledge of advanced calculus, ordinary differential equations, linear algebra, mathematical statistics, and transport theory. Chapters conclude with references and problems.

Syski, Richard. INTRODUCTION TO CONGESTION THEORY IN TELEPHONE SYSTEMS. Foreword by Sir Thomas Eades. London: Oliver & Boyd, for Automatic Telephone and Electric Co., 1960. xvi, 742 p. Mathematical Appendix, pp. 661-703. References, pp. 705-28. Name Index, pp. 729-32. Subject Index, pp. 733-42.

A comprehensive reference and supplementary text on congestion theory easily accessible to the practical engineer. Considerable use made of stochastic processes, storage theory, queueing theory, and operations research. Topics include review of probability theory and stochastic processes; telephone traffic characteristics; loss systems, including birth and death processes; waiting systems, including single channel and many channel servers; limited availability, including equation of state; link systems; random servicing; bulk service; repeated calls; Erland loss formulas; hunting problems; and exchange problems.

Topping, J. ERRORS OF OBSERVATION AND THEIR TREATMENT. Science Paperbacks. London: Chapman and Hall, 1962. 119 p. References, p. 115. Bibliography, p. 116. Index, pp. 117-19.

A monograph on the statistical analysis of measurements obtained in experimental work for use in technical colleges particularly in physics and science. Types of errors include accidental and systematic errors, errors and fractional errors, estimate of error, error in a product and a quotient, and error in a sum or difference. Statistical topics used in error analysis include the mean and standard deviation; Sheppard's correction; Charlier's checks; frequency distribution, such as the normal and Poisson; Bessel's formulas; and Peter's formulas. Theory of errors include normal Gaussian law of error, standard error of a compound quantity, least squares, weighted or mean, and accuracy of coefficients. Chapters conclude with problems. Elementary calculus used in a few sections.

Tribus, Myron. RATIONAL DESCRIPTIONS, DECISIONS, AND DESIGNS. Foreword by R.S. Silver. Pergamon Unified Engineering Series. New York: Pergamon, 1969. xix, 478 p. Index, pp. 473-78.

A text and reference on engineering design based on probability concepts and Bayesian statistics. Topics include probability and probability distributions, including multinomial, exponential, gamma, beta, and uniform; Bayes' formulas; contingency tables; principle of maximum entropy; hypothesis testing; prior information; decision theory; and applications to a variety of engineering systems and designs. Chapters conclude with references. Assumes knowledge of advanced calculus.

Tuma, Jan J. ENGINEERING MATHEMATICS HANDBOOK: DEFINITIONS, THEOREMS, FORMULAS, TABLES. New York: McGraw-Hill, 1970. xiii, 334 p. Appendix A: Numerical Tables, pp. 295-312. Appendix B: Conversion Tables, pp. 313-16. Appendix C: Glossary of Symbols, pp. 317-22. Appendix D: References and Bibliography, pp. 323-26. Index, pp. 327-34.

A reference for engineers, scientists, architects, teachers and students, on the major tools of engineering mathematics. Subject matter arranged in twenty chapters corresponding to undergraduate and graduate courses in mathematics and science and engineering curricula. Topics include algebra, geometry, trigonometry, elementary functions, differential calculus, infinite series, vector algebra, complex variables, ordinary differential equations, partial differential equations, Laplace transform, numerical methods, probability and statistics.

Volk, William. APPLIED STATISTICS FOR ENGINEERS. 2d ed. New York: McGraw-Hill, 1969. xii, 415 p. Tables, pp. 401-9. Index, pp. 411-15.

A text for a course in applied statistics for engineers and a reference for engineers engaged in applied statistics in industry. Topics include probability and Bayes' theorem; permutations and combinations; binomial, normal, and Poisson distributions;

measures of variability; chi-square; t test for means and differences between two means; analysis of variance; 2^n factorial experiments; correlation and regression; sequential analysis; nonparametric tests; and computer applications. Assumes knowledge of college algebra. Many examples taken from the chemical industry. Chapters conclude with problems.

Wade, Oliver R. TOLERANCE CONTROL IN DESIGN AND MANUFACTURING. New York: Industrial Press, 1967. x, 190 p. Index, pp. 189-90.

A working text for courses in machine design or in industrial or tool engineering, a supplementary text in engineering drawing, and a reference for the working product engineer, quality control engineer, and others interested in tolerance design. Topics include tolerance charts and programs; determination of required balance and mean working dimensions; analysis of stock removal as expressed in the equal bilateral form; statistical aspects of design and production; value engineering; and education and organization of tolerance charting.

Wine, Russell Lowell. STATISTICS FOR SCIENTISTS AND ENGINEERS. Englewood Cliffs, N.J.: Prentice-Hall, 1964. xvi, 671 p. Statistical Tables, pp. 623-59. Index, pp. 661-71.

A text for a one-year course in theoretical or applied elementary statistics with engineering calculus as the main prerequisite. Includes numerous examples, with exercises at the ends of the sections designed to give readers practice in applying and extending the concepts and in developing new concepts. Topics include descriptive statistics; probability and random variables; sampling distributions; point estimators; maximum likelihood; expectation and other moments of random variables; chi-square; estimation and hypothesis testing; F distribution; one- and multiple-way analysis of variance; Latin squares; factorial designs; simple and multiple regression; analysis of counted data; and nonparametric tests. Chapters conclude with exercises.

Wortham, A.W., and Smith, T.E. PRACTICAL STATISTICS IN EXPERIMENTAL DESIGN. Columbus, Ohio: Charles E. Merrill, 1959. viii, 128 p. Index and Glossary of Terms, p. 128.

A text for a one-semester course in applied statistics for engineers and scientists who have little formal training in mathematics and statistics. Topics include descriptive statistics; derived distributions and confidence limits using standard normal and t distributions; two-sample problem; analysis of variance; randomized block experiments; the Latin square experiment; Graeco-Latin square design; split plot experiment; and factorial arrangements. Emphasizes applications using numerical examples, with no extensive derivations. Chapters conclude with supplementary readings and exercises.

Yevjevich, Vujica M. PROBABILITY AND STATISTICS IN HYDROLOGY. Fort Collins, Colo.: Water Resources Publications, 1972. vii, 302 p. References, pp. 287-94. Index, pp. 295-302.

A reference for practitioners in hydrology, water resources, and allied fields, graduate students, and specialists interested in applying probability and mathematical statistics in hydrology. Contains no proofs, derivations, computer programs, or statistical tables. Selection of topics based on author's experience, and include characteristics of hydrologic phenomena; random variables and probability distributions; limit theorems and Markov processes; law of large numbers; expectation and variance; empirical distributions of hydrologic variables; mathematical statistics models; parameters and order-statistics as descriptors of distributions (descriptors of asymmetry, flatness, etc.); probability distribution functions in hydrology (binomial, Poisson, lognormal, gamma, etc.); estimation methods (least squares, moments, maximum likelihood); sampling theory; hypothesis testing, including composite; simple and multiple regression and correlation; spurious correlation; and multivariate analysis (principal component, factor, and canonical). Assumes knowledge of calculus.

_____. STOCHASTIC PROCESSES IN HYDROLOGY. Fort Collins, Colo.: Water Resources Publications, 1972. vii, 276 p. References, pp. 261-68. Index, pp. 269-76.

A monograph on the various methods of analyzing stochastic processes in hydrology for use by practicing hydrologists, students studying hydrology, and specialists in related fields. including statisticians and geophysicists. Excludes proofs and derivations, and includes concepts, formulas, techniques, and applications. Does not differentiate between general stochastic processes and time series. Many classical stochastic processes omitted. Topics include autocorrelation and lag cross correlation; spectral and cross spectral analysis; range analysis of hydrological series; analysis of hydrologic series by runs; transient components in hydrologic series; analysis of intermittent hydrologic processes; and computer technology and the experimental method in hydrology. Chapters conclude with problems and conclusions.

Chapter 10

STATISTICAL QUALITY CONTROL

Allan, Douglas H.W. STATISTICAL QUALITY CONTROL: AN INTRODUCTION FOR MANAGEMENT. Reinhold Management Series. New York: Reinhold, 1959. x, 129 p. Index, pp. 127-29.

> A reference for managers who wish to become familiar with statistical quality control without becoming involved in the mathematical details. Topics include quality control objectives and techniques; process capabilities; control charts; acceptance sampling; statistical methods for investigation and experimentation; and sources of quality control information.

Amstadter, Bertram L. RELIABILITY MATHEMATICS: FUNDAMENTALS; PRACTICES; PROCEDURES. New York: McGraw-Hill, 1971. viii, 408 p. Appendix A: Mathematical Derivations, pp. 309-25. Appendix B: Statistical Tables and Failure-Rate-Data Sources, pp. 327-52. Appendix C: Reliability Tables, pp. 353-97. Index, pp. 398-408.

> A text and reference for undergraduates and practitioners who have had a basic course in statistics or a related subject such as statistical quality control. Knowledge of calculus desirable. Emphasizes applications. Useful to supervisory and management personnel as a ready reference. Topics include distributions used in reliability; tests of hypotheses; data considerations; logic diagrams; prediction of component reliability system prediction; apportionment; reliability growth; assessment methods; reliability demonstration; and system reliability considerations. Chapters conclude with references.

Bazorsky, Igor. RELIABILITY: THEORY AND PRACTICE. Prentice-Hall International Series in Engineering. Englewood Cliffs, N.J.: Prentice-Hall, 1961. xii, 292 p. Index, pp. 287-92.

> A reference for engineers who are confronted with reliability problems. Includes an abundance of reliability formulas useful in predicting system reliability, establishing reliability goals, and determining procedures necessary to achieve them. Topics

include the exponential case of chance failures; useful life of components; wearout and reliability; early failures and the life function of components; the exponential and Poisson distributions; reliability of series systems; reliability of parallel systems; reliability of stand-by systems; Bayes' theorem in reliability; component modes of failure and system reliability; component failure rates at system stress levels; reliability of aircraft and airborne systems; reliability design analysis; overhaul and part replacements; sequential reliability tests; and implementation of reliability.

Burr, Irving W. STATISTICAL QUALITY CONTROL METHODS. Statistics: Textbooks and Monographs, vol. 16. New York: Marcel Dekker, 1976. xii, 522 p. Answers to Odd-Numbered Problems, pp. 465-74. Appendix: Tables, pp. 475-506. Glossary of Symbols, pp. 507-14. Author Index, pp. 515-17. Subject Index, pp. 519-22.

A text for a course in quality control for undergraduates and graduates in engineering, industrial management, statistics and science who have had a course in basic statistics. Also useful as a reference for practitioners in industry. Emphasizes data analysis and decision making, with nearly all problems and examples taken from actual cases based on the author's experience in industry. Topics include review of statistical concepts; control charts for measurements; control charts for attributes; relative efficiency of different types of control charts; applications of control charts; acceptance sampling by attributes; acceptance sampling by measurements; standard plans for attributes; sequential analysis; and statistics of combinations. Chapters conclude with references and problems.

Butterbaugh, Grant Illion. A BIBLIOGRAPHY OF STATISTICAL QUALITY CONTROL. Seattle: University of Washington Press, for the Bureau of Business Research, College of Business and Economics, 1946. viii, 114 p. Index of Authors, pp. 111-14.

An annotated bibliography of 712 articles, manuals, and books on statistical quality control by 340 authors from 1924 to 1945 in 137 different periodicals published in the United States, Canada, England, and Australia. Consists of three parts: "Periodical Literature"; "Manuals, Monographs, Pamphlets"; and "Books." Within part I, entries arranged alphabetically by title of periodical, and within parts II and III, entries arranged alphabetically by author or organization.

______. BIBLIOGRAPHY OF STATISTICAL QUALITY CONTROL: SUPPLEMENT. Seattle: University of Washington Press, 1951. 141 p. Index of Authors, pp. 130-34. Index of Subjects, pp. 135-41.

A continuation of the original annotated bibliography of 1946.

Contains 725 items covering the period 1946 through June 1949. Indexes cover both the original bibliography and the supplement.

Calabros, S.R. RELIABILITY PRINCIPLES AND PRACTICES. New York: McGraw-Hill, 1962. xii, 371 p. Appendix 1: Definitions Frequently Used, pp. 293-304. Appendix 2: Special Techniques, pp. 305-15. Appendix 3: Reliability Control and Acceptance Procedures, pp. 316-21. Appendix 4: Quality Control System Requirements, pp. 322-26. Appendix 5: Reliability Monitoring Programs, pp. 327-34. Appendix 6: Guides for Reliability Organization, pp. 335-42. Appendix 7: Tables, pp. 343-60. Bibliography, pp. 361-63. Index, pp. 365-71.

A reference for engineers, managers, and others who have some knowledge of statistics and reliability analysis. Presents the basic concepts underlying reliability theory and illustrates their applications to the solution of practical problems. Topics include descriptive statistics; probability and its application to series and parallel reliability binomial, Poisson, and normal distributions; reliability data; maintainability and availability; maintenance time constraint; sampling methods; control charts; prediction methods; reliability design and specification; U.S. government requirements; and management of a reliability program. Chapters conclude with problems.

Caplen, Rowland. A PRACTICAL APPROACH TO QUALITY CONTROL. London: Business Books, 1969. viii, 278 p. Appendix: Tables, pp. 269-72. Index, pp. 273-78.

A practical introduction to statistical quality control for the practitioner. Consists of four parts: "An Introduction to Quality Control and Quality Costs"; "Preparing for Satisfactory Quality"; "Quality Control of the Actual Production Operations"; and "The Design, Organization and Introduction of a Quality Control System." Knowledge of basic statistics helpful.

Chorafas, Dimitris N. STATISTICAL PROCESSES AND RELIABILITY ENGINEERING. Foreword by Clifford M. Ryerson. New York: Van Nostrand, 1960. xiv, 438 p. Bibliography, pp. 431-32. Index, pp. 433-38.

An early reference, supplementary text, and handbook on mathematical statistics and reliability for engineers, applied mathematicians, and managers who have a working knowledge of calculus. Presentation not as rigorous as that found in most mathematical statistics texts and derivations not as extensive or detailed. Consists of six parts: "Engineering Statistics"; "Statistical Experimentation"; "Stochastic Processes"; "Information Processes"; "Quality Control"; and "Reliability Engineering." Topics include tests of sign; operating characteristic curve; interval estimation; regression and correlation; analysis of variance; experimental design; Latin squares;

centroid and diagonal methods of factor analysis; combinatorial analysis; beta and gamma functions; Monte Carlo simulation; Markov chains; queueing cybernetics; transmission and regulation; communication theory; noise; quality control; reliability and product assurance mathematical models for reliability studies; designing and testing for reliability; and application of reliability to weapons systems and electronic equipment. Applications taken mainly from engineering.

Cowden, Dudley J. STATISTICAL METHODS IN QUALITY CONTROL. Englewood Cliffs, N.J.: Prentice-Hall, 1957. xxiv, 727 p. Glossary of Important Symbols, pp. 704-11. Index, pp. 713-27.

A text for a one-year course in statistical techniques of quality control for students who have had basic statistics and calculus. Topics include probability distributions; maximum likelihood estimation; tests of hypotheses and confidence limits; analysis of variance; likelihood ratio tests; chi-square; control charts; analysis of a process subject to sporadic change; one- and two-sided specification limits; use of control charts; charts for non-normal distributions; control charts for variances; analysis of defectives; the Poisson distribution; sloping control charts; lot acceptance sampling for attributes; the hypergeometric distribution; single sampling plans for attributes; double sampling; item-by-item sequential sampling; multiple sequential sampling; and analysis of pattern of variability.

Drury, C.G., and Fox, J.G. HUMAN RELIABILITY IN QUALITY CONTROL. New York: Wiley, Halsted Press, 1975. xii, 315 p. Author Index, pp. 303-7. Subject Index, pp. 309-15.

Eighteen papers presented at an international symposium on human factors in quality control held at the State University of New York, Buffalo, in 1974, grouped under the following headings: "Models of Inspector Performance" (six papers); "Factors Affecting Inspection Performance" (six papers); and "Industrial Applications" (six papers). Use of mathematics limited.

Duncan, Acheson J. QUALITY CONTROL AND INDUSTRIAL STATISTICS. 4th ed. Homewood, Ill.: Irwin, 1974. xix, 1,047 p. Appendix L: Selected Mathematical Proofs and Technical Material, pp. 889-941. Appendix II: Special Tables and Charts, pp. 942-89. Appendix III: Glossary of Symbols, pp. 990-96. Appendix IV: Glossary of Special Technical Terms, pp. 997-1003. Cumulative List of References, pp. 1004-30. Index, pp. 1031-47.

A text for a one-year course in statistical quality control in five parts: "Fundamentals"; "Lot Acceptance Sampling Plans"; "Rectifying Inspection"; "Control Charts"; and "Some Statistics Useful in Industrial Research." Includes such topics as tests of hypotheses pertaining to proportions, means, and variances, and differences between proportions, means, and variances; chi-square; analysis of variance; regression and correlation; analysis of covariance; and the design of experiments, including confounding in factorial experiments; acceptance sampling by attributes; acceptance sampling by variables to control fraction defectives; sampling plans for continuous production; control charts for fraction defective and number defective; and cumulative sum control charts. Uses numerous charts and numerical examples to illustrate the various quality control methods. Knowledge of basic statistics helpful. Chapters conclude with problems and references.

Enrick, Norbert Lloyd. QUALITY CONTROL AND RELIABILITY: PRACTICE-TESTED METHODS AND PROCEDURES BASED ON SCIENTIFIC PRINCIPLES AND SIMPLIFIED FOR IMMEDIATE APPLICATION IN A VARIETY OF MANUFACTURING PLANTS. 7th ed. New York: Industrial Press, 1977. ix, 306 p. Appendix 1: Methods of Computing Standard Deviations, pp. 267-72. Appendix 2: Operating Characteristics for Lot-by-Lot Sampling Plans, pp. 273-78. Appendix 3: Cases and Problems, pp. 279-90. Glossary, pp. 291-303. Index, pp. 305-6.

A reference for managers, inspectors, engineers, and students on quality control and product reliability with emphasis on reliability design, evaluation and assurance. Presents a large number of illustrations in a variety of practical, industrial operations, many based on the author's consulting experience. Topics include lot-by-lot inspection; process inspection with control charts; control of variability; statistical basis of control charts; process capability and product tolerances; analysis of variance; optimizing processing through evolutionary operation; multiple choice chains; and reliability assurance and design. Knowledge of basic statistics helpful. Chapters conclude with review questions.

Feigenbaum, Armand Vallin. TOTAL QUALITY CONTROL-ENGINEERING AND MANAGEMENT: THE TECHNICAL AND MANAGERIAL FIELD FOR IMPROVING PRODUCT QUALITY, INCLUDING ITS RELIABILITY, AND FOR REDUCING OPERATING COSTS AND LOSSES. New York: McGraw-Hill, 1961. xi, 627 p. Index, pp. 621-27.

A survey of the field of quality control from the business viewpoint for managers and engineers. Consists of six parts: "Business Quality Management"; "Quality-Control Management"; "Engineering Technology of Quality Control"; "Statistical Technology of Quality Control"; "Applying Total Quality Control in the Company"; and "Quality-Control Education and Training." Presentation primarily descriptive, relying on tables and charts instead of mathematical formulas. Useful as a text for in-company training courses.

Fetter, Robert B. THE QUALITY CONTROL SYSTEM. Irwin Series in Operations Management. Homewood, Ill.: Irwin, 1967. vii, 141 p. Appendix I: Glossary of Symbols, pp. 99-100. Appendix II: Computer Programs, pp. 101-28. Appendix III: Tables, pp. 129-37. Index, pp. 139-41.

A short reference on statistical methods relevant to the design of statistical quality control from both the technical and economic viewpoints. Topics include technical design of sampling; variable sampling plans; economics of sampling inspection; economic acceptance plans; control charts; process control and process capability; and techniques of statistical quality control, including regression, analysis of variance, sequential sampling plans, and continuous sampling plans. Includes several computer programs. Assumes knowledge of elementary statistics. Chapters conclude with problems and references.

Gedye, Rupert. A MANAGER'S GUIDE TO QUALITY AND RELIABILITY. Foreword by B.H.P. Rivett. New York: Wiley, 1968. xi, 127 p. Books Recommended for Further Reading, pp. 122-23. References, p. 124. Index, pp. 125-27.

A guide for managers for improving statistical quality control and reliability. Topics include inspection and quality control; statistical concepts; control charts; design and organization for quality control and reliability; and economic aspects. Assumes knowledge of basic statistics.

Grant, Eugene L., and Levenworth, Richard S. STATISTICAL QUALITY CONTROL. 4th ed., rev. and enl. New York: McGraw-Hill, 1972. xv, 694 p. Appendix 1: Glossary of Symbols, pp. 627-33. Appendix 2: Bibliography, pp. 634-40. Appendix 3: Tables, pp. 641-82. Name Index, pp. 683-85. Subject Index, pp. 686-94.

A practical working manual which deals primarily with various types of Shewart control charts and various types of acceptance sampling systems and procedures that have found wide use in industry. Also useful as a text or supplementary text for courses in statistical quality control. Liberal use made of descriptions of actual cases from a number of industries, as well as hypothetical examples. Consists of four parts: "What Will Statistical Quality Control Do?"; "Shewart Control Charts"; "Acceptance Sampling"; and "Some Related Topics." Topics include X-bar and R charts; control charts for attributes; process control procedures; specifications and tolerances; the Dodge-Romig and AQL systems for lot-by-lot acceptance sampling by attributes; acceptance sampling by variables; life testing and reliability; and economic aspects of quality decisions. Assumes knowledge of basic statistics. Chapters conclude with problems on applications.

Hansen, Bertrand L. QUALITY CONTROL: THEORY AND APPLICATIONS. Englewood Cliffs, N.J.: Prentice-Hall, 1963. xii, 498 p. Appendixes, pp. 435-84. Bibliography, pp. 485-88. Name Index, pp. 489-90. Subject Index, pp. 491-98.

A text for introductory and intermediate courses in engineering and management and for accelerated industrial training programs in quality control, as well as a reference for managers, engineers, technicians, and others. Includes developing concepts, applications, and sources for further study, and consists of six parts: "Introduction to Quality Control Theory"; "Quality Control in Process"; "Acceptance Control"; "Quality Engineering"; "Quality Management"; and "Discussion Topics and Practice."

Harris, Douglas H., and Chaney, Frederick B. HUMAN FACTORS IN QUALITY ASSURANCE. Wiley Series in Human Factors. New York: Wiley, 1969. xiii, 234 p. Index, pp. 231-34.

Analyzes human factors in the attainment of quality objectives in the production process. Provides a source of information and ideas for supervisors, engineers, and specialists concerned with quality objectives in industrial operations. Topics include human performance in industry; nature of quality assurance; designing the quality engineering job; industrial inspection; measuring inspecting performance; inspector selection; and quality motivation. Useful to industrial psychologists and human factor specialists. Uses no formulas. Chapters conclude with references.

Hopper, A. Graham. BASIC STATISTICAL QUALITY CONTROL. New York: McGraw-Hill, 1969. x, 171 p. Revision Problems, pp. 136-40. Glossary, pp. 141-43. Tables, pp. 144-59. Answers to Problems, pp. 160-67. Index, pp. 169-71.

A text for an introductory statistics course for engineers in technical colleges and a reference for practitioners in statistical quality control. Mathematical arguments kept to a minimum with proofs included as notes at the ends of the chapters. Includes numerous worked examples. Problems included at the ends of the chapters. Topics include probability; sampling inspection schemes; control charts for sample means, range, proportion defective, and for defects per unit; confidence limits and significance tests; and chi-square.

Huitson, Alan, and Keen, Joan. ESSENTIALS OF QUALITY CONTROL. London: William Heinemann, 1965. xii, 128 p. Appendix I: Statistical Tables, pp. 108-21. Appendix II: Answers to Exercises, pp. 122-23. Appendix III: Definitions, pp. 124-26. Index, pp. 127-28.

A text and reference on applications of statistical quality

control for students, executives, and technical personnel in industry. Topics include control charts for variables and qualitative data and sampling inspection schemes. Chapters conclude with exercises. Knowledge of basic statistics helpful.

Ireson, W. Grant, ed. RELIABILITY HANDBOOK. New York: McGraw-Hill, 1966. xiii, 692 p. Appendix A: Tables, pp. 617-57. Appendix B: Charts, pp. 658-68. Appendix C: Selected References, pp. 669-77. Index, pp. 678-92.

A reference for reliability, quality, design, and production engineers and a text for undergraduates and graduates. Consists of a large collection of principles, examples, tables, sources of reliability data, statistical and mathematical models, data systems, forms, charts, and techniques all grouped into seventeen sections. Cross references provided in all sections to indicate where topics are discussed. Index provides a rapid reference to all entries for speed in locating specific information. Topics include life patterns and their uses; selecting reliability test plans; reliability estimation; testing programs; failure analysis; design and development for reliable systems; human factors in reliability; acceptance sampling; and cost aspects of a reliability and quality assurance program.

Juran, Joseph M., and Gryna, Frank M., Jr. QUALITY PLANNING AND ANALYSIS: FROM PRODUCT DEVELOPMENT THROUGH USAGE. New York: McGraw-Hill, 1970. xx, 684 p. Appendix: Cases and Tables, pp. 643-64. Index, pp. 665-84.

A comprehensive text on quality planning and analysis for students and practitioners who have a college algebra background. Emphasizes the relation of quality planning to other company activities. Topics include history of quality control; economics of quality; measurement and analysis of quality costs; organization for quality; statistical aids to reliability; statistical tests of hypotheses; quality specification; statistical aids in limits and tolerances; reliability; manufacturing planning; inspection; acceptance sampling; vendor relations; process control; finished goods acceptance; customer relations; quality assurance; and quality control engineering. Chapters conclude with problems which emphasize applications.

Juran, Joseph M.; Gryna, Frank M., Jr.; and Bingham, R.S., Jr., eds. QUALITY CONTROL HANDBOOK. 3d ed., rev. and enl. New York: McGraw-Hill, 1974. xii, 1,750 p. Appendix I: Glossary of Symbols, pp. 1607-11. Appendix II: Tables and Charts, pp. 1612-59. Name Index, pp. 1660-73. Subject Index, pp. 1674-1750.

A reference for managers, supervisors, and engineers in industry and a training text for courses in statistical quality control. Consists of fifty-two sections written by forty-two authors arranged in the following three broad groupings: "Managing the Quality Function"; "Statistical Methods"; and "Industries and Processes." Methods of locating information in this handbook consist of: Table of Contents, the Index, and Cross References. Section titles: "Quality Costs"; "New Product Quality"; "Vendor Relations"; "Production of Quality"; "Manpower"; "Sampling by Attributes"; "Bulk Sampling"; "Regression Analysis"; "Evolutionary Operation"; "Chemical Process Industries"; "Plastic Molding"; "Textiles"; "Automotive Industry"; "Job Shop Quality"; "Service Industries"; and "Complex Systems."

Kirkpatrick, Elwood G. QUALITY CONTROL FOR MANAGERS AND ENGINEERS. New York: Wiley, 1970. xiii, 422 p. Appendixes A to C: Tables, pp. 346-53. Appendix D: Military Standard MIL-STD-105D, pp. 354-417. Index, pp. 419-22.

A text for a course in quality control, with emphasis on the quality system and the economics of quality, in engineering, management, and business schools. Topics include elements of the quality system; technical specifications; process capability; interchangeability alternatives; production tolerances; process control; sampling inspection; inspection and gaging; and quality control trends. One year of basic statistics helpful for comprehension. Chapters conclude with references, review questions, and problems.

Knowler, Lloyd A.; Howell, John M.; Gold, Benk; Coleman, Edward P.; Moan, Obert B.; and Knowler, William C. QUALITY CONTROL BY STATISTICAL METHODS. New York: McGraw-Hill, 1969. x, 139 p. Appendix 1: References, p. 103. Appendix 2: Tables, pp. 105-28. Answers to Exercises, pp. 129-33. Index, pp. 135-39.

A combination text and training manual with emphasis on the production of a usable product. Topics include elements of probability and statistics; control charts for measurements and attributes; and acceptance sampling by attributes and variables. Chapters conclude with exercises. Blank as well as completed data sheets, tables, and forms for control charts.

Mann, Nancy R.; Schafer, Ray E.; and Singpurwalla, Nozer D. METHODS FOR STATISTICAL ANALYSIS OF RELIABILITY AND LIFE DATA. Wiley Series in Probability and Mathematical Statistics. New York: Wiley, 1974. ix, 564 p. Appendix: Tables, pp. 529-45. Index, pp. 547-64.

A text for a one-semester course and a reference for reliability engineers who have knowledge of calculus. Includes probability and statistical models; failure models; and various methods for estimation. Concludes with a discussion of Bayesian methods in reliability and accelerated life testing. Chapters conclude with exercises and references.

Myers, Richard H.; Wong, Kam L.; and Gordy, Harold M., eds. RELIABILITY ENGINEERING FOR ELECTRONIC SYSTEMS. New York: Wiley, 1964. viii, 360 p. Appendix I: Reliability Definitions, pp. 325-37. Appendix II: Most Used Tables, pp. 338-54. Index, pp. 355-60.

A reference manual for electronic design and reliability engineers and a text for industry training programs. Consists of nine chapters by different specialists, and begins with basic reliability principles and progresses through the sequential areas, and product design, development, and operational phases. Topics include reliability mathematics, reliability prediction, reliability testing, environmental testing, and reliability reporting and analysis. Chapters conclude with references, problems, and answers.

Naus, Joseph I. DATA QUALITY CONTROL AND EDITING. Statistics Series, vol. 10. New York: Marcel Dekker, 1975. ix, 202 p. Appendix of Tables, pp. 191-96. Bibliography, pp. 197-200. Index, pp. 201-2.

Presents in detail the principles and techniques for monitoring and editing data for errors. Useful for professionals in universities, industry, and government who deal with large quantities of data. Topics include dictionary of deterministic tests; techniques for probabilistic tests; monitoring and improving the quality of data; automatic data correction; locating errors; and cost effectiveness of data validation. No mathematical prerequisites. Includes examples.

O'Brien, James Jerome. SCHEDULING HANDBOOK. New York: McGraw-Hill, 1969. x, 605 p. Index, pp. 599-605.

A reference on operational scheduling techniques. Emphasizes techniques, methods of applications, and in some cases case histories, rather than on the philosophy of the applications. Techniques include networks, PERT, resources scheduling, cost schedule optimization, inventory scheduling, line of balance, close-order scheduling, graphical scheduling, capital scheduling, design scheduling, maintenance scheduling, construction scheduling, systems scheduling, hospital scheduling, and commerce and administrative scheduling. Useful primarily to managers and schedulers. Presentation of each technique concludes with references.

Peach, Paul. QUALITY CONTROL FOR MANAGEMENT. Englewood Cliffs, N.J.: Prentice-Hall, 1964. 204 p. Appendix: Tables, pp. 195-97. Index, pp. 198-204.

A reference for managers on basic concepts in statistical quality control. Topics include probability and expected values; review of mathematics; probability distributions; statistical tests; sampling; sampling inspection; process quality control;

gages, tests, and measurements; and quality control and operations research. Provides managers with a broad grasp of the field of quality control.

Samson, Charles; Hart, Philip; and Rubin, Charles. FUNDAMENTALS OF STATISTICAL QUALITY CONTROL. Reading, Mass.: Addison-Wesley, 1970. xi, 144 p. Glossary, p. 131-33. Tables, pp. 135-41. Index, pp. 143-44.

A nontechnical introduction to quality control mainly for the practitioner as an aid in the solution of industrial problems. Examples presented in a clear style. Includes problems. Topics include control charts; acceptance sampling; operating characteristic curves; reliability; setting tolerances; and design of experiments.

Sandler, Gerald H. SYSTEM RELIABILITY ENGINEERING. Foreword by M.M. Tall. Englewood Cliffs, N.J.: Prentice-Hall, 1963. xiii, 221 p. Bibliography, pp. 211-18. Index, pp. 219-21.

Primarily a reference for practicing engineers on concepts and techniques for designing large-scale systems for reliability. Assumes some knowledge in mathematical probability. Also useful as a supplementary text in systems engineering, operations research, and reliability engineering. Emphasizes the development of the differential-difference equations arising from situations where equipment failure takes place at a constant rate, with repair rates constant. Topics include review of Markov processes; reliability models of nonmaintained and maintained systems; reliability models with rewards; allocation of redundancy; system maintenance policies; and allocating failure and repair rates.

Sarkadi, Károly, and Vincze, I. MATHEMATICAL METHODS OF STATISTICAL QUALITY CONTROL. Probability and Mathematical Statistics: A Series of Textbooks and Monographs, vol. 18. New York: Academic Press, 1974. 415 p. Appendix: Tables, pp. 379-400. Bibliography, pp. 401-8. Index, pp. 409-15.

A mathematically oriented text for a course in statistical quality control for students who have had advanced calculus. Consists of two parts: "Theoretical Foundations" and "Methods of Statistical Quality Control." First part equivalent to a course in mathematical statistics. Includes mathematical derivations and numerous examples. Topics include probability theory and random variables; theorem of Chebyshev and related inequalities; laws of large numbers; special types of distributions; sampling; theory of order statistics; theories of estimation, hypothesis testing, and regression; process control by variables; control by attributes; acceptance sampling; sequential sampling; and reliability theory. Exercises provided.

Shewart, Walter Andrew. ECONOMIC CONTROL OF QUALITY OF MANUFACTURED PRODUCT. New York: Van Nostrand, 1931. xiv, 501 p. Appendix I: Resultant Effects of Constant Cause Systems, pp. 425-36. Appendix II: Experimental Results, pp. 437-71. Appendix III: Bibliography, pp. 473-91. Index of Names, pp. 493-95. Index of Subjects, pp. 497-501.

> An early text for a course in statistical quality control and a reference for practitioners in seven parts: "Introduction"; "Ways of Expressing Quality of Product"; "Basis for Specification of Quality Control"; "Sampling Fluctuations in Quality"; "Allowable Variability in Quality"; "Quality Control in Practice"; and "Statistical Basis for Specification of Standard Quality." Topics include maximum control; sampling fluctuations in simple statistics, including correlation coefficient; design limits on variability; detection of lack of control; and the control program. Based on the author's experience in research at Bell Telephone Laboratories. Assumes knowledge of basic statistics.

Shewart, Walter Andrew, and Deming, W. Edwards. STATISTICAL METHOD FROM THE VIEWPOINT OF QUALITY CONTROL. Washington, D.C.: Department of Agriculture, 1939. ix, 155 p. Some Comments on Symbols and Nomenclature, pp. 152-55. No index.

> An exposition of some elementary principles and techniques on statistical quality control, the establishment of tolerance limits, the presentation of data, and the specification of accuracy and precision. Based on lectures presented at the Graduate School of the Department of Agriculture, and assumes knowledge of basic statistics.

Shooman, Martin L. PROBABILISTIC RELIABILITY: AN ENGINEERING APPROACH. Brooklyn Polytechnic Institute Series. New York: McGraw-Hill, 1968. xix, 524 p. Appendix A: Analog Computation, pp. 489-93. Appendix B: Numerical Analysis and Digital Computation, pp. 494-502. Appendix C: Some Useful Integrals, pp. 503-6. Appendix D: Number of Monte Carlo Trails, pp. 507-8. Bibliography, pp. 509-16. Name Index, pp. 517-18. Subject Index, pp. 519-24.

> A text for a course in reliability for undergraduates and graduates in engineering who have knowledge of differential equations and introductory probability. Emphasizes the formulation and interpretation of probabilistic reliability models in analysis and their utilization in reliability design. Topics include combinatorial properties; discrete and continuous random variables; moments and moment-generating functions; Markov models; several random variables; properties of point estimators; combinatorial reliability; catastrophic-failure models; system reliability and reliability improvement; drift failures, component tolerance, and parameter variation; and reliability physics models and statistical parameter estimation. Chapters conclude with problems.

Simmons, David A. PRACTICAL QUALITY CONTROL. Reading, Mass.: Addison-Wesley, 1970. xiv, 240 p. Glossary, pp. 231-32. Index, pp. 235-40.

A reference for practitioners on how to utilize statistical tools in making quality management decisions that are based on data. Consists of five parts: "Organization and Control"; "Vender Quality Control"; "Statistical Quality Control"; "Manufacturing Quality Control"; and "Reliability." Assumes knowledge of basic statistics.

Stok, Theodorus Leonardus. THE WORKER AND QUALITY CONTROL. Foreword by J. von Ettinger. Ann Arbor: University of Michigan, Bureau of Industrial Relations, 1965. xi, 207 p. Appendix, pp. 177-201. Footnotes, pp. 203-7. No index.

A nontechnical investigation of the relationship between workers in industry and statistical quality control which makes use of visual aids of quality control to the worker. Useful to anyone interested in quality control and job satisfaction.

Tippett, Leonard Henry Caleb. TECHNOLOGICAL APPLICATIONS OF STATISTICS. Foreword by John E. Burchard. Wiley Series in Probability and Mathematical Statistics. New York: Wiley, 1950. ix, 189 p. Bibliography, pp. 185-86. Index, pp. 187-89.

A supplementary text for a course in basic statistics in two parts: "The Routine Control of Quality" and "Investigation and Experimentation." Exposition developed from examples using authentic procedures rather than mathematical proofs. Topics include statistical and technical details in applying the control chart procedures; fraction defective; acceptance sampling; application of the statistical theory of errors; application of analysis of variance; and planning an investigation. Assumes knowledge of basic statistics.

Tsokos, Chris P., and Shimi, I.N., eds. THE THEORY AND APPLICATIONS OF RELIABILITY: WITH EMPHASIS ON BAYESIAN AND NONPARAMETRIC METHODS. Vol. 1. New York: Academic Press, 1977. xvi, 549 p. No index.

Twenty-nine papers presented at a conference on the theory and application of reliability held at the University of South Florida in Tampa, December 15-18, 1977. Topics include Bayesian approach for testing increasing failure rates; nonparametric estimation of distribution functions; Wilcoxon Mann-Whitney statistic with applications to reliability; the asymptotic theory of extreme order statistics; shock and wear models and Markov additive processes; bounds for the distributions and hazard gradients of multivariate random minimums; structural inference on reliability in a lognormal model; uniformly most powerful unbiased tests for the parameters of the gamma distribution; stochastic characterization of multivariate survival; optimal replacement policies for devices subject to a gamma wear process; opportunistic replacement policies; and optimal sampling procedures for selection problems.

_____. THE THEORY AND APPLICATIONS OF RELIABILITY WITH EMPHASIS ON BAYESIAN AND NONPARAMETRIC METHODS. Vol. II. New York: Academic Press, 1977. xvi, 582 p. No index.

Twenty-seven papers presented at a conference on the theory and application of reliability held at the University of South Florida in Tampa, December 15-18, 1975. Topics include Bayesian confidence bounds for the Poisson failure model; Bayes' estimation of reliability for the lognormal distribution; robustness and the prior distribution in Bayesian estimation; estimation of nonlinear models and specification of the errors; reliability estimation under competing causes of failure; reliability analysis of three-state Markov models; least squares analysis of accelerated life tests for the power rule and Arrhenius models; analysis of variance for Weibull populations; estimation of a multi-parameter failure rate using a general replacement testing plan; system reliability using Bernoulli sampling of components; application of nonparametric methods in the statistical and economic analysis of warranties; nonparametic tests of exponential distributions with unknown parameters; and Bayesian estimation of system reliability for Weibull distributions using Monte Carlo simulation.

Wetherill, G. Barrie. SAMPLING INSPECTION AND QUALITY CONTROL. 2d ed., rev. New York: Halsted Press, 1977. viii, 146 p. Papers and Books for Further Reading, p. 126. Appendix I: Theoretical Models for Industrial Processes, pp. 127-28. Appendix II: Statistical Tables, pp. 129-36. References, pp. 137-43. Index, pp. 145-46.

A supplementary text and a reference which gives broad coverage of sampling inspection and quality control with emphasis on the principles of various quality control plans. Exercises provided at the ends of most sections, with the more difficult ones marked with an asterisk. Topics include acceptance sampling; control charts; cumulative sum charts; and continuous sampling plans. Knowledge of basic statistics assumed.

Chapter 11

BIOMETRICS AND MEDICAL STUDIES

American Mathematical Society. SOME MATHEMATICAL PROBLEMS IN BIOLOGY. Foreword by Murray Gerstenhaber. Lectures on Mathematics in the Life Sciences. Providence, R.I.: 1968. vi, 117 p. Author Index, pp. 113-14. Subject Index, pp. 115-17.

> Three papers presented at the first symposium on mathematical biology held in Washington, D.C., in December 1966: "The Ecological Role of Volterra's Equations," by Egbert R. Leigh; "Evolution of Complex Genetic Systems," by Richard C. Lewontin; and "Studies on the Biological Clocks: A Model for the Circadian Rhythms of Nocturnal Organisms," by Theodosios Pavlidis.

Armitage, P. SEQUENTIAL MEDICAL TRIALS. 2d ed., rev. New York: Halsted Press, 1975. xi, 194 p. Appendix: Notes on Statistical Theory, pp. 170-76. Index to Principal Tables, p. 177. References, pp. 179-89. Index, pp. 191-94.

> Presents sequential methods of design and analysis by means of which the results of one trial can be examined continuously as they become available and can thus form the basis of a decision to stop the trial at a suitable point. Assumes knowledge of at least basic statistics, and preferably intermediate statistics. Topics based on their usefulness in practical applications and include the nature of medical trials; sequential experimentation; evaluation by preference; comparison of two proportions; measurement with known and unknown variability; and sequential models. Proofs excluded.

______. STATISTICAL METHODS IN MEDICAL RESEARCH. New York: Wiley, 1971. xv, 504 p. Appendix: Tables, pp. 458-75. Some Books for Further Reading, pp. 476-77. References, pp. 478-85. Author Index, pp. 486-88. Subject Index, pp. 489-504.

> A reference for the medical research worker who has very little mathematical expertise and for the professional statistician interested in medical applications. Proofs usually omitted or

relegated to small type. Calculus used occasionally for explanation. Topics include probability distributions; sampling errors of the mean, proportion, and variance; statistical inference; regression and correlation; planning of statistical investigations; comparison of several groups, including analysis of variance; Latin squares and other incomplete designs; analysis of covariance; simple and multiple regression and multivariate analysis; data editing; distribution-free methods; sequential methods; statistical methods in epidemiology; and biological assay. Numerous short illustrative examples provided.

Ashton, Winifred Diana. THE LOGIT TRANSFORMATION WITH SPECIAL REFERENCE TO ITS USES IN BIOASSAY. Griffin's Statistical Monographs and Courses, no. 32. London: Charles Griffin, 1972. viii, 88 p. Appendix 1: Standard Errors of Functions of Random Variables, pp. 77-78. Appendix 2: Tables of Logits, Antilogits, and Logistic Weights, pp. 79-84. References, pp. 85-87. Index, p. 88.

Covers the theory of linear transformations, and the method of logits in particular, including the maximum likelihood and minimum chi-square methods for fitting the parameters of the logistic function, and worked examples from bioassay. Also discusses the advantages and disadvantages of the more important types of transformations, such as the angular transformation. Assumes knowledge of basic statistics. Useful to research workers in biology.

Atkins, Gordon Leslie. MULTICOMPARTMENT MODELS FOR BIOLOGICAL SYSTEMS. London: Methuen, 1969. xiii, 153 p. Appendixes: Mathematical Methods, pp. 117-47. References, p. 147. Index, pp. 149-53.

Describes certain biological systems in terms of multicompartment models where the rate of transfer of a material out of a given compartment is proportional to the amount or concentration of the material within the compartment. Systems described by a set of linear differential equations. Topics include systems in steady state; systems not in steady state; simulation techniques; treatment of experimental data; and curve fitting and model fitting. Appendixes present an account of the mathematics useful in compartment analysis, including the differential operator, the Laplace transform, matrices and determinants, kinetics of systems in a steady state, and references. Assumes knowledge of linear differential equations. Applications included.

Bailey, Norman T.J. THE MATHEMATICAL THEORY OF INFECTIOUS DISEASES AND ITS APPLICATIONS. 2d rev. ed. Books on Cognate Subjects. London: Charles Griffin & Co., 1975. xvi, 413 p. Appendix: Tables, pp. 376-82. References, pp. 383-403. Index of Authors, pp. 405-8. Index of Subjects, pp. 409-13.

A systematic treatment of the mathematical and statistical theory of epidemics in three parts: "Orientation"; "General Theory"; and "Specific Applications." Topics include simple and general epidemics; recurrent epidemics and endemicity; discrete-time, spatial, and carrier models; host vector and venereal disease models; detection of infectiousness; chain-binomial models; simple multistage models; parasitic diseases; interference models; geographical spread; immunization programs; and public health control. Includes both deterministic and stochastic models. Assumes knowledge of intermediate probability theory, linear algebra, mathematical statistics, and advanced calculus.

______. STATISTICAL METHODS IN BIOLOGY. New York: Wiley, 1959. ix, 200 p. Suggestions for More Advanced Readings, p. 161. Summary of Statistical Formulas, pp. 163-91. Appendix: Tables, pp. 192-97. Index, pp. 198-200.

Primarily a reference for workers in the biological and medical sciences who already have some acquaintance with statistical concepts. No trigonometry or calculus used, and fully worked examples of each type of analysis provided. Topics include frequency distributions, including normal, binomial, and Poisson; confidence limits and significance tests; including comparisons of means of two samples; t distribution for small samples; chi-square and contingency tables; correlation of measurements; experimental design and analysis of variance; factorial experiments; random samples; partial correlation and regression; and the use of calculus for computations.

Balaam, L.N. FUNDAMENTALS OF BIOMETRY. New York: Wiley, Halsted Press, 1972. xiv, 259 p. Answers to Exercises, pp. 238-42. Statistical Tables, I-V, pp. 243-55. Index, pp. 256-59.

A text for an introductory undergraduate course for students in the biological and agricultural sciences who possess knowledge of college algebra. More rigorous than most elementary textbooks, with many simple theorems proved and illustrated with examples. Topics include variables and variation, including linear transformation of variables; probability and probability distributions; properties of distributions, including expected values; sampling theory, including estimation and hypothesis testing; the t distribution and the F test; nonparametric tests; analysis of variance; and chi-square. Exercises throughout the text intended to give practice in biometrical techniques. Each chapter also concludes with collateral reading.

Banks, H.T. MODELLING AND CONTROL IN THE BIOMEDICAL SCIENCES. Lecture Notes in Biomathematics, vol. 6. New York: Springer-Verlag, 1975. 114 p. Bibliography, pp. 104-14. No index.

A monograph on the use of optimization and control in biomedical science. Topics include models for enzymatically active membranes and enzyme cascades; control of epidemics; modeling of the control system in glucose homeostasis; probability and deterministic models of tumor growth; and patient care and diagnostic models. Assumes knowledge of differential equations and elementary probability.

Bartlett, Maurice Stevenson, and Hiorns, R.W., eds. THE MATHEMATICAL THEORY OF THE DYNAMICS OF BIOLOGICAL POPULATIONS. New York: Academic Press, 1973. xii, 347 p. Author Index, pp. 337-40. Subject Index, pp. 341-47.

Nineteen papers presented at a conference held at Oxford University in 1972 grouped under the following five parts: "Population Processes in Time" (three papers); "Population Processes in Space" (four papers); "Population Genetics" (four papers); "Estimation and Simulation Problems" (four papers); and "Population Distributions and Commodity Structure" (four papers). Topics include simulation model for studying the population dynamics of fish; predator-prey models; geographic variation in host-parasite specificity; stochastic processes in artificial selection; dynamics of migration and selection in human populations; capture-recapture studies; estimation of parameters from epidemic models; stochastic formulation for life tables; and species diversity in ecological communities.

Batschelet, Edward. INTRODUCTION TO MATHEMATICS FOR LIFE SCIENTISTS. 2d ed. New York: Springer-Verlag, 1976. xv, 643 p. Appendix: Tables, pp. 572-86. Solutions to Odd-Numbered Problems, pp. 587-609. References, pp. 610-21. Author and Subject Index, pp. 623-43.

A text for a one-year course in mathematics for the life sciences for students who have a college algebra background. Each concept introduced in an intuitive style, and all procedures illustrated by examples. Topics include real numbers; sets and symbolic logic; relations and functions; power, periodic logarithmic, and exponential functions; limits; differential and integral calculus; ordinary differential equations; functions of two or more independent variables; probability; matrices and vectors; and complex numbers. Graphs and charts used freely to supplement the mathematical exposition. Chapters conclude with problems.

Benjamin, Bernard. ELEMENTS OF VITAL STATISTICS. Chicago: Quadrangle Books, 1959. 352 p. Index, pp. 348-52.

A text for a course in vital and health statistics for students who have a high school algebra background, although calculus occasionally used. Excludes mathematical derivations. Numerical examples illustrate U.K. conditions. Topics include population census; measures of fertility and mortality, and morbidity; statistics of infectious diseases; maternity and child welfare; public health statistics; hospital statistics; cancer statistics; mental health statistics; and general practitioner statistics. Chapters conclude with references.

Bernstein, Leon, and Weatherall, M. STATISTICS FOR MEDICAL AND OTHER BIOLOGICAL STUDENTS. Edinburgh, Scot.: E. & S. Livingstone, 1952. xii, 180 p. Appendix A: Biological Normality, pp. 155-56. Appendix B: The Choice of Statistical Tests, pp. 157-60. Supplementary Tables, pp. 161-73. Index, pp. 175-80.

A reference and supplementary text on the logical and mathematical bases of selected statistical procedures used in medical and biological research for students who have knowledge of elementary algebra. Emphasizes verbal explanation and examples with only a few short derivations provided. Topics include descriptive statistics; chance differences; regression and correlation; transformations; analysis of variance; experimental design; therapeutic experiments; and interpretation of observations.

Blesser, William B. A SYSTEMS APPROACH TO BIOMEDICINE. McGraw-Hill Series in Bioengineering. New York: McGraw-Hill, 1969. xv, 615 p. Appendix A: Modal Analysis and Computer Elements, pp. 569-80. Appendix B: Source Representations, pp. 581-87. Appendix C: Partial-Fraction Expansion, pp. 588-92. Appendix D: Table of Laplace Transforms, p. 593. Glossary of Terms, pp. 594-600. Index, pp. 601-15.

A text for a course in systems analysis for students of biomedicine who understand the rudiments of calculus, as well as an introduction for engineering students preparing for a more advanced course. Emphasizes the verbal style. Uses few formulas and derivations. Topics include system properties of resistance and storage; simulation; systems with combined properties; transfer function; impedance concept; periodic signals; relation between phase log and time log; transient oscillations and resonance; and feedback. Chapters conclude with problems and references. Includes simple physiological examples.

Bliss, Chester I. STATISTICS IN BIOLOGY: STATISTICAL METHODS FOR RESEARCH IN THE NATURAL SCIENCES. Vol. One. New York: McGraw-Hill, 1967. xiii, 558 p. Glossary, pp. 479-86. Appendix: Tables, pp. 487-537. Name Index, pp. 539-43. Subject Index, pp. 545-58.

A text for a one-year course in basic statistics for students of biology and related fields (forestry, agriculture, medicine, oceanography, etc.) who have a college algebra background. Worked examples and exercises based on real data supplemented by data generated by random sampling. Few derivations included. Emphasizes assumptions in the use of the formulas. Topics include binomial and chi-square distributions; analysis of four-fold tables; normal distribution, descriptive statistics; lognormal distribution; intervals in statistical estimating; analysis of variance; comparison of several groups; experimental designs; split-plot designs; and linear regression. Chapters conclude with references and examples.

______. STATISTICS IN BIOLOGY. METHODS FOR RESEARCH IN THE NATURAL SCIENCES. Vol. Two. New York: McGraw-Hill, 1970. xii, 639 p. Appendix: Tables, pp. 543-612. Name Index, pp. 613-19. Subject Index, pp. 621-39.

Topics include polynomial regression; exponential and hyperbolic regression; periodic regression; multivariate regression; factorial experiments; and covariance. Chapters conclude with exercises and references. Assumes knowledge of basic statistics.

Bourke, Geoffrey Joseph, and Gilvray, James. INTERPRETATION AND USES OF MEDICAL STATISTICS. Oxford: Blackwell Scientific Publications, 1969. viii, 162 p. Index, pp. 159-62.

A text on the scope, logic, and technique of statistical methods in medicine and related subjects for graduates and undergraduates who have had no formal training in medical statistics, and a reference for research workers. Emphasizes interpretation rather than calculation, with no mathematical derivations. Topics include descriptive statistics; samples and populations; normal distribution; tests of significance and estimation concerning the difference between two means; simple and multiple regression and correlation; dichotomous populations; sequential sampling; analysis of variance; and life tables and cohort analysis.

Brown, Byron William, and Hollander, Myles. STATISTICS: A BIOMEDICAL INTRODUCTION. Wiley Series in Probability and Mathematical Statistics. New York: Wiley, 1977. xiii, 456 p. Appendix A: Glossary, pp. 361-74. Appendix B: Answers to Selected Questions and Solutions to Selected Problems, pp. 375-406. Appendix C: Mathematical and Statistical Tables, pp. 407-50. Index, pp. 451-56.

A text for a one-semester course in basic statistics for students of biology and medicine who have knowledge of college algebra. Chapters begin with data sets arising from studies in the biomedical sciences. Topics include rules of probability; analysis of matched pairs using sample means; analysis of the two-sample location problem; surveys in medical research; statistical inference for dichotomous variables; comparing two success probabilities; chi-square; analysis of variance; linear regression and correlation; analysis of matched pairs using ranks; two-sample location problem using ranks; and methods for censored data. Chapters conclude with references and sources of basic data sets.

Brown, J.H.U.; Jacobs, John E.; and Stark, Lawrence. BIOMEDICAL ENGINEERING. Philadelphia: F.A. Davis, 1971. xvi, 435 p. Appendix 1: Control Theory by George A. Bekey and Matthew B. Wolf, pp. 379-95. Appendix 2: Pattern Recognition by Daniel Bertoux, pp. 396-404. Appendix 3: Introduction to Analog/Hybrid Programming by James Mitchell, pp. 405-19. Index, pp. 421-35.

Fourteen general contributions, by different authors, on the basic principles of modeling, system theory, control, biological systems analysis, instrumentation, and engineering in the delivery of health services grouped under the following five headings: "Engineering Concepts in Biomedicine" (four papers); "Engineering in the Analysis of Physiological Systems" (five papers); "Instrumentation" (one paper); "Biomaterials" (one paper); and "Engineering and Health Care" (three papers). Useful to the novice and beginning student in engineering and biology.

Buckland, William R. STATISTICAL ASSESSMENT OF THE LIFE CHARACTERISTICS: A BIBLIOGRAPHIC GUIDE. Griffin's Statistical Monographs and Courses, no. 13. New York: Hafner, 1964. 125 p. Appendix: Select List of Additional References Occurring Principally During the Period 1961 to 1963, pp. 121-25. No index.

An annotated bibliography and guide to a large portion of the literature in life testing up to 1961 in the following four chapters: Some General Problems, Problems of Estimation, Tests of Hypotheses, and Analysis of Fatigue Tests. Includes explanation of references on right-hand page, with actual references on left-hand page. References during 1961-63 provided in a separate five-page appendix. Annotation qualitative, providing a good starting point for statisticians and others seeking information on life testing.

Byrkit, Donald R. ELEMENTS OF STATISTICS: AN INTRODUCTION TO PROBABILITY AND STATISTICAL INFERENCE. 2d ed., rev. New York: D. Van Nostrand, 1975. x, 431 p. Appendix A: Mathematical Review, pp. 311-21. Appendix B: Nonparametric Tests, pp. 323-37. Tables, pp. 338-76. Answers, pp. 377-426. Index, pp. 427-31.

A text for a one-semester course in basic statistics for students in the biological and social sciences. Emphasizes the use of statistical inference in decision-making, with presentation based on demonstration by example, rather than on mathematical exposition. Consists of five parts: "Descriptive Methods"; "Probability and Probability Distributions"; "The Binomial and Normal

Distributions"; "Samples"; and "Decisions." Topics include confidence intervals for means and proportions; tests concerning means and proportions and differences between two means and two proportions; analysis of variance; correlation and regression; and chi-square. Sections conclude with problems; chapters with review problems.

Campbell, Richard Colin. STATISTICS FOR BIOLOGISTS. 2d ed. New York: Cambridge University Press, 1974. xiv, 385 p. Further Reading, p. 340. References, pp. 341-42. Appendix: Tables and Figures for Statistical Tests and Exercises, pp. 343-79. Index, pp. 381-85.

A text for a one-semester course in basic statistics for students of biology who have knowledge of high school algebra. Emphasizes the exposition of ideas using mathematical symbols, and topics include descriptive statistics; interval estimation of population median; comparison of two and several samples using nonparametric tests; measures of association, including chi-square; decision theory, including utility, minimax, and Bayes' rules; normal distribution; tests of significance concerning differences between two population means; analysis of variance; regression and correlation; binomial and Poisson distributions; and transformation of variables. Chapters conclude with exercises.

Chambers, E.G. STATISTICAL CALCULATION FOR BEGINNERS. 2d ed., rev. Cambridge: Cambridge University Press, 1964. x, 168 p. Answers to Exercises, pp. 148-52. Appendixes A to K, pp. 153-66. Index, pp. 167-68.

Presents the calculations involved in basic statistical methods accompanied by enough statistical theory to enable the student to understand the use and application of the methods. Addressed chiefly to students in the biological sciences, and uses only arithmetic. Topics include averages; scatter or dispersion; the normal and binomial distributions; difference between means; simple, product-moment, partial, rank, biserial, and fourfold correlations; regression; chi-square; contingency, and goodness of fit; ranking and the agreement of judges; and introduction to analysis of variance. Appendixes consist of statistical tables.

Clarke, Geoffrey M. STATISTICS AND EXPERIMENTAL DESIGN. New York: Elsevier, 1969. xi, 161 p. References and Bibliography, p. 137. Answers to and Comments Upon Exercises, pp. 138-48. Tables, pp. 149-56. Index, pp. 157-61.

Mainly a supplementary text for a course in basic statistics for biology students. Stresses the use of symbols and notation in explaining basic statistical concepts, and emphasizes elementary aspects of experimental design. Topics include normal, Poisson, and binomial probability distributions; tests of hypotheses, including difference between two means; chi-square; F distribution;

confidence interval estimates of population means and proportions; regression and correlation; completely randomized designs; randomized blocks; Latin squares; factorial experiments; missing observations and non-normality; and nonparametric tests. Worked examples and exercises follow the chapters. Based on lectures given to biology students in an honors degree course at the University of Sussex.

Cowan, Jack D., ed. SOME MATHEMATICAL QUESTIONS IN BIOLOGY II. Lectures on Mathematics in the Life Sciences, vol. 3. Providence, R.I.: American Mathematical Society, 1972. vii, 121 p. Author Index, pp. 117-18. Subject Index, pp. 119-21.

Three papers presented at the fourth symposium on mathematical biology presented in Boston in December 1969. Papers concerned with the molecular and cellular control of differentiation and development in multicellular organisms. Topics include models of clocks and maps in developing organisms; periodic wave propagation and pattern formation with applications to problems in development; and the organization of cellular genetic control systems.

______. SOME MATHEMATICAL QUESTIONS IN BIOLOGY III. Lectures on Mathematics in the Life Sciences, vol. 4. Providence, R.I.: American Mathematical Society, 1972. vi, 151 p. Author Index, pp. 145-47. Subject Index, pp. 148-51.

Four papers presented at the fifth symposium on mathematical biology held in Chicago, in December 1970. Papers deal with the theoretical biology of development, and topics include control of development in cellular slime molds; analysis of the retino-tectol projection of the amphibian visual system; and the application of Lotka-Volterra equations for ecological kinetics.

Cutbill, J.L., ed. DATA PROCESSING IN BIOLOGY AND GEOLOGY. Systematics Association Special, vol. 3. New York: Academic Press, 1971. xv, 346 p. Author Index, pp. 331-33. Subject Index, pp. 335-46.

Twenty papers presented at a symposium held at the University of Cambridge, September 24-26, 1969. Includes an introduction by John L. Cutbill. Topics include mark sensing for recording and analysis of sedimentological data; source data automation; a computer program package for experimental data banking; machine languages for representation of geological information; geological data structure; automatic data handling in geochemistry; and data processing for museums.

Dahlberg, Gunnar. MATHEMATICAL METHODS FOR POPULATION GENETICS. Basle, Switz.: S. Karger, 1947. viii, 182 p. Bibliography, pp. 176-79. Index, pp. 180-82.

A survey of elementary mathematical applications in population genetics using only simple college algebra with graphic and numerical illustrations. Areas studied include forms of inheritance; composition of populations in panmixia; effect of mutatins on the composition of a population in panmixia; effect of selection on a population; effect of inmarriage on a population; assortative mating; isolates and race, and isolates and inmarriage. First attempt at a synthetic presentation of problems of heredity from the population aspect. Comprehensible to persons with no mathematical training.

Daniel, Wayne W. BIOSTATISTICS: A FOUNDATION FOR ANALYSIS IN THE HEALTH SCIENCES. New York: Wiley, 1974. xvi, 448 p. Appendix: Tables, pp. 381-439. Answers to Odd-Numbered Exercises, pp. 439-43. Index, pp. 445-48.

A text for a two-semester course in biostatistics for graduates and undergraduates in the health services field who have knowledge of college algebra, and a reference for a wide range of professionals. Includes examples and exercises of interest to the public health nurse, the hospital administrator, the laboratory technologist, the health educator, the pharmacist, and others. Emphasizes appealing to the student's intuition instead of on mathematical derivations. Topics include sampling distributions; set theory and probability; binomial, Poisson and normal distributions; estimation and hypothesis testing concerning differences between two means and two proportions; completely randomized designs; factorial experiments; simple and multiple regression and correlation; chi-square and goodness of fit; nonparametric statistics; and vital statistics. Chapters conclude with exercises, review questions, and references.

Defares, J.G., and Sneddon, I.N. With the assistance of M.E. Wise. AN INTRODUCTION TO THE MATHEMATICS OF MEDICINE AND BIOLOGY. 2d ed. Foreword to the first edition by J.W. Duyff. Chicago: Year Book Medical Publishers, 1970. xv, 675 p. Appendix: Determinants, pp. 633-43. Further Reading, pp. 644-54. Answers to Problems, pp. 655-65. Addenda and Corrigenda, p. 666. Name Index, pp. 667-68. Subject Index, pp. 669-75.

A reference on mathematical techniques and applications for research workers in the biological and medical sciences. Topics include algebra; functions of a single variable; limits and derivatives; differential calculus; integration; logarithms and exponential functions; functions of more than one variable; differential equations; and applications to medicine and biology. Includes probability distributions but excludes statistical methods. Presentation consists of explanation of concepts, theorems with proofs, and examples and illustrations. Sections conclude with problems.

Deutsch, Sid. MODELS OF THE NERVOUS SYSTEM. New York: Wiley, 1967. ix, 266 p. Index, pp. 261-66.

Presents a number of mathematical models of the nervous system for use by engineers, although biologists who have knowledge of calculus, matrix algebra, linear system theory, and Laplace transforms can follow. Topics include models of neuron function; neuron networks of the spinal chord; multisynoptic chains with and without feedback; the local feedback loops of skeletal muscle; stimulus-amplitude discrimination; learning and memory; recognition of auditory and visual patterns; and somatic, motor, and thought patterns. Mathematical derivations kept to a minimum, and chapters conclude with problems and references.

Dunn, Olive Jean. BASIC STATISTICS: A PRIMER FOR THE BIOMEDICAL SCIENCES. Foreword by Wilfrid J. Dixon. Series on Quantitative Methods for Biologists and Medical Scientists. New York: Wiley, 1964. xiii, 184 p. Appendix: Tables, pp. 161-75. Answers to Some of the Exercises, pp. 177-80. Index, pp. 181-84.

A text for a one-semester course in statistics for students in the biomedical field who have knowledge of high school algebra and a reference for the physician and others engaged in research. Topics include population and samples; descriptive statistics; normal distribution; confidence intervals for means, variances, proportions, and differences between two means; tests of hypotheses concerning means and differences between two means and two proportions; chi-square; and regression and correlation. Sections conclude with exercises.

Dyke, Bennett, and MacCluer, Jean Walters. COMPUTER SIMULATION IN HUMAN POPULATION STUDIES. Studies in Anthropology. New York: Academic Press, 1973. xx, 518 p. Bibliography, pp. 505-13. Index, pp. 515-18.

Twenty-four papers presented at a conference held at the Pennsylvania State University, June 12-14, 1972. Conference divided equally between techniques and applications, with papers grouped under the following four headings: "Anthropology and Social Systems" (six papers); "Genetics and Adaptive Systems" (six appers); "Demography" (seven papers); and "Simulation Methdology" (five papers). Topics include simulating human reproduction; migrating model; empirical perspective on simulation models of human population; simulation over space; research and experience with demographic simulation models; the mathematics of population simulation models; computer generation of random variates; and computer programs for simulation.

Elandt-Johnson, Regina C. PROBABILITY MODELS AND STATISTICAL METHODS IN GENETICS. Wiley Series in Probability and Mathematical Statistics. New

York: Wiley, 1971. xviii, 592 p. Appendix I: Elements of Matrix Algebra, pp. 555-68. Appendix II: Minima and Maxima of Functions, Taylor's Expansion, pp. 569-75. Index of Statistical and Mathematical Terms, pp. 577-88. Index of Authors, pp. 589-92.

A text for a course in probability and statistics for students of genetics who have knowledge of the rudiments of calculus. Emphasizes genetical applications and formal definitions, rather than detailed proofs, with major emphasis given to discrete random variables, rather than continuous ones. Consists of the following two parts: "Population Genetics: Probability Models" and "Experimental Genetics: Estimation of Genetic Parameters and Testing Genetic Hypotheses." Topics include genotypes and phenotypes in experimental populations; equilibrium laws in panmictic populations; inbreeding and non-random mating; natural selection and mutation; estimation of genetic parameters; estimation of parameters associated with multinomial distributions; testing genetic hypotheses; human blood groups; autosomal linkage in experimental populations; statistically equivalent models of inheritance; complex segregation analysis; and histocompatibility testing. Chapters conclude with references and problems.

Elashoff, Robert M., ed. PERSPECTIVES IN BIOMETRICS. Vol. 1. New York: Academic Press, 1975. xii, 200 p. Index, pp. 199-200.

Six heretofore unpublished papers on research and methodological aspects of biometrical data analysis. Emphasizes computer-based interactive data analysis using APL. Chapter titles: "Interactive Statistical Computation with Large Data Structures," by M. Schatzoff, P. Bryant, and A.P. Dempster; "A Survey of Adaptive Sampling for Clinical Trials," by D.G. Hoel, M. Sobel, and G.H. Weiss; "Computer-Aided Prognosis," by H.D. Brunk, D.R. Thomas, R.M. Elashoff, and C. Zippin; "The Use and Interpretation of Multivariate Methods in the Classification of Stages in Serious Infectious Disease Processes in the Critically Ill," by H.P. Friedman, R.M. Goldwyn, and J.H. Siegel; "Approximate Tests and Confidence Intervals Using the Jacknife," by J.N. Arvesen and D.S. Salsburg; and "Estimation Procedures for Simulation Applications," by M.E. Tarter.

Emmens, C.W. PRINCIPLES OF BIOLOGICAL ASSAY. Foreword by Percival Hartley. London: Chapman and Hall, 1948. xv, 206 p. Appendix: Notation, pp. 203-4. Index, pp. 205-6

A monograph on statistical methods in biological essay (the design and analysis of tests made for the purpose of assigning limits within which the potency of preparations may be presumed to fall in comparison with a standard) for research workers and practitioners. No proofs given and examples taken from actual assays. Topics include applications of mathematics to biological assay; means, variances, and degrees of freedom; comparison between groups using analysis of variance; dose-response lines using regression; Latin designs; polynomial coefficients; covariance; estimation of relative potency; 2x4-point assay with restrictions in design; chi-square; variance of a probit; probit assay; assays based on reaction times; and choosing and measuring the response.

Falconer, Douglas Scott. INTRODUCTION TO QUANTITATIVE GENETICS. London: Oliver & Boyd, 1960. ix, 365 p. Glossary of Symbols, pp. 346-48. Indexed List of References, pp. 349-60. Subject Index, pp. 361-65.

An introduction to quantitative genetics with emphasis on principles rather than on applications for students of biology who have a good high school algebra background and one year of basic statistics, as well as an elementary knowledge of Mendelian genetics. Topics include changes in gene frequency; pedigreed populations and close inbreeding; means and variances; heritability; selection; inbreeding and crossbreeding; scale; threshold characters; correlated characters; and metric characters under natural selection. Examples used to illustrate the theory.

Finney, David John. PROBIT ANALYSIS. 3d ed., rev. New York: Cambridge University Press, 1971. xv, 333 p. References, pp. 269-82. Tables, pp. 283-324. Index of Authors, pp. 325-27. Index of Subjects, pp. 328-33.

Presents statistical techniques needed in the analysis of quantal response data (all-or-nothing response), rather than with the general theory of biological assay (the measurement of the potency of any stimulus by means of reactions which it produces in living matter). Most material presented in terms of tests of the potencies of intesticides. Topics include quantal responses and the dose-response curve; estimation of median effective doses; maximum likelihood estimation; comparison of effectiveness; adjustments for natural responsiveness; factorial experiments and other designs; and quantal responses to mixtures using correlation analysis. Includes forty-one detailed examples, and an example of probit calculations by computer. Includes detailed derivations with emphasis on computation of results. Assumes knowledge of basic statistics.

Fleiss, Joseph L. STATISTICAL METHODS FOR RATES AND PROPORTIONS. Wiley Series in Probability and Mathematical Statistics. New York: Wiley, 1973. xiii, 223 p. Appendix: Tables, pp. 173-208. Author Index, pp. 209-12. Subject Index, pp. 213-23.

A reference for research workers which deals solely with comparisons of qualitative or categorical data with emphasis and examples from clinical medicine, epidemiology, psychiatry and psychopathology, and public health. Prerequisites include high school algebra, one year of applied statistics and a thorough grounding of chi-square and correlation. Topics include significance in a four-fold table; determination of sample sizes needed to detect a difference between two proportions; sampling methods for cross-sectoral studies, prospective and retrospective studies, and controlled comparative trials; analysis of data from matched samples; the measurement and control of misclassification errors; and the standardization of rates. Chapters also conclude with references.

Franklin, D.A., and Newman, G.B. A GUIDE TO MEDICAL MATHEMATICS. New York: Wiley, Halsted Press, 1973. xii, 453 p. Appendix, pp. 389-423. Notes for Preparation of Mathematical Papers, pp. 425-27. References, pp. 429-32. Tables, pp. 433-41. Symbol Index, p. 443. Index, pp. 444-53.

An exposition of mathematical notation and methods in medical work. Topics include graphs and functions; indexes; the binomial theorem and logarithms; limits and continuity; ordered sets of data; vector and matrix algebra; co-ordinate geometry; calculus; series; computational methods and curve fitting; and differential equations. The appendix contains many formulas not discussed in the chapters. Intended for the medical research worker and student whose study of mathematics stopped at an early stage in their careers.

Friedenberg, Robert M. UNEXPLORED MODEL SYSTEMS IN MODERN BIOLOGY. Pioneering Concepts in Modern Science, vol. 1. New York: Hafner, 1968. ix, 98 p. Index, pp. 93-98.

Uses simplified mathematics to explore new ideas and concepts in model systems of modern biology in three parts: "A Criterion for Biological Model Systems"; "Exobiology (Outer Space Biology)"; and "Long Range Forces in Biology." Topics include classification and analysis of biological models; applications of thermodynamics to living systems; applications of quantum mechanics to living systems; and electrostatics of biological cell membranes. Portions assume knowledge of differential equations.

Gani, Joseph Mark. STOCHASTIC MODELS FOR BACTERIOPHAGE. Methurn's Review Series in Applied Probability, vol. 4. London: Methuen, 1966. 46 p. References, pp. 42-44. Index, pp. 45-46.

A pamphlet which develops mathematical models for the following biological processes: biological processes of phage; phage reproduction and mutation in a bacterium; age distribution of vegetative phage; extinction of bacterial colonies; and attachment models. Assumes knowledge of advanced calculus and differential equations.

Gelfand, I.M.; Gurfinkel, V.S.; Fomin, S.V.; and Tseflin, M.L., eds. STRUCTURAL-FUNCTIONAL ORGANIZATION OF CERTAIN BIOLOGICAL SYSTEMS. Foreword by Peter H. Greene. Translation by Carol R. Beard. Translation reviewed by John S. Barlow. Cambridge, Mass.: MIT Press, 1971. xxxviii, 405 p. Index, pp. 396-405.

Thirteen papers originally published in Russian in 1966 on theoretical and experimental studies conducted at the Institute of Problems of Information Transmission in Moscow. Topics include mathematical models of the central nervous system; functional properties of dendrites in relation to their structure; electrical behavior of the myocardium as a system and the characteristics of the cellular membrane of the heart; electrical properties of syncytia; respiratory neurons; model of a system of neurons with periodic volley activity; organization of the cerebellar cortex; regulation and analysis of movements; analysis of physiological tremor by means of computers; and control of movements of the joints and kinesthetic afferentation.

George, Frank Honywill. CYBERNETICS AND BIOLOGY. San Francisco: Freeman, 1965. vii, 138 p. References, pp. 132-36. Index, pp. 137-38.

A brief introduction to cybernetics for biologists, especially for ethologists, or biologists with special interest in behavioral problems. Deals verbally (only a few formulas are used) with the following topics: automata theory; logic and information theory; biological models; digital computers; theorems of cognition; cybernetics modeling of perception; models of cognition; language and artificial intelligence; and models of the nervous system.

Gerstenhaber, Murray, ed. SOME MATHEMATICAL QUESTIONS IN BIOLOGY. I. Lectures on Mathematics in the Life Sciences, vol. 2. Providence, R.I.: American Mathematical Society, 1970. vii, 156 p. Author Index, pp. 151-52. Subject Index, pp. 153-56.

Four papers presented at the second symposium on mathematical biology held in New York in December 1967, and the third symposium held in Dallas in December 1968. Topics include statistical mechanics of nervous activity; graphical analysis of ecological systems; models of extinction of species; and the temporal morphology of a biological clock.

Goel, Narendra S., and Dyn, Nira Richter. STOCHASTIC MODELS IN BIOLOGY. New York: Academic Press, 1974. x, 269 p. Appendixes A to H, pp. 245-65. Index, pp. 267-69.

A monograph for both professionals and amateurs on the theory of stochastic processes in biology from the molecular to the ecological level. Knowledge of stochastic processes assumed.

Topics include random processes continuous in time and both discrete and continuous in state space; population growth and extinction; population growth of two-species systems; dynamics of a population of interacting species; population genetics; firing of a neuron; chemical kinetics; and photosynthesis. Appendixes contain additional mathematical results and calculations. Chapters conclude with references.

Gold, Harvey J. MATHEMATICAL MODELING OF BIOLOGICAL SYSTEMS--AN INTRODUCTORY GUIDEBOOK. New York: Wiley, Interscience, 1977. xv, 357 p. Appendix A: Examples, pp. 266-307. Appendix B: Mathematical Review, pp. 308-35. Appendix C: Mathematical Approximation, pp. 336-39. Appendix D: Linearity and the Use of Averages, pp. 340-45. Appendix E: Discussion of Exercises, pp. 346-50. Index, pp. 351-57.

A text for a one-semester course in mathematical modeling for students of biology who are familiar with calculus. Assists in understanding how biological concepts and systems can be formulated in mathematical terms and how these formulations may be used in research. Examples drawn from a wide variety of areas. Topics include mathematical models; modeling process, including variables, parameters, and the state of the system; dimension and similarity; probability, expected values, and probability models; dynamic processes, including simple linear rate processes; feedback control and stability of biological systems, including Lotka-Volterra model for two species; sensitivity analysis; curve fitting and correlation; and computer simulation of systems. Exercises scattered throughout text.

Goldstein, Avram. BIOSTATISTICS: AN INTRODUCTORY TEXT. New York: Macmillan, 1964. xi, 272 p. Answers to Problems, pp. 196-233. Tables, pp. 234-65. Index, pp. 267-72.

An early text for a course in applied biostatistics for medical students who have a college algebra background and descriptive statistics, and a reference for research workers. Few derivations provided. Topics include aspects of experimental design; statistical hypotheses and decision rules; confidence intervals for two means; comparison of single means, including the two-sample rank test; analysis of variance with bioassay data; interval estimate of a ratio; and parallel-line bioassay with quantal responses. Chapters conclude with problems.

Greville, Thomas Nall Eden, ed. POPULATION DYNAMICS. New York: Academic Press, 1972. ix, 445 p. Subject Index, pp. 435-40. Name Index, pp. 441-45.

Fourteen papers presented at a symposium held at the University of Wisconsin, Madison, in June 1972, under the auspices of the Mathematics Research Center. Topics include properties of a stochastic attraction model; the sampling frame as a determinant of observed distributions of duration variables; comparison of alternative marriage models; contraceptive impact over several generations; estimating the risk of conception from censored data; inhomogeneous semi-Markov processes, select actuarial tables, and duration-dependence in demography; a general migration process; the PLATO system population dynamics course; and the main results of optimal control theory.

Griffith, John Stanley. MATHEMATICAL NEUROBIOLOGY: AN INTRODUCTION TO THE MATHEMATICS OF THE NERVOUS SYSTEM. New York: Academic Press, 1971. ix, 161 p. Appendix: Lagrange's Method of Undetermined Multipliers, pp. 146-47. References, pp. 148-57. Subject Index, pp. 159-61.

A self-contained introduction to the study of mathematical problems of the nervous system and especially of the brain. Provides a critical discussion of experimental facts, mathematical models, and techniques, and draws attention to such mathematical topics as the theory of nonlinear equations and differential-difference equations which are likely to be used in future work in this field. Useful to students of chemistry, biochemistry, physics, and mathematics. Topics include properties of nerve cells, mathematical models of neurones, time series of action potentials; randomly connected networks of neurones; information theory and memory; and nonlinear equations.

Grodins, Fred S. CONTROL THEORY AND BIOLOGICAL SYSTEMS. New York: Columbia University Press, 1963. xii, 205 p. Index, pp. 201-5.

A monograph useful mainly as a reference for students and researchers interested in the system approach to the study of biological systems. Includes an introduction to systems, including first and second order physical systems and the mathematical theory of linear lumped-constant physical systems; transient and frequency analysis of physical systems; and two examples of biological control systems: the respiratory and the cardiovascular. Mathematical derivations kept to a minimum, and knowledge of ordinary differential equations and systems theory necessary. Numerous graphs and charts used for illustrative purposes.

Gross, Alan J., and Clark, Virginia A. SURVIVAL DISTRIBUTIONS: RELIABILITY APPLICATIONS IN THE BEHAVIORAL SCIENCES. Wiley Series in Probability and Mathematical Statistics. New York: Wiley, 1975. xvi, 331 p. Appendix: Tables, pp. 289-304. Annotated Bibliography, pp. 305-23. Index, pp. 325-31.

A text for a one-semester course for students who have knowledge of mathematical statistics and matrix algebra. Includes many of the parametric models used in both reliability and survivability, illustrating their applications in survival studies, with estimation for censored and noncensored distributions a primary consideration. Distributions include exponential, gamma, Weibull, and Rayleigh. Exercises occur at the ends of the sections.

Grossman, Stanley I., and Turner, James E. MATHEMATICS FOR THE BIOLOGICAL SCIENCES. New York: Macmillan, 1974. xi, 512 p. Appendix A: Trigonometry, pp. 399-405. Appendix B: Differential Calculus, pp. 407-37. Appendix C: Integral Calculus, pp. 439-55. Appendix D: The Exponential Function, pp. 457-60. Appendix E: Complex Numbers, pp. 461-64. Appendix F: Mathematical Notation, pp. 465-67. Tables, pp. 469-75. Answers to Selected Problems, pp. 477-506. Index, pp. 507-12.

A text for a course in mathematics for students of biology and medicine who have a college algebra background. General topics include probability; vector spaces; linear programming; Markov chains; game theory; differential equations; and difference equations. Specific topics include Bayes' theorem; random variables and their moments; eigenvalues and eigenvectors; games; Chebyshev's inequality; and mathematical models in biology, including survival and extinction of species, selection and fitness, and Lotka-Volterra equations. Includes examples and some derivations. Sections conclude with problems.

Gurland, John, ed. STOCHASTIC MODELS IN MEDICINE AND BIOLOGY. Madison: University of Wisconsin Press, 1964. xvi, 393 p. Index, pp. 387-93.

Thirteen papers presented at a symposium conducted by the mathematics Research Center and held at the University of Wisconsin June 12-14, 1963. Knowledge of advanced mathematics including mathematical statistics and stochastic processes necessary. Topics include stochastic models of epidemics and of competing risks of illness and competing risks of death; the general catalytic queue process; oscillations of nonlinear systems; stochastic processes in evolution and genetics; a stochastic model for Prisoner's dilemma; and stochastic approximation to the median effective dose in bioassay.

Heath, Oscar Victor Sayer. INVESTIGATION BY EXPERIMENT. Institute of Biology's Studies in Biology, no. 23. London: Edward Arnold, 1970. vi, 74 p. Further Reading and References, pp. 73-74. No index.

A largely nontechnical exposition of various methods of scientific inquiry using only algebra. Topics include prediction and design of experiments, including factorial and serial experiments and experiments in pairs; levels of interpretation; dating experiments; random variation in measurements; normal distribution; confidence limits and tests of significance; analysis of variance; randomized block methods; Latin squares; split plot designs and groups and class experiments. Knowledge of basic statistics helpful, but not necessary.

Heinments, Ferdinand, ed. CONCEPTS AND MODELS OF BIOMATHEMATICS: SIMULATION TECHNIQUES AND METHODS. Vol. 1. Biomathematics Series, vol. 1. New York: Marcel Dekker, 1969. xiv, 287 p. Author Index, pp. 275-82. Subject Index, pp. 283-87.

Eight heretofore unpublished contributions on mathematical modeling and simulation of biological processes arranged in the following sequence; specific biological reactions, compartment analysis; physiological phenomena, growth process and its regulation, and ecological problems. Topics include simulation of glycolytic systems; Fourier transform analysis of tracer data; blood glucose regulation and diabetes; cellular growth process; and systems of species competition. Uses calculus and differential equations in a few places.

Hill, Sir Austin Bradford. PRINCIPLES OF MEDICAL STATISTICS. 9th rev. ed. New York: Oxford University Press, 1971. ix, 390 p. Definitions, pp. 324-34. Exercises, pp. 335-45. Answers to Exercises, pp. 346-63. Random Sampling Numbers, pp. 364-82. Tables of "t_p", p. 383. Tables of Chi-Square, pp. 384-85. Index, pp. 386-90.

A reference for research workers in the medical field and a supplementary text for a course in basic statistics for medical students. Excludes derivations but includes the use and limitations of basic statistical formulas with numerical examples taken from medical publications. Topics include measures of dispersion and central tendency; problems of sampling; chi-square; correlation; death rates; life tables; measures of morbidity; clinical trials; fallacies and difficulties; and statistical inference.

______. STATISTICAL METHODS IN CLINICAL AND PREVENTIVE MEDICINE. Foreword by Sir Robert Platt. London: E. and S. Livingstone, 1962. viii, 610 p. Bibliography, pp. 605-10. No index.

Twenty-six reprints of articles published by the author during the period 1948-1960 (some are published jointly with other authors) on statistical methods in clinical and preventive medicine. The articles grouped under the following three headings: "Clinical Trial of Treatment" (nine articles); "The Field Trial of Vaccines" (five articles); and "The Epidemiological Approach" (twelve articles). Statistical applications limited to the use of descriptive statistics and considers such topics as tuberculosis; prevention and treatment of the common cold; prevention of whooping-cough by vaccination; trials of an Asian influenza vaccine; lung cancer; incidence of lukemia after exposure to diagnostic radiation; and incidence of cancer in a factory handling inorganic compounds of arsenic.

Hills, Michael. STATISTICS FOR COMPARATIVE STUDIES. New York: Wiley, Halsted Press, 1974. viii, 194 p. Tables I and II, p. 183. Appendix: Exponents and Logarithms, pp. 184-89. References, pp. 190-91. Index, pp. 193-94.

A monograph on the large sample theory of the relationship between two variables with extensions to more than two variables with illustrative examples from epidemiology. Topics include probability distributions; factors, levels, and effects, including sampling errors and tests of hypotheses; linear regression and least squares; growth curves; and incidence rates, mortality ratios, and survival studies. Assumes knowledge of basic statistics. Chapters conclude with references.

Huntsberger, David V., and Leaverton, Paul E. STATISTICAL INFERENCE IN THE BIOMEDICAL SCIENCES. Boston: Allyn and Bacon, 1970. xv, 269 p. Appendix: Tables, pp. 233-60. Index, pp. 261-69.

A text for a one-semester course in basic statistics for students in medicine who have knowledge of only high school algebra and a reference for research workers in the biomedical sciences. Uses hypothetical examples to illustrate real world problems. Topics include empirical distributions; descriptive statistics; probability; random variables and expected values; random samples; confidence interval estimation for means and proportions; tests of significance, including nonparametric tests; regression and correlation; analysis of variance; two-sample problem; covariance analysis; and epidemiology and data analysis. Chapters conclude with problems and references.

International Encyclopedia of Pharmacology and Theropeutics. BIOSTATISTICS IN PHARMACOLOGY. Section 7, Vol. I. New York: Pergamon, 1973. xivii, 610 p. Author Index, pp. xix-xxvi. Subject Index, pp. xxvii-xliv.

An encyclopedia on sampling, data, preparation and reduction of data, graphs, and distributions and transformations in the medical science field, for research workers, physicians, and students. Knowledge of mathematical statistics essential for understanding the theory. Emphasizes intuitive reasoning. Topics include simple random sampling, confidence interval estimation; ratio estimate method; stratified random sampling; two-stage sampling; organization of sample surveys; sampling with probability proportionate to size; mortality and morbidity data; descriptive statistics; discrete and continuous random variables and their distributions; and the binomial, Poisson, logarithmic, and hypergeometric probability distributions.

_____. BIOSTATISTICS IN PHARMACOLOGY. Section 7, Vol. II. New York: Pergamon, 1973. pp. 611-1060. Author Index, pp. xv-xxii. Subject Index, pp. xxiii-xl.

Deals with interval estimation, hypothesis testing, analysis of variance, regression and correlation, sequential analysis, nonparametric tests, biological assay with applications in medicine for research workers, physicians, and students. Topics include central limit theorem; point estimation; maximum likelihood method; method of moments; least squares; chi-square; power function; simple and composite hypotheses; likelihood ratio tests; F-distribution; noncentral distributions; two-sample problem; Graeco-Latin squares; orthogonal contrasts; hierarchial classification; orthogonal polynomials; analysis of covariance; U-test of Mann and Whitney; sign test; Kruskal and Wallis test; and probit and logit methods.

Jacquez, John A. COMPARTMENTAL ANALYSIS IN BIOLOGY AND MEDICINE: KINETICS OF DISTRIBUTION OF TRACER-LABELLED MATERIALS. New York: Elsevier, 1972. xiv, 237 p. References, pp. 217-33. Index, pp. 234-37.

A text for a course in compartmental analysis for graduate students in biophysics, bioengineering, and physiology. Fairly detailed mathematically without the rigorous theorem-lemma-proof approach. Applications developed in detail to illustrate usefulness of compartmental analysis. The first eight chapters cover classical compartmental analysis while the remaining six chapters extend the analysis to biology, stochastic processes, and control systems. Assumes knowledge of advanced calculus, differential equations, and stochastic processes. Chapters conclude with exercises.

Jagers, Peter. BRANCHING PROCESSES WITH BIOLOGICAL APPLICATIONS. Wiley Series in Probability and Mathematical Statistics. New York: Wiley, 1975. xiii, 268 p. Appendix, pp. 259-63. Index, pp. 265-68.

Analyzes the growth of biological populations, often by probabilistic models. Topics include classical continuous time demography as part of branching process theory; Galton-Watson process; multi-type processes; Martingales; renewal theorems; point processes; and general branching process. Concludes with a chapter on branching models of cell kinetics. Assumes knowledge of probability theory. Chapters conclude with references. The appendix presents proofs of two important theorems.

Jardine, Nicholas, and Sibson, Robin. MATHEMATICAL TAXONOMY. Wiley Series in Probability and Mathematical Statistics. New York: Wiley, 1971. xviii, 286 p. Appendix 1: Estimation of Information Radius, pp. 189-201. Appendix 2: Information Radius for Normal Distributions, pp. 202-26. Appendix 3: Computation of B_k, pp. 227-34. Appendix 4: Computation of C_u, pp. 235-37. Appendix 5: A Cluster Listing Method, pp. 238-39. Appendix 6: Fast Hierarchic Clustering, pp. 240-43. Appendix 7: Illustrative Applications, pp. 243-58. Appendix 8: Bibliographic Sources, pp. 259-61. Glossary, pp. 263-75. Index of References, pp. 277-80. Subject Index, pp. 281-86.

Presents a mathematical account of some of the methods of data simplification involved in the practice of biological taxonomy. Consists of the following three parts: "The Measurement of Dissimilarity"; "Cluster Analysis"; and "Mathematical and Biological Taxonomy." Develops an automatic classificatory system in biological taxonomy. Topics include information theory; K-dissimilarity; correlation and weighing of attributes; hierarchic cluster methods; an axiomatic approach to cluster analysis; flat cluster methods; and application of methods of automatic classification. Assumes knowledge of set theory, elementary calculus, and linear algebra.

Kempthorne, Oscar. AN INTRODUCTION TO GENETIC STATISTICS. Wiley Series in Probability and Mathematical Statistics. New York: Wiley, 1957. xvii, 545 p. Index, pp. 517-45.

A fairly complete introductory account of the basic statistical concepts and tools used in genetic research and in the study of quantitative inheritance. Topics include random mating populations; stochastic theory of genetic populations; selection problems; inbreeding tests of genetic hypotheses and estimation of genetic parameters; planning of experiments; statistical problems of human genetics; inheritance of quantitative characteristics in a random mating population; one-locus polyploid populations; diploid populations with an arbitrary number of segregating loci and arbitrary epistacy; infinitesimal equilibrium theory of assortative mating; and selection for quantitative characters. Statistical techniques include means, variances, and covariances. Essential statistical techniques included to give completeness and continuity, making this book accessible to anyone with a high school algebra background.

Kempthorne, Oscar; Bancroft, Theodore A.; Gowen, John W.; and Lush, Jay L., eds. STATISTICS AND MATHEMATICS IN BIOLOGY. New York: Hafner, 1954. ix, 632 p. Bibliography, pp. 573-614. Index, pp. 617-32.

A text for a seminar course devoted to the synthesis of biological, statistical, and mathematical concepts. Consists of forty-four papers presented at a conference on biostatistics held at Iowa State College in June and July of 1952. Papers grouped under the following five headings: "General Biometrical Principles and Procedures" (twelve papers); "Changes in Population Number" (three papers); "Estimation of Populations" (eight papers); "Determination of Biological Response" (ten papers); and "General Analysis of Populations" (eleven papers).

Kojima, Ken-Ichi, ed. MATHEMATICAL TOPICS IN POPULATION GENETICS. Biomathematics, vol. 1. New York: Springer-Verlag, 1970. x, 400 p. No index.

Fifteen heretofore unpublished contributions in mathematical genetics dealing with topics such as models in populations genetics; theory of limits to selection with line crossing; the evolution of dominance; survival of MUTANT genes as a branching process; the incomplete binomial distribution; and fitness and optimization. Assumes knowledge of calculus and probability theory.

Lancaster, Henry Oliver. AN INTRODUCTION TO MEDICAL STATISTICS. Wiley Series in Probability and Mathematical Statistics. New York: Wiley, 1974. xiv, 305 p. Bibliography, pp. 264-90. Appendix: Tables, pp. 291-97. Author Index, p. 299. Subject Index, pp. 300-305.

An introduction to medical statistics for students, graduates, and scientists who have knowledge of college algebra, although knowledge of calculus helpful for chapters dealing with probability distributions, set theory, and statistical inference. Provides an elementary review of vital statistics and the application of statistical methods to the understanding of clinical and laboratory medicine. Topics include descriptive statistics, sampling distributions, including binomial and normal; measurement of probability; the life table; mortality in human populations in developing countries; fertility and population dynamics; statistical aspects of human genetics; problems of inference; power of a test; distribution theory, including bivariate normal; clinical trials and observations; statistical epidemiology; stochastic processes; the taxonomy and diagnosis of diseases; and the history and scope of medical statistics.

Landis, Paul H. POPULATION PROBLEMS: A CULTURAL INTERPRETATION. 2d ed. American Sociology Series. New York: American Books, 1954. xiv, 597 p. Appendix: Essential Statistical Concepts and Methods in Demography by Leo Silberman, pp. 529-69. Index of Names, pp. 570-75. Index of Subjects, pp. 576-97.

A treatment of population problems in five parts: "Population Facts and Population Theories"; "Cultural and Demographic Factors in Population Replacement"; "Differential Population Replacement"; "Structural and Spatial Distribution and Movement of Population"; and "International Aspects of the Demographic Position of the United States: Problems and Policy." Appendix reviews statistical concepts used in demography and the construction of life tables. Useful as a reference for students and general readers.

Ledley, Robert Steven. With the Assistance of James Bruce Wilson. USE OF COMPUTERS IN BIOLOGY AND MEDICINE. Foreword by Lee B. Lusted. New York: McGraw-Hill, 1965. xxii, 965 p. Name Index, pp. 927-29. Subject Index, pp. 931-65.

A comprehensive text and handbook on biological and medical research applications of electronic computer for the mature biomedical research worker who wishes to use the computer in his work. Consists of the following four parts: "Introduction"; "Use of Computers"; "Applications of Computers in Biology and Medicine"; and "Mathematical Background for Data-Processing Techniques." Topics include description and programming of digital computers; analog computers; application to the analysis of biochemical systems, biocontrol systems engineering, solutions to biomathematical equations, simulation of biomedical systems, the synthesis of biomedical systems, biomedical data-processing, medical diagnosis, and medical-record keeping; and review of matrices, determinants, equations, numerical analysis, Boolean algebra and partitions, calculus of propositions, probability, and statistics.

Levin, Simon A., ed. MATHEMATICAL PROBLEMS IN BIOLOGY. Foreword by P. van den Driessche. Lecture Notes in Biomathematics, vol. 2. New York: Springer-Verlag, 1974. 280 p. A Bibliography of Mathematical Biology by G.W. Swan, pp. 273-80. No index.

Thirty-four papers presented at a conference on mathematical problems in biology held at the University of Victoria, B.C., Canada, from May 7 to 10, 1973. Topics include models of large-scale nervous activity; coexistence of species in a discrete system; probabilistic limit cycles; a model of morphogenesis; qualitative behavior of stochastic epidemics; stochastic models for cell proliferation; ecological and growth processes; and stochastic growth processes. Knowledge of calculus and mathematical statistics necessary for most papers.

______. SOME MATHEMATICAL QUESTIONS IN BIOLOGY VI. Lectures on Mathematics in the Life Sciences, vol. 7. Providence, R.I.: American Mathematical Society, 1974. vi, 232 p. No index.

Eight papers presented at the eighth symposium on mathematical biology held in San Francisco in February 1974. Topics include relative importance of selection and chance in evolution; mathematical and statistical problems arising in the non-Darwin theory; selection and evolution in chemical networks; primary and secondary waves in development biology; biological pattern formation involving lateral inhibition; a diffusion model of pattern formation in the insect cuticle; and the geometry of color perception. Knowledge of differential equations necessary to follow the derivations.

______. SOME MATHEMATICAL QUESTIONS IN BIOLOGY VII. Lectures on Mathematics in the Life Sciences, vol. 8. Providence, R.I.: American Mathematical Society, 1976. viii, 182 p. No index.

Six papers presented at the ninth symposium on mathematical

biology held in New York in January 1975. First three papers deal with problems in ecology and evolutionary biology with emphasis on the role of population structure. Topics include spatial structure, age structure, and the relation between demographic and evolutionary parameters. The second three papers deal with problems in neurobiology, and include such topics as mathematical developments in Hodgkin-Huxley theory, and models for active nerve conduction and passive nueronal integration. Calculus necessary to follow the derivations.

_____. SOME MATHEMATICAL QUESTIONS IN BIOLOGY VIII. Lectures on Mathematics in the Life Sciences, vol. 9. Providence, R.I.: American Mathematical Society, 1977. vi, 186 p. No index.

Six papers presented at the tenth symposium on mathematical biology held in Boston on Febraury 24, 1976 under sponsorship of the American Mathematical Society and the Society for Industrial and Applied Mathematics. Topics include mathematical models in immunology, including a model designed to explain critical phenomena in the activation of the cells which can secrete antibodies and a survey assay methods for circulating antibodies and for antibody-producing cells; theories of pattern formation; dynamic models of the mitotic cycle; fluid mechanic problems with emphasis on blood flow in arteries and veins; and theories of axoplasmic transport.

Lewis, Alvin E. BIOSTATISTICS. Reinhold Books in the Biological Sciences. New York: Reinhold Publishing Co., 1966. xi, 227 p. Appendix: Tables, pp. 211-23. Recommended Reading List, p. 224. Index, pp. 225-27.

A text for a one-semester course in biostatistics for students in biology and medicine who have reached the stage where they are ready to judge data and begin their own investigations and experiments. Algebraic developments linked to examples in biological work or hypothetical illustrations. Exposition relies heavily on the intuitive approach. Topics include probability and randomization; normal curve; regression and correlation; enumeration statistics; chi-square; analysis of variance; tolerance limits; quality control and its application to biological problems; alternatives to the null hypothesis; sequential analysis; and nonparametric statistics. Chapters conclude with problems.

Lieberstein, H. Melvin. MATHEMATICAL PHYSIOLOGY: BLOOD FLOW AND ELECTRICALLY ACTIVE CELLS. Modern Analytic and Computational Methods in Science and Engineering: A Group of Monographs and Advanced Textbooks, vol. 40. New York: Elsevier, 1973. xiv, 377 p. Historical References, pp. 351-52. Index, pp. 353-77.

A monograph on mathematical physiology for mathematics students who have knowledge of mathematics through differential equations. Rigorous theorem-proof presentation avoided wherever feasible in order to attract mathematically oriented readers from other disciplines. Consists of the following two parts: "Flow, Pressures, and Tension in the Arteries" and "Toward a Mathematical Description of the Electrical Behavior of Electrically Active Cells." Chapters conclude with references.

Locker, A., ed. QUANTITATIVE BIOLOGY OF METABOLISM. New York: Springer-Verlag, 1968. xvi, 296 p. Author Index, pp. 281-86. Subject Index, pp. 287-96.

Sixteen papers presented at the third international symposium on quantitative biology of metabolism held in Helgoland, Holland, September 26-29, 1967, grouped under the following headings: "Models of Metabolism" (four papers); "Metabolic Parameters" (three papers); "Damage to Metabolism" (three papers); "Metabolic Control" (five papers); and "Conclusion" (one paper). Includes contributions from mathematics, computer science, physics, biophysics, psychology, biochemistry, and pharmacology. Topics include discrete and continuous representations of metabolic models; epistemological significance of models in science; a model for sustained rhythmic binary logic in biochemical systems; functioning of a cell model; computation of equilibria and kinetics of chemical systems with many species; analysis of heart rate adaption to temperature; models of growth of organisms under nutrient limiting conditions; models to study thermoregulation in man; memory and cellular control processes; and analysis by computer of some oscillatory features of the red cell system.

Lundberg, Ove. ON RANDOM PROCESSES AND THEIR APPLICATIONS TO SICKNESS AND ACCIDENT STATISTICS. 2d ed., rev. Uppsala, Sweden: Almqvist and Wiksells Boktryckeri, 1964. viii, 172 p. Bibliography, pp. 171-72. No index.

An account of the theory and application of random processes to sickness and accident statistics and the subsequent duration of incapacity. Based on Kolmogoroff's theory of random processes called stochastically definite. Processes and models include Bernoulli, Polya-Eggenberger, and Lexis; random processes with continuous time parameter, particularly those of the discontinuous type; elementary random processes (those in which the number of events--sickness and accidents--is a variable); time homogeneous processes; the compound Poisson process; and characteristic function, moment relations, and asymptotic properties for large t of the compound Poisson process. Concludes with applications of the theory to some recent smallpox cases and sickness and accident cases.

Mainland, Donald. ELEMENTARY MEDICAL STATISTICS. Philadelphia: W.B. Saunders, 1963. xiii, 381 p. References, pp. 353-56. Appendix: Tables, pp. 357-74. Index, pp. 365-81.

An introduction to medical statistics from the point of view of statistical investigations. First ten chapters arranged in the form of questions which may be of concern to a project, or research undertaking. Topics include method of investigation, population and sampling, skeleton layouts, interpretation of experiments, sample size, data analysis, and lost information. Remaining six chapters consider statistical analysis, and include such topics as estimating population percentages from samples of frequency data; comparison of samples of frequency data; variation between measurements; comparisons by measurement; and concomitant variation and trends. Nonparametric methods emphasized. No previous knowledge of statistics required. Useful as a supplementary text for a course in basic medical statistics.

Malécot, Gustave. THE MATHEMATICS OF HEREDITY. Rev. ed. Translation by D.M. Yermanos. San Francisco: W.H. Freeman, 1969. xv, 88 p. Bibliography, pp. 85-86. Index, pp. 87-88.

Originally published in French. Uses probability theory to prove a number of classical formulas pertaining to genetics and the mathematical theory of evolution. The three chapter titles: "The Mendelian Lottery"; "Correlation Between Relatives in an Isogamous Stationary Population"; and "Evolution of a Mendelian Population."

Mather, Kenneth. STATISTICAL ANALYSIS IN BIOLOGY. 5th ed. Foreword by R.A. Fisher. London: Methuen, 1964. iv, 267 p. Glossary of Terms, pp. 253-57. Tables, pp. 258-63. Index, pp. 265-67.

A text or supplementary text for a course in basic statistics for students of biology who have knowledge of high school algebra. Topics include probability; distributions; tests of significance; chi-square; degrees of freedom and the analysis of variance, including interaction; planning experiments; regression and correlation; polynomial regression; the analysis of frequency data; and estimation and information. Most derivations kept simple and short, supplemented by extensive verbal explanation and numerical illustrations.

Maxwell, A.E. BASIC STATISTICS FOR MEDICAL AND SOCIAL SCIENCE STUDENTS. New York: Wiley, Halsted Press, 1972. 126 p. Appendixes: Tables, pp. 117-21. References, pp. 122-23. Index, pp. 125-26.

A text for a short course in basic statistics for students of psychiatry. Emphasizes experimental design and data analysis, and includes no derivations. Topics include descriptive statistics;

probability; sampling; contingency tables; regression and correlation; analysis of variance; and recording data on punch cards.

Meehl, Paul E. CLINICAL VERSUS STATISTICAL PREDICTION: A THEORETICAL ANALYSIS AND REVIEW OF THE EVIDENCE. Minneapolis: University of Minnesota Press, 1954. x, 149 p. References, pp. 139-43. Index, pp. 144-49.

Treats philosophically two types of prediction: actuarial or statistical prediction based on observed facts and data of an individual in the same class; and clinical prediction, based on some psychological hypothesis regarding the structure and the dynamics of the individual. Topics include the rationality of inference from class membership; probability in prediction; the logic of clinical activity; clinical intuition; empirical comparisons of clinical and actuarial prediction; and quantification of clinical material.

Milsum, John H. BIOLOGICAL CONTROL SYSTEMS ANALYSIS. New York: McGraw-Hill, 1966. xiv, 466 p. Problems, pp. 426-43. References and Bibliography, pp. 444-56. Index, pp. 457-66.

A text for a course in control theory for biologists, physicists, engineers, and others interested in biological control systems who have knowledge of ordinary differential equations and the Laplace transform. Emphasizes linear theory with much of the book devoted to the development of basic tools of linear dynamic analysis and control theory. Topics include first- and second-order linear lumped models and their transient response and frequency response characteristics; high-order, nonlinear, and spatially distributed models; computer simulation and numerical solutions; feedback control, including first- and second-order closed-loop dynamics; thermoregulatory control systems for the human body; models of the human operator in manual tracking; stabilization system for visual fixation; skeletal-muscle servomechanism; biological receptors; statistical signals and biological performance criteria; and adaptive control.

Moran, P.A.P. THE STATISTICAL PROCESS OF EVOLUTIONARY THEORY. London: Oxford University Press, 1962. vii, 200 p. Bibliography, pp. 187-97. Author Index, p. 198. Subject Index, pp. 199-200.

A monograph on the mathematical aspects of the genetics of natural populations, with no extensive discussion of applications. Topics include the structure of a breeding population; deterministic models of random mating populations; mutation and selection; tendency to homozygosity in finite populations; the survival of a single mutant, haploid and diploid models, self-sterility; and the effects of geographical distribution. Assumes knowledge of calculus and mathematical statistics.

Mosimann, James Emile. ELEMENTARY PROBABILITY FOR THE BIOLOGICAL SCIENCES. New York: Appleton-Century-Crofts, 1968. xv, 255 p. Answers, pp. 239-55. No index.

A text for a course in probability theory for students of biology who have a high school algebra background. Limited to probability on finite sample spaces. Optional sections deal with specific biological topics, including excellent treatments of biostatistics. Topics include rule of counting; permutations; sets and sample spaces; probability, including hypergeometric probability; use of tree diagrams to assign probabilities; and binomial probabilities. Applications include genetics, chromosomes, nucleic and sequences, smoking and lung cancer, faunal similarities, zoogeography, population, pollen analysis, and vegetation changes. Sections conclude with exercises; chapters, with references.

Muench, Hugo. CATALYTIC MODELS IN EPIDEMIOLOGY. Cambridge, Mass.: Harvard University Press, 1959. xi, 110 p. Appendix A: Nomograms, pp. 98-100. Appendix B: Table of Negative Exponentials, p. 101. Appendix C: Mathematical Notes, pp. 101-7. References, p. 108. Index, pp. 109-10.

Presents a number of deterministic catalytic models dealing with the relationship between forces of infection and the population on which they act. Assumes knowledge of ordinary differential equations. Useful as a reference in a course in biostatistics.

Orkin, Michael, and Drogin, Richard. VITAL STATISTICS. New York: McGraw-Hill, 1975. x, 388 p. Tables, pp. 331-86. Index, pp. 387-88.

A text for a one-semester course in basic statistics for students with minimal mathematics background. Includes both classical and nonparametric statistics and topics include descriptive statistics; probability and tree diagrams; random variables; binomial and normal distributions; comparisons of two sample means; nonparametric tests; chi-square; analysis of variance; regression and correlation; conditional probability and decision theory. Sections conclude with problems and chapters conclude with summaries of terms, additional problems and true-false tests.

Pavlidis, Theodosios. BIOLOGICAL OSCILLATORS: THEIR MATHEMATICAL ANALYSIS. New York: Academic Press, 1973. xv, 207 p. References, pp. 187-204. Index, pp. 205-7

A monograph on dynamic properties of selected biological oscillators (systems) and the mathematical techniques necessary for their investigation; rigorous proofs omitted. Knowledge of ordinary differential equations sufficient for comprehension. Topics include mathematical theory of oscillators, including phase plane asymptotic techniques; examples of biological rhythms, including circadian rhythm and neural oscillators; phase response curves; entrainment of oscillators by pulses; dynamics of circadian oscillators; populations of interacting oscillators, including their synchronization; and biological phenomena attributable to populations of oscillators. Mathematical derivations kept to a minimum, and supplemented by verbal description, graphs, pictures, and numerical examples.

Pearce, S.C. BIOLOGICAL STATISTICS: AN INTRODUCTION. McGraw-Hill Series in Probability and Statistics. New York: McGraw-Hill, 1965. xiii, 212 p. Suggestions for Further Reading, pp. 197-200. Appendix I: Critical Values of t, pp. 201-2. Appendix II: Critical Values of pp. 203-8. Index, pp. 209-12.

A reference on the analysis of experiments for biologists who have a limited background in statistics or no formal training at all. Uses very little mathematics, and covers such topics as analysis of variance for orthogonal, nonorthogonal, and arbitrary designs; missing data, interactions, and confounding; correlation and regression; analysis of covariance; and component analysis.

Pollard, J.H. MATHEMATICAL MODELS FOR THE GROWTH OF HUMAN POPULATIONS. New York: Cambridge University Press, 1973. xii, 186 p. References, pp. 150-54. References According to Chapter and Section, pp. 155-57. Solutions to Exercises, pp. 158-74. Australian Life Tables, 1961, pp. 175-77. Author Index, pp. 179-80. Subject Index, pp. 181-86.

A reference for demographic research workers and a text for undergraduate mathematics majors and graduate demography students with knowledge of calculus, matrix algebra, and basic statistics. Emphasizes stochastic models. Topics include mathematics for the life table; deterministic models of T. Malthus, A.J. Lotka, and F.R. Sharp; deterministic theory of H. Bernardelli, P.H. Leslie, and E.G. Lewis; simple birth and death processes; stochastic models of M.S. Bartlett and D.G. Kendall; the extinction of surnames; the stochastic version of Leslie's model; and hierarchial population models and recruitment. The estimation of numerical values for the life table omitted. Chapters conclude with exercises.

Proschan, Frank, and Serfling, R.J., eds. RELIABILITY AND BIOMETRY: STATISTICAL ANALYSIS OF LIFELENGTH. Philadelphia: Society for Industrial and Applied Mathematics, 1974. xiv, 815 p. No index.

Thirty-two papers presented at a conference on reliability and biometry held at the Florida State University, Tallahassee,

July 9-27, 1973, grouped under the following headings: "Classes of Life Distributions and Their Properties" (four papers); "Stochastic Processes" (four papers); "Linear Models" (two papers); "Competing Risks" (four papers); "Prediction and Estimation of System Reliability" (two papers); "Life Testing" (three papers); "Comparisons of Populations: Ranking, Selection, Classification and Similarity Measurement" (five papers); "Applications in Reliability and Biometry" (four papers); and "Statistical Theory and Methods not Specifically Directed Towards Reliability and Biometry" (four papers). Topics include stochastic characterization of wear; a compound Poisson process; bounds and inequalities on the rate of population growth; parametric approaches to the theory of competing risk; nonparametric tests of independence for censored data with applications to heart transplant studies; negative exponential lifetime distributions; and problems in cell kinetics and the early detection of disease.

Rashevsky, Nicolas. MATHEMATICAL BIOLOGY OF SOCIAL BEHAVIOR. Chicago: University of Chicago Press, 1951. xii, 256 p. Index, pp. 241-56.

Develops the mathematical biology of social behavior in six parts: "Brain Mechanism and Behavior"; "Social Hierarchies"; "Imitative Behavior"; "Motivational Behavior"; "Learned Behavior"; and "Miscellaneous Problems." Part I devoted to the mathematical biology of the central nervous system, and Part II develops a mathematical approach to the problem of social hierarchies. Parts III, IV, and V apply to equations to the behavior of an individual in a social group. Based on the mathematical biophysics of the central nervous system. Assumes knowledge of advanced calculus and differential equations. Applications include hereditary effects of social changes and social dynamics.

______. MATHEMATICAL BIOPHYSICS: PHYSICO-MATHEMATICAL FOUNDATIONS OF BIOLOGY. Vol. 1. 3d rev. ed. New York: Dover, 1960. xxvi, 488 p. Index, pp. 463-88.

Develops the foundations for a mathematical biology, analogous in its methods to mathematical physics in two parts: "Mathematical Biophysics of Vegetative Cells and Cellular Aggregates" and "Mathematical Biophysics of Excitation and Conduction in Peripheral Nerves." Derivations require knowledge of calculus and differential equations. Concepts explained both verbally and graphically. Topics include diffusion equation; spherical cell; periodicities in metabolizing systems; diffusion fields; active transport; metabolizing systems; theory of cell division; elastic stresses in elongation and division of a cell; osmotic pressures as a cause of cell division; factors influencing the stability and spontaneous division of cells; theory of mitosis;

molecular theory of cell division; dynamics of artifically deformed cells; cellular growth; mathematical approach to the cancer problem; probabilistic aspects of the cancer problem; mathematical molecular biophysics; Blair's theory of excitation; Rashevsky's theory of excitation and inhibition; fluctuations of thresholds and of response times in nerve fibers; nerve conduction; and a physical mechanism of excitation. Useful as a reference and a text. Chapters conclude with references.

_____. MATHEMATICAL BIOPHYSICS: PHYSICO-MATHEMATICAL FOUNDATIONS OF BIOLOGY. Vol. 2. 3d ed., rev. New York: Dover, 1960. xii, 462 p. Index, pp. 439-62.

Develops a systematic abstract mathematical theory of the functions of the central nervous system in two parts: "Mathematical Biophysics of the Central Nervous System" and "General Mathematical Principles in Biology." Assumes knowledge of calculus and the rudiments of differential equations. Mathematical derivations kept to a minimum. Topics in part I include central excitation and inhibition; simple neurological structures with applications to reaction times; discrimination of intensities; hysteresis phenomena; conditional and delayed reflexes; Gestalt problem; color vision and flicker phenomena; mental phenomena; Boolean algebra of neural nets; random nets. Topics of part II include outline of a new mathematical approach to general biology; locomation and forms of snakes; flight of birds and insects in relation to their form; internal structure of animals; organisms mappings; comparison of the set-theoretical and combinatorial approaches; the organism as a set of mappings; categories and equivalence; and the geometrization of biology. Useful as a reference and supplementary text. Chapters conclude with references.

_____. MATHEMATICAL THEORY OF HUMAN RELATIONS: AN APPROACH TO A MATHEMATICAL BIOLOGY OF SOCIAL PHENOMENA. Mathematical Biophysics Monograph Series, no. 2. Bloomington, Ind.: Principia Press, 1947. xiv, 202 p. Index, pp. 196-202.

Outlines a system of mathematical sociology in the spirit of mathematical physics and mathematical biology. Topics include mathematical relations useful in describing the structure and behavior of a society; mathematical treatment of interaction of social classes; periodic fluctuations in the behavior of a social group; mathematical theory of individuals in a society; spatial distribution of individuals; theory of the sizes of cities; distribution of sizes of cities; constant profile variations of society; change in degree of organization of society with time; and mathematical theory of individualistic and collectivistic societies. Assumes knowledge of advanced calculus and differential equations. Includes a few graphs but omits numerical examples. Chapters conclude with references.

______, ed. PHYSICOMATHEMATICAL ASPECTS OF BIOLOGY. New York: Academic Press, 1962. viii, 524 p. No index.

Seventeen papers presented at the International School of Physics meeting in Varenna, Italy, July 1-30, 1960. The papers dealt with the physical aspects of biology from a mathematical viewpoint and the topics include mathematical models for the representation of neural interaction; mathematical models of pharmacological systems; role of diffusion in biological phenomena; a mathematical model of the human heart; mathematical principles in biology; and discrimination and learning in terms of neural net models. Models based on differential equations.

______. SOME MEDICAL ASPECTS OF MATHEMATICAL BIOLOGY. Foreword by I. Newton Kugelmass. Publications no. 550, American Lecture Series. Springfield, Ill.: Charles C Thomas, 1964. xii, 314 p. Appendixes 1 to 15, pp. 241-300. References, pp. 301-8. Index, pp. 309-14.

A reference and supplementary text on selected topics in mathematical biology for medical men and biologists who have knowledge of calculus and ordinary differential equations. Consists of the following six parts: "Retention of Particulate Material in Respiratory Passages"; "The Cardiovascular System"; "Pharmacological Problems"; "The Endocrine System"; "The Central Nervous System"; and "Some Abstract Speculations and Their Potential Value." Topics include mathematics of breathing through mouth and nose; elastic reservoir model of the circulatory system; theory of the circulatory system; volume elasticity of the blood vessels; mathematical approach to drug effects; the endocrine system in periodic psychoses; thyroid pituitary interaction and its implication; mental disorders and social stratification; and relational biology.

Reiss, Richard F. NEURAL THEORY AND MODELING: PROCEEDINGS OF THE 1962 OJAI SYMPOSIUM. Palo Alto, Calif.: Stanford University Press, 1964. xiii, 427 p. Index, pp. 423-27.

Twenty-one papers presented at a symposium held in Ojai, Calif., in December 1962. Purpose was to bring together a variety of theorists and model builders, half being biologists and remainder from various fields of engineering and the physical sciences. Papers grouped under the following two headings: "General Theory and Modeling" (eleven papers) and "Theories and Models of Specific Systems" (ten papers). The second group emphasizes invertebrate nervous systems. Topics include computer techniques in neural research, brain models, theory of resonant networks; pulse processing by neuron models; peripheral organization of sensory systems; visual-information processing in the beetle; and use of gas-ion processes in modeling excitable membrane.

Remington, Richard D., and Schork, M. Anthony. STATISTICS WITH APPLICATIONS TO THE BIOLOGICAL AND HEALTH SCIENCES. Englewood Cliffs, N.J.: Prentice-Hall, 1970. xiii, 418 p. References, pp. 352-55. Appendix: Tables, pp. 357-411. Index, pp. 413-18.

A text for a course in biostatistics for students of medicine, public health, dentistry, veterinary medicine, nursing, pharmacy, and other health sciences who have knowledge of high school algebra. Emphasizes explaining concepts, and topics include descriptive statistics; sets and probability; permutations and combinations; population and sample; binomial, Poisson, and normal probability distributions; estimation and hypothesis testing concerning differences between two proportions and two means; chi-square; regression and correlation; analysis of variance; nonparametric statistics; demography; and vital statistics.

Reyment, R.A. INTRODUCTION TO QUANTITATIVE PALEOECOLOGY. New York: Elsevier, 1971. xii, 226.p. Appendixes 1 to 5: Tables, pp. 187-96. Appendix 6: FORTRAN Programs for Some of the Statistical Methods Used in this Book, pp. 197-208. References, pp. 209-12. Index, pp. 213-26.

A monograph on quantitative paleoecology organized and presented by case histories. Statistical treatment kept at an elementary level, and knowledge of basic statistics assumed. Topics include orientation analysis; environmental effects; predators, prey, and population dynamics; spatial paleoecology; and quantitative analysis of fossel assemblages. Statistical topics include analysis of variance; life tables; and regression and correlation.

Riggs, Douglas Shepard. THE MATHEMATICAL APPROACH TO PHYSIOLOGICAL PROBLEMS: A CRITICAL PRIMER. Cambridge, Mass.: MIT Press, 1963. xiv, 445 p. References, pp. 357-62. Appendix A: Discussion of Exercises, pp. 363-420. Appendix B: Logarithms, pp. 421-23. Appendix C: Approximations, pp. 424-26. Appendix D: Symbols, pp. 427-29. Index, pp. 431-45.

A guide to students of biology and related disciplines who are just starting to apply mathematical reasoning to the solution of physiological problems. Some results assume knowledge of differential equations and calculus. Topics include dimensions and units; constants, variables, and functional relationships; feedback relationships; homeostasis; exponential growth; transfer of substances between biological compartments; simple diffusion; kinetic problems; fluid flow and metabolic transformations; law of mass action; substrate-enzyme and drug-receptor interactions; derivation of equations; and checking the validity of equations. Includes applications to biology and biological systems. Shows how to use simple mathematics to describe living systems. Chapters conclude with exercises.

Roberts, Fred S. DISCRETE MATHEMATICAL MODELS WITH APPLICATIONS TO SOCIAL, BIOLOGICAL, AND ENVIRONMENTAL PROBLEMS. Englewood Cliffs, N.J.: Prentice-Hall, 1976. xvi, 559 p. Author Index, pp. 549-50. Subject Index, pp. 551-59.

A text for a variety of undergraduate courses, including mathematical models in the social and biological sciences, graphs, games, and their applications. Also a reference for the mathematically mature social scientist, biologist, and environmental scientists. Topics include graphs; weighted digraphs and pulse processes; Markov chains; n-person games; group decision making, including Arrow's impossibility theorem; and measurement and utility. Assumes knowledge of logical symbols, elementary linear algebra, probability theory, and one year of calculus. Numerous exercises included at the ends of the sections, and the chapters conclude with references and glossaries of frequently used terms.

Rosen, Robert. DYNAMICAL SYSTEM THEORY IN BIOLOGY. Vol. I: STABILITY THEORY AND ITS APPLICATIONS. Wiley Series in Probability and Mathematical Statistics. New York: Wiley, 1970. xiii, 302 p. Index, pp. 297-302.

A supplementary text for a graduate course in mathematical biology and a reference on basic concepts of dynamical systems in biology that can be described by a finite set of ordinary differential equations. Heuristic discussions of biological systems included, as well as graphs and charts. Topics include linear and nonlinear dynamical systems, including Poincaré-Bendixon theory; stability of dynamical systems; nonautonomous linear dynamical systems; dynamical aspects of morphogenesis and excitation; and statistical dynamics, including Liouville's theorem. Chapters conclude with notes and references.

_____. OPTIMALITY PRINCIPLES IN BIOLOGY. New York: Plenum, 1967. xi, 198 p. Index, pp. 195-98.

A text for a course in mathematical biology for graduates and undergraduates who have knowledge of calculus and open loop control systems. Emphasizes breadth of topics, rather than depth, and interrelationships that exist between mathematics, physics, biology, and the social sciences, and the mathematical tools that may be used to solve problems. Topics include the vascular system; ontogeny and phylogeny; optimality and the allometric law; D'Arcy Thompson's theory of transformations; homeostasis; input-output systems; biological regulators; adaptive systems in biology; and biology and the social sciences.

_____, ed. FOUNDATIONS OF MATHEMATICAL BIOLOGY. Vol. 1: SUBCELLULAR SYSTEMS. New York: Academic Press, 1972. xxv, 287 p. Author Index, pp. 279-83. Subject Index, pp. 284-87.

Four heretofore unpublished contributions on the place of mathematical biology in relation to the other biological, physical, and organizational sciences with the following titles: "The Nature of Hierarchial Control in Living Matter," by Howard H. Pattee; "Chemical Kinetics and Enzyme Kinetics," by Anthony H. Bartholomay; "Quantum Genetics," by Robert Rosen; and "Excitability Phenomena in Membranes," by D. Agin. Topics include stochastic approach to microscopic chemical kinetics; stochastic models of the unimolecular reaction; equations for the axon membrane; equations of electrodiffusion; and properties of language and control hierarchies in living matter. Assumes knowledge of differential equations, probability theory, and quantum theory.

_____. FOUNDATIONS OF MATHEMATICAL BIOLOGY. Vol. II: CELLULAR SYSTEMS. New York: Academic Press, 1972. xviii, 330 p. Author Index, pp. 323-25. Subject Index, pp. 326-30.

Five heretofore unpublished contributions on simple biological units and their properties. Four contributions devoted to the properties of cells, while the remaining contribution takes up the properties of compartment--a unit larger than a cell. Titles include: "Morphogenesis," by Robert Rosen; "Mechanics of Epigenetic Control," by Robert Rosen; "Automata Theory in the Context of Theoretical Embryology," by Michael A. Arbib; "Some Relational Cell Models: The Metabolism-Repair Systems," by Robert Rosen; and "Compartments" by Aldo Rescigna and James S. Beck. Assumes knowledge of advanced calculus, differential equations, and matrix algebra.

_____. FOUNDATIONS OF MATHEMATICAL BIOLOGY. Vol. III: SUPERCELLULAR SYSTEMS. New York: Academic Press, 1973. xvii, 412 p. Author Index, pp. 395-98. Subject Index, Volume I, pp. 399-402. Subject Index, Volume II, pp. 403-7. Subject Index, pp. 408-12.

Five heretofore unpublished contributions on the mathematical theory of behavior of whole organisms and groups of organisms with the titles: "Physiological Regulation and Control," by J.H. Milsum and F.A. Roberge; "Mathematical Aspects of Some Cardiovascular Phenomena," by N. Rashevsky; "The Principle of Adequate Design," by N. Rashevsky; "A Unified Approach to Physics, Biology, and Sociology," by N. Rashevsky; "Automata Theory in the Context of Theoretical Neurophysiology," by Michael A. Arbib; "The Deterministic Theory of Population Dynamics," by Aldo Rescigno and I.W. Richardson; and "Is There a Unified Mathematical Biology?" by Robert Rosen. Assumes knowledge of advanced calculus, differential equations, and matrix algebra. Mathematical derivations brief and accompanied by much verbal description.

Rubinow, S.I. INTRODUCTION TO MATHEMATICAL BIOLOGY. New York: Wiley-Interscience, 1975. xiii, 386 p. Solutions to Problems, pp. 278-341. References, pp. 342-47. Appendix A: Brief Review, pp. 348-63. Appendix B: Determinants, Vectors, and Matrixes, pp. 364-74. Author Index, pp. 375-77. Subject Index, pp. 379-86.

A text for a graduate course in mathematical biology for students of biology who have knowledge of calculus. Based primarily on differential equations, with some linear algebra and graph theory included. Main topics include cell growth, enzyme kinetics, tracers in physiological systems, biological fluid dynamics, and diffusion in biology. Includes technical aspects of biology for the benefit of students in mathematics, physics, and engineering. Chapters conclude with problems. Sixty-three pages devoted to a discussion of problems.

Schefler, William C. STATISTICS FOR THE BIOLOGICAL SCIENCES. Reading, Mass.: Addison-Wesley, 1969. viii, 231 p. Appendix A: Bibliography, pp. 184-85. Appendix B: Solutions to Even-Numbered Problems, pp. 186-208. Appendix C: Tables, pp. 209-28. Index, pp. 229-31.

A text for an introductory course in biometrics for students, researchers, and teachers of biology who have knowledge of high school algebra and a good background in biology. Emphasizes the uncertainty attached to scientific findings and conclusions. Theory logically, rather than mathematically, derived. Topics include descriptive statistics; normal distribution; probability; sampling and inference; hypothesis testing, including the two sample problem; two-group experimental design; chi-square and Poisson distributions; analysis of variance; factorial designs; nonparametric tests; correlation and regression; and analysis of covariance. The problems at the ends of the chapters kept simple, and the solutions to even numbered problems worked out in detail in appendix B.

Schwan, Herman P., ed. BIOLOGICAL ENGINEERING. Inter-University Electronic Series, vol. 9. New York: McGraw-Hill, 1969. x, 556 p. Index, pp. 547-56.

Five heretofore unpublished contributions in biomedical engineering: "Mathematical Models of Excitation and Propagation in Nerves," by Richard FitzHugh; "Biolgoical Control Mechanisms," by Richard W. Jones; "Absorption and Dispersion of Ultrasound in Biological Media," by Floyd Dunn, Peter D. Edmonds, and William J. Fry; "Electrocardiography," by David B. Geselowitz and Otto H. Schmitt; and "Hemodynamics," by Abraham Noordergaaf. Assumse knowledge of elementary calculus and differential equations. May be used as a text or supplementary text in biomedical engineering courses.

Seal, Hilary L. MULTIVARIATE STATISTICAL ANALYSIS FOR BIOLOGISTS. New York: Wiley, 1964. xiii, 209 p. Appendix I: Useful Computer Routines, pp. 184-88. Appendix II: General Block Designs and Missing Observations, pp. 189-99. Author Index, pp. 200-204. Subject Index, pp. 205-9.

A text for a one-semester course in multivariate analysis for students who have had a course in basic statistics and matrix algebra. Consists of the following two parts: "A Single Dependent Variable" and "Several Dependent Variates." Emphasizes theory and topics include least squares analysis; orthogonal vectors and the analysis of variance; the analysis of covariance; multiple regression; the p-variate linear model; principal component analysis; canonical analysis; and factor analysis. Examples included, and theorems proved. Chapters conclude with problems and references.

Sheldon, Alan; Baker, Frank; and McLaughlin, Curtis P., eds. SYSTEMS AND MEDICAL CARE. Cambridge, Mass.: MIT Press, 1970. xv, 360 p. Index, pp. 349-60.

Fourteen papers presented to a symposium on systems and medical care held at Harvard University in 1968. Presents a variety of systems theories and techniques, and includes such topics as general systems; systems analysis; cybernetics; systems models of disease and medical care; evolution of medical care systems; interorganizational systems models; and health systems planning. Presentation verbal with no formulas used.

Sheps, Mindel C., and Menken, Jane A. With the Assistance of Annette P. Radick. MATHEMATICAL MODELS OF CONCEPTION AND BIRTH. Chicago: University of Chicago Press, 1973. xxii, 429 p. Bibliography, pp. 387-95. Answers to Selected Exercises, pp. 396-406. Appendix: Tables, pp. 407-8. Index, pp. 409-29.

A unified approach to the derivation of mathematical models of conception and birth with substantive applications. Intended as a reference and text, particularly for students of demography, statistics, and biology. Includes models in three major areas: models of conception risks at each month of marriage or after the end of a previous pregnancy; family-building models which describe the reproductive history of a couple as shown in the sequence and spacing of consecutive conceptions and birth; and models of the distribution of intervals between successive births. Assumes knowledge of mathematical statistics.

Simon, William. MATHEMATICAL TECHNIQUES FOR PHYSIOLOGY AND MEDICINE. New York: Academic Press, 1972. xi, 267 p. Appendix I: The Rules of Differentiation, pp. 239-45. Appendix II: Table of Laplace Transforms, pp. 246-47. Appendix III: Derivatives of Sine and Cosine

Functions, p. 248. Appendix IV: Solutions to Selected Problems, pp. 249-57. References, pp. 259-61. Subject Index, pp. 263-67.

A text for a one-semester course in mathematics for biology students who have knowledge of calculus. Proofs rigorous wherever possible. Biological examples somewhat sketchy because of the complexity of biological situations. Topics include differential equations in biology; guessing the solution of a differential equation; the Laplace transform; compartmental problems; numerical methods; regulation and oscillation; diffusion; theory of blood flow measurement; and curve fitting by least squares. Chapters conclude with problems.

Smith, Cedric A.B. BIOMATHEMATICS: THE PRINCIPLES OF MATHEMATICS FOR STUDENTS OF BIOLOGICAL AND GENERAL SCIENCE. Vol. I. ALGEBRA, GEOMETRY, CALCULUS. 4th ed. New York: Hafner, 1966. xii, 523 p. Appendix: Tables, pp. 493-503. Answers to Problems, pp. 505-14. Index, pp. 515-23.

A text for a course in mathematics for students of biology and medicine, as well as those in the physical sciences, psychology, economics, and social sciences, who have knowledge of high school algebra. Topics include measurements of outcomes, volume, areas, velocities, rates of change, etc.; graphic presentation of data and functions; series; differential and integral calculus; differential equations; partial differentiation; and physical and chemical magnitudes. The mathematical derivations brief, and much verbal and graphic used. Most examples from biology.

______. BIOMATHEMATICS: THE PRINCIPLES OF MATHEMATICS FOR STUDENTS OF BIOLOGICAL AND GENERAL SCIENCES. Vol. 2. NUMERICAL METHODS, MATRICES, PROBABILITY, STATISTICS. 4th ed. New York: Hafner, 1968. x, 682 p. Appendix: Tables, pp. 625-61. Answers to Problems, pp. 662-74. Index, pp. 675-82.

A text for a course in mathematics and statistics for students of biology and medicine, as well as students in economics, psychology, and physics. Presupposes some knowledge of standard results in algebra and calculus. Topics include matrices; solutions of simultaneous equations; probability; probability distributions; random variables; multivariate distributions; chi-square; statistical inference; regression; analysis of variance; and the Colson notation. Verbal explanation accompanies the mathematical derivations. Sections conclude with problems.

Smith, David, and Keyfitz, Nathan, eds. MATHEMATICAL DEMOGRAPHY: SELECTED PAPERS. Biomathematics, vol. 6. New York: Springer-Verlag, 1977. xi, 514 p. References, pp. 501-6. Author Index, pp. 507-9. Subject Index, pp. 510-14.

Fifty-six reprints of articles on mathematical demography grouped under the following seven headings: "The Life Table" (nine reprints); "Stable Population Theory" (twelve reprints); "Attempts at Prediction and the Theory They Simulated" (eight reprints); "Parameterization and Curve Fitting" (ten reprints); "Probability Models of Conception and Birth" (four reprints); "Branching Theory and Other Stochastic Processes" (five reprints); and "Cohort and Period, Problem of the Sexes, Sampling" (eight reprints). Some articles assumed knowledge of mathematical statistics and differential equations.

Smith, J. Maynard. MATHEMATICAL IDEAS IN BIOLOGY. Cambridge: Cambridge University Press, 1968. vii, 152 p. Appendixes: Tables, pp. 127-43. Suggestions for Further Reading, pp. 144-45. Answers to Examples, pp. 146-47. Index, pp. 147-52.

A monograph on special mathematical concepts (mainly differential equations, recurrence relations, and probability theory) useful in describing biological processes for biologists who need to read papers containing mathematical reasoning. Emphasizes the formulation of equations, rather than solutions, and assumes knowledge of only algebra. Includes solutions to equations by both numerical and analytical methods. Topics include consequences of scale (power output, running, jumping, diving, flying); population regulation; generations separate and not separate (density-dependent reproduction, delayed regulation, logistic equations, predator-prey, logarithmic growth, competing species, age structure); genetics of families (binomial, conditional, and inverse probability); genetics of populations (Hardy-Weinberg ratio, selection, inbreeding); target theory (multi-hit theories, Poisson, ecological applications); regulation and control (control of muscular movement, kinetics of chemical reactions, control of protein synthesis); and diffusion and similar processes (diffusion and morphogenesis). Chapters conclude with somewhat difficult exercises.

Sokal, Robert R., and Rohlf, F. James. BIOMETRY: THE PRINCIPLES AND PRACTICES OF STATISTICS IN BIOLOGICAL RESEARCH. A Series of Books in Biology. San Francisco: W.H. Freeman, 1969. xxi, 776 p. Appendixes, pp. 643-49. Bibliography, pp. 751-57. Index, pp. 759-76.

A text for graduate students of biology, zoology, botany, and genetics. Develops the subject from an elementary introduction up to the advanced methods necessary for biological research and for an understanding of published literature. Represents the minimum required knowledge in statistics for the Ph.D. in the biological sciences. Emphasizes practical applications. Topics include descriptive statistics; simple distributions (binomial, normal, and Poisson); statistical tests, including nonparametric; analysis of variance through factorial experiments; regression and correlation; and application of digital computers to the solution of problems. Appendixes include mathematical reviews, operation of desk calculators, FORTRAN programs, and a tabular guide to statistical methods. Chapters conclude with exercises.

_____. INTRODUCTION TO BIOSTATISTICS. A Series of Books in Biology. San Francisco: W.H. Freeman, 1969. xv, 368 p. Appendix A1: Mathematical Appendix, pp. 305-12. Appendix A2: Statistical Tables, pp. 313-54. Bibliography, pp. 355-57. Index, pp. 359-68.

A text for a course in biostatistics for students in the biological sciences who have a high school algebra background. Emphasizes practical applications to biology, with discussions of statistical theory kept to a minimum. Topics include data in biology; descriptive statistics; probability; binomial, Poisson, and normal distributions; estimation and hypothesis testing; one- and two-way analysis of variance; simple regression and correlation; and analysis of frequencies. Exercises at the ends of the chapters consist of real research problems, and some of them require extensive computations.

Sokal, Robert R., and Sneath, P.H. PRINCIPLES OF NUMERICAL TAXONOMY. San Francisco, 1963. xvi, 359 p. Appendix: Computational Methods for Numerical Taxonomy, pp. 290-319. References, pp. 320-38. Index, pp. 339-59.

A reference for practitioners in botany, zoology, biology, and related sciences who have knowledge of statistics through correlation and regression. Restricted to methods intended to demonstrate taxonomic relationships and to create taxonomic groupings. Topics include aims and principles of numerical taxonomy; estimation of taxonomic resemblance using correlation techniques; the construction of a taxonomic system using cluster analysis; phylogenetic considerations; and problems of nomenclature.

Stacy, Ralph W., and Waxman, Bruce D., eds. COMPUTERS IN BIOMEDICAL RESEARCH. Vol. 1. Foreword by James A. Shannon. New York: Academic Press, 1965. xxii, 562 p. Author Index, pp. 547-56. Subject Index, pp. 557-62.

Twenty-two heretofore unpublished contributions on the use of computers in biomedical research grouped under the following six headings: "Computer Simulation of Life Processes" (two papers); "Computers and Mathematics in the Life Sciences" (five papers); "Computer Analysis of Specific Biosystems" (two papers); "Computer Uses in Neurophysiology" (three papers); "Computers in Clinical Medicine" (six papers); and "Computation in Psychology and Psychiatry" (four papers). Knowledge of computer programming helpful. Some contributions utilize differential equations. Topics include statistical packages in biomedical computation; the analog computer in the biological laboratory; computer simulation of life processes and cybernetic systems; computational methods in protein structure analysis; application of computers in multiphasic screening, electroenephology, and neurophysiology; and computer aids in evaluating fetal distress.

______. COMPUTERS IN BIOMEDICAL RESEARCH. Vol. II. Foreword by James A. Shannon. New York: Academic Press, 1965. xxi, 363 p. Author Index, pp. 351-54. Subject Index, pp. 355-63.

Fourteen heretofore unpublished contributions on the use of computers in biomedical research grouped under the following headings: "Computer Technology in the Life Sciences" (four papers); "Programming for Life Sciences Research" (three papers); "Biological and Physiological Applications of Computers" (four papers); "Computers in Hospital Automation" (one paper); and "Computers in Psychology and Psychiatry" (two papers). Differential equations and FORTRAN programming used in some of the papers. Topics include analog-digital conversion systems; programs as theories of higher mental processes; compartmental analysis in kinetics; simulation of ecological systems; computer techniques of value for study of circulation; and computer analysis of psychopharmacological psychology and psychiatric data.

______. COMPUTERS IN BIOMEDICAL RESEARCH. Vol. III. Foreword by Paul J. Sanazato. New York: Academic Press, 1969. x, 288 p. Author Index, pp. 277-79. Subject Index, pp. 280-88.

Ten heretofore unpublished contributions (by twenty-three authors) on the use of computers in medical care, with emphasis on the technological aspects of clinical computing. Two phases of computer technology stressed: on-line computing facilities, and computers dedicated to the task at hand and often not used for any other purpose. Topics include on-line data acquisition in the clinical laboratory; cell identification and sorting; processing radioisotope scintiscan matrices; analysis of tumor registry data; data transformation useful in electrocardiography; and patient monitoring.

Stanley, John. THE ESSENCE OF BIOMETRY. Montreal: McGill University Press, 1963. xiii, 147 p. Bibliography, p. 141. Index, pp. 142-47.

A text for a one-semester course in biometry for graduates and undergraduates who have knowledge of college algebra. Calculus and differential equations used in a few places. Topics include theory of probability, including multiple successes in multiple trials; simple regression; samples and universes;

normal distribution; binomial and Poisson; rank correlation; chi-square; analysis of variance; and fifty percent lethal dose.

Steel, Robert G.D., and Torrie, James H. PRINCIPLES AND PROCEDURES OF STATISTICS WITH SPECIAL REFERENCE TO THE BIOLOGICAL SCIENCES. New York: McGraw-Hill, 1960. xvi, 481 p. Selected Symbols, pp. xv-xvi. Appendix: Tables, pp. 427-71. Index, pp. 473-81.

A text for a graduate course in applied statistics for students in biometry who have knowledge of high school algebra, but no basic statistics. Topics include descriptive statistics; probability and probability distributions; sampling from a normal distribution; comparisons involving two-sample means; principles of experimental design; one-way and multi-way experiments; split-plot designs and analysis; analysis of variance for unequal subclass numbers; multiple and partial regression and correlation; analysis of covariance; nonlinear regression; chi-square; contingency tables; discrete probability distributions; nonparametric statistics; and sampling finite populations. Also useful to scientists with no special training in mathematics. Most examples chosen from biology and allied fields. Chapters conclude with references.

Sterling, Theodor D., and Pollack, Seymour V. COMPUTERS AND THE LIFE SCIENCES. New York: Columbia University Press, 1965. x, 342 p. Glossary, pp. 315-28. Suggested Readings, pp. 329-36. Index, pp. 337-42.

A general introduction to the use of computers in the life sciences in four parts: "The Anatomy and Physiology of the Robot"; "Robot Data Processing"; "Biomedical Robots"; and "Whether Now?" Based largely on the computer's ability to scan, describe, display, and classify information. Limited use of mathematics. Topics include statistics in the world of computers; not-so-routine statistical applications; simulation; computers in nuclear medicine; the electroballistographic robot; and establishing computing facilities.

Stibitz, George R. MATHEMATICS IN MEDICINE AND THE LIFE SCIENCES. Chicago: Year Book Medical Pub. Inc., 1966. 391 p. Index, pp. 381-91.

An elementary introduction to mathematical concepts and models in medicine and the life sciences with little statistics included. Topics include survey of models, postulational methods, and symbolic logic; Boolean numbers; multi-dimensional numbers; variables and functions; rates and derivatives; integrals and averages; solutions of algebraic equations; solution of ordinary differential equations; weighted averages and hidden information; feedback; operators and Fourier transforms; and diagnosis by computers. Presentation largely verbal and descriptive, using charts and graphs for illustrative purposes, and almost no derivations. Useful as a reference for a variety of elementary mathematics courses as well as quantitative courses in medicine and the life sciences.

Tanur, Judith M.; Mosteller, Frederick; Kruskal, William H.; Link, Richard F.; Pieters, Richard S.; Rising, Gerald R.; and Lehman, E.L., eds. A GUIDE TO THE STUDY OF THE BIOLOGICAL AND HEALTH SCIENCES. Holden-Day Series in Probability and Statistics. San Francisco: Holden-Day, 1977. ix, 140 p. Index, pp. 137-40.

Twelve heretofore unpublished contributions on the application of basic statistics and probability in the biological and health sciences. Applications include epidemics, smoking, plight of the whales, inheritance and disease, deathday and birthday, population explosion, drug screening, and success of innovations in surgery and anesthesia. Useful as a reference for basic statistics courses in the health sciences.

Taylor, Thomas R. THE PRINCIPLES OF MEDICAL COMPUTING. Oxford, Engl.: Blackwell, 1967. xii, 154 p. Appendix A: Binary Notation, pp. 128-29. Appendix B: Programming, pp. 130-35. Glossary, pp. 136-42. Bibliography, pp. 143-51. Index, pp. 152-54.

A simple straight-forward guide to computers and their potential value in clinical and academic medicine for the clinical research worker with previous knowledge of computing. Emphasizes laboratory research. Topics include computer layout; input and outputs; data preparation; medical records; hospital management; clinical laboratory; applications in treatment and research; computers in diagnosis; special purpose computers; information storage and retrieval systems; and future development. Glossary based on the Honeywell glossary of computer terms. Chapters conclude with references.

Van Den Driessche, Pauline, ed. MATHEMATICAL PROBLEMS IN BIOLOGY: VICTORIA CONFERENCE. Lecture Notes in Biomathematics, vol. 2. New York: Springer-Verlag, 1974. vi, 280 p. A Bibliography of Mathematical Biology, pp. 273-80. No index.

Twenty-two papers presented at a conference on mathematical problems in biology held in Victoria, B.C., from May 7 to 10, 1973. Assesses the rapid growth of mathematical interaction with the biosciences and exposes the problems of communication between mathematicians and biological scientists. Topics include models of nervous activity; habitat selection and a Liapunov function; coexistence of species in a discrete system; asymptotic behavior and stability in epidemic models; thresholds for deterministic epidemics; probability limit cycles; oscillations in biochemistry; model of morphogenesis; random sets mosaics; and stochastic models for cell proliferation.

Waltman, Paul. DETERMINISTIC THRESHOLD MODELS IN THE THEORY OF EPIDEMICS. Lectures in Biomathematics, vol. 1. New York: Springer-Verlag, 1974. No index.

A monograph which develops a deterministic threshold model for the spread of an infection. Computational aspects of the model are provided. Also includes a two-population threshold model, and a model with age dependence and an open population. Concludes with a consideration of the problem of control of a predicated epidemic.

Waterman, Talbot H., and Morowitz, Harold J., eds. THEORETICAL AND MATHEMATICAL BIOLOGY. A Blaisdell Book in the Pure and Applied Science. New York: Blaisdell, 1965. xvii, 426 p. Author Index, pp. 409-14. Subject Index, pp. 415-26.

Seventeen contributions on theoretical and mathematical biology most of which were presented at a seminar at the Zoology Department at Yale University in the spring of 1962, grouped under the following four headings: "Introduction" (three papers); "Physical and Chemical Analysis" (four papers); "Statistical Analysis and Computer Applications" (four papers); and "System Analysis" (six papers). Contributions represent case histories on quantitative methods in the life sciences and include such topics as thermodynamics and chemical kinetics; molecular structure; theory; experiment, and the nerve impulse; cochlear mechanics; morphometrics; computer simulation in biochemistry and ecology; transients in metabolism; nervous processing of sensory information; and genetic consequences of natural selection. Main reliance placed on verbal description and graphs.

Witts, Leslie John, ed. MEDICAL SURVEYS AND CLINICAL TRIALS: SOME METHODS AND APPLICATIONS OF GROUP RESEARCH IN MEDICINE. 2d ed. New York: Oxford University Press, 1964. x, 367 p. Index, pp. 365-67.

Eighteen heretofore unpublished contributions in medical surveys and clinical research grouped under the following two headings: "Methods" (nine contributions); and "Applications" (nine contributions). Topics include prevalence surveys, questionnaires, operational research, retrospective and prospective studies, prophylactic trials, follow-up studies, and applications in genetics, child development, chest diseases, mental illness, cancer, and tropical diseases. Presentation primarily descriptive with no mathematical or statistical prerequisites. A few charts and simple numerical examples provided. Useful for clinical research workers.

Woolf, Charles M. PRINCIPLES OF BIOMETRY: STATISTICS FOR BIOLOGISTS. New York: D. Van Nostrand, 1968. xiii, 359 p. References, pp. 324-25. Appendix: Tables, pp. 327-40. Answers to Problems, pp. 341-53. Index, pp. 355-59.

Zar, Jerrold H. BIOSTATISTICAL ANALYSIS. Prentice-Hall Biological Sciences Series. Englewood Cliffs, N.J.: Prentice-Hall, 1974. xvi, 620 p. Appendix A: Glossary of Mathematical and Statistical Symbols, pp. 329-36. Appendix B: Mathematical Equivalence of Certain Statistical Formulas, pp. 337-40. Appendix C: Factorial Analysis of Variance Hypothesis Testing, pp. 341-55. Appendix D: Mathematical and Statistical Tables, pp. 356-580. Appendix E: Answers to Odd-Numbered Exercises, pp. 581-92. Literature Cited, pp. 593-99. Index, pp. 601-20.

A text for a one-semester course in biostatistics for students with no prior knowledge of statistics, and a reference for research workers. Topics include descriptive statistics; goodness of fit; contingency tables; normal distribution; one- and two-sample hypotheses; paired-sample hypotheses; multisample hypotheses; multiple comparisons; two-factor analysis of variance; data transformations; simple and multiple correlation and regression; binomial distribution; testing for randomness; circular distributions; and nonparametric statistics. Chapters conclude with exercises.

Chapter 12

STATISTICAL DECISION THEORY

Aigner, Dennis J. PRINCIPLES OF STATISTICAL DECISION MAKING. Foreword by J.L. McKenney. Macmillan Decision Series. New York: Macmillan, 1968. xii, 145 p. Tables, pp. 133-40. Index, pp. 141-45.

A supplementary text devoted to an elaboration of the methodology of inference. Bridges the gap between classical and modern methods of decision making under uncertainty and assumes knowledge of calculus. Topics include calculus of probability; probability distributions; moments of single variate distributions; sampling and estimation; classical hypothesis testing; and the relationship between classical and Bayesian decision making. Excludes problems, and derivations kept to a minimum.

Aitchison, John. CHOICE AGAINST CHANCE: AN INTRODUCTION TO STATISTICAL DECISION THEORY. Behavioral Sciences: Quantitative Methods Series. Reading, Mass.: Addison-Wesley, 1970. ix, 284 p. Further Reading, pp. 265-68. Appendixes, pp. 269-75. Index, pp. 276-84.

A text for a one-year course in decision theory for students with a high school algebra background. Concepts motivated by realistic examples taken from a variety of fields, from golf to medical practice, from gem cutting to locating machine faults, from water diving to wage and price contracting. Topics include game theory; statistical inference; Bayesian decision theory; and sequential decision making. Appendixes include mathematical derivations. Sections conclude with exercises.

Atchison, Thomas A., and Martz, Harry F., Jr., eds. EMPIRICAL BAYES ESTIMATION AND COMPUTING IN STATISTICS. Mathematics Series, no. 6. Lubbock: Texas Technical University, 1969. viii, 255 p. No index.

Seventeen papers presented at a symposium on empirical Bayes' estimation and computing held at the Department of Mathematics, Texas Technical University, in 1969. Part I, consisting of ten papers, devoted to recent advancements in empirical Bayes' decision theory; part II, consisting of seven papers, takes up applications of numerical and computing techniques in statistics. Topics include empirical Bayes' techniques in point estimation; empirical Bayes estimation of queuing parameters; smooth empirical Bayes' estimators; computer implementation of distribution function algorithms; a technique for reducing multivariate normal integrals; and representations of the multivariate t and multivariate F distribution.

Bell, David E.; Kenney, Ralph L.; and Raiffa, Howard, eds. CONFLICTING OBJECTIVES IN DECISIONS. Foreword by Jermen Gvishiani and Roger Levien. International Series on Applied Systems Analysis, 1. New York: Wiley, 1977. x, 442 p. Index, pp. 439-42.

Nineteen papers presented at a workshop on decision making with multiple conflicting objectives held at the International Institute for Applied Systems Analysis in Laxenburg, Austria, October 20-24, 1975. Grouped under the following two headings: "Methodology" (eleven papers) and "Applications" (eight papers). Topics include vector optimization in multi-objective decision making; conjoint measurement; multiattribute utilities in expected utility theory; multicriterion problems with subjective criteria; on the elicitation of preference; state-dependent time preference; use of decision analysis in capital investment problems; selecting nuclear power plant sites in the Pacific Northwest using decision analysis; decision analysis of objectives for a forest pest problem; and a community information feedback system with multiattribute utilities. Knowledge of calculus, decision theory, and probability helpful.

Box, George E.P., and Tiao, G.E. BAYESIAN INFERENCE IN STATISTICAL ANALYSIS. Reading, Mass.: Addison-Wesley, 1973. xviii, 588 p. Tables, pp. 554-70. References, pp. 571-79. Author Index, pp. 581-84. Subject Index, pp. 585-88.

A text for a two-semester course in Bayesian inference for students in statistics who have knowledge of calculus, matrix algebra, mathematical statistics, and elementary probability. Explores the use and relevance of Bayes' theorem to problems that arise in scientific work in which inferences must be made concerning parameter values about which little is known a priori. Topics include choice of prior distributions; problems of nuisance parameters; role and relevance of sufficient statistics; standard problems concerned with the comparison of location and scale parameters, including inferences concerning the difference between two means and inferences concerning a variance ratio; effect of non-normality on inference about a population mean; comparison of variances; Bayesian analysis of hierarchical classifications with two variance components; analysis of cross classification designs; inference about means with information from more than one source; multivariate analysis; estimation of regression coefficients; and transformation of data. Includes extensive derivations and some simple numerical illustrations.

Braverman, Jerome D. PROBABILITY, LOGIC, AND MANAGEMENT DECISIONS. New York: McGraw-Hill, 1972. xii, 474 p. Suggested References, p. 448. Appendix: Tables, pp. 449-69. Index, pp. 471-74.

A text for a two-semester course in decision theory for students who have little or no background in probability and statistics but who are familiar with intermediate algebra and finite mathematics. Consists of four parts: "Logic"; "Probability"; "Statistics"; and "Decision Theory." Topics include Boolean algebra; logical networks; sets, functions, and combinatorial analysis; probability, including Bayes' rule; random variables; probability networks; descriptive statistics; statistical estimation and tests of hypotheses; correlation and regression; risk and uncertainty in decision making; preposterior analysis; revision of probabilities; extensive and normal forms; use of bets, normal and gamma distributions in decision analysis; and decision trees and sequential analysis. Includes numerous examples, and chapters conclude with problems.

Brown, Rex V.; Kahr, Andrew S.; and Peterson, Cameron. DECISION ANALYSIS: AN OVERVIEW. Series in Quantitative Methods for Decision Making. New York: Holt, Rinehart and Winston, 1974. x, 86 p. Bibliography, pp. 81-83. Index, pp. 85-86.

A brief summary of the fundamentals of applied decision analysis. Includes a detailed case study of a decision analysis application, the iron ore case, and the experience of major companies in applying decision analysis. Suitable for independent study for students and managers, also a text for a short course in a masters degree program. Chapters conclude with exercises.

______. DECISION ANALYSIS FOR THE MANAGER. Series in Quantitative Methods for Decision Making. New York: Holt, Rinehart and Winston, 1974. xxii, 618 p. Bibliography, pp. 605-7. Glossary, pp. 609-10. Index, pp. 611-18.

A text for a one-semester course in decision analysis for students in business schools who have knowledge of high school algebra. Approach personalistic (inputs and outputs refer to a specified person, the decision maker). Emphasizes practical, rather than theoretical topics, and excludes rigorous proofs. Consists of five parts: "Decision Analysis in Application"; "Modeling"; "Using Decision Analysis to Make a Specific Decision"; "Information and Assessment"; and "Decision Analysis for the Organization." Topics include expected value; decision-tree caselet; a case study in the application of decision analysis (by G. Eskin); certainty models with examples; uncertainty models with examples; complex decision tree models; direct and indirect assessment of probabilities; information gathering decisions; and the decision to seed hurricanes. Includes numerous case studies. Chapters conclude with assignments.

Chacko, George K. APPLIED STATISTICS IN DECISION-MAKING. New York: Elsevier, 1971. xv, 493 p. Appendixes: Tables, pp. 459-65. Index, pp. 467-71. Answers to Problems, pp. 473-91. About the Author, p. 493.

A problem-oriented exposition of statistical reasoning, structure and methods for model-building in decision-making requiring knowledge of high school algebra. Consists of seven parts: "Events and Relations: Alternative Views"; "Events and Relations: Linear Representations"; " Events and Relations: Nonlinear Representations"; "Events and Relations: Underlying Processes"; "Decisions and Consequences: Experimental and Physical"; "Decisions and Consequences: Inference and Implications"; "Decisions and Consequences: Randomness and Risks." Topics include types of causality; types of probability and measure theoretic notions; specification of relations; simple regression descriptive statistics; product moment correlation; time series; chi-square; normal curve; binomial distribution; generating functions; Poisson processes; stochastic processes; point and interval estimation; tests of hypotheses; tests of randomness; Shewart cycles of control of product quality; sequential analysis; and adaptive control. Emphasizes illustrative examples. Useful as a text and reference for graduates and undergraduates.

Chernoff, Herman, and Moses, Lincoln E. ELEMENTARY DECISION THEORY. Wiley Series in Probability and Mathematical Statistics. New York: Wiley, 1959. xv, 364 p. Appendixes, pp. 298-352. Partial List of Answers to Exercises, pp. 353-57. Index, pp. 359-64.

A text for a first course in statistics based on decision theory. Omits classical methodology. Topics include probability and random variables; utility; uncertainty; Bayes' strategies; and estimation and hypothesis testing. Appendixes include tables and proofs of basic results of decision theory. Chapters conclude with references and problems. Nonrigorous style employed and few proofs included.

Diamond, Peter, and Rothschild, Michael, eds. UNCERTAINTY IN ECONOMICS: READINGS AND EXERCISES. Economic Theory and Mathematical Economics. New York: Academic Press, 1978. xi, 556 p. No index.

Thirty heretofore unpublished articles, as well as reprints of articles published elsewhere, grouped under the following three headings: "Individual Choice in a Static Setting" (ten articles); "General Equilibrium in a Static Setting" (fourteen articles);

and "Sequential Choice and Equilibrium with Limited Information" (six articles). Topics include axiomatic theories of choice; risk aversion; precautionary demand for saving; effect of uncertainty on resource allocation; competitive equilibrium under uncertainty; role of stock market in a general equilibrium model with technological uncertainty; job market signaling; insurance; uncertainty and the evaluation of public investments; models of market organization with imperfect information; and equilibrium distribution of sales and advertising prices.

Edwards, Ward, and Tversky, Amos, eds. DECISION MAKING: SELECTED READINGS. Baltimore: Penguin Books, 1967. 413 p. Acknowledgements, pp. 399-400. Author Index, pp. 401-7. Subject Index, pp. 408-13.

Fifteen reprints of papers and excerpts on decision theory written between 1954 and 1966 grouped under the following four headings: "Theory of Decision Making: A General Review" (four articles); "Utility and Subjective Probability" (four articles); "Riskless Choice" (three articles); and "Choice Models" (four articles).

Farrar, Donald E. THE INVESTMENT DECISION UNDER CERTAINTY. Foreword by Dyke Brown. Englewood Cliffs, N.J.: Prentice-Hall, 1962. x, 90 p. Bibliography, pp. 83-90. No index.

Develops a quadratic programming model of portfolio investment for maximizing expected utility. Model tested by company portfolios. Data includes Standard and Poor's price indices on a monthly basis. Assumes knowledge of mathematical programming.

Gupta, Shanti Swarup, and Yackel, James. STATISTICAL DECISION THEORY AND RELATED TOPICS. New York: Academic Press, 1971. xiv, 303 p. No index.

Twenty papers presented at a symposium held at Purdue University November 23-25, 1970. Topics include asymptotically efficient estimation of nonparametric regression coefficients; contribution to multiple decision theory; the role of symmetry and approximation in exact design optimality; detection of outliers; empirical Bayes' slippage tests; search strategies for Wiener processes; optimal confidence intervals for the largest location parameter; and nonoptimality of likelihood ratio tests for sequential detection of signals in Gaussian noise.

Halter, Albert N., and Dean, Gerald W. DECISIONS UNDER UNCERTAINTY: WITH RESEARCH APPLICATIONS. Cincinnati, Ohio: South-Western, 1971. vi, 266 p. Appendix A: Probability that t Lies Between -t and +t, pp. 249-54. Appendix B: Answers to Chapter Questions, pp. 255-66. No index.

A text for a one-semester course in decision theory; a supplementary text for courses which include decision theory; and a reference for researchers in natural resources and other applied fields. Topics include probability theory; decisions involving expected utility; decision problems with prior distribution on the states; decision problems with posterior distributions on the states; Bayesian decision making; application to agriculture, geology, forest management, and climatology; and guidelines for application of decision making. Assumes knowledge of intermediate statistics and calculus, although the more complex empirical applications use advanced topics such as quadratic programming and Lagrangian multipliers.

Jones, J. Morgan. INTRODUCTION TO DECISION THEORY. Irwin Series in Quantitative Analysis for Business. Homewood, Ill.: Irwin, 1977. xiv, 369 p. Tables, pp. 338-64. Index, pp. 365-69.

A text for an introductory course in decision theory for undergraduates and graduates who have a background in college algebra. Includes three aspects of decision theory: use of sampling strategies, applications, and use of computer programs in APL and BASIC. Topics include probability; payoff and loss approaches for solving decision problems; expected value criterion; binomial sampling; use of probability distributions; prior and beta distributions; decisions involving means when sampling occurs; and methods of establishing distributions empirically. Includes some derivations.

Keeney, Ralph L., and Raiffa, Howard. With Contributions by Richard F. Meyer. DECISIONS WITH MULTIPLE OBJECTIVES: REFERENCES AND VALUE TRADEOFFS. Wiley Series in Probability and Mathematical Statistics. New York: Wiley, 1976. xxviii, 569 p. Bibliography, pp. 549-60. Index, pp. 561-69.

A comprehensive treatment of decision theory treating such topics as the structuring of multiple-objective problems; the theory of quantifying preferences over multiple objectives; applications, including air pollution control, instructional programs, fire department operations, computer systems, nuclear power facilities, sewage disposal, job selection, and foreign policy. Applications include airport development, the evaluation of preference over time under conditions of uncertainty and uncertainty, and aggregation of individual preferences. Useful to a wide range of readers, including analysts, policymakers, economists, engineers, and managers. Assumes knowledge of decision theory, but no advanced mathematics.

Levy, Haim, and Sarnat, Marshall, eds. FINANCIAL DECISION MAKING UNDER UNCERTAINTY. Economic Theory and Mathematical Economics. New York: Academic Press, 1977. xii, 301 p. Author Index, pp. 293-96. Subject Index, pp. 297-301.

Thirteen papers presented at the Israel Scientific Research Conferences held at Em Bokek in Israel in March 1975, grouped under the following five parts: "Utility and Risk Analysis" (two papers); "Investment Decisions Under Uncertainty" (three papers); "Portfolio Analysis and Capital Market Theory" (three papers); "Inflation and Financial Decisions" (one paper); and "Applications of Risk Analysis" (four papers). Topics include an algorithm for finding undominated portfolios; generalized logarithmic utility model as the premier model of financial markets; demand for risky assets; optimal timing of capital expenditures; leasing and buying with reference to capital services; capital asset pricing model; portfolio efficiency criteria; efficient paths toward efficient capital markets in large and small countries; equivalence among alternative portfolio selection criteria; and optimal investment and financing patterns under alternative methods of regulation.

Lindley, Dennis Victor. BAYESIAN STATISTICS: A REVIEW. Regional Conference Series in Applied Mathematics. Philadelphia: Society of Industrial and Applied Mathematics, 1972. vi, 83 p. Bibliography, pp. 75-83. No index.

A monograph on Bayesian statistics based on lectures given by the author at Oregon State University in July 1970. Presents a subjective view and includes such topics as sequential experimentation, sampling from finite populations, robustness, multiparameter problems, tolerance regions and predictive distributions, multinomial data, asymptotic results, nonparametric statistics, invariance theories, information, probability, assessments, and comparison of Bayesian and orthodox procedures. Assumes knowledge of mathematical statistics and linear algebra.

______. MAKING DECISIONS. New York: Wiley, 1971. x, 195 p. Appendix, pp. 181-86. Answers to Exercises, pp. 187-89. Glossary of Index, p. 191. Subject Index, pp. 193-95.

A theoretical approach to decision making for business executives, scientists, and college students who have knowledge of basic statistics. Topics include uncertain events; numerical measures of uncertainty; laws of probability; the utility of money; Bayes' theorem; value of information; and decision trees. Chapters conclude with exercises on hypothetical applications of the concepts.

Maritz, J.S. EMPIRICAL BAYES METHOD. New York: Barnes and Noble, 1970. viii, 159 p. Bibliography, pp. 153-55. Subject Index, pp. 157-58. Author Index, p. 159.

A monograph on empirical Bayes' techniques accessible to users of Bayes' techniques. Assumes knowledge of the standard non-Bayesian methods as presented in a course in mathematical statistics. Emphasizes the performance of empirical Bayes' procedures relative to non-Bayesian methods. Topics include estimation of prior distributions; empirical Bayes' point estimation; testing of hypotheses; two-parameter problem; and the compound decision problem.

Miller, James R. III. PROFESSIONAL DECISION-MAKING: A PROCEDURE FOR EVALUATING COMPLEX ALTERNATIVES. New Directions in Management and Economics. New York: Praeger, 1970. xii, 305 p. Appendixes, pp. 257-305. No index.

Develops a nonmonetary assessment procedure for choosing among decision alternatives to replace profit as a universal measure. Consists of three parts: "The Procedure"; "Testing the Procedure"; and "Implications for Decision Making." Procedure tested by questionnaire interviews with sixty officers and civilian personnel of the Defense Weapons System Management Center at Wright-Patterson Air Force Base, Dayton, Ohio. Appendixes include the questionnaire.

Morales, J.A. BAYESIAN FULL INFORMATION STRUCTURAL ANALYSIS: WITH AN APPLICATION TO THE STUDY OF THE BELGIAN BEEF MARKET. Lecture Notes in Operations Research and Mathematical Systems. New York: Springer-Verlag, 1971. vi, 154 p. References, pp. 149-54. No index.

An introduction to Bayesian analysis of the simultaneous equations model in two parts: "Bayesian Full Information Analysis of the Simultaneous Equations Model" and "Empirical Illustration of a Bayesian Full Information Analysis." Assumes knowledge of calculus, statistical decision theory, and probability.

Morgan, Bruce W. AN INTRODUCTION TO BAYESIAN STATISTICAL DECISION PROCESSES. Englewood Cliffs, N.J.: Prentice-Hall, 1968. 116 p. Suggestions for Further Reading, p. 111. Index, pp. 113-16.

A nontechnical introduction to Bayesian statistics in the context of a binomially distributed random variable. Topics include inference problems with rectangular or normally distributed random variables, and sequential decision procedures. Sections conclude with questions.

Newman, Joseph W. MANAGEMENT APPLICATIONS OF DECISION THEORY. New York: Harper & Row, 1971. 210 p. Appendix: Background on Bayesian Analysis of Business Decisions, pp. 205-7. Index, pp. 209-10.

A nontechnical introduction to Bayesian decision theory for use as a supplementary text in decision theory courses and for independent study in two parts: "Introduction to the Bayesian Approach" and "Applications of the Bayesian Approach." Three FORTRAN programs on applications available from the publisher. Latter part consists of three sections: "A Decision Problem for Prior and Posterior Analysis"; "A Decision Problem for Prior Analysis"; and "Concluding Comments on Applying the Bayesian Approach." Includes problems faced by Maxwell House Coffee and General Foods Corp.

Raiffa, Howard, and Schlaifer, Robert. APPLIED STATISTICAL DECISION THEORY. Foreword by Bertrand Fox. Studies in Managerial Economics. Boston: Graduate School of Business, Harvard University, 1961. xxviii, 356 p. Tables, pp. 354-56. No index.

An introduction to the mathematical analysis of decision making under uncertainty based on Bayesian principles. Consists of three parts: "Experimentation and Decision: General Theory"; "Extensive-Form Analysis When Sampling and Terminal Utilities are Additive"; and "Distribution Theory." Assumes knowledge of mathematical probability and statistics, advanced calculus, and matrix theory. Topics include sufficient statistics and noninformative stopping; additive utility, opportunity loss, and the value of information; linear terminal analysis; problems in which the act and state spaces coincide; posterior analysis; univariate normalized mass and density functions; multivariate normalized density functions; Bernoulli process; Poisson process; and normal regression process. Accessible to a heterogeneous audience, including statisticians interested in practical applications.

Schmitt, Samuel A. MEASURING UNCERTAINTY: AN ELEMENTARY INTRODUCTION TO BAYESIAN STATISTICS. Addison-Wesley Series in Behavioral Science: Quantitative Methods. Reading, Mass.: Addison-Wesley, 1969. xvi, 400 p. Suggestions for Further Reading, pp. 341-43. Bibliography, pp. 345-48. Appendix A: Mathematical Details, pp. 351-63. Appendix B: Logarithms, pp. 364-69. Appendix C: Random Numbers, pp. 370-72. A Gallery of Standard Distributions, pp. 375-95. Index, pp. 397-400.

A text for a one-semester course in basic statistics for students who have a good background in high school mathematics. Emphasizes Bayesian statistics leading to the modern concepts of decision theory and information theory. Includes numerous examples. Topics include rules of probability; joint and marginal probabilities; sampling experiments; Bayes' theorem and prior probabilities; continuous distributions; inferences about the Gaussian distribution; nonnormality; goodness of fit; sequential decisions; simple regression; reliability; and entropy and information.

Wald, Abraham. STATISTICAL DECISION FUNCTIONS. Wiley Series in Probability and Mathematical Statistics. New York: Wiley, 1950. ix, 179 p. Bibliography, pp. 169-72. Index, pp. 173-79.

Presents the foundations of a general theory of statistical decision functions, including multi-stage experimentation and the general multi-decision problem. Emphasizes general ideas and results rather than specific methods or techniques. Assumes knowledge of probability distributions in infinite dimensional spaces, measure theory, and set theory, but previous knowledge of mathematical statistics unnecessary. Topics include zero-sum two-person games with infinitely many strategies; a general theory of statistical decision functions; properties of Bayes' solutions when chance variables are independent and identically distributed; and applications to sequential and nonsequential decision problems.

Weiss, Lionel. STATISTICAL DECISION THEORY. McGraw-Hill Series in Probability and Statistics. New York: McGraw-Hill, 1961. viii, 195 p. Exercises, pp. 165-84. Appendix, pp. 187-92. Index, pp. 193-95.

A text for a one-semester course in decision theory for students who have had calculus through partial differential equations and multiple integration, and matrix algebra. Includes a brief and simple discussion of probability theory. Topics include discrete and continuous random variables; multivariate distributions; important expected values and distributions; Bayes' decision rules; sequential decision procedures; linear programming; empirical cumulative distribution functions; and classical statistical theory. Presentation rigorous with no numerical examples provided.

White, Douglas John. DECISION METHODOLOGY: A FORMALIZATION OF THE OPERATIONS RESEARCH PROCESS. New York: Wiley, Intersciences, 1975. xii, 274 p. References, pp. 260-65. Index, pp. 267-74.

Deals with the economic problems surrounding the applications of operations research techniques for students of decision analysis, as well as practicing managers, who have knowledge of decision theory and operations research. Topics include origins and nature of decision analysis; steps in setting up a decision problem; and methodological decisions and suboptimization. Concludes with a chapter containing a set of exercises.

Wilcox, Jarrod W. A METHOD FOR MEASURING DECISION ASSUMPTIONS. Cambridge, Mass.: MIT Press, 1972. x, 252 p. Appendix A: Derivation of Factor Measure Transforms, pp. 203-5. Appendix B: Simple Questionnaire and Interview Materials, pp. 206-13. Appendix C: Individual Factor Analysis Results, pp. 214-37. Appendix D: Individual Predictive Models, pp. 238-40. Bibliography and Reference List, pp. 241-47. Index, pp. 249-52.

A handbook on a method for experimentation on why people choose among alternatives for students of the social sciences who have knowledge of basic statistics. Method called measuring decision assumptions. Based on factor analysis and applied to a study of stock market participants in the following steps: eliciting attribute scales, algorithmic estimation of decision assumptions, and predictive validation of assumption measures.

Wilhelm, Jochen. OBJECTIVES AND MULTI-OBJECTIVE DECISION MAKING UNDER UNCERTAINTY. Lecture Notes in Economics and Mathematical Systems, vol. 112. New York: Springer-Verlag, 1975. iv, 111 p. References, pp. 106-11. No index.

A formal mathematical development of the problems of intrapersonal objectives and of multi-objective decision making under uncertainty. Results applied to production by a firm, financing, sales, and indifference against objective risks. Assumes knowledge of topology and probability theory.

Willner, Dorothy, ed. DECISIONS, VALUES AND GROUPS. Vol. 1. Foreword by Charles E. Hutchinson. New York: Pergamon, 1960. xxix, 348 p. No index.

Nineteen papers presented at the first interdisciplinary research conference held at the University of New Mexico June 17-August 10, 1957, grouped under the following five headings: "Mathematical Models in Decision Processes" (four papers); "Conceptualizations and Designs for Research in Values and Evaluative Processes" (four papers); "Theoretical Contributions to Small Group Research" (five papers); "Psychodynamic Patterns of Behavior" (four paper); and "Special Military Problems" (two papers). Covers such topics as stochastic choice and subjective probability; formation of hypotheses and styles; a theory of the structure of conscience; values in person cognition; common fate similarity and other indexes; a scale to measure individual prominence; the problem of vicarious experience; and human parameters in space. Some papers assume knowledge of basic statistics, and several required knowledge of intermediate probability theory.

Winkler, Robert L. AN INTRODUCTION TO BAYESIAN INFERENCE AND DECISION. Series in Quantitative Methods for Decision Making. New York: Holt, Rinehart and Winston, 1972. xi, 563 p. Additional Reference and Suggestions for Further Reading, pp. 446-47. Tables, pp. 448-530. Bibliography, pp. 531-50. Answers to Selected Exercises, pp. 551-55. Index, pp. 557-63.

A text for an introductory course in statistical inference from a Bayesian viewpoint for students who have knowledge of high school algebra. Includes numerous problems at ends of chapters ranging from applications of the textual material to extensions of the concepts. Topics include Bayesian inference for discrete and continuous probability models, decision theory, value of perfect information, preposterior analysis, sequential analysis, posterior distribution and estimation, posterior hypothesis testing, and likelihood ratio tests. Chapters conclude with references.

Chapter 13

STATISTICAL GEOGRAPHY, GEOLOGY, AND ECOLOGY

Agterberg, Frederik Pieter. GEOMATHEMATICS: MATHEMATICAL BACKGROUND AND GEO-SCIENCE APPLICATIONS. Developments in Geomathematics. Foreword by S.C. Robinson. New York: Elsevier, 1974. xvi, 596 p. Bibliography, pp. 553-78. Index, pp. 579-96.

> A text for a course in geomathematics for advanced students, research workers, and teachers who possess competence in calculus and intermediate statistics. Consists mainly of case histories based on the author's research with the Geological Survey of Canada. Assumes knowledge of matrix algebra and regression. Topics include reviews of calculus, matrix algebra, and geometry; factor analysis; random variables and probability distributions; statistical dependence; multiple regression; trend analysis; stationary random variables; harmonic analysis and power spectra; powers of matrices and Markov chains; multivariate stochastic process models with applications to the petrology of basalts; and calculation of preferred orientations from vectorial data.

Bartlett, Maurice Stevenson. THE STATISTICAL ANALYSIS OF SPATIAL PATTERNS. Wiley, Halsted Press, 1975. ix, 90 p. Appendix: Tables, pp. 82-83. References, pp. 84-88. Index, pp. 89-90.

> A monograph on the statistical techniques for analyzing patterns in two parts: "Survey of Underlying Theory" and "Examples of Statistical Analyses." Topics include continuous, point and line processes; and nearest neighbor systems on a lattice. Examples of continuous and point processes include Mead's randomization test, spectral analysis, and nearest-neighbor distances between gulls' nests. Examples of processes on a lattice include simulation and conditional models, discrete variables, and simple chi-square analyses. Omits problems of robust estimation in ecology, multivariate measurements, and the detection of space-time interactions in epidemiology. Useful to statisticians and biometricians.

Berry, Brian Joe Lobley, and Marble, Duane F., eds. SPATIAL ANALYSIS: A READER IN STATISTICAL GEOGRAPHY. Englewood Cliffs, N.J.: Prentice-Hall, 1968. xiv, 512 p. Index, pp. 499-512.

Thirty-seven reprints of articles on quantification in geography grouped under the following six headings: "Methodology" (five articles); "Spatial Data and Spatial Statistics" (eight articles); "Analysis of Spatial Distributions" (ten articles); "Study of Spatial Association" (seven articles); "Regionalization" (three articles); and "Problems in the Analysis of Spatial Series" (four articles). Topics include geography and analog theory; geographic sampling; physics of population distribution; statistical study of the distribution of scattered villages; maps based on probabilities; trend-surface mapping in geographical research; Fourier analysis in geology; regression analysis applied to farm population; distribution of forested areas in Southeast Brazil; geographical distribution of crop productivity in England; ecological correlation; and the contiguity ratio and statistical mapping. Assumes knowledge of one year of basic statistics.

Blinder, Alan S., and Friedman, Philip, eds. NATURAL RESOURCES, UNCERTAINTY, AND GENERAL EQUILIBRIUM SYSTEMS: ESSAYS IN MEMORY OF RAFAEL LUSKY. Economic Theory and Mathematical Economics Series. New York: Academic Press, 1977. xv, 255 p. No index.

Fifteen heretofore unpublished contributions dedicated to the memory of Professor Rafael Lusky grouped under the following four headings: "Natural Resources" (two contributions); "Uncertainty" (five contributions); "General Equilibrium Systems: Stability Optimality and Distribution" (four contributions); "Policy and Applications" (four contributions). Topics include resource depletion with technological uncertainty and the Rawlsian Fairness Principle; monopoly, uncertainty, and exploration; price discrimination and uncertainty; insurance theoretic aspects of workers' compensation; adverse selection and optimum insurance policies; an exchange model of bilaterial trade; optimal taxes on foreign lending; an extended permanent expenditure system; and multiperiod stochastic dominance in the log-normal case. Assumes knowledge of calculus, econometrics, and mathematical economics.

Chorley, Richard J., and Haggett, Peter, eds. MODELS IN GEOGRAPHY. Second Madingley Lectures. London: Methuen, 1967. 816 p. Index by D.R. Stoddart, pp. 795-816.

Eighteen heretofore unpublished contributions on the role of model building in various fields of geographical research grouped under the following five headings: "The Role of Models" (two contributions); "Models of Physical Systems" (three contributions); "Models of Socio-Economic Systems" (six contributions); "Models of Mixed Systems" (four contributions); and "Information Models" (three contributions). Topics include models in geomorphology, meteorology, and climatology; hydrological models; demographic models; models of urban geography, economic development, and industrial location; models of agricultural activity; models of evolution of spatial patterns in human geography; network models in geography; and hardware models. Articles nonmathematical and treat conditions under which various models can be applied.

Clark, Colin W. MATHEMATICAL BIOECONOMICS: THE OPTIMAL MANAGEMENT OF RENEWABLE RESOURCES. New York: Wiley, 1976. xi, 352 p. Supplementary Reading, pp. 336-37. Bibliography, pp. 338-46. Index, pp. 347-52.

An introduction to the mathematical theory of conservation with applications largely to commercial fishery and forestry, rather than to the recreational uses of natural resources. Emphasizes the productive aspects of renewable resources in which economics and biology play important roles. Uses dynamic models of biological processes to establish the theory. Assumes knowledge of differential equations and calculus. Topics include capital-theoretic aspects of resource management; optimal control theory; dynamical systems; discrete-time or metered models; and multispecies problems. Methods entirely analytic with examples used to illustrate the theory. Chapters conclude with exercises and notes.

Cliff, A.D., and Ord, J.K. SPATIAL AUTOCORRELATION. Monographs in Spatial and Environmental Systems Analysis. London: Pion, 1973. xi, 178 p. Appendix 1: Models for Spatial Autocorrelation, pp. 161-62. Appendix 2: Tables of Unstandardised and Standardised Weights for the Eire County System, pp. 163-64. Appendix 3: Calculation of Maximum Likelihood Estimates for the Autoregressive Model, p. 165. Glossary of Notation, pp. 166-72. References and Author Index, pp. 173-76. Subject Index, pp. 177-78.

A monograph on statistical methods for analyzing the spatial patterns inherent in geographically located data with insights into the stochastic processes forming the patterns. Useful to researchers and practitioners in economics, ecology, geography, geology, planning, statistics, and regional science. Assumes knowledge of mathematical statistics. Topics include measures and tests for autocorrelation; distribution theory for joint count, I, and c statistics; application of the spatial autocorrelation measures to Geary's Irish data and in quadrat count analysis; map comparison with application to diffusion processes; the Hagerstand model; analysis of regression residuals with empirical examples; comparisons of tests for spatial autocorrelation; Monte Carlo studies; and partial correlations and autocorrelations.

Cole, John P., and King, Cuchlaine, A.M. QUANTITATIVE GEOGRAPHY: TECHNIQUES AND THEORIES IN GEOGRAPHY. New York: Wiley, 1968. x, 692 p. Glossary, pp. 645-70. Mathematical and Statistical Signs, pp. 671-77. Author Index, pp. 679-81. Subject Index, pp. 683-92.

A text for a course in quantitative geography and a reference for research workers. Consists of four parts: "Introduction, Mathematics, and Statistics"; "Spatial Distributions and Relationships"; "Dimensions of Space and Time"; and "Models, Theories and Organization." Topics include methods of describing single distributions; comparisons; correlations between two or more distributions in the same area and between different areas; geography and three space dimensions; geography and time; networks and classification; and data retrieval. Chapters conclude with references.

Davis, John C. STATISTICS AND DATA ANALYSIS IN GEOLOGY. FORTRAN programs by Robert J. Sampson. New York: Wiley, 1973. xiii, 550 p. Appendix, pp. 537-43. Index, pp. 545-50.

A text for an intermediate course in statistics for geology students who have knowledge of computer programming, elementary statistics, and matrix algebra. Emphasizes operational aspects of data analysis, and includes a large number of FORTRAN programs throughout. Topics include review of geomathematics; analysis of sequences of data, including run tests, least squares, time-trend analysis, and transition matrices; map analysis, including contouring, four-dimensional trend surfaces, and double Fourier series; and analysis of multivariate data, including multiple regression, discriminant functions, cluster analysis, and factor analysis. Chapters conclude with selected readings. Uses the verbal style with graphs, charts, and numerical examples.

Dogan, Mattei, and Rokkan, Stein, eds. QUANTITATIVE ECOLOGICAL ANALYSIS IN THE SOCIAL SCIENCES. MIT Studies in Comparative Politics. Cambridge, Mass.: MIT Press, 1969. xv, 607 p. Index of Persons, pp. 589-94. Index of Institutions, pp. 595-97. Geographical Index, pp. 598-600. Index of Subjects, pp. 601-7.

Twenty-four heretofore unpublished contributions grouped under the following six headings: "The Logic of Ecological Inference" (four contributions); "Individual Behavior and Collective Properties" (five contributions); "Multivariate Analysis in Political Ecology" (two contributions); "Factor Analysis and Ecological Typologies" (five contributions); "Historical Dimensions of Ecological Analysis" (three contributions); and "The Organization of Ecological Data Archives" (five contributions). Techniques used include regression and covariance analysis, factor analysis, causal path analysis, and systems of simultaneous equations.

Duncan, Otis Dudley; Cuzzort, Ray P.; and Duncan, Beverly. STATISTICAL GEOGRAPHY: PROBLEMS IN ANALYZING AREAL DATA. Glencoe, Ill.: Free Press, 1961. xiv, 191 p. Bibliography, pp. 175-87. Subject Index, pp. 189-91.

A monograph on selected methodological problems of statistical geography based on the research experience of the author. Includes detailed examinations of the ways in which areal data are generated, with attention to the problem of quality of areal data, and the actual manipulation of quantitative data by statistical methods.

Fenner, Peter, ed. QUANTITATIVE GEOLOGY. Special Paper, no. 146. Boulder, Colo.: Geological Society of America, 1972. viii, 101 p. Index, pp. 95-101.

Eight papers presented at a symposium held at the eighty-second annual meeting of the Geological Society of America in Atlanta City, November 10, 1969. Topics include probabilistic models and the quantification process in geology; estimating lithologic components in stratigraphic sequences under uncertainty; statistical meaning in geologic field work; trend surface analysis and spatial correlation; systems analysis and model building; and cybernetic geomathematics interaction. Assumes knowledge of basic statistics.

Gregory, Stanley. STATISTICAL METHODS AND THE GEOGRAPHER. 3d ed., rev. New York: Longman, 1973. xviii, 271 p. A Selected Bibliography, pp. 252-60. Formulas Index, pp. 261-64. General Index, pp. 265-71.

A text for a course in basic statistics for students of geology with examples from the United Kingdom. Topics include descriptive statistics; probability assessments, including binomial and Poisson; methods of sampling; interval estimation; testing hypotheses; analysis of variance; nonparametric tests; Kolmogorov-Smirnov test; simple regression and correlation; and fluctuations and trends. Uses the intuitive approach with illustrative examples.

Greig-Smith, Peter. QUANTITATIVE PLANT-ECOLOGY. 2d ed. London: Butterworth, 1964. xii, 256 p. Appendixes A and B, pp. 220-25. References, pp. 225-46. Author Index, pp. 248-52. Subject Index, pp. 253-56.

A monograph on the practical techniques of quantitative plant ecology. Topics include methods of describing vegetation in quantitative terms; testing for significance of patterns; patterns of different species; correlation between vegetation and environmental factors; delineation of plant communities; and classification of vegetation. Appendixes include examples of correlations with meteorological data, and area and spread of species, and statistical tables.

Griffiths, John Cedric. SCIENTIFIC METHODS IN THE ANALYSIS OF SEDIMENTS. McGraw-Hill Series in the Earth and Planetary Sciences. New York: McGraw-Hill, 1967. xvi, 508 p. References, pp. 485-502. Index, pp. 503-8.

A text for a course in petrography for students of geology who have a high school algebra background and a reference for practitioners. Topics include sampling sedimentary rocks; measurement of grain size; descriptive statistics of measured data; measurement of grain shape, grain fabric, grain packing, mineral composition, and derived properties; data processing with computers; probability distributions, including normal, binomial, Poisson, and hypergeometric; coefficient of variation; tests of significance, including comparison of the means of two samples; chi-square; one- and two-way analysis of variance; Latin square and incomplete block designs; and regression and correlation. Includes examples from petrographic analysis of detrital sediments.

Haining, Robert P. SPECIFICATION AND ESTIMATION PROBLEMS IN MODELS OF SPATIAL DEPENDENCE. Studies in Geography, no. 4. Evanston, Ill.: Department of Geography, Northwestern University, 1978. xi, 231 p. Bibliography, pp. 227-31. No index.

An exposition of multidimensional processes using observations at a single period of time over one or more spatial dimensions. Structure falls within the category of a two dimensional finite stochastic field with the spatial pattern of the midpoints of the subregions forming a square lattice within a rectangular region. Develops temporal and spatial autoregressive models, estimates them by ordinary least squares and maximum likelihood procedures; and tests hypotheses about parameters of the regression model with autocorrelated errors. Includes applications to crop yields. Assumes knowledge of mathematical statistics helpful.

Hall, Charles A.S., and Day, John W., Jr., eds. ECOSYSTEM MODELING IN THEORY AND PRACTICE: AN INTRODUCTION WITH CASE HISTORIES. New York: Wiley, 1977. xxvi, 684 p. No index.

Twenty-five heretofore unpublished contributions by different authors suitable for an introductory course in modeling ecosystems in four parts: "Basic Principles"; "Case Histories: Understanding Natural Systems"; "Case Histories: Assessing Environmental Impact"; and "Case Histories: Designing Optimal Interactions of Man and Nature." Topics include mathematical construction of ecological models; environmental modeling; natural ecosystems; life and death of a forest with the aid of a computer; model of a thermal spring flood chain; Baltic ecosystem modeling; modeling and nature in southern Louisiana; applications of an ecosystem model to water quality management;

pest management models of crop ecosystems; population optima; and modeling Narragansett Bay estuary in New England.

Harbaugh, John Warvelle, and Bonham-Carter, Graeme. COMPUTER SIMULATION IN GEOLOGY. New York: Wiley, 1970. xiv, 575 p. Appendix: Solution of Simultaneous Linear Equations, pp. 558-65. Annotated Bibliography, pp. 565-66. Index, pp. 567-75.

A text and a reference on computer simulation in geology from a systems viewpoint for students of geology who have a working knowledge of computer programming, basic statistics, linear algebra, and numerical analysis. Topics include construction of simulation models; mathematical and computational tools of simulation; application to sedimentation, ecology and paleoecology, evolution, and morphology, structural geology, hydrology, and petrology; FORTRAN IV computer programs; generating random variables; Markov chains; flow and transportation system control; and optimization using direct-search, linear programming least squares, calculus, and simplex methods. Chapters conclude with problems and annotated bibliographies.

Harbaugh, John W[arvelle]., and Merriam, Daniel F. COMPUTER APPLICATIONS IN STRATIGRAPHIC ANALYSIS. New York: Wiley, 1968. xi, 282 p. References, pp. 261-76. Appendix, pp. 277-78. Index, pp. 279-82.

A reference and supplementary text on computer applications in stratigraphic analysis for students of geology who have knowledge of algebra and basic statistics. Emphasizes techniques useful in dealing with stratigraphic and structural problems involving spatial relationships in sedimentary basins. Methods based on statistics largely excluded. Topics include mapping techniques, including contour mapping, directional data mapping, and facies mapping; time-trend analysis in stratigraphic correlation; polynomial trend analysis; including trend-surface analysis and four-variable trend hypersurfaces; harmonic trend analysis; cluster, factor, and discriminant function analysis; and dynamic deterministic and probabilistic simulation of various types of sedimentation. Appendixes include use of computers, review of statistics, sources of computer programs, and references.

Innis, George S., ed. GRASSLAND SIMULATION MODEL. Foreword by George M. Van Dyne. New York: Springer-Verlag, 1978. xxv, 298 p. Author Index, pp. 283-87. Subject Index, pp. 289-98.

Ten heretofore unpublished contributions dealing with the ELM grasslands simulation model of the U.S. Grassland Biome program. Model developed from 1971 through 1974 by the contributors and include such topics as structure of the model; abiotic section of ELM; mammalian consumer component of ELM; simulation of grasshopper populations; ELM decomposition submodel; simulation of nitrogen flow; simulation of phosphorus cycling in semiarid grasslands; sensitivity analysis of the ELM model; and critique and analysis. Most concepts illustrated by graphs and numerical examples, including simulation results, but knowledge of calculus, matrix algebra, and differential equations helpful for derivations. Also includes flowcharts and printouts of computer programs.

Jeffers, John Norman Richard, ed. MATHEMATICAL MODELS IN ECOLOGY. London: Blackwell, 1972. viii, 398 p. Author Index, pp. 389-92. Subject Index, pp. 393-98.

Nineteen papers presented at the twelfth symposium of the British Ecological Society held in Grange-Over-Sands, Lancashire, March 23-26, 1971. Topics include philosophical aspects of mathematical modelling in empirical science; developments in the Leslie matrix model; models and analysis of descriptive vegetation data; models for large-scale vegetation surveys; ecosystem models; population models as a basis for pest control; parameter estimation and interdependence in hydrological models; computer simulation in conservation management; stochastic model fitting by evolutionary operation; and points of view of the agriculturalist, statistician, and ecologist.

Jöreskog, K.G.; Klovan, J.E.; and Reyment, R.A. GEOLOGICAL FACTOR ANALYSIS. Methods in Geomathematics, 1. New York: Elsevier, 1976. xi, 178 p. References, pp. 175-78. No index.

A supplementary text and reference on the use of factor analysis in geology for geologists working in mining geology, sedimentology, and petrology. Knowledge of basic statistics helpful. Topics include basic concepts of multivariate algebra; rotation of coordinate systems; role of engenvalues and eigenvectors; concepts of factor analysis; and the statistical interpretation of models; principal components; R-Mode Methods; Q-Mode Factor Analysis; correspondence analysis; steps in the analysis and the selection of methods; and examples in numerical chemistry, sedimentology, subsurface brine geochemistry; foraminiferal palaeoecology; metamorphic rocks; and actuopalaeoecology.

Kershaw, Kenneth Andrew. QUANTITATIVE AND DYNAMIC ECOLOGY. New York: Elsevier, 1964. viii, 183 p. References, pp. 171-78. Author Index, pp. 179-80. Subject Index, pp. 181-83.

A monograph on the use of statistics in describing vegetation. Topics include sampling plant communities to make inferences; use of statistical measures to study plant succession; cyclic vegetation change; correlation and causal factors in positive and negative association between species; Poisson series and the detection of nonrandomness; contagious distributions; and the detection of natural groupings of species. Uses few formulas, but includes many pictures, graphs, and charts for illustrating statistical techniques. Useful as a supplementary text in ecology courses and as a reference.

King, Leslie J. STATISTICAL ANALYSIS IN GEOGRAPHY. Englewood Cliffs, N.J.: Prentice-Hall, 1969. xii, 288 p. Appendix A: Some Mathematical Guidelines, pp. 233-56. Appendix B: Glossary of Terms and Symbols, pp. 257-59. References, pp. 260-81. Index, pp. 283-88.

A text for a course in quantitative analysis in geography for graduate students who have a minimum training in mathematics and statistics. Topics include numerical data in geographic research; central tendency and variance; sets and probability; discrete and continuous probability distributions, including Poisson, negative binomial, and exponential; stratified areal sampling; chi-square; comparison of two variances and two means; regional method of nearest-neighbor analysis; randomness in the arrangement of points by quadrats; statistical considerations in choropleth patterns; simple and multiple correlation and regression in geography; principal components analysis; factor analysis; classification and linear discriminant functions; applications of canonical correlation analysis; and advanced analysis of spatial series. Chapters conclude with suggested readings.

Koch, George S., and Link, Richard F. STATISTICAL ANALYSIS OF GEOLOGICAL DATA. Vol. 1. New York: Wiley, 1970. xii, 376 p. Appendix: Tables, pp. 339-61. Index, pp. 363-76.

A reference for practitioners and a text for a formal course. Also useful to mining and petroleum engineers, geochemists, and mineral economists. Consists of three parts: "Introduction"; "Univariate Statistical Methods"; and "Sampling and Variability in Geology." Topics include descriptive statistics; sampling distributions, statistical inference; Bayesian statistics; analysis of variance; distributions and transformations; geological sampling; and variability in geological data. Assumes knowledge of high school algebra. Chapters conclude with references.

_____. STATISTICAL ANALYSIS OF GEOLOGICAL DATA. Vol. 2. New York: Wiley, 1971. x, 438 p. Appendix: Tables, pp. 418-21. Partial List of Symbols, pp. 423-25. Index, pp. 427-38.

A monograph on statistical analysis of geological data with a prerequisite of basic statistics. Consists of three parts: "Geological Trends"; "Some Problems in Applied Geology"; and "Electronic Computers and Geology." Examples use real data from structural geology and petrology. Useful to mining and petroleum engineers, geochemists, geophysics, mineral economists, as well as geologists. Topics include analysis of multivariate data; ratios and variables of constant sum; exploration; delineation of ore deposits; operations research; geological sampling; and gold and the lognormal distribution. Includes a brief introduction to the use of computers in geology.

Krumbein, William Christian, and Graybill, Franklin A. AN INTRODUCTION TO STATISTICAL MODELS IN GEOLOGY. International Series in Earth Sciences. New York: McGraw-Hill, 1965. xvi, 475 p. Appendix: Tables, pp. 415-60. Author Index, pp. 461-65. Subject Index, pp. 467-75.

A guide for the geologist (rather than a text) for formalizing ideas that arise from data and for testing concepts. Based on statistical inference and assumes knowledge of calculus and basic statistics. Topics include geological foundation on which statistical studies are based; models in geology; geological populations; sampling distributions and statistical inference; chi-square; analysis of variance; linear economic model with application to map analysis; and data evaluation. Chapters conclude with references in two parts: "Statistical" and "Geological and Related References." Includes applications to sedimentation.

McCammon, Richard B., ed. CONCEPTS IN GEOSTATISTICS. New York: Springer-Verlag, 1975. xv, 168 p. References, p. 163. Index, pp. 164-68.

Seven papers presented at a summer course entitled current statistical methods in geology held at the University of Illinois, Chicago, June 19-30, 1972. Prepares geology college students for teaching computer and statistical applications in geology. Topics include probability with applications to searching for dike; factor analysis; time series analysis, including polynomial curve fitting and Fourier analysis; Markov models; correlation and regression; and computer applications.

Matern, Bertil. SPATIAL VARIATION: STOCHASTIC MODELS AND THEIR APPLICATION TO SOME PROBLEMS IN FOREST SURVEYS AND OTHER SAMPLING INVESTIGATIONS. Stockholm: Meddelanden, Fran, 1960. References, pp. 140-44. No index.

A review of some basic theory of spatial variation based on static stochastic models with applications to problems in sampling, many associated with forest surveys. Restricted to variance-covariance properties of processes in n-dimensional Euclidean space R_n. Topics include moving average models with constant and stochastic weight functions, errors of observation, stratified random sampling and sampling by Latin square design, systematic sampling, allowance for border effects in estimating the sampling error, linear sampling units in R_2, comparison between strip surveys and plot surveys and size and shape of sample plots. Assumes knowledge of calculus and mathematical statistics. Excludes detailed derivations. Includes simple examples based on Swedish forestry conditions. Useful as a text on spatial variation in forestry and geography, and as a reference.

Merriam, Daniel F., ed. GEOSTATISTICS: A COLLOQUIUM. Computer Applications in the Earth Sciences Monographs. New York: Plenum, 1970. xiii, 177 p. Index, pp. 175-77.

Twelve papers presented at a colloquium on geostatistics, held at the University of Kansas June 7-9, 1970. Topics include statistical treatment of orientation data; application of random functions in geology; autocorrelation functions in geology; component estimation under uncertainty; numerical classification; random kriging; and the effect of a single nonzero open covariance on the simple closure test.

Miller, Robert L., and Kahn, James Steven. STATISTICAL ANALYSIS IN THE GEOLOGICAL SCIENCES. New York: Wiley, 1962. xiii, 483 p. Appendix A: Differentiation of a Collection of Fossils, pp. 440-46. Appendix B: Models for Fossil Populations, pp. 447-54. Appendix C: F Distributions, pp. 455-57. Appendix D: Chi-Square Distribution, pp. 458-61. Appendix E: Cumulative Chi-Square Distribution, p. 462. Appendix F: The Addition Theorem for Chi-Square Distributions, p. 463. Appendix G: The Kolmogorov-Smirnov Statistic: Charts for 0.95 and 0.99 Confidence Regions, pp. 464-70. Author Index, pp. 471-75. Subject Index, pp. 477-83.

A reference for research workers in the earth sciences and a text for a graduate course on applications with emphasis on a survey of the literature. Assumes knowledge of one year of basic statistics and calculus. Includes applications to a wide variety of problems in the earth sciences. Topics include probability and probability distributions; random variables and their moments; statistical inference; regression with emphasis on paleobiometrics; analysis of variance; multivariate analysis; factor analysis; one-dimensional trends including time series; distribution of points on a plane and higher dimensions; and statistical approaches to mapping problems. Chapters conclude with references.

Minshull, Roger. AN INTRODUCTION TO MODELS IN GEOGRAPHY. New York: Longman, 1975. vi, 162 p. Bibliography, pp. 155-58. Index, pp. 159-62.

A nontechnical exposition on models in geography using no formulas. Topics include types of models; uses of models in research and exposition; problems and dangers of the use of models; and aims of models in geography. Useful as a reference to anyone interested in models in geography.

Neft, David S. STATISTICAL ANALYSIS FOR AREAL DISTRIBUTIONS. Philadelphia: Regional Science Research Institute, 1966. viii, 172 p. Appendix A: List of Symbols Used in the Study Specifically for the Analysis of Areal Distributions, pp. 149-54. Appendix B: Demonstration of Bias Due to Grouping in the Calculation of Positive Areal Moments, pp. 155-56. Appendix C: Proof that the Density and Volume Values of the Normal Probability Surface are Complementary at any Given Distance from the Center, pp. 157-58. Bibliography, pp. 159-66. Index, pp. 167-72.

Presents a statistical methodology of areal distributions using standard statistical measures of central tendency, dispersion, skewness, kurtosis, correlation, confidence limits, and selected tests.

Panofsky, Hans A., and Brier, Glenn W. SOME APPLICATIONS OF STATISTICS TO METEOROLOGY. University Park: College of Mineral Industries, Pennsylvania State University, 1965. ix, 224 p. Appendix, pp. 209-19. Index, pp. 220-24.

A text for a course in statistics for meteorology students and a reference for forecasters and research personnel. Emphasizes explanation of techniques and the assumptions on which the techniques are based. Topics include classical statistics, including descriptive statistics, sampling theory, simple and multiple regression and correlation; time series; and applications to weather forecasting and forecast verification. Appendixes include proofs and derivations.

Patil, Ganapati P.; Pielou, E.C.; and Waters, W.E., eds. STATISTICAL ECOLOGY. Vol. 1. SPATIAL PATTERNS AND STATISTICAL DISTRIBUTIONS. University Park: Pennsylvania State University Press, 1971. xxvii, 582 p. No index.

Twenty-three papers presented at an international symposium on statistical ecology held in New Haven, Conn., in August 1969. Emphasizes analytical approaches useful to the solution of man-environment problems. Assumes knowledge of mathematical statistics. Topics include properties of discrete ecological distributions; paleoecological pollen studies; stirling numbers in discrete distributions; doubly stochastic Poisson processes in the plane; spatial patterns in some Australian dryland plant communities; aggregation of species within spatial units; measures of spatial patterns in ecological populations; mathematical models of contagion and their relation to density and basal area sampling techniques; and estimation of fish population distributions using acoustic methods.

_____. STATISTICAL ECOLOGY. Vol. 2. SAMPLING AND MODELING BIOLOGICAL POPULATIONS AND POPULATION DYNAMICS. University Park: Pennsylvania State University Press, 1971. viii, 420 p. No index.

Nineteen papers presented at an international symposium held in New Haven, Conn., in August 1969. Emphasizes analytical approaches and techniques to man-environment problems. Topics include walk models for animal behavior; forest sampling in the absence of a well-defined frame; techniques for sampling western pine beetle populations; sampling techniques for estimation of mite incidence in the field with special reference to the tea crop; numerical comparisons of deterministic and stochastic predation models; population fluctuations of grey larch bud moth; robustness of estimating density by distance measurements; and the center-satellite concept as a basis for ecological sampling.

______. STATISTICAL ECOLOGY. Vol. 3. MANY SPECIES POPULATIONS, ECOSYSTEMS, AND SYSTEMS ANALYSIS. University Park: Pennsylvania State University Press, 1971. ix, 462 p. No index.

Twenty papers presented at the international symposium on statistical ecology held in New Haven, Conn., in August 1969. Topics include simulation models in ecology; systems of equations for predicting forest growth and yield; stochastic model of energy flow in predator compartments of an ecosystem; analysis of wilderness ecosystem; application of numerical methods to tropical forests; information theory techniques for classifying plant communities; contingency-table analysis of rain forest vegetation; simulation of dispersal in desert rodents; uses and limitations of mathematical analysis in plant ecology and land management; and a test of difference between clusters. Includes a bibliography on population dynamics, mathematics, and statistics in ecology, by V. Schultz.

Patten, Bernard C., ed. SYSTEMS ANALYSIS AND SIMULATION IN ECOLOGY. Vol. I. New York: Academic Press, 1971. xv, 607 p. Author Index, pp. 585-90. Subject Index, pp. 591-607.

Ten heretofore unpublished contributions to systems analysis and simulation in ecology grouped under the following three headings: "Introduction to Modeling" (two papers); "One-Species Models" (three papers); and "The Ecosystem; Simulation" (five papers). Emphasizes modelling and simulating by use of analog and digital computers and description of FORTRAN programs for modelling. Models based on a system of differential equations. Topics include dynamics of microbial populations; ecological bioenergetics of a terrestial isopod; computer analysis of predation energetics in the large mouth bass; systems approaches to the study of forest floor arthropods; compartment model simulation; simulation of energy flow in cedar bog lake; and analog computer models of the wolves of Isle Royale.

_____. SYSTEMS ANALYSIS AND SIMULATION IN ECOLOGY. Vol. II. New York: Academic Press, 1972. xvi, 592 p. Author Index, pp. 571-77. Subject Index, pp. 578-92.

Twelve heretofore unpublished contributions in systems analysis and simulation in ecology grouped under four headings: "Introduction to Systems Science" (one paper); "The Ecosystem: Systems Analysis" (two papers); "Theory" (four papers); and "Applications and Prospects" (five papers). Topics include introduction to systems science for ecologists; sensitivity analysis of energy flow in a marine ecosystem; frequency response analysis of magnesium cycling in a tropical forest ecosystem; steady-state equilibrium in simple nonlinear food webs; niche quantification and niche pattern; systems analysis applied to fishery problems; digital simulation modeling in resource management; and systems methods in environment court actions. Assumes knowledge of matrix algebra, differential equations, and computer programming.

_____. SYSTEMS ANALYSIS AND SIMULATION IN ECOLOGY. Vol. III. New York: Academic Press, 1975. xv, 601 p. Index, pp. 589-601.

Twelve papers based on a symposium held during March 1-3, 1973, at the University of Georgia grouped under two headings; "Ecosystem Modeling in the U.S. International Biological Program" (seven papers) and "Models of Freshwater-Estuarine Ecosystems" (five papers). Emphasizes interaction between U.S. International Biological Program (IBP) BIOME and selected non-IBP investigations involving systems approaches to ecosystem analysis. Topics include total systems models in the grassland BIOME study; modeling in the Eastern deciduous forest BIOME; modeling in desert, tundra, and conferous forest BIOME; modeling of the Algal-fly components of a thermal ecosystem; modeling for small woodland streams; and phytoplakton-zooplankton-nutrient interaction model for Western Lake Erie.

_____. SYSTEMS ANALYSIS AND SIMULATION IN ECOLOGY. Vol. IV. New York: Academic Press, 1976. xx, 593 p. Index, pp. 581-93.

Seventeen papers presented at a conference held at the University of Georgia March 1-3, 1973, grouped under the following five parts: "Models of Estuarine-Marine Ecosystems" (three papers); "Models of Terrestrial Ecosystems" (three papers); "Models of Human Ecosystems" (three papers); "Special Problems in Ecosystem Modelling" (three papers); and "Theory in Ecosystem Analysis" (five papers). Topics include conceptual ecological model of the Delaware Estuary; Mangrove ecosystem analysis; role of species interaction in the response of a forest ecosystem to environmental perturbation; human ecosystem design and management; simulating a world ecosystem; linear and nonlinear approaches for ecosystem modeling; the aggregation and validation problems; engineering systems analysis; control theory and regulation of ecosystems; patterns of biological control in ecosystems; and propagation of course in ecosystems.

Pielou, E.C. AN INTRODUCTION TO MATHEMATICAL ECOLOGY. New York: Wiley, 1969. viii, 286 p. Bibliography, pp. 273-79. Author Index, pp. 281-82. Subject Index, pp. 283-86.

A text for a one-semester graduate course in mathematical ecology for students who have knowledge of calculus and introductory mathematiaal statistics. Derivations formed in detail for use as a self-study. Emphasizes charts, verbal explanation, and numerical examples. Topics include birth and death processes; logistic population growth; dynamics of host-parasite population; the pattern of individuals in a continuum; studying pattern by distance sampling; patterns resulting from diffusions; patterns of ecological maps; segregation between two species and among many species; measurement of diversity; classification of communities; canonical variate analysis; and the ordination of continuously varying communities.

Poole, Robert W. AN INTRODUCTION TO QUANTITATIVE ECOLOGY. McGraw-Hill Series in Population Biology. New York: McGraw-Hill, 1974. xii, 532 p. Appendix: Mathematical Symbols, pp. 513-15. Literature Cited, pp. 515-25. Index, pp. 527-32.

A text for an introductory or advanced course in quantitative ecology for students with a background in high school algebra. Knowledge of basic statistics helpful. Emphasizes statements of problems, methods of solving problems, the analysis of examples, and implications. Topics include mathematics of population changes in an unlimited environment; probability distributions and stochastic processes; dispersal patterns and spatial distributions; competition between two species; predator-prey and host-parasite interactions; epidemics and disease; modeling of natural populations; sampling; and estimation of population parameters; association within pairs of species; community classification and ordination; measurement of species diversity; interaction of three or more species; production, biomass, and energy in single populations; and energy flow and nutrient cycling through an ecosystem.

Pratt, John W., ed. STATISTICAL AND MATHEMATICAL ASPECTS OF POLLUTION PROBLEMS. Statistics: Textbooks and Monographs, vol. 6. New York: Dekker, 1974. xxvii, 392 p. Index, pp. 387-92.

Twenty-six papers presented at a symposium held at the Harvard Business School August 31-Sept. 3, 1971, under sponsorship of the International Association for Statistics and Physical Sciences. Grouped under the following headings: "Collection and Dissemination of Basic Data: (four papers); "Indices, Economic and Policy Perspectives" (five papers); "Mathematical Models" (five papers); "Statistical Studies Using Regression and Related Methods" (five papers); and "Other Statistical Methods" (seven papers). Topics include environmental monitoring; design and operation of the National Aerometric data bank; water quality control; development of environmental indices; modelling current movements within bodies of water; and statistical problems in aerosol studies.

Prodan, Michail. FOREST BIOMETRICS. Translation by Sabine H. Gardiner. New York: Pergamon, 1968. xi, 447 p. Bibliography, pp. 432-44. Index, pp. 445-47.

Originally published in German in 1961. A text for students, practical workers, and research project leaders in forestry. Uses methods of mathematical statistics. Includes derivations. Topics include mathematical aids; descriptive statistics; errors caused by grouping of observations; probability; normal distributions; distribution of rare events; generalized frequency distribution; lognormal negative binomial and Pearson distribution curves; combined distributions; sampling distributions and tests of hypotheses; analysis of variance; sample surveys; experimental design; regression and correlation; curve fitting by orthogonal polynomials; fitting of regression subject to periodic variation; multiple regression and correlation; various growth functions; time series; and linear programming. Assumes knowledge of calculus.

Rogers, Andrei. INTRODUCTION TO MULTIREGIONAL MATHEMATICAL DEMOGRAPHY. New York: Wiley, 1975. xiii, 203 p. Bibliography, pp. 197-99. Index, pp. 201-3.

A monograph on the mathematics of multiregional population systems for readers familiar with the mathematics of single-region demographic analysis. Intended as a reference for mathematically oriented demographers, sociologists, geographers, economists, and regional planners, and as a text for a graduate course in demography. Includes numerical illustrations for two-region population systems, with a few on five- and nine-region population systems. Based on four concepts: life table, continuous and discrete models of population growth, and estimation of demographic measures using model life tables and stable populations. Topics include multiregional life tables, Lexis diagrams; multiregional renewal equation and stable growth; reconciliation of the discrete and continuous models; and selecting the appropriate model. Assumes knowledge of linear algebra and calculus.

Romanova, Mariîa Andreevna, and Sarmanov, O.V., eds. TOPICS IN MATHEMATICAL GEOLOGY. Translation by J.P. Fitzsimons. New York: Consultants Bureau, 1970. viii, 281 p. No index.

Twenty-four heretofore unpublished contributions in mathematical geology (probability models of geological processes) grouped according to type of problem as defined by A.B. Vistelius as follows: "Geologic Hypothesis and Probability Distributions" (three papers); "Use of the Specific Properties of Multidimensional Space in Solving Geological Problems" (three papers); "Paragenetic Analysis" (four papers); "Analysis of Geologic Sections" (five papers); "Mapping Geological Characteristics" (two papers); "Various Geological Problems" (five papers); and "Chronicle and Bibliography" (two papers). Topics include log-normal frequency distribution in sediments; correlation of joint trends with the elements of tectonic structure; linear paragenetic associations in rocks and minerals; stochastic models of stratification; use of a harmonic model for analysis of the dynamic system of sedimentation in the Jatulian of Central Karelia; use of the computer for quantitative analysis of fossil distribution; variance of some selected attributes in granitic rocks; and trend analysis of geologic data.

Schwarzacher, Walther. SEDIMENTATION MODELS AND QUANTITATIVE STRATIGRAPHY. Developments in Sedimentology 19. New York: Elsevier, 1975. xi, 382 p. References, pp. 371-77. Index, pp. 379-82.

A text for a course in stratigraphy and sedimentology for geology students who are familiar with calculus and elementary probability theory, stochastic processes, spectral analysis, and the Laplace transform. Topics include deterministic, stochastic, and Markov models used in these areas; stationary stochastic processes and time series; spectral analysis of geological data; analysis of stratigraphical trends and the smoothing of data; sedimentary cycles; stratigraphical correlation; and problems of three-dimensional analysis. Treatment geologically oriented with mathematical background developed as needed.

Smith, J. Maynard. MODELS IN ECOLOGY. New York: Cambridge University Press, 1974. xii, 146 p. References, pp. 137-42. Index, pp. 143-46.

A monograph on mathematical models in ecology for anyone with a serious interest in ecology who have knowledge of the rudiments of calculus. Includes models of exponential logistic growth, Volterra's and Leslie's equations, Rosenzweig-MacArthur equations, delayed feedback, delays due to development over time, population growth, migration, predator-prey systems with age structure, competition, stability and complexity, ecosystems, genetic feedback, natural selection, and behavioral models.

Till, Roger. STATISTICAL METHODS FOR THE EARTH SCIENTIST: AN INTRODUCTION. New York: Wiley, Halsted Press, 1974. xxii, 154 p. References, pp. 145-48. Further Reading, pp. 149-50. Index, pp. 151-54.

A text for a course in basic statistics for graduates and undergraduates in the earth sciences, including geology, geophysics, and soils. Statistical procedures illustrated by examples based on real data. Topics include probability, including Markov processes, normal, Poisson, and binomial; sampling; testing hypotheses; chi-square; correlation; regression and F tests; and nonparametric tests. Concludes with a chapter on a non-technical guide to advanced statistics. Assumes knowledge of high school algebra.

Vistelius, Andrew B. STUDIES IN MATHEMATICAL GEOLOGY. New York: Consultants Bureau, 1967. xv, 294 p. Index, pp. 293-94.

Twenty-six reprints of articles previously published by the author in English and Russian grouped under the following headings: "General Problems" (three articles); "Frequency Distributions" (four articles); "Paragenesis" (eight articles); "Analysis of Geologic Sections" (eight articles) and "Problems of Mapping" (three articles). Topics include linear-correlation analysis of paragenesis; programming of geological and geochemical problems for all-purpose electronic computers; frequency distributions and the law of geochemical processes; correlations in minerology and petrology; geochemical problems and measures of information; sedimentary time trend functions; and basic features of porosity distribution in a typical section of paleozoic rocks in the Volga region. Assumes knowledge of mathematical statistics for some papers.

Watt, Kenneth E.F. ECOLOGY AND RESOURCE MANAGEMENT--A QUANTITATIVE APPROACH. New York: McGraw-Hill Publications in the Biological Sciences. New York: McGraw-Hill, 1968, xi, 450 p. Author Index, pp. 440-43. Subject Index, pp. 444-50.

A text for a course in resource management or biomathematics for students of biology, agronomy, mathematics, zoology, biochemistry, forestry, genetics, and related fields who have knowledge of calculus, differential,equations, and basic statistics. Derivations kept to a minimum. Consists of four parts: "The Problem of Resource Management"; "The Theory of Resource Management"; "The Principles of Resource Management"; and "The Methods of Resource Management." Topics include maximum biomass productivity; pest control; oceanic fisheries; overexploitation of a population; sea lamprey in the Great Lakes; hatchery operations; extraction of a population: bighorn and bighorn sheep; pressure on one sex: deer management; mathematical models of effect of density on fecundity; predators and predation; water-management; application of FORTRAN to biology; science of sampling; stepwise and mixed-mode multiple regression; interactive regression; maximizing rate of convergence on best parameter values; models for describing population systems; attack and dispersal; and optimization methods; including dynamic programming and adaptive control processes.

Chapter 14

DATA ANALYSIS

Bendat, Julius S., and Piersol, Allan G. MEASUREMENT AND ANALYSIS OF RANDOM DATA. New York: Wiley, 1966. xv, 390 p. Glossary of Symbols, pp. xii-xv. References, pp. 379-81. Index, pp. 383-90.

> A reference for practicing engineers and scientists, as well as a textbook for students who have knowledge of probability theory, differential and integral calculus, statistics, and transform methods of applied mathematics. Emphasizes problems of defining, measuring, analyzing, and interpreting random data, regardless of the intended applications; excludes specific applications. Topics include properties of random data; response characteristics of physical systems, including constant parameter and time-varying linear systems; mathematical theory for analyzing random data; statistical techniques for evaluating data, including analysis of variance procedures; data processing procedures and errors; analog measurement techniques; digital computer techniques; analysis of nonstationary data; and illustration of experimental procedures.

______. RANDOM DATA: ANALYSIS AND MEASUREMENT PROCEDURES. New York: Wiley, Interscience, 1971. xv, 407 p. Glossary of Symbols, pp. xiii-xv. References, pp. 381-83. Appendix: Statistical Tables, pp. 385-96. Index, pp. 397-407.

> A reference for practicing engineers and scientists and a supplementary text for a variety of statistics courses. Assumes knowledge of basic statistics, probability, and transform methods of applied mathematics. Topics include classification and properties of random data; review of physical system response properties; review of stationary random processes theory; review of statistical properties, including normal, chi-square, t, and F distributions; ordinary, partial, and multiple coherence functions; multiple-input linear systems; statistical errors in random data analysis; data acquisition and processing; analog data analysis procedures; digital data analysis procedures, including filtering methods, Fourier transforms, and autocorrelation functions; and nonstationary, transient, and multidimensional data. Chapters conclude with problems.

Bevington, Philip R. DATA REDUCTION AND ERROR ANALYSIS FOR THE PHYSICAL SCIENCES. New York: McGraw-Hill, 1969. xv, 336 p. Appendix A: Calculus, pp. 277-85. Appendix B: Matrices, pp. 286-303. Appendix C: Graphs and Tables, pp. 304-23. References, pp. 325-26. Solutions to Odd-Numbered Exercises, pp. 327-30. Index, pp. 331-36.

A text for an introductory course in the techniques of data reduction and error for both graduates and undergraduates in the physical sciences who have had no previous exposure to statistics, but who are familiar with matrix algebra and differential calculus. Emphasizes applications using FORTRAN IV computer routines. Topics include descriptive statistics; binomial, Poisson, normal, and Lorentzian distributions; simple and multiple linear and nonlinear regression and correlation; chi-square and goodness of fit; least-squares fit to an arbitrary function, including searching parameter space, parabolic extrapolation of chi-square, linearization of function, and error determination; fitting composite curves, including area determination and background determination; and data manipulation, including smoothing, interpolation and extrapolation, and area integration. Chapters conclude with formulas and exercises.

Bisco, Ralph L., ed. DATA BASES, COMPUTERS, AND THE SOCIAL SCIENCES. Information Sciences Series. New York: Wiley, Interscience, 1970. xvi, 291 p. Index, pp. 287-91.

Sixteen papers presented at the Fourth Annual Conference of the Council of Social Science Data Archives held at the University of California, Los Angeles, grouped under the following headings: "Problems and Prospects" (three papers); "Government as the Major Producer, User, and Archivist of Social Science Data Bases" (two papers); "Case Studies in the Development and Use of Complex Data Bases" (two papers); "Computer Systems for Managing Complex Data Structures" (two papers); "Handling Missing-Data Problems" (two papers); "Data-Linkage Problems and Solutions" (three papers); and "The Protection of Privacy" (two papers). Aimed at a diverse audience, including social and behavioral scientists, librarians, and archivists.

Box, George E.P.; Hunter, William G.; and Hunter, J. Stuart. STATISTICS FOR EXPERIMENTERS: AN INTRODUCTION TO DESIGN, DATA ANALYSIS, AND MODEL BUILDING. Wiley Series in Probability and Mathematical Statistics. New York: Wiley, 1978. xviii, 653 p. Appendix: Tables, pp. 629-44. Index, pp. 645-53.

A text for a one-semester course in data analysis with emphasis on the philosophy of experimentation and the part that statistics plays in experimentation. Introduces statistical theory as needed. Consists of three parts: "Comparing Two Treatments"; "Comparing More Than Two Treatments"; and "Measuring the Effects of Variables." Uses both real and hypothetical data in examples. Effects of violations of assumptions pointed out. Useful to those assessing research results, managers who direct research projects, and statisticians who work with experiments. Topics include random sampling and the declaration of independence; blocking with paired comparisons; tests and confidence intervals for means, variances, proportions, and frequencies; randomized blocks and two-way factorial designs; design with more than one block (Latin squares and Graeco-Latin squares); factorial designs at two levels; fractional factorial designs; response surface methods; model building; and time series. Chapters conclude with questions and references, and parts conclude with problems on applications.

Brandt, Siegmund. STATISTICAL AND COMPUTATIONAL METHODS IN DATA ANALYSIS. New York: Elsevier, 1970. xii, 323 p. List of Frequently Used Symbols, pp. xi-xii. Appendixes, pp. 237-315. Bibliography and References, pp. 316-18. Subject Index, pp. 319-22. Index to FORTRAN Statements and FORTRAN Subroutines Used in This Book, p. 323. No index.

A reference on statistical data analysis for students of mathematics and research workers in science, medicine, engineering, and economics, who are faced with the problem of evaluating experimental data. Assumes knowledge of calculus and matrix algebra. Topics include random variables; sampling; method of maximum likelihood; tests of hypotheses, including the Neyman-Pearson theorem; least squares regression; and analysis of variance. Includes FORTRAN programs for regression and analysis of variance. Includes examples, but no problems. Appendixes include an introduction to computer programming, matrix calculus, combinatorial analysis, Euler's gamma function, collection of formulas, and tables. Includes extensive mathematical derivations.

Chambers, John M. COMPUTATIONAL METHODS FOR DATA ANALYSIS. Wiley Series in Probability and Mathematical Statistics. New York: Wiley, 1977. xi, 268 p. References, pp. 228-47. Appendix: Available Algorithms, pp. 248-56. Index, pp. 257-68.

A relatively complete picture of computing for data analysis. Includes an appraisal of currently competitive methods and references to selected algorithms. Topics include program and program evaluation; data management, including arrays and their indexing; data structure, order statistics, and sorting; numerical computations, including error analysis, approximation by rational functions, spline approximations, numerical integration, and Fourier transforms; methods for linear models orthogonal-triangular decompositions, singular value decomposition, weighted least squares, principal components, and analysis of variance; methods for nonlinear models (quasi-Newton, nonlinear least squares, and constrained optimization);

simulation of random processes, including congruental generators, modifying generators, and Monte Carlo methods; and graphical methods, including geometry of plotting several dimensions, plotting surfaces, contour plotting, and probability plots. Useful for anyone involved in the planning, selection, and development of computational support for data analysis. Assumes knowledge of computer programming.

Coombs, Clyde H. A THEORY OF DATA. New York: Wiley, 1964. xviii, 585 p. Bibliography, pp. 567-76. Author Index, pp. 577-80. Subject Index, pp. 581-85.

An account of the foundations of psychological measurement based on geometrical models for the inferential classification of stimuli and people. Presents important ideas in verbal terms, although knowledge of algebra, geometry, and calculus helpful. Consists of six parts: "Basic Concepts"; "Preferential Choice Data"; "Single Stimulus Data"; "Stimuli Comparison Data"; "Similarities Data"; and "Interrelations." Topics include parallelogram analysis; one- and multi-dimensional unfolding techniques; factor analysis of preference; alternative theories of preferential choice; multidimensional stimulus models; nonmetric multidimensional scaling; Thurstone's comparative judgement model; and the scale grid. Chapters conclude with references.

Deming, William Edwards. STATISTICAL ADJUSTMENT OF DATA. New York: Dover, 1964. x, 261 p. Appendix: Tables, pp. 252-55. Index, pp. 257-61.

Originally published in 1938 by Constable and Company (London). A reference on data analysis in five parts: "Some Simple Adjustments"; "Least Squares Solutions of More Complicated Problems"; "Conditions Without Parameters"; "Conditions Containing Parameters"; and "Exercises and Notes." Topics include least squares; method of Lagrange multipliers; and geometric conditions and adjustment of sample frequencies to expected marginal totals. Uses calculus for portions of the presentation. Sections conclude with exercises.

Dixon, Wilfrid J., and Nicholson, W.L., eds. EXPLORING DATA ANALYSIS: THE COMPUTER REVOLUTION IN STATISTICS. Berkeley and Los Angeles: University of California Press, 1974. xvi, 409 p. Citation Index, pp. 401-9.

Eight papers presented at workshops on statistical computing for the purpose of examining the frontiers of data analysis by computer held at the University of California, Los Angeles, in September 1971. Topics include analysis of breast cancer data; block voting in the United Nations; robustness study analysis; soil fertility experiments for prediction response to an audio tone; and density estimates based on orthogonal expansions.

Ehrenberg, A.S.C. DATA REDUCTION: ANALYSING AND INTERPRETING STATISTICAL DATA. New York: Wiley, Interscience, 1975. xvii, 391 p. List of Exercises, pp. 371-76. References, pp. 377-80. Name Index, pp. 381-82. Subject Index, pp. 383-91.

A text on how to handle and interpret statistical data for use by anyone who encounters data in ordinary work. Consists of five parts: "Data Handling"; "Lawlike Relationships"; "Statistical Variation"; "Sampling"; and "Empirical Generalisation." Topics include descriptive statistics; tables and graphs; linear relationships and their uses; nonlinear relationships; normal, binomial, Poisson, and other frequency distributions; probability models; correlation and regression; multivariate techniques; sampling distributions; statistical inference; and design of experiments. Chapters conclude with exercises.

Eskin, Gerald J., and Montgomery, David B. DATA ANALYSIS: CASES IN COMPUTER AND MODEL ASSISTED MARKETING. Palo Alto, Calif.: Scientific Press, for Hewlett Packard, 1975. vi, 98 p. No index.

A computer-assisted case book of consumer marketing problems. Includes microsimulation model of a company to analyze reactions to a competitive product; regression analysis to study the relation between advertising and sales; decision analysis to determine whether a new product should be test marketed; regression and decision analysis to study the reaction to competitive price cuts by service stations; and trial and repeat modes for projecting test market panel data for sales results. Includes BASIC COMPUTER PROGRAMS.

Gnanadesikan, R. METHODS FOR STATISTICAL DATA ANALYSIS OF MULTIVARIATE OBSERVATIONS. Wiley Series in Probability and Mathematical Statistics. New York: Wiley, 1977. x, 311 p. References, pp. 286-96. Appendix: Computer Programs and Software, pp. 297-99. Author Index, pp. 301-3. Subject Index, pp. 305-11.

Describes and discusses multivariate statistical techniques and concepts according to the following five objectives for analyzing multiresponse data: reduction of dimensionality, multivariate dependence, multidimensional classification, assessment of statistical models, and summarization and exposure. Emphasizes methodology and data-based interpretation relevant to the needs of data analysis with examples throughout. Assumes knowledge of advanced calculus, mathematical statistics, and linear algebra. Excludes exercises.

Hartigan, John A. CLUSTERING ALGORITHMS. Wiley Series in Probability and Mathematical Statistics. New York: Wiley, 1975. xiii, 351 p. Index, pp. 347-51.

A text for a course in data analysis and a reference for those actively working in the field. Each chapter devoted to a single algorithm and includes purpose of algorithm on a small data set, discussion and evaluation of algorithm, suggestions for applying the algorithm, discussion of relevant literature, and a listing of FORTRAN programs. Algorithms include quick partition, the K-mean, ditto, drawing trees, quick tree calculation, triads, single-linkage, distance and amalgamation, minimum tree, factor analysis, and prediction.

McNeil, Donald R. INTERACTIVE DATA ANALYSIS: A PRACTICAL PRIMER. New York: Wiley, Interscience, 1977. xii, 186 p. Index, pp. 181-86.

A text for a course in exploratory data analysis with computer routines in APL and FORTRAN. Topics include displays, including plottings of data; comparisons; relations, including time series plottings; assays; tables, including sizes of residuals; smoothing, including multiple regression, and fitting. Assumes knowledge of APL and FORTRAN. Chapters conclude with exercises.

Milton, Roy C., and Nelder, John A., eds. STATISTICAL COMPUTATION. New York: Academic Press, 1969. xii, 462 p. No index.

Nineteen papers presented at a conference held at the University of Wisconsin April 28-30, 1969, grouped under the following five headings: "Specifications for Statistical Data Structure" (four papers); "Statistical Systems and Languages" (seven papers); "Statistical Data Screening with Computers" (one paper); "Teaching of Statistics with Computers" (two papers); and "Current Techniques in Numerical Analysis Related to Statistical Computation" (five papers). Topics include autocodes for the statistician; language design; interactive statistics; use of APL in statistics; robot data screening; matrix decomposition and statistical calculations; algorithms for data maintenance and for multivariate analysis; and computer optimization of second order response surface designs. Useful in statistical theory, applied statistics, numerical analysis, computer management, programming, language design, and computer science.

Tukey, John W. EXPLORATORY DATA ANALYSIS. Addison-Wesley Series in Behavioral Science: Quantitative Methods. Reading, Mass.: Addison-Wesley, 1977. xvi, 688 p. Glossary, pp. 667-76. Index to Reference Tables, p. 677. Alphabetical Index, pp. 677-88.

A monograph on exploratory data analysis using only simple arithmetic and pictures. Exposes readers to a variety of techniques for looking more effectively at data. Emphasizes general principles, rather than specific problems. Topics include scratching down numbers, schematic summaries; plots of relationships; straightening out plots; smoothing sequences;

parallel and wandering schematic plots; two-way analyses; advanced fits; three-way fits; counted fractions; filter smoothing; product-ratio plots; shape of distributions; and mathematical distributions. Includes review questions and problems.

Wike, Edward L. DATA ANALYSIS: A STATISTICAL PRIMER FOR PSYCHOLOGY STUDENTS. Psychonomic Perspectives Series. Chicago: Aldine-Atherton, 1971. x, 256 p. Answers to Even-Numbered Problems, pp. 177-79. References, pp. 181-85. Appendix: Tables, pp. 187-248. Index, pp. 249-56.

A text and reference for undergraduate psychology students undertaking research for the first time. Devoted to elementary statistical techniques with examples based on real data. Emphasizes the philosophy of data analysis, and includes such topics as descriptive statistics; inferences concerning a single mean, two means, means of k independent groups, multiple comparisons of means and variances from k independent samples, means of two and of k matched groups, and multiple comparisons of means from k matched groups; location tests for two and for k independent groups; location tests for two and for k matched groups; multiple comparison location tests for k matched groups; class frequencies of two and of k independent comparisons of class frequencies with k matched groups; linear and curvilear relationships; and testing statistical hypotheses vs. confidence intervals. Chapters conclude with problems.

Chapter 15

NONPARAMETRIC STATISTICS

Andrews, David F., et al. ROBUST ESTIMATES OF LOCATION: SURVEY AND ADVANCES. Princeton, N.J.: Princeton University Press, 1972. ix, 372 p. Appendixes, pp. 261-368. References, pp. 369-72. No index.

> A survey of some sixty-eight robust estimation procedures of location found in the literature with the aid of augmenting the properties of robust estimation. Estimates include trimmed means; adaptive estimates; Huber estimates; and skipped procedures and the Hodges-Lehmann estimate. Topics include asymptotic characteristics of the estimates; finite-sample calculations; and a detailed analysis of the variances. Appendixes include computer programs for implementing the estimating procedures; random number generators; dual-criterion problems in estimation; integration formulas; and Monte Carlo methods for contaminated Gaussians. Assumes knowledge of nonparametric statistics. Presentation not rigorous mathematically. Omits proofs.

Bradley, James V. DISTRIBUTION-FREE STATISTICAL TESTS. Englewood Cliffs, N.J.: Prentice-Hall, 1968. xii, 388 p. Appendix: Tables for the Test Statistics, pp. 313-79. Author Index, pp. 380-81. Subject Index, pp. 382-88.

> A text for a course in distribution-free statistics with emphasis on the logic and mathematical rationale of the underlying theory for students who have knowledge of high school algebra, the rudiments of calculus, elementary statistical theory, and parametric tests of significance. Tests grouped into families having a common type of derivation (all tests whose test statistic is binomially distributed are included in one chapter). Topics include comparison of distribution-free and classical tests; formulas for permutations, combinations, and the probability fraction; Fisher's method of randomization; tests based on the method of randomization applied to ranks; normal score tests; test based on the binomial, hypergeometric, and multivariate hypergeometric distribution; runs up and down; and miscellaneous tests, including Mann-Kendall test for trends

and Smirnov's maximum deviation tests for identical populations. Includes proofs of some theorems, examples, and applications. Chapters conclude with references.

Conover, W.J. PRACTICAL NONPARAMETRIC STATISTICS. New York: Wiley, 1971. xii, 462 p. Appendix: Tables, pp. 365-427. References, pp. 428-49. Answers, pp. 450-53. Index, pp. 455-62.

A text for a one-year course and a reference for applied research workers with a prerequisite of college algebra and basic statistics. Includes applications from psychology, biology, statistics, engineering, business, education, economics, medicine, agriculture, and jurisprudence. Topics include probability theory and random variables; statistical inference; tests based on the binomial; contingency tables; use of ranks, including confidence intervals for the median and difference between two means; rank correlation; Kolmogorov-Smirnov type tests for two and several independent samples; slippage test for several independent samples; tests based on runs, and Fisher's method of randomization. Sections conclude with problems.

David, Herbert Aron. ORDER STATISTICS. Wiley Series in Probability and Mathematical Statistics. New York: Wiley, 1970. xi, 272 p. Appendix: Guide to Tables, pp. 225-33. References, pp. 235-66. Index, pp. 267-72.

Presents order statistics combining features of both a textbook and a guide through the literature. Assumes knowledge of intermediate statistical theory. Topics include distributions of order statistics; expected values and moments; bounds and approximations for moments of order statistics; order statistics in estimation and hypothesis testing; short-cut procedures; the treatment of outliers; and asymptotic theory. Includes proofs of theorems, with fairly extensive algebraic derivations. Also includes numerical illustrations. Chapters conclude with exercises.

Ferguson, George Andrew. NONPARAMETRIC TREND ANALYSIS. Montreal: McGill University Press, 1965. viii, 61 p. References, p. 61. No index.

A monograph intended as a guide to nonparametric analysis of experimental data for research workers. Useful for applications to ordinal data. Includes sampling distributions of the S statistic as used by M.G. Kendall; ranks of orthogonal polynomials; monotonic trends for correlated data and for independent samples; nonmonotonic rank correlation; and higher-order trend analysis for correlated data and for independent samples. Includes examples, and assumes knowledge of basic statistics.

Fraser, Donald Alexander Stuart. NONPARAMETRIC METHODS IN STATISTICS. New York: Wiley, 1957. x, 299 p. Index, pp. 297-99.

A text for a second course in mathematical statistics for students familiar with calculus and a first course in mathematical statistics. Measure theory introduced as needed. Topics include probability measures; properties of sufficiency and completeness of a statistic; statistical inference, including confidence and tolerance regions; single sample and randomness nonparametric problems; estimation of real parameters; most powerful rank tests; limiting distributions; and large sample properties of tests. Chapters conclude with references and problems.

Gibbons, Jean Dickinson. NONPARAMETRIC METHODS FOR QUANTITATIVE ANALYSIS. International Series in Decision Processes. New York: Holt, Rinehart and Winston, 1976. xv, 463 p. Appendix: Tables, pp. 383-444. Bibliography, pp. 445-52. Answers to Even-Numbered Problems, pp. 453-56. Index, pp. 457-63.

An applied text for a one-semester course in nonparametric statistics for students who have knowledge of basic statistics and high school algebra, and a reference for research workers. Introduces each technique by means of examples, and hypothesis testing concludes with the associated p-value rather than with a decision as to whether to accept or to reject the hypothesis. Statistical tables provide complete probability distributions, rather than critical values for tests and selected levels. Topics include goodness-of-fit tests; inference concerning location based on one-, two-, or more than two-samples; inferences concerning such parameters; distribution tests for two or more independent samples; association analysis; and tests for randomness. Chapters conclude with problems.

______. NONPARAMETRIC STATISTICAL INFERENCE. McGraw-Hill Series in Probability and Statistics. New York: McGraw-Hill, 1971. xiv, 306 p. References, pp. 295-99. Index, pp. 301-6.

A text for a one-semester course in nonparametric statistics for students with varied backgrounds who have knowledge of one year of probability and parametric statistical inference. Lies between a handbook style and a highly rigorous mathematical style. Provides a compendium of nonparametric techniques for a variety of problem situations. Includes proofs of simple theorems with references to the more advanced proofs. Topics include order statistics; tests based on runs; chi-square and goodness of fit; rank order statistics; sign test; general two-sample problem; linear rank tests for location and scale problems; tests of the equality of k independent samples; measures of association for bivariate samples and multiple classifications; and asymptotic relative efficiency. Chapters conclude with problems.

Hájek, Jaroslav. A COURSE IN NONPARAMETRIC STATISTICS. San Francisco: Holden-Day, 1969. viii, 184 p. Tables I to XVIII, pp. 158-77. Bibliography, pp. 179-82. Index, pp. 183-84.

> A text for an undergraduate course in nonparametric statistics for students who have knowledge of elementary probability and statistics. Concentrates on rank tests, leaving untouched such topics as nonparametric estimation, invariance considerations, and permutation tests. Rank tests labeled according to the null hypothesis (randomness, independence, paired samples, random blocks, symmetry) and secondarily according to alternatives (two samples, regression, location, scale). Results formulated as theorems with emphasis on proofs. Includes examples based on simulated and real-life data.

Hájek, Jaroslav, and Sidak, Zbynek. THEORY OF RANK TESTS. New York: Academic Press, 1967. 297 p. Bibliography, pp. 281-90. Indes, pp. 291-97.

> Presents the theory of rank tests for specialists, teachers, and advanced students in statistics who are already acquainted with the theory of testing hypotheses, measure theory, stochastic processes, and the central limit theorem. Emphasizes problems concerning location and scale parameters and on contiguous alternatives. Little attention given to the noncontiguous alternatives and to the Chernoff-Savage theorem, and omits entirely rank tests. Includes the following tests: randomness, symmetry, independence, random blocks, permutation, linear rank tests, location, scale, tests of the Kolmogorov-Smirnov types, rank tests of the chi-square types, Wilcoxon, and Kruskal-Wallis. Other topics include exact distributions of test statistics under the hypotheses and their computations; limiting distributions of test statistics under the hypotheses; limiting distributions of test statistics under the alternatives; and asymptotic optimality and efficiency of rank tests. Chapters conclude with problems and complements.

Hollander, Myles, and Wolfe, Douglas A. NONPARAMETRIC STATISTICAL METHODS. Foreword by Ralph A. Bradley. Wiley Series in Probability and Mathematical Statistics. New York: Wiley, 1973. xviii, 503 p. Appendix A: Tables and Charts, pp. 255-434. Appendix B: Glossary, pp. 435-66. Bibliography, pp. 467-90. Author Index, pp. 491-96. Subject Index, pp. 497-503.

> A text for a course in applied nonparametric statistics for students who have knowledge of basic statistics, and a reference for researchers. Presentation centered around actual experiments, and examples taken from astronomy, biology, criminology, education, engineering, environmental science, geology, home economics, medicine, oceanography, physics, psychology, sociology, and space science. Topics include one- and two-sample problems; one-way and two-way layouts; independence

problems; regression; two regression lines; and tests designed to detect broad alternatives. Procedures selected have desirable efficiency properties. Sections conclude with problems.

Kraft, Charles H., and Van Eeden, Constance. A NONPARAMETRIC INTRODUCTION TO STATISTICS. New York: Macmillan, 1968. x, 342 p. Solutions to Exercises, pp. 331-40. Index, pp. 341-42.

A text for a one-semester course in nonparametric statistics for students who have a college algebra background. Consists of the following three parts: "Elementary Theory of Statistical Analysis"; "Descriptions of Particular Analyses"; and "Tables." Topics include models for the effect of treatment; relating the observations to the class of models; randomization; basing decisions on experiments; the binomial, hypergeometric, normal distributions; optimum analyses; two-sample problems based on the Wilcoxon, Fisher-Pitman, and median tests; one-sample problem based on the Wilcoxon, Fisher, and sign tests; k-sample problems based on the Kruskal-Wallis Rijkoort tests, and the Mood-Brown median test; randomized blocks; goodness-of-fit tests; and independence, correlation, and regression. Chapters conclude with exercises.

Lehmann, Erich Leo. With the Special Assistance of H.J.M. D'Abrera. NONPARAMETRICS: STATISTICAL METHODS BASED ON RANKS. Holden-Day Series in Probability and Statistics. San Francisco: Holden-Day, 1975. xvi, 457 p. Acknowledgements for Tables, p. 434. Answers to Selected Problems, pp. 435-44. Data Guide (Titles for Data Presented in the Text), pp. 445-46. Author Index, pp. 447-50. Subject Index, pp. 451-57.

A text for an introductory course in nonparametric methods for students who have knowledge of algebra and elementary probability theory. Assumes knowledge of calculus. Limited mainly to tests of the Wilcoxon type. Topics include normal score procedure; permutations tests; sequential methods; optimum theory; tests for two-way contingency tables; large sample theory underlying approximations where tables are unavailable and where exact computations are too laborious; block comparisons for two treatments; paired comparisons; comparisons of more than two treatments; randomized complete blocks; and tests of randomness and dependence. Includes illustrative examples. Chapters conclude with problems and references.

Marascuilo, Leonard A., and McSweeney, Maryellen. NONPARAMETRIC AND DISTRIBUTION-FREE METHODS FOR THE SOCIAL SCIENCES. Monterey, Calif.: Brooks/Cole, 1977. xvii, 556 p. Appendix: Tables, pp. 481-528. References, pp. 529-34. Answers to Selected Exercises, pp. 535-48. Index, pp. 549-56.

A text for a course in nonparametric statistics for undergraduates and graduates in the social sciences, and a reference for researchers. Topics include binomial and sign tests; statistical efficiencies of nonparametric tests; Irwin-Fisher tests; chi-square of homogeneity of proportions; chi-square tests of independence in contingency tables for three or more variables; two- and multiple-sample methods for quantitative variables based on ranks and normal scores; nonparametric tests for repeated measures and matched samples for multiple samples; block designs; and tests on aligned observations. Includes examples and problems.

Noether, Gottfried Emanuel. ELEMENTS OF NONPARAMETRIC STATISTICS. The SIAM Series in Applied Mathematics. New York: Wiley, 1967. x, 104 p. References, pp. 97-99. Index, pp. 101-4.

A reference for statisticians who are already familiar with the basic concepts of nonparametric statistics and who have gone through a course in mathematical statistics. Omits examples and exercises. Examines the mathematical bases of nonparametric statistics with emphasis on the translation of test procedures into confidence intervals and/or point estimates. Procedures based on the assumption that the appropriate mathematical model involves random variables with continuous distribution functions. Topics include methods based on empirical distribution functions; order statistics; rank sums and the two-sample problem; confidence intervals for location parameters; two-sample dispersion tests; and efficiency of nonparametric methods.

Pierce, Albert. FUNDAMENTALS OF NONPARAMETRIC STATISTICS. With Problems by Jay Beaman. Belmont, Calif.: Dickenson, 1970. xviii, 301 p. Appendix A: Distribution of Chi-Square Probability, pp. 279-80. Appendix B: ALGOL Computer Program for 2x3 Cell Fisher Exact Test, pp. 281-87. Appendix C: BASIC Language Program for the 3-Dimensional Chi-Square Contingency Table, pp. 289-94. Appendix D: BASIC Language Program for the 2x3 Cell Fisher Exact Probability Model, pp. 295-98. Index, pp. 299-301.

A text for a one-semester course in nonparametric statistics for students of the social and behavioral sciences who have knowledge of high school algebra. Emphasizes statistical literacy, rather than techniques. Graduated mathematical prerequisites introduced as an integral part of the exposition. Topics include set theory, sample spaces, events and their probabilities; dependent trial experiments; the ball-and-cell model for the analysis of sample spaces; the hypergeometric and binomial distributions and their applications, including median test and statistical inference; occupancy problem; the space for unordered samples taken with replacement; chi-square and the multinomial model; Poisson distribution; and two-sample tests. Chapters conclude with problems.

Puri, Madan Lal, and Sen, Pranab Kumar. NONPARAMETRIC METHODS IN MULTIVARIATE ANALYSIS. Wiley Series in Probability and Mathematical Statistics. New York: Wiley, 1971. xi, 440 p. Appendixes, pp. 400-414. References, pp. 415-32. Index, pp. 433-40.

A text for specialists, teachers, and advanced graduate students on the theory of nonparametric multivariate statistical analysis assuming a background in parametric multivariate statistical theory and probability theory. Topics include univariate nonparametric theory; multivariate one-sample tests of location and scale; point and interval estimates in linear models; nonparametric procedures in multifactor designs; testing independence of subsets of a stochastic vector; and testing the identity of dispersion matrices. Appendixes include proofs of results for one- and two-sample cases, and of aligned rank order statistics. Emphasizes Hoeffding's U-statistic and suitable families of rank-order statistics. Presentation consists largely of proofs of theorems and lemmas. Chapters conclude with problems requiring additional proofs and applications of the theory.

Rey, William J.J. ROBUST STATISTICAL METHODS. Lecture Notes in Mathematics, 690. New York: Springer-Verlag, 1978. vi, 128 p. References, pp. 88-99. Appendixes, pp. 100-122. Author Index, pp. 124-26. Subject Index, pp. 127-28.

A monograph on methods for designing robust estimators with emphasis on preventing bias due to the selection of an erroneous model or to spurious data in the sample. Also emphasizes type M estimators and computational aspects. Assumes knowledge of the jacknife and the influence function. Applications include location estimation and regression. Appendixes include derivations on consistent estimators, contaminated normal distributions, Prokhorov metric, and von Mises derivatives.

Runyon, Richard P. NONPARAMETRIC STATISTICS: A CONTEMPORARY APPROACH. Reading, Mass.: Addison-Wesley, 1977. vi, 218 p. Appendix: Tables, pp. 145-91. Answers, pp. 192-216. Index, pp. 217-18.

A text, supplementary text, and self-study for basic statistics courses with emphasis on the relevance of statistics to a broad spectrum of disciplines using few formulas and no proofs. Consists of three parts: "Nominal Scales of Measurement"; "Ordinal Scales of Measurement"; and "Interval and Ratio Scales." Includes exercises in right hand margin. Chapters conclude with tests, and reviews appear repeatedly throughout the text. Topics include type I and type II errors; power of tests; nominal, ordinal, and interval scales in one sample, independent samples, and related samples.

Ruymgaart, F.H. ASYMPTOTIC THEORY OF RANK TESTS FOR INDEPENDENCE. Mathematisch Centre Tracts, 43. Amsterdam: Mathematisch Centrum, 1973. iv, 151 p. References, pp. 109-11. Index, pp. 112-15.

Presents a method for proving asymptotic normality of rank statistics for testing the hypothesis of independence in a two-sample problem. Method imposes a relatively weak condition on the limiting score function, i.e. the function may exhibit discontinuities on a finite number of lines in the unit square. Results applied to the proof of asymptotic normality under converging sequences of underlying distribution functions, to the proof of consistency, and to the proof of asymptotic relative efficiency. Concludes with a consideration of discrete distributions.

Sarhan, Ahmed E., and Greenberg, Bernard G., eds. CONTRIBUTIONS TO ORDER STATISTICS. Foreword by H.O. Hartley. Wiley Series in Probability and Mathematical Statistics. New York: Wiley, 1962. xxv, 482 p. References, pp. 454-67. Index, pp. 469-82.

Twenty-nine heretofore unpublished contributions arranged in two parts: "General Theory" and "Specific Applications." Topics include distribution and moments of order statistics; generalized least squares theorem; approximation to the best linear estimates; estimation of location and scale parameters by sample quantiles (for large samples); statistical theory of extreme values; testing hypothesis; nonparametric confidence intervals and tolerance regions; and multiple decisions and multiple comparisons. Includes applications to normal, exponential, rectangular, gamma, symmetric, and right triangular distributions. Assumes knowledge of multivariate calculus and the elements of mathematical statistics.

Savage, I. Richard. BIBLIOGRAPHY OF NONPARAMETRIC STATISTICS. Cambridge, Mass.: Harvard University Press, 1962. xii, 284 p. Cross References for Multiple-Authored Entries, pp. 279-84. No index.

Entries listed alphabetically by author and include year of publication, title of article or book, name and volume of journal, or name and location of publisher, inclusive page number of articles or total number of pages of book, sources for abstracts and reviews, notes, citations, and classification (indicated by code letters at end of entry). Current through April 1961. Includes detailed description of entries, literature searched, abbreviations, and guide to volumes and years of statistical journals.

Siegel, Sidney. NONPARAMETRIC STATISTICS FOR THE BEHAVIORAL SCIENCES. New York: McGraw-Hill, 1956. xvii, 312 p. Glossary of Symbols, pp. xv-xvii. References, pp. 241-44. Appendix: Tables, pp. 245-301. Index, pp. 303-12.

A text for an introductory course in nonparametric statistics for behavioral scientists who have knowledge of high school algebra. One-sample tests include Kolmogorov-Smirnov, binomial, chi-square, and runs. Two-sample tests include McNemar, sign, Wilcoxon, Walsh, Fisher exact probability, chi-square, median, Mann-Whitney, Kolmogorov-Smirnov, Wald-Wolfowitz, Moses, and randomization test for two independent samples. The k-sample tests include Cochran Q, Friedman two-way analysis of variance, chi-square, extensions of the median test, and the Kruskal-Wallis one-way analysis of variance by ranks. Correlation measures include Spearman and Kendall rank correlation coefficients, Kendall partial rank correlation coefficient, and Kendall coefficient of concordance. Omits problems.

Tate, Merle W., and Clelland, Richard C. NONPARAMETRIC AND SHORT-CUT STATISTICS IN THE SOCIAL, BIOLOGICAL, AND MEDICAL SCIENCES. Danville, Ill.: Interstate, 1957. ix, 171 p. References, pp. 123-24. Appendix I: Tables and Charts, pp. 125-53. Appendix II: Solutions to Exercises, pp. 154-68. Index, pp. 169-71.

A manual for graduate students and researchers on nonparametric statistical methods with emphasis on their limitations. Exercises at the ends of the sections and examples utilize real data. Topics include inferences from a single sample (run, Kolmogorov-Smirnov, corner, contingency, and coefficient of concordance tests); inferences from two samples; and inferences from k samples. Assumes knowledge of basic statistics.

Walsh, John E. HANDBOOK OF NONPARAMETRIC STATISTICS I: INVESTIGATIONS OF RANDOMNESS, MOMENTS, PERCENTILES, AND DISTRIBUTIONS. New York: D. Van Nostrand, 1962. xxvi, 549 p. Tables, pp. 480-95. Abbreviations for Place of Publication, p. 496. Bibliography-Author Index for References, pp. 497-524. Subject Index, pp. 525-49.

Presents a large number of nonparametric probability information procedures in use up to 1958. Assumes knowledge of mathematical statistics. Topics include standardized notation, special terminology, and statistical procedures; tests of randomness, including runs up and down; tests based on signs of differences, most powerful tests, sequential tests, and multivariate tests of randomness; estimates and tests for expected values; estimates and tests for population percentiles; distribution-free tolerance regions; nonsequential results for distributions from ungrouped data; sequential, decision, and categorical data results for distributions; and chi-square goodness of fit. Provides only a few numerical examples.

______. HANDBOOK OF NONPARAMETRIC STATISTICS II: RESULTS FOR TWO AND SEVERAL SAMPLE PROBLEMS, SYMMETRY, AND EXTREMES. New

York: D. Van Nostrand, 1965. xxvi, 686 p. Tables, pp. 630-45. Abbreviations for Place of Publication, p. 646. Bibliography-Author Index for References, pp. 647-61. Subject Index, pp. 663-86.

Topics include the two-sample problem where the data are not converted to categorical form; the several sample problems for noncategorical and categorical forms; population symmetry; and results for extreme populations and observations. Results for population symmetry limited to the univariate case. Analysis of extreme populations concerned with the rejection of outlying observations and the development of asymptotic expressions for distributions of extremes and with methods for estimating the unknown quantities of these expressions. Chapters conclude with a discussion of problems and characteristics of the procedures presented. Includes numerical examples.

Part II

ECONOMETRICS

Chapter 16

ECONOMETRICS—TEXTS AND REFERENCES

Aigner, Dennis J., and Goldberger, Arthur S., eds. LATENT VARIABLES IN SOCIO-ECONOMIC MODELS. Contributions to Economic Analysis, vol. 103. New York: Elsevier, 1977. xiv, 383 p. No index.

> Nineteen recent papers, some heretofore unpublished, on the use of latent variables in econometrics, psychometrics, and sociology. Includes both empirical and methodological papers. Topics include errors in variables and other unobservables; asymptotic bias from errors of omission and measurement; estimation of regression relationships containing unobservable independent variables; a model for an unobservable variable with endogenous causes; identification of simultaneous equation models with measurement error; response errors of non-black males in models of the stratification process; methods for analysis of longitudinal data; and identification of the dynamic shock-error model. Useful as a supplementary text for an advanced econometrics course, and as a reference.

Allard, R.J. AN APPROACH TO ECONOMETRICS. New York: Wiley, 1974. viii, 227 p. Appendix A: Mathematical Notes, pp. 207-13. Appendix B: Statistical Tables, pp. 214-20. Further Reading, pp. 221-22. Numerical Answers to Odd-Numbered Exercises, pp. 223-24. Index, pp. 225-27.

> A text for an introductory course in econometrics for students who have little knowledge of statistics, but have a good grounding in algebra and the summation notation. Uses calculus sporadically. Emphasizes the logic behind econometric techniques to enable the reader to appreciate their use and (and misuse). Topics include data analysis without models; least squares regression, including stepwise regression; probability and random variables; statistical inference; likelihood function; prediction; multicollinearity; dummy variables; disturbances and residuals; autocorrelation; hetersocedasticity; errors in the variables; lagged endogenous variables; simultaneous equations; identification; reduced form; indirect least squares; and two-stage least squares. Chapters conclude with problems.

Texts and References

Andrews, J.G., and McLone, R.R., eds. MATHEMATICAL MODELLING. Woburn, Mass.: Butterworths, 1976. xvii, 260 p. Index, pp. 259-60.

Brings together many different aspects of mathematical modelling through case studies from a wide range of applications. Consists of sixteen chapters each written by a different author; each chapter begins with a short list of prerequisites for comprehension and ends with references and problems for further study. Prerequisites include matrix algebra, set theory, modern algebra, mathematical analysis, probability theory, statistics, Laplace transform, ordinary differential equations, and elementary mechanics. Topics and applications include steering problems; liquid flowing from a container; molecular models; drilling holes with laser; population models; stochastic models for road traffic conditions; business planning models; mathematical model of motor insurance; military applications of game theory; network flow models; and urban structure.

Aykac, Ahmet, and Brumat, Carlo. NEW DEVELOPMENTS IN THE APPLICATIONS OF BAYESIAN METHODS. Contributions to Economic Analysis, 119. Amsterdam: North-Holland, 1977. xxiv, 385 p. No index.

Twenty-one papers presented at the first European conference held at Fontainebleau, France, in June 1976. Topics include a statistical model of a financial conglomerate; Bayesian approach to simultaneous equations models; maximal data information prior distributions; Bayesian regression analysis using poly-T densities; Markov processes with exchangeable interarrival times and increments; cognitive processes and the assessment of subjective probability distributions; theory of expected inequity; analysis of language and information; and Bayesian approach to the optimal control of continuous industrial processes. Some papers use only a few mathematical formulas.

Balsley, Howard Lloyd. QUANTITATIVE RESEARCH METHODS FOR BUSINESS AND ECONOMICS. New York: Random House, 1970. viii, 339 p. Appendixes, pp. 293-331. Index, pp. 333-39.

Presents the most generally applicable research methods used in business and economics. Omits formal derivations and proofs. Useful as a text for a graduate course in research in schools of business. Topics include statistical inference; statistical tests, experimental design; correlation and regression; time series; and linear programming. Chapters conclude with exercises and references. Appendixes include statistical tables.

Brennan, Michael J. PREFACE TO ECONOMETRICS: AN INTRODUCTION TO QUANTITATIVE METHODS IN ECONOMICS. 3d rev. ed. Cincinnati: South Western, 1973. viii, 448 p. Bibliography, pp. 429-32. Answers to Odd-Numbered Problems, pp. 433-36. Tables, pp. 437-40. Index, pp. 441-48.

A largely nontechnical text for an introductory course in econometrics for undergraduates who have some knowledge of elementary economic theory, college algebra, and basic statistics. Consists of the following five parts: "Elementary Mathematical Formulation"; "Elements of Calculus"; "Econometric Models"; "Statistical Inference"; and "Econometric Models Reconsidered." Topics include systems of equations; determinants and matrices; economic applications of derivatives; partial derivatives and economic applications; static and dynamic models, including cobweb; random variables; and expected value; regression and correlation; and the identification problem. Chapters conclude with problems.

Bridge, J.L. APPLIED ECONOMETRICS. New York: Elsevier, 1971. xi, 422 p. References, pp. 406-13. Author Index, pp. 415-17. Subject Index, pp. 419-22.

A text for a graduate course in applied econometrics for students already familiar with J. Johnston, ECONOMETRIC METHODS (McGraw-Hill, 1972). Consists of a survey of the literature on applied econometrics in the following fields: consumption, demand functions, investment, inventories, and production functions.

Brown, Tillman Merritt. SPECIFICATION AND USES OF ECONOMETRIC MODELS. New York: Macmillan, 1970. 487 p. Appendix A: Bibliography and References, pp. 463-68. Appendix B: Glossary of Symbols, pp. 469-82. Index, pp. 483-87.

Deals with the specification of a detailed macro-economy which includes systems of production functions and technology; money and finance; demands, supplies, markets, and income; and savings, assets, liabilities, and wealth. Consists of four parts: "Foundations for Specification"; "Detailed Specification of a Macro-Model of the Economy"; "Examples of Specification and Testing: Some Actual Econometric Models"; and "Uses and Applications of the Econometric Macro-Model." Examples consist of three Canadian econometric models. Uses and applications of the model include short-run forecasting and policy, optimal growth paths, and the analysis of the dynamic properties of an economy. Considerable verbal description accompanies mathematical formulations. Based on the author's experience in econometrics with the Canadian government.

Chiswick, Barry R., and Chiswick, Stephen J. STATISTICS AND ECONOMETRICS: A PROBLEM SOLVING TEXT. Baltimore: University Park Press, 1975. xiii, 261 p. Statistical Appendix, pp. 241-57. Subject Index, pp. 259-61.

A text for an introductory econometric course for students who possess knowledge of elementary algebra (no matrix algebra or calculus is used). Consists of two parts: "Descriptive Statistics, Probability, and Hypothesis Testing" and "Regression Analysis." Each chapter provides a brief review of the theory and formulas followed by problems applying the theory. Chapter titles: "Descriptive Statistics"; "Probability and Random Variables"; "Hypothesis Testing"; "Means and Proportions"; "Hypothesis Testing"; "Variances and Goodness of Fit"; "Simple Regression Analysis"; "Multiple Regression Analysis"; and "Simultaneous Systems of Equations." Statistical appendix consists of tables. Useful as a self-study and as a supplement in basic statistics courses as well as for undergraduate courses in econometrics.

Chow, Yuan-shih; Robbins, Herbert; and Siegmund, David. GREAT EXPECTATIONS: THE THEORY OF OPTIMAL STOPPING. Boston: Houghton Mifflin, 1971. xii, 141 p. Bibliographical Notes, pp. 130-32. Bibliography, pp. 133-38. List of Symbols, p. 139. Index, p. 141.

A monograph on the theory of discrete time optimal stopping together with examples illustrating the application of the theory. Accessible to anyone possessing knowledge of measure-theoretic probability, including conditional expectation. Topics include martingales with application to sequential probability ratio tests; monotone case; application to martingale theory; and the Markov and independent case. Uses the theorem-lemma-proof sequence with examples. Chapters conclude with problems on applications and extensions of the theory.

Christ, Carl F. ECONOMETRIC MODELS AND METHODS. Foreword by Jocob Marschak. New York: Wiley, 1966. xxiii, 705 p. Appendix A: Some Rudiments of Algebra, pp. 629-66. Appendix B: Probability Tables, pp. 667-72. Appendix C: References, pp. 673-88. Index, pp. 689-705.

A text for a one-year graduate course in econometrics requiring knowledge of differential calculus, statistical inference, and matrix algebra. Consists of three parts: "Making the Acquaintance of Econometrics"; "Theoretical Models"; and "Empirical Methods." Style intuitive, and derivations short. Topics include two-equation national income model; solutions of linear equations; probability and expectation; stochastic structures, models, and reduced forms; cross-section models; lagged variables; linear difference equations; random variables; hypothesis testing and statistical inference; identification; simple and multiple regression and correlation; maximum-likelihood; limited information; full-information; two-stage least squares; serial correlation; Aitken's generalized least squares; predictive and nonpredictive tests; and illustrative model of the U.S. economy, 1929-41 and 1946-59. Chapters conclude with questions and problems.

Clark, John; Cole, Sam; Curnow, Ray; and Hopkins, Mike. GLOBAL SIMULATION MODELS: A COMPARATIVE STUDY. New York: Wiley, Interscience, 1975. x, 135 p. Appendix A: Interactive Simulation Modelling, pp. 117-20. Appendix B: Technical Tools of Modelling, pp. 121-24. References, pp. 125-30. Index, pp. 131-35.

A monograph on the problems, prospects, and criticisms of computer models for forecasting with emphasis on world computer models for anyone currently engaged in modeling or anyone who has an interest in future studies. Style verbal with no mathematics prerequisites. Topics include description of world computer models, including Forrester's model; tools of world modeling; use of world models in forecasting urban problems, ecology, policy, demography, and macroeconomics; systems analysis and modeling; and theoretical foundations.

Cramer, Jan Salomon. EMPIRICAL ECONOMETRICS. New York: Elsevier, 1969. xii, 277 p. Appendix A: Notes to the Tables, pp. 254-60. Appendix B: Notes to the Figures, pp. 261-63. References, pp. 264-70. Index of Names, pp. 271-73. Index of Subjects, pp. 274-77.

A collection of examples and models illustrating methods and results in the following areas: random arrivals and related events; attributes of consumer behavior; the distribution of personal income and other size distributions based on the log-normal; linear regression; simultaneous equations and the problem of identification; analysis of family budgets; the consumption function; demand analysis; and production functions, including CES. Empirical results in the form of estimated coefficients of the models and their standard errors, as well as other derived data. Omits development of the statistical basis of econometrics. Assumes knowledge of intermediate statistics. Useful as a supplement for econometric courses.

Cuddy, J.D.A. QUANTITATIVE METHODS IN ECONOMICS: AN INTRODUCTION TO STATISTICAL INFERENCE, ESTIMATION,AND MODELLING. Rotterdam, The Netherlands: Rotterdam University Press, 1974. viii, 180 p. Bibliography, pp. 178-80. No index.

A supplementary text for an introductory course in econometrics for undergraduates who have knowledge of calculus and matrix algebra, but no familiarity with statistics. Consists of two parts: "Statistical Inference" and "Econometric Thoery and Applications." Topics include the simple linear model; generalized least squares; autocorrelation; heteroscedasticity; multiple-equation models; indirect least squares; simultaneous equation models; three-stage least squares; and analysis of variance in regression. Style informal with emphasis on clarity rather than on vigor. Stress placed on use of simple numerical examples and results of empirical research in econometrics. Exercises not included.

Day, Richard H., and Groves, Theodore, eds. ADAPTIVE ECONOMIC MODELS. New York: Academic Press, 1975. ix, 581 p. Index, pp. 575-81.

Twenty-three papers presented at a symposium on adaption economic models sponsored by the Mathematics Research Center at the University of Wisconsin, October 21-23, 1974. Topics include biological systems as paradigms for adaption; market adaption of the firm; learning by firms about demand conditions; adaptive utility; Bayesian equilibrium under uncertainty; demand for labor in a dynamic theory of the firm; diffusion of innovations under imperfect competition; autonomous control of the economic system; modelling discrete adaptive behavior in the chemical process industries; equilibrium in stochastic economic models; and temporary Walrasian equilibrium in a monetary economy. Some papers require no formal mathematics training, while others assume knowledge of linear algebra, mathematical analysis, advanced calculus, and mathematical programming.

Desai, Meghnad. APPLIED ECONOMETRICS. London: Philip Allan, 1976. x, 277 p. References, pp. 269-75. Index, pp. 276-77.

A text for an applied econometrics course for students who have had a course in theoretical econometrics. Emphasizes the combination of economic theory and econometric theory with stress on the testing of restrictions and on specification of the stochastic terms. Illustrates single-equation models with demand analysis, and simultaneous equations models with production functions. Uses technical change to illustrate the interaction of theory and measurement. Includes both single-equation and multiple equation dynamic models with emphasis on the specification of error and autoregressive influence in the error terms. Concludes with an analysis of simulation and policy making with large macro-economic models. Derivations kept to a minimum.

Dhrymes, Phoebus J. DISTRIBUTED LAGS: PROBLEMS OF ESTIMATION AND FORMULATION. Mathematical Economics Texts, no. 8. San Francisco: Holden-Day, 1971. viii, 414 p. Appendix: Some Monte Carlo Experiments, pp. 355-401. Bibliography, pp. 402-10. Index, pp. 411-14.

A discussion of the problems of formulation and estimation in distributed lag models of various orders of complexity including geometric, polynomial, and general rational lag models. Other topics include spectral techniques in the estimation of these models and a brief overview of the theory of variance stationary processes. Appendix contains results of Monte Carlo experiments to study the asymptotic properties of estimates. Deals only peripherally with the theoretical bases of models. Derives asymptotic distributions for maximum likelihood estimators and for other estimators claimed to be computationally easier than maximum likelihood estimators. Prerequisites of mathematical statistics and econometrics assumed. Useful as a reference for graduate students and specialists in econometrics.

_____. ECONOMETRICS: STATISTICAL FOUNDATIONS AND APPLICATIONS. New York: Harper & Row, 1970. xii, 592 p. Mathematical Appendix, pp. 545-84. Index, pp. 585-92.

A text for a graduate course in the theory of econometrics for students who have knowledge of calculus, linear algebra, and elementary mathematical statistics. Extensive derivations and proofs provided. Includes a limited number of numerical examples. Topics include multivariate analysis with applications to principal components; discriminant analysis, and factor analysis; simultaneous equations systems, including two- and three-stage least squares with applications; recursive systems, indirect least squares, and the identification problem; maximum likelihood methods, including reduced form and full maximum and limited information estimation; relations among estimators; Monte Carlo method; spectral analysis; cross-spectral analysis; and applications of spectral analysis to simultaneous equations systems. Chapters conclude with references.

_____. MATHEMATICS FOR ECONOMETRICS. New York: Springer-Verlag, 1978. viii, 136 p. References, pp. 132-33. Index, pp. 134-36.

A supplementary text and reference for econometrics courses. Reinforces the student's mathematical training, and includes proofs in the majority of cases. Topics include vectors and vector spaces; matrix algebra (rank and inverse, trace, partitioned, Kronecker product, characteristic roots, orthogonal and symmetric, idempotent); linear systems of equations and generalized inverses of matrices; vectorization of matrices and matrix functions; and systems of difference equations with constant coefficients. Assumes knowledge of college algebra and calculus.

Dowling, John Malcolm, and Glahe, Fred R., eds. READINGS IN ECONOMETRIC THEORY. Boulder: Colorado Associated University Press, 1970. xxi, 560 p. No index.

Twenty-seven reprints of classic articles on econometrics grouped under the following four headings: "Methodology" (one article); "Single Equations" (fourteen articles); "Simultaneous Equations" (seven articles); and "Small Sample Properties" (five articles). Topics include autocorrelation; lagged variables; aggregation; multicollinearity; errors in variables; dummy variables; single equation bias; identification; estimating methods; recursive systems; theoretical analysis; and Monte Carlo techniques.

Duncan, Otis Dudley. INTRODUCTION TO STRUCTURAL EQUATION MODELS. New York: Academic Press, 1975. ix, 180 p. References, pp. 169-73. Author Index, pp. 175-76. Subject Index, pp. 177-80.

A survey of the use of recursive and nonrecursive models in sociological research and a discussion of the methodological questions pertaining to such models. Topics include correlation and causation; identification, overidentification, and underidentification in nonrecursive models; specification and identification errors; and multiple indicators. Assumes knowledge of random variables and their moments, regression and correlation, college algebra, and determinants. Chapters conclude with references.

Dutta, Manoranjan. ECONOMETRIC METHODS. Cincinnati: South-Western, 1975. vi, 382 p. Appendix: Tables, pp. 369-76. Index, pp. 378-82.

A text for an undergraduate course in econometrics for students who have had one semester of statistics and one semester of linear algebra. Emphasizes the role of economics in econometrics, and includes the following topics: serial correlation and heteroscedasticity; multicollinearity; lag structures; instrumental variables; identification; interdependent systems of linear equations; and full information maximum likelihood method and three-stage least squares. Chapters conclude with problems on both theory and applications, and also references.

Fienberg, Stephen E., and Zellner, Arnold, eds. STUDIES IN BAYESIAN ECONOMETRICS AND STATISTICS. ESSAYS IN HONOR OF LEONARD J. SAVAGE. Contributions to Economic Analysis, vol. 86. New York: Elsevier, 1975. ix, 676 p. Appendix: Programs of the NBER-NSF Seminars on Bayesian Inference in Econometrics, pp. 655-62. Author Index, pp. 663-68. Subject Index, pp. 669-76.

Thirty heretofore unpublished contributions arranged under the following eleven headings: "Econometrics and Bayesian Inference" (four contributions); "Bayes' Theorem and Economic Theory" (two contributions); "Assessing Prior Distributions" (one contribution); "Identification and Bayesian Analysis" (two contributions); "Applications of Bayesian Regression" (three contributions); "Missing Observations" (three contributions); "Time Series Problems" (three contributions); "Analyses of Simultaneous Equation Models" (three contributions); "Control Problems" (two contributions); "Reporting Results" (two contributions); and "New Developments in Estimation" (five contributions).

Fisher, Walter Dummer. CLUSTERING AND AGGREGATION IN ECONOMICS. Baltimore: Johns Hopkins, 1969. xii, 195 p. References, pp. 139-47. Appendixes, pp. 151-87. Index, pp. 189-95.

A presentation of the aggregation problem of economics for the purpose of recommending specific procedures for econometric research. Problems include reduced form, input-output matrix, and linear programming. Includes a step-wise clustering procedure to solve the problems. Knowledge of econometric methods and mathematical analysis necessary. Appendixes include tables and further mathematical results.

Fishman, George S. SPECTRAL METHODS IN ECONOMETRICS. Cambridge, Mass.: Harvard University Press, 1969. xi, 212 p. References, pp. 200-206. Index, pp. 207-12.

Presents spectral methods and their applications to the estimation and testing of distributed lag models for graduate students and econometricians who have knowledge of probability theory, difference equations, matrix algebra, and multivariate statistical analysis; familiarity with complex variables also helpful. Results restricted to the class of covariance stationary stochastic processes. Topics include spectral representation of a covariance stationary process; relationship between autocorrelation and spectral density functions; first- and second-order autoregressive processes; bivariate and multivariate spectral analyses; correlation between spectrum estimates; asymptotic covariances of cross-spectrum estimates; testing the zero coherence hypothesis; multivariate testing and estimation procedures; and estimation and testing in distributed lag models. Concludes with the application of spectral methods to quarterly U.S. disposable personal income and personal comsumption expenditures from 1947 through 1965.

Fisk, P.R. STOCHASTICALLY DEPENDENT EQUATIONS: AN INTRODUCTORY TEXT FOR ECONOMETRICIANS. Griffin's Statistical Monographs and Courses, no. 21. New York: Hafner, 1967. viii, 181 p. Appendix, pp. 144-54. Notation Used in Text, pp. 155-60. References, pp. 161-65. Bibliography, pp. 166-73. Author Index, pp. 175-76. Subject Index, pp. 177-81.

A monograph on simultaneous equations models with emphasis on theory for students who have knowledge of calculus, matrix algebra, and statistical theory, including multivariate analysis. Topics include identification, full and limited information maximum likelihood estimation; k-class and related estimators; measures of correlation; and numerical illustrations.

Fox, Karl A. ECONOMETRIC ANALYSIS FOR PUBLIC POLICY. Ames: Iowa State University Press, 1958. xi, 288 p. Appendix: Accuracy of Price Forecasts from 1922 to 1941 Demand Functions During the Postwar Period, pp. 275-79. Index, pp. 283-88.

Presents a number of previously published articles on demand analysis and econometric models together with some heretofore unpublished material. Consists of two parts: "The Analysis of Demand" and "The Use of Econometric Models." Demand analysis based on graphs, rather than sets of equations, for nonmathematical readers. Second part deals with the use of econometric models in appraising economic policies in foreign trade, spatial equilibrium of the livestock-feed economy in the United States, and on the contributions of farm prices support programs to general economic stability. Concludes with an analysis of three econometric models of the U.S. economy. Based on research undertaken between 1951 and 1955.

Giles, D.E.A. ESSAYS ON ECONOMETRIC TOPICS: FROM THEORY TO PRACTICE. Research Paper, no. 10. Wellington: Federal Reserve Bank of New Zealand, 1973. 81 p. References, pp. 80-81. No index.

Seven essays by the author on a variety of topics linking the theory and practice of econometric analysis. Essays linked together by the need for specification of econometric models. Useful to econometricians who desire to employ econometric analysis in their work, but who do not have the time to do extensive reading of the literature. Chapter titles: "The Kitchen Sink Dilemma"; "The Use and Abuse of R^2"; "The Multicollinearity Problem"; "Non-Linear Models: The Intrinsically Linear Case"; "Switching Regressions: Testing and Estimating, with Structural Instability"; "The Problem of Serial Correlation in Regression"; and "The Estimation of Large Econometric Systems."

Glickman, Norman J. ECONOMETRIC ANALYSIS OF REGIONAL SYSTEMS: EXPLORATIONS IN MODEL BUILDING AND POLICY ANALYSIS. Foreword by L.R. Klein. Studies in Urban Economics. New York: Academic Press, 1977. xi, 210 p. References, pp. 197-206. Index, pp. 207-10.

An exploration of the application of econometric models to regional problems, rather than input-output analysis, with emphasis on macroeconomic forecasting for metropolitan regions. Topics include review of methods of regional economic analysis; a 228 equation econometric model of the Philadelphia metropolitan area consisting of forty-seven exogenous and forty-four lagged endogenous variables for the 1947-71 sample period; and tests, forecasting, and simulations using the Philadelphia model.

Goldberger, Arthur S. ECONOMETRIC THEORY. New York: Wiley, 1964. xi, 399 p. Bibliography, pp. 389-92. Index, pp. 393-99.

A text for a one-year graduate course in econometrics with a prerequisite of one semester of matrix algebra and one semester of mathematical statistics, and a reference for those engaged in empirical economic research. Unity of treatment provided by the classical regression model with weakened assumptions.

Topics include review of matrix algebra and mathematical statistics; classical regression; extensions of linear regression (analysis of variance, nonspherical distributions, functional forms, and use of extraneous information); linear regression with stochastic regressors; autoregressive linear regression; uncorrelation linear regression; and simultaneous equation systems, including identification, reduced-form and indirect least squares, two-stage least squares, three-stage least squares, maximum likelihood estimation, and comparison of alternative structural estimation methods. Presentation rigorous with extensive derivations, and brief numerical examples.

Goldfeld, Stephen M., and Quandt, Richard E. NONLINEAR METHODS IN ECONOMETRICS. Contributions to Economic Analysis, vol. 77. Amsterdam: North-Holland, 1972. vi, 280 p. Appendix A: Comparison of Maximization Algorithms: Some Numerical Results, pp. 27-38. Appendix B: The Peak Test of Heteroscedascicity, pp. 120-23. Appendix C: The Density Function for Dependent Error Structures, p. 146. Appendix D: Additional Tables for Sampling Experiments, pp. 215-18. Index, pp. 278-80.

A contribution to the analysis of nonlinear problems in econometrics treating such topics as maximization techniques; least squares; maximum likelihood; nonlinear estimation in the case of heteroscedasticity; regressions with dummy dependent variables; Cobb-Douglas type functions with multiplicative and additive errors; estimator behavior for a nonlinear model of production; autocorrelation in simultaneous equation systems; nonlinear simultaneous equations; and estimation of discontinuous parameter changes. Assumes knowledge of linear algebra, and mathematical statistics. Compares the estimates of the various techniques discussed.

______, eds. STUDIES IN NONLINEAR ESTIMATION. Cambridge, Mass.: Ballinger, 1976. xiv, 279 p. Index, pp. 273-78. About the Author, p. 279.

Eleven papers presented at a seminar on nonlinear estimation held at Princeton University in 1974, grouped under the following four headings: "Switching Regression Models" (four papers); "Estimation of Production Functions" (two papers); "Estimation of Expenditure Systems" (three papers); and "Limited Dependent Variables" (two papers). Topics include estimation of structural change in simultaneous equation models; aggregation and structural shifts; specification and testing of error structure in nonlinear simultaneous equation models; quadratic utility; small sample properties of demand system estimates; a Monte Carlo study of limited dependent variable estimation; and simultaneous equations models with continuous and endogenous variables and structural shifts.

Gujarati, Damodar. BASIC ECONOMETRICS. New York: McGraw-Hill, 1978. xvii, 462 p. Appendix A: A Review of Some Statistical Concepts, pp. 389-408. Appendix B: Rudiments of Matrix Algebra, pp. 409-23. Appendix C: A List of Some Packaged Computer Programs, pp. 424-26. Appendix D: Statistical Tables, pp. 427-41. Answers and Hints to Solutions of Selected Exercises, pp. 442-50. Selected Bibliography, pp. 451-55. Name Index, pp. 457-58. Subject Index, pp. 459-62.

> A text for a course in econometrics for undergraduates and graduates who have knowledge of basic statistics. Emphasizes learning econometrics by doing, and knowledge of matrix algebra and calculus not essential. Consists of four parts: "Single-Equation Regression Models"; "Violations of the Assumptions of the Classical Model"; "Topics in Econometrics"; and "Simultaneous-Equation Models." Topics include classical simple and multiple regression; Gauss-Markov theorem; analysis of variance approach; matrix approach; multicollinearity; heteroscedasticity; autocorrelation; autoregression and distributed lag models; dummy variables; restricted least squares; nonlinear regression; identification; indirect least squares; and two-stage least squares. Chapters conclude with exercises. Includes some numerical examples.

Harkema, Rinse. SIMULTANEOUS EQUATIONS: A BAYESIAN APPROACH. Foreword by T. Kloek. Rotterdam, The Netherlands: Rotterdam University Press, 1971. viii, 108 p. References, pp. 105-6. Index, pp. 107-8.

> A monograph on a Bayesian inference method for estimating the parameters of simultaneous equation systems. Attempts to find a mathematically traceable informative prior density on the space of the structural parameters such that the resulting posterior density on the space of the reduced-form parameters is mathematically traceable as well. Replaces reduced form point estimates by interval estimates. Applied to Klein's model I in ECONOMIC FLUCTUATIONS IN THE U.S., 1921-1941 (New York: Wiley, 1950). Assumes knowledge of mathematical statistics.

Hood, William C., and Koopmans, Tyalling C., eds. STUDIES IN ECONOMETRIC METHOD. Cowles Foundation, monograph 14. New Haven, Conn.: Yale University Press, 1953. xiii, 323 p. References, pp. 305-10. Index of Names, p. 311. Subject Index, pp. 313-23.

> A collection of ten essays, some reprinted articles and others heretofore unpublished studies, on some of the problems of econometrics dealt with in Cowles Foundation Monograph 10, STATISTICAL INFERENCE IN DYNAMIC ECONOMIC MODELS. Topics include criteria of identifiability of the parameters of economic behavior; examples of specification errors in two-equation systems; application of maximum-likelihood estimation procedures to sets of equations for demand for and supply of

food; large-sample theory of maximum-likelihood estimation; the use and misuse of the least-squares method of estimation in simple models involving the consumption function; and asymptotic properties of limited-information estimates under generalized conditions.

Hooper, John W., and Nerlove, Marc, eds. SELECTED READINGS IN ECONOMETRICS FROM ECONOMETRICA. Cambridge, Mass.: MIT Press, 1970. viii, 498 p. Index, pp. 495-98.

Reprints of twenty-one classic articles previously published in ECONOMETRICA between 1933 and 1964. Balance struck between articles in methodology and in applications. Useful as a reference for students and practitioners in econometrics. Topics include simultaneous equations; demand for durable goods; econometric models as a guide to economic policy; identification; generalized least squares; international comparison of household expenditure patterns; canonical correlation; three-stage least squares; and alternative estimators for simultaneous equations.

Hu, Teh-wei. ECONOMETRICS: AN INTRODUCTORY ANALYSIS. Baltimore: University Park Press, 1973. viii, 172 p. Appendix A: Notation, pp. 153-54. Appendix B: Tables, pp. 155-61. References, pp. 163-67. Index, pp. 169-72.

A self-contained development and explanation of econometric methods for students and researchers who do not have a background in matrix algebra but who possess knowledge of elementary statistics and high school algebra. Topics include statistical inference and hypothesis testing; two- and three-variable regression models; inference and hypothesis testing in regression; dummy variables; problems of single-equation models, including multicollinearity, autocorrelation, heteroscedasticity, errors in variables, and lagged variables; application of single-equation models to demand, cost, supply, consumption, and production functions; and simultaneous-equation models, including identification and applications. Derivations kept to a minimum.

Huang, David S. REGRESSION AND ECONOMETRIC METHODS. Wiley Series in Probability and Mathematical Statistics. New York: Wiley, 1970. xiii, 274 p. Appendix A: Statistical Tables, pp. 249-57. Appendix B: Some Concepts and Results of Matrices, pp. 258-65. Bibliography, pp. 267-71. Index, pp. 273-74.

A text for a one-semester course in regression analysis or econometrics for graduates and undergraduates who have knowledge of basic statistics and calculus. Emphasizes applications and intuitive appreciation with proofs and derivations supplied only where necessary. Also stresses assumptions of the various models. Topics include fundamentals of simple regression; multiple regression in matrix form, including the general linear hypothesis; generalized least squares; autocorrelation; multicollinearity; heteroscedasticity; errors in the variables; dummy variables; nonlinear regression; multivariate analysis, including sets of regression equations; stepwise least squares; indirect least squares; two-stage squares; three-stage least squares; and simulation.

Intriligator, Michael D. ECONOMETRIC MODELS, TECHNIQUES, AND APPLICATIONS. Englewood Cliffs, N.J.: Prentice-Hall, 1978. xv, 638 p. Appendix A: An Econometric Project, pp. 561-68. Appendix B: Matrices, pp. 569-98. Appendix C: Probability and Statistics, pp. 599-629. Index, pp. 631-38.

A comprehensive text for a one-year course in econometrics for advanced undergraduates and graduates and a supplementary text for courses in economic statistics, sociometrics, engineering, public administration, and other social sciences. Prerequisites include basic statistics, calculus, and matrix algebra. Consists of the following seven parts: "Introduction"; "Models and Data"; "Single-Equation Estimation"; "Applications of Single-Equation Estimation"; "Simultaneous Equations"; "Applications of Simultaneous-Equations Estimation"; and "Uses of Econometrics." Applications in new areas of labor economics, industrial organization, and health economics, as well as the traditional areas. Includes survey of several large econometric models, and uses of econometrics for forecasting and policy evaluation. Chapters conclude with problems and references.

Intriligator, Michael D., and Kendrick, D.A., eds. FRONTIERS OF QUANTITATIVE ECONOMICS. Vol. II. Contributions to Economic Analysis, vol. 87. New York: Elsevier, 1974. xi, 580 p. Subject Index, pp. 571-80.

Nine heretofore unpublished studies presented to the North American Winter Meeting of the Econometric Society held in Toronto, December 1972, grouped under the following three headings: "Economic Methodology and Theory" (three studies); "Econometric Techniques" (two studies); and "Quantitative Approaches to Traditional Topics in Economics" (four studies). Paper titles: "The Design of Mechanisms for Resource Allocation," by Leonard Hurwicz; "Market Equilibrium and Uncertainty: Concepts and Problems," by Roy Radner; "Applications of Duality Theory," by W.E. Diewart; "Exact Finite Sample Distributions for Some Econometric Estimators and Test Statistics: A Survey and Appraisal," by R.L. Basmann; "Distributed Lags," by Christopher A. Sims; "Investment and Production: A Review," by Dale W. Jorgenson; "Econometric Studies of Health Economics," by Martin S. Feldstein; "Multi-

Sector Models for Development Planning: A Survey," by Alan S. Manne; and "Labor Market Discrimination: Analysis, Findings, and Problems," by R.B. Freeman.

Jang, Young Sik. ECONOMETRIC MODEL BUILDING: A COMPARATIVE STUDY OF SIMULTANEOUS EQUATION SYSTEMS. Seoul, Korea: Yonsei University Press, 1973. 170 p. Bibliography, pp. 157-65. Index, pp. 166-70.

Emphasizes two opposing approaches to structural model building: the Cowles Commission system of simultaneous equations, initiated by T. Haavelmo, and the Woldian causal chain (recursive) system of simultaneous equations first initiated by J. Tinbergen. Begins with a historical review and concludes with the current state of the controversy. The U.S. tin can industry, 1950-1967, used as a case study of the two systems. Assumes knowledge of a graduate course in econometrics. Useful as a supplementary test for a graduate course where the identification problem is stressed as well as the Lundberg-Lindahl type of disequilibrium dynamic process and the Walras-Keynes type of equilibrium process.

Johnston, John. ECONOMETRIC METHODS. 2d ed., rev. and enl. New York: McGraw-Hill, 1972. x, 437 p. Appendix, pp. 424-33. Index, pp. 434-37.

A text for a one-year course in econometric methods at the graduate or advanced undergraduate levels with a prerequisite of one year of mathematical statistics. Also suitable for a one-semester undergraduate course with a prerequisite of only matrix algebra and basic statistics (matrix algebra is reviewed in chapter 4). Topics include the general linear model and its extensions in matrix form, including multicollinearity, prediction, and specification error; generalized least squares; heteroscedasticity; autocorrelation, including conventional tests and the Theil BLUS procedure; lagged variables; principal components, canonical correlations, and discriminant analysis; and identification and estimation in simultaneous-equation models, including recursive systems, two- and three-stage least squares, k-class estimators, limited information estimators, full information maximum-likelihood methods, and simultaneous confidence intervals. Emphasizes the rationale of the various methods and the assumptions underlying the techniques. Useful to readers with diverse backgrounds. Includes number of numerical examples and most chapters conclude with theoretical and numerical exercises, as well as references. The appendix consists of statistical tables.

Kane, Edward J. ECONOMIC STATISTICS AND ECONOMETRICS: AN INTRODUCTION TO QUANTITATIVE ECONOMICS. New York: Harper & Row, 1968. xvi, 437 p. Appendix I: Notes on Electronic Data Processing, pp.

387-409. Appendix II: A Program of Independent Reading, pp. 410-12. Appendix III: Statistical Tables, pp. 413-26. Index, of Names, pp. 429-30. Index of Subjects, pp. 431-37.

A text for a one-semester introductory course in statistics and econometrics for economics students who have knowledge of elementary calculus, but no basic statistics. Emphasizes motivation rather than rigor, the meaning and significance of basic concepts rather than the extent of available techniques, and the methodological steps by which econometric research proceeds, rather than the richness of its field of application. Consists of five parts: "Quantitative Economics: A Preliminary Look"; "Descriptive Statistics"; "Probability and Inference"; "Regression in Action"; and "The Least-Squares Assumptions: Tests and Transformations." Topics include basic elements of models, including consumption function, structural and reduced form; sources of error; descriptive statistics; principal of moments; covariance; probability calculus; random variables and their distributions; expected value; multivariate distributions; estimators and estimation; bivariate regression and correlation; analysis of variance table for regression; multiple regression; identification; simultaneous equation estimation using indirect least squares; autocorrelation; and heteroscedasticity. Omitted or stressed very little, are such topics as F, chi-square, and Poisson distributions; design of experiments; cross section, and index number problems. Chapters conclude with problems.

Kelejian, Harry H., and Oates, Wallace E. INTRODUCTION TO ECONOMETRICS: PRINCIPLES AND APPLICATIONS. New York: Harper & Row, 1974. xi, 300 p. Supplementary Readings, p. 269. Statistical Tables, pp. 271-78. Answers to Questions, pp. 279-97. Index, pp. 299-300.

A text for an introductory course in econometrics for undergraduates and beginning graduate students who have a modest background in mathematics. Presentation intuitive; use made of calculus or matrix algebra; and the basic results derived using the instrumental variable approach and applied to actual studies taken from the literature. Topics include simple and multiple regression and correlation, including the Koyck and Almon lags, dummy variables, and logarithmic transformations; problems of regression analysis, including multicollinearity, autocorrelation, and heteroscedasticity; and systems of equations, including the identification problem and two-stage least squares with applications to demand and supply and public finance. Chapter appendixes devoted to the more advanced mathematical derivations and concepts. Chapters conclude with questions and problems.

Klein, Lawrence R. AN INTRODUCTION TO ECONOMETRICS. Englewood Cliffs, N.J.: Prentice-Hall, 1962. viii, 280 p. Index, pp. 271-80.

An early supplementary text designed for students who lack the college mathematics necessary to understand the author's A TEXTBOOK OF ECONOMETRICS (Row, Peterson, 1953). Use of calculus, matrix algebra, and mathematical analysis omitted. Reliance placed on simple equations, numerical examples, and diagrams. Topics include statistical demand analysis, including use of cross-section data and pooling of cross-section and time series data; cobweb analysis; cost and supply functions; input-output analysis; distribution of income and wealth; models of growth and trade cycles, including the great ratios of economics; forecasting; simulation of business cycles; sample surveys; and a critic of model building.

_____. A TEXTBOOK OF ECONOMETRICS. Evanston, Ill.: Row, Peterson, 1953. ix, 355 p. Appendix: Introduction to Algebra of Matrices and Determinants, pp. 324-46. Index, pp. 347-55.

An early text for a one-year course in econometrics for graduate students who have not yet studied matrix algebra, probability, and statistics; self-contained for students familiar with calculus. Intuitive approach used throughout and derivations not extensive. Topics include statistical groundwork, including distributions, moments, and inference; identification, maximum likelihood and limited information estimates; least squares; disaggregation; sector models; cross-section data with application to railroad service; pooling of cross-section and time series data; prediction; application of input-output models; and weighted least squares. Sections conclude with questions and problems, and chapters conclude with references.

Kmenta, Jan. ELEMENTS OF ECONOMETRICS. Macmillan Series in Economics. New York: Macmillan, 1971. xiii, 655 p. Appendix A: Algebra of Summations, pp. 601-3. Appendix B: Elements of Matrix Algebra, pp. 604-12. Appendix C: Computational Designs for Least Squares Estimation, pp. 613-19. Appendix D: Statistical Tables, pp. 620-37. Suggested Further Readings, pp. 639-44. Index, pp. 645-55.

A text for a one-year course in econometrics for graduates and undergraduates who have knowledge of intermediate economic theory, basic calculus, and descriptive statistics. Also useful as a reference for economists of all specializations, who want to keep up with current applied economic research. Last two chapters require knowledge of matrix algebra. Consists of two parts: "Basic Statistical Theory" and "Basic Econometric Theory." Topics include random variables and their distributions; theoretical derivations of sampling distributions; tests of hypotheses; distributed lag models; point and interval estimation; simple and multiple linear and nonlinear regression; autocorrelation; multicollinearity; specification errors; pooling of cross-section and time series data; simultaneous equation methods; two- and three-stage least squares; and the identification problem. Chapters conclude with exercises.

Koehler, Gary J.; Whinston, Andrew B.; and Wright, Gordon P., eds. OPTIMIZATION OVER LEONTIEF SUBSTITUTION SYSTEMS. Amsterdam: North-Holland, 1975. x, 221 p. References, pp. 209-16. Subject Index, pp. 217-19. Author Index, pp. 220-21.

A monograph on matrix iterative procedures (supersparse) for solving large scale mathematical programming problems with economic applications. Advantages of such iterative procedures include control of rounding errors, absence of inverse, and the detection and elimination of sub-optimal variables as the solution progresses. Topics include hidden Leontief systems; recursive integral solutions over Leontief substitution systems, and concave minization over Leontief substitution systems. Addressed to anyone interested in the solutions of large scale linear programming problems and who have some expertise in dynamic programming and stochastic control.

Koopmans, Tyalling C. STATISTICAL INFERENCE IN DYNAMIC MODELS. Introduction by J. Marschak. Cowles Foundation, monograph 10. New York: Wiley, 1950. xiv, 438 p. References, pp. 423-28. Index, pp. 429-38.

A collection of nineteen essays dealing with the formulation, identification, and estimation of economic models grouped under the following headings: "Simultaneous Equation Systems in which the Problem of Identification and Estimation are Considered"; "Problems Specific to Time Series"; and "Specification of Hypotheses."

Koutsoyiannis, A. THEORY OF ECONOMETRICS: AN INTRODUCTORY EXPOSITION OF ECONOMETRIC METHODS. Foreword by C.F. Carter. New York: Harper & Row, 1973. 601 p. Appendix I: Elements of Statistical Theory, pp. 503-62. Appendix II: Determinants and the Solution of Systems of Equations, pp. 563-76. Appendix III: Statistical Tables, pp. 577-86. Bibliography, pp. 587-95. Index, pp. 597-601

A text for an introductory course in econometrics for students who have knowledge of high school algebra and basic statistics. Emphasizes economic aspects with the assumptions and their economic meaning treated in great detail. Consists of three parts: "Correlation Theory: The Simple Linear Regression Model"; "Econometric Problems: Second-Order Tests of the Assumptions of the Linear Regression Model"; and "Models of Simultaneous Equations." Matrix algebra omitted and proofs presented in small print. Topics include autocorrelation, multicollinearity, errors in variables, dummy variables, identification, maximum likelihood, three-stage least squares; and Monte Carlo studies. Chapters conclude with exercises.

Lange, Oskar. INTRODUCTION TO ECONOMETRICS. New York: Pergamon, 1959. 384 p. Appendix I: On the Dependence Between Accumulation and Growth of Production by K. Porwit, pp. 384-68. Appendix II: Input-Output

Tables, pp. 369-72. References, pp. 373-77. Index, pp. 379-82. Content, pp. 383-84.

Based on lectures presented at the University of Warsaw. Emphasizes econometric methods useful in the socialistic economy for planning and management. Topics include forecasting business conditions, including seasonal fluctuations; market analysis, including statistical methods for determining demand and supply curves; input-output analysis, including dynamic analysis; and linear programming. Presentation not rigorous mathematically but knowledge of matrix algebra, calculus, and econometric methods helpful for thorough understanding. Most applications taken from the Polish economy.

Leser, Conrad Emanuel Victor. ECONOMETRIC TECHNIQUES AND PROBLEMS. Griffin's Statistical Monographs and Courses, no. 20. New York: Hafner, 1966. viii, 119 p. References, pp. 113-16. Index, pp. 117-19.

A monograph devoted to an introduction to econometrics. Topics include heteroscedasticity; serial correlation of errors; errors in variables; multicollinearity; reduced form equations; two-stage least squares; and applications to production functions, demand analysis (using budget data), consumption function, and medium-size macro models of an economy. Emphasizes reasoning and the underlying assumptions of the methods, rather than mathematical rigor, with numerical examples based on actual data. Assumes knowledge of elementary statistical theory, such as random variables, standard errors, hypothesis testing, and regression analysis. Includes exercises.

Łoś, M.W.; Łoś, J.; and Wieczorek, A., eds. WARSAW FALL SEMINARS IN MATHEMATICAL ECONOMICS 1975. Lecture Notes in Economics and Mathematical Systems, 133. New York: Springer-Verlag, 1976. 159 p. No index.

Ten contributions on mathematical models in economics presented at a seminar of the Polish Academy of Sciences in the fall of 1975. Topics include an open von Neumann model with consumption; existence of von Neumann equilibrium; von Neumann models of open economies; quasi-Leontief models; coalition games without players; and Lagrange multipliers for the problem of stochastic programming.

Madansky, Albert. FOUNDATIONS OF ECONOMETRICS. Advanced Textbooks in Economics, vol. 7. New York: Elsevier, 1976. viii, 266 p. Index, pp. 125-66.

A theoretical text for a one-year graduate course in econometrics for students with substantial background in linear algebra, statistics, and calculus. Presentation confined to derivations, proofs of theorems, and verbal discussions of the concepts, with no illustrations or applications. Provides an understanding of the basis for the techniques learned in a first course in econometrics. Topics include matrix theory; multivariate statistical analysis; hypothesis testing theory; linear expected value models; simultaneous equation estimation; and a brief discussion of econometric modelbuilding. Also includes a new notation for simultaneous equation models. Chapters conclude with references.

Maddala, G.S. ECONOMETRICS. Economics Handbook Series. New York: McGraw-Hill, 1977. xii, 516 p. Appendix A: Matrix Algebra, pp. 434-47. Appendix B: The Linear Model in Matrix Notation, pp. 448-69. Appendix C: Simultaneous Equation Models, pp. 470-92. Appendix D: Some Exercises, pp. 493-502. Appendix E: Tables, pp. 503-11. Index, pp. 513-16.

A text for undergraduates and graduates who have knowledge of differential and integral calculus, and a reference for applied econometricians in government and industry. Consists of four parts: "Introduction"; "Introduction to Probability and Statistical Inference"; "Introduction to Econometric Methods"; and "Further Discussions of Selected Topics." Strikes a balance between theory and empirical applications, with proofs and algebraic details contained in the appendixes. Comprehensive and includes topics not found in other texts, including proxy variables; limited and dummy dependent variables; missing observations and aggregation problems; analysis of grouped data; pooling of cross section and time series data; aggregation over time; Hannan's estimator and Shiller's method in distributed lag models; forecasting; varying parameter models; and Bayesian inference. Matrix notation relegated largely to the appendixes. Chapters conclude with exercises.

Malvinvaud, E. STATISTICAL METHODS OF ECONOMETRICS. Translation by Mrs. A. Silvey. Studies in Mathematical and Managerial Economics, vol. 6. Chicago: Rand McNally, 1966. xvi, 631 p. References, pp. 615-26. Subject Index, pp. 627-28. Author Index, pp. 629-31.

Originally published by Dunod, Paris, 1964. A theory-oriented text for a graduate course in econometrics for students who have knowledge of probability, calculus, and mathematical statistics. Proofs usually included with detailed guidance on practical applications. General theories of estimation and testing omitted since they appear in general textbooks on mathematical statistics. Consists of five parts: "Introduction"; "Linear Estimation"; "Two Important Stochastic Models"; "Fitting Time Series"; and "Simultaneous Equation Models." Topics include simple and multiple regression; the consumption function; analysis of variance and covariance; errors in the variables; linear filters; autocorrelation; distributed lag models; multicollinearity; identification two-stage least squares; recursive models; principle component analysis; and limited information estimation.

Meyer, Donald L., and Collier, Raymond O., Jr. BAYESIAN STATISTICS. Ninth Annual Phi Delta Kappa Symposium on Educational Research. Itasca, Ill.: F.E. Peacock, 1970. xii, 138 p. References, pp. 127-32. Index, pp. 133-38.

Five papers presented at a symposium held in Syracuse, New York, on January 12, 1968. Topics include contrasts between Bayesian and classical inference in the analysis of variance; Bayesian analysis in regression; discriminatory practices; and frequency theory of probability, Bayes' theorem, and sequential trials. Knowledge of mathematical statistics helpful. Emphasizes verbal description and numerical examples.

Murphy, James L. INTRODUCTORY ECONOMETRICS. Homewood, Ill.: Irwin, 1973. xii, 524 p. Appendixes of Tables and Symbols, pp. 498-511. Index, pp. 515-24.

A text for a one-semester course in econometrics for graduates and undergraduates in economics, as well as in geography, city and regional planning, sociology, psychology, and political science who have knowledge of the rudiments of calculus, matrix algebra, and intermediate statistics. Style conversational, with much repetition of subject matter, and with chapters that vary in length and technical details. Emphasizes applied econometrics in estimating and testing linear models, proceeding from the simple regression model, to multiple regression models with a general variance-covariance matrix of distributions, to a simultaneous equations econometric model. Other topics include stepwise regression, multicollinearity, autocorrelation, generalized least squares, dummy variables, distributed lags, identification, and two-stage least squares. Numerical examples selected as an aid in explaining econometric methods, rather than the results of economic theory. Chapters conclude with exercises.

Neeleman, D. MULTICOLLINEARITY IN LINEAR ECONOMIC MODELS. Foreword by J.J.J. Dalmulder. Tilburg Studies in Economics, 7. A Study on Econometrics. Tilburg, The Netherlands: Academic Book Service, for Tilburg University Press, 1973. viii, 103 p. Appendix A, pp. 90-97. Appendix B, pp. 98-99. Literature, pp. 100-103.

A theoretical study of multicollinearity in linear multiple equation models which proposes, in the case of nonperfect multicollinearity, the approximation of the full-rank (though ill-conditioned) matrices by good-conditioned ones of the desired rank. Proposed method leads to two closely related solutions; the estimation of stable linear combinations of coefficients, or the dropping of the unbiasedness assumption and working instead with minimum variance minimum bias estimators. Procedure compares favorably with two-stage least square estimators in a two-equation Monte-Carlo simulation. Appendix A gives a short review of generalized inverse, and Appendix B derives three properties of the Kronecker product of matrices.

Pindyck, Robert S., and Rubinfeld, Daniel L. ECONOMETRIC MODELS AND ECONOMIC FORECASTS. New York: McGraw-Hill, 1976. xix, 576 p. Statistical Tables, pp. 551-56. Solutions to Selected Problems, pp. 557-68. Indexes, pp. 569-76.

A text for introductory courses in econometrics, business forecasting, and quantitative methods for policy analysis for a varied group of undergraduates and graduates who have knowledge of calculus (no matrix algebra) and a good background in basic statistics. Most chapters have appendixes devoted to reviews of mathematics and statistics. Consists of three parts. Part I, "Single-Equation Regression Models," considers simple and multiple regression, including multicollinearity, heteroscedasticity, errors in variables, two-stage least squares, Zellner's estimation in matrix form, distributed lags, and pooling of cross-section and time-series data. Part II, "Multi-Equation Simulation Models," includes simultaneous equation estimation, dynamic behavior of simulation models, an industry-wide econometric model, and a model for corporate financial planning. Part III, "Time Series Models," consider properties of stochastic time series, linear time series models, estimation and forecasting, and examples of time series applications in inventories, forecasting seasonal telephone data, short-term interest rates, and savings deposit flows. Emphasizes the science and art of model building and forecasting, rather than theory, using a wide variety of numerical examples. Chapters conclude with exercises.

Pitchford, John D., and Turnovsky, Stephen J., eds. APPLICATIONS OF CONTROL THEORY TO ECONOMIC ANALYSIS. Contributions to Economic Analysis, 101. New York: Elsevier, 1977. xii, 363 p. No index.

Twelve heretofore unpublished studies on theoretical problems encountered in practical economic research grouped under the following two headings: "Non-Linear Models" (eight studies); and "Linear Stabilization Models" (four studies). Papers illustrate the wide range of applications of control theory to economic problems, some incorporating difference and differential equations. Topics include resource depletion with possible non-convexities in production; two-state variable problem; optimal control theorems; optimal exploitation and replenishment of a natural resource; the adjustment cost problem with jumps in the state variable; existence, uniqueness, and stability of linear optimal stabilization policies; and optimal control of linear systems with stochastic coefficients and additive disturbances.

Rao, Potluri, and Miller, Roger LeRoy. APPLIED ECONOMETRICS. Belmont, Calif.: Wadsworth, 1971. x, 235 p. Special References, p. 221. Tables, pp. 222-30. Index, pp. 231-35.

A text for an introductory econometrics course with emphasis on explanation of the applied aspects, with few numerical examples, rather than theory. Derivations kept to a minimum. Verbal description employed freely. Topics include simple and multiple regression; dummy variables; time as a trend variable; analysis of residuals, including heteroscedasticity; hypothesis testing in regression; lagged variables; autocorrelation; errors in variables; simultaneous equations; indirect least squares; and two-stage least squares.

Richard, Jean Francois. POSTERIOR AND PREDICTIVE DENSITIES FOR SIMULTANEOUS EQUATION MODEL. Lecture Notes in Economics and Mathematical Systems, vol. 90. New York: Springer-Verlag, 1973. vi, 226 p. References, pp. 223-26. No index.

A monograph which shows how to perform a full information analysis of the two-equation, simultaneous equation model under a reasonably flexible prior density. Posterior analysis for both the structural and the reduced form coefficients obtained, and procedure for computing predictive moments outlined.

Rowley, J.C.R. ECONOMETRIC ESTIMATION. Foreword by S.G.B. Henry. London School of Economics Handbook in Economic Analysis. New York: Wiley, 1973. viii, 234 p. Appendix I: The Partitioned Inverse, pp. 226-28. Appendix 2: Idempotent Matrices, pp. 229-30. Index, pp. 232-34.

A text for a one-semester course in theoretical econometrics for graduates and undergraduates who are familiar with mathematical statistics and matrix algebra. Covers the main problems encountered in estimating the parameters of single equations or individual equations from larger systems. Concerned with derivations and explanation of results, with little emphasis on numerical examples. Topics include classical linear model; generalized linear model, including first-difference transformation and autoregressive processes; interdependent systems and identification; indirect least squares and two-stage least squares; maximum likelihood (single equation) estimation; stepwise least-squares; method of least lines; and distributed lags. Chapters conclude with references.

Schmidt, Peter. ECONOMETRICS. Statistics: Textbooks and Monographs, vol. 18. New York: Marcel Dekker, 1976. vi, 269 p. Appendix A1: Convergence of Random Variables, pp. 249-50. Appendix A2: Estimation Theory, pp. 251-56. Appendix A3: Central Limit Theorems, pp. 257-59. Notes, p. 260. References, p. 261. Author Index, p. 263. Subject Index, pp. 265-69.

A supplementary text for graduate studies and a reference for research workers who have knowledge of calculus, matrix algebra, and classical statistics. Consists of a collection of econometric results with proofs, except for the appendixes which give results from statistics without proofs. Topics include least squares; generalized least squares; multicollinearity; asymptotically uncooperative regressions; autoregressive models; instrumental variables; errors in variables; reduced form; identification; indirect least squares; two-stage least squares; limited information maximum likelihood; three-stage least squares; full information likelihood; and the derived reduced form. Chapters conclude with references, notes, and exercises. Numerical examples omitted.

Streissler, Erich W. PITFALLS IN ECONOMETRIC FORECASTING. Research Monograph, no. 23. Westminster, Engl.: Institute for Economic Affairs, 1970. 80 p. Further Reading, pp. 75-80. No index.

A critic on the use of econometric models for macroeconomic forecasting. Deals with two dangers of forecasts; forecasting in areas not amenable to forecasts, and treating econometric forecasts as inspired guesses. Considers the large forecasting error when going beyond the limits of the data, and the problems of formulating exact mathematical relations of complex social systems.

Sullins, Walter L. MATRIX ALGEBRA FOR STATISTICAL APPLICATIONS. Danville, Ill.: Interstate, 1973. viii, 108 p. Exercises, pp. 97-103. References, pp. 105-6. Index, pp. 107-8.

A supplementary text for statistics courses, a self-study, or a text for a short course in applied matrix algebra for advanced students or research workers in the behavioral, social, biological, and physical sciences. Emphasizes applications of matrix algebra in multiple regression, factor analysis, discriminant analysis, multivariate analysis of variance, and canonical analysis. Development intuitive and rigorous proofs included only when they aid in understanding for applications. Assumes knowledge of algebra and basic statistics.

Surrey, M.J.C. AN INTRODUCTION TO ECONOMETRICS. London: Oxford University Press, 1974. 77 p. Statistical Tables, pp. 72-76. Index, p. 77.

A brief account of the main aspects of classical regression analysis without using matrix algebra. Intended for students who wish to pursue econometrics in greater depth later, and working economists who wish to know something about econometrics without becoming expert econometricians. Presentation limited to two and three variable models with extensions. Derivations, such as normal equations, included. Topics include simple and multiple regression, hypothesis testing and prediction, multicollinearity, principal components, errors in variables, heteroscedasticity, autocorrelation, distributed lags, identification, indirect least squares, and two-stage least squares. Chapters conclude with references.

Theil, Henri. PRINCIPLES OF ECONOMETRICS. New York: Wiley, 1971. xxx, 736 p. Appendix A: Elements of Consumer Demand Theory, pp. 674-78. Appendix B: Derivation of the Limited-Information Maximum-Likelihood Estimation, pp. 679-86. Bibliography, pp. 687-715. Tables, pp. 717-29. Index, pp. 731-36.

A text for a one-year course in theoretical econometrics for students who have knowledge of mathematical statistics and matrix algebra. Topics include review of matrix algebra and mathematical statistics; least squares and the standard linear model; partial and multiple correlation; statistical analysis of distributions; generalized least squares and linear constraints; combination of several linear relations; asymptotic distribution theory, including asymptotic properties of estimators; simultaneous equations models; including two- and three-stage least squares; full-information maximum likelihood; limited-information maximum likelihood; specification and aggregation analysis; robust and distribution free procedures; probit analysis and logit analysis; Bayesian inference; and specific econometric models. Derivations extensive, verbal discussion accompanies the formulas, and graphs and illustrations used freely. Chapters conclude with problems.

______. STATISTICAL DECOMPOSITION ANALYSIS: WITH APPLICATIONS IN THE SOCIAL AND ADMINISTRATIVE SCIENCES. Studies in Mathematical and Managerial Economics, vol. 14. New York: Elsevier, 1972. xvi, 337 p. Bibliography, pp. 325-28. Hints for Selected Problems, pp. 329-32. Index, pp. 333-37.

A text and reference on applications of statistical decomposition to a variety of problems in economics, management science, regional science, sociology, political science, accounting, and other areas for students who have knowledge of calculus and elementary mathematical statistics. Matrix algebra used in chapter 5 on Markov chain applications to social mobility. Topics include information and dividedness in racial integration, industrial diversity and the combining of assets on balance sheets; extensions to decomposition in racial composition in Chicago's public schools, industrial diversity of American cities; and income inequality; multidimensional extensions; and decompositions and their determining factors. Emphasis on verbal description, and on numerical and graphic illustrations. Chapters conclude with problems on further applications and derivations.

Tintner, Gerhard. ECONOMETRICS. A Wiley Publication in Economics. New York: Wiley, 1952. xiii, 370 p. Appendix A1: Elements of Matrices and Determinants, pp. 331-41. Appendix A2: Methods of Numerical Computation, pp. 342-58. Index of Names, pp. 359-63. Index of Subjects, pp. 364-70.

A survey of the statistical aspects of econometrics for students having a background in economic theory, calculus, and mathematical statistics. Consists of three parts: "A Non-technical Introduction to Econometrics"; "Introduction to Multivariate Analysis"; and "Some Topics in Time Series Analysis." Topics include regression analysis; discriminant analysis; principal components; canonical correlations; identification; orthogonal polynomials; periodogram analysis; autocorrelation; ratio of mean square successive difference to the variance; stochastic difference and differential equations; transformation of observations; and correlogram analysis.

______. THE VARIATE DIFFERENCE METHOD. Cowles Commission, monograph, no. 5. Bloomington, Ind.: Principia Press, 1940. xiii, 175 p. Appendix I: Summary of Computations, pp. 133-35. Appendix II: Mathematical Notes, pp. 136-49. Appendix III: Seasonal Variation, pp. 150-52. Appendix IV: The Standard Errors of Some Derived Statistical Series, pp. 153-54. Appendix V: Alternative Methods, pp. 155-60. Appendix VI: The Variability of the Random Variance Through Time, pp. 161-64. Appendix VII: The Normality of the Random Element, pp. 165-67. Index of Authors, pp. 171-72. Index of Subjects, pp. 173-75.

A contribution to the analysis of the random element of economic time series. Takes up review of concepts; calculation of variances of finite difference series; standard error of the difference between the variances of two consecutive series of finite differences; criteria for stability and tests of significance for the variances of the series of finite differences; and reduction of the random variation by Sheppards's smoothing formulas. Useful as a reference to mathematical economists and statisticians.

Valavanis, Stefan. Edited from a manuscript by Alfred H. Conrad. ECONOMETRICS: AN INTRODUCTION TO MAXIMUM LIKELIHOOD METHODS. Economics Handbook Series. New York: McGraw-Hill, 1959. xv, 223 p. Appendixes A to E, pp. 197-215. Index, pp. 217-23.

A reference and supplementary text in econometrics with emphasis on maximum likelihood and limited information techniques of estimation rather than hypothesis testing. Introduces concepts by means of examples with emphasis on limitations and criteria for estimation. Excludes formal proofs. Topics include least squares; bias in models of decay; pitfalls in simultaneous interdependence; many-equation linear models; identification; instrumental variables; Theil's method of reduced form; models not exactly identified; partial correlation; bunch map analysis; linear vs. ratio models; testing for linearity; unspecified variables; testing orthogonality; factor analysis and analysis of variance; and time series, including serial correlation, correlograms, autoregression, leading indicators, and cross-section and time series estimates. Appendixes devoted to stepwise regression, proof of least squares bias, completeness and stochastic independence, subsample variance as estimators, and layout of computations.

Van Arkadie, Brian, and Frank, Charles R., Jr. With the Assistance of Clifford Russell. ECONOMIC ACCOUNTING AND DEVELOPMENT PLANNING: AN INTRODUCTION TO GENERAL PRINCIPLES OF ACCOUNTING, INPUT-OUTPUT TABLES, AND NATIONAL INCOME ACCOUNTS AND THEIR APPLICATION TO PLANNING ECONOMIC DEVELOPMENT WITH SPECIAL REFERENCE TO THE PROBLEMS OF TROPICAL AFRICA. Vol. II in the Series of Undergraduate Teaching Works in Economics Being Developed at Makerere College, University of East Africa. New York: Oxford University Press, 1966. xiv, 390 p. Index of Names, pp. 389-90.

An introduction to a number of accounting approaches to national income accounts in four parts: "Basic Principles of Accounting"; "Inter-Industry Analysis"; "National Accounts"; and "Planning and Economic Accounting." Topics include input-output tables for developing countries; national accounts in African countries; balance of payments accounts; measurement of capital stock; and linear programming model of the planning process. Compares the various accounting approaches, emphasizing problems in developing countries. Useful as a text for economic theory courses for undergraduates interested in problems of African countries. Examples of balance of payments, input-output tables, and national accounts include East Africa, Ghana, Uganda, Nigeria, Rhodesia, Tanganyika, and Zambia.

Wallis, Kenneth F. INTRODUCTORY ECONOMETRICS. Lectures in Economics, 2. Chicago: Aldine, 1972. viii, 124 p. Review Problems, pp. 117-18. Outline Solutions, pp. 119-24.

A text for an introductory econometrics course for students possessing knowledge of matrix algebra and elementary statistics. Encourages an appreciation of the problems of empirical measurement of economic relationships and of the techniques of solving them, rather than the statistical theory underlying the techniques. Numerical examples omitted. Topics include dynamic systems, including lagged models and others that can be represented by difference equations; identification problem; reduced form; and estimation, including autocorrelation, indirect least squares, recursive systems, and instrumental variables. Chapters conclude with exercises.

Walters, A.A. AN INTRODUCTION TO ECONOMETRICS. 2d ed. New York: Macmillan, 1968. 377 p. Selected Bibliography, pp. 370-74. Index, pp. 375-77.

An introduction to statistics and econometrics for students who wish to acquire a working knowledge of econometrics as an aid to applied economics. Assumes knowledge of basic statistics, and calculus. Consists of four parts: "Methodology, Probability and Sampling"; "Regression and Correlation"; "Econometric Models"; and "Application." Topics include statistical inference; probability; identification; equation systems; consumer expenditures and elasticities; and econometric studies of production, including the Cobb-Douglas production function. Multiple regression limited to three variable single-equations and no matrix algebra is used. Emphasizes the use of U.K. data in the numerical examples. Chapters conclude with questions for discussion.

Wynn, R.F., and Holden, K. AN INTRODUCTION TO APPLIED ECONOMETRIC ANALYSIS. New York: Wiley, Halsted Press, 1974. x, 245 p. Author Index, pp. 239-41. Subject Index, pp. 242-45.

A text for a course in applied econometrics for advanced undergraduates who have knowledge of elementary economic theory, basic statistics, algebra, calculus, introductory econometrics, and matrix algebra. Includes a review of econometric techniques, and applications in investment, production function, wage-price models, specification and related issues in macro-economic models, and preparation and analysis of forecasts. Models discussed include Cobb-Douglas and C.E.S., Phillips curve, Klein III, Klein-Goldberger II, Canadian model IX, the Dutch forecasting and policy model, the Michigan RSQE model, and the Wharton and Brookings models. Chapters conclude with references.

Yotopoulos, Pan A., and Nugent, Jeffrey B. ECONOMICS OF DEVELOPMENT: EMPIRICAL INVESTIGATIONS. New York: Harper & Row, 1976. xxiii, 478 p. Bibliography and Author Index, pp. 431-57. Index, pp. 459-78.

A text for a one-year course in economic development for graduates and undergraduates who have knowledge of calculus and econometric techniques. Consists of six parts: "Introduction"; "Development Statics"; "Development Dynamics"; "Development Disequilibrium: International Trade and Growth"; "Development Disequilibrium: Sectoral Articulation and Structure"; and "Development Disequilibrium: Planning." Topics include Rostow's stage theory; application of factor analysis to the identification of stages; Cobb-Douglas production functions; linear programming production functions; diagonal regression model for errors-in-variables relationships; general equilibrium analysis of welfare; technical change; human capital; measurement of surplus labor; the Gini coefficient and other measures of inequality; estimates of structural equations of the general equilibrium model for the household sector; determinants of commodity composition of exports; and practical approaches to project evaluation. Emphasizes deriving equations and estimating parameters from numerical data.

Zellner, Arnold. AN INTRODUCTION TO BAYESIAN INFERENCE IN ECONOMETRICS. Wiley Series in Probability and Mathematical Statistics. New York: Wiley, 1971. xv, 431 p. Appendix A: Properties of Several Important Univariate Probability Distribution Functions, pp. 363-78. Appendix B: Properties of Some Multivariate Probability Distribution Functions, pp. 379-99. Appendix C: FORTRAN Programs for Numerical Integration, pp. 400-14. Bibliography, pp. 415-25. Subject Index, pp. 427-31.

A text for a graduate course in Bayesian influence in econometrics for students who have knowledge of probability theory, calculus, matrix algebra, and econometrics. Topics include Bayesian approach in scientific inference; application of Bayesian analysis to simple problems; Bayesian analysis of models often encountered in econometrics with emphasis on estimation; problems of comparing and testing hypotheses; and control problems. Presentation rigorous consisting of proofs with few numerical examples. Chapters conclude with questions and problems.

_____, ed. READINGS IN ECONOMIC STATISTICS AND ECONOMETRICS. Boston: Little, Brown, 1968. xiv, 718 p. No index.

Twenty-nine previously published articles and other works on applied econometrics grouped under the following headings: "Problems of Economic Measurement" (five articles); "Analyses of Consumer Behavior" (eight articles); "Aspects of Firm Behavior" (nine articles); and "Econometric Models of Economies" (seven articles). Topics include seasonal adjustment of price indexes; additive preferences; cross-section analysis; permanent-income hypothesis; life-cycle theory of savings; specification and estimation of Cobb-Douglas production function models, technical change; returns to scale in electricity supply; determinants of business investments; forecasting with an econometric model; and dynamic properties of the Klein-Goldberger model.

Chapter 17

ECONOMETRICS—STUDIES AND ANALYSES

Aber, John W. BETA COEFFICIENTS AND MODELS OF SECURITY RETURN. Lexington, Mass.: Heath, Lexington Books, 1973. xv, 90 p. Appendix: The Unconditional Distribution of r, p. 87. References, pp. 89-90. No index.

> Develops linear multi-index assessment models of security returns and examines them with respect to two major assumptions: that index parameters exhibit temporal stability, and that the indexes account for all the dependencies among security returns whose distribution is under analysis. Estimates six index coefficients by least squares, each set corresponding to one of six regression models, for each of seventy-five stocks. Employs monthly data from July 1962 to June 1969.

Adams, F. Gerard, and Behrman, Jere R. ECONOMETRIC MODELS OF WORLD AGRICULTURAL COMMODITY MARKETS: COCOA, COFFEE, TEA, WOOL, COTTON, SUGAR, WHEAT, RICE. Cambridge, Mass.: Ballinger, 1976. xi, 160 p. Appendix A: List of Variables, pp. 114-26. Appendix B: Data, pp. 127-37. Appendix C: Charts of Dynamic Simulations, pp. 139-56. Bibliography, pp. 157-60. No index.

> Develops a common econometric model for eight agricultural commodity markets consisting of supply and demand relations, world inventory relation, and a world price determination relation with applications to each of three subgroups of countries--developed, developing, and centrally planned. Each model consists of eight equations (if a commodity is not produced in all three regions, the number of equations is less than eight). Estimated by ordinary least squares using annual data from 1956 to 1973.

Adams, F. Gerard, and Behrman, Jere R., eds. ECONOMETRIC MODELING OF WORLD COMMODITY POLICY. Wharton Econometric Studies Series. Lexington: Lexington Books, 1978. viii, 227 p. About the Contributors, pp. 225-26. About the Editors, p. 227. No index.

> Eight heretofore unpublished contributions on commodity modeling for policy analysis with emphasis on the evaluation of alternative approaches to commodity market stabilization. Topics

include theory of supply and demand; price determination; specification equations; elasticities; estimation of market models; optimal control methods; application of econometric models; policy evaluation with an econometric model of coffee; stochastic simulations; econometric models covering ten commodities to appraise the cost of UNCTAD "Integrated Programme," and bibliography on commodity modeling.

Adams, F. Gerard; Eguchi, H.; and Meyer-Zu-Schlochtern, F. AN ECONOMETRIC ANALYSIS OF INTERNATIONAL TRADE: AN INTERRELATED EXPLANATION OF IMPORTS AND EXPORTS OF OECD COUNTRIES. Paris: OECD, 1969. 143 p. Appendix A: Charts, pp. 63-103. Appendix B: Data, pp. 105-43. No index.

A monograph which presents multiple regression models of imports and exports for each of nine OECD countries using quarterly data for the period 1955-65. Extensions to other OECD countries and non-OECD countries made. Equations for the individual countries combined into a single simultaneous equation model of trade and income flows. The parameters are estimated and their implications for policy considered.

Adams, F. Gerard, and Klein, Sonia A., eds. STABILIZING WORLD COMMODITY MARKETS: ANALYSIS, PRACTICE, AND POLICY. Lexington, Mass.: Heath, Lexington Books, 1978. xvii, 335 p. Index, pp. 323-35.

Sixteen papers presented at a conference held at Airlie, Virginia, March 17-20, 1977, under sponsorship of the Ford Foundation. Papers grouped under the following headings: "Modeling World Commodity Markets" (five papers); "Theoretical Considerations of Commodity Market Stabilization" (four papers); "Economics, Political, and Institutional Considerations in Commodity Policy" (three papers); and "Integrated Commodity Stabilization Programs" (four papers). Topics include simulation of market intervention in coffee markets; simulation of international rice buffer stock operation; potentials of econometrics for commodity stabilization policy analysis; commodity instability and market failure; producers' associations; commodity agreements; and an alternative common fund proposal. Assumes knowledge of econometrics.

Agarwala, Ramgopal. AN ECONOMETRIC MODEL OF INDIA 1948-1961. Foreword by R.J. Ball. London: Frank Cass, 1970. xvi, 188 p. Appendix 1: The Compilation of the Data, pp. 163-74. Bibliography, pp. 175-84. Index, pp. 185-88.

Presents a macro model of the Indian economy using time series from 1948-49 to 1960-61 with emphasis on the relationship between the agricultural and nonagricultural sectors and in particular, on the problem of the transfer of food surplus from agriculture to the rest of the economy. Consists of twenty-four equations and forty-four variables, including twenty predetermined or exogenous. Includes seven constraints (identities) and seventeen behavioral equations. Cobb-Douglas type production function used and past and present incomes of India assumed to be the most important determinant of private investment. Model used to simulate the Indian economy in order to test various policy instruments. Estimated by ordinary least squares, two-stage least squares, and limited information maximum likelihood methods. Knowledge of econometric techniques comparable to J. Johnston, ECONOMETRIC METHODS (McGraw-Hill, 1972) helpful.

Al-Bashir, Faisal Safooq. A STRUCTURAL ECONOMETRIC MODEL OF THE SAUDI ARABIAN ECONOMY: 1960-1970. New York: Wiley, 1977. x, 134 p. Statistical Appendix, pp. 94-121. References, pp. 122-25. Index, pp. 127-34.

A twenty-five equation simultaneous equation model of the Saudi Arabian economy containing twenty-five endogenous variables and nineteen predetermined variables. Estimated by ordinary least squares and two-stage least squares using time series from 1959 to 1975. Forecasting of the 1971 variables also included.

Allen, R.I.G., and Gossling, W.F., eds. ESTIMATING AND PROJECTING INPUT-OUTPUT COEFFICIENTS. Foreword by I.G. Stewart. London: Input-Output, 1975. xvii, 104 p. References, pp. 99-102. Index, pp. 103-4.

Five papers presented at several input-output seminars held at Edinburgh University and the University of East Anglia in 1971 on the biproportional method of revising and projecting (updating) input-output relationships over time using a minimum of information. Method also compared to various other methods such as the ex ante approach which utilizes expert knowledge and judgement rather than precise statistics. A sixth paper analyzes the technological assumptions in U.K. input-output tables.

Amstutz, Arnold E. COMPUTER SIMULATION OF COMPETITIVE MARKET RESPONSE. Cambridge: MIT Press, 1967. xii, 457 p. Index, pp. 445-57.

Develops and implements a behavioral theory of market interaction based on computer simulation with applications in consumer and industrial product markets. Includes simulation models of consumer behavior, retail behavior, distribution behavior, salesman behavior, and the marketing manager. Model constructed in four steps: description of factors in the marketing environment; design of gross macroflow models encompassing previously defined elements and processes; quantification of relevant behavior and development sector models; and validating simulation performance against data obtained from the actual environment. Simulation models useful in undergraduate, graduate, and executive development courses in marketing management and market-oriented information systems. Assumes knowledge of FORTRAN programming.

Artle, Roland. THE STRUCTURE OF THE STOCKHOLM ECONOMY: TOWARD A FRAMEWORK FOR PROJECTING METROPOLITAN COMMUNITY DEVELOPMENT. Foreword to the Swedish edition by Folke Kristersson. Foreword to the American edition by Barclay G. Jones. Ithaca, New York: Cornell University Press, 1965. xlii, 197 p. Appendix 1: Definition of the Stockholm Area, pp. 140-41. Appendix 2: The Intersectoral Flow Datum Table: Definitional and Computational Procedures, pp. 142-65. Appendix 3: Special Estimates and Compilation, pp. 166-70. Appendix 4: Tables, pp. 171-77. References, pp. 178-91. Name Index, pp. 193. Subject Index, pp. 195-97.

A reprint of a work originally published in Sweden under the title STUDIES IN THE STRUCTURE OF THE STOCKHOLM ECONOMY (Stockholm Business Research Institute, Stockholm School of Economics, 1959). Combines the traditional methods of national and regional accounting with the concepts of input-output analysis to develop a detained balance of payments accounts for an urban region as well as to assess Stockholm's contribution to Swedish national income. Concludes with a probabilistic approach to the study of locational distribution using standard regression analysis and a random technique for studying the location of certain kinds of business firms in the Stockholm region.

Askin, A. Bradley, and Kraft, John. ECONOMETRIC WAGE AND PRICE MODELS: ASSESSING THE IMPACT OF THE ECONOMIC STABILIZATION PROGRAM. Lexington, Mass.: Heath, 1974. xi, 152 p. Appendix A: Definition of Variables, pp. 107-11. Appendix B: Sources of Data, pp. 113-16. Appendix C: Correlation Matrices for Wage and Price Equations, pp. 117-25. Appendix D: Preliminary Estimates of Alternative CPA Wage and Price Equations, pp. 127-31. Appendix E: Additional Tables Related to Chapter 6 Evaluation of the 90-Day Freeze and Phase II, pp. 133-41. Appendix F: Data Used to Forecast 1973 and 1974 Wage and Price Changes in Chapter 7 Simulations, pp. 143-44. Notes, pp. 145-48. References, pp. 149-52. No index.

An analysis of the estimates of wages and prices of three recently published models using quarterly data for the private nonfarm economy from 1955 to 1971. Models include the distributed lag adjustment model by R.J. Gordon; the imposed lag adjustment model of O. Eckstein and R. Brinner; and the current period adjustment model by C. Siebert and M. Zaidi. Includes the following for each model: the wage and price equations; empirical estimates using ordinary least squares; simulation of the model over the period; and the solutions of the long run Phillips curve implied by the model. Concludes with an evaluation of the results of the 90-day wage-price freeze and phase-II of the Economic Stabilization Program.

Bain, Andrew David. THE GROWTH OF TELEVISION OWNERSHIP IN THE UNITED KINGDOM SINCE THE WAR: A LOGNORMAL MODEL. University of Cambridge, Department of Applied Economics Monographs, no. 12. New York: Cambridge University Press, 1964. 72 p. References, pp. 70-71. Index, p. 72.

The growth rate in the proportion of households owning a TV set approximated by a cumulative lognormal density function with time as the independent variable. Uses cross-section analysis to investigate the effects of social class and household size on ownership of TV, and time series data to investigate the effects of purchase restrictions, changes in price, and the provision of TV programs. Useful to researchers as an example of a growth model for new durable goods.

Balestra, Piestro. THE DEMAND FOR NATURAL GAS IN THE U.S.: A DYNAMIC APPROACH FOR THE RESIDENTIAL AND COMMERCIAL MARKET. Contributions to Economic Analysis, vol. 46. Amsterdam: North-Holland, 1967. xiv, 153 p. Appendix A: The Effect of the Rate of Growth of Stocks on the Depreciation Rate, pp. 137-43. Appendix B: The Algebra of P-Matrices and its Relation to the Variance-Covariance Matrix of the Residual Model, pp. 144-46. Bibliography, pp. 147-50. Index, pp. 151-53.

Develops both single-equation and two-equation dynamic demand models for natural gas in the residential and commercial sectors of the U.S. economy during 1950-1962 with price, income, and population as the main independent variables. Estimated by ordinary least squares and two stage least squares using both time series and cross-section data (i.e., pooled observations).

Balopoulos, Elias T. FISCAL POLICY MODELS OF THE BRITISH ECONOMY. Introduction by R.J. Ball. Contributions to Economic Analysis, vol. 47. Amsterdam: North-Holland, 1967. xviii, 313 p. Statistical Appendix, pp. 285-99. Bibliography, pp. 301-5. Index, pp. 307-13.

Develops and tests an econometric model of fiscal policy for the United Kingdom consisting of fourteen stochastic equations, three special equations (consumption function, personal income tax liability, and the taxes on expenditure equation) computed outside the model, and eight definitional equations. Relationships determine the values of twenty-five endogenous variables given the values of fourteen instruments of fiscal policy and fifteen predetermined variables. Estimated by two-stage least squares using observations over the period 1949-60. Forecasts made for the years 1958, 1959, and 1961.

Banks, Ferdinand E. THE WORLD COPPER MARKET: AN ECONOMIC ANALYSIS. Cambridge, Mass.: Ballinger, 1974. xvii, 149 p. Appendixes A to E, pp. 125-40. References, pp. 141-43. Index, pp. 145-49.

A monograph on the economics of the world copper market. Topics include production and consumption trends, price trends; structure of ownership in the industry; trade in copper, including copper exchanges and hedging; secondary copper; and costs of production. Single equation regression models formulated to estimate demand adjustments in response to price changes or changes in aggregate variables, inventories, expectations, and supply. Supply equations established for each of several countries (Canada, Chile, France, Peru), and demand equations established for the United States, United Kingdom, France, Germany, Italy, and Japan. Appendixes include additional mathematical developments and derivations.

Baum, Emanuel L.; Heady, Earl O.; and Blackmore, John, eds. METHODOLOGICAL PROCEDURES IN THE ECONOMIC ANALYSIS OF FERTILIZER USE DATA. Foreword by Leland G. Allenbaugh. Ames: Iowa State University Press, 1956. xx, 218 p. Index, pp. 215-18.

Fourteen papers presented at a symposium held in Knoxville, Tenn., in June 1955 under sponsorship of the TVA grouped under the following five headings: "Over-all Methodological Considerations" (two papers); "Fundamental Design and Prediction Problems" (three papers); "Agronomic and Related Considerations in Experiments and Fitting Functions to Existing Data" (four papers); "Applications of Data" (four papers); and "Trends in Use and Manufacture of Fertilizer" (one paper). Topics include discrete and continuous econometric models in agriculture production functions (regression models); discrete models with qualitative restrictions; models and designs for surfaces; fertilizer and moisture variables; fitting functions to data; application of fertilizer production functions; input-output data in farm planning; selecting fertilizer programs by activity analysis; and trends in use and manufacture of fertilizer.

Behrman, Jere R. SUPPLY RESPONSE IN UNDERDEVELOPED AGRICULTURE: A CASE STUDY OF FOUR MAJOR CROPS IN THAILAND, 1937-1963. Contributions to Economic Analysis, vol. 55. Amsterdam: North-Holland, 1968. xx, 446 p. Appendix A: Basic Changwad Data for the Estimation of the Nerlovian Dynamic Total Supply Model, pp. 338-74. Appendix B: Miscellaneous Data, pp. 375-85. Appendix C: Miscellaneous Regression Estimates, pp. 386-411. Appendix D: Other Miscellaneous Statistical Analysis, pp. 412-14. Appendix E: Definitions of Symbols, pp. 415-21. Bibliography, pp. 422-39. Index of Persons to Whom Reference is Made, pp. 440-42. Subject Index, pp. 443-46.

A research report on the responsiveness of four major crops in the agricultural sector of Thailand to various incentives, including malaria control, agricultural population, time of planting and harvesting, and harvest price using a Nerlovian dynamic total supply model. Estimated by reduced form using time series data from 1937 to 1964, and census of population for 1937, 1947, and 1960. Also estimates certain price elasticities. Assumes knowledge of econometric techniques and matrix algebra.

Berger, Laurence B., and Sullivan, Paul R. MEASURING HOSPITAL INFLATION: A COMPOSITE INDEX FOR THE MEASUREMENT AND DETERMINATION OF HOSPITAL COSTS IN THE COMMONWEALTH OF MASSACHUSETTS. Lexington, Mass.: Lexington Books, 1975. xv, 200 p. Appendix A: Member Hospital Survey Report, pp. 77-85. Appendix B: Testing the Index, pp. 87-179. Appendix C: Procedures for Computing Values for the Economic Change Indicators Used in the Composite Index, pp. 181-98. Notes, pp. 199-200. No index.

A report on the development and implementation of a composite index for measuring the effects of inflationary pressures on hospital costs. Index composed of three elements: a set of hospital cost categories; a set of weights to be factored against the individual cost categories; and a set of economic change indicators that appropriately measures the annual rate of inflation (deflation) associated with elements of each cost category. Surveys thirty Massachusetts hospitals to assist in the selection of the following seven cost categories: salaries, wages, fees, and fringe benefits; supplies; utilities; purchased services; depreciation and leased equipment; interest; and other reimbursable costs. Index established a cost threshold, based on unique characteristics of individual hospitals, in which cost beyond the threshold will require justification. Index developed for Blue Cross of Mass., Inc., and the Massachusetts Hospital Association, Inc., under provisions of the Hospital Reimbursement Agreement. Appendix B discusses the validity of the index in fifteen representative Massachusetts hospitals.

Bergstrom, A.R., ed. STATISTICAL INFERENCE IN CONTINUOUS TIME ECONOMIC MODELS. Contribution to Economic Analysis, no. 99. New York: Elsevier, 1976. x, 333 p. Index, pp. 329-33.

Nine papers, five previously published, on the statistical theory of identification and estimation of parameters of a continuous system from discrete observations of the variables. Contributions can be classed into three parts; relatively simple, discrete simultaneous equation models yielding asymptotically biased estimates; methods yielding consistent estimates or asymptotically efficient estimates; and the problem of identification. Concludes with a chapter on fitting a disequilibrium neoclassical growth model to U.K. data. Estimated by two-stage and three-stage least squares.

Bibby, John, and Toutenburg, Helge. PREDICTION AND IMPROVED ESTIMATION IN LINEAR MODELS. Foreword to German Edition by H. Toutenburg. New York: Wiley, 1977. xiii, 188 p. Appendix A: Matrix Algebra, pp. 164-69. Appendix B: Matrix Differentiation, pp. 170-76. Bibliography, pp. 177-82. Index, pp. 183-86. Glossary, pp. 187-88.

Originally published in German. Brings together from widely scattered sources the problems of estimation and prediction using prior restrictions and auxiliary information on the parameters of the model, and the extension of point estimators to estimation regions of various types. Provides a basis for application of the techniques in economics, technology, biology, agriculture, and medicine. Assumes knowledge of mathematical statistics and linear algebra. Theorems proved in detail. Topics include classical methods of linear models, including generalized least squares and the Gauss-Markov theorem; heteroscedasticity; covariance; optimal estimation; classical and optimal prediction; relationship between estimation and prediction; prediction with linear constraints; prediction and modal choice; prediction intervals; prediction in econometric models; and minimax linear estimation. Covers many topics useful to econometricians.

Birnberg, Thomas B., and Resnick, Stephen A. COLONIAL DEVELOPMENT: AN ECONOMETRIC STUDY. Foreword by Gustav Ranis. New Haven, Conn.: Yale University Press, 1975. xiii, 347 p. Appendix, pp. 259-322. Sources, pp. 323-29. Index, pp. 331-47.

Uses an aggregate annual econometric model to examine historically and quantitatively the process of colonial development for selected Asian, African, and Latin American countries with diverse historical characteristics. Consists of simultaneous equation system with five behavioral equations and seven definitional equations, which together describe the trade and government sectors of the colonial economy. Model applied to ten countries.

Bos, G.G.J. A LOGISTIC APPROACH TO THE DEMAND FOR PRIVATE CARS. Tilburg Studies on Economics, no. 5. Rotterdam, The Netherlands: Tilburg University Press, 1970. x, 165 p. Appendixes, pp. 123-60. Literature, pp. 161-65. No index.

Uses a logistic growth function for making a long-term forecast of vehicle numbers in the Netherlands for 1994 when the saturation level of forty-five cars to every one-hundred individuals will be reached. Demand components include replacement demand, new car demand, and used car demand. Independent variables of the logistic function include time, income (real, net per capita national income), and car prices. Parameters estimated using annual data from 1950 to 1967. Useful to anyone interested in forecasting durable goods demand, and also interested in traffic and ecological problems, particularly air pollution.

Bradley, Paul Grant. THE ECONOMICS OF CRUDE PETROLEUM PRODUCTION. Contributions to Economic Analysis, vol. 48. Amsterdam: North-Holland, 1967. xiv, 149 p. Appendix A: Extraction Costs Long-Run Estimated Value Compared with Initial Period Value, pp. 126-27. Appendix B: Allocation of Investment Among Reservoirs, pp. 128-30. Appendix C: Incremental Development Cost Within the Reservoir, pp. 131-32. Appendix D: Estimation of Development Costs: Abqaiq, Saudi Arabia, pp. 133-39. Appendix E: The Effect of Investment-Capacity Ratios on Optimal Exploitation Rates, pp. 140-43. Bibliography, pp. 144-47. Index, pp. 148-49.

Develops a formula for estimating development cost per barrel of crude output based on actual outlays and discounted reservoir production for individual reservoirs. Formula applied to three regions: Middle East, Africa, and Venezuela. Regression analysis for the period 1948-64 provides estimates for the production decline rates and development investment in these regions, with estimated development cost per barrel of between $.12 and $1.14 per barrel. Forecasts of costs for 1978, assuming a lognormal distribution for reservoir size, yield equivocal results for Venezuela, but suggest stability for the Persian Gulf.

Bruckmann, Gerhart, and Weber, W., eds. CONTRIBUTIONS TO THE VON NEUMANN GROWTH MODEL. New York: Springer-Verlag, 1971. xv, 216 p. No index.

Eighteen heretofore unpublished papers presented at a conference organized by the Institute for Advanced Studies and held in Vienna, Austria, July 6-7, 1970, grouped under the following four headings: "Equilibrium Models Which Have Their Origins in Von Neumann's Model" (six papers); "Optimization Models Based on Von Neumann's Model" (six papers); "Methods of Computation of Optimal Prices and Intensities in a Von Neumann Model" (two papers); and "Topics Related to Von Neumann Model" (four papers). Topics include the period of production in a Von Neumann world; balanced stochastic growth at the maximum rate; lags in growth models; economic efficiency in an infinite horizon model; a twisted turnpike theorem; calculating Von Neumann Trajectories by simulated market adjustments; Von Neumann model solutions are generalized eigen-systems; maximal growth when food output is uncertain; and the Von Neumann growth model and Socialist planning.

Brunner, Karl, ed. PROBLEMS AND ISSUES IN CURRENT ECONOMETRIC PRACTICE. College of Administrative Science, monograph no. AA-6. Columbus: Ohio State University, 1972. vii, 284 p. No index.

Eight heretofore unpublished contributions based on two conferences held in 1967 and 1968 at Ohio State University. Examines whether or not econometrics violates the basic principle of scientific methods in light of the proliferation of large-scale model building. Topics include a critical review of the Brookings model; a review of the notions of causality in economics; on cognitive content of econometric models; and econometrics, model construction, and predictive testing.

Burrows, James C. COBALT: AN INDUSTRY ANALYSIS. A Charles River Associate Research Study. Lexington, Mass.: Heath, Lexington Books, 1971. xvii, 218 p. Appendix A: Cobalt Production in the United States, pp. 185-89. Appendix B: Production of Cobalt by Chibuluma Mines, Ltd., p. 190. Appendix C: Summary of Equations Reported in the Text, pp. 191-95. Appendix D: Variables Used in the Analysis, pp. 196-99. Appendix E: Data Used in the Econometric Analysis, pp. 200-205. Bibliography, pp. 206-10. Notes, pp. 211-18.

A comprehensive analysis of the cobalt industry aimed at an understanding of the forces which affect price, consumption, and production of cobalt. Aimed at a general audience with no prior experience in the cobalt industry or training in economics, although knowledge of econometrics helpful for understanding the econometric models. Single-equation regression models (linear and log-linear) used to estimate price of cobalt using annual data for 1947-1968. Explains over 90 percent of the variance of the cobalt price, with the estimated coefficients of the price equations highly significant. Independent variables include total U.S. consumption, U.S. government stock piles, U.S. purchases, time, and dummy variable formagnet demand shift. Also includes industry structure, including descriptive analyses of production, consumption, stocks, and price trends.

______. TUNGSTEN: AN INDUSTRY ANALYSIS. A Charles River Associates Research Study. Lexington, Mass.: Heath, 1971. xxv, 287 p. Calculations of Test Statistics for a Special Case of Two-Stage Least Squares, pp. 239-42. Appendix B: Geology of the Major Commercial Tungsten Deposits, pp. 243-49. Appendix C: Variables Used in the Econometric Model of the Tungsten Industry, pp. 251-55. Appendix D: Summary of Equations in the Tungsten Model, pp. 257-61. Appendix E: Data Used in the Econometric Analysis, pp. 263-70. Bibliography, pp. 271-77. Notes, pp. 279-87. No index.

A detailed analysis of the tungsten market with emphasis on the determinants of the level of price and the rate of consumption and production of tungsten for the general audience with no prior experience in the industry or training in economics, although knowledge of econometrics helpful. Model contains twenty-five behavioral equations, one market identity, and twenty-six endogenous variables, used to predict prices, production, and consumption of various types of tungsten products.

Estimated by reduced form using data from 1947 to 1968. Other topics include industry structure, price history, government policies affecting the market, and a number of single-equation demand and supply models.

Burrows, James C.; Metcalf, Charles E.; and Kaler, John B. INDUSTRIAL LOCATION IN THE UNITED STATES. A Charles River Associates Research Study. Lexington, Mass.: Heath, Lexington Books, 1971. ix, 123 p. Appendix A: The National Employment Forecasts, pp. 85-91. Appendix B: Correspondence Between OBE 118-Industry Classification and the 1957 Standard Industrial Classification, pp. 92-93. Appendix C: Correspondence Between OBE 32- and 118-Industry Lists, pp. 94-97. Appendix E: Estimated Equations, pp. 98-116. Appendix E: Forecasting Equations, pp. 117-23. No index.

Presents the results of a study to obtain long-term forecasts of economic growth in each of 3,097 counties in the contiguous United States. Analyzes factors associated with industrial location decisions and economic growth in small geographic and economic areas, rather than actual predictions of industrial activity for these areas. Includes one general simultaneous equation model, as well as special models, for analyzing data for each county in the United States to provide a 1970 projection of county employment by industry.

Burstein, Meyer L., et al. THE COST OF TRUCKING: ECONOMETRIC ANALYSIS. Dubuque, Iowa: Wm. C. Brown, for the Transportation Center at Northwestern University, 1965. xix, 137 p. No index.

Consists of the following three papers: "Cost Models, Measurement Errors, and Economies of Scale in Trucking," by Stanley L. Warner; "The Optimal Use of Truck Fleets," by A. Victor Cabot and Arthur P. Hurter, Jr.; and "Economics of Private Carriage: A Case Study," by M.L. Burstein and John W. Egan. First paper develops a model to estimate economies of scale in trucking operations. Second paper concerned with the development of techniques to analyze and solve linear programming problems of optimal scheduling of transport equipment. Third paper uses standard regression techniques to deal with the question of why a firm would use its own trucking fleet when private trucking firms are available to do the job.

Choudhry, Nanda K.; Kotowitz, Yehuda; Sawyer, John A.; and Winder, John W.L. THE TRACE ECONOMETRIC MODEL OF THE CANADIAN ECONOMY. Studies in Social and Economic Policy. Toronto: University of Toronto Press, 1972. x, 166 p. Appendixes, pp. 126-61. References, pp. 162-66. No index.

A nonlinear econometric model of the Canadian economy consisting of 67 stochastic equations and 120 identities of which 52 are essential identities. All equations, with the exception of the export and foreign exchange equation, estimated by two-stage least squares using annual data for 1928-66 (excluding 1941-46). Designed to forecast most of the figures appearing in the principal tables of the accounts. Appendixes include names, definitions, and sources of variables; method of estimating the stock of capital; estimates of interindustry input-output coefficients, 1956-1959 (by T.I. Matuszewski, P.R. Pitts, and J.A. Sawyer); and import content of gross domestic product, 1959.

Chow, Gregor C. DEMAND FOR AUTOMOBILES IN THE UNITED STATES: A STUDY IN CONSUMER DURABLES. Contributions to Economic Analysis, XIII. Amsterdam: North-Holland, 1957. xi, 110 p. Appendix I: A Note on the Stochastic Limits and the Expectations of the Least Squares Estimators in a Multiple Linear Regression When One Independent Variable is Subject to Error, pp. 94-98. Appendix II: Source of Data, pp. 99-110. No index.

Presents a theory of demand for new car sales based on single-equation regression models with independent variables consisting of total money stock per capita, per capita automobile stock of cars, automobile price, disposable income per capita, expected income per capita, and personal money stock per capita. Includes a time lag in the adjustment of stock to its equilibrium level. Estimated using annual time series data from 1920 to 1953.

Cicchetti, Charles J.; and Seneca, Joseph J.; and Davidson, Paul. THE DEMAND AND SUPPLY OF OUTDOOR RECREATION: AN ECONOMETRIC ANALYSIS. Foreword by Lawrence N. Stevens. New Brunswick, N.J.: Bureau of Economics Research, Rutgers, The State University, 1969. vi, 30; p. No index.

Develops projections of participation in outdoor recreation on the basis of projections of the specific socioeconomic variables (age, income, sex, education, etc.). By means of regression, relates participation in various forms of outdoor recreation to a range of socioeconomic variables and supply characteristics. Develops a conditional probability for participation in an activity as a function of the socioeconomic factors and supply configurations. Evaluates the number of days of participation for individuals previously determined as participants. Data taken from the 1960-61 National Recreation Survey, consisting of 16,000 persons and conducted by the Bureau of the Census; and the 1965 survey of outdoor recreation, consisting of 7,200 respondents and conducted by the Bureau of Outdoor Recreation. Projects outdoor recreation activity for 1980 and 2000.

Cicchetti, Charles J., and Smith, V. Kerry. THE COSTS OF CONGESTION: AN ECONOMETRIC ANALYSIS OF WILDERNESS RECREATION. Cambridge,

Mass.: Ballinger, Lippincott, 1976. xi, 112 p. Appendix A: Questionnaire and Related Materials, pp. 97-106. Appendix B: Aitken Estimation in R^2, pp. 107-8. Bibliography, pp. 109-10. Index, pp. 111-12.

Presents a methodology for estimating the congestion costs associated with crowding using ordinary least squares and generalized least squares. A single-equation linear model developed to measure the determinants of a representative individual's willingness to pay for a wilderness recreation experience at the Spanish Peak Primitive Area in Montana. Data obtained by sampling about 600 wilderness users of the area. Consists of ten variables, including length of stay of the trip in days, income, willingness to pay per trip when the encounters are with backpacker (hiker) parties (in dollars), number of nights of camp encounters, sex, education, age, and willingness to pay per trip when the encounters are with horseback parties. Established the relationship between an individual's willingness to pay for wilderness experience and a set of variables describing the quantity and quality of those experiences.

Coates, C. Robert. THE DEMAND FOR MONEY BY FIRMS. Business and Economics and Finance. New York: Marcel Dekker, 1976. vi, 183 p. Appendix A: Sources and Description of Data, pp. 165-71. Appendix B: The Relationship Between Nominal and Real Rates of Interest, pp. 173-74. Bibliography, pp. 175-79. Index, pp. 181-83.

Uses multiplicative inventory and production regression models, with sales (production) and treasury bill rates as independent variables, for estimating the firm's demand for money from quarterly data of 102 manufacturing corporations provided by the Securities and Exchange Commission covering the period 1961-I to 1970-IV. Estimated by ordinary least squares, dummy least squares, and modified generalized least squares with estimates taking the form of elasticities using both time series and cross section data. Concludes that the elasticity of demand for money with respect to sales is equal to unity, whereas the elasticity of demand for money with respect to treasury bill rates does not differ significantly from -1/2.

Cohen, Elchanan. Assisted by Stephen D. Millman. INPUT-OUTPUT ANALYSIS IN PUBLIC EDUCATION. With a contribution by It-Keong Chew. Cambridge, Mass.: Lippincott, Ballinger, 1975. v, 137 p. Appendix: Tables, pp. 99-120. Glossary, pp. 121-23. Bibliography, pp. 125-31. Index, pp. 133-35. About the Author, p. 137.

Chapters 1-4 provide an overview of the input-output concept as a technique of educational planning designed to reduce costs. Second part explores the production process of secondary education for a sample of up to 500 Pennsylvania schools for 1970-73, followed by a simultaneous equation analysis (using two-stage least squares), and an input-output index based upon the technique of canonical correlations. Concludes with a chapter on the use of mathematical programming, in particular goal programming, as an alternative tool for educational input-output analysis. Useful to anyone interested in educational planning and the application of regression and mathematical programming in the planning process.

Cohen, Kalman J. COMPUTER MODELS OF THE SHOE, LEATHER, AND HIDE SEQUENCE. Foreword by Thomas H. Carroll. The Ford Foundation Doctoral Dissertation Series. Englewood Cliffs, N.J.: Prentice-Hall, 1960. xii, 156 p. Appendix A: Models III and IIIE, pp. 84-88. Appendix B: Obtaining Actual Data on the Shoe, Leather, Hide Sequence, pp. 89-92. Charts, pp. 95-153. Bibliography, pp. 155-56. No index.

Presents two simultaneous equation models describing the aggregate behavior of shoe retailers, shoe manufacturers, and cattlehide leather tanners using monthly data between 1930 and 1940. Estimated by ordinary least squares and designed for simulation rather than for analytical solution. Computer used to trace out the time paths from 1930 to 1940 for each endogenous variable. One-period-change model intended to explain values of endogenous variables for only one time period; process model designed to simulate endogenous variables for only one time period; process model designed to simulate endogenous variables for an arbitrary large number of future time periods. Exogenous variables include consumer prices, disposable personal income, and stocks of hides held by dealers. Endogenous variables include selling price, sales, production, shoe and leather receipts, hide wettings, and hide receipts.

Cole, H.S.D.; Freeman, Christopher; Jahoda, Marie; and Pavitt, K.L.R., eds. MODELS OF DOOM: A CRITIQUE OF THE LIMITS TO GROWTH. New York: Universe Books, 1973. x, 244 p. Index, pp. 241-44.

Fourteen heretofore unpublished nontechnical contributions on forecasting the future in two parts: "The World Models and Their Sub-Systems" (nine contributions) and "The Ideological Background" (five contributions). Analyses undertaken at the Social Policy Research Unit of the University of Sussex. Topics include structure of world models; the non-renewable resources, agriculture, capital, and pollution of subsystems; energy resources; population forecasting; and system dynamics. No mathematical prerequisites.

Cole, Rosanne. ERRORS IN PROVISIONAL ESTIMATES OF GROSS NATIONAL PRODUCT. Studies in Business Cycles, 21. New York: Columbia University Press, for the NBER, 1969. xiv, 109 p. Appendix: An Error Model, pp. 97-103. Index, pp. 104-9.

A report on the nature of the difference between the provisional and the revised estimates of GNP and its major components. Considers measurement error only, with no attention given to errors created by limitations of concepts, definitions, and coverage. Seven chapter titles: "Errors in Estimates of GNP and Its Components"; "Characteristics of Revisions"; "Relative Accuracy of the Provisional Estimates"; "Gains in Accuracy from Additional Information"; "Expenditures Estimates Compared with Income Estimates"; "Revisions in Major Patterns of Change"; and "Summary." Uses data extending from 1947 to 1965.

Collins, Norman R., and Preston, Lee E. CONCENTRATION AND PRICE-COST MARGINS IN MANUFACTURING INDUSTRIES. Berkeley: University of California Press, 1970. xvi, 163 p. Appendix A: Data Employed in Statistical Analysis, Four-Digit Industries, 1958, pp. 119-48. Appendix B: Stigler Dataon Concentration and Rates of Return for Industries Classified by Geographic Scope of Market, pp. 149-60. Index, pp. 161-63.

Examines statistically the relationship between conventional measures of industrial concentration and the percentage margin between prices and costs using a simple regression model with price the dependent variable and concentration ratio the independent variable, and a multiple regression model with price as dependent and concentration ratio, index of geographic dispersion, and capital-output ratio as independent variables. Uses cross-section data for 20 two-digit industries and 288 four digit industries for the period 1956-1960 obtained from the 1958 Census of Manufacturers.

Cooper, J. Phillip. DEVELOPMENT OF THE MONETARY SECTOR, PREDICTION AND POLICY ANALYSIS IN THE FRB-MIT-PENN MODEL. Lexington, Mass.: Lexington Books, 1974. xv, 225 p. References, pp. 211-17. Index, pp. 219-25.

Four essays on specification of economic structure, methodology, forecasting, and policy analysis of the FRB-MIT-PENN macroeconometric model of the U.S. economy. Topics include development of the monetary sector; ex post and as ante predictive performance; stochastic simulation; and policy analysis. Includes one-quarter-ahead forecasts when exogenous variables are known without error and when they must be predicted using time series model of the Box-Jenkins autoregressive moving-average type. Policy analysis concerned with the relationship between money supply and the rate of inflation and unemployment.

Cootner, Paul H., and Löb, George O.G. WATER DEMAND FOR STEAM ELECTRIC GENERATION: AN ECONOMIC PROJECTION MODEL. Baltimore: Johns Hopkins, for the Resources of the Future, 1966. xi, 144 p. Appendix

A: The Physics of Thermal Efficiency, pp. 87-120. Appendix B: The Supply Curve of Thermal Efficiency, pp. 121-40. Appendix C: References and Literature Citation, pp. 141-44. No index.

Identifies the main factors that determine the demand for water by steam electric power plants and constructs a model for forecasting water demand in 1980 for the West South Central region (Arkansas, Louisiana, Oklahoma, and Texas) using data for the period 1957-1962. Thermal efficiency for 1980 estimated from the equation of demand and supply curves for thermal efficiency and water use calculated from this estimate.

Coupé, B.E.M.G. REGIONAL ECONOMIC STRUCTURE AND ENVIRONMENTAL POLLUTION. Foreword by J. Paelinck. Studies in Applied Regional Science, vol. 5. The Netherlands, Leiden: Steinfert Kroese B.V., 1976. Bibliography, pp. 158-66. No index.

Constructs a simple input-output table for two regions in The Netherlands, each region assumed to have two sectors: a relatively polluting sector and a relatively nonpolluting sector. Determines equilibrium in terms of production and pollution. Each region assumed to have its own consumption function in terms of expenditures for the goods produced by each sector, and in terms of the incomes available to households and prices. Model estimated using data for the two regions for 1960.

Cresswell, W.L., and Foggatt, P. THE CAUSATION OF BUS DRIVER ACCIDENTS: AN EPIDEMIOLOGICAL STUDY. New York: Oxford University Press, 1963. xvii, 298 p. Appendix, pp. 261-98. No index.

A statistical analysis of causes of bus driver accidents in Northern Ireland in the period 1952-55 using techniques commonly applied to epidemiological problems. Includes a review of the literature, comparisons of actual frequency distributions with theoretical distributions, such as the Poisson and negative binomial, and an examination of the relationships between variables by such techniques as chi-square, analysis of variance, correlation, averages, and standard deviations. Variables include accident rates by routes, and the age, experience, personality, and health of drivers. Knowledge of basic statistics helpful, although conclusions do not require this knowledge. Appendix contains data and analysis, including some derivations.

Cummins, J. David. AN ECONOMETRIC MODEL OF THE LIFE INSURANCE SECTOR OF THE U.S. ECONOMY. Lexington, Mass.: Heath, Lexington Books, 1975. xii, 254 p. Appendix A: Variables Appearing in the Model, pp. 191-96. Appendix B: Simultaneous Sample Period Solution Results, pp. 197-225. Notes, pp. 227-42. Bibliography, pp. 243-50. Index, pp. 251-54.

A comprehensive disaggregated model of the life insurance

sector in the Federal Reserve Flow of Funds Account. Useful for explaining fluctuations in the major sources and uses of insurance sector funds, and examining the linkages between the insurance sector and other sectors of the economy. Includes simulations to indicate the effects of proposed economic policies on the insurance sector and on other segments. Consists of thirteen behavioral equations and eleven identities with the behavioral equations estimated by ordinary least squares using data over the period 1955-1972, and adjustments made for autocorrelated errors through the use of the Cochrane-Orcutt iterative technique. Model includes extensive lag distributions.

Cutt, James. A PLANNING, PROGRAMMING, AND BUDGETING MANUAL: RESOURCE ALLOCATION IN PUBLIC SECTOR ECONOMIES. Foreword by T.L. Johnston. Praeger Special Studies in International Economics and Development. New York: Praeger, 1974. viii, 150 p. Appendix A: Structural Aspects of Program Budgeting, pp. 111-36. Appendix B: Output Indicators, pp. 137-41. Notes, pp. 142-50.

An examination of attempts over the last decade to introduce a more systematic managerial approach to public sector decision making based on experience in Canada, United States, United Kingdom, India, and Australia. Emphasizes cost-benefit and cost-effectiveness analysis. Topics include models and system design; inputs and outputs; time; uncertainty; constraints; the establishment of national criteria for program design selection and ranking; and suboptimization. No mathematical prerequisites.

David, Paul A., and Reder, Melvin W., eds. NATIONS AND HOUSEHOLDS IN ECONOMIC GROWTH: ESSAYS IN HONOR OF MOSES ABRAMOVITZ. New York: Academic Press, 1974. xvi, 411 p. Author Index, pp. 407-11.

Fourteen heretofore unpublished contributions written in honor of Moses Abramovitz on his sixtieth birthday. Includes a wide range of Abramovitz's interest in economics and economic history in two parts: "Microeconomic Foundations" (seven contributions) and "Macroeconomic Performance: Growth and Stability" (seven contributions). Topics include measurement of real value added; microeconomics of migration; economic theory of imperialism; demand theory and the maximum principles; monetary policy in developing countries; building cycle economic indicator analysis during 1969-72; and long swings and the Atlantic economy.

Dean, Joel. STATISTICAL COST ESTIMATION. Bloomington: Indiana University Press, 1976. xi, 499 p. Index, pp. 493-99.

Nine statistical cost studies made by the author--seven reprints of studies previously published and two published for the first time. Grouped under the following four headings: "Cost and Output Rate" (four papers); "Cost and Plant Size" (two papers); "Cost and Plant Location" (one paper); and "Cost and Real Profits" (two papers). Includes the following industries: furniture, hosiery mills, belt shop, department stores, finance chain, shoe chain, drug chain, electronics, and machinery manufacturers.

______. STATISTICAL DETERMINATION OF COSTS, WITH SPECIAL REFERENCE TO MARGINAL COSTS. Studies in Business Administration, vol. VII, no. 1. Chicago: University of Chicago Press, 1936. xi, 145 p. Appendix A: Behavior of Components of Average Combined Cost, pp. 109-29. Appendix B: Behavior of Components of Marginal Combined Cost, pp. 130-45. No index.

Presents various practical procedures for deriving average and marginal costs using cost and output data from a furniture factory. Methods include: graphic (visual curve fitting); first-difference; least squares; and graphic-least squares.

Deaton, Angus. MODELS AND PROJECTIONS OF DEMAND IN POST-WAR BRITAIN. Foreword by Richard Stone. Cambridge Studies in Applied Econometrics, vol. 1. New York: Wiley, Halsted Press, 1975. x, 261 p. Appendix: The Program RIDGE, pp. 240-50. List of Works Cited, pp. 251-57. Index, pp. 258-61.

Assesses techniques for measuring, understanding, and predicting the response in purchasing behavior of households to the stimuli of changing prices and incomes in the United Kingdom since WW II. Linear expenditure system model applied simultaneously to the full disaggregation of thirty-seven categories of expenditures using time series data from 1854 to 1970. Categories include meat and bacon, bread and cereals, fish, dairy, produce, fruit, footwear, and clothing. Estimates based on a single-equation model and compared with those offered by the linear expenditure system. Includes demand forecasts for 1975 and 1980.

Drake, Alvin W.; Keeney, Ralph L.; and Morse, Philip M. ANALYSIS OF PUBLIC SYSTEMS. Cambridge: MIT Press, 1972. x, 532 p. Index, pp. pp. 527-32.

Twenty-three heretofore unpublished contributors by analysts at MIT and the New York City Rand Institute on applications of modeling for the improvement of the delivery of public services. Applications include New York City fire project, allocating urban emergency units, blood bank inventory control, library models, post office mail processing operations, driver accident models, water quality management, air pollution, health planning, operations research in university planning, and airport development for Mexico City.

Duijn, Jacob Johan van. AN INTERREGIONAL MODEL OF ECONOMIC FLUCTUATIONS. Lexington, Mass.: Lexington Books, 1972. x, 187 p. List of Symbols, pp. viii-ix. List of References, pp. 179-81. Index, pp. 183-87.

The construction and analysis of an interregional model of economic fluctuations to determine how regional and national fluctuations of output and unemployment are influenced by the economic characteristics of region and trade among them, and in what ways the central government can attain its goal of interregional equality of unemployment and economic stability. Interrelationships among regions established through two trade matrices (one for private consumption and one for private investment), with fluctuations in the model generated by a flexible-accelerator type private investment function. Model contains buffers (ceilings and floors) which keep the movement of output in check over a period of time, with simulation used to study the behavior of the model over time. Includes simulations for a hypothetical three-region economy. Chapters conclude with notes.

Duprez, Colette, and Kirschen, E.S., eds. MEGISTOS: A WORLD INCOME AND TRADE MODEL FOR 1975. New York: Elsevier, 1970. xxix, 668 p. Commodities Index, pp. 659-60. Geographical Index, pp. 661-68.

Nineteen chapters written in English by fifteen authors on a system of projections for 1975 for the main economic aggregates at the world level grouped into the following four parts: "The Model" (three papers); "The Developed Capitalistic Countries" (five papers); "The Communistic Countries" (three papers); and "The Underdeveloped Zones" (eight papers). Includes projections for the twenty-two capitalistic countries based on a production function with labor and investment (but not capital) as independent variables with parameters estimated by a cross-section regression. Other projections include the volume of goods which each underdeveloped zone will export to the capitalistic countries in 1975; export of services by underdeveloped countries; aid from capitalistic countries; and private capital flows to underdeveloped countries. Includes projection of net materials products for the USSR and seven other communistic countries for 1975, as well as projections of imports of goods from the underdeveloped countries and aid to these countries. Projections for the 105 underdeveloped countries based on production functions developed for the following zones: communistic Asia, Africa, non-Communistic Asia, Latin America, the oil producing countries, and the Mediterranean zone.

Earl, Paul H., ed. ANALYSIS OF INFLATION. Lexington, Mass.: Lexington Books, 1975. xx, 232 p. No index.

Nine papers presented at a conference on the analysis of inflation held at Georgetown University July 15-18, 1974. Provides a broad coverage of the history, theory, measurement, analysis, and policy considerations concerning inflation. Topics include accuracy of price indices; econometric considerations; consumer and wholesale prices in a model of price behavior by stage-of-processing; disaggregated approach to forecasting prices; forecasts of aggregate price behavior using macroeconomic models; and policy choices in combating inflation.

Eckstein, Otto, ed. THE ECONOMETRICS OF PRICE DETERMINATION CONFERENCE, OCTOBER 30-31, 1970. Washington, D.C.: Board of Governors of the Federal Reserve System and the Social Science Research Council, 1972. x, 392 p. No index.

Thirteen heretofore unpublished papers and discussions of the papers on the econometrics of price determination presented at a conference held in Washington, D.C., October 30-31, 1970. Topics include econometric testing of the natural rate hypothesis; the structure of serial dependence of some U.S. price series; industry price equations; the relationship between monetary variables and the behavior of prices and unemployment; price determination and simulations with large aggregative models such as the Wharton model; price formation in European countries; wage and price formation in some selected Canadian econometric models; and the objectives for price and wage statistics at the Bureau of Labor Statistics.

______. PARAMETERS AND POLICIES IN THE U.S. ECONOMY. Data Resources Series, vol. 2. New York: Elsevier, 1976. viii, 389 p. Index, pp. 379-89.

Thirteen previously published studies conducted by Data Resources designed to identify key parameters of the structure of the U.S. economy and to analyze the impact of public policies on economic performance. Topics include distribution of earned income; determinants of interest rates; causes of inflation; determinants of personal savings; reducing the unemployment rate; the investment of tax credit and countercyclical policy; value added tax and the U.S. economy; analysis of wage-price freeze of 1971-72; impact of a value added tax on the economy; analysis of President Ford's package for energy; and the analysis of the Ways and Means Committee's energy proposals.

Elliott-Jones, M.F. LONG-TERM PROJECTIONS OF PRIMARY METALS MARKETS. Foreword by John W. Kendrick. New York: The Conference Board, 1972. iv, 52 p. Appendix, pp. 50-52. No index.

Presents forecasts for 1975 and 1980 in constant 1969 dollars for six primary metals: iron, steel, copper, lead, zinc, aluminum, and other nonferrous metals, using an input-output table (Maryland Interindustry Forecasting Model) for 1969.

Epple, Dennis N. PETROLEUM DISCOVERIES AND GOVERNMENT POLICY: AN ECONOMETRIC STUDY OF SUPPLY. Cambridge, Mass.: Ballinger, Lippincott, 1975. xv, 139 p. Appendix A: Reduced Form Estimates of the Parameters of the Model, pp. 109-13. Appendix B: Data Preparation, pp. 115-19. Notes, pp. 121-29. Bibliography, pp. 131-35. Index, pp. 137-39.

Develops and tests a nonlinear three-equation simultaneous equation model of the supply of petroleum and natural gas discoveries in the United States which takes into account the role of market incentives and government policies. Includes full information maximum likelihood estimates of the parameters of the model using data for 1947-68. Includes estimates of price elasticity of supply of new discoveries of crude oil and natural gas, the percent change in the ratio of discoveries of oil and gas in response to a given change in the ratio of the prices of the outputs when the level of inputs are held constant, and the net effects of two opposing influences; technical progress which tends to increase the productivity of exploratory drilling, and exhaustion of undiscovered deposits which tends to reduce the productivity of drilling.

Evans, Michael K. AN ECONOMETRIC MODEL OF THE FRENCH ECONOMY: A SHORT-TERM FORECASTING MODEL. Foreword by Thorkil Kristensen. Economic Studies Series. Paris: OECD, 1969. 103 p. Appendix A: List of of Equations, pp. 61-65. Definition of Variables, pp. 67-69. Graphs of Equations, pp. 71-103. No index.

A fifty-five equation annual short-term forecasting model of the French economy estimated by ordinary least squares for the period 1952-1965. Equations estimated in percentage differences instead of levels of the variables, and forecasts made for 1966 and 1967. Equations classified into groups as follows: consumption (three equations); investment (four equations); foreign trade (seven equations); factor share (nine equations); cyclical variables (three equations); prices (eight equations); and identities (twenty-one equations). Includes ninety-two variables (thirty-seven exogenous and fifty-five endogenous) and graphs for the actual and estimated values of each of thirty-five nonidentity equations.

Feige, Edgar L. THE DEMAND FOR LIQUID ASSETS: A TEMPORAL CROSS-SECTION ANALYSIS. Foreword by Clarence H. Faust. Englewood Cliffs, N.J.: Prentice-Hall, 1964. xii, 91 p. Appendix A: Demand Function Estimates, pp. 45-64. Appendix B: Basic Data, 1949-1959, pp. 65-87. Bibliography, pp. 88-91. No index.

Uses single equation regression models, and cross-section data for forty-nine states for each of the years 1949-1959, to estimate demand deposits, time deposits, and savings and loan association shares as functions of four interest rates (commercial bank demand and time deposits, rate on savings and loan association shares, and rate on mutual savings bank deposits) and per capita advertising. Includes restricted efficient cross-section regressions to estimate price, cross, and income elasticities. Regression results presented in appendix A, and the basic data used in the regressions in appendix B.

Fisher, Franklin M. In Association with Carl Kaysen. A STUDY IN ECONOMETRICS: THE DEMAND FOR ELECTRICITY IN THE UNITED STATES. Contributions to Economic Analysis, XXVII. Amsterdam: North-Holland, 1962. xii, 190 p. Appendix A: Aggregation of Individual Demand Functions, p. 153. Appendix B: Consumers' Stocks by States of Selected Major Appliances, 1944-57, pp. 154-82. Bibliography, pp. 183-86. Index, pp. 187-90.

Performs single-equation multiple regressions (in first differences of logarithms) of electricity consumption on real price and real income per capita for each state for the years 1946 to 1957 and uses analysis of covariance to test the hypothesis that the regressions fall into homogeneous groups. Also uses regression to determine demand for various household appliances which use gas and electricity. Estimates elasticity of demand by cross-section analysis over states for 1955 and 1956 for each of the ten two-digit industries. Estimated elasticities vary from 0 in the fabricated metal products and transportation equipment to 2.6 for the chemical industry.

Fox, James Alan. FORECASTING CRIME DATA: AN ECONOMETRIC ANALYSIS. Foreword by Marvin E. Wolfgang. Lexington, Mass.: Heath, Lexington Books, 1978. xvi, 141 p. Appendix A: List of the Data, pp. 81-86. Appendix B: Segmented Functions, pp. 87-94. Appendix C: The HUDSON program, pp. 95-112. Appendix D: Technical Notes on the Police Expenditure Equation, pp. 113-16. Appendix E: Selection of the Exogenous Variables, pp. 117-24. Notes, pp. 125-30. References, pp. 131-38. Index, pp. 139-40. About the Author, p. 141.

A monograph on applications of econometric methods to crime data. Presents a simultaneous equation model of national crime leading to the generation of forecasts for the years through 2000. Model consists of eight behavioral equations and one identity. Estimated by two-stage least squares using annual data for 1950-1974. Variables include crime data rates, such as violent crime and property crime; and police data, such as size of police force and police expenditures; and arrest rates, including arrest for violent crimes and for property crime; population; income; and consumer price index.

Frank, Ronald E., and Massy, William F. AN ECONOMETRIC APPROACH TO A MARKETING DECISION MODEL. Cambridge, Mass.: MIT Press, 1971. xiv, 224 p. Appendix A: Coding Conventions, pp. 186-87. Appendix B: pp. 188-219. Bibliography, p. 220. Index, pp. 221-24.

Develops a multiple-regression simulation model of a test market for experimenting with a wide range of alternative marketing programs for a manufacturer of a branded, frequently purchased food product. Model incorporates the retailer's response to allowances offered by the manufacturers and the customer's response to the resulting retailer promotional activities. Model also describes the demand for the product by a separate equation for each size and brand (three sizes and four brands) relating sales to the retailer price discounts, media advertising, special promotion, and to the sales of other sizes and brands. Uses ordinary least squares and instrumental variables estimation methods with the residuals examined to estimate the effects upon sales of special offers, signs, displays, changes in a brand's normal price, and different time intervals between major promotions for the same size and brand. Model designed for use with a time-sharing computer facility.

Freedman, Charles. THE FOREIGN CURRENCY BUSINESS OF THE CANADIAN BANKS: AN ECONOMETRIC STUDY. Staff Research Studies, 10. Ottawa: Bank of Canada, 1974. xvi, 233 p. Notes on Empirical Variables, pp. 218-20. List of Variables, pp. 221-25. References, pp. 227-33. No index.

Studies the factors and causes of the rapid expansion of foreign currency assets and liabilities of the Canadian chartered banks over the decade 1961-1971. Uses multiple regression equations with various interest rates (rate on 90-day foreign currency deposits at Canadian banks, rates on instruments competing for rest-of-world funds, for example) as dependent variables. Other models include profit from transactions in foreign currency and various foreign currency deposits at Canadian banks as dependent variables. Develops and tests empirically a model of chartered bank behavior. All estimation by ordinary least squares.

Friedman, Benjamin M. ECONOMIC STABILIZATION POLICY: METHODS OF OPTIMIZATION. Foreword by H. Theil. Studies in Mathematical and Managerial Economics, vol. 15. New York: Elsevier, 1975. xviii, 375 p. Appendix A: List of Wharton Model Variables Symbols, pp. 317-22. Appendix B: Linearized Coefficient Values for the Wharton Model, pp. 323-33. Appendix C: Proof of Piecewise Quadratic Convergence in the Scalar Case, pp. 335-40. Appendix D: The TRIOPT Algorithm, pp. 341-49. Appendix E: Card Input Guide for TRIOPT, pp. 351-58. References and Selective Bibliography, pp. 359-67. Index, pp. 369-75.

Develops a methodology for applying econometric models to problems in government policy for economic stabilization. Reviews the available econometric models of the U.S. Wharton model employed throughout to illustrate the application of the various methods developed. Uses the linearization approach to generate several distinct sets of linear constraints from a nonlinear model which renders the model's nonlinear function to piecewise linear functions. Concludes with a chapter on applications of piecewise quadratic optimization and endogenous time horizon optimization to the experience of the U.S. economy in the 1957-58 recession. Assumes knowledge of linear algebra and econometric methods.

Friend, Irwin, and Jones, Robert, eds. CONSUMPTION AND SAVING. Vol. II. Study of Consumer Expenditures, Income and Savings. Philadelphia: Wharton School of Finance and Commerce, University of Pennsylvania, 1960. ii, 498 p. No index.

Nine papers, most of which employ regression analysis, presented at a conference on savings held at the University of Pennsylvania in 1959 grouped under the following headings: "General Saving Relations: Permanent Income and Other Theories" (three papers); "Specific Aspects of Saving Behavior" (three papers); and "Income, Debt, and Methodology" (three papers). Topics include consumer expenditure and the capital account; windfall income; entrepreneurial saving; relative income shares; cross-section analysis of consumer debt; and an appraisal of consumer expenditures studies.

Frisch, Ragnar. NEW METHODS OF MEASURING MARGINAL UTILITY. Tubingen, Ger.: Verlog von J.C.B. Mohr, 1932. viii, 142 p. No index.

Develops a method of isoquants for measuring utility statistically and applies the method using time series on price and quantity for goods in Paris during the period 1920-22. Constructs a marginal utility of money curve for the average consumer. Uses the quantity variation method to construct the marginal utility curve from family budget data. A third method called the translation method applied to U.S. family budget data for 1918-19. Assumes knowledge of differential and integral calculus.

Fuchs, Victor R., and Kramer, Marcia J. DETERMINANTS OF EXPENDITURES FOR PHYSICIANS' SERVICES IN THE UNITED STATES 1948-1968. NBER Occasional Paper, 117. DHEW Publication No. (HSM) 73-3013. Washington, D.C.: Health Services and Mental Health Administration, National Center for Health Services Research and Development, 1972. vi, 63 p. Appendix A: Time Series: Sources and Methods, pp. 43-46. Appendix B: Time Series: Derivation of Average Price, pp. 47-53. Appendix C: Cross-Section: Sources and Methods, pp. 54-60. Bibliography, pp. 61-63. No index.

Using time series data from 1948 to 1968 and cross section data by state for 1966, one part provides a statistical decomposition of the growth of per capita expenditures with the focus on different rates of change in expenditures between subperiods 1948-56 (4.1 percent per year) and 1956-66 (6.6 percent per year). Second part uses cross section data to test a regression model for studying variations in quantity of services per capita, physicians per capita, quantity of services per physician, and insurance coverage.

Fuss, Melvin, and McFadden, Daniel, eds. PRODUCTION ECONOMICS: A DUAL APPROACH TO THEORY AND APPLICATIONS. Vol. I: THE THEORY OF PRODUCTION. Contributions to Economic Analysis, vol. 110. Amsterdam: North-Holland, 1978. xx, 482 p. Appendix A.1: Definite Quadratic Forms Subject to Constraints, pp. 365-73. Appendix A.2: Necessary and Sufficient Conditions for the Classical Programming Problem, pp. 375-82. Appendix A.3: Convex Analysis, pp. 383-408. Appendix A.4: Testing and Imposing Monotonicity, Convexity and Quasi-Convexity Constraints, pp. 409-53. Bibliography, pp. 455-69. Author Index, pp. 471-74. Subject Index, pp. 475-82.

Seven contributions (some heretofore unpublished) on the theoretical analysis of the duality of cost, profit, and production, as well as a number of specific empirical investigations. Assumes knowledge of economic theory, advanced calculus, linear algebra, mathematical economics, and econometrics. Topics include Cobb-Douglas and C.E.S. production functions; restricted profit functions; symmetric duality and polar production functions; design of functional forms; nonlinear forms; separability; and flexibility vs. efficiency in plant design. Emphasizes the empirical implications of production theory and the relationship between economic theory and econometrics.

______. PRODUCTION ECONOMICS: A DUAL APPROACH TO THEORY AND APPLICATIONS. Vol. 2: APPLICATIONS OF THE THEORY OF PRODUCTION. Contributions to Economic Analysis, vol. III. Amsterdam: North-Holland, 1978. xviii, 338 p. Bibliography, pp. 311-25. Author Index, pp. 327-29. Subject Index, pp. 331-38.

Emphasizes empirical applications in three parts: "An Analysis of the Concept of Real Value-Added"; "Empirical Applications of Production Theory: Micro-Economic Data"; and "Empirical Applications of Production Theory: Macro-Economic Data." Topics include duality, intermediate inputs, and value-added; aggregation theorem and the existence of a real-value-added function; homotheticity and real value-added in Canadian manufacturing; estimation techniques for elasticity of factor substitution; identification of technical change in the electricity generating industry; putty-clay hypothesis and factor substitution in electricity generation; an aggregation model with multi-product technologies; and factor substitution in the interindustry model and the use of inconsistent aggregation.

Gearing, Charles E.; Swart, William W.; and Var, Turgut. PLANNING FOR TOURISM DEVELOPMENT: QUANTITATIVE APPROACHES. Foreword by Tunay Akoglu. Praeger Special Studies in International Economics and Development. New York: Praeger, 1976. xiv, 221 p. Appendix: General Information Regarding Organizations Engaged in Tourism and Travel Research Activities, pp. 202-11. Index, pp. 212-17. About the Contributors, pp. 218-21.

A collection of contributions on the construction and application of tourism decision models, some published here for the first time. Consists of the following three parts: "Tourism Planning in Perspective"; "Seeking a Structure for Tourism Planning"; and "Applying Tourism Decision Structures." Quantitative approaches include linear programming, input-output analysis, multiple regression, and dynamic programming. Includes much descriptive material on tourist trade in several countries, such as Mexico, Turkey, Spain, Japan, United Kingdom, and the OECD countries. Assumes knowledge of regression analysis and mathematical programming, although much of the book can be read by those without much mathematical training.

Georgiadis, Hourmouzis George. BALANCE OF PAYMENTS EQUILIBRIUM: A THEORETICAL AND EMPIRICAL STUDY. Pittsburgh: University of Pittsburgh Press, 1964. xi, 220 p. Appendix A: The Microeconomic Relationships of the Model of Chapter 2, pp. 179-202. Appendix B: The Trade Intermodel Reestimated, 1949-60, pp. 203-14. Index, pp. 215-20.

Points out the shortcomings of Keynes-like models of balance of payments-equilibrium, and reformulates and tests a large empirical equilibrium model for the U.S. economy for 1949-56 involving eight sectors (consumer, corporate business, farm business, federal government, state and local governments, banking, insurance, and rest of world) with the consumer sector alone consisting of thirty-nine behavioral equations and fifty-eight variables. Offers a reformulation of the criteria of international equilibrium. Estimated by ordinary least squares, and knowledge of regression assumed.

Ghali, Moheb, and Renaud, Bertrand. THE STRUCTURE AND DYNAMIC PROPERTIES OF A REGIONAL ECONOMY: AN ECONOMETRIC MODEL FOR HAWAII. Lexington Books Regional Science Monograph Series. Lexington, Mass.: Heath, Lexington Books, 1975. xv, 158 p. Appendix: The Data, pp. 141-48. References, pp. 149-54. Index, pp. 155-58.

Presents a large-scale econometric forecasting model for Hawaii for the period 1958-68 consisting of seventy-four stochastic equations and twenty-six identities. Estimated by a modified two-stage least squares. Includes five equations for consumption, nine for private investment, eight for imports and exports, twenty-five for state and local governments' current expenditures, eleven for state and local governments' investment, one for total expenditures, twenty-nine for employment and labor force, and twelve for income. Simulations run for 1961-68 for evaluating the impact of policy changes.

Goldberger, Arthur S. IMPACT MULTIPLIERS AND DYNAMIC PROPERTIES OF THE KLEIN-GOLDBERGER MODEL. Contributions to Economic Analysis, XIX. Amsterdam: North-Holland, 1970. viii, 138 p. Appendix: The Approximate Linearity of the K-G Model, pp. 136-38. No index.

Develops the reduced form version of the structural Klein-Goldberger model of the United States using data for 1929-52 to estimate the endogenous variables for the years 1929-41 and 1946-52.

Goldfeld, Stephen M. COMMERCIAL BANK BEHAVIOR AND ECONOMIC ACTIVITY: A STRUCTURAL STUDY OF MONETARY POLICY IN THE POSTWAR UNITED STATES. Contributions to Economic Analysis, vol. 43. Amsterdam: North-Holland, 1966. xii, 212 p. Data Appendix, pp. 198-202. Index, pp. 209-12.

Presents a thirty-two equation quarterly macroeconometric model (twenty-one stochastic, six identities, and five definitional equations) of the banking, consumption, and investment sectors of the American economy in order to show how monetary variables affect aggregate demand and to access various policy instruments by means of impact multipliers. Estimated by two-stage least squares from forty-eight consecutively quarterly observations beginning with the third quarter of 1950.

Gossling, W.F. PRODUCTIVITY TRENDS IN A SECTORAL MACRO-ECONOMIC MODEL: A STUDY OF AMERICAN AGRICULTURE AND SUPPORTING INDUSTRIES, 1919-1964. London: Input-Output Publishing Co., 1972. xxii, 296 p. Appendix A: Mathematical Proofs for the Determination of Subsystems, pp. 165-79. Appendix B: Mathematical Addenda for the Stone and Brown, and Sraffa Systems, pp. 180-200. Appendix C: Input-Output Tables and Related Employment and Capital Data, pp. 201-88. Bibliography, pp. 289-93. Index, pp. 294-96.

A monograph on the mathematical development and empirical application of a subsystems in agriculture of the U.S. economy in the form of an input-output table for the purpose of measuring its technical progress (productivity). Applications include a North Central mixed farm and a corn grain subsystem. Mathematical derivations require knowledge of linear algebra. Useful as a reference and supplementary text for courses in input-output analysis.

______, ed. CAPITAL COEFFICIENTS AND DYNAMIC INPUT OUTPUT MODELS. Foreword by Wm. H. Miernyk. London: Input-Output Publishing Co., 1975. xvi, 157 p. Index, pp. 143-57.

Six papers, originally presented at different meetings, on dynamic input-output analysis. Topics include investment matrices for the United Kingdom; capital replacement; prices and wages under steady growth; and developing ex ante input-output glow and capital coefficients.

______. INPUT-OUTPUT AND THROUGHPUT. Foreword by Richard Stone. London: Input-Output Publishing Co., 1975. xiv, 142 p. Subject Index, pp. 135-42.

Ten papers presented at the Norwich Conference on input-output analysis held September 13-16, 1971, at the University of East Anglia, Norwich, Engl. Topics include errors in data; input-output analysis in urban planning and international trade; investment matrices for the United Kingdom, a dynamic model of capital replacement; forecasting; and updating the coefficients. Emphasizes the time dimension, and concludes that the time taken by an input (for example, raw materials) in passing through various states to its ultimate disappearance can produce deficiencies in normal input-output projections of input coefficients and output.

Granger, Clive William John, and Morgenstern Oskar. PREDICTABILITY OF STOCK MARKET PRICES. Lexington, Mass.: Heath, 1970. xxiii, 303 p. Bibliography, pp. 283-96. Index, pp. 297-303.

An empirical approach to the predictability of stock market prices. Includes predictions for one day, one week, and one month in advance. Also includes a chapter on predictions over a longer period, and another chapter on predictions of less than a day, i.e., between adjacent transactions. Employs spectral techniques for analyzing time series. Also includes random walk models. Assumes knowledge of differential and integral calculus and statistical estimation theory. Chapters conclude with summaries.

Green, Donald W., and Higgins, Christopher I. SOVMOD I: A MACRO-ECONOMETRIC MODEL OF THE SOVIET UNION. Foreword by Lawrence R. Klein and Herbert S. Levine. New York: Academic Press, 1977. xxii, 312 p. Appendix A: Documentation of SOVMOD I: Variables and Equations, pp. 191-251. Appendix B: Data Sources and Methodology, pp. 253-68. Appendix C: Glossary of Dummy Variables in SOVMOD I, pp. 269-74. Appendix D: Control Simulation to 1990, pp. 275-94. Appendix E: SRI-WEFA Project Working Papers and Colloquia Participants, pp. 295-302. Bibliography, pp. 303-9. Index, pp. 311-12.

The first large scale econometric model of a centrally planned economy developed by the Stanford Research Institute and the Wharton Econometric Forecasting Association in 1974 and 1975. Model consists of eighty-four stochastic equations and thirty-five identities; 119 endogenous and seventy-four exogenous variables of which twenty-nine are dummy. Estimated by ordinary least squares. Endogenous variables organized into fourteen sectors, including investment, agriculture, wages, income, prices, exports and imports. Simulations reveal an error about what one would expect in model building efforts for advanced Western countries. Most errors under three percent.

Gronau, Reuben. THE VALUE OF TIME IN PASSENGER TRANSPORTATION: THE DEMAND FOR AIR TRAVEL. NBER Occasional Paper, 109. New York: Columbia University Press, for the NBER, 1970. xiv, 74 p. Bibliography, pp. 69-71. Index, pp. 72-74.

Uses single-equation regression models to estimate price and income elasticities of demand for the number of domestic air travel trips using data for 1963-64.

Grossman, Gregory. SOVIET STATISTICS OF PHYSICAL OUTPUT OF INDUSTRIAL COMMODITIES: THEIR COMPILATION AND QUALITY. Foreword by G.W. Nutter. General Series, no. 69. Princeton, N.J.: Princeton University Press, 1960. xiii, 151 p. Abbreviations, pp. 135-36. Bibliography, pp. 137-48. Index, pp. 149-51.

An inquiry into the reliability and general usability of Soviet statistics of the physical output of industrial commodities, with reference to the period beginning with the five-year plans. Includes the following two parts: "The Soviet Statistical System" and "The Quality of Data." Covers such topics as types of data and their flows, errors in the data, reporting at the enterprise level, processing at intermediate levels, and publication. Descriptive in nature, with no examples of statistical data provided.

Grossman, Michael. THE DEMAND FOR HEALTH: A THEORETICAL AND EMPIRICAL INVESTIGATION. NBER Occasional Paper, 119. New York: Columbia University Press, for the NBER, 1972. xvii, 115 p. Appendix A: Utility Maximization, pp. 84-86. Appendix B: Derivation of Investment Model Formulas, pp. 87-93. Appendix C: Derivation of Consumption Model Formulas, pp. 94-96. Appendix D: Statistical Properties of the Model, pp. 97-101. Appendix E: Additional Empirical Results, pp. 102-9. Appendix F: Sources and Methods: Mortality Analysis, pp. 110-11. Index, pp. 112-15.

A study of the demand for health care (as distinguished from the demand for medical care) which treats health as a durable item demanded as both a consumption and investment good. Constructs a shadow price of health care using many variables besides the price of medical care. Model consists of demand functions fitted by ordinary least squares and production functions estimated by two stage least squares. Data obtained from the 1963 health interview survey conducted by the National Opinion Research Center and the Center for Health Administration Studies of the University of Chicago. Independent variables in the regression model include age of the individual, number of years of schooling, weekly wage, and family income.

Hamilton, Henry R.; Goldstone, S.E.; Milliman, J.W.; Pugh, A.L. III; Roberts, E.B.; and Zellner, Arnold. SYSTEMS SIMULATION FOR REGIONAL ANALYSIS: AN APPLICATION TO RIVER-BASIN PLANNING. Cambridge, Mass.:

MIT Press, 1969. xii, 407 p. Appendix A: The Management of a Multidisciplinary Research Project, pp. 276-88. Appendix B: Classification and Estimation of Employment, pp. 289-305. Appendix C: Computation of Access Factors, pp. 306-25. Appendix D: Technical Description of the Model, pp. 326-93. Index, pp. 395-407.

Develops a methodology for analyzing regional and water resource phenomena of the Susquehanna River Basin. Model consists of three sectors: demographic, employment, and water. Incorporates explicit feedbacks and lagged relationships among the sectors and variables. River basin divided into eight subregions. Includes extensive sensitivity analyses. Model used to make projections of population, employment, income, water use, etc., and includes a fifty-year simulation of the Wilkes-Barre-Scranton subregion. Appendix D includes equations of one subregion of the entire model.

Hanna, R.S. COMPOSITE LOG DISTRIBUTIONS IN THE FINANCIAL SECTOR. Lexington, Mass.: Lexington Books, 1975. xv, 179 p. Appendix A: Data Used-Description and Sources, pp. 137-40. Appendix B: Statistical Appendix, pp. 141-50. Bibliography, pp. 151-72. Index, pp. 173-79.

Presents two models of the monetary sector. A frequency response reduced form model based on multivariate cross-spectra of weekly data, and a structural regression model estimated from monthly data with lag responses over second-order pascal distributions. Concludes that money supply responds to policy changes with a lag of about ten months and long-term interest rates with a lag within six months.

Hart, P.E.; Mills, G.; and Whitaker, J.K. ECONOMETRIC ANALYSIS FOR NATIONAL ECONOMIC PLANNING. Foreword by R.S.W. Clarke. Preface by R.C. Tress. London: Butterworths, 1964. xi, 297 p. No index.

Twelve papers presented at a symposium on econometrics sponsored by the Colston Research Society of England held at the University of Bristol, April 6-9, 1964, classified into the following five headings: "Econometric Methodology" (two papers); "Econometric Application" (two papers); "Aggregate Econometric Models" (four papers); "Economic Theory" (one paper); and "Optimizing Models" (three papers). Emphasizes econometric problems of Western industrial nations and include such topics as inflation in the United Kingdom; estimating parameters of a production function model for the United Kingdom; estimation of a family consumption function; a linear optimizing model of the French economy; optimum saving and growth in a two-sector model with a finite planning horizon; optimal economic organization for national planning; and progress on large scale national econometric model building in the United States, the United Kingdom, and the Netherlands.

Hasenkamp. Georg. SPECIFICATION AND ESTIMATION OF MULTIPLE-OUTPUT PRODUCTION FUNCTIONS. Lecture Notes in Economics and Mathematical Systems, vol. 120. New York: Springer-Verlag, 1976. vi, 151 p. References, pp. 146-51. No index.

> A contribution to applied work in production treating the measurement problem whenever several outputs are jointly produced and presenting an econometric model for estimating production function parameters whenever relative prices of outputs vary. Model estimated using U.S. railroad cross-section data for 1928-1936 and time series for the U.S. private domestic economy for the years 1929-69.

Hawkins, R.G.; Kelly, Margaret R.; and Lightfoot, R.E. FACTOR DEMANDS, STOCKS AND PRICES: AN INTER-RELATED APPROACH. Occasional Paper, no. 3H. Sidney: Reserve Bank of Australia, 1972. 67 p. References, pp. 48-52. Appendix A: The Algebra of Cost Minimization, p. 53. Appendix B: Factor Demand Identities, pp. 54-57. Appendix C: Notations and Data Sources, pp. 58-62. Appendix D: Data Listing, pp. 63-67. No index.

> The eight in a series of papers on a project designed to develop quarterly models of the Australian economy. Presents a model of the inter-related factor demands in which the desired inputs of fixed capital, employment, and hours worked conform to a single explicitly specified production function. Factor adjustment paths related to one another by means of a set of assumptions about relative factor adjustment speeds. Model tested using quarterly data from 1958 to 1970.

Heady, Earl O., and Dillon, John L. AGRICULTURAL PRODUCTION FUNCTIONS. Ames: Iowa State University Press, 1961. viii, 667 p. Bibliography, pp. 645-63. Index, pp. 665-67.

> A text and reference on formal production function concepts in agriculture with summaries of results from selected production function studies. Includes linear Cobb-Douglas; Spillman exponential; quadratic forms; resistance formula; power; square root; and certain surface functions. Includes collection and analysis for estimation, multicollinearity, autocorrelation, experimental design, and results of studies for hogs fed in drylot, hogs on pasture, broilers, turkeys, milk, and beef. Concludes with a formal analysis of crop response surfaces in fertilizer use, functions for fixed farm size, and a comparison of production function estimates from farm samples over the world.

Henderson, James M. THE EFFICIENCY OF THE COAL INDUSTRY: AN APPLICATION OF LINEAR PROGRAMMING. Cambridge, Mass.: Harvard University Press, 1958. xii, 146 p. Appendix A: Data: Sources and Rectification, pp. 119-32. Appendix B: A Short-Run Model for Agriculture, pp. 133-37. A Selected Bibliography, pp. 139-44. Index, pp. 145-46.

A monograph devoted to the study of the deviation of the bituminous coal industry from perfectly competitive norms using the transportation problem model of linear programming and data for the years 1947, 1949, and 1951. Objective function minimizes the total cost of extraction and transportation from twenty-two coal deposits and fourteen consuming areas. Linear program includes thirty-seven equations and 190 variables. Information used includes spatially distributed demands for coal, capacities of spatially distributed coal deposits, and unit costs of deliveries from deposits to consuming locations.

Henderson, James M., and Krueger, Anne O., with the collaboration of Rodd, R. Stephen, and Adams, John S. NATIONAL GROWTH AND ECONOMIC CHANGE IN THE UPPER MIDWEST. A Publication of the Upper Midwest Economic Study. Minneapolis: University of Minn. Press, 1965. xiii, 231 p. Appendix A: Projection Methods, pp. 159-65. Appendix B: Basic Data and Projections for 1960 and 1975, pp. 167-77. Appendix C: Maintenance of Upper Midwest Data, pp. 178-81. Appendix D: Upper Midwest County Indicators, pp. 182-227. Appendix E: UMES Publications, p. 228. Index, pp. 229-31.

A summary of the Upper Midwest Economic Study (UMES) with emphasis on future development and action alternatives. Includes projections of income and employment for 1960 and 1975 for thirty-eight income-generating sectors plus agriculture in six upper midwest states by a system of simultaneous equations containing 690 equations, 921 variables, and 2,784 parameters. Defines nine regions outside the upper midwest for classification of external purchases and trade flows--seven within the United States and Canada with the rest of the world forming the remaining two.

Henripin, J., and Asimakopulos, A., eds. CONFERENCES ON STATISTICS 1962 and 1963. Toronto: University of Toronto Press, for the Canadian Political Science Association, 1964. vii, 260 p. No index.

Eight papers presented at the third and fourth conferences on statistics held at McMaster University in Hamilton, Ontario, June 10-11, 1962, and at Laval University (Quebec), June 8-9, 1963. Topics include quantitative analyses of Canadian election results; historical statistics on growth and structure in manufacturing in Canada; an econometric study of the reliability of Canadian annual national accounts; short-term forecasting of nonresidential construction; and ratio estimates and sample surveys.

Hickman, Bert G., ed. ECONOMETRIC MODELS OF CYCLICAL BEHAVIOR. Vol. I. Studies in Income and Wealth, no. 36. New York: Columbia University Press, for the NBER and the Social Science Research Council Committee on Economic Stability, 1972. xiii, 598 p. Appendix to Part I: Equations and

Definitions of Variables for the FRB-PENN Econometric Model, November 1969, by A. Ando, F. Modigliani, and R. Rosche, pp. 543-98. No index.

Four out of ten papers presented at a conference on econometric models of cyclical behavior held at Harvard University November 14-15, 1969: "Short- and Long-Term Simulations with the OBE Econometric Model," by G.R. Green, in association with M. Liebenberg and A.A. Hirsch; "Short-Run Prediction and Long-Run Simulation of the Wharton Model," by M.K. Evans, L.R. Klein, M. Saito, and M.D. McCarthy; "Short- and Long-Run Simulations with the Brookings Model," by G. Fromm, L.R. Klein, and G.R. Schink; and "Business Cycle Analysis of Econometric Model Simulations," by V. Zarnowity, C. Boschan, G.H. Moore, and J. Su.

_____. ECONOMETRIC MODELS OF CYCLICAL BEHAVIOR. Vol. II. Studies in Income and Wealth, no. 36. New York: Columbia University Press, for the NBER, 1972. xi, pp. 601-1246. Author Index, pp. 1219-21. Subject Index, pp. 1223-46.

Six papers out of eleven presented at a conference on econometric models of cyclical behavior held at Harvard University November 14-15, 1969: "Dynamic Properties of a Condensed Version of the Wharton Model," by E.P. Howrey; "Effects of Aggregation Over Time on Dynamic Characteristics of an Econometric Model," by R.F. Engle and Ta-chung Lio; "An Econometric Model of Business Cycles," by G.C. Chow and G.H. Moore, assisted by An-loh Lin; "The Predictive Performance of Quarterly Econometric Models of the United States," by R.L. Cooper: "An Analysis of the Forecasting Properties of U.S. Econometric Models," by M.K. Evans, Y. Haitovsky, and G.I. Treyz, assisted by V. Su; and "Forecasting with Statistical Indicators," by D.J. Dale.

Hildebrand, George H., and Liu, Ta-chung. MANUFACTURE PRODUCTION FUNCTIONS IN THE UNITED STATES: AN INTERINDUSTRY AND INTERSTATE COMPARISON OF PRODUCTIVITY. Cornell Studies in Industrial and Labor Relations, no. XV. New York: New York School of Industrial and Labor Relations, Cornell University, 1965. xi, 224 p. Appendix I: Output-Labor, Capital-Labor, and Certain Other Important Data on Seventeen Manufacturing Industries in 1957, pp. 160-86. Appendix II: Estimated Marginal Physical and Revenue Products of Labor and Capital by Industry and by State, 1957, pp. 187-201. Appendix III: Results of a Sample Study of Manufacturing Production Functions for New York State, pp. 202-13. Appendix IV: Rejected Estimates for the Textile and the Furniture and Fixtures Industries, pp. 214-16. Bibliography, pp. 217-21. Index, pp. 223-24.

Uses a seven equation simultaneous equation model to estimate production functions and labor demand functions for fifteen two-digit industries in American manufacturing using cross-section data from the Census of Manufacturers for 1957. Estimated by ordinary least squares and two-stage least squares.

Hildreth, Clifford, and Jarrett, F.G. STATISTICAL STUDY OF LIVESTOCK PRODUCTION AND MARKETING. Cowles Commission for Research in Economics, monograph no. 15. New York: Wiley, 1955. xiii, 156 p. Appendix, pp. 130-51. Index, pp. 153-56.

Formulates a simultaneous equation model of livestock and marketing consisting of the following seven equations: production relation, demand for feed grain, demand for protein, supply of livestock products, demand for livestock products, supply of feed grains, supply of protein feeds, and an inventory relation. Estimated by ordinary least squares and limited-information maximum likelihood techniques using annual data from 1920 to 1949.

Hilton, Kenneth, and Heathfield, David H., eds. THE ECONOMETRIC STUDY OF THE UNITED KINGDOM: PROCEEDINGS OF THE 1969 SOUTHHAMPTON CONFERENCE ON SHORT-RUN ECONOMETRIC MODELS OF THE UNITED KINGDOM ECONOMY. New York: Augustus M. Kelley, 1970. xvi, 514 p. Appendix I: Papers Discussed but not presented to the Conference, pp. 479-94. Appendix II: Summaries of Other Papers Presented to the Conference, pp. 497-503. Index, pp. 505-14.

Seventeen heretofore unpublished papers presented to the conference grouped under the following four headings: "Large-Scale Econometric Models" (two papers); "Sector Studies" (nine papers "Methods" (four papers); and "Current Forecasting Methods" (two papers). Also includes two nonconference papers and summaries of four other papers. Topics include the Southhampton and National Institute of Economic and Social Research Econometric Models of the United Kingdom; forecasting of consumption, imports, dividends, investment, and monetary sectors; a computerized data bank; fiscal policy simulation of the U.K. economy, 1955-56; serial correlation in econometric models; short- and long-term econometric models; an interim report on a quarterly statistical model of the U.K. economy; and an economic analysis of the U.K. balance of payments on current account.

Hood, William C., and Sawyer, John A., eds. CONFERENCE ON STATISTICS 1961. Toronto: University of Toronto Press, for the Canadian Political Science Association, 1963. viii, 170 p. No index.

Ten papers presented at the second conference on statistics held at Sir George William University, Montreal, June 11-12, 1961. Topics include inter-industry estimates of Canadian imports, 1949-58; regional table of inter-industry flows for Province of Quebec; characteristics of persons looking for work; and regional aspects of Canadian labor mobility.

Houck, James P.; Ryan, Mary E.; and Subotnik, Abraham. SOYBEANS AND THEIR PRODUCTS: MARKETS, MODELS AND POLICY. Minnesota: University of Minnesota Press, 1972. x, 284 p. Appendix A: Description and Sources of Data, pp. 261-72. Appendix B: Effective Support Prices and Acreage Supply Functions: A General Approach, pp. 273-75. Index, pp. 276-84.

A research report on analytical and statistical supply and demand models of postwar markets for U.S. soybeans and products. Demand model includes thirteen simultaneous relationships, seven behavioral and six physical and technical (identities) equations. Estimated by ordinary least squares, two-stage least squares, and three-stage least squares using data from 1946 to 1967. Supply model includes six regional supply response equations (each equation is a multiple regression model with soybean acreage the dependent variable) and a national aggregate identity. Demand and supply models joined together by a market-clearing equation which assures that crop-year demand equals crop-year supply available from current production and carryover stocks.

Houthakker, Hendrik S., and Taylor, Lester D. CONSUMER DEMAND IN THE UNITED STATES: ANALYSES AND PROJECTIONS. 2d ed., rev. and enl. Harvard Studies, vol. CXXVI. Cambridge, Mass.: 1970, xii, 321 p. Data Sources, pp. 311-12. References, pp. 313-16. Index, pp. 317-21.

Estimates demand equations for each of eighty-one items of consumption. Includes forecasts for 1970 and 1975. Seventy-nine out of eighty-one equations dynamic in the sense that quantity of a particular item depends on price, income, and the pre-existing inventory of the item in question. Demand equations include past values of the predetermined variables as independent variables. Uses a three-pass least squares estimation procedure to overcome the effect of autocorrelation. Uses annual per capita data in constant dollars from 1929 to 1964 and provides regression estimates for each item of expenditure. Models include linear, semi-logarithm, double-logarithms, and inverse semi-logarithms.

Ingram, Gregory K.; Kain, John F.; and Ginn, J. Royce. With Contributions by H. James Brown and Stephen P. Dresch. THE DETROIT PROTOTYPE OF THE NBER URBAN SIMULATION MODEL. Foreword by J.R. Meyer. Urban and Regional Studies, 1. New York: Columbia University Press, for the NBER, 1972. xix, 233 p. Appendix A: Programming Considerations and Printed Output from the Model, pp. 175-91. Appendix B: The Choice of Housing Types Made by San Francisco Households (with H. James Brown), pp. 192-211. Appendix C: Analysis of the Two-Stage Procedure for Estimating Gross Price Effects (with Stephen P. Dresch), pp. 212-15. Appendix D: A Summary of Major Variables and Program Operations, pp. 216-24. Bibliography, pp. 225-28. Index, pp. 229-33.

A monograph which describes the Detroit prototype of the NBER Urban Simulation Model. Topics include the comparison of the NBER model with existing models, including the RAND model for the study of urban transportation; structure of the NBER model; theoretical issues and practical alternatives in model design; Detroit and the modeled city; modeling demographic behavior; modeling the housing market; gross price effects and estimation of submarket demand parameters; problems of calculating the Detroit Prototype; and characteristics of Pittsburgh I and II models. Appendix B summarizes submarket demand equations for San Francisco households.

Isard, Walter, and Langford, Thomas W. REGIONAL INPUT-OUTPUT STUDY: RECOLLECTIONS, REFLECTIONS, AND DIVERSE NOTES ON THE PHILADELPHIA EXPERIENCE. Regional Science Studies Series, 10. Cambridge: MIT Press, 1971. xvii, 228 p. Index, pp. 223-28.

Consists of comments and discussions on the 496-sector, 1959 input-output table of the Philadelphia region. Topics include choice of region, choice of base year, selection of a sector classification system, general survey procedures, secondary production and margins, construction of coefficients, estimation, final demand sectors, reconciliation and the undistributed and dummy sectors, subarea analysis, measurement of indirect effects and the use of the inverse, impact of Vietnam war expenditures on the Philadelphia economy, environmental quality analysis and standardization, and new directions. Useful to anyone interested in input-output analysis.

Jacobsson, Lars. AN ECONOMETRIC MODEL OF SWEDEN. Stockholm: J. Beckmans Bokforlag, 1972. 348 p. Appendix I: Estimates, Symbols, and Sources for the Model Estimates, pp. 237-60. Appendix II: The Revised Model-List of Equations, pp. 313-40. Bibliography, pp. 341-48. No index.

Presents a semiannual, simultaneous equation model for the Swedish economy consisting of both a nominal and real part designed for forecasting economic development and illustrating the effects of different measures of economic policy and other exogenous changes in the economy. Consists of eleven categories: labor market, wages, income of private entrepreneurs, household taxes, household disposable income, private consumption, production in mining and manufacturing, inventories, importa, exports, and investments. Estimated by two-stage least squares and ordinary least squares using data from 1955 to 1965. Includes forecasts for 1969-1972.

Johnston, John. STATISTICAL COST ANALYSIS. Economics Handbook Series. New York: McGraw-Hill, 1960. x, 197 p. Index, pp. 195-97.

An integrated survey of the field of statistical cost functions, including the mathematical formulation of various hypotheses, problems involved in statistical analyses, and an assessment of the results in such industries as electricity, road passenger transport, food processing, insurance, and mining. Employs both simple and multiple regression models. Intended as a reference for courses in economic theory, theory of the firm, business economics, business administration, operations research, and accounting. Assumes knowledge of regression analysis.

Jorgenson, Dale W., ed. ECONOMETRIC STUDIES OF U.S. ENERGY POLICY. Data Resources Series, vol. 1. New York: Elsevier, 1976. xvi, 251 p. References, pp. 243-48. Index, pp. 249-51.

Consists of the following econometric studies, not previously published, of the Energy Policy Project, sponsored by the Ford Foundation: "Tax Policy and Energy Conservation," by Edward A. Hudson and Dale W. Jorgenson; "A World Oil Model," by Michael Kennedy; and "A Study of the Demand for Gasoline," by Philip K. Verleger, Jr. and Dennis P. Sheehan. Includes an interindustry model of the U.S. economy that relates economic growth and energy utilization to demand and supply for energy resources. Presents a regional multi-market general equilibrium model of the international oil industry, consisting of four segments (crude production, transportation, refining, and consumption of products) relating the growth in world trade and pricing policies of petroleum exporters to world trade in petroleum and U.S. petroleum imports. Presents a single-equation model of U.S. demand for gasoline using quarterly data from 1963 to 1972 focusing on the impact of price changes on gasoline demand and its regional distribution within the United States.

Katz, Jorge M. PRODUCTION FUNCTIONS, FOREIGN INVESTMENT AND GROWTH: A STUDY BASED ON THE ARGENTINE MANUFACTURING SECTOR 1946-1961. Contributions to Economic Analysis, vol. 58. Amsterdam: North-Holland, 1969. 203 p. Bibliography, pp. 195-203. No index.

An inquiry into the sources and nature of economic growth in the manufacturing sector of Argentina and into the distribution between the factors of production of the benefits of economic growth. Uses the CES production function to derive cross-regional estimates of the elasticity of substitution between capital and labor for fifteen Argentine industries for 1946 and 1954. Elasticities, as well as the rate of technical progress for each industry, also derived by the CES production function using time series for 1943 to 1953, and from 1954 to 1961. Other estimates include returns to scale in manufacturing, productivity, and unit labor and unit material costs. Assumes knowledge of mathematical economics and econometrics.

Kendrick, John W. Assisted by Maude R. Peck. PRODUCTIVITY TRENDS IN THE UNITED STATES, 1948-1969. NBER General Series, no. 18. Princeton, N.J.: Princeton University Press, for the NBER, 1961. xx, 369 p. Appendix: Sources and Methods, pp. 145-359. Index, pp. 361-69.

Derives postwar productivity trends for thirty-two industry groupings for the period 1948-66 with preliminary estimates through 1969. Includes estimates of correlations among rates of change in productivity, output, and associated variables.

Kettunen, Lauri. DEMAND AND SUPPLY OF PORK AND BEEF IN FINLAND. Publications of the Agricultural Economics Research Institute, no. 11. Helsinki: Agricultural Economics Research Institute, 1968. 93 p. References, pp. 84-85. Appendix I: List of Variables and Sources of Data, pp. 86-87. Appendix II: Linear Correlation Coefficients of the Variables Included in Each Function, pp. 88-89. Appendix III: Observed Values of the Variables in the Analysis, pp. 90-92. Appendix IV: Deflators and Population, Quarterly Values, 1954-65, p. 93. No index.

Uses quarterly time series data for 1956 to 1965 and recursive and block recursive simultaneous equations models to estimate the demand and supply of pork and beef in Finland by ordinary least squares and two-stage least squares. Dependent variables include production, net imports, consumption, deflated retail price, price margins, and producer prices. Selection of independent variables based on a careful analysis of the beef and pork sectors and include predetermined variables for many equations. Useful to the Finnish government for setting target prices for beef and pork.

Klein, Lawrence R. ECONOMIC FLUCTUATIONS IN THE UNITED STATES, 1921-1941. Cowles Commission Monographs, no. 11. New York: Wiley, 1950. xii, 174 p. Appendix, pp. 135-68. Index, pp. 169-74.

An extension of Jan Tinbergen's earlier League of Nations investigations on statistical testing and measurement of business cycles in the United States. Develops mathematically the theories of the firm and the consumer relevant to model building. Includes three econometric models: a three-equation system (with three endogenous variables) consisting of consumption, investment, and labor demand equations plus three definitional equations estimated by maximum likelihood, reduced form (limited-information), and ordinary least squares; a reduced form model estimated by ordinary least squares; and a twelve stochastic equation model estimated by reduced form. Uses data for the years 1921-41.

_____. AN ESSAY ON THE THEORY OF ECONOMIC PREDICTION. Markham Economic Series. Chicago: Markham, 1971. 140 p. Appendix, pp. 105-33. Index, pp. 135-40.

Based on the Yrjo Jahnsson lectures delivered by the author at the University of Helsinki, April 1-5, 1968. Represents the author's experience in model building during the 1960s and include such topics as types of prediction, prediction error, improvement of prediction, degree of aggregation, and predictive vs. structural models. Formulas and equations used for illustrative purposes, but no numerical examples provided.

______, ed. ESSAYS IN INDUSTRIAL ECONOMETRICS. Vol. I. Studies in Quantitative Economics, no. 3. Philadelphia: University of Pennsylvania, Economic Research Unit, 1969. x, 172 p. No index.

Three heretofore unpublished contributions to econometric analysis of industries: "A Dynamic Supply and Demand Model of the United States Automobile Industry, Together with a Simulation Experiment," by Hiroya Ueno and Hiroki Tsurumi; "An Econometric Study of Oligopolistic Competition Among American Automobile Firms, Together with a Forecast Exercise," by Hiroki Tsurumi; and "An Econometric Model of the United States Petroleum Refining Industry," by F. Gerard Adams and James M. Griffin.

______. ESSAYS IN INDUSTRIAL ECONOMETRICS. Vol. II. Studies in Quantitative Economics, no. 4. Philadelphia: University of Pennsylvania, Economic Research Unit, 1969. x, 202 p. No index.

The following three heretofore unpublished contributions on the econometrics of American industry: "An Econometric Description of the U.S. Steel Industry," by Christopher I. Higgins; "An Agricultural Submodel for the U.S. Economy," by Michael K. Evans; and "Capacity Balance in the Chemical Industry," by Helen Malenbaum.

______. ESSAYS IN INDUSTRIAL ECONOMETRICS. Vol. III. Studies in Quantitative Economics, no. 5. Philadelphia: University of Pennsylvania, Economic Research Unit, 1969. 211 p. No index.

The following three heretofore unpublished econometric studies of industries: "Econometric Model Simulations of the World Rubber Market, 1950-1980," by Jere R. Behrman; "An Econometric Study of the Japanese Steel Industry," by Tsunehiko Watanabe and Soshichi Kinoshita; and "A Dynamic Demand-Supply Model of the Japanese Automobile Industry, 1955-1966," by Hiroya Ueno and Hiromichi Muto.

Klein, Lawrence R.; Ball, R.J.; Hazlewood, A.; and Vandome, P. AN ECONOMETRIC MODEL OF THE UNITED KINGDOM. Oxford University of Statistics Monographs, 6. Oxford, Engl.: Basil Blackwell, 1961. xii, 312 p. Appendix I: Diagrams of the Quarterly Estimates, pp. 223-53. Appendix II: Least Squares Estimates of Equations Estimated in Chapter III by the Method of Limited Information Maximum Likelihood, pp. 255-59. Appendix III: Some Dynamics of the Price Level, pp. 261-75. Appendix IV: The Numerical Data, pp. 277-304. Index, pp. 305-12.

Presents a prototype eleven equation simultaneous equation annual model of the United Kingdom, containing eleven endogenous variables and thirteen predetermined (lagged endogenous or exogenous) variables estimated from sample data for the period 1947-56 for explaining movements in industrial production. Annual prototype extended to a thirty-seven equation quarterly model using thirty-six observations from the period 1948-56 with the period 1946-47 used to provide initial lagged values in some of the equations. Estimated by both least squares and by limited information maximum likelihood methods.

Klein, Lawrence R., and Burmeister, Edwin, eds. ECONOMETRIC MODEL PERFORMANCE: COMPARATIVE STUDIES OF THE U.S. ECONOMY. Philadelphia: University of Pennsylvania, 1976. vi, 407 p. No index.

Eighteen papers presented at various symposia held by the Conference on Econometrics and Mathematical Economics sponsored by the NBER and NSF. Considers eleven models with emphasis on comparing simulations results in their respective sample periods (ex ante forecasting) as well as extrapolations beyond the sample period (ex post forecasting). Models include Wharton Mark III St. Louis Model, Data Resources Model, BEA model, Michigan Quarterly Econometric Model of the U.S. Economy, Hickman-Coen Annual Growth Model, Brookings Quarterly, NBER/NSF, MIT/PENN/SSRC (MPS), and LIU-HWA models. Other topics include testing the predictive performance of models; rate of expectations of price and technological change; asymptotic theory and large models; and birth control in an econometric simulation.

Klein, Lawrence R., and Goldberger, Arthur S. AN ECONOMETRIC MODEL OF THE UNITED STATES 1929-1952. Contributions to Economic Analysis, IX. Amsterdam: North-Holland, 1955. xv, 165 p. Explanation of Symbols, pp. xiv-xv. Appendix I: The Basic Time Series, pp. 115-41. Appendix II: The Tax-Transfer Functions, pp. 142-55. Appendix III: Residuals from Estimated Equations, pp. 156-59. Index, pp. 161-65.

Presents a twenty equation econometric model of the United States which others could apply to practical economic problems of business cycle forecasting. Model consists of twenty endogenous variables, including gross private domestic capital formation, national income, and an index of hourly wages, and eighteen exogenous variables including population, number of government employees, and government expenditures. Includes a table of the differences between actual values of the main endogenous variables and those estimated by the structural equations for 1953 and 1954 with the observed values of the explanatory variables inserted for the years 1949-54.

Klein, Lawrence R., and Summers, Robert. THE WHARTON INDEX OF CAPACITY UTILIZATION. Studies in Quantitative Economics, no. 1. Philadelphia: University of Pennsylvania, Economics Research Unit, Wharton School of Finance and Commerce, 1966. vii, 94 p. References, pp. 93-94. No index.

An exploration on the construction of indices of utilization of industrial and service capacities for thirty-six industries consisting of: (1) method of estimating capacity; (2) data used; (3) method of implementing the index for each industry; and (4) procedure used for combining industry indices into an aggregate index. Data obtained from government sources and from trade associations for 1946-1966. Measures of capacity utilization useful in econometrics forecasting models where they appear in the investment function, price equation, hours worked equation, and production function.

Komiya, Ryūtaro, ed. POSTWAR ECONOMIC GROWTH IN JAPAN. Translation by Robert S. Ozaki. Publications of the Center for Japanese and Korean Studies. Berkeley and Los Angeles: University of California Press, 1966. xviii, 260 p. Bibliography of Japanese Sources With Their English Titles, pp. 253-56. Index, pp. 257-60.

Originally published in Japanese. Eleven papers of the seventeen papers presented at the first conference of the Tokyo Economic Research Center held in Tokyo in January 1963, and ten comments. Deal with the nature and causes of Japan's postwar economic growth. Grouped under the following five headings: "Public Finance and Monetary Policy" (three papers); "The Balance of Payments" (two papers); "Income Distribution and Savings" (three papers); "Business Fluctuations and Stabilization Policy" (two papers); and "Management" (one paper). Includes simulation analysis of the Japanese economy by Kei Mori using the econometric model developed by Uchids and Associates for the year 1955-1960; technical innovations and the balance of payments crisis; labor's share of income; the role of savings; and the stabilization role of fiscal policy.

Kravis, Irving B., et al. Assisted by Sultan Ahmad. A SYSTEM OF INTERNATIONAL COMPARISONS OF GROSS NATIONAL PRODUCT AND PURCHASING POWER: UNITED NATIONS INTERNATIONAL COMPARISON PROJECT: PHASE ONE. Baltimore: Johns Hopkins University Press, for the World Bank, 1975. xi, 294 p. Glossary, pp. 287-89. Index, pp. 291-94.

Constructs a framework for intercountry comparisons of national accounts aggregates on a comparable basis other than the officially set exchange rates. Six countries compared for 1967 and ten (four in addition to the original six) for 1970. Also tests and describes suitable techniques for a more comprehensive comparison for future stages of research. Concludes that per capita income using official exchange rates were underestimated by 15 percent to 249 percent as compared to the United States.

Kuh, Edwin. CAPITAL STOCK GROWTH: A MICRO-ECONOMETRIC APPROACH. Contributions to Economic Analysis, XXXI. Amsterdam: North-Holland, 1963. xvi, 341 p. Subject Index, pp. 337-39. Author Index, pp. 340-41.

A sequel to an earlier study on investment behavior, THE INVESTMENT DECISION (Harvard University Press, 1957) by the author, in which an attempt is made to explain investment by stock of capital, sales, profits, and a capital intensity index using both time series and cross-section data for sixty firms for the period 1935-1955. Evaluates the relative importance of profits compared to sales and investment, with particular attention given to the problems of specification and aggregation. Employs single-equation regression models and provides regression estimates.

Labys, Walter C. DYNAMIC COMMODITY MODELS: SPECIFICATION, ESTIMATION, AND SIMULATION. Lexington, Mass.: Heath, Lexington Books, 1973. xvii, 350 p. Appendix A: Stability Conditions for First and Higher Order Systems, pp. 247-50. Appendix B: Spectral Validation of Commodity Markets, pp. 251-55. Appendix C: An Inventory of Commodity Models, pp. 256-71. Bibliography, pp. 272-346. Index, pp. 347-50.

A monograph on the theory and methods for specifying, estimating, validating, and applying commodity models which describe behavior of a quarterly, annual, or monthly phenomena, as well as simulating the models for historical explanation and prediction. Includes components or separate behavioral relationships necessary for constructing a model (i.e., demand, supply, inventories, and prices); considers how these different relationships can be incorporated into a complete econometric model, taking into account model specification, estimation, and validation; and illustrates the applications of commodity models to a variety of policy problems utilizing multiplier analysis and simulation. Useful as a reference for commodity model builders, price theorists, and econometricians.

______, ed. QUANTITATIVE MODELS OF COMMODITY MARKETS. Cambridge, Mass.: Lippincott, Ballinger, 1975. xxi, 404 p. Appendix: Bibliography of Commodity Models, pp. 379-99. Index, pp. 401-4.

Eleven contributions on quantitative studies pertaining to the economic behavior of commodity markets, treating such topics as a linear programming model of the U.S. petroleum refining industry, simulation of the world coffee economy, estimation of continuous-time models of the sugar market, feedback control for cocoa market stabilization, model of living marine resources, and the price structure of the U.S. beef, pork, and broiler markets. Useful to commodity price makers, commodity economists, students, and research workers.

Labys, Walter C., and Granger, C.W.J. SPECULATION, HEDGING AND COMMODITY PRICE FORECASTS. Lexington, Mass.: Heath, Lexington Books, 1970. xxv, 320 p. Appendix A: Data, pp. 275-80. Appendix B: Computations, pp. 281-82. Notes, pp. 283-93. Bibliography, pp. 295-314. Index, pp. 317-20.

Presents a short-term price behavior model capable of both explanation and prediction using weekly, daily, and monthly prices of selected commodities traded on American domestic markets from 1950 to 1966 with forecasts through 1967. Includes methods of spectra and cross-spectra analysis, stepwise regression, random walk, Box-Jenkins, exponential smoothing, and simultaneous equations. Speculative influences found dominant in price behavior. Useful to a wide audience, including statisticians, econometricians, price theoreticians, commodity economists, graduate students, and research workers.

Laughhunn, D.J. ON THE PREDICTIVE VALUE OF COMBINING CROSS-SECTION AND TIME SERIES DATA IN EMPIRICAL DEMAND STUDIES. University of Illinois Bulletin Series, no. 92. Urbana: University of Illinois, Bureau of Economics and Business Research, 1969. x, 152 p. Appendix A: Definitions of Expenditure Categories, pp. 117-24. Appendix B: Significance Tests for Model III, pp. 125-34. Appendix C: Marginal Distributions, pp. 135-40. Appendix D: Time-Series Data, 1929-1964, pp. 141-46. Appendix E: Predictive Test Results, pp. 147-52. No index.

Presents a series of tests to investigate whether the combination of time series and cross-section data will increase the predictive accuracy of demand functions relative to that obtainable for demand functions estimated from time series alone. Includes three single-equation models. Model I relies on time series data alone; model II utilizes a marginal propensity to consume estimate from cross-section data; and model III combines an extraneous consumption budget estimate with a distributional effect.

Lerner, Daniel, ed. QUANTITY AND QUALITY. Glencoe, Ill.: Free Press, 1961. 221 p. Notes on Contributors, pp. 213-15. Guide to Further Reading, pp. 217-21.

Eight nontechnical papers presented at the second Hayden Colloquium on scientific method held at MIT. Topics include mathematics without numbers; quantification of sensation; and quantification in quantum physics, electrical activity of the nervous system, political and legal analysis, and economics. Includes a lengthy paper on the history of quantification in economics, by Joseph J. Spengler.

Lin, Steven A.Y., ed. THEORY AND MEASUREMENT OF ECONOMIC EXTERNALITIES. Economic Theory and Mathematical Economics. New York: Academic Press, 1976. xiv, 265 p. Index, pp. 261-65.

Twelve papers presented at a conference on externalities held at Southern Illinois University at Edwardsville, April 19-20, 1974. Emphasized analytical formulation and empirical applications to current problems. Grouped under four headings: "The Nature of Externalities" (two papers); "Externalities in

General Equilibrium" (three papers); "Externalities in Collective and Decentralized Decision Making" (three papers); and "Measurement of Externalities" (four papers). Topics include externality taxes and subsidies; information, incentives, and the internalization of production externalities; a generalized cost allocation scheme; collective choice and the Lindohl allocation method; noncooperative general exchange; an economic model of airport noise pollution in an urban environment; and externality production functions. Many papers assume knowledge of set theory, calculus, matrix algebra, and econometrics.

Linnemann, Hans. AN ECONOMETRIC STUDY OF INTERNATIONAL TRADE FLOWS. Contributions to Economic Analysis, vol. 42. Amsterdam: North-Holland, 1966. xiii, 234 p. Appendix: Sources of Data Used in the Empirical Analysis, pp. 217-28. Author Index, pp. 229-30. Subject Index, pp. 231-34.

A quantitative analysis of trade flows among countries to determine why the size of international trade differs so much between different pairs of countries. Utilizes data on trade flows in 1959 among eighty countries and log-linear regression model to estimate the elasticities. Explanatory variables include nominal and real GNP, population, distance, and preference factor (preference for the United Kingdom and U.K. associates, preference for France and French associates, and Portuguese and Belgian colonial preference.

Lioi, Vittorio Corbo. INFLATION IN DEVELOPING COUNTRIES: AN ECONOMETRIC STUDY OF CHILEAN INFLATION. Contributions to Economic Analysis, vol. 84. New York: Elsevier, 1974. xix, 286 p. Appendixes A to C, pp. 247-75. References, pp. 277-81. Index, pp. 283-86.

Presents a microeconomic model to study the interaction among the main economic variables responsible for inflation in a developing country in three parts: "Monetarism, Structuralism and Past Studies of Chilean Inflation"; "A Quarterly Model for Industrial Prices, Industrial Wages and Inflation"; and "An Annual Study of Inflation." Model consists of forty-four behavioral equations, twenty-six identities and miscellaneous equations, and 101 variables, including thirty-three exogenous. Estimated using data in Chile from 1950 to 1970 by means of an iterative procedure available in the TROLL system at MIT Simulations made for the period 1963-1970 under different assumptions regarding unemployment and real wages, and foreign exchange accumulation and use. Appendixes contain the data used in the estimation of the quarterly model, the methods used to derive the different variables in the annual model, and an empirical study of the Kmenta approximation of the CES production function.

Lippitt, Vernon G. DETERMINANTS OF CONSUMER DEMAND FOR HOUSE FURNISHING AND EQUIPMENT. Cambridge, Mass.: Harvard University Press, 1959. xvii, 172 p. Appendix A: Types of Functional Relations and Aggregation Problems, pp. 145-51. Appendix B: Calculations of Income and Family-Type Effects when Cell Frequencies are Unequal, pp. 152-56. Bibliography, pp. 157-62. Index, pp. 163-72.

> An empirical analysis of the determinants of demand for kitchen equipment, cleaning equipment, laundry equipment, floor coverings, furniture, linens, glass, china and silverware, and miscellaneous items using cross-section budget data for 1,200 families from the 1935-36 Study of Consumer Purchases. Combines the results from budget data with time series for 1929-56 in constant 1935-36 prices. Includes twenty determinants of demand in two groups: family characteristics, and market conditions.

Lukacs, Eugene. STOCHASTIC CONVERGENCE. Heath Mathematical Monographs. Lexington, Mass.: Heath, 1968. x, 142 p. References, pp. 137-38. Index, pp. 139-42.

> A monograph on the convergence of numerically valued sequences of random variables based on strong limit theorems. Includes infinite series of random variables and discusses applications of such series; stochastic integrals and derivations; characterization of the normal distribution by properties of infinite sums of random variables; and characterizations of the Wiener process.

Lukacs, Eugene, and Laha, R.G. APPLICATIONS OF CHARACTERISTIC FUNCTIONS. Griffin's Statistical Monographs and Courses, no. 14. New York: Hafner, 1964. 202 p. Appendixes A to F, pp. 171-93. References, pp. 194-97. Index, pp. 199-202.

> A monograph on the application of characteristic functions to problems of theoretical statistics. Some topics studied primarily for their intrinsic mathematical interest. Includes proofs of theorems, but omits applications to probability theory. Topics include multivariate distributions, including normal, Poisson, and gamma types; the distribution problem of statistics; independence; regression problems; stochastic processes; identically distributed statistics; and stability theorems. Appendixes include basic concepts of probability, Fourier transforms of probability measures, stochastic convergence, determinants and matrices, and proofs of lemmas. Assumes knowledge of mathematical statistics and advanced calculus.

Lund, P.J., and Miner, D.A. AN ECONOMETRIC STUDY OF THE MACHINE TOOL INDUSTRY. Government Service Occasional Papers, 4. London: Her Majesty's Stationery Office, 1973. iii, 90 p. References, pp. 76-78. Appendix A: Calculation of Capacity Utilization and Business Optimism Series

Using CBJ Industrial Trends Survey Results, p. 79. Appendix B: The Rate of Tax on Company Profits, p. 80. Appendix C: The Value of Investment Inventories, p. 82. Appendix D: Quantity and Value Elasticities in Trade Equations, pp. 83-84. Appendix E: World Demand for U.K. Exports, p. 85. Bibliography, pp. 86-90. No index.

> Attempts to identify the factors determining the home production, imports, and exports for the U.K. machine tool industry in order to examine the structural relationships affecting the industry and to assist in forecasting. Specifies and estimates thirty-six regression equations for the 1958 IV-1968 II period. Variables include capital stock adjustment, expectations, the tax rate, and investment incentives. Incorporates two definitions of the dependent variables, two lag schemes, three measures of the capital stock in use, and three measures of expectations. Dependent variables include total market demand (twenty-two equations), import share (eight equations), and export share (six equations). Other regression equations developed for estimating home market and export market waiting times for deliveries of machine tools.

Maciariello, Joseph A. DYNAMIC BENEFIT-COST ANALYSIS: EVALUATION OF PUBLIC POLICY IN A DYNAMIC URBAN MODEL. Lexington, Mass.: Heath, xv, 184 p. Appendix A: The Basic Model, pp. 143-45. Appendix B: Tertiary Variables of the Basic Model, pp. 147-48. Appendix C: Cost and Benefit Evaluation of the Sacramento Transit Authority, pp. 149-63. Glossary, pp. 165-67. Index, pp. 181-84.

> Develops a dynamic benefit-cost technique with application to an urban simulation model. Model designed to overcome many deficiencies of static methods of benefit-cost procedures. Extensive sensitivity analysis used to locate key parameters and to evaluate the uncertainty in the net benefits. Knowledge of difference equations helpful to understand model development and results.

Mackrell, N.C. EQUATIONS FOR TAX PAYMENTS. Occasional Paper, no. 3C. Sydney: Reserve Bank of Australia, 1970. 28 p. References, p. 23. Data Appendix, pp. 24-27. Reserve Bank of Australia Publications, p. 28.

> Develops equations to explain quarterly tax payments in Australia. Tax payments disaggregated into three broad categories: personal income taxes; company income taxes; and indirect taxes. Equations developed to explain payments of P.A.Y.E. (pay-as-you-earn), non-P.A.Y.E. and total personal income taxes, company income taxes, total indirect taxes, and several important Commonwealth indirect taxes.

Malca, Edward. BANK-ADMINISTERED COMMINGLED PENSION FUNDS: PERFORMANCE AND CHARACTERISTICS, 1962 TO 1970. Lexington, Mass.:

Heath, Lexington Books, 1973. xiii, 93 p. Appendix: Distribution Tables, pp. 65-69. Notes, pp. 70-82. Bibliography, pp. 83-89. Index, pp. 91-93.

An attempt to measure by regression models true investment performance (based on rates of return and risk) of thirty-seven bank administered commingled private pension funds using quarterly data provided by about seventy-five banks during the nine-year period 1962-70. Performance measure calculated for each fund equals quarterly rate of return minus the rate that would have been earned on an equivalent-risk combination. Estimates the average beta coefficient for the commingled equity fund as 0.96 with a range of from 0.70 to 1.16. Suggests an inferior performance of commingled funds relative to unmanaged portfolios of similar risk.

Mansfield, Edwin. INDUSTRIAL RESEARCH AND TECHNOLOGICAL INNOVATION: AN ECONOMETRIC ANALYSIS. New York: W.W. Norton, for the Cowles Foundation for Research in Economics at Yale University, 1968. xviii, 235 p. Appendixes A to C, pp. 211-21. References, pp. 222-30. Index, pp. 231-35.

A monograph which brings together econometric studies of industrial research and technological innovation undertaken by the author over the years. Consists of five parts: "Introduction"; "Industrial Research and Development"; "Technological Innovation"; "Diffusion of Innovations"; and "Conclusions." Tests a number of single-equation regression models using data from 1919 to 1961 for industries such as steel, coal, petroleum, food, apparel, etc. Measures the influence of size of firm and market structure on research and development expenditures, and such factors as speed of response to innovation by individual firms, intrafirm rates of diffusion, and the rate of imitation. Knowledge of regression analysis necessary to interpret the research results.

Meadows, Dennis L. DYNAMICS OF COMMODITY PRODUCTION CYCLES. Cambridge, Mass.: Wright-Allen Press, 1970. xi, 104 p. Appendix A: The Dynamic Commodity Cycle Model, pp. 89-91. Appendix B: The Dynamic Hog Cycle Model, pp. 92-94. Appendix C: Cattle System Parameter Values, pp. 95-98. Bibliography, pp. 99-101. Index, pp. 103-4.

Reviews the literature of commodity cycles, analyzes the limitations of the cobweb model, and presents tests of a dynamic commodity cycle model using the U.S. hog cycle. Model formulated in terms of the BASIC computer language. Includes simulation of monthly prices and production for hogs, cattle, and chickens for the period 1958-1963.

Medgyessy, Pál. DECOMPOSITION OF SUPERPOSITIONS OF DISTRIBUTION FUNCTIONS. Revised by Károly Tandori and András Prekopa. Budapest: Hungarian Academy of Sciences, 1961. Appendixes 1 to 11, pp. 165-219.

Bibliography, pp. 221-22. Symbols and Notations, pp. 223-24. Name Index, p. 225. Subject Index, pp. 226-27.

A systematic treatment of the problem of the decomposition of superpositions of probability distribution functions of one variable with emphasis on practical applications. The presentation employs characteristic functions, Fourier-Stieltjes transforms, and Riemann-Stieltjes integration. Omits decomposition of continuous mixtures of distribution functions. Useful not only to mathematicians, but also to a wide circle of scientists. Assumes knowledge of classical analysis and probability theory.

Meyer, John R., and Glauber, Robert R. INVESTMENT DECISIONS, ECONOMIC FORECASTING, AND PUBLIC POLICY. Foreword by Bertrand Fox and John Lintner. Boston: Division of Research, Harvard Business School, 1964. xix, 280 p. Appendix A: The Sample, Industry Groupings, and Individual Firms, pp. 259-65. Appendix B: Time-Series Data, pp. 266-72. Selected Bibliography on Investment Decisions, pp. 273-76. Index, pp. 277-80.

Employs simple and multiple regression analysis to test the accelerator-residual funds hypothesis of the determinants of plant and equipment investment at different stages of cycle using cross-section data for twenty manufacturing industries for each of the years 1951-54 and quarterly time series data for 1948-60. Dependent variable is investment outlays, and the independent variables include profit, sales, changes in sales, and lagged investment. Results support the accelerator-residual funds theory of investment.

Meyer, John R., and Kuh, Edwin. THE INVESTMENT DECISION: AN EMPIRICAL STUDY. Harvard Economics Studies, vol. CII. Cambridge, Mass.: Harvard University Press, 1957. xv, 284 p. Appendix A: The Sample: Industry and Firm Coverage, pp. 209-32. Appendix B: Cross-Section Correlation and Regression Estimates, pp. 233-57. Appendix C: Correlation and Regression Estimates When the Data are Ratios, pp. 258-67. List of Works Cited, pp. 269-77. Index, pp. 279-84.

Uses cross-section data of about 600 individual firms in a multiple regression model for 1946-50 to test various hypotheses of investment behavior and the social consequences of that behavior in three parts: Introduction, Methods and Techniques, and Empirical Results. Explanatory variables for investment include depreciation, age of equipment, change in sales, capacity, liquidity stock, sales, and profit. Appendix B presents the correlation and regression estimates for each year for each of the fifteen industries. Assumes knowledge of regression analysis.

Minhas, Bagicha Singh. AN INTERNATIONAL COMPARISON OF FACTOR COSTS AND FACTOR USE. Contributions to Economic Analysis, vol. XXXI. Amsterdam: North-Holland, 1963. xii, 124 p. Appendix I: International

Data on Labor Inputs and Wage Rates, pp. 99-106. Appendix II: Rate of Return on Capital before Corporate Taxes, pp. 107-18. Bibliography, pp. 119-22. Index, pp. 123-24.

Attempts to explain international differences in factor inputs, for twenty-four industrial classifications, by assuming that different countries in the sample are on different points of a common production function. Also compares rates of return on capital from data collected in fifty countries. Uses constant elasticity of substitution production function to estimate the elasticities using cross-section data for 1950 and 1955. Rates of return on capital computed annually between 1949 and 1958 for twenty-two industrial groups for the United States, Canada, the United Kingdom, Japan, and India.

Miyazawa, Kenichi. INPUT-OUTPUT ANALYSIS AND THE STRUCTURE OF INCOME DISTRIBUTION. Lecture Notes in Economics and Mathematical Systems, vol. 116. New York: Springer-Verlag, 1976. ix, 135 p. References, pp. 129-31. Index, pp. 133-35.

Consists of three parts: "Input-Output and Income Formation"; "Internal and External Multipliers"; and "Dual Economic Structure." Relates input-output analysis to income analysis by means of a synthesis of the Leontief interindustry matrix multiplier and the Keynesian income multiplier in disaggregated form to introduce a new concept called the interrelational income multiplier. Designed to analyze the interrelationships among various income groups in the process of income formation through the medium of industrial production activity.

Morgenstern, Oskar, ed. ECONOMIC ACTIVITY ANALYSIS. New York: Wiley, 1954. xviii, 554 p. Index of Names, pp. 551-54.

Thirteen papers on activity analysis and linear programming made by the Economics Research Project, Princeton University, grouped under the following three headings: "Economic Properties of Input-Output Systems" (four papers); "Mathematical Properties of the Input-Output System" (seven papers); and "Meta-Economics" (two papers). Topics include models of general equilibrium; aggregation in input-output models, treatment of foreign and domestic trade and transportation; changes in the Leontief input-output table, properties of linear systems, characteristic roots of input-output models, matrices and trees, and large scale computation in economics.

Morgenstern, Oskar, and Thompson, Gerald L. MATHEMATICAL THEORY OF EXPANDING AND CONTRACTING ECONOMIES. Lexington, Mass.: Heath, Lexington Books, 1976. xvi, 275 p. Appendix 1: Matrix Games, pp. 225-32. Appendix 2: Linear Programming, pp. 233-38. Appendix 3: "A Model of General Economic Equilibrium," by John von Neumann, pp. 239-49. Appendix 3: "Game-Theoretic Solution of an Economic Problem," by John G.

Kemeny, pp. 251-55. Bibliography, pp. 257-68. Author Index, pp. 271-72. Subject Index, pp. 273-75.

A text for a course in mathematical programming economics for students who have knowledge of linear programming, game theory, matrix algebra, and set theory. Integrates both new and previously published material on expanding and contracting economic models relevant to the economy of any country, employing linear programming in large scale uses and game theory as a technique of proving theorems, as a device for computation, and as a model of economic activity when there is interaction among players. Topics include the idea of profitable industries supporting unprofitable industries; the combination of several open single country models to obtain an expanding world economy; and the identification of control variables and their uses in long-term world planning models, trading-blocks, international transactions balance of profit, etc. Numerous examples included throughout the text. Exercises follow the chapters.

Mulvaney, John Edward, and Mann, C.W. PRACTICAL BUSINESS MODELS. New York: Wiley, Halsted Press, 1976. viii, 171 p. No index.

A practical, oriented monograph on model building in the United Kingdom and Europe for managers (not for specialists in model building) with limited mathematics knowledge, based on the author's consulting experience since the mid-1960s for the Whitehead Consulting Group, Ltd. Topics include types of models and how and where to use them; market models; new-product models; planning models for an industrial economy; models for international investment; and managing with models.

National Council of Applied Economic Research. ALL INDIA RURAL HOUSEHOLD SURVEY. Vol. II. INCOME, INVESTMENT AND SAVING. New Delhi: 1965. xvii, 139 p. Tables, pp. 102-29. Appendix I: The Project Team, p. 132. Appendix 2: The Sampling Errors, pp. 133-38. Appendix 3: Computation of Depreciation, p. 139. No index.

Presents the findings of the Rural Household Survey which was launched in 1963 covering about 9,000 households in places below 10,000 population. Includes the following topics: sample design and household characteristics; components of tangible reproducible wealth; composition and distribution of income; sources of capital formation; financial assets; and patterns of savings.

The NBER. INPUT-OUTPUT ANALYSIS: AN APPRAISAL. Studies in Income and Wealth, vol. 18. Princeton, N.J.: Princeton University Press, for the NBER, 1955. x, 371 p. Index, pp. 369-71.

Seven papers dealing with the general problems, methods, and results of input-output analysis, and also a report on an input-output study for Puerto Rico presented at the conference on research in income and wealth held in October 1952. Topics include data problems, survey of current input-output models, comparisons of three social accounting systems, and interindustry economics and national income.

Nerlove, Marc. THE DYNAMICS OF SUPPLY: ESTIMATION OF FARMERS' RESPONSE TO PRICE. Johns Hopkins University Studies in Historical and Political Science. Series LXXVI, no. 2. Baltimore: Johns Hopkins University Press, 1958. 267 p. Bibliography, pp. 255-59. Index, pp. 261-67.

Reports on research undertaken to estimate short- and long-run elasticities and cross-elasticities of supply for corn, wheat, and cotton in the United States using single-equation distributed lag models and data from 1910 to 1951. Concentrates on acreage decisions rather than output decisions and deals primarily with the role which farmers' expectations of future relative prices play in shaping their decisions as to how many acres to devote to each crop.

Norton, W.E. A MODEL OF THE AUSTRALIAN ECONOMY: A PROGRESS REPORT. Occasional Paper, no. 3A. Sydney: Reserve Bank of Australia, 1970. 28 p. Notation, pp. 22-25. References, pp. 26-27. Reserve Bank of Australia Publications, p. 28. No index.

A progress report on the contribution of a quarterly neo-Keynesian model of the Australian economy containing thirty-two behavioral equations and fifteen identities. Identities include a government budget identity, and definitional, institutional, and balance sheet identities. Model incorporates lagged responses of investment, employment, and imports to changes in gross national product and relative prices using the Almon variable technique and the probability distribution method. Uses data from 1959 to 1967 with estimation by ordinary least squares.

______, ed. THREE STUDIES OF PRIVATE FIXED INVESTMENT. Occasional Paper, no. 3E. Sydney: Reserve Bank of Australia, 1971. 39 p. No index.

Contains the following three papers: "Equations for Business Fixed Investment," by N.C. Mackrell, J. Frisch, and P. Roape; "Equipment Investment: An Alternative Approach," by K.R. McLaren; "Investment in Dwellings: An Econometric Analysis," by G.P. Kelly and W.E. Norton. Indicates long lags between investment and its assumed determinants, the average lag being ten quarters for equipment investment and eight quarters for construction investment.

Norton, W.E., and Broadbent, Jillian R. EQUATIONS FOR PERSONAL CONSUMPTION EXPENDITURES. Occasional Paper, no. 3B. Sydney: Reserve

Bank of Australia, 1970. 28 p. References, pp. 24-25. Data Appendix, pp. 26-27. Reserve Bank of Australia Publications, p. 28.

Develops equations to explain quarterly movements in personal consumption expenditures disaggregated into three categories: motor vehicles, other durables (electrical goods and other household durables), and nondurables as aggregates of the other ten categories of personal consumption expenditures. Equations form part of the quarterly model of Australian economy.

Norton, W.E.; Cohen, A.M.; and Sweeny, K.M. A MODEL OF THE MONETARY SECTOR. Occasional Paper, no. 3D. Sydney: Reserve Bank of Australia, 1970. 32 p. References, p. 29. Data Appendix, pp. 30-31. Reserve Bank of Australia Publications, pp. 32. No index.

Develops a quarterly model of the Australian monetary sector as part of the quarterly model of the Australian economy. Variables include holdings by banks of notes, coin and cash balances, loans to the money market, advances and government securities, and the holdings by the non-bank private sector of currency, current deposits and fixed deposits. Consists of six behavioral equations and five are identities.

Norton, W.E., and Henderson, J.F. A MODEL OF THE AUSTRALIAN ECONOMY: A FURTHER REPORT. Occasional Paper, no. 3G. Sydney: Reserve Bank of Australia, 1972. 48 p. References, pp. 23-25. Appendix, pp. 26-48. No index.

Describes a revised version of the neo-Keynesian model of the Australian economy containing thirty-eight identities and forty-one behavioral equations. Uses quarterly seasonally adjusted data from 1958 to 1969 to test the model. Behavioral equations estimated by two stage least-squares.

Norton, W.E.; Schott, Kerry E.; and Sweeny, K.M. EMPLOYMENT AND PRICES. Occasional Paper, no. 3F. Sydney: Reserve Bank of Australia, 1971. 28 p. Data Appendix, pp. 25-27. Reserve Bank of Australia Publications, p. 28. No index.

The first part develops an equation to explain quarterly movements in civilian employment based on the neo-classical theory of factor demand with attention given to lags in the response of employment to changes in its determinants. Second part develops equations for the implicit deflators for gross national expenditure and its main private expenditure component.

Oi, Walter Y., and Shuldiner, Paul W. AN ANALYSIS OF URBAN TRAVEL DEMANDS. Metropolitan Transportation Series. Chicago: Northwestern University Press, for the Transportation Center, 1962. x, 281 p. Appendix A: Summary Statistics for the Modesto Study, pp. 197-218. Appendix B: Summary

Statistics for the Follow-up Detroit Study, pp. 219-30. Appendix C: Linear Regression Analysis of Trip Generation Rates, pp. 231-43. Appendix D: Growth Factor Methods for Computing Future Interzonal Traffic Volume, pp. 244-54. Notes, pp. 255-73. Bibliography, pp. 275-78. Index, pp. 279-81.

> An empirical analysis of trip generation using simple and multiple regression, analysis of variance, and analysis of covariance based on data collected in Modesto, Calif., in 1956 and in Detroit, Michigan. Explanatory variables include household size, car ownership, central business district distance, population density, income of household, occupational status of household head, and dwelling unit type. Main determinants of travel expenditure include income and city size.

Oldham, Peter David. MEASUREMENT IN MEDICINE: THE INTERPRETATION OF NUMERICAL DATA. Modern Medicine Series. London: English Universities Press, 1968. viii, 216 p. References, pp. 203-5. Glossary, pp. 206-9. Index, pp. 211-16.

> A monograph which attempts to explain why particular statistical techniques fulfill practical needs in medicine. Assumes knowledge of basic statistics and calculus. Uses no lengthy mathematical arguments. Topics include scales and transformations; estimation; tests of significance; significance of measurements; significance of frequencies; clinical trials; and the specification of normal values. Applications of the following probability distributions discussed: Poisson, lognormal, negative binomial, and fiducial.

ON POLITICAL ECONOMY AND ECONOMETRICS: ESSAYS IN HONOUR OF OSKAR LANGE. New York: Pergamon, 1965. viii, 661 p. Bibliography of Works, 1925-1963, pp. 651-61. No index.

> Forty-two essays commemorating Oskar Lange's sixtieth birthday in 1964 and a bibliographical memoir by Tadeusz Kowalik. Includes topics in economic analysis, statistical theory, economic ideology and planning practice, philosophy of history, and econometrics. Papers written in five languages (English, French, German, Italian, and Russian), with English synopses of non-English papers.

Oury, Bernard. A PRODUCTION MODEL FOR WHEAT AND FEEDGRAINS IN FRANCE (1946-1961). Contribution to Economic Analysis, vol. 40. Amsterdam: North-Holland, 1966. xviii, 306 p. Selected Bibliography, pp. 215-16. Appendix A: Part One: The Wheat Model, Regression Equations, Yield Acreage, Production, pp. 219-52. Appendix A: Part Two: The Feedgrain Model, Regression Equations, Yield, Acreage, Production, pp. 253-86. Appendix B: Time Series Data Related to the Construction and the Discussion of the Wheat and Feedgrain Models Proposed for France, pp. 287-303. Appendix C: Accidental Interchange Within Time Series X_3, pp. 305-6. No index.

Estimates three single-equation regression models (production, acreage, and yield) by ordinary least squares for wheat and feedgrains in France using annual data for 1946-1961. Consists of five parts: "Introduction"; "Considerations Underlying the Specification of the Regressors for the Preparation of the Model"; "Construction of a French Model"; "Evaluation of the Model"; and "An Application of the Model." Predicts the impact upon French production of alternative grain price adjustment policies within the European Economic Community.

Parkin, Michael, and Zis, George, eds. INFLATION IN THE WORLD ECONOMY. Studies in Inflation. Toronto: University of Toronto Press, 1976. xvii, 334 p. Index of Names, pp. 326-29. Subject Index, pp. 330-34.

Twelve heretofore unpublished papers, with comments, on inflation presented at a conference on inflation in the world economy at the University of Manchester, July 17-19, 1974. Topics include inflationary expectations; the failure of stable inflation; world demand for money function; inflation rates under fixed exchange rates; empirical study of the monetary approach to the balance of payments in fourteen industrial countries; international transmission of inflation; and money and prices in Sweden, 1732-1972.

Parsons, Leonard J., and Schultz, Randall L. MARKETING MODELS AND ECONOMETRIC RESEARCH. New York: Elsevier, 1976. xiii, 300 p. References, pp. 273-93. Author Index, pp. 295-98. Subject Index, pp. 299-300.

Uses econometric methodology to develop marketing decision models for marketing researchers and practitioners who have knowledge of calculus, matrix algebra, mathematical statistics, and elementary econometrics. Consists of four parts: "Introduction"; "The Econometric Model-Building Approach"; "Econometric Research in Marketing"; and "Policy and Research Implications." Topics include simultaneous equations and structural equation models; ordinary least squares and generalized least squares; recursive equation systems; two- and three-stage least squares; combining cross-section and time series data; sales response models; lag structure models; empirical decision models and their implementation; and industry advertising effects.

Pavlopoulos, P. A STATISTICAL MODEL FOR THE GREEK ECONOMY, 1949-1959. Contributions to Economic Analysis, vol. 44. Amsterdam: North-Holland, 1966. xi, 333 p. Appendix A, pp. 313-18. Appendix B, pp. 319-23. Bibliography, pp. 324-29. Index, pp. 330-33.

Presents a seventeen-equation model of the Greek economy consisting of eight behavioral, two institutional (tax equations), and seven identities with seventeen endogenous variables and twenty-seven exogenous (including lagged values of the indogenous variables). Intended to describe consumers' and investors' behavior and to cast some light on the working of the agricultural sector. Equations classified into the following groups: expenditure, income formation, price, government revenue, and supply of agricultural products. Estimated by ordinary least squares and Theil's two-stage least squares using annual data covering the period 1949-59. Prediction made for the sample period and for 1960-61. Eight behavioral equations include consumption, imports, investment in plant and equipment; investment in residential construction, agriculture and non-agriculture income determination, agricultural prices, and consumer prices.

Peacock, Alan T., ed. With the Assistance of Dieter Biehl. QUANTITATIVE ANALYSIS IN PUBLIC FINANCE. Praeger Special Studies in International Economics and Development. New York: Praeger, 1969. xii, 266 p. Notes, pp. 213-38. Supplementary Bibliography, pp. 239-66. No index.

Seven papers presented at a conference in public finance held in Turin in September 1968 in conjunction with the annual meeting of the International Institute of Public Finance, and two papers which were not presented. Topics include survey research in public finance; statistical measures for analyzing the size of the public sector; cost-benefit analysis in public finance; measuring efficiency in government service; econometric analysis of the incidence of measurement of fiscal performance in developing countries.

Pearce, Ivor F. A CONTRIBUTION TO DEMAND ANALYSIS. Oxford, Engl.: Claredon Press, 1964. viii, 258 p. Index, pp. 255-58.

A contribution to demand analysis based upon the work of the Stanford school of preference and rational choice as put forth by Uzawa. Develops the theory of demand for the individual, then turns to the problem of developing a community demand function. Includes complementarity, substitutability, and independence, with applications in international trade theory. Presents three experiments in demand analysis based on national income and expenditures in the United Kingdom for 1958. Assumes knowledge of partial derivatives, matrix algebra, and set theory.

Pearce, Ivor F.; Trivedi, P.K.; Stromback, C.T.; and Anderson, G.J. MODEL OF OUTPUT, EMPLOYMENT, AND PRICES IN THE U.K. New York: Cambridge University Press, 1976. vii, 172 p. References, pp. 164-68. Index, pp. 169-72.

An overview of the Southampton econometric model of the United Kingdom of fifteen sectors and almost 200 equations or identities. Model formulated in stages, each sector tested for tracking performance at first separately and then together.

Estimated by ordinary least squares using quarterly data for the period 1955-72.

Perry, George L. UNEMPLOYMENT, MONEY WAGE RATES, AND INFLATION. MIT Monographs in Economics. Cambridge: MIT Press, 1966. xv, 143 p. Appendix, pp. 126-34. Bibliography, pp. 135-37. Index, pp. 139-43.

Develops a single-equation regression model for explaining changes in aggregate wage levels using as explanatory variables, unemployment, the profit rate, the change in cost of living, change in profit rate, and the direction of a change in unemployment using quarterly data from 1942 to 1963 for all manufacturing, durable-goods industries, and nondurable goods industries. Uses wage change equation in a wage-price-profit subsystem for the economy with separate equations for explaining profit rates, manufacturing output prices, and living costs using ordinary least squares and two-stage least squares as the estimating procedures. Appendix presents the basic data and the construction of the variables and equations.

Pessemier, Edgar A. EXPERIMENTAL METHODS OF ANALYZING DEMAND FOR BRANDED CONSUMER GOODS WITH APPLICATIONS TO PROBLEMS IN MARKETING STRATEGY. Pullman: Washington State University Press, 1963. x, 165 p. Technical Appendix: Experimental Methods of Estimating Demand for Branded Consumer Goods with Applications to Problems in Marketing Strategy, pp. 142-62. Bibliography, pp. 163-65. No index.

Presents the results of an experiment performed in Pullman in 1961 involving five simulated shopping experiments using a random sample of 320 nonstudent buyers of branded consumer goods designed to study the demand for these goods, specifically, to derive estimates of cross elasticities of demand. Results of the experiment displayed in tables and charts throughout the monograph, and the technical appendix describes many of the details of the experiment. Useful to anyone interested in undertaking controlled experiments to study economic behavior.

Polenske, Karen R., et al. STATE ESTIMATES OF THE GROSS NATIONAL PRODUCT 1947, 1958, 1963. Vol. I of Multiregional Input-Output Analysis. Lexington, Mass.: Lexington Books, 1972. xiii, 459 p. Appendix A: Classification Tables, pp. 165-71. Appendix B: Alignment of 1960 Consumer Expenditures Survey Categories with the 80-Order Input-Output Industrial Classification, pp. 173-211. Appendix C: 1947, 1958, and 1963 State Estimates of Final Demands (MRIP Data Set 1), pp. 213-447. Bibliography, pp. 449-59. No index.

Presents estimates of six components of final demand (personal consumption expenditures, gross private capital formation, net inventory change, net foreign exports, state and local government purchases of goods and services, and federal government purchases) for eighty-seven industries in each of fifty-one states for 1947, 1958, and 1963, the three years for which comparable national input-output tables are presently available from the Office of Business Economics. Explains the methodology for making the estimates. Estimates of final demand compiled for use in the multiregional input-output model of the Harvard Economics Research Project.

Polenske, Karen R., and Skolka, Jiri V. ADVANCES IN INPUT-OUTPUT ANALYSIS. Cambridge, Mass.: Ballinger, 1976. Lii, 604 p. No index.

Twenty-nine papers presented at the Sixth International Conference on input-output techniques held in Vienna in April 22-26, 1974, grouped under the following seven headings: "National Economic Development Studies" (six papers); "Applications in Developing Countries" (four papers); "Regional and Interregional Studies" (four papers); "Industrial Applications" (three papers); "Studies on Energy and the Environment" (four papers); "International Trade Studies" (three papers); and "Optimization Models and Production Functions" (five papers).

Pontificia Accademia delle Science. STUDY WEEK ON THE ECONOMETRIC APPROACH TO DEVELOPMENT PLANNING. Pontificiae Academiae Scientiarum Scripta, Varia, 28. Amsterdam: North-Holland, 1965. xivii, 1,259 p. No index.

Eighteen technical papers on some early econometric approaches to development planning presented at a study week held in Vatican City, July 7-13, 1963. Papers printed in English, and treat such topics as assessing the efficacy of public investment by econometric analysis; optimal economic growth; dynamic structure and estimation in economy-wide econometric models; simulation techniques in development programming; balanced growth and technical progress in a log-linear multisectoral economy; role of capital in economic development; spatial organization and regional planning; statistical tools and techniques in planning in India; and econometric analysis and agricultural and development planning.

Powell, Alan A., and Williams, Ross A., eds. ECONOMETRIC STUDIES OF MACRO AND MONETARY RELATIONS. New York: Elsevier, 1973. viii, 358 p. List of Papers Presented at the Second Australian Conference of Econometricians, Monash University, August 9-13, 1971, pp. 349-50.

Thirteen papers presented at the conference grouped under the following two headings: "Macroeconometrics" (eight papers); and "Monetary Sector Models" (five papers). Topics include treatment of undersized samples in econometrics; the Canadian quarterly model RDX2; model of the Australian economy; wage-price sector for a quarterly Australian model; simulation with a quarterly macroeconomic model of the U.S. economy; dynamic properties of a nonlinear econometric model; a productivity model of a monetary economy; a continuous disequilibrium model of U.K. financial markets; and short-run adjustments in the Australian economy.

Prachowny, Martin F.J. A STRUCTURAL MODEL OF THE U.S. BALANCE OF PAYMENTS. Contributions to Economic Analysis, vol. 60. Amsterdam: North-Holland, 1969. 176 p. Appendix I: Data Sources, pp. 125-41. Appendix II: Diagrams of Actual and Predicted Values of the Dependent Variables, pp. 143-57. Appendix III: A Theoretical Framework of the Monetary-Fiscal Policy Mix for the Balance of Payments, pp. 159-64. Appendix IV: Changes in the Endogenous Variables Caused by the Assumed Monetary-Fiscal Policy Mix, pp. 165-66. Appendix V: A Hypothetical Model of Capital Movements Based on Portfolio Adjustments, pp. 167-70. Bibliography, pp. 171-74. Subject Index, pp. 175-76.

Presents an econometric model of the foreign sector of the U.S. economy. Consists of three import equations: consumer goods, investment goods, and raw materials; an export equation for merchandise and the following categories: foreign travel, transportation and services, including private remittances; direct foreign investment; long-term portfolio capital movements; repatriation of dividends and interest; short-term capital movements; and other long-term capital movements. Estimated by ordinary and two-stage least squares using seasonally adjusted quarterly data from 1953 to 1965. Relates all three import items to an income-type variable and relative prices, using lagged variables and dummy variables. Relates merchandise exports to a world income variable, relative prices, U.S. investments abroad, and lagged values of U.S. exports. Develops a rudimentary model of the domestic sector to estimate the multipliers involved in the foreign sector.

Pyatt, F. Graham. PRIORITY PATTERNS AND THE DEMAND FOR HOUSEHOLD DURABLE GOODS. University of Cambridge, Department of Applied Economics, monograph 11. Cambridge: Cambridge University Press, 1964. xv, 147 p. Definitions and Notation, pp. 137-40. Appendix: The British Market Research Bureau Limited Survey, pp. 141-42. References, pp. 143-44. Index, pp. 145-47.

A monograph on the empirical demand analysis for household durable goods based on a survey of the ownership of durable goods by households in Great Britain conducted in May 1958. by British Market Research Bureau Limited. Incorporates priority and probability pattern estimates of accumulation of durable goods into a set of differential equation models with variable parameters in the probabilities that a household own each of the durable goods in some set at a given time. No attempt made to evaluate the factors which determine a household's demand for, and ownership of, durable goods. Provides three applications of the model. Assumes knowledge of probability theory, calculus, and ordinary differential equations.

Quandt, Richard E., ed. THE DEMAND FOR TRAVEL: THEORY AND MEASUREMENT. Lexington, Mass.: Heath, Lexington Books, 1970. xii, 304 p. Author Index, pp. 303-4.

Twelve essays including ten reprints of articles originally published in various journals, on the demand for passenger transportation. Topics of other essays include statistical theory of spatial distribution models; demand theory for abstract transport modes; cross-sectional travel demand models; estimation of modal splits; aggregation and estimation in the nonlinear model; the subsidy issue in urban transportation; value of time spent in travel; and choice of travel mode for the journey to work.

Rao, Calylmpudi Radhakrisna. In Collaboration With D.B. Lahiri, K.R. Nair, P. Pant, and S.S. Shrikhande. ESSAYS ON ECONOMETRICS AND PLANNING. Foreword by C.D. Deshmukh. New York: Pergamon, 1965. iv, 354 p. Scientific Contributions of Professor P.C. Mahalanobis, pp. 321-28. Messages, pp. 329-54. No index.

Twenty-one essays, with planning as the central theme, presented to Professor P.C. Mahalanobis of the Indian Statistical Institute on the occasion of his seventieth birthday. Topics include planning in Britain; the national balance sheet of the Soviet Union; a philosophical view of civilization; a theory of system behavior; planning and economic growth; project appraisal; capital formation and its financing in the private corporate sector of India; parametric solution and programming of the Hicksian model; and measure, quality, and optimum scale.

Rasmussen, P. Nørregaard. STUDIES IN INTER-SECTORAL RELATIONS. Amsterdam: North-Holland, 1957. 217 p. Appendix A: The Measurement of Gains and Losses from Changes in the Terms of Trade, pp. 161-82. Appendix B: The Basic Data, 183-200. Resume (Summary in Danish), pp. 201-8. Bibliography, pp. 209-14. Index, pp. 215-17.

A monograph on the theory of input-output analysis with illustrative examples from the Danish economy for 1947 and 1949. Topics include the open static model with extensions, interindustry terms of trade, and structural change in an input-output model.

Renton, G.A., ed. MODELLING THE ECONOMY. Foreword by Alan T. Peacock. New York: Crane, Russak, 1975. xiii, 676 p. Index, pp. 670-76.

Twenty papers with discussions presented at the Social Science Research Council Conference on Modelling of the U.K. economy held at the London Graduate School of Business Studies in July 1972, grouped under the following nine headings: "Econometric Models of the U.K. Economy" (four papers); "Forecasting Methods" (two papers); "Simulations with Models" (three papers); "Econometric Methods" (three papers); "Control Models of the Economy" (two papers); "Monetary Sector" (two papers); "Dividend Behavior" (one paper); "Policy Analysis and Consumption" (two papers); and "International Linkage of Models" (one paper). Topics include the London School of Business Quarterly, treasury short-term forecasting, and Southampton Models; National Institute experience with econometric models; leading indicators of cycles in unemployment; simulation with the Federal Reserve-MIT-Penn model of the United States; estimates of a simple control model of the U.K. economy; the demand for financial assets by the personal sector of the U.K. economy; and the LINK research project.

Ricks, R. Bruce, ed. NATIONAL HOUSING MODELS: APPLICATION OF ECONOMETRIC TECHNIQUES TO PROBLEMS OF HOUSING RESEARCH. Lexington, Mass.: Heath, Lexington Books, 1973. xii, 185 p. About the Contributors, pp. 177-79. Index, pp. 181-85.

Five papers presented at a conference on housing models held in Washington, D.C., March 4-5, 1971, under sponsorship of the Federal Home Loan Bank System. Papers achieve a balance between diversity of the econometric approach and the homogeneity of the subject. Titles: "An Econometric Analysis of the U.S. Residential Housing Market," by Eugene A. Brady; "Housing Starts in 1966 and 1969: A Comparison Using an Econometric Model," by James B. Burnham; "Monthly Housing Starts," by Ray C. Fair; "A Summary of the Current Financial Intermediary, Mortgage, and Housing Model," by John H. Katchbrenner; and "Econometric Models of the Residential Construction Sector: A Comparison," by Gary Fromm.

Rodgers, John M. STATE ESTIMATES OF INTERREGIONAL COMMODITY TRADE, 1963. Multiregional Input-Output Analysis, vol. 1. Lexington, Mass.: Lexington Books, 1973. xix, 447 p. Appendix A: Classification Tables, pp. 47-52. Appendix B: Miscellaneous Tables, pp. 53-64. Appendix C: Estimation of Consumption in Destination Area, pp. 65-66. Appendix D: 1963 Interregional Trade Flows (MRIO Data Set 5), pp. 67-443. Bibliography, pp. 445-47. No index.

A compilation of state estimates of commodity freight shipments in 1963 for use in the multiregional input-output model of the Harvard Economics Research Project. Trade estimates in terms of value and tons prepared for sixty-one industries. Documents the procedures used to construct statistics on the value of trade between states, sources of data, and adjustments of the estimates for consistency with other MRIO accounts. Bulk of the book (nearly 400 pages) gives the estimated value of 1963 trade flows between fifty-one states. Data sources include Census of Transportation, 1963; Carload Waybill statistics, 1963; Minerals Yearbook, 1963; and Waterborne Commerce of the United States, 1963.

Rothenberg, Thomas J. EFFICIENT ESTIMATION WITH A PRIOR INFORMATION. Cowles Foundation, monograph 23. New Haven, Conn.: Yale University Press, 1973. viii, 180 p. References, pp. 173-76. Index, pp. 177-80.

Attempts to unify certain aspects of econometric theory, in particular the simultaneous equations problem and the identification problem, by the use of a priori information with the basic tool being the Cramér-Rao inequality. Assumes knowledge of elementary mathematical statistics and matrix algebra. Many difficult results stated without proof. Topics include exact and inexact priori information; efficient estimation of simultaneous equation systems; Bayesian approach to econometrics; and value of Bayesian structural information. Bayesian approach omits unbiasedness assumption, allows for flexibility in describing a priori information, and places the decision aspect of estimation in a decision theory context.

Rowley, J.C.R., and Trivedi, P.K. ECONOMETRICS OF INVESTMENT. Wiley Monographs in Applied Econometrics. New York: Wiley, 1975. xii, 205 p. References, pp. 183-98. Author Index, pp. 199-202. Subject Index, pp. 203-5.

A survey of critical issues and potential approaches using primarily single-equation models to illustrate practical problems in fixed capital formation and inventory adjustments. Useful supplement to books on applied econometrics with emphasis on numerical results and their interpretation. Describes economic theories associated with empirical studies of real fixed capital formation and inventories and the main technical aspects of estimation, including the structure of temporal response, problems of specification, partial and temporal aggregation, and spatial autocorrelation. Concludes with econometric evidence for several alternative specifications of inventory equations which are found in the literature, including a large quarterly aggregative model of Canada.

Sahota, Gian S. FERTILIZER IN ECONOMIC DEVELOPMENT: AN ECONOMETRIC ANALYSIS. Foreword by Theodore W. Schultz. Praeger Special Studies in International Economics and Development. New York: Praeger, 1968. xxii, 240 p. Appendix A: Detailed Regression of Relation(1) and Some Additional Computations, pp. 128-38. Appendix B: The Data: Sources, Definitions, Adjustments, pp. 139-61. Appendix C: An Analysis of the Sources of Pure Technical Change, pp. 163-88. Appendix D: A Comparison of Technical Change and Scale Economies Computed by Alternative Methods, pp. 189-200. Notes, pp. 201-26. Bibliography, pp. 229-40. No index.

Examines the causes of the decline in the real price of fertilizer in the United States during 1936-60. Employs a single-equation regression model with price/ton of fertilizer as the dependent variable and quantities of nitrogen, phosphorus, and potassium as independent variables using semi-annual cross-section data for the years 1949 to 1964.

Schaffer, William A., ed. With the Assistance of E.A. Laurent, C.F. Floyd, E.M. Sutter, Jr., C.K. Hamby, and R.C. Herbert. ON THE USE OF INPUT-OUTPUT MODELS FOR REGIONAL PLANNING. Statistics in Applied Science volume 1. The Netherlands, Leiden: Stenfert Kroese B.V., 1976. xviii, 170 p. Appendix A: Income and Product Accounts for Georgia, 1970, pp. 122-33. Appendix B: Projections of Employment Growth in Georgia: A Shift and Share Analysis (by Charles F. Floyd), pp. 134-43. Appendix C: Tables, pp. 145-66. Selected References, pp. 167-70. No index.

Illustrates the use of a twenty-eight industry input-output table for Georgia for 1970 with emphasis on the computation of various multiplier, projections with an input-output table, analysis of the impact of public policy, and the use of input-output tables in market analysis. Appendixes devoted to notes on constructing regional income and product accounts for use in input-output tables, and shift and share analysis. Also included logic of input-output models and procedures for constructing the transaction table.

Schotter, Andrew, ed. SELECTED ECONOMIC WRITINGS OF OSKAR MORGENSTERN. New York University Series in Selected Economic Writings. New York: New York University Press, 1976. xv, 539 p. Bibliography, pp. 513-27. Author Index, pp. 529-32. Subject Index, pp. 533-39.

Thirty reprints of articles and three excerpts from books in economic theory written since 1933 by Oskar Morgenstern. Grouped under the following headings: "Game Theory and Utility Theory" (four articles); "Linear Economic Systems" (four articles); "Economic Theory" (six articles); "Economic Statistics" (four articles); "Methodology" (four articles); and "History of Theory" (eight articles).

Schultz, Henry. THE THEORY AND MEASUREMENT OF DEMAND. Chicago: University of Chicago Press, 1938. xxix, 817 p. Appendixes, pp. 669-75. Bibliography, pp. 779-803. Indexes, pp. 807-17.

A comprehensive empirical analysis of demand functions of sixteen agricultural commodities with both elasticities and time shifts in the functions estimated. Consists of three parts: "Theoretical Foundations"; "Statistical Findings"; and "Interrelations of Demand." Includes a review of modern demand theory. Appendixes consist of the basic data used for estimation, summary of statistical methods useful in demand analysis, and standard errors of the coefficients of elasticity of demand.

Scott, Maurice Fitzgerald. A STUDY OF UNITED KINGDOM IMPORTS. Cambridge, Engl.: Cambridge University Press, 1963. xvi, 269 p. Appendix I: The Problem of Grouping, pp. 188-208. Appendix II: Statistical Sources and Methods, pp. 209-56. List of Works Cited, pp. 257-61. General Index to Parts I and II, pp. 263-67. Index of Names, pp. 268-69.

An empirical study of the determinants of demand for U.K. imports using simple and multiple single-equation models with annual time series data from 1900 to 1955. Includes regressions in log-linear form giving rise to direct estimates of various price, production, and trend elasticities. Consists of two parts: "General Survey and Main Conclusions" and "The Behavior of Imports of Food, Materials, and Manufacturers." Useful to individuals interested in early econometric analysis, including economic historians.

Sellekaerts, Willy, ed. ECONOMETRICS AND ECONOMIC THEORY. ESSAYS IN HONOUR OF JAN TINBERGEN. New York: Macmillan, 1974. viii, 298 p. Bibliography of Jan Tinbergen, pp. 285-95. Index, pp. 297-98.

A collection of thirteen heretofore unpublished articles arranged under the following headings: "Econometrics" (seven articles) and "Economic Theory and Miscellaneous" (six articles). Topics include maximum likelihood estimators of autocorrelation in disturbances; aggregation theory; estimation and prediction in dynamic models; economic policy simulation; models explaining trends and cycles in India; economic theory of replacement depreciation; multidimensional pricing, and size distribution of labor incomes derived from the distribution of aptitudes.

Shapiro, Arlene K. INPUT-OUTPUT ANALYSIS AS A PREDICTIVE TOOL. Washington, D.C.: Bureau of Economic Analysis, Department of Commerce, 1972. 77 p. No index.

Compares projections obtained through input-output analysis with projections obtained through two regression methods, a GNP blowup method, a final demand blowup method, and a combined GNP and final demand blowup method. Concludes that input-output analysis is at least as good and is generally better than alternative methods.

Simon, Herbert A., ed. MODELS OF MAN: SOCIAL AND RATIONAL MATHEMATICAL ESSAYS ON RATIONAL HUMAN BEHAVIOR. New York: Wiley, 1957. xiv, 287 p. Index, pp. 281-87.

Collection of sixteen articles on the theory of the rational and nonrational aspects of human behavior previously published in thirteen journals, including ECONOMETRICS, QUARTERLY JOURNAL OF ECONOMICS, and the PSYCHOLOGICAL REVIEW, during the period 1947-1956. Grouped under the following four headings: "Causation and Influence Relations" (five articles); "Social Processes" (four articles); "Motivation: Inducements and Contributions" (two articles); and "Rationality and Administrative Decision Making" (five articles). Topics include spurious correlations; definition of causal relation; measurement of political power; a theory of interaction in social groups; a class of skew distribution functions; a theory of employment relation; application of servomechanism theory to production control; and a comparison of game theory and learning theory. Useful as a supplementary text in graduate courses in mathematical social theory.

Sletmo, Gunnar K. DEMAND FOR AIR CARGO: AN ECONOMETRIC APPROACH. Bergen: Institute for Shipping Research, The Norwegian School of Economics and Business Administration, 1972. 125 p. Bibliography, pp. 97-100. Appendix A: Price Elasticity for Transportation Demand, pp. 101-2. Appendix B: Derivation of the Gompertz Curve, p. 103. Appendix C: Need for Additional Data on Air Freight, p. 104. Data Appendix, pp. 105-25.

Presents a study of demand for air frieght with emphasis on estimation of price and income elasticities. Estimates obtained for separate geographical areas, including North Atlantic, Pacific, Latin America, and the United States. Employs both single equation models and simultaneous equation models, using two-stage least squares. Uses aggregate time series published by the International Civil Aviation Organization for 1949 to 1969.

Slovin, Myron B., and Sushka, Marie Elizabeth. INTEREST RATES ON SAVINGS DEPOSITS: THEORY, ESTIMATION, AND POLICY. Lexington, Mass.: Lexington Books, 1975. xiii, 173 p. Glossary, pp. 161-63. Bibliography, pp. 165-68. Index, pp. 169-73.

Presents several models to explain the deposit rate setting behavior of commercial banks, mutual saving banks, and saving and loan associations, and evaluates the impact of savings deposit rates on the level of economic activity and on the effectiveness of monetary policy using single-equation regression models. Includes a cross-section analysis for 544 banks for each of the years 1961-67 and time series analysis for the period 1955-68. Other topics include development of a model to explain behavior of the market for certificates of deposit; the relation between interest rates and demand for money; and an empirical analysis of saving deposit rates using the Federal Reserve-Penn-MIT econometric model.

Smith, Lawrence Berk. THE POSTWAR CANADIAN HOUSING AND RESIDENTIAL MORTGAGE MARKETS AND THE ROLE OF GOVERNMENT. Toronto: University of Toronto Press, 1974. x, 178 p. Appendix: Summary of Symbols and Sources of Data, pp. 154-58. Notes, pp. 159-78. No index.

Examines the organization of the postwar Canadian housing and residential mortgage markets for the purpose of assessing the role and scope of government policy. Consists of the following four parts: "Introduction"; "The Housing Market"; "The Mortgage Market"; and "Housing and Government Policy."

Housing market model consists of fourteen equations estimated by ordinary least squares using seasonally adjusted quarterly data from 1955 to 1967. Mortgage market represented by a single-equation model, with interest rates the key variable. Applied to a number of lenders, using quarterly data from 1955 to 1968 for lenders and from 1954 to 1959 for others. Housing market simulated with respect to housing starts, house prices, stock of houses, construction costs, mortgage rates, mortgage approvals, and inflow of funds.

Smith, Ron P. CONSUMER DEMAND FOR CARS IN THE USA. University of Cambridge, Applied Economics Occasional Paper, 44. New York: Cambridge University Press, 1975. ix, 108 p. Appendix A: The Basic Data, pp. 89-93. Appendix B: Estimation Methods in Chapter 3, pp. 94-97. Appendix C: Alternative Specifications of Expectations, pp. 98-105. Bibliography, pp. 106-8. No index.

Presents three econometric demand models for automobiles in the U.S. to explain ownership, replacement, and purchase, with a considerable amount of background material on the automobile market in the USA. Estimates regression models from data covering the period 1950-70 and the inter-war years. Ownership model utilizes a time series of cross-sections between 1952 and 1969 to decompose the observed growth in stock into that resulting from income changes, population growth, and the movement of the parameters over time. Replacement demand model based on the trade-in behavior of new car buyers.

Smith, V. Kerry. TECHNICAL CHANGE, RELATIVE PRICES, AND ENVIRONMENTAL RESOURCE EVALUATION. Foreword by J.V. Krutilla. Baltimore: Johns Hopkins University Press, for the Resources for the Future, 1974. x, 106 p. No index.

A monograph which provides an analytical framework for linking relative price behavior of goods and services to the forces of technical change and intertemporal externalities. Links the rise in the relative prices of a class of goods or services directly to the rate of general technological progress. Presentation theoretical and excludes empirical applications or numerical examples. Useful primarily to economic theoreticians who are familiar with the rudiments of differential calculus. Chapters conclude with references.

Stone, Donald N. INDUSTRIAL LOCATION IN METROPOLITAN AREAS: A GENERAL MODEL TESTED FOR BOSTON. Foreword by Benjamin Chinitz. New York: Praeger, 1974. xvii, 91 p. Appendix A: Excerpts from Boston Industrial Survey Questionnaire, pp. 73-77. Appendix B: Supplemental Industrial Questionnaire, pp. 78-79. Appendix C: Description of Statistical Tests, pp. 80-84. Bibliography, pp. 85-89. Index, pp. 90-91.

Develops a single-equation cost model of intrametropolitan industrial location based on the assumption that firms choose their location within the metropolitan area in an effort to minimize their costs. Model tested using data from a sample of 311 firms employing twenty or more employees which out-migrated from Boston over a nine-year period and those firms remaining in the city. Independent variables of the cost equation include the prices of land, labor, government services, transportation, and business services. Chapters conclude with notes and references.

Straszheim, Mahlon R. AN ECONOMETRIC ANALYSIS OF THE URBAN HOUSING MARKET. National Bureau of Economic Research Urban and Regional Studies, no. 2. New York: Columbia University Press, for the National Bureau of Economic Research, 1975. xv, 203 p. Appendix A: Demand Elasticities for White Households by Life Cycle, pp. 174-86. Appendix B: Demand Estimates for Black Households by Life Cycles, pp. 187-94. Bibliography, pp. 195-98. Index, pp. 199-203.

Uses data from a household interview survey in the San Francisco area to formulate an econometric model to estimate household demand functions with price, income, race, geographic area, age of structure, and lot size as variables. Model based on Alonso's theory of household behavior in which utility is maximized subject to a budget constraint.

Suits, Daniel B. AN ECONOMETRIC MODEL OF THE GREEK ECONOMY. Research Monographs Series, no. 7. Athens: Center of Economic Research, 1964. 131 p. No index.

Presents a thirty-five linear equation model of the Greek economy: six investment demand equations, six import demand equations, six consumer demand equations, two stock equations, eight production and income equations (of which four are identities); and seven tax and transfer equations. Estimated by ordinary least squares using data for the period 1950-1960, and used to make forecasts for 1961. The variables divided into four groups: endogenous, quasi-predetermined, predetermined, and exogenous. Estimates a number of multipliers and analyzes their policy implications.

Teekens, Rudolf. PREDICTION METHODS IN MULTIPLICATIVE MODELS. Foreword by J. Koerts. Rotterdam, The Netherlands: Rotterdam University Press, 1972. viii, 121 p. Appendixes, pp. 97-117. References, pp. 118-19. Index, pp. 120-21.

A monograph on practical problems that a research worker may have in using multiplicative single-equation regression models. Analyzes and compares existing methods, such as least squares, maximum likelihood, and minimum variance unbiased estimates, and introduces a new generalized minimal mean square error estimator. Useful as a reference for anyone dealing with regression models. Assumes knowledge of linear algebra and mathematical statistics. Appendixes include additional topics such as the lognormal distribution, properties of certain estimators, second order conditions for a maximum of the likelihood function of the independent variables, the mean and variance of the logarithm of a gamma distributed random variable, and simulation.

Terleckyj, Nestor E., ed. HOUSEHOLD PRODUCTION AND CONSUMPTION. Studies in Income and Wealth, vol. 40. New York: Columbia University Press, for the NBER, 1975. xiii, 669 p. Index, pp. 653-69.

Thirteen papers presented at a conference held in Washington, D.C., November 30-December 1, 1973, grouped under four headings: "Demographic Behavior of the Household" (three papers); "Market and Nonmarket Aspects of Real Earnings" (two papers); "Level of Aggregation in Consumer Analysis" (four papers); and "Measurement and Policy Issues in Consumption Analysis" (four papers). Topics include estimation of a stochastic model of reproduction; correlation between health and schooling; estimates of a human capital production function; the value of saving a life; demand for housing; risk measurement and safety standards in consumer products; measurement of product quality; and measuring real consumption from quantity data, Canada, 1935-1968. Assumes knowledge of regression and econometrics.

Thompson, Wilbur R., and Mattila, John M. AN ECONOMETRIC MODEL OF POSTWAR STATE INDUSTRIAL DEVELOPMENT. Detroit: Wayne State University Press, 1959. vii, 116 p. Appendix A: Dependent Variables, pp. 87-91. Appendix B: Independent Variables: Industry General Form, pp. 92-95. Appendix C: Independent Variables: Industry Specific Forms, pp. 96-103. Appendix D: The Correlation Matrices of the Independent Variables, pp. 104-5. Appendix E: Figures: Maps Showing Relocation of Manufacturing, pp. 106-16. No index.

A cross-section (interstate) multiple correlation and regression analysis of employment trends embracing twenty manufacturing industry groups, forty-eight states, and the years 1947-50. Annual change in employment (the dependent variable) correlated with five sub-groups of independent variables; local market variables (average annual change in state population 1940-47, and average annual change in state personal income); industrialization variables (expenditures on plant and equipment, patents issued, average annual change in total manufacturing employment); state and local tax variables; labor market characteristics variables; and educational levels and facilities; and industry-specific variables. Computes over 1,000 separate correlations. Includes a summary and interpretation of findings.

Thorbecke, Erik, ed. THE ROLE OF AGRICULTURE IN ECONOMIC DEVELOPMENT. Universities-National Bureau Conference Series. New York: Columbia University Press, for the NBER, 1969. x, 480 p. Index, p. 451-80.

Ten papers presented at a conference of the Universities-National Bureau Committee for Economic Research grouped under the following three parts: "Agriculture in the World Economy" (three papers); "The Relationship Between Agriculture and Other Sectors" (three papers); and "Transformation of Traditional Agriculture" (four papers). Topics include an application of Frisch's theorem on cross-elasticities to food and non-food prices in Peru; an econometric projection of agricultural exports from the less-developed countries using both log-inverse equations and log-log inverse equations ($\log y = a - b/x - c \log x$); and a linear programming model for a dual economy.

Todaro, Michael P. DEVELOPMENT PLANNING: MODELS AND METHODS. New York: Oxford University Press, 1971. x, 101 p. No index.

An introduction to the most common and widely used economic models of development planning in poor nations with emphasis on static and dynamic input-output models. Uses no mathematics beyond elementary algebra. Useful as a reference in undergraduate courses in economic development and planning.

Treml, Vladimit G., and Hardt, John P., eds. SOVIET ECONOMIC STATISTICS. Durham, N.C.: Duke University Press, 1972. xii, 457 p. Index, pp. 447-57.

Eighteen papers presented at a conference held at Duke University in November 1969, grouped under the following headings: "Statistics in the Soviet Union" (three papers); "National Income Statistics" (three papers); "Industry Statistics" (three papers); "Agricultural Statistics" (three papers); "Real Income and Consumption Statistics" (three papers); and "Statistics on Prices and Money" (three papers).

Ulmer, Melville J. THE ECONOMIC THEORY OF COST OF LIVING INDEX NUMBERS. Studies in History, Economics and Public Law. New York: Columbia University Press, 1949. 106 p. Appendix A: The Derivation of Methods for Constructing Cost of Living Index Numbers from Family Budget Data, pp. 77-93. Appendix B: Additional Practical Implications: The Income and Space Dimensions of Cost of Living Index Numbers, pp. 94-97. Appendix C: A Note on Wartime Experience, pp. 98-100. Selected Bibliography, pp. 101-4. Index, pp. 105-6.

Explains the problem of measuring changes in living costs over time for the purpose of determining methods for approximating these changes, and a method of estimating the reliability of such measurements. Shows that the Laspeyre's index approximates the "true" measure of change in living costs. Includes methods for estimating error and the assumptions underlying cost of living formulas. Appendixes assume knowledge of calculus.

Uselton, Gene C. LAGS IN THE EFFECTS OF MONETARY POLICY: A NON-PARAMETRIC ANALYSIS. Business Economics and Finance Series, vol. 2. Marcel Dekker, 1974. xii, 174 p. Appendix, pp. 149-59. Bibliography, pp. 161-66. Author Index, pp. 167-69. Subject Index, pp. 171-74.

Argues that data concerning monetary policy changes and subsequent changes in a particular target variable (such as income, employment, and interest) are original or nominal at best, and hence are unsuited for parametric analysis. Demonstrates that data can be used in a nonparametric analysis to estimate the average length of lag of monetary policy. Topics include a review of parametric methods for estimating lags; a theoretical framework for monetary policy lag analysis using nonparametric statistical methods; nonparametric estimates of monetary policy lags on income, nominal wages, prices, and interest rates; and policy recommendations. Chapters conclude with notes.

Vartia, Pentti L.I. AN ECONOMETRIC MODEL FOR ANALYZING AND FORECASTING SHORT-TERM FLUCTUATIONS IN THE FINNISH ECONOMY. Series A2. Helsinki, Finland: Research Institute of the Finnish Economy, 1974. 249 p. References, pp. 208-17. Appendixes, pp. 218-49. No index.

Develops a short-term annual econometric model of the Finnish economy consisting of twelve behavioral equations and thirty definitional equations, with the estimation period being 1951-1970. Model designed for demand oriented analyses of the business cycle. Sectors include domestic expenditures (consumption, private investment, and inventory changes); the foreign sector, labor input and unemployment; and wages and prices. Model tested by providing ex post predictions for the period 1950 through 1973 and by simulations to obtain ex ante predictions for 1974 and 1975. Appendixes present data on resources and expenditures and for the main variables for 1948-1974, and also the model matrices.

Werin, Lars. A STUDY OF PRODUCTION, TRADE AND ALLOCATION OF RESOURCES. Stockholm Economic Studies. New Series, VI. Stockholm: Almqvist & Wiksell, 1965. 191 p. Bibliography of Works Cited, pp. 184-86. Name Index, p. 188. Subject Index, pp. 189-91.

Uses a linear programming model to estimate the effects on internal prices, production, and other variables of a change in terms of trade, world market price of a given commodity, rate of indirect taxes on a commodity, increase of capacity in a production sector, etc., for Sweden in 1957. Constraints include input coefficients of domestic production, capacity limit in each sector, the possibility for importation or exportation of products of some sectors at given prices, the absence of such for products of other sectors, and a given export surplus. Shadow prices also computed--the shadow price for labor being 1.30-1.45, implying that labor was paid less than the value of its marginal contribution in 1957. Useful to anyone interested in application of linear programming to economics.

Weymer, F. Helmut. THE DYNAMICS OF THE WORLD COCOA MARKET. MIT Monographs in Economics, 9. Cambridge, Mass.: MIT Press, 1968. xvi, 253 p. Appendix 2A: Monthly History of the Cocoa Market, 1953-1963, pp. 151-87. Appendix 3A: The FAO Cocoa Price Model, pp. 189-94. Appendix 4A: The Data for Chapter 4, pp. 195-217. Appendix 4B: Seasonal Inventory Behavior: Regressions pp. 219-22. Appendix 5A: The Data for Chapter 5, pp. 223-37. Appendix 5B: Quarterly and Monthly Consumption Equations, pp. 239-40. Appendix 5C: Consumption: Indirect Estimation Regression Results, pp. 241-43. Selected Bibliography, pp. 245-47. Index, pp. 249-53.

A monograph on the dynamics of the cocoa industry aimed at describing and explaining the nature of the response of the world cocoa industry to annual fluctuations in world cocoa production. Includes a system of equations to estimate intermediate-term fluctuations in the world price, consumption rate, and inventory level of cocoa in response to exogenous changes in producer sales of cocoa, and in world production forecasts using monthly data from 1952 to 1963 and ordinary and generalized least squares. Also includes simulations of price and consumption. Useful to price theoreticians, econometricians, and cocoa enthusiasts.

Wheat, Leonard F. REGIONAL GROWTH AND INDUSTRIAL LOCATION: AN EMPIRICAL VIEWPOINT. Lexington, Mass.: Heath, Lexington Books, 1973. xii, 223 p. Notes, pp. 213-17. Index, pp. 219-23.

Uses regression analysis to identify and evaluate the relative importance of factors that cause one region to grow faster than another. Uses data for the forty-eight contiguous states from 1947 to 1963 with three growth variables (absolute, per capita, and percentage growth) as dependent variables. Obtains correlations between each of the three dependent variables and hundred of independent variables, with all but thirteen independent variables generated by the computer. The thirteen original variables include personal income, value added, farm population, land area, January mean temperature, and average hourly earnings. Uses simple correlations to identify the dominant influences and to refine the variables measuring them. Uses partial correlations to measure the influence of a given variable with all other influences remaining constant. Uses multiple correlation to indicate which combination of variables best explain the interregional differences in manufacturing growth.

Wilson, Alan Geoffrey. PAPERS IN URBAN AND REGIONAL ANALYSIS. London: Pion, 1972. x, 261 p. Author Index, pp. 253-56. Subject Index, pp. 257-61.

Twelve reprints of articles published by the author during the period 1968-1971 grouped under the following four headings: "Models and Planning Methodology" (two papers); "Problems in Modelling" (four papers); "Modelling Techniques" (five papers); and "Models in Planning" (one paper). Topics include entropy in system modelling; use of accounting frameworks in the development of location models; spatial interaction models; Lowrey models; planning for ports and transportation; and micro-economic approaches to modelling household behavior. Useful to postgraduate students and research workers in a wide range of disciplines. Knowledge of input-output analysis and macro-economic mathematical models helpful for some of the papers.

_____. URBAN AND REGIONAL MODELS IN GEOGRAPHY AND PLANNING. New York: Wiley, 1974. xiv, 418 p. Appendix 1: Entropy-Maximizing Methods, pp. 393-96. Appendix 2: The Interviewing Opportunities Model, pp. 397-99. Appendix 3: The Algebra of the Contragredient (or Companion Matrix) Transformation, pp. 400-418. Author Index, pp. 405-7. Subject Index, pp. 409-18.

A text for a course in urban and regional analysis for graduates and undergraduates in geography, economics, environment science, regional planning, and applied mathematics who have knowledge of matrix algebra and introductory mathematical modelling, including input-output analysis, and a reference for research workers. Gives an elementary account of the range of models used in analysis and planning of cities and regions, in four parts: "Models and Urban Problems"; "Techniques for Constructing Urban and Regional Models"; "Urban and Regional Models"; and "The Use of Models in Planning." Topics include relationship between models and sub-models; rules for model construction; mathematical prerequisite; theory of spatial interaction; demographic, input-output, econometric, and transport models and examples; the Lowry spatial interaction model; principles for building a general model, and a hypothetical example of a general model; and use of models in planning. Chapters conclude with references.

Wold, Herman O.A. In Association with Lars Jureen. DEMAND ANALYSIS: A STUDY IN ECONOMETRICS. Wiley Series in Probability and Mathematical

Statistics. New York: Wiley, 1953. xvi, 358 p. Appendix: Notes, pp. 323-36. Bibliography, pp. 337-46. List of Author References, pp. 347-49. Subject Index, pp. 350-58.

A monograph written in the dual form of a research report and a specialized textbook. Provides a systematic account of demand analysis, employing empirical studies of the authors into the structure of consumer demand in Sweden. Consists of five parts: "A Broad Survey of Topics and Findings"; "The Paretoan Theory of Consumer Demand"; "Some Topics in the Theory of Stationary Random Processes"; "Theory and Methods of Regression Analysis"; and "Empirical Findings." Topics include the theoretical requisites of demand analysis; specification of demand patterns; types of stationary processes; structural problems in time-series analysis; analyses of family budgets and market statistics; income elasticities obtained from family budget data; and elasticity calculations based on market statistics.

______, ed. ECONOMETRIC MODEL BUILDING: ESSAYS ON THE CAUSAL CHAIN APPROACH. Contributions to Economic Analysis, vol. XXXVI. New York: Elsevier, 1964. xiii, 419 p. No index.

A collection of thirteen reports on causal chains and interdependent systems approaches to model building under the following four parts: "The Causal Chain Approach, An Orientation" (two reports); "Mathematical and Theoretical-Statistical Contributions" (four papers); "Econometric Contributions" (three papers); and "Empirical Contributions" (four papers). Topics include forecasting by chain principle, wavelet composition of time series, recursive decomposition of stochastic processes, price strategies of a monopolist, and productivity studies in Swedish agriculture.

Wonnacott, Ronald J. CANADIAN-AMERICAN DEPENDENCE: AN INTER-INDUSTRY ANALYSIS OF PRODUCTION AND PRICES. Contributions to Economic Analysis, XXIV. Amsterdam: North-Holland, 1961. xiv, 143 p. Selected Bibliography, pp. 141-43. No index.

An input-output analysis using a 2x2 interregional model of trading relations between the United States and Canada in two parts: "The Structure of Production in Canada and the United States" and "The Effect of External Inflation on the Canadian Price Structure." Input-output tables consists of thirty-five industry sectors for 1949 (the 1947 U.S. input-output table was transformed to 1949). Shows the extent to which the changes in U.S. prices affect the Canadian price structure.

Zarembka, Paul, ed. FRONTIERS OF ECONOMETRICS. Economic Theory and Mathematical Economics Series. New York: Academic Press, 1974. ix, 252 p. Author Index, pp. 245-49. Subject Index, pp. 250-52.

Eight chapters contributed by different authors, each dealing with recent innovations in econometrics, grouped under the following headings: "Model Selection" (two chapters); "Linear Models" (four chapters); and "Multiple-Equation Models" (two chapters). Topics include tests for specification errors in regression models; Bayesian and non-Bayesian methods for discrimination among alternative models; transformation of variables in econometrics; conditional logit analysis of quantitative choice behavior; linear models with random coefficients; estimation by minimizing the sum of absolute errors; and consistent and efficient estimation of systems of simultaneous equations by means of instrumental variables.

Ziemba, W.T.; and Vickson, R.G., eds. STOCHASTIC OPTIMIZATION MODELS IN FINANCE. Economic Theory and Mathematical Economics Series. New York: Academic Press, 1975. xvi, 719 p. Bibliography, pp. 701-14. Index, pp. 715-19.

Thirty-three reprints of articles grouped under the following five headings: "Mathematical Tools" (four articles); "Qualitative Economic Results" (five articles); "Static Portfolio Selection Models" (eight articles); "Dynamic Models Reducible to Static Models" (three articles); and "Dynamic Models" (thirteen articles). Topics include expected utility theory; convexity and the Kuhn-Tucker conditions; dynamic programming; stochastic dominance; measures of risk aversion; separation in portfolio analysis; mean-variance and safety first approaches in portfolio analysis; existence and diversification of optimal portfolio policies; effects of taxes on risk taking; models that have a single decision point; myopic portfolio policies; two-period consumption models and portfolio revision; models of optimal capital accumulation; models of option strategy; and the capital growth criterion and continuous-time models.

INDEXES

AUTHOR INDEX

In addition to authors, this index includes all editors, translators, compilers, and other contributors to works cited in the text. References are to page numbers and alphabetization is letter by letter.

A

Author Index

B

C

D

E

G

H

Author Index

I

J

K

Author Index

Author Index

N

Q

R

S

T

Author Index

TITLE INDEX

This index is alphabetized letter by letter. It includes all titles of books, monographs, and published reports cited in this text. Individual chapters, articles, and essay titles are not included. References are to page numbers.

A

Title Index

B

Title Index

C

D

E

Title Index

G

H

Title Index

Title Index

N

O

P

Q

T

Title Index

U

V

W

SUBJECT INDEX

In this index, emphasis is on key concepts and topics of general interest, as well as the use of techniques, such as linear programming, in specific areas of research. References to authors indicate that their theories or concepts are the subject of discussion. This index is alphabetized letter by letter. Numbers refer to page numbers.

A

Subject Index

B

Subject Index

C

Subject Index

Subject Index

D

F

G

H

J

K

L

Q

R

S

Subject Index

Subject Index

U

V

W

Z